BERLIN
THEN AND NOW

So I shall not now, or ever, say 'goodbye'.
For Berlin is too much a part of me to ever leave.
I shall only say 'so long, thank you, and God bless you'.

GENERAL LUCIUS D. CLAY, MAY 1, 1962

2

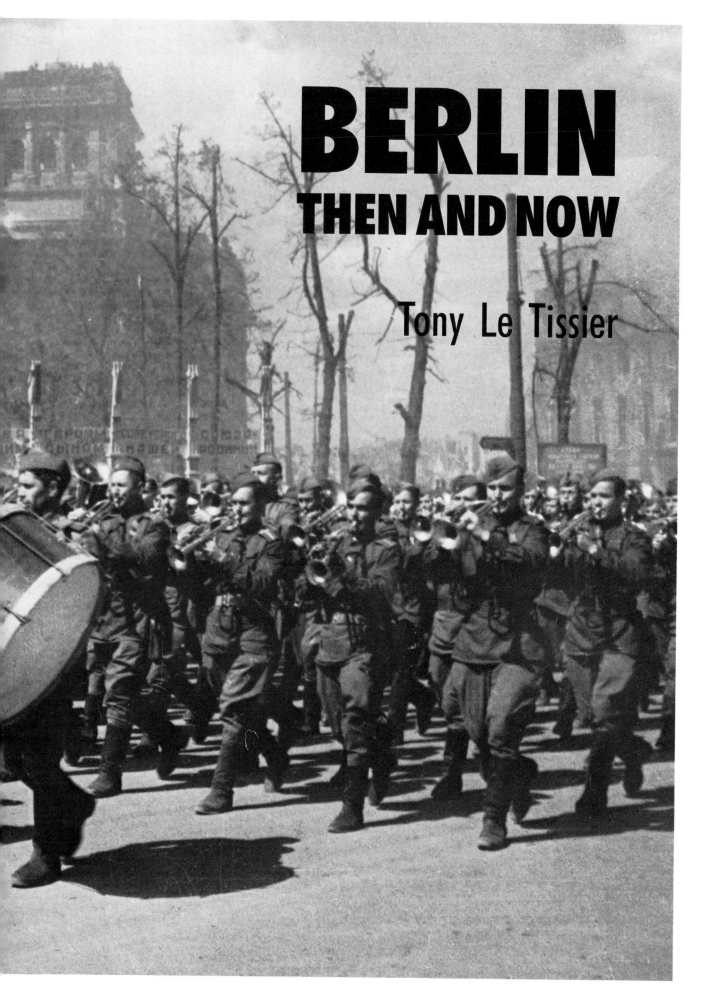

BERLIN
THEN AND NOW

Tony Le Tissier

Credits

© *After the Battle* 1992
ISBN: 0 900913 72 X
Second Impression 1997
Third Impression 2000
Edited and designed by Winston G. Ramsey
Editor-in-Chief *After the Battle*

PUBLISHERS
Battle of Britain International Limited,
Church House, Church Street,
London E15 3JA
An After the Battle publication

PRINTERS
Printed in Great Britain by Heronsgate Ltd,
Basildon, Essex

PHOTOGRAPHS
Copyright is indicated for all original illustrations where known. Present day photographs
are the copyright of *After the Battle* magazine
unless otherwise stated. (See Photographic
Credits.)

EXTRACTS
Acknowledgement is given to the following
authors and their publishers for permission
to quote from published works:
As It Happened, C. R. Attlee, William
   Heinemann, 1954.
Wer weiss ob wir uns Wiedersehen, Dieter
   Borkowski, Fischer Taschenbuch Verlag,
   1983.
Berlin '45 — The Grey City, Richard Brett-
   Smith,
The End of the Third Reich, V. I. Chuikov,
   Progress Publishers, 1978.
The Second World War, Winston S.
   Churchill, Cassell, 1952.
The Berlin Wall, Pierre Galante, Arthur
   Barker Ltd, 1965.
The Goebbels Diaries, Hamish Hamilton,
   1948.
Berlin Command, Brigadier General Frank
   Howley, Putnam, 1950.
Year of Victory, I. Koniev, Progress
   Publishers, 1969.
The Russians and Berlin, Erich Kuby,
   William Heinemann, 1968.
Götterdämmerung — La Prise de Berlin,
   Pierre Rocolle, Indo-China, 1954.
Defeat in the West, Milton Scuhmann, Secker
   and Warburg, 1947.
A Woman in Berlin, Secker and Warburg,
   1955.
Berlin Diary, William L. Shirer, Hamish
   Hamilton, 1941.
End of a Berlin Diary, William L. Shirer,
   Hamish Hamilton, 1947.
Das Ende zwischen Oder und Elbe, Wilhelm
   Tieke, Motorbuch Verlag, 1981.
Triumph und Tragödie, Colonel-General
   Dimitri Volkognov, Classen Verlag, 1989.
The Defense of Berlin, Willan Willemer, HQ
   USAREUR 1953.
Reminiscences and Reflections, G. Zhukov,
   Progress Publishers, 1974.

FRONT COVER
Reproduced from a painting by George A.
Campbell depicting the raising of the Soviet
flag on the roof of the Reichstag just before
midnight on April 30, 1945 (see also pages
238-240).

BACK COVER
Midnight 45 years later. The Unification Flag
is raised outside the Reichstag on October 2,
1990, marking the reunification of the two
Germanys.

FRONTISPIECE
Soviet victory parade in May 1945. In the
background lies the shattered Reichstag,
already a burnt-out shell following the fire in
February 1933.

FRONT ENDPAPER
Wilhelmstrasse: centre of government until
1945. Crowds watch the arrival of Adolf
Hitler at the palace of President Paul von
Hindenburg in 1933.

REAR ENDPAPER
Top racing cars parade in Wilhelmstrasse to
publicise the 1938 Berlin Motor Show.

PART I   PAGES 8–9
Napoleon's triumphal entry into Berlin on
October 27, 1806. From a painting by
Charles Meynier.

PART II   PAGES 40–41
The night of January 30, 1933 — the Third
Reich is born in Germany.

PART III   PAGES 114–115
September 1, 1939 — Hitler announces to
the Reichstag that Germany is at war.

PART IV   PAGES 286–287
Military leaders of the Four Power Allied
Control Council photographed in August
1945 outside its headquarters located in the
Kammergericht on Potsdamer Strasse.

PART V   PAGES 402–403
The parade held on October 7, 1989 to mark
the 40th — and last — anniversary of the
founding of the German Democratic Republic. Troops pass the reviewing stand on Karl-
Marx-Allee.

ACKNOWLEDGEMENTS
The Author would like to thank the follow-
ing for their help and advice:
Ludwig Freiherr and Dorothée Freifrau
von Hammerstein-Equord; Dr Alfred
Kernd'l; the staff of the Landesbildarchiv in
Berlin, and the staff of the Soviet Army
Museum, Karlshorst.
   At the same time, the Editor is indebted to
many organisations and individuals for their
assistance:
   Arno E. Abendroth; Rupert Allason, MP;
E. Russell Anderson, Chief of Public
Affairs, US HQ Berlin; Peter Chamberlain;
Brian L. Davis; Michael Davis; Terry
Gander; Martin Gilbert, CBE; David O.
Hale; Alan Hall, Editor, *Aviation News*;
Peter Hoffmann, McGill University; Major
M. R. P. James and Mervyn Wynne-Jones of
HQ Berlin Infantry Brigade; Specialist Kyle
Lamson; Clifforde Mark; Lieutenant-
Colonel R. W. Obbard; Jean Paul Pallud;
Sabine Preuss and Klaus-Dieter Pett of the
Landesarchiv; Richard Raiber, MD; Dr
Peter Schenk; The Lady Soames, DBE;
Peter Thompson; Bart Vanderveen; Elmar
Widmann and Trevor Wignall.
   Special thanks are extended to Andrew
Mollo for his very generous help in the loan
of research material and photographs from
his extensive Third Reich collection, and to
Roger Freeman, the Eighth Air Force histor-
ian, who also loaned photographs from his
archive. Denis Bateman cast his eagle eye
over the proofs and picked up many points,
and Jan Heitmann helped at the last minute
with comparison photography. Throughout
the whole period of research and production,
Roger Bell has been a staunch ally, carrying
out research and providing support on the
photographic side, joining us in Berlin
shortly before the reunification.

Contents

Berlin — then and now — where even the present-day scene is changing rapidly with the upheaval caused by Unification in October 1990. However, many of the 20th century changes have been politically inspired, both the National Socialists and the Communists seeking to promote their régimes through architectural aggrandisement. The old Schloss — the King's Palace in the city centre — dated back to the 17th century. *Above:* Wilhelm I (1861–88) unveils a monument in front of the palace to his father, Friedrich Wilhelm III (1797–1840), on June 16, 1871, six months after the Prussian victory over France.

As a result of the French defeat at Sedan the previous September, Napoleon III had lost his throne with the declaration of the new French Republic. The Prussians then rubbed salt into the wound by using Napoleon's palace at Versailles for the ceremony to proclaim their King, Wilhelm I, Emperor (or Kaiser) of Germany. Eighty years on, the newly-created German Democratic Republic (GDR) gave orders for the demolition of the castle in 1950 as a political statement to sever ties with Germany's Second Republic. The Communists then used the site to erect their own Palace of the Republic *(opposite).*

Introduction

BERLIN. What visions the word conjures up. For those old enough to remember, it may recall the 'twenties when Berlin was a contrast: of fashionable boulevards and gay abandon on the one hand, and an upheaval of warring political factions on the other.

For others it may be synonymous with the rise of Adolf Hitler whose manoeuverings brought him to the centre of power; a power which became all-pervading after the fortuitous fire in the parliament building — the Reichstag — in February 1933.

The architectural connoisseur may express profound regret at many fine buildings lost in bombing and battle and their aftermath. The fact that the Soviets inherited the old cultural centre of Berlin within their Sector was a double-edged sword, for while much was restored after the war, much was also swept away for ideological reasons.

BERLIN. The 'Big B' for the Eighth Army Air Force in its massive daylight raids carried out with all the scenario and drama of a Cecil B. de Mille extravaganza. For the Royal Air Force it meant the 'Battle of Berlin' as crews fought their way across a thousand miles of hostile territory, through fighters, searchlights and flak — at night to reach a target so often hidden by cloud.

To the Russians it meant the end of the bitter, pitiless war in the East; an awful no-quarter struggle for survival in which man's inhumanity to man reached new depths of depravity on both sides. Then, when they reached the German capital, the Red Army reaped the spoils of war in an orgy of vengeance.

'We have won the German war,' said Field-Marshal Montgomery in his final message to the men of the 21st Army Group. 'Let us now win the peace.' But that peace, as far as Berlin was concerned, was forty-five years in the making as one war was exchanged for another between East and West. In 1948 the skies over Berlin became a battleground once again as new waves of aircraft fought the Soviet blockade — and won.

The Wall will probably remain the long-lasting vision of the city with its inhuman division of lives and property which accentuated the striking differences between the 'haves' in West Berlin and the 'have nots' in the East. It focussed the minds of politicians for decades, from the immortal 'Ich bin ein Berliner' from John F. Kennedy and the shoe-banging of Nikita Kruschev, to the day when the impossible suddenly became possible: the Wall was breached and with it communism crumbled before the astonished eyes of the world.

Ever since I produced the first issue of *After the Battle* way back in 1973, Berlin was always high on our list of priorities. However, to do justice to the story, extensive comparison photography was necessary, but a camera and communism just did not go together as all East European regimes banned photography of things like railway stations and bridges which are part and parcel of our story. I attempted to get round the problem by seeking the assistance of the official East German press agency but, while they were happy to supply 'tourist' type shots, as soon as I asked them to take more specific comparisons for us, they clammed up. Thus there was no alternative but to put the story on the back burner until a breakthrough could be achieved in some way or another.

November 1989 — the turning point for Berliners and much of Eastern Europe — provided the opportunity, and in the following months we paid several visits to the city, spending many days seeking out the 'nows' to set to the 'thens' that we had been collecting for fifteen years. But our concept also changed. *After the Battle* has a simple raison d'être: to depict the battlefields of the Second World War as they are today, but Berlin was somehow different in that the battle in 1945 was only one small part in the overall story. In this instance I felt that more was required of us; that the Berlin story could not just be shoe-horned into 56 pages of one issue of the magazine. And so we set about widening the picture, deciding to illustrate all the meaningful events in the life of a city which has been at the heart of European history for the last 75 years. Thus our story covers the period from the end of the First World War right up to Unification.

Our author, Tony Le Tissier, has served for over twenty years in the British Army and has lived in Berlin for the past sixteen years. He has therefore been in a unique position to study the battle for the city from the military point of view at close quarters, and readers desiring even more detail than is given here are recommended to consult Tony's own book, *The Battle of Berlin 1945*, published in 1988. He is also ideally qualified to write on post-war Berlin, having served in the British Military Government in the city for fourteen years before Unification.

Berlin Then and Now has been a joint effort between Tony Le Tissier and your Editor, and we would both like to record our appreciation to the many official bodies who have assisted us, particularly the British Army for providing the facility of a helicopter flight for aerial photography. It has been a memorable association for us both and we hope you enjoy the result of our two years' work.

WINSTON G. RAMSEY

7

PART I
FROM REICH TO REPUBLIC

Early history

The guide books describe Berlin as lying in a glacier valley on the great plain of the Mark of Brandenburg, but the general impression one gets is of a gently undulating landscape with few significant geographical features other than the waterways.

Berlin was first established during the last third of the 12th century on the north bank of the River Spree at a conveniently narrow crossing point for the overland trade routes and half-way between the waterway controlling the fortresses of Spandau and Köpenick. The twin township of Cölln grew up on the southern bank and was the first to be mentioned in a document, this being dated 1237, the date now celebrated for the foundation of the city of Berlin.

Under the Ascanian Margraves of Brandenburg the two townships flourished as trading centres, exporting rye, wool and oak as far afield as England, and also dealing in hides and furs from the lands to the east.

In 1307 the two towns, faced with increasing insecurity in the area, agreed upon a common alliance in self defence. The local situation in the Mark deteriorated even further with the extinction of the Ascanian dynasty in 1319 and the twin towns turned to membership of the Hanseatic League with the great trading cities like Hamburg and Bremen for security. This ensured their continuing prosperity and a growing political prominence that enabled them to combine with Margrave Frederick of Hohenzollern in subduing the banditry in the

Previous pages: **Napoleon's triumphant entry into Berlin on October 27, 1806. The Brandenburg Gate had been constructed between 1789 and 1791 to a design by Carl Gotthard Langhans. The Quadriga, designed by Johann Gottfried Schadow, was added in 1793. Napoleon had the Quadriga removed to Paris as war booty, but it was returned in triumph in 1814, having meanwhile become a significant symbol in the German wars of liberation. Before the ceremonial unveiling on June 30, 1814, Schinkel modified the charioteer from Irene, Goddess of Peace, to Victoria, Goddess of Victory, equipping her with a spear and the emblem of the Iron Cross in a wreath surmounted by a Prussian eagle. The Gate and its Quadriga were badly damaged during the Second World War (above), and in the 1950s the authorities in the Eastern and Western Sectors surprisingly agreed on a joint venture of restoration. While the GDR saw to the repair of the Gate, the Senate sponsored the casting of a new Quadriga from the original moulds that had been discovered in the city. However, when the Quadriga was replaced in 1956, the East German authorities first removed the Prussian eagle and Iron Cross as unacceptable symbols of militarism (below).**

Mark in 1414. However, as Elector of Brandenburg, Frederick took advantage of internal civic disputes to dissolve the union of the two towns and take over personal control. He then began building his palace in Cölln.

The formation of a sovereign court with its officials and attendants brought a new form of life into the towns, and between 1450 and 1600 the population doubled to 12,000.

The next major change to effect the city was the spread of Lutherism, at first bitterly resisted by the then Elector, Joachim I, but then embraced by his successor, Joachim II, in 1539 at the behest of the councillors of the two towns. The Thirty Years War (1618-48) that ensued in Europe as the adherents of the main religions fought their bloody crusades also extended its miseries to Berlin-Cölln. Occupation by Imperial troops of the Roman Catholic cause, taxation, plague, smallpox and dysentry, all served to devastate the lives of the inhabitants and halve their number.

In 1658 it was decided to fortify the towns, a task that took seven years to complete. Townsfolk and peasants were conscripted to the task of erecting an 80-metre-wide rampart surrounded by a moat and surmounted by an eight-metre wall with 13 bastions and six gates.

To compensate for the loss of population the Great Elector, Friedrich Wilhelm (reigned 1640-88), decided to encourage immigration, offering preferential terms to the French Calvinists, or Huguenots, then fleeing France. Six thousand alone came to Berlin and by 1700 about one Berliner in five was of Huguenot extraction. The Huguenots were to have a profound and lasting impact on Berlin, influencing public life, the armed forces, administration, arts and sciences, language, education and fashion.

In 1618 the Electors of Brandenburg inherited the Duchy of Prussia, then part of the Kingdom of Poland, but were unable to do much about it until 1701, by which time Poland was being ruled by the Elector of Saxony. Elector

In preparation for the 200th anniversary of the inauguration of the Gate, the stonework was renovated and the Quadriga removed for repair following damage caused to it by joyous revellers on December 31, 1989 — the first New Year's Eve following the demise of the Berlin Wall.

Frederick III (1688-1713) then obtained the consent of his peers to crown himself Frederick I, King in Prussia, as opposed to King of Prussia, in return for his promise to help in the impending War of the Spanish Succession (1701-14). Thus Berlin became the royal capital of Brandenburg-Prussia and an important political, economic and cultural centre. The population consequently rose from 29,000 in that year to 172,000 by the end of the century, and by 1850 had reached 428,000.

However, Berlin's vulnerability to attack and invasion remained, and so a fifth to a quarter of these figures represented the military garrison. Frederick Wilhelm I, famous for his regiment of giant grenadiers, was responsible for

founding and enlarging the Prussian Army that was to become such a powerful weapon in his son's hands. As the expanding population could not be contained within the old walls, new suburbs sprang up and eventually a new 14-kilometre-long perimeter wall with 14 gates was completed in 1736 and the old wall demolished.

Nevertheless these measures failed to stop Napoleon's entry on October 27, 1806 through the Brandenburg Gate, whose Quadriga he then had removed to the Louvre in Paris as war booty. Two years of French occupation then followed. The Quadriga was eventually recovered in 1814 and restored to its former position with the addition of an Iron Cross and a Prussian Eagle.

When remounted in July 1991 in time for the anniversary celebrations on August 6, amid considerable controversy, the Goddess of Victory once again held aloft her spear complete with Iron Cross topped with the Prussian eagle.

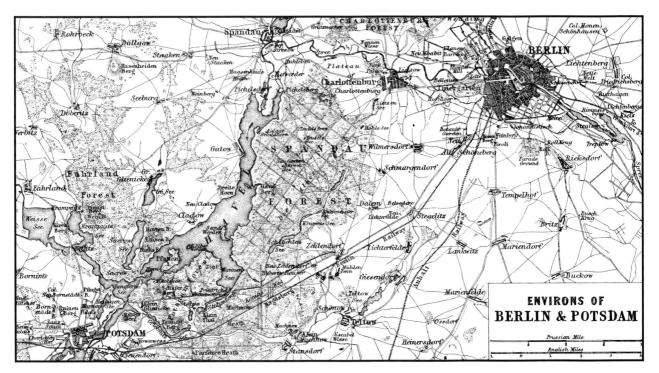

Berlin in 1860 with Potsdam — the true cradle of the Prussian Army — some thirty kilometres to the south-west. It was at Potsdam that Frederick Wilhelm I (1713–40) personally instructed his soldiers on drill and discipline.

The city seen looking westwards in 1886: 1 – The Schloss; 2 – The Dom (Cathedral); 3 – Lustgarten; 4 – Altes Museum; 5 – Zeughaus (armoury); 6 – Krönprinz Palais (Palace of the Crown Prince); 7 – Opera; 8 – French church; 9 – Schauspielhaus (theatre); 10 – New Church; 11 – Palace of Kaiser Wilhelm I; 12 – Königswache (Royal Guard House); 13 – University; 14 – Library; 15 – Brandenburger Tor; 16 – Reichstag (parliament); 17 – Friedrichstrasse station; 18 – Unter den Linden; 19 – Tiergarten; 20 – Charlottenburger Chaussee; 21 – The Siegessäule; 22 – River Spree.

Above: **Prussian parade in the reign of Frederick Wilhelm III. The year is 1835; the place, at the eastern end of Unter den Linden. The building in the centre background is the King's Palace — which later became the Palace of the Crown Prince. The march of the Dragoon Guards and Uhlan Guards (Lancers) has ended by the Zeughaus (on the left).** *Right:* **Even with the demise of the Schloss, the scene has many similarities 150 years later.**

The foundation of the Academy of Arts in 1696 and the Academy of Sciences in 1700 provided a tremendous stimulous to intellectual life. This was continued by Frederick II (Frederick the Great, 1740-86), who made Berlin the focal point in the 'Age of Enlightenment'. This era saw the founding of such landmarks as the Charité Hospital (1726), the Supreme Court, now the Berlin Museum (1735), and the Opera House (1740).

This picture was taken in front of the Königswache (later renamed the Neue Wache) built in 1816–18. Following the victory in the Franco-Prussian War, a large cannon, 'La belle Joséphine', was brought from Fort Mont Valérien and displayed alongside. At the same time, the interior of the Zeughaus in the background was altered and reopened as the Hall of Fame of the Prussian Army. After the Second World War when the Zeughaus was gutted, it became the GDR's Museum of German History but is now the home of the German Historical Museum whose outlook is somewhat different!

The view from the opposite side of the street. On the left the eastern wing of the Friedrich-Wilhelm University, the Königs-wache, with the dome of the Cathedral showing above the Zeughaus. Part of the Royal Palace can be seen on the far right across the Schloss Bridge with the clock tower of the Rotes Rathaus showing above. (The name 'Red Town Hall' was in use long before the Communists took it over in 1945 and is simply indicative of its red-brick construction.) The statues on either side of the Guard House are of Graf Bülow von Dennewitz, Prussian general and military theorist of the late 18th century, and the General Gerhard von Scharnhorst who distinguished himself in campaigns in the 1790s against French Revolutionary forces.

The 18th century also saw Berlin prosper under state promotion and protection, particularly with regard to wool and silk processing. By the turn of the century the industrial revolution was beginning with the installation of steam engines, and the opening of the Royal Iron Foundry. By the 1830s numerous machine tool factories had been opened and then the Customs Union of 1834 enabled the construction of railways, linking the various parts of Germany to

We took the comparison on October 3, 1990 — the Tag der Einheit or Day of Unification when Berliners turned out in their tens of thousands to celebrate the reunification of the two Germanys. Only the lamp-posts have changed, with the Royal Palace replaced by the modern structure of the Volkskammer (the GDR parliament) — immediately closed upon Unification because of asbestos contamination. The television tower on Alexanderplatz is another modern intrusion. In 1949, the University acquired the new title of Humboldt after its founders, Wilhelm and Alexander von Humboldt, and to distinguish it from the post-WWII Free and Technical Universities founded in the western sectors of the city.

Both statues survived the destruction of World War II, but they were later removed by the East German authorities. Bülow has since disappeared, but Scharnhorst was re-erected across the road in the small park beside the Opera House, joining three Prussian field-marshals: Graf Yorck von Wartenburg, Gebhard von Blücher and Graf Neidhardt von Gneisenau.

As a powerful European nation with a highly effective conscript army, Prussia extended its territory to the east under Frederick the Great with gains from Austria in 1740 and Poland in 1772, 1793 and 1795. Much of the latter, along with other territory, was lost following Prussia's defeat at the hands of Napoleon in 1807. However, the final victory over Napoleonic France led to the Congress of Vienna restoring many of Prussia's former holdings. Thereafter Prussia rivalled Austria as one of the two leading states of the German confederation. Seeking unification in Prussia's favour, Prime Minister, or Chancellor, Otto von Bismarck sought a showdown with Austria which came to a head in the Seven Weeks War of 1866. Prussian ascendancy was assured following victory in the Battle of Königgrätz on July 3. *Above:* This is the disbandment parade of the Royal Prussian Cadet Corps on March 9, 1920 at the barracks at Lichterfelde to the south of the city centre (see map page 20).

As we shall see in a later chapter, these barracks were destined to become the home of Adolf Hitler's own praetorian guard, the Leibstandarte-SS, but today it is American forces who hold sway at what is now Andrews Barracks.

the hub of Berlin. The industrial revolution reached its peak between 1850 and 1870 with over a thousand new factories in Berlin alone, and the waterways were extended by canals to facilitate the heavy goods traffic involved. (A century later these same waterways were still carrying 40 per cent of West Berlin's goods traffic.)

However, the political background was not so harmonious. Attempts at social reform were ignored and in March 1848 fighting broke out in the streets between the citizens and the troops causing the King to agree to granting the freedom of the press, the rights of association, assembly and vote, and for a popular militia to be raised. But the King's supporters were against this and by the end of the year the National Assembly had been dispersed and martial law introduced.

The population continued to increase, reaching 826,000 by 1871, tens of thousands being either homeless or crammed into barrack-like tenements, many of which can still be found in the poorer parts of the city, with up to six shaft-like inner courts one behind the other.

These wretched conditions did not improve when Berlin became capital of the Second German Reich in 1871 with Wilhelm I as the new Kaiser after the defeat of France in the Franco-Prussian War. The city's population continued to grow to over two million by 1905 and yet government was still imposed from above and voices in the Reichstag ignored as of no consequence, for the system of government instituted by Bismarck placed all the power in the hands of the Kaiser and the ministers he appointed. The people's elected deputies in the Reichstag, or lower parliament, were only empowered to approve legislation and the military budget, and even that representation was so arranged that the rural constituencies outweighed the urban ones, whose deputies were often socialists too tainted with Marxism to suit the regime.

On September 2, 1873, the third anniversary of the Battle of Sedan, a mighty Victory Monument — the Siegessäule — was erected on a parade ground originally laid out by Frederick Wilhelm I just west of the Brandenburg Gate on the northern side of the Charlottenburger Chaussee (see page 12). In 1864 the parade ground had been renamed the Königsplatz (King's Square) and the 200-foot column designed by Johann Strack was topped by a 48-foot gilded figure of Victory by Friedrich Drake. Sixty captured Danish, Austrian and French cannon were mounted in three rows of flutings around the column. Four relief panels were inlaid in bronze around the square pedestal portraying Prussian victories. On the east face a scene depicted victory in the Danish War of 1864, and to the north the 1867 Battle of Königgrätz. The Battle of Sedan in 1870 and the triumphal entry into Paris was mounted on the western side, while the return of the troops to Berlin in 1871 faced south (illustrated above left). This was the direction in which the figure of Victory was orientated to look out along a Victory Avenue (the Siegesallee) which in 1889–1901 was adorned with 32 marble statues of Prussian heroes (right).

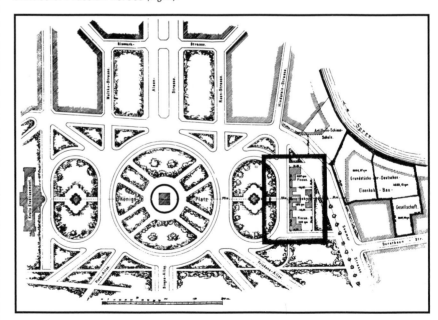

The Königgrätz victory paved the way for the establishment of a German house of representatives or parliament and this was inaugurated on February 5 the following year in the White Salon of the Schloss. A provisional home for the Reichstag was found at the Herrenhaus (see map page 21) located at Number 3 Leipziger Strasse, while moves were made to find a more suitable permanent location. Considerable debate ensued as to whether to use an existing building or construct a purpose-built one; meanwhile the Reichstag moved to other temporary quarters along the street at Number 75 in March 1871 and Number 4 later that year. The arguments rumbled on for ten years before agreement was finally reached to build on the east side of the Königsplatz on a site then occupied by the Raczinsky Palace.

The choice of a suitable location was only the first problem. Numerous designs for the actual building were submitted, considered and rejected before Paul Wallot's winning submission in the Italian Renaissance style was agreed. The foundation stone was laid on June 9, 1884 by Kaiser Wilhelm I four years before his death. When completed in 1894 the building measured 430 feet in width, 290 feet in depth and 225 feet to the tip of the imperial crown on top of the glass dome. Although von Bismarck never entered the new building, his memory was enshrined in a monument erected in 1901 between the Reichstag-Gebäude (literally Hall of the Imperial Diet) and the Siegessäule. The picture *above* was taken from the observation platform at the top. That *below* shows the Königsplatz in 1929 as photographed from Zeppelin LZ 127.

What Whitehall is to Great Britain, so Wilhelmstrasse was to Germany. At the turn of the century not only was the street considered the most aristocratic quarter of the city, it was also dubbed 'Diplomatstrasse' due to the number of official buildings located there. In this view looking south from the top end near Unter den Linden, the British Embassy at No. 70 on the right seems to be sporting an advertisement for the Hotel Adlon which lay to its rear fronting the Pariser Platz just east of the Brandenburg Gate. No. 72 was the Palace of Prince George of Prussia; No. 73 the office of the Minister of the Household with the Reichsamt des Innern at No. 74. Opposite the Ministry of the Interior was the Justice Ministry at No. 65 with the Privy Council at No. 64 and the Ministry of State at No. 63. On the right-hand side next to the Interior Ministry lay the Foreign Office at Nos. 75–76, with the Chancellery at No. 77 and Palace of the Prince of Pless at No. 78.

Today only the former Ministry of State building remains on the left, the line of palatial buildings on the right having been replaced by the GDR government with blocks of prestige apartments.

No. 77 Wilhelmstrasse — the 'old' Chancellery (Reichskanzlei) as it became after 1939 — looking rather sorry for itself in 1945.

Midway along the Wilhemstrasse, at the crossroad with Voss-strasse, lay the Wilhelmplatz. *Above:* In this view we are looking east across the square and down Mohrenstrasse. The building on the left is the Kur & Neumärkische Haupt-Ritterschafts-Direction with the Hotel Kaiserhof opposite. Above the hotel roof, the top of the Church of the Trinity (Dreifaltigkeits-Kirche) can just be seen. The square was originally landscaped with gardens adorned by the statues of six heroes from the Silesian wars of Frederick the Great. *Left:* In 1945 Allied troops found the square only a shadow of its former glory and by 1975 *(below left)* the Kaiserhof had been demolished and replaced by a modern block. *Below right:* The Czechoslovakian Embassy was then built on the southern portion of the Wilhelmplatz and by 1990 flats covered the square on its northern side. The entrance to the underground railway system — the U-Bahn — remains although the station name was later changed from Wilhelmplatz to Kaiserhof. Currently it is Otto-Grotewohl-Strasse.

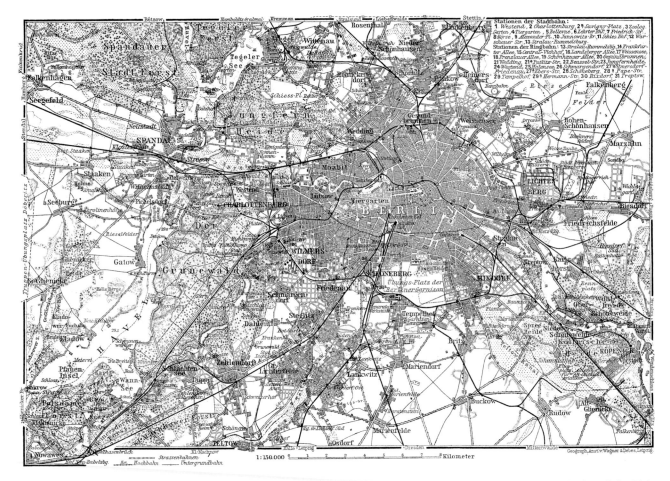

Stationen der Stadtbahn: 1 Westend, 2 Charlottenburg, 3 Zoolog. Garten, 4 Tiergarten, 5 Bellevue, 6 Lehrter Bhf, 7 Friedrich-Str. 8 Börse, 9 Alexander-Pl., 10 Jannowitz-Br., 11 Schles. Bhf, 12 Warschauer-Str., 13 Stralau-Rummelsburg.
Stationen der Ringbahn: 13 Stralau-Rummelsbg, 14 Frankfurter Allee, 15 Central-Viehhof, 16 Landsberger Allee, 17 Weissensee, 18 Prenzlauer Allee, 19 Schönhauser Allee, 20 Gesundbrunnen, 21 Wedding, 21ᵃ Putlitz-Str. 22 Beussel-Str.23 Jungfernheide, 24 Westend, 25 Halensee, 26 Schmargendorf, 27 Wilmersdorf-Friedenau, 27ᵃ Ebers-Str, 28 Schöneberg, 28ᵃ Pape-Str. 29 Tempelhof, 29ᵃ Hermann-Str, 30 Rixdorf, 31 Treptow.

The U-Bahn underground railway (which, just to confuse the issue, also has above-ground elevated sections) was built by Siemens & Halske, founded by Werner Siemens, the inventor of the electric tram. The street trams provided yet another means of transport run by the Grosse Berliner Strassenbahn Aktien Gesellschaft running on tramlines usually sited down the centre of main roads. The trams were discontinued in the western part of the city after WWII but still run in the east.

The public transportation systems at the beginning of the 20th century also included the Stadtbahn (the city railway, usually abbreviated to S-Bahn and not to be confused with the Strassenbahn) which was constructed in 1874–82 and linked into the Ringbahn built in 1867–77. The S-Bahn had four lines of rails of which two were shared by mainline trains which had their own separate termini or 'Bahnhof': Anhalter, Potsdamer, Lehrter, Stettiner and Görlitzer.

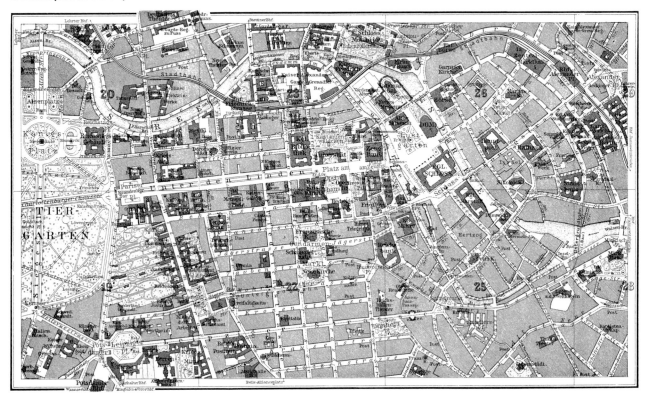

The Prussian War Ministry *(above)* lay on Leipziger Strasse next to the Herrenhaus. Its garden extended for several hundred yards to the south beyond the Museum of Industrial Arts and Crafts (Kunst-Museum) erected in 1877–81 on Prinz-Albrecht-Strasse. *Below left:* The wall to the War Office garden provided an effective barrier across the road until the Abgeordnetenhaus, or Prussian Chamber of Deputies, was built facing the museum on the opposite side of the street in 1893–98. The War Office could then no longer maintain its stubborn defence of its property and the road was driven through to link Königgrätzer Strasse (renamed Saarland Strasse during the Third Reich period but now changed to Stresemannstrasse) to Wilhelmstrasse. The map shows the situation in 1913. *Below right:* After WWII, the boundary between the Soviet and American Sectors ran along the southern side of the street and, when the East Germans decided to erect the Berlin Wall in 1961, Prinz-Albrecht-Strasse was blocked yet again — but in this case longitudinally! (See also page 27.)

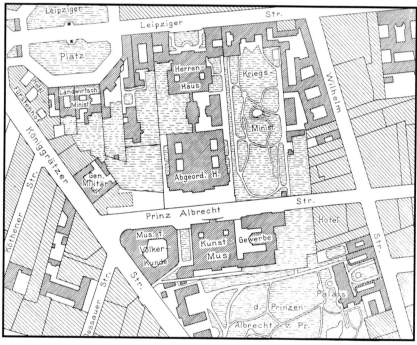

For hundreds of years, Britain and the German states had been at peace — in fact at Waterloo German forces had fought alongside the British. The British Crown was closely entwined with that of Germany, King George I, who came to the British throne in 1714, being Hanoverian. This bond had been reinforced in the 19th century when Queen Victoria's eldest daughter married the future Emperor Frederick III. Their son, Wilhelm II *(left)*, of a British mother and German father, had become Emperor in 1888 at the age of 29 and was impatient to promote Germany to the status of a world power. Young and headstrong, he quickly alienated his Chancellor, von Bismarck, who resigned in 1890. The German Reichstag was still subservient to the will of the Emperor and the current Kaiser was imbued with the image of the Prussian warrior king. His ambitions were undoubtedly fired by the immense power of his grandmother's empire on which, it was said, the sun never set. With possessions spread around the globe, and the most powerful navy in the world, Britain was the example to which he aspired. When Queen Victoria died in 1901, her son, Edward VII, was welcomed on a state visit to Berlin in 1909 *(right)*.

The origins of the First World War were many and would take several pages to describe in detail. At this distance in time they appear all the more petty, especially bearing in mind Wilhelm's desire for a close bond with Britain. However, Britain looked more to its Empire than to Europe and sought 'splendid isolation' rather than commitments on the Continent. This was a time when mutual assistance treaties were all the rage, and a series of agreements, some secret, were concluded by Germany, Austria-Hungary, Italy, Russia and France. By 1914, although Britain was more friendly with her natural enemy, France, than Germany, she had little interest in European squabbles, and when the heir to the Austro-Hungarian throne was assassinated that June in Bosnia, Britain had no concern over the goings-on in a minor Balkan state. Russia and France were quickly involved due to their cross-guarantees of mutual aid, but these agreements did not obligate Great Britain to take any set course of action. On July 31, Germany sent an ultimatum to Russia to halt their mobilisation, and a demand to France to keep out of any war between Germany and Russia. *Left:* Anxious Berliners sit on the steps of the cathedral facing the Lustgarten on August 1. Ever since their victory over France in 1871, Germans had feared a return match: Will it be peace . . . or war? *Right:* Only recently released from the yoke of communism, the Dom presents a sad face to the world in 1991.

Above: The crossroads at Unter den Linden and Friedrich-strasse. Throughout the years this has been the pulsating centre of social life in Berlin, where Kranzler's coffee shop and the Hotel Bauer with its café were world-famous. *Below:* The Grand Hotel, with its internal reconstruction of 'Café Bauer' imitating the splendour of the original lost during the post-WWII years, was opened in 1987 in time for the 750th anniversary of the founding of Berlin.

And it was here that these crowds were pictured watching the Army march off to war. When both Russia and France ignored the German ultimatum, Germany mobilised her forces against both countries and entered Luxembourg on August 2, demanding of Belgium — which had declared her neutrality — free passage. Having declared war against Russia on August 1, on August 3 Germany did likewise against France and later that day crossed into Belgium. Now Britain was involved because of the guarantee she had given to defend Belgium's neutrality, and war was declared against Germany on August 4. Eventually, the whole world became involved as one declaration followed another: Austria-Hungary against Russia on August 5; Serbia against Germany the following day; Montenegro (a Balkan state) against Austria-Hungary on August 7; France against Austria-Hungary on August 10. Two days later Britain declared war against Austria-Hungary; Japan came in against Germany on August 23, Austria-Hungary reciprocating against Japan on the 25th and against Belgium on August 28. Russia declared war on Turkey on November 1. During the next three years, many other nations entered the fight: Italy was persuaded to join the Allies in return for the promise of Austro-Hungarian territory. Greece was drawn in during 1916, as was Rumania, the United States declaring war in 1917 together with Liberia and China. By July 1918, a host of others including Costa Rica, Cuba, Brazil, Guatemala, Haiti, Honduras and Nicaragua were all at war against Germany.

Like many wars, the original motives of the First World War got lost along the way, although the British laid the blame for starting it fairly and squarely on Kaiser 'Bill'. As the war ground on, Wilhelm divorced himself more and more from everyday life, spending much time at the German HQ at Spa in Belgium and at the front. Germany fell increasingly under the control of its military leaders and by 1918 the monarchy was so discredited that he was forced to abdicate, finding asylum in the Netherlands where he died in June 1941.

Surprisingly the military budget required upon the outbreak of war in 1914 was almost unanimously approved in a spirit of patriotism, for the deputies believed this was for the defence of the realm. But as the war progressed and the real power passed into the hands of General Erich Ludendorff, Generalfeldmarschall Paul von Hindenburg's Chief-of-Staff, who expected even the Imperial Chancellor to comply with his instructions, dissatisfaction and disillusionment grew as it became more and

Within Germany, unrest surfaced as early as January 1915 when a member of the German Social Democrats (SPD), Karl Liebknecht *(left)*, spoke out in the Reichstag against the war. Liebknecht's father, Wilhelm, had joined the Communist League back in the 1850s in London and had led German socialism in the latter part of the century. When Wilhelm died in 1900, Karl, 29 years old, took up his father's mantle, entering the Reichstag as a deputy in 1912. However, in 1916 Liebknecht was expelled from the SPD party for his outspoken views, a move which resulted in him joining forces with a like-minded 35-year-old woman of Polish birth, Rosa Luxemburg, to promote the socialist cause. Together they formed the underground Spartacus League (Spartakusbund) to disseminate their views against the war. On May 1, 1916, in a May Day demonstration in the Potsdamer Platz — one of the busiest and bustling corners of Berlin — Liebknecht addressed the crowd from the terrace of the Café Josty *(above)*.

more obvious both that Germany was fighting a war of aggression and that the country could not stand the strain of maintaining such large armies in the field.

The Russian Revolution inspired considerable unrest among the workers in Germany, and in January, 1918, 400,000 Berlin ammunition workers went on strike demanding more food and a speedy end to the war. Ludendorff concluded that he should go over to the attack before the Americans arrived in Europe in strength, and his Spring Offensive nearly carried the day before it petered out in July. In September the Allies counter-attacked, remorselessly pushing the Germans back. Ludendorff called for a temporary armistice with a view to obtaining a breathing space in which a favourable peace treaty could be negotiated, failing which war would be resumed. Thus, early on the morning of Saturday, November 9, 1918, a German delegation was apprised of the terms for an armistice in a railway carriage in the Forest of Compiègne, which called on the Germans to quit France and retire behind the Rhine. This retirement was carried out by the German Army in

excellent order, but the rear areas were already heavily infected with the revolutionary virus and morale in the armed forces began to crack. By that Saturday, the revolution that had begun five days earlier in the fleet at Kiel had spread to

Berlin. Kaiser Wilhelm II, who had so rashly led his country to war, abdicated the same day when it was discovered that even his own bodyguards were no longer trustworthy. He departed for exile in the Netherlands.

His slogan was simple: 'Down with the war, down with the government,' a stance which quickly led to his trial and imprisonment for the duration. Charges were also trumped up against Rosa Luxemburg and she too was sent to prison. *Above:* Although we are jumping ahead somewhat in our story, it is too good an opportunity to miss including this comparison of Soviet tanks enforcing Liebknecht's words of wisdom on the self-same spot on Potsdamer Platz in June 1953. The final irony: the infuriated demonstrators have set fire to information stands set up by the SED — the Communist government party in East Berlin!

Official moves for a cessation of hostilities had surfaced early in 1916 when the United States offered to mediate between the belligerents. However, the process was slow and, in the interim, Generalfeldmarschall Paul von Hindenburg, the German Chief of Staff, supported by General Erich Ludendorff, announced the 'Hindenburgprogramm' for all-out military victory. Both Britain and Germany presented each other with offers of peace, but the terms were so unacceptable to both sides that it was a foregone conclusion that they would be rejected. Unrestricted submarine warfare followed, precipitating the entry of the United States to the conflict. Not until October 1918 was Germany forced to ask for a cease-fire, although her forces were far from beaten on the field of battle. Hindenburg and Ludendorff merely wanted a breathing space to regroup on a reduced front, and were quite prepared to continue the war when the Allied terms for an armistice appeared more like a demand for unconditional surrender. However, events on the home front cut the ground from beneath their feet with the German public calling for an end to hostilities. Even worse, sailors at Kiel openly refused to take the High Seas Fleet out for a final, decisive battle against the Royal Navy. What began as a mutiny quickly developed into armed insurrection and within days open revolution swept across Germany. When the German delegation met the Allies at Compiègne they were unable to negotiate from a position of strength, and the armistice was signed two days later (left).

In Berlin, the Reichstag members had been surprised by the request for an armistice, not having been informed how close the armies were to collapse. Now, with the abdication of the Kaiser, the leader of the largest political party, Friedrich Ebert of the Socialist Party (SPD), suddenly found himself pushed forward to take over the Chancellorship from the imperial incumbent. So it came about that on that same fateful November 9, his colleague, Philipp Scheidemann, announced Ebert's appointment as Chancellor to a crowd assembled outside the Reichstag and then impetuously cried: 'Long live the great German republic!' Ebert would have preferred a constitutional monarchy, but the die was now cast.

Later that day Karl Liebknecht of the Communist-inspired Spartacus League proclaimed a 'Free Socialist Republic' from a balcony of the Royal Palace, by then occupied by revolutionary sailors, but government troops were shortly able to stifle this attempt to seize power on Soviet lines.

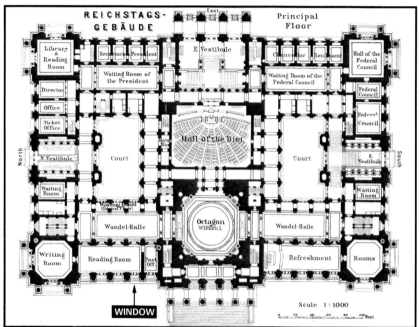

On October 3, Prince Max of Baden had been appointed Chancellor of a new coalition government, one of his first acts being to grant an amnesty to political prisoners. Karl Liebknecht was released and he immediately began to capitalise on recent events to try to foment a German revolution on the lines of the Bolshevik one the previous November. With the abdication of the Kaiser on November 9, Prince Max handed over the Chancellorship to Friedrich Ebert of the Social Democrat Party, and at 2.00 p.m. Philipp Scheidemann proclaimed the new German Republic from the Reichstag.

The interesting exhibition of political and industrial items, 'Questions of German History', to be found in the northern part of the Reichstag, surprisingly failed to indicate the window within it from which Scheidemann made his momentous announcement until only very recently. But now a newly erected plaque confirms our research into this matter as indicated above, and is located inside roughly where the partition wall dividing the Reading Room from the Post Office used to be. (The plan dates from 1910 and shows the building before the post World War II reconstruction.)

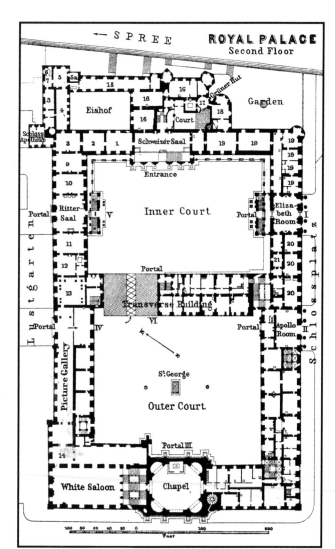

ROYAL PALACE
Second Floor

The Weimar Republic

The ensuing period of the Weimar Republic, was an unhappy, turbulent time for the city and Germany as a whole.

The first task of the new republic was to make peace, an incredibly difficult task against a background of domestic revolution and with a dominant officer corps that did not accept that they had been defeated, still felt they owed their allegiance to the Kaiser, and had nothing but contempt for the politicians now having to try to govern the shattered country.

The peace terms when eventually presented on May 7, 1919, were both outrageous and impractical. However, the German delegation had no option but to accept them, and the treaty was signed in the Hall of Mirrors at Versailles on June 28, 1919. The General Staff had taken no part in either this or the preceding armistice agreement and so they were able to create the myth of the 'Stab in the Back', implying that they would not have lost the war or accepted such dishonourable terms had it not been for the Socialist-Marxist politicians at home. The ensuing widespread condemnation of the Versailles Treaty was one of the major factors that led to the creation of Nazi Germany.

As Philipp Scheidemann was announcing the new German Republic at the Reichstag, just a mile away to the east Karl Liebknecht was proclaiming his own Free Socialist Republic at the Schloss. He had been given a rapturous welcome on his release from prison just over two weeks before by his Spartacus supporters who had planned a general strike in Berlin for November 9. Soldiers' councils had already taken over their barracks and the police headquarters, and a red flag was already flying over the Schloss when Liebknecht arrived. His vantage point was the balcony above Doorway Four (Portal IV on plan) overlooking the Lustgarten (the same doorway visible on the right of the picture on page 6). *Right:* To give them their due, the post-WWII Communist regime was mindful of history when it suited their style. Before demolishing the Royal Palace, the whole of Portal IV was carefully dismantled and built into the façade of the Staatsratsgebäude, the official seat of the head of state of the GDR, constructed on the southern side of the new Marx-Engels Platz facing the Palace of the Republic. Its most recent incumbent, since deposed: Erich Honecker.

These terms included the loss of all the German colonies, as well as Alsace-Lorraine and some frontier districts to France and Belgium; large areas in the East to the re-emergent nation of Poland, including Danzig as a 'free city'; a plebiscite to be held in Silesia to determine between German and Polish sovereignty, and the coal-mining area of the Saar to be placed under French protection for a minimum of 15 years to compensate for the destruction of the French coal-mining industry. The army, the Reichswehr, was to be cut to 100,000 men and deprived of all offensive weaponry, the air force eliminated and the navy reduced to impotence. Further, as a guarantee of compliance, the Allies would be able to occupy parts of the Rhineland for at least 15 years.

Devastating as these conditions appeared, German industry soon began to recover. Despite a temporary setback in 1923, within four years the gross national product had already exceeded that of 1913.

However, it was the resulting political demoralisation within the country that was to cause the greatest damage. Those moderates that might have supported the republic were now easily swayed against it. Of particular consequence was the 'war guilt' that the Allied-dictated terms foisted on the Germans and which the latter did their best to refute.

To crush the revolutionary forces now threatening the city and the republic, the new Defence Minister in Ebert's government used volunteer units raised

Von Hindenburg was still head of the army, an army which felt it had not been defeated but merely betrayed by events in Berlin and elsewhere. Having called the shots for two years, von Hindenburg was hardly going to resign like the Kaiser, and Friedrich Ebert quickly received a telephone call from army headquarters at Spa in Belgium. Von Hindenburg's Quartermaster-General, Wilhelm Groener, was on the line. The question was, would the new government be prepared to protect Germany againt anarchy and restore order. When assured by Ebert that it was, Groener replied that the High Command would therefore maintain discipline, deal with the mutinous sailors and the soldiers' councils, and the officer corps would co-operate in the suppression of Bolshevism. Thus a secret pact was struck by the army to preserve military power.

by the General Staff and paid for by the Prussian War Ministry. These Freikorps were usually the remains of famous regiments led by officers violently opposed to the revolution and contemptuous of the government. The extreme left-wing Spartacus uprising in Berlin in January 1919 was brutally repressed by Freikorps units, whose methods were violent and led to many atrocities, including political assassinations. However, when the Freikorps backed the extreme right-wing so-called Kapp Putsch in March 1920, the Berlin trade unions were able to call a general strike that soon restored the situation.

Despite all this turbulence, the future of Berlin was significantly advanced at this time by the decision of the Prussian government to reorganise Berlin as a metropolis. In 1920, seven other towns and 59 villages were merged into Greater Berlin, which was then divided into the 20 districts or boroughs that still form the basis of the city administration today. This gave Berlin a population approaching four million, and made it the second largest city in Europe.

However, it was because of the prevalent danger in the city that it was decided to convene the new National Assembly on February 6, 1919, in the little town of Weimar, some hundred miles south of Berlin, where it could more easily be protected.

For a few days both republics — those of Ebert and Liebknecht — existed side by side but, after the armistice came into effect, the anti-war aims of the Spartacus League began to lose their meaning. In December, a congress of German workers' and soldiers' councils was held in the Prussian Chamber of Deputies (the Abgeordnetenhaus — see map page 21) which led to the decision to form the German Communist Party from January 1. Its founder members were Karl Liebknecht, Rosa Luxemburg, released from prison and now editing the party's newspaper *Der Rote Fahne* (The Red Flag), and Wilhelm Pieck. Here Liebknecht addresses members of the Spartakusbund and the Group of Revolutionary Shop Stewards crowding the Prinz-Albrecht-Strasse at the opening of the conference on December 16.

Our comparisons are taken a year apart to illustrate the demolition of the wall and to show how a section has been left for preservation. *Above:* August 1990 and *below right* October 1991.

The view in the opposite direction where we see the corner of the Industrial Arts Museum (page 21) on the right. The road of course now runs right through. The building in the left background is the museum's school building constructed between 1901 and 1905. It will reappear later in our story under new masters — the Gestapo!

27

Under the terms of the armistice, German forces had just 31 days to evacuate France, Belgium, Luxembourg and the Rhineland (which was due to be occupied by the Allies until 1930–35). Although Berlin was spared the ignominy of a victory parade, as had been inflicted on Paris in 1871, or the removal of the Quadriga again as in 1806, Germany lost Alsace-Lorraine which had been incorporated into the German Empire for nearly 50 years. By Christmas 1918 some two million soldiers had been brought home, a huge body of dispirited and disillusioned men highly susceptible to the political storm then sweeping Germany. Many of the officers, out of a job and lacking purpose, formed themselves into volunteer groups, called the Freikorps, to be used to restore law and order. With all the weapons of war at their disposal, 'Free Corps Law' was ruthless and bloody, and the streets of Berlin were turned into a battlefield.

Above: This armoured car is at the top end of Oranienburger Strasse in an area which is, or rather was, part of East Berlin — hence the tram lines in our comparison *below.* Linienstrasse lies on the right.

Having so successfully masterminded his own revolution, Lenin was already exasperated by the pussyfooting of his German Communist comrades, commenting that 'they would not even storm a railway station unless they had bought a platform ticket first'. Although the Spartacists could claim control of public utilities, transportation and the like, not until the chief of police was dismissed on January 3 by the government did Liebknecht act. Now openly calling themselves Communists, the call went out for a mass demonstration and general strike for Monday the 6th. However, although upwards of 200,000 supporters massed in central Berlin, there was no clear plan of action as Liebknecht was still in closed conference with his Revolutionary Council, arguing as to how they should best go about seizing power. The prerequisite of any revolution is normally the take-over of government buildings, and finally Liebknecht ordered a column of naval mutineers who were supporting the Communist cause to enter the army's General Staff office on the northwestern corner of the Königsplatz *(top)*. However, when the sailors reached the building the situation became farcical, confirming all Lenin's beliefs. When the naval petty officer in charge presented the duty officer with a typed statement from the Revolutionary Council, after scrutinising the document the officer pointed out that it was not signed. True to his military training, the petty officer agreed that the document was invalid without a signature and promptly turned his men about! Probably the best-known image of the period was taken from the best vantage-point of all — the top of the Brandenburg Gate *(right)*. However, accounts conflict as to which side these particular soldiers belong, as military men in uniform were part and parcel of Liebknecht's uprising.

With arms and ammunition freely available to the demonstrators, it was a nightmare situation for the fledgling Ebert government which was bound to lead to armed confrontation. Factory workers and soldiers supporting Liebknecht marched on the newspaper district of Berlin, taking over the offices of the SPD newspaper *Vorwärts* (Forwards) at No. 3 Lindenstrasse. Barricades were set up ready to do battle and the Freikorps were pleased to oblige. On January 11, hundreds of troops descended on the area equipped with field guns, mortars, machine guns and flame-throwers. Even though the outcome was a foregone conclusion, nevertheless 400-odd Spartacists gave a good account of themselves. In the end, Freikorps troops managed to assault the building and get inside under the cover of smoke, capturing 390 of the defenders. Today the site of the *Vorwarts* building has been lost as the configuration of the streets has changed (see page 154).

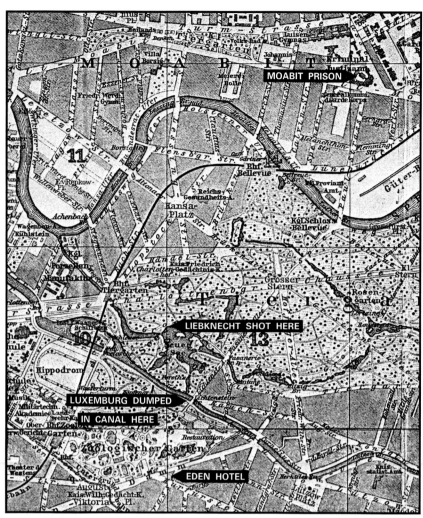

MOABIT PRISON

LIEBKNECHT SHOT HERE

LUXEMBURG DUMPED
IN CANAL HERE

EDEN HOTEL

With the failure to capture important government buildings, and the abortive stand at the *Vorwärts* offices, the Spartacus 'putsch' came to an end. Karl Liebknecht and Rosa Luxemburg went into hiding but were soon hunted down by the Freikorps. They were discovered at the home of a sympathetic businessman, Siegfried Markussohn, on January 15 and taken to the headquarters of the Cavalry Guards Division temporarily located in the Eden Hotel on the Kurfürstendamm for interrogation. Hauptmann Waldemar Pabst then ordered that the two prisoners were to be taken to Moabit prison but that they were to be shot en route on the pretext of trying to escape.

Liebknecht was driven away in the leading vehicle and into the unlit Tiergarten. On the northern side of the large lake (the Neuer See) a breakdown was staged and the car ran to a halt. Liebknecht was ordered out and promptly shot. *Above:* The location of the murder became a Communist shrine, being formally marked with a memorial in 1987 *(right).*

As she was being escorted from the Eden, Rosa Luxemburg was knocked unconscious with a rifle butt before being bundled into the back of the car. Although this set off following the lead vehicle containing Liebknecht, she was shot inside the car within a hundred yards of the hotel and her body dumped into the Landwehr Canal from the Lichtenstein Bridge. *Above:* This picture of the hotel was taken several years later after the part of the Kurfürstendamm on which it stood had been renamed Budapester Strasse. After the Second World War what was left of the Eden was expunged from the map when a realignment of the junction with Kurfürsten Strasse cut through the island site. The map extract *(right)* shows the original location, and the overlay the modern road layout. *Below:* In concert with the memorial erected to Karl Liebknecht, a plaque and bronze name panel were placed beside the Lichtenstein Bridge in 1987. The deaths of the two founders of the German Communist Party, just fifteen days after it had been born, was a severe setback, yet causes thrive on martyrs and their murder inspired others to rally to the flag. Chancellor Ebert was horrified when he heard of the killings, yet the perpetrators were dealt with lightly — only one serving a few months in prison for 'attempted manslaughter'.

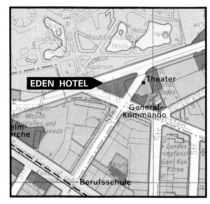

With the Communist threat temporarily averted, Chancellor Ebert called for an immediate general election and, instead of Berlin, chose Weimar, 200 kilometres away to the south-west, as the venue for the new National Constituent Assembly. It was hoped that the little town would be easier to defend against reactionaries and reasonably isolated to avoid the spill-over from the street confrontations which had swept the country. Although the result was a landslide for the SPD, proportional representation meant that the party did not have a working majority. On February 11, the new Assembly elected Friedrich Ebert for a seven-year term as President, with sweeping dictatorial powers, and Philipp Scheidemann as his Reichs Chancellor. Through all its ups and downs, the new 'Weimar Republic' was to last for just fourteen turbulent years.

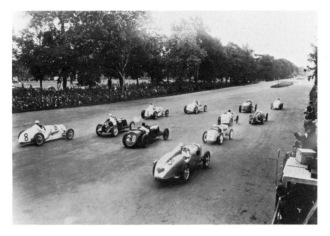

Back in Berlin, let us break from political strife for a moment to savour the beginning of what later would become known in the capital as the 'Goldene Zwanziger' — Berlin's Golden Twenties'. One of the era's earliest pleasures was the 'AVUS' — the Automobilvekehrs und Übungsstrasse, opened in 1920. *Left:* At the time it was the longest motor racing and test track in the world — the twin 8-metre tracks running virtually dead straight for 20 kilometres with loops at either end. It had been first mooted as far back as 1909 until the war interrupted plans, but when completed in September 1920 it was still Germany's first race-track. The first race that year was won at a speed of 129 kph (80 mph). *Right:* The Roaring Twenties having given way to the Motorway Nineties, the AVUS is now part of Berlin's autobahn network — as much a race-track as it ever was! The stand still survives and the road is still closed for the occasional race.

Start of the Grand International Motor Race on May 21, 1933.

That year, 1920, also saw another attempt to seize power, this time by right-wing elements in the army. The 'Kapp Putsch' had its origins in the punitive terms demanded by the Allies at the Peace Conference at Versailles the previous May. Scheidemann and his government resigned rather than agree to the onerous conditions, but his successor, Mathias Erzberger, took a more pragmatic view in the knowledge that 'there was a world of difference between signing and fulfilling an agreement'. The French took the opportunity to turn the tables once again by holding the signing ceremony in the Hall of Mirrors where Prussia had proclaimed the Second Reich fifty years earlier. The Germans' outrage was compounded on February 3, 1920 when the Allies published their list of 900 names, including General-feldmarschall von Hindenburg, the ex-Crown Prince and two of his brothers, all of whom were to be surrendered for trial as war criminals. The Kapp Putsch was led by Hauptmann Pabst (who we met on page 30), General Ludendorff *(left)*, and Dr Wolfgang Kapp of the extreme right-wing Nationale Vereinigung. On the night of March 12–13, some 12,000 men of the Freikorps marched on Berlin but, failing to gain any strategic objectives, and thwarted by a general strike called by President Ebert which paralysed the city, the whole thing was a disaster. *Right:* With Berlin, virtually every event in its history features the Brandenburg Gate in some way or other. These Kapp troops were pictured there on March 19 when it was all over bar the shouting.

By now another man had entered the stage; a man who was to end up changing the face of Germany — and Berlin — like no one had ever done before. As soon as news of the attempted coup reached Bavaria, Adolf Hitler, a 30-year-old corporal in the Reichswehr, arrived hot-foot from Munich where he had already begun to make a name for himself as a political agitator with the Deutsche Arbeiter Partei (German Workers' Party). At the begining of that month the DAP had added the word 'Nationalsozialistische' (conveniently abbreviated in German to 'Nazi'), transforming it into the NSDAP, and it simultaneously adopted the swastika as its emblem. However by the time Hitler arrived in Berlin, having been flown to the capital in a small plane by the war ace Leutnant Robert Ritter von Greim (a name which will crop up again later), Kapp had fled and the putsch was at an end. Hitler's own coup d'état, also supported by Ludendorff, was launched against the Bavarian government in November 1923. The previous October in Italy, Benito Mussolini had marched on Rome and successfully installed a Fascist government, and Hitler believed that he could duplicate the act in Germany with a 'March on Berlin'. Hitler's 2,000-strong column of stormtroopers began their putsch from the Bürgerbräu beer hall on the morning of November 9 but had marched only some two kilometres before coming up against a police road-block beside the Feldherrnhalle *(left)* — a monument to the Bavarian army. Firing broke out from both sides and the marchers scattered, including Hitler, leaving behind fourteen Nazi dead. *Right:* When Hitler came to power, one of his first acts was to erect a memorial on the wall of the Feldherrnhalle and to ceremonially retrace his footsteps on the anniversary of the putsch.

Hitler was tried and sentenced to five years imprisonment, but he had served barely a year before he was released on parole. He immediately set about gaining control of the NSDAP and promoting his ideals, made easier in February 1925 when the Bavarian government lifted its ban on the party. That same month, Reichs President Friedrich Ebert died and, after national elections, Ludendorff's old chief, the 78-year-old Generalfeldmarschall Paul von Hindenburg, was installed as the new President. *Above:* This early NSDAP march in Berlin was pictured in November of that year.

For administrative purposes, Hitler adopted the old German term for a village community — the 'Gau' — to denote the various provinces of the country, each being controlled by a Gauleiter. Joseph Goebbels was appointed Berlin's Gauleiter in November 1926.

This is the exact spot today, the marchers having just crossed the Schloss Bridge. The picture shows the evening rush-hour travelling eastwards — a recent phenomenon since large numbers of east Berliners now travel to the west for work.

Meanwhile the economic situation was worsening. On January 11, 1921, the French and Belgians announced their intention of occupying the Ruhr, Germany's most important industrial complex, in addition to the Frankfurt/Main area they had already seized the previous year, because of the German government's failure to meet their reparation demands. In retaliation, the German government sponsored passive resistance to the occupation, but the outcome was a massive financial and economic burden which Germany was ill-equipped to bear, for the world was slipping into recession and the Mark had already fallen to a tenth of its pre-

war value. Inflation now escalated and many people were ruined by it. With the final collapse of the Mark the parties on the extreme right and left of the political spectrum began to gain ground and increase their membership.

Currency reform introduced in 1923, followed by the adoption of the Dawes Plan establishing a more reasonable scale of reparation payments helped to revive the economy. This had particular impact in Berlin, where from 1924 to 1929, freed from the authoritarian trappings of the past, the city revelled in the period known as 'The Golden Twenties' as Europe's leading cultural and intellectual centre.

The year of 1929 brought the Wall Street stock market crash in the United States, and the Great Depression that ensued. Germany was badly affected with nearly two million unemployed. By 1930, the situation was reflected in the election results in which there had been a further reinforcement of the extreme right and left wings. The Nazi Party, which had first appeared in the Reichstag in 1928 with twelve seats now had 107, and the Communist Party had risen from 54 to 77.

The Nazi Party, or the German National Socialist Workers' Party to give it its full title, had originated in Munich, which had gone through similar post-war throes of political upheaval, left-wing take-overs, violent repression by the Freikorps and political assassinations. The oratory of Adolf Hitler with its anti-Marxist, anti-Semitic themes, its condemnation of the Versailles Treaty, the Socialist government, reparations and the Allied occupation of the Ruhr, attracted a growing audience. Many Freikorps aspects were introduced into the movement, such as uniforms and the title of 'Führer'. By 1926, discipline and total allegiance had replaced political debate within the party, and the Nazi deputies taking their places in the Reichstag following the 1930 elections marched in wearing their brown uniforms with Swastika armbands.

In November 1923, Hitler and General Ludendorff had tried with a grouping of nationalist-minded parties to take over the Bavarian government, but this so-called Munich Putsch had ended in bloodshed and Hitler's incarceration under privileged conditions in Landsberg Prison, where he wrote his rambling political thesis, *Mein Kampf.*

With its strong Communist leanings, Berlin would be a tough nut to crack and Hitler's appointment of Goebbels as its Gauleiter was a shrewd move. Goebbels was a brilliant propagandist, a captivating orator and a skilled writer, and soon began his own weekly newspaper *Der Angriff* (The Attack). *Left:* The Communist Party headquarters was located on Bülowplatz, the building being appropriately named Karl Liebknecht House. *Right:* Today, a plaque records its place in history that the leader of the Communist Party, Ernst Thälmann, worked there from 1926 to 1933.

Hitler was released on parole at the end of 1924, banned from addressing public meetings because of the inflammatory nature of his speeches, but he continued to address meetings in the private houses of his wealthier adherents and to plan the strategic growth of the party. One result of this was the dispatch of Dr Joseph Goebbels to win over Berlin as Gauleiter of the then 1,000 strong Nazi membership within what was broadly recognised as a Communist and Social Democratic stronghold.

A staunch advocate of Stalinism after Lenin's death in 1924, Thälmann twice opposed von Hindenburg in the elections for President (in 1925 and 1932) and within the Communist Party his popularity was such that it gave him a cult status to rival that of Hitler. In this picture taken on June 13, 1926, Thälmann salutes the fallen — Communist style — at the dedication of the memorial erected in the cemetery at Friedrichsfelde to those killed in the uprising.

There was really no difference between the Communists and the Nazis when it came to honouring fallen heroes and when Horst Wessel was shot by a Communist supporter in January 1930, Gauleiter Goebbels capitalised on the event to maximum effect. *Left:* Wessel (standing on the right) was leader of Sturmabteilung (SA) Unit No. 5 in the predominantly Communist borough of Friedrichshain and was living with his girl-friend, Erna Jänicke, at No. 62 Grosse Frankfurter Strasse *(right)*, where he was shot in the mouth by Albrecht Höhler on January 14. Gravely wounded, he was rushed to hospital.

A principal feature of the Party was its private army, the uniformed Sturmabteilung (SA), which reached a strength of some 60,000 under Ernst Röhm. In addition, a bodyguard unit, known as the Schutzstaffel (SS) was formed to protect the leadership. The SA were used to demonstrate the might and orderly discipline of the party, but also to engage the private armies of their political opponents in the many street battles that occurred, particularly in Berlin.

Goebbels proved a brilliant propagandist, speaker and organiser. In May 1927, he was one of the first twelve Nazi deputies elected to the Reichstag. Eighteen months later he had Hitler addressing a 10,000 strong meeting in the Sportpalast. Then in 1930 Goebbels scored a major propaganda coup from the murder of a young SA man, Horst Wessel, who had written a poem, later set to music, *Raise High the Flag*. Stemming from a respectable background, against which he rebelled, Wessel had fallen in love and was living

In 1949 the street was renamed Stalinallee and reconstruction began to transform it into a huge eight-lane highway lined with apartment blocks in the Soviet style. Number 62 stood here, just yards away from the spot selected as a saluting base for the parades of the GDR. (When Stalin fell from favour the street name was changed yet again to Karl-Marx-Allee. We await further developments!)

Wessel lingered for five weeks before finally succumbing to his wound on February 23. Goebbels wanted to stage an elaborate show funeral to be attended by the Nazi hierarchy, including Hitler. However, Hermann Göring, who had marched with Hitler at the Feldherrnhalle in Munich and had been shot and wounded in the mêlée, declared categorically that if Hitler came to Berlin it would be a red rag to the Communists. As one of the Party's twelve deputies (with Goebbels) in the Reichstag since the election of May 1928, Göring argued against anything which might jeopardise their fragile parliamentary toe-hold. Although Hitler stayed away, the funeral still turned into a running battle as the Communists tried to break up the procession to the small cemetery of St Nikolai and St Marien *(left)* on the corner of Prenzlauer Allee. *Right:* The entrance survives unchanged to this day.

At the graveside Goebbels announced the roll-call for the departed: 'Horst Wessel?' to which the assembled SA mourners replied with a rousing 'Hier!' — a piece of drama later adopted as part of Nazi ceremonial for the annual remembrance service for the Munich martyrs. When the NSDAP Ehrenliste — the Nazi Roll of Honour — was compiled of those who had died for the cause, Horst Wessel, became the 56th to have lost his life since 1923. *Right:* Wessel's remains were disinterred in 1955 — German custom dictating that, unless the family chooses to maintain the grave, the bones of the dead are removed and cremated after 25 years. The present occupant of his grave is Pauline Mertsching.

with a former prostitute, whose land-lady wanted her evicted. The latter called on the Communists for help and Wessel was shot dead by one of them when they burst into the lovers' room. The Communists then tried to label Wessel a pimp, which he was not, but Goebbels used the occasion to turn him into a Nazi hero and adopted his song with its attractive melody (possibly from the opera *Joseph* by Étienne-Nicolas Méhul) as the Party anthem.

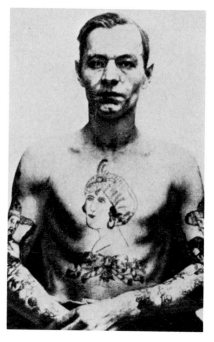

Above: On February 18, while Wessel was dying in hospital, Berlin police turned over the Communist Party headquarters. 'Ali' Höhler *(right)*, a previously convicted thug and Communist, was sentenced for the crime, only to be snatched from his cell and murdered when the Nazis came to power.

Horst Wessel was quickly elevated to the status of the Nazis' greatest martyr, his song becoming the anthem of the party. On a national level, the following year saw the establishment of a memorial in Berlin to the dead of the First World War. Britain and France had been first to establish specific memorials to their dead of the 1914-18 war, when in 1920 the idea was conceived to bury the remains of an 'unknown warrior' as a symbol to which all those who had lost a loved one could relate. The idea was taken up by the United States the following year, but it was another ten years before Germany copied the Allies. The Royal Guard House on Unter den Linden was chosen for its location and the architect, Heinrich Tessenau, was commissioned to convert it into Germany's national war memorial with its central sarcophagus of black stone. It was dedicated on June 2, 1931.

Left: Changing the guard on the occasion of the anniversary of the Battle of Skaggerak (as the Germans refer to the Jutland naval action of 1916). *Right:* After wartime damage had been repaired, the memorial was re-opened by the GDR in 1960, but with a new theme: as 'The Memorial for the Victims of Fascism and Militarism'. In 1969, urns were interred bearing soil from Buchenwald and Mauthausen concentration camps, El Alamein, Monte Cassino, Moscow and Stalingrad, to symbolise both an unknown soldier and an unknown resistance fighter.

The Prussian Paradeschritt or goose-step was retained by the East German Army (the Nationale Volksarmee or NVA) — somewhat of an anachronism, bearing in mind the antipathy of the Communists towards the days of the Kaisers. Perhaps it was adopted as a deliberate snub against their counterparts in the Americanised army of West Germany. Whatever the reason, it was performed with the utmost smartness and precision by the members of the Friedrich Engels Honour Guard until the NVA was disbanded in October 1990.

By now the sands were running out for Weimar Germany. Proportional representation in the Reichstag had led to weak government, unable to command any sort of majority whatever the policy, and political schisms had created upwards of a dozen different political parties, ten of which polled over a million votes in the 1930 election. Having abandoned the concept of armed revolution, Hitler was now seeking power through the ballot box and crafty manoeuverings behind the scenes. Apart from the Kaiserhof Hotel, which we have already seen (page 19), Hitler also used the Hotel Prinz Albrecht (left) as a base while in Berlin. Right: The hotel at No. 9 Prinz-Albrecht-Strasse (see map page 21) no longer exists. It was demolished in the 1950s, and when we took this photograph in August 1990, youngsters were doing their best to hack their own souvenir from a later piece of history built directly outside its front door.

Against a background of almost three million unemployed, and with Hitler offering something to almost every kind of voter, whether farmer, industrial worker, industrialist or student, patriot, racist or simple bourgeois, the Nazi Party continued to grow in influence. In the September elections of 1930 it won 107 seats in the Reichstag with 18 per cent of the vote, which was to increase to 37.4 per cent with 230 seats, the largest party representation in the Reichstag, in the July elections of 1932. Hitler wanted the Chancellorship, which President Hindenburg would not give him. Instead Franz von Papen continued in office until he found the Reichstag so uncooperative that he was obliged to call another election in the November. This time the Nazis gained only 196 seats but still remained the largest party. Von Papen was eventually forced to resign, to be followed briefly and equally unsuccessfully by General Karl von Schleicher, so that Hindenburg finally appointed Hitler as Chancellor on January 30, 1933.

Hitler and Goebbels leave the hotel after a meeting on May 19, 1932.

And still the violence in the streets went on as the Communists and Nazis pursued their vendetta of hate towards each other. Left: January 22, 1933 — just a week before Hitler achieved his goal — the SA marched on the Communist headquarters on Bülowplatz. Right: The Karl Liebknecht House is just hidden behind the Volksbühne Theatre on the left.

PART II
THE THIRD REICH

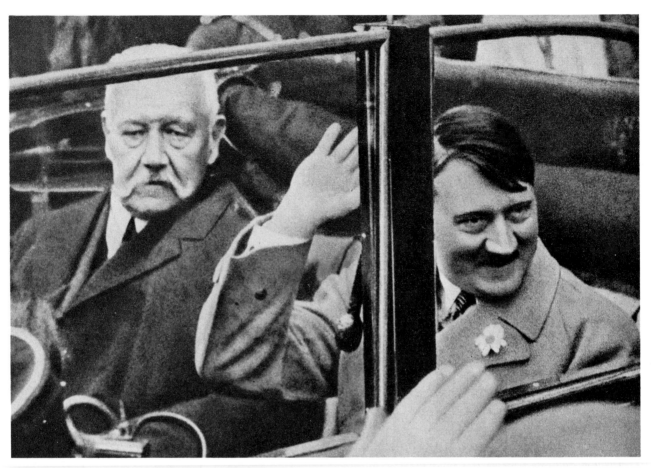

The First Five Years

Hitler assumed office with von Papen as his Vice-Chancellor and only two other Nazis in his Cabinet, Hermann Göring and Hans Frank. The event was celebrated by a mass parade with thousands of torch-bearing SA troopers marching through the Brandenburg Gate and down the Wilhelmstrasse to salute first, President Hindenburg on the balcony of his palace, then Hitler, who was leaning out of a window of the Reichs Chancellery in response to the tumultuous applause of thousands.

Events moved fast that January as the Weimar Republic thrashed about in its final death throes, searching for a solution to its problems. There was even the rumour of yet another coup d'état in the making, this time by the military against von Hindenburg personally. Hitler was informed on the evening of Sunday, January 29. 'My immediate counter-action to this planned putsch,' Hitler recalled later, 'was to send for the commander of the Berlin SA, Count von Helldorf, and through him alert the whole of the SA of Berlin . . . and instruct . . . the police . . . to prepare for a sudden seizure of the Wilhelmstrasse.' In the event, none of that was necessary. General Werner von Blomberg, then in Geneva representing Germany at the Disarmament Conference, was summoned to Berlin and sworn in on Monday morning as the new Minister of Defence with the authority to put down any attempted coup by the army. At 10.50 a.m. Hitler, together with the seven members of the proposed new Cabinet, arrived at the President's Palace. By noon the deed had been done: Generalfeldmarschall Paul von Beneckendorff und Hindenburg, acting under the constitutional powers vested in him as President, appointed Adolf Hitler Chancellor of Germany. Hitler was just 43 years old.

Monday evening and the Wilhelmstrasse erupts into joyous adulation — for President von Hindenburg at a window of his palace *(left)* and Chancellor Hitler, acknowledging the crowd from the Chancellery. Perhaps at last there would be stability; perhaps at last an end to the bitter years of strife . . . Surely with a strong man in charge there was hope?

The new Reichs Cabinet. Standing L–R: Franz Seldte, former leader in the Stahlhelm (the 'Steel Helmet' organisation of nationalistic war veterans), became the new Minister of Labour; Graf Lutz von Schwerin-Krosigk, Minister of Finance; Dr Wilhelm Frick, Minister of the Interior; General von Blomberg who remained Minister of Defence, and Dr Alfred Hugenberg who combined the Ministry of Economics with Food and Agriculture. Seated: Hermann Göring, nominally Minister Without Portfolio but heir-apparent to the Ministry of Aviation as soon as Germany revived its air force, and also Minister of the Interior for Prussia. This appointment was highly significant as for the moment each German state ran its own police force and it meant that the Prussian force, the largest by far, was now under the control of the Nazis. The Vice-Chancellor of the Reich and Premier of Prussia, Franz von Papen, sits on the right. The Nazis were not long in showing their true colours. Five hours after being appointed Chancellor, Hitler called his first Cabinet meeting at which Göring proposed the dissolution of the Reichstag and the holding of fresh elections.

We are determined, as leaders of the nation, to fulfil as a national Government the task which has been allotted to us, swearing fidelity only to God, our conscience, and the nation.

The inheritance which has fallen to us is a terrible one. The task with which we are faced is the hardest which has fallen to German statesmen within the memory of man. But we are all filled with unbounded confidence, for we believe in our people and their imperishable virtues. Every class and every individual must help us to found the new Reich.

The National Government will regard it as their first and foremost duty to revive in the nation the spirit of unity and co-operation. They will preserve and defend those basic principles on which our nation has been built up. They regard Christianity as the foundation of our national morality, and the family as the basis of national life. They are determined, without regard for class and social status, to restore the nation to a consciousness of its political and national unity and of the duties consequent upon this realisation. They intend to make respect for our glorious past and pride in our ancient traditions the ground principles for the education of German youth. In this way *they will wage a pitiless warfare upon spiritual, political and cultural Nihilism. Germany must not, Germany shall not, go under in the chaos of Communism.*

Turbulent instincts must be replaced by a national discipline as the guiding principle of our national life. All those institutions which are the strongholds of the energy and vitality of our nation will be taken under the especial care of the Government. . . .

Fourteen years of Marxism have ruined Germany: one year of Bolshevism would destroy her. If, however, Germany is to experience this political and economic revival and conscientiously fulfil her duties towards the other nations, one decisive step is absolutely necessary first: the overcoming of the destroying menace of Communism in Germany.

May God Almighty give our work His blessing, strengthen our purpose and endow us with wisdom and the trust of our people, for we are fighting not for ourselves, but for Germany!

PROCLAMATION TO THE NATION,
BERLIN, FEBRUARY 1, 1933

After initial protests from Hugenberg and von Papen, the following day they caved in and polling was fixed for March 5. Now, with the benefit of all the resources of the media at his disposal, Goebbels was overjoyed: 'We shall stage a masterpiece of propaganda with no lack of money.' Hitler had agreed that they should not come out with direct countermeasures against the Communists just yet. 'The Bolshevik attempt at revolution must first burst into flame,' wrote Goebbels in his diary. 'At the proper time we shall strike.' Ten days later, on February 10, Hitler addressed the faithful assembled in the Sportpalast indoor stadium on Potsdamer Strasse: 'Marxism means tearing in pieces of the nation . . . Marxism is a fight against culture and the idea of freedom, a war against tradition and honour. It is an attack upon all the foundations of our community life and thus an attack upon the basis of our life as a whole.'

When the expected Communist backlash failed to materialise, the Nazis became impatient for a showdown. On February 24, with the election less than two weeks away, Göring decided to try to bring matters to a head and he ordered a raid on the Karl Liebknecht House to seek evidence of subversion. The building had already been abandoned by the Communists but the propaganda literature and files found on the premises were good enough. That same day Göring issued his official statement that the police had discovered evidence of an intention by the Communists to mount a revolution. However, Göring's indictment was received with not a little scepticism and it was obvious that even more drastic measures would be necessary — yet there was now only a week to go before the election. Something had to be done — and quickly. The following day, a Saturday, the fire brigade was called out three times to control

fires which had burst out in government buildings, including one in the Schloss, which were clearly the work of an arsonist. Although the identity of the culprit was not known, the germ of an idea was undoubtedly sown in Göring's fertile brain. Goebbels, too, may have conferred with him to see how the situation could be turned to their advantage. Some dramatic incident had to be pulled out of the hat. An attack on the Reichstag *(left)*, the very heart of the government — just as Guy Fawkes had attempted on the British Parliament more than three hundred years earlier — would surely be the answer. *Right:* After remaining a burned-out shell for twenty years, the interior was restored in modern style between 1959 and 1971. However, for some reason the President's rostrum (see plan page 25) was completely reversed so that today the Chancellor speaks from the opposite side of the chamber.

What was actually discussed that weekend will probably never be known with certainty, as those closest to the action have all taken their secrets to their graves. However, evidence presented at the Nuremberg Military Tribunal laid the blame for starting the Reichstag fire firmly on the shoulders of the Nazis. Gestapo chief Rudolf Diels stated that 'Göring knew exactly how the fire was to be started' and had already ordered him in advance to prepare a list of people who were to be arrested. An official in Göring's ministry, Hans Gisevius, also testified that 'it was Goebbels who first thought of setting the Reichstag on fire'. General Franz Halder, Chief of the Army General Staff from

1938–1942, recalled at Nuremberg: 'At a luncheon on the birthday of the Führer in 1942 the conversation turned to the topic of the Reichstag building and its artistic value. I heard with my own ears when Göring interrupted the conversation and shouted: "The only one who really knows about the Reichstag is I, because I set it on fire!" With that he slapped his thigh with the flat of his hand.' *Left:* Picture taken on Tuesday morning, February 8, 1933. *Right:* In order that we do not jump too far ahead in our story, our comparison is one taken before October 3, 1990, as it was on this spot that the flag-pole was installed for raising the Flag of Unity.

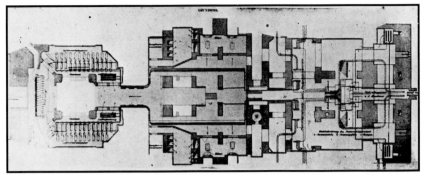

There is even one report that the SA picked up a young, rather simple, Dutch Communist, Marinus van der Lubbe *(left)*, who had been boasting in a bar that he was the phantom arsonist and that his next target was the Reichstag building. One can only speculate whether news of this encounter ever reached the ears of Göring and Goebbels, but it was an amazing coincidence that the Dutchman was caught red-handed by police while still in the burning building on Monday night. *Above:* Later in 1933 the university in Basel provided the clue as to how it could have been done by publishing a plan of the cellars showing the tunnel link with Göring's Reichstag President's Palace across Sommer Strasse at the rear of the parliament building.

From his own researches, William Shirer, an American correspondent in Berlin during the Third Reich period, believed that 'through this tunnel Karl Ernst, a former hotel bell-hop who had become the Berlin SA leader, led a small detachment of stormtroopers [who] scattered petrol and self-igniting chemicals and then made their way quickly back to the palace by the way they had come'. Possibly the half-witted van der Lubbe was set up by the SA to enter the building and start a fire while they carried out their own work. Whatever the truth of the matter, the Dutchman was a heaven-sent scapegoat for the Nazis.

Then, within a month of taking office, a fortuitous event occurred that gave Hitler the opportunity he needed to promote his plans. On February 27, 1933, the Reichstag was set on fire by a mentally-unbalanced Dutchman of extreme left-wing opinions. Hitler declared this to have been an attempt at a Communist coup and next day persuaded von Hindenberg to issue a presidential decree 'to protect the German People and the State', which enabled the gradual imposition of Nazi tyranny by removing all the existing constitutional safeguards against arbitrary arrest and the suppression of free speech. Communists were promptly arrested, beaten up and incarcerated in improvised concentration camps.

Göring was one of the first on the scene. 'This is the beginning of the Communist uprising,' he ranted. 'Now they are going to strike.' Turning to his police chief, Rudolf Diels, who had just arrived, he ordered that, 'Not a minute must be lost'. Now that the deed had been done, it was essential that the blame be laid fairly and squarely on the Communists, and that night hundreds on the prepared hit-list were pulled from their beds. *Right:* The debating chamber pictured on Tuesday.

Hitler, who had been dining with Goebbels at the latter's apartment on the Reichskanzlerplatz (see page 84), some five miles away. arrived at the height of the blaze. 'Now there can be no mercy,' he shouted. 'Whoever gets in our way will be cut down. The German people will not put up with leniency. Every Communist functionary will be shot wherever we find him. The Communist deputies must be hanged this very night. Everyone in alliance with the Communists is to be arrested. We are not going to spare the Social Democrats and members of the Reichsbanner either!' *Right:* In the end, three Bulgarian Communists and the parliamentary leader of the Communists, Ernst Torgler, together with van der Lubbe, were given the semblance of a trial in Leipzig in November. The evidence of course was flimsy and all were found not guilty save for van der Lubbe who paid the supreme penalty.

The burning of the Reichstag was intended to be the signal for a bloody uprising and civil war. Large-scale pillaging in Berlin was planned for as early as four o'clock in the morning on Tuesday. It has been determined that starting today throughout Germany acts of terrorism were to begin against prominent individuals, against private property, against the lives and safety of the peaceful population, and general civil war was to be unleashed. . . . Warrants have been issued for the arrest of two leading *Communist Reichstag deputies on grounds of urgent suspicion. The other deputies and functionaries of the Communist Party are being taken into protective custody. Communist newspapers, magazines, leaflets and posters are banned for four months throughout Prussia. For two weeks all newspapers, magazines, leaflets and posters of the Social Democratic Party are banned. . . .*
OFFICIAL PRESS RELEASE,
FEBRUARY 27, 1933

The bandwagon immediately began to roll against the Communists. First the press release already pre-dated for February 27 (above). Then the emergency decree, already pre-prepared, which Hitler presented to von Hindenburg on Tuesday for signature. This suspended seven sections of the constitution providing for 'restrictions on personal liberty, on the right of free expression of opinion, including freedom of the press; on the rights of assembly and association; and violations of the privacy of postal, telegraphic and telephonic communications.' It also gave power for 'warrants for house searches, orders for confiscations as well as restrictions on property, beyond the legal limits otherwise prescribed . . . ' The death sentence was extended to a number of crimes including serious disturbances of the peace by armed individuals. Thus, within a month of taking office, Hitler had constitutionally been given dictatorial powers to deal with his opponents, and he made the most of them. Throughout that week, all over Germany, police and storm-troopers, now with full government backing, descended on the homes of any likely dissidents, be they Communists, Social Democrats, or whatever, and thousands were carted off to interrogation centres which had been set up in storm-trooper barracks and pub cellars across Berlin to be questioned in the only way the SA knew: with beatings and torture. One of the first to be run in was the Communist leader, Ernst Thälmann *(right)*, who was arrested on March 3, two days before the election. In Berlin itself, Sefton Delmer, the Berlin correspondent of the *Daily Express*, interviewed Hitler and boldly suggested that the Reichstag fire was a put-up job to give the German leader the excuse of waging war against the Communists: 'It is nothing but a damned lie and a malicious libel', retorted Hitler, 'as base as it is ridiculous. Of course, there is one way in which I could settle these reports once and for all. I could have the Communist who was caught hanged from the nearest tree. That would dispose for ever of this vile insinuation that he is an agent of ours. But these lies are really too absurd even to discuss seriously. But I will tell you another thing. Europe, instead of suspecting me of false play, should be grateful to me for my drastic action against the Bolsheviks. If Germany went Communist, as there was every danger of her doing until I became Chancellor, it would not have been long before the rest of civilised Europe fell a prey to this Asiatic pest. The onslaught on the Reichstag was just one of a whole series of terrorist atrocities which the police are able to prove were planned by the Communists. The fire in the Berlin Royal Castle,

which was only just discovered in time, was to have raised the curtain on an orgy of destruction. We have seized hundredweights of material in the secret cellar of the Communist headquarters, proving that these fires were to be the beacon signals for a nationwide campaign of dynamiting, incendiarism, and mass murder. Why, those Bolshevist criminals had even made preparations to poison the water reservoirs! Suppose that there had been a similar situation in Britain. Suppose that the Communists had tried to set Buckingham Palace on fire, and had actually succeeded in setting on fire the House of Commons and gutting this national shrine! Your Government would have acted just as I have acted.'

This is not the place to discuss the merits or demerits of various parliamentary voting systems but, by any standards, the Nazi victory at the polls of March 5 was outstanding. Hitler achieved a majority of ten million votes over his next nearest rival, the SPD, receiving 44 percent of all votes cast. This gave him, under the proportional representation system then in use, 288 out of the Reichstag's 647 seats. (By comparison, Britain's 'first past the post' system of voting means that the government very often achieves office with a much smaller majority of votes.) One of the most visible signs of the Nazi victory was the immediate raising of the National Socialist flag on all public buildings. When the Centre Party protested, Göring replied that 'I am responsible for seeing that the will of the majority of the German people is observed, but not the wishes of a group which apparently has failed to understand the signs of the times.'

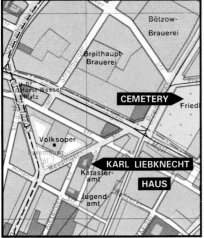

Then on Wednesday, March 8, SA Troop 6/6 entered the Karl Liebknecht House and, hoisting the Nazi flag, claimed the Communist Party headquarters for themselves. Situated as it was no more than 200-odd metres from the cemetery where Horst Wessel lay buried, the building was then converted into a shrine for Wessel.

An additional doorway was cut in the north-western face and decorative emblems added. This picture was taken in March 1938 and shows the standards of the Berlin SA being paraded from the building to the Sportpalast on the incorporation of Austria into the Greater German Reich.

The street on which it stood — Weiding Strasse — was renamed Horst-Wessel-Strasse and the square at the end altered from Bülowplatz to Horst-Wessel-Platz. Likewise the Volksoper opposite (page 39) was renamed 'Theater am Horst Wessel Platz', and the name of the U-Bahn station also changed. The alterations were completed with the establishment of a small memorial park *(left)* facing the building.

Right: In the end, the Communist Party had the last laugh. When they came to power after the war, the exterior was changed back to its original pre-Nazi configuration; the 'SA' doorway was eliminated, and of course it reverted to being called the Karl Liebknecht Haus. The square and underground station were renamed after their other martyr, Rosa Luxemburg. Nevertheless a few of the Horst Wessel trees still survive.

Hitler's first big public occasion following the election was Volkstrauertag — Germany's Remembrance Sunday — held in 1933 on March 12. Where France and Britain honoured their war dead on Armistice Day, November 11, to the Germans this was a day of disgrace, and instead the fifth Sunday before Easter was chosen for People's Memorial Day. The following year Hitler changed the name to Heldengedenktag — Heroes' Memorial Day — but for the present he was out on the Unter den Linden in his Sunday best as he greeted Generalfeldmarschall von Hindenburg for the 'service' at the Staatsoper.

Following the Totengedenkfeier — the thanksgiving celebration for the dead — the principal players moved outside to where units of the Reichswehr were drawn up for inspection. This is the Honour Guard — the building in the background being the old palace of Prince Henry, converted in 1809 for the Friedrich Wilhelms University. (It will feature in less favourable circumstances a few pages on.)

The reason that the Opera was chosen for the service was no doubt because of its convenience as it lies almost directly opposite the war memorial, dedicated not two years earlier. There the President took the salute for the march past.

Left: The political entourage stood quietly in the background although at least one young admirer managed to get close to the new Chancellor. *Right:* Five decades later, Communist forces on the same spot — Hitler would turn in his grave!

Having achieved success at the polls, the next stage in Hitler's plan for his legalised revolution was to improve his majority within the Reichstag. However, in order to pass an 'enabling act' to confer absolute executive powers on Hitler's Cabinet, i.e. a dictatorship, he needed a two-thirds majority, and even with the support of the Nationalist Party he had only an overall majority of 16. The solution, discussed at a Cabinet meeting on March 15, was easy. Under powers conferred on him by the decree signed by the President after the Reichstag fire, Hitler could have as many deputies arrested as would give him the necessary majority. The Communists would not be voting anyway, because of their 'enforced absence', and Göring was confident they could make the numbers up by refusing admittance to a few Social Democrats. Such was the plan, but first there had to be the ceremonial. Goebbels (who had been appointed Propaganda Minister on March 13) had dubbed election day as the 'Day of the Awakening Nation'; now he announced that the state opening of the new Reichstag would be held on Tuesday, March 21, which he called the 'Day of the National Rising'. The date was perfect for Goebbels' purposes as it was the 62nd anniversary of the day in 1871 on which von Bismarck had opened his inaugural Reichstag of the Second Reich. Now for the birth of the Third Reich Goebbels wanted a perfect setting where history, solemnity and tradition would blend in perfect harmony. The choice fell on Potsdam (see map page 12) — so favoured by the Prussian kings with whom Goebbels now sought to link the new charter. The main ceremony would take place in the Garnison (Garrison) Church *(above)*, and was to be staged directly over the tomb in the crypt of Prussia's Frederick the Great.

Above: Almost like the final act of a Wagnerian drama, thunder-clouds threaten Breite Strasse as if to bear down on those responsible for despoiling history. We are standing on the old Paradeplatz, but of the church there is no trace, thanks to the post-war Communist authorities who deliberately razed it as an unequivocal political statement.

Goebbels personally planned the spectacle of what became known as the 'Tag (Day) von Potsdam' right down to the last detail; indeed, after his recce trip he explained that 'with such great state ceremonies, the smallest touches matter.' The proceedings were opened at 6.30 a.m. by a Reichswehr band giving an open-air concert in the square *(left)* in front of the

Potsdam Schloss. *Right:* Then, shortly after 10.00 a.m., the first cars began to arrive, driving though the crowded streets hung with garlands and flags. In deference to the old Empire, the National Socialist flag alternated with the black-white-red tricolour adopted in 1867 — Hitler having already abolished the Weimar colours of black, red and gold on March 12.

Above: Von Hindenburg, Göring, the Reichstag deputies, the SA leaders and Reichswehr generals, attended a thanksgiving

service at the Protestant Nikolaikirche (just behind the Schloss), while Catholics worshipped in the Hedwigskirche.

Left: The Nikolaikirche, with its Doric columns, can be seen on the left of the picture. *Right:* The old castle also suffered the

destructive attentions of the Communist regime and it, too, was destroyed after the war.

Hitler and Goebbels, nominal Catholics, were conspicuously absent from the thanksgiving service, the official excuse being 'because of the hostile attitude of the Catholic episcopate'. They had, in fact, gone to pay their respects 'at the graves of National Socialists murdered in Berlin' in the Luisenstädtische Friedhof near Spittelmarkt.

Left: They then drove to Potsdam and are seen here in the company of other Cabinet members walking along Breite Strasse to the Garrison Church. The corner of the church can just be seen on the left. *Right:* Not so today as a Communist youth club, complete with Marxist slogans in mosaic, now occupies the site.

Above: After having been driven around Potsdam, von Hindenburg then arrived to inspect the Guard of Honour drawn up on the other side of the road. He had first come to the Garrison Church in 1866 when, as a young Guards officer, he returned from the war which gave Germany its first unification; now he was to be the figurehead in a dramatic spectacle to join 'old greatness with new strength'. *Right:* Hitler, the former Austrian corporal, was waiting at the church to pay due homage to the Generalfeldmarschall. Hitler said that he would not have wanted to come to power without 'the Old Gentleman's blessing' — now that blessing had been sealed with a handshake — the symbol of a nation reconciled reproduced on a million postcards. *Below:* Where history was made. From the unification then . . . to the year of unification now. In between, the Communists have done their best to destroy Breite Street with almost all the buildings on this side demolished. At this point we are looking across Breite Strasse to the buildings beyond.

In the company of the assembled dignitaries of Army, State and Party, the act of union began. It was in fact more like a betrothal as both President and Chancellor pledged the future to each other. After the opening chorale *Nun danket alle Gott*, von Hindenburg stood to give his blessing to the new government: 'May the old spirit of this celebrated shrine permeate the generation of today, may it liberate us from selfishness and party strife and bring us together in national self-consciousness to bless a proud and free Germany, united in herself.' Hitler replied in similar vein: 'By a unique upheaval in the last few weeks our national honour has been restored and, thanks to your understanding, Herr Generalfeldmarschall, the union between the symbols of the old greatness and the new strength has been celebrated. We pay you our homage. A protective Providence places you over the new forces of our nation.'

Goebbels recorded his feelings in his diary: 'At the end everyone is profoundly moved. I am sitting close to Hindenburg and see tears filling his eyes. All rise from their seats and jubilantly pay homage to the grey-haired Generalfeldmarschall who is extending his hand to the young Chancellor. A historic moment. The shield of German honour is once again washed clean. The standards with our eagles rise high. Hindenburg places laurel wreaths on the tombs of the great Prussian kings. Outside, the cannon thunder. Now the trumpets sound; the President of the Reich stands upon a podium, baton in hand, and salutes the Reichswehr, the SA, SS and Stahlhelm, which march past. He stands and salutes . . .'

Left: The Garrison Church in 1964, gutted but still repairable. *Above:* The Communist authorities did a thorough job to destroy this aspect of German history. Not only did the church disappear, but also the bridge and the canal. The dome of the Nikolaikirche can just be seen peeping from behind the flats.

With the Reichstag building burned out, an alternative location had to be urgently found to house the new German parliament. On the western side of the Königsplatz stood Kroll's Establishment built in 1852 and leased after the turn of the century by the Berlin authorities for use as the New Opera House — better known by 1933 as the Krolloper.

The premises were quickly commandeered and the stage suitably converted for its new rôle. Goebbels added a backdrop of a huge swastika flag as a unmistakable demonstration of the new National Socialist order. As soon as the activities at Potsdam were over, everyone trooped back to Berlin for the opening of parliament scheduled for 5.00 p.m. Here the Reichstag President, Hermann Göring, greets the NSDAP delegates with the Nazi salute — the 'Hitlergruss'.

The day's proceedings terminated with a gala performance of 'Die Meistersinger von Nurnberg', Richard Wagner's opera of 1868, when once again the 'royal' box of the 'Lindenoper' was host to Hitler's party. Outside, torchlight columns transformed the Unter den Linden into a river of fire as Germany's historic Day of Potsdam came to an end.

We are determined to create a new community out of the German peoples — a community formed of men of every status and profession and of every so-called class — which shall be able to achieve that community of interests which the welfare of the entire nation demands. All classes must be welded together into a single German nation.

The splitting up of the nation into groups with irreconcilable views, systematically brought about by the false doctrines of Marxism, means the destruction of the basis of a possible communal life. The disintegration attacks all the foundations of social order. The completely irreconcilable views of different individuals with regard to the terms State, society, religion, morals, family, and economy give rise to differences that lead to internicine war. Starting from the liberalism of the last century, this development is bound by natural laws to end in communistic chaos . . .

It is only the creation of a real national community, rising above the interests and differences of rank and class, that can permanently remove the source of nourishment of these aberrations of the human mind.

ADOLF HITLER,
REICHSTAG, MARCH 21, 1933

However, it was hardly an end but a whole new beginning. Norman Baynes who, probably more than any other person, has minutely studied Hitler's speeches of the period, wrote that 'the theme of the destruction of all political parties save the National Socialist Party recurs constantly throughout [his] speeches; the interests of party and of class had to be merged in the one common interest of the "Volksgemeinschaft", the "Community of the People". The people must become the unified "Gefolgschaft" — the "followers of the Führer" with whose will they must identify their own wills which will henceforth be "zusammengeballt" — "compressed into the single will of the Nation".' The euphemistic word conjured up to describe the whole process was 'Gleichschaltung' or 'co-ordination'.

In the war that was now just six years away, the Opera House would be severely damaged *(left)*, but it would rise again *(right)*, painstakingly restored to Knobelsdorff's original by the East

Berlin authorities, save that the former inscription above the entrance: 'Fridericus Rex Apollini et Musis' became simply 'Deutsche Staatsoper'.

With Tuesday's formalities over, the ruthless take-over of the state quickly followed. On Thursday afternoon (March 23), having thrown off the formal attire of past days, Hitler appeared before the Reichstag in his true colours: the brown shirt of the SA. No longer the wolf in sheep's clothing; from now on he was to wear uniform at virtually every public occasion. In outlining his government's programme, he announced that he required an 'Enabling Act' to put his plans into effect. Dressed up under the disguise of 'The Law for Relieving the Distress of People and Reich', the act transferred the power to make laws from the Reichstag to himself as Chancellor. When put to the vote, the result was 441 for and 94 (all SPD) against. 'Thus,' wrote William Shirer, 'was parliamentary democracy finally interred in Germany. Except for the arrest of the Communists and some of the Social Democratic deputies, it was all done quite legally, though accompanied by terror. Parliament had turned over its constitutional authority to Hitler and thereby committed suicide, although its body lingered on in an embalmed state to the very end of the Third Reich, serving infrequently as a sounding board for some of Hitler's thunderous pronunciamentos, its members henceforth hand-picked by the Nazi Party, for there were to be no more real elections. It was this Enabling Act alone which formed the legal basis for Hitler's dictatorship. From March 23, 1933, on, Hitler was the dictator of the Reich, freed of any restraint by Parliament or, for all practical purposes, by the weary old President.'

With the demise of the German parliament, the building it then occupied has also now faded into oblivion. *Left:* Almost as if it was an embarassment, the Krolloper was never repaired after the war. One corner lingered on for a time as a café, but then the whole structure was swept away. *Right:* Not a stone remains today to mark its passing.

With parliament out of the way, the next to go were the local governments, each state having a Nazi governor appointed on April 7 with sweeping powers. Then came the trade unions, and a secret plan of action to deal with them was drawn up on April 21 by Dr Robert Ley, appointed by Hitler to establish the German Labour Front. The 'co-ordination' of the unions would come on May 2, but first May Day was declared a public holiday as the 'Day of National Labour'. Goebbels masterminded the publicity and staged the greatest outdoor demonstration ever witnessed in Germany on the old Prussian parade ground at Tempelhofer Feld, where Hitler addressed a crowd of over 100,000 workers and trade unionists flown specially to Berlin.

'This first of May', announced Hitler, 'is intended to bring to the realisation of the German nation that diligence and labour alone do not create life, unless they are united to the strength and will of a people. Diligence and labour, strength and will, even if they work together, still need behind them the protection of the mighty fist of the nation in order that real blessings may result. . . . Germans! You are a strong nation, if you yourselves wish to be strong . . . Forget the fourteen years of decay and think of the two thousand years of German history.' The following day the SS struck at trade unions throughout Germany, arresting their leaders, confiscating their funds and dissolving the organisations.

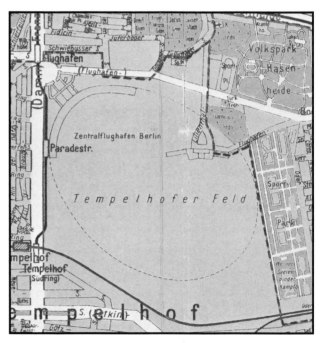

Before the First World War, Tempelhofer Feld was the training area for the Berlin garrison and also the location of the Kaiser's embryo air transport unit. *Left:* In 1923 the eastern part was earmarked for Berlin's commercial airport, leaving a smaller parade ground to the west, but it was not until 1928 that a

purpose-built terminal building had been constructed on the northern side. *Right:* The Third Reich brought about a massive enlargement of the airport to the south, north and west, completely obliterating the Tempelhofer Feld. (We will see the new airport terminal buildings later on.)

And then there was another aspect — even more sinister — which spelt the beginning of the suppression of free thought and the Nazification of culture. It began on March 26 when a list was published of those books deemed to be 'un-German and deserving to be burned', the majority by Jewish authors, Communists or pacifists. Goebbels followed this up by declaring April 1 as 'Boycott Day' putting Julius Streicher, publisher of the inflammatory *Der Stürmer* (The Stormer), in charge. Goebbels addressed a large crowd at the Lustgarten as the SA placarded Jewish shops. Their war cry, chanted everywhere: 'Deutsche, kauft nicht bei Juden!' (Germans, don't buy from Jews.) *Far right:* The 1933 picture was taken from the terrace of the Schloss. We took our comparison from the terrace of the Palace of the Republic on a similar, auspicious day: the 'Tag der Einheit' October 3, 1990.

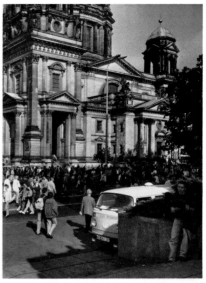

Operating within the framework of the law and thus calming any public fears about unconstitutional behaviour, Hitler began a quiet revolution under the innocuous name of Gleichschaltung, or co-ordination, much to the annoyance of Röhm and his SA who were looking for a more violent outcome. In April, decrees were issued banning Jews from all Civil Service posts and restricting the liberty of the legal profession. Jewish businesses had SA guards posted at their doors to remind customers that they were dealing with Jews, and Heinrich Himmler was appointed head of the Prussian Secret Police which then began to operate throughout the whole of the Reich. In May, the trade unions were suppressed and the German Labour Front established. The following month the Social Democratic Party was outlawed, its leaders arrested and sent off to the concentration camps, and then in July Germany was formally declared a one-party state.

During this honeymoon period people from right across the social spectrum flocked to join the Nazi Party, seeing Hitler as the new Messiah that would save Germany. That autumn, Hitler obtained a plebiscite to withdraw the country from the League of Nations, and by the end of the year the country was ready to accept the totalitarianism and conformity that his leadership demanded.

On April 13, the pro-Nazi German Students' Association published a proclamation 'Against the un-German Spirit' calling for the public burning of all un-German literature throughout Germany on May 10. In Berlin it was later reported that 500 tonnes of objectionable material had been removed from libraries and universities. *Centre:* Bonfire night in Berlin outside the Royal Library on the Operaplatz (just to the right of the Opera in the pictures on page 57). *Right:* Our comparison was taken from the roof although it was not possible to get right up to the same precarious vantage point. The library in the background — where Lenin studied in 1895 — is now part of the university across the road.

The pressure continued on the Jewish population and was growing on the Christian churches. Despite a concordat signed with the Vatican in March 1933, the Catholics were soon dismayed and upset by the dissolution of the Catholic Youth League and the passing of a sterilisation law. Any protests by priest or layman were met with prosecution and incarceration. The Protestants too were attacked. The Lutherans, who formed the largest group, at first welcomed the order and discipline heralded by the Nazis. Then Hitler tried to gain control of the various sects through a new Reichs Church, whose constitution was formally recognised by the Reichstag on July 14, 1933, but his nominee as the Bishop to head this organisation, Army Chaplain Ludwig Müller, was rejected by the leaders of the existing Church Federation in favour of a more eminent divine, and it took a wide-ranging programme of intimidation to secure the eventual election of Müller. One of the Protestant Pastors that had welcomed Hitler's appointment as Reichs Chancellor was Dr Martin Niemöller of the Dahlem village church in Berlin, a former U-boat commander turned clergyman with a widely popular following, but he soon became a leading opponent as the government started intervening in church affairs with a view to further nazifying the congregations through the churches. Niemöller was one of over 800 clergymen arrested in 1937 for their opposition to these measures and was to remain imprisoned in concentration camps for another eight years. From 1942 onwards Cardinals von Galen of Münster and Preysing of Berlin were particularly outspoken from the pulpit against the Nazis, von Galen attacking and actually succeeding in bringing the euthanasia programme to an end, but it was their seniority and standing in the international hierarchy of the Catholic Church that saved these clerics from persecution.

As soon as the trade unions had been crushed, Hitler turned his attention to his political opponents. On May 10 the SPD had its buildings and property confiscated, the party itself being dissolved on June 22. The German National Party, which had supported Hitler thus far, was 'co-ordinated' on June 21, with the German National Front and the State Party being banned on the 28th. The remaining parties were all dealt with during the following week, so that by July 14 the government was in a position to issue a decree stating that the NSDAP was henceforth the sole legal political party. In the same wide-ranging decree, a new Lutheran 'Reich' Church was established with Adolf Hitler deemed as 'a gift from the hand of God', with perhaps the ultimate sacrilege of the swastika imposed upon the Cross. *Above:* German Christians (DC) on the march beside the cathedral. *Below:* The Dom reflected in the bronze glass of the Volkskammer which replaced the Schloss.

Meanwhile, as the Nazi leaders consolidated their positions and built up their individual empires, there was increasing unease in the SA, which saw the chances of the socialist revolution they wanted and for which they had sacrificed so much in the past slipping away from them. This mutinous attitude Hitler could not accept, and so he eventually decided to bring them to heel in what became known as the Röhm Putsch or purge, the so-called 'Night of the Long Knives'. With the connivance of Himmler, Hess, Goebbels and Göring, some two hundred senior members of the SA and other potential political opponents were murdered in

On March 17, 1933, Josef 'Sepp' Dietrich created a special personal bodyguard for Hitler called the 'Stabwache Berlin'. It initially comprised 160 hand-picked individuals from the Schutzstaffel (SS) — the protection squads already formed by the party to 'police' political meetings. Six months later Hitler's personal protection squad was renamed the 'Leibstandarte (or Bodyguard Regiment)-SS Adolf Hitler' which by 1935 had grown to over 2,500 with its own quarters in the south of the city at Lichterfelde.

three days commencing on June 30, 1934. Among them were General von Schleicher (Hitler's immediate predecessor as Reichs Chancellor) and his wife, his friend, General Kurt von Bredow, von Papen's press attaché and many others. In Berlin the execution of prisoners was mainly carried out at the Lichterfelde barracks and at the Gestapo headquarters in Prinz-Albrecht-

Strasse or at the so-called Columbia-haus, a military detention centre near Tempelhof Airport. This barbarism was legalised with full Cabinet approval, with the exception of von Papen, who remained under house arrest and wanted to resign, but Hitler would not allow this as he still could use von Papen's services as Minister to Austria. Surprisingly, in their relief at the sup-

The black-uniformed Leibstandarte made its first public appearance in strength at the NSDAP rally at Nuremberg in September 1934, just two months after it had been called upon by Hitler to do his dirty work and eliminate the leadership of the SA. At this time, the parent organisation of the Leibstandarte was called the SS-Verfügungstruppe; later it expanded a thousand-fold, becoming a second fighting force alongside the Army — the Waffen-SS. It was in the cellars here that the SS executed forty leaders of the SA in the Röhm Purge during the

weekend of June 30, 1934. *Left:* An undated photograph showing Hitler arriving at the entrance located on Finckenstein Allee. *Right:* Some fifty-odd years later the barracks are under new management. Located in the borough of Steglitz, the complex came within the American Sector of Berlin — this is now the main entrance to Andrews Barracks, named after Lieutenant General Frank Andrews, the wartime commander of the US European Theater of Operations, who was killed in a plane crash in May 1943.

pression of the SA, who had been challenging their position as guardians of the state, the Army docilely accepted the murder of the two generals. Following the putsch the SS was made independent of the SA and its rôle elevated as an armed force within the state.

Then the Nazi Party in Austria staged their own putsch in the course of which they murdered the Austrian Chancellor, Engelbert Dolfuss. Although Hitler intended to incorporate Austria into a Greater Germany in due course, he had only recently promised Mussolini that he would observe Austrian neutrality at the latter's request, and consequently this independently-staged putsch proved an acute embarrassment further compounded by the fact that Dolfuss's wife was a house-guest of Mussolini at the time. The putsch failed but this, together with the purge of the SA, appeared to have expedited the decline of President von Hindenburg, who expired on August 2, 1934.

Even before von Hindenburg was dead Hitler had the Cabinet draft a law combining the offices of Chancellor and President. He then summoned Generalfeldmarschall Blomberg and the three chiefs of the armed forces to his office to swear the oath: 'I swear before God to give my unconditional obedience to Adolf Hitler, Führer of the Reich and

Although at first glance the architecture of the gate-house appears modern, it is, like the main block *(left)* facing the forecourt, of genuine Third Reich origin, having been rebuilt specifically for the Leibstandarte headquarters from 1935–38. The eagle was remounted above the central façade, but by the time the Americans took over in July 1945 *(right)*, the Russians had already removed it. *Below:* American alterations include the addition of a central stairway to what is now the burger bar and pizza pub.

its people, Supreme Commander of the Armed Forces, and I pledge my word as a brave soldier to observe this oath always even at the risk of my life.' This oath was unprecedented in that it replaced one of loyalty and obedience to

the constitution and the President for one of personal loyalty. Yet it was accepted without question by all concerned. Hitler's succession to von Hindenburg met with a 90 per cent vote of approval from the population.

The 'Flensburg Lion'. This was a Danish monument commemorating their victory over the Schleswig-Holsteiners and a weak Prussian contingent at the Battle of Isted on July 23, 1850, and brought back in triumph by the Prussians after their defeat, in conjunction with the Austrians, of the Danes in 1864 and placed centrally at the eastern end of the parade ground at the cadet school (see also page 15). The Leibstandarte emblazoned it with the SS runes but all has now disappeared.

Least of all were justice and the law immune from Nazi interference. Membership of the League of Nazi German Jurists was made compulsory for all judges to ensure their compliance in making judicial decisions in accordance with Nazi principles. So-called Special Courts were established as early as March 1933 to deal with crimes that were regarded as political, and People's Courts to deal with cases of treason. Both kinds of courts were designed to ensure the conviction of opponents of the regime with the minimum of fuss. One of the special responsibilities of Rudolf Hess, Hitler's deputy, was to monitor all such cases and in turn ensure that the punishments awarded had been sufficient; if not he was empowered to take 'merciless action' to effect the desired result.

As head of the Prussian State Police, Göring had founded the Geheime Staatspolizei, the Secret State Police, better known by its abbreviation 'Gestapo', in April 1933 from their political police department, and started using it as his own instrument of terror to murder and imprison political opponents. Then a year later he handed the Gestapo over to Heinrich Himmler in a deal which obtained him the latter's support in the power struggle within the party that ended with the 'Night of the Long Knives'. Under Himmler, the Gestapo then rapidly expanded nationwide as a wing of the SS in close cooperation with the latter's Security Service, the Sicherheitsdienst, or SD for short, which had originally been responsible for internal security within the Party under Reinhard Heydrich. This now became the intelligence department of the Gestapo. On February 10, 1936, the government decreed the Gestapo to be above the law, forbidding the courts to intervene in its activities in any way, and two years later extended the SD's rôle to cover the whole country, enabling the creation of a comprehensive spying system to keep the population in thrall.

This enthrallment began with the

With any totalitarian state, the creation of a secret police force to act against its political opponents is of paramount importance. It was Göring, acting in his official position of Prussian Minister of the Interior, who was instrumental in establishing a 'Secret State Police' force — the Geheime Staatspolizei — on April 26, 1933. *Above:* **He did not have to look far for premises for the new organisation as a building was immediately available, just along from the hotel, at No. 8, Prinz-Albrecht-Strasse (see map page 21 where No. 8 is referred to as 'Gewerbe'). In 1924, the Museum of Industrial Art had relinquished its school building which had then been let commercially, but that lease had fortunately just expired. Göring snapped up the building and appointed Rudolf Diels** *(left)* **as Director of the 'Gestapo'.**

education process and control of the teachers, professors and students, and the re-writing of the text books, the history ones in particular being heavily falsified, to conform to Nazi ideology in producing fit young eighteen-year-olds for six months labour service with the Reichsarbeitsdienst, the RAD, before military service or for bearing children

for the glory of the Reich. This process was eventually to result in a decline in university graduates and other highly qualified technically and scientifically trained personnel. The party did provide alternative channels of education, such as the ten Adolf Hitler schools which took selected twelve-year-olds for six years intensive training for party

Sixty years separates these two photographs, the intervening period a dreadful catalogue of pain, suffering, torture and death. Following Berlin's penchant for changing street names according to the political persuasion of those in power at the time, Prinz Albrecht Strasse was renamed in 1951 by the East Berlin authorities Niederkirchnerstrasse, after Käthe Niederkirchner, a German Communist who had emigrated to the Soviet Union in 1933. In 1943 she was parachuted into Poland but was captured and executed in Ravensbrück concentration camp in September 1944. Repaired and restored from the damage it suffered in the Second World War, the old museum building on the right is now used as an exhibition hall, and has been renamed the Martin-Gropius-Bau after one of its original architects. The school building is noticeably absent.

leadership or the public service, leading up to university entrance, and the Napola (National Political Institute of Education) schools, which were run under SS supervision on military lines, but with a grammar school curriculum, and intended to produce an elite type of leadership in all spheres of German life.

Simultaneously, the children and youngsters of the country were expected to be members of the various categories of Hitler Jugend (Youth) from the age of ten until they started

Left: **The innocuous-looking Gestapo reception area at the top of the main staircase displayed busts of Hitler and Göring alongside the National Socialist flag. Prisoners being escorted up the stairs would be carefully guarded in case they tried to make a suicide bid by diving over the balcony.** *Right:* **Today, all has been demolished, save for a fragment of the front wall, recently protected against further deterioration by the addition of a wooden canopy.**

their labour service. During this time they were even further indoctrinated with Nazi ideology and trained to drill, march and play war games in preparation for their warrior future. The girls too learned how to march and were

expected to do a year of work on the land at eighteen in the Bund-Deutsche-Mädel, or League of German Maidens, and then a 'Household Year' of domestic service, all as preparation for their destiny as child-bearers for the Reich.

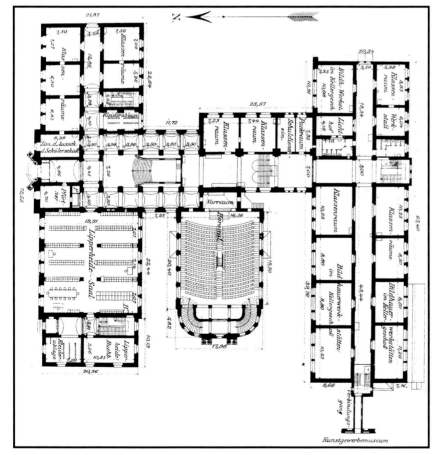

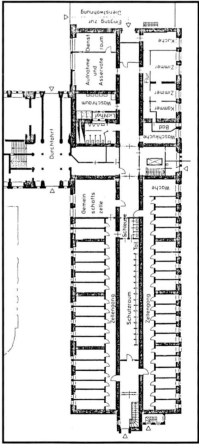

Diels, who, it may be recalled, was one of the first police officers on the scene when the Reichstag was fired, immediately set about adapting the building for its new rôle. The main change

was the conversion of the former sculptors' studios on the ground floor of the southern wing into a cell block *(right),* **while classrooms in the northern wing became offices.**

Left: One Communist, then aged 23, who was arrested and taken to Prinz Albrecht Strasse in December 1935, has since become more well known as the deposed leader of the DDR, Chairman Erich Honecker (right).

Some were not so lucky. Ernst Thälmann, the Communist leader arrested on March 3 (see page 46), suffered what the Gestapo euphemistically called 'intensive interrogation' at their new HQ. He was finally liquidated at Buchenwald concentration camp in August 1944.

It is nearly impossible to relate what happened for four and a half hours, from 5 p.m. to 9.30 p.m. in that interrogation room. Every conceivable cruel method of blackmail was used against me to obtain by force and at all costs confessions and statements both about comrades who had been arrested, and about political activities. It began initially with that friendly 'good guy' approach as I had known some of these fellows when they were still members of Severing's Political Police [during the Weimar Republic]. Thus, they reasoned with me, etc., in order to learn, during that playfully conducted talk, something about this or that comrade and other matters that interested them. But the approach proved unsuccessful. I was then brutally assaulted and in the process had four teeth knocked out of my jaw. This proved unsuccessful too. By way of a 'third act' they tried hypnosis which was likewise totally ineffective. But the actual highpoint of this drama was the final act. They ordered me to take off my pants and then two men grabbed me by the back of the neck and placed me across a footstool. A uniformed Gestapo officer with a whip of hippopotamus hide in his hand then beat my buttocks with measured strokes. Driven wild with pain I repeatedly screamed at the top of my voice. Then they held my mouth shut for a while and hit me in the face, and with a whip across the chest and back. I then collapsed, rolled on the floor, always keeping face down and no longer replied to any of their questions. I received a few kicks yet here and there, covered my face, but was already so exhausted and my heart so strained, it nearly took my breath away.

ERNST THÄLMANN,
PRISONER AT No. 8 PRINZ ALBRECHT STRASSE,
JANUARY 9–23, 1934

Left: The cell block built in 1933 as it appeared in 1948. The Gestapo headquarters remained more or less intact right up to 1953 when demolition work began. The façade was dropped by explosives in June 1956 and the site cleared over the next two years. The subsequent restoration of the museum building next door awakened public interest in the area and a historical exhibition was mounted in 1981 which subsequently led to demands to erect some form of memorial on the site. Right: In 1986 excavation work uncovered the floor of the cell block on which wreaths were laid on September 1.

With Berlin's 750th anniversary looming the following year, it was agreed that further archaeological work should be carried out with the whole site made available to visitors as a 'Topography of Terror'. In the spring of 1987, cellars of the former kitchen block were discovered behind the main building, and a museum erected above the walls, both to preserve them from the elements and to provide suitable premises for a photographic exhibition. At the same time sign boards were erected on the 'Prinz Albrecht Terrain' and an observation platform created on top of the sole remaining heap of rubble.

Back in January 1929, Heinrich Himmler *(left)*, one of the early recruits to the Schutzstaffel in Bavaria, was appointed head of the organisation with the title of Reichsführer-SS. As a counter-force to the unruly storm-troopers *(centre)*, Himmler set exacting racial and physical standards for his own men, although the SS was still nominally part of the SA led by Ernst Röhm *(above right)*. However, by now, heady with power, the SA were an increasing embarrassment to the Nazi government. Having swept away or imprisoned the opposition, Hitler's need for street-fighters was over, and the SA sensed that their usefulness was on the wane. Röhm had even pushed for his force to become the new Nazi Army with himself as Minister of War. By June 1934 the situation had become intolerable, and Hitler decided to act while Röhm was on a month's furlough with the rest of the SA. On June 30 Hitler personally led an SS squad to Bavaria to arrest Röhm while Himmler and Göring handled the Berlin end. In this picture the latter's police have occupied the Columbushaus on Potsdamer Platz.

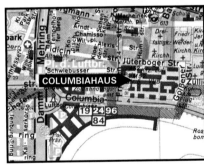

The Columbus House no longer stands (we shall see its demise later in the 1950s) but it is often confused with the SS 'detention centre' of like-sounding name — the Columbiahaus — which had achieved a notorious reputation as a place of torture and execution long before the Röhm Purge. It lay beside the Columbiastrasse on the north side of Tempelhof airport *left*. Today the site is occupied by the Vehicle Registration Office administered by the Berlin police.

The success of the operation against the SA was largely due to intelligence carried out beforehand by the SS, and in particular by its own internal Security Service — the Sicherheitsdienst (SD). Himmler had set up this special department in 1931 under an ex-naval officer, Reinhard Heydrich. When, in April 1934, Himmler was promoted from his official position of Chief of Police in Munich to command the political police in Berlin, he brought Heydrich with him and one of their first jobs had been to prepare the lists of names in anticipation of the clampdown on the SA. While Himmler based himself in the Gestapo HQ in Prinz-Albrecht-Strasse, Heydrich took over the Prinz Albrecht Palais as Director of the Secret State Police Office. *Right:* Its ornate arched entrance was just round the corner on Wilhelmstrasse.

Göring relinquished his executive position vis-à-vis the secret police in 1934, and in 1936 Himmler was given carte blanche to reorganise the entire police force in his new position of Chief of Police. After reorganisation, Heydrich *(left)* headed the Reichs-sicherheitshauptamt (RSHA), the Reich Security Main Office, which included the Gestapo and the 'Kripo' (Criminal Police) until he was assassinated in Prague in June 1942. *Right:* In this picture his casket is drawn up outside the RSHA headquarters on June 9 on its way to the Invaliden Cemetery on the Invalidenstrasse.

Lying in the American Sector, the Palais, which had stood since 1735, having been rebuilt to plans by Schinkel in 1832, was unceremoniously blown up in April 1949. The lack of any protest over the loss of such an historic building now appears rather hypocritical when viewed against the outrage which followed the demolition of the Schloss by the East Berlin administration the following year. Further down the street, Göring's Air Ministry in the Soviet Sector was spared by the Communist authorities who used it for several of their ministries. The Berlin Wall crossed the road just this side of it.

In September 1934 the annual Nazi Party Congress held at Nuremberg was notable for two important aspects. Hitler's speech on Wednesday afternoon (September 5) gave birth to the slogan the 'Thousand-Year Reich' when he stated that 'the nervous 19th century has reached its end. There will not be another revolution in Germany in the next 1,000 years.' It was also the rally featured in Leni Riefenstahl's highly acclaimed film *Triumph des Willens* (Triumph of the Will).

The Friday evening climax on the Zeppelinwiese was stage-managed by the young architect, Albert Speer, using 130 searchlights borrowed from Göring's Luftwaffe which formed columns of light, transforming the arena into a vast pagan temple. The final day saw a mock battle conducted by the Reichswehr to demonstrate its modern equipment and its capabilities.

Shortly afterwards Hitler issued instructions for the trebling of the size of the Reichswehr. Previously restricted to a strength of 100,000 by the Versailles terms, the Reichswehr had nevertheless been designed for rapid expansion and was quickly able to produce nine corps headquarters, fourteen infantry divisions and seven motorised battalions. Conscription was re-introduced the following March to enable further expansion.

The expansion of the armed forces naturally alarmed Germany's neighbours, particularly France, as well as Great Britain, but Hitler managed to persuade visiting delegations that his actions were purely defensive, even though the rate of expansion was actually far greater than they realised.

Dr Hjalmar Schacht, an economic wizard, was first appointed Minister of Economics and then, more specifically, Plenipotentiary for War Economy to prepare the way. Göring tasked the aircraft manufacturers with producing designs for military use and had thousands of enthusiastic young pilots trained under cover of the League of Air Sports. In May 1935 the title of the Reichswehr was changed to Wehrmacht

Göring's extensive Air Ministry building — the Reichsluftfahrtministerium — spanned the entire western side of the Wilhelmstrasse between the Prinz-Albrecht-Strasse and the Leipziger Strasse. Although, as we have seen, civil aviation was allowed to flourish in Germany between the wars, military aircraft were banned under the Treaty of Versailles. Nevertheless, a pilot is a pilot, whatever aircraft he flies, and the nucleus of an air force was already in being long before 1933. When Göring was made Air Minister, his deputy was Erhard Milch, then the head of the German national airline, Lufthansa. His official title was Secretary of State for Air, and it was on his shoulders that the burden of expanding the air force mainly fell over the next two years. This, of course, had to be carried out behind the scenes, but in March 1935 Hitler threw all caution to the winds and announced the inauguration of the new German Air Force — to be called the 'Luftwaffe'. Work began immediately to demolish the existing buildings opposite the Prinz Albrecht Hotel to lay the foundations for a headquarters building which befitted the new service.

At noon on May 28, 1936, a large crowd watched as sentries of the Luftwaffe in their new blue-grey uniforms mounted guard outside the building for the first time. The troops are lined up in the courtyard on the corner of Leipziger Strasse. The Oberfeldwebel wears marksmanship stripes and a sniper chevron.

Of all the Third Reich-era buildings in Berlin, the Air Ministry is one of the largest to have survived. Bomb damage was repaired and it was then occupied by several East German ministries for forty-odd years. When we photographed it in October 1991, it was being refurbished for the Bonn government.

and the Minister of Defence became Minister of War. Then at a naval conference in London, Joachim von Ribbentrop, the Foreign Minister, managed to get British agreement to an increase in the size of the German Navy to equal 35 per cent that of the Royal Navy, much to the annoyance of the other major naval powers, France and the Soviet Union.

On March 7, 1936, German troops marched into the de-militarised part of the Rhineland, an event which followed the reincorporation of the Saarland into Germany the previous year as a result of a massive vote in favour by the population of that state. Despite strong French protests at this latest move, no counter action was taken and eventually the British also acquiesced. Four days later, following the public announcement of the re-establishment of compulsory national military service and the expansion of the army, the freeing from the Versailles shackles was marked by a mass turn out of the leaders of all three armed services in the State Opera House on the occasion of Heldengedenkentag, or Heroes' Memorial Day on March 11. What was normally a solemn occasion became one of jubilant national pride in the faces of the participants.

The Wilhemstrasse entrance. *Above:* **Generaloberst Göring takes the salute at a march-past of Luftwaffe personnel on March 16, 1937, the second anniversary of 'Wehrfreiheit' — the day on which the German armed forces were officially reborn.**

We are now inside former East Berlin, looking north towards Unter den Linden in the far distance. The eagles of course have long gone, but the other embellishments undoubtedly survive . . .

Then in July Hitler received a request from General Franco to assist him with aircraft to fly troops from Africa to engage the Communist forces in Spain. Göring was keen to test his new equipment in combat, so part of the transport fleet was sent to aid Franco, together with some fighter, bomber and anti-aircraft units. This expeditionary force became known as the Condor Legion, which later took part in the infamous terror bombing raid on Guernica.

This is a close-up of the pedestrian entrance (also visible in the top picture) with its engraved symbolism.

The swastikas and Latin crosses were chiselled off in 1945 before the disfigured stonework was hidden by the cladding.

Meanwhile the Nazis' grip on the people's everyday life steadily increased. In February 1935, the Work Book was introduced for all employees, being a civilian version of a soldier's pay book, in which all employment and training details were recorded and without which no one could find employment or change jobs. Then in June 1935 the state employment offices were empowered to decide who did what work and where. The next stage came in June 1938 with labour conscription, one of the measures introduced under the Four Year Plan that had been launched under Göring in September 1936 to prepare the economy for war so that Germany would not be hamstrung by a blockade. This new law enabled the fining and imprisonment of workers absent without good cause, but also protected them from dismissal without prior consultation with the state employment office by the employer.

The German Labour Front was staffed solely by Nazi party functionaries and was out to get the most work possible out of its members. There were no more trade unions, strikes were unlawful and pay was low, but for the first time in decades there was enough work for all as the nation prepared for war. Also the 'Beautification in Every Place' scheme was introduced to improve the workplace by such measures as adding more windows for light, keeping it neat and tidy, and adding flowers wherever possible to enliven the scene. The Labour Front provided a major sweetener in the form of the

Much of the undercover training for the air force in the 1920s had been carried out in commercial flying schools and the Deutsche Luftsportverband which circumvented the Treaty by organising courses in gliding. A military flying training school was also set up in secret in Russia. As far as our Berlin story is concerned, a combined Luftwaffe Academy, School of Air Warfare, Aeronautical Technical Institute and Flying Training School, was established to the west of the city at Gatow. Built in record time on forest land, it was opened by Hitler in November 1935. *Above:* The 1. Flugbetriebs Kompanie parade outside the accommodation blocks *(below)*.

Gatow became a Luftwaffe showpiece in the same way that Cranwell was to the Royal Air Force, so it was ironic that in later years the RAF itself would take over the base as the spoils of war. *Above:* Pay parade outside what is now the RAF

Sergeants' Mess, and *below* a dance held by the 2. Flugbetriebs Kompanie in the present RAF Junior Ranks' Club. (We shall see the actual airfield itself in 1948 when it became a vital staging post during the Berlin Airlift.)

Two other notable events concerning Hermann Göring which took place in Berlin in April 1935 should be covered — the unification of the Reich judicial system under Dr Franz Gürtner, and Göring's marriage a week later to a popular actress of the period, Emmy Sonnemann. Göring had already handed over the Prussian Ministry of the Interior to Wilhelm Frick in May 1934 and the following month Gürtner had assumed responsibility for the Prussian Ministry of Justice, an office which had been absorbed by the Reich Ministry of Justice by the end of the year with those of the other States. The 'Basic Law of the Nazi State' was drawn up in January 1935, effective as of April 1. *Left:* Here Hitler arrives at the Opera House on Unter den Linden to attend the official ceremony on April 2. *Right:* The characteristic overhanging canopy has since been dispensed with.

'Kraft durch Freude', or 'Strength through Joy', movement covering all leisure activities and organised on a massive scale. Much was made of getting out and seeing the beauties of the countryside, of cheap, subsidised sponsored marine cruises, holidays by the sea or in the mountains, concerts and the like, all of which brightened peoples' lives. Hitler even proposed a scheme for a cheap people's car, the Volkswagen, which the Labour Front undertook to manufacture for its members with the idea that once a member's contribution to this scheme had reached a certain sum a serial delivery number would be allocated him. However, the factory had to switch to war production before any such deliveries were made, and the war was to be over before the first Volkswagen cars came off the production line under the temporary British management struggling to restore German industry.

Göring's first wife, Carin, had died in October 1931 and his private estate, 40 miles north of Berlin, was named Carinhall in her memory. His second wife was well-known in theatrical circles and, as Sir Eric Phipps, the British Ambassador who attended the nuptials as Britain's representative, reported to the Foreign Office, 'a visitor to Berlin might well have thought that the monarchy had been restored and that he had stumbled upon the preparations for a royal wedding. The streets were decorated; all traffic in the interior of the city was suspended; over thirty thousand members of the para-military formations lined the streets, whilst two hundred military aircraft circled in the sky and, at a given moment, escorted the happy couple from the Brandenburger Tor to the Cathedral.' To Sir Eric, 'General Göring would seem to have reached the apogee of his vainglorious career: I see for him and his megalomania no higher goal . . . unless indeed it be the scaffold.' Prophetic words indeed, written over ten years before Göring cheated the gallows by committing suicide at the eleventh hour. *Right:* Emmy Göring in November 1950, four years after her husband's death. She died in June 1973.

Within two years of having been appointed Chancellor, Hitler had, in the idiom of the 'nineties', 'turned Germany around'. Not only did he control every facet of the government, but after the death of von Hindenburg in August 1934, he even proclaimed himself Head of State as well, combining the duties of both Chancellor and President under his Nazi Party title of 'Der Führer' (Leader). The heart of the regime, 'Der Regierungsviertel', or government quarter, was firmly centred on the Wilhelmstrasse. In this contemporary sketch, circa 1936, the new Air Ministry has been completed, Göring having then renamed the old Prussian Chamber of Deputies (we saw it on page 27) Haus der Flieger or 'Airmen's House'.

The farmers and peasants working on the land were in a poor way when the Nazis came to power. The Nazis had wooed them with promises of land reform, but the Hereditary Farm Law they then introduced covered only one aspect of this in declaring all farms of up to 125 hectares (308 acres) capable of reasonably sustaining a family nominated hereditary estates under the old entailment laws, which prevented their sale, division, mortgage or foreclosure in case of debt. When the owner died the property was to be passed on to the oldest or youngest son in accordance with local custom, or the nearest male relative, who was then responsible for

The only building of significance not included on the plan which should be mentioned is Angriff House *(below)* at Wilhelmstrasse 106. This had been the editorial office of the NSDAP newspaper *Der Angriff* until Viktor Lutze moved in in July 1934 *(below right)* on his appointment as SA Chief of Staff following the killing of his predecessor, Ernst Röhm. Thereafter, it became the SA-Gruppen führung — the headquarters of the Stormtrooper Division Command for Berlin-Brandenburg. (No comparison as the building no longer exists. Its location is indicated on the aerial photograph *opposite*.)

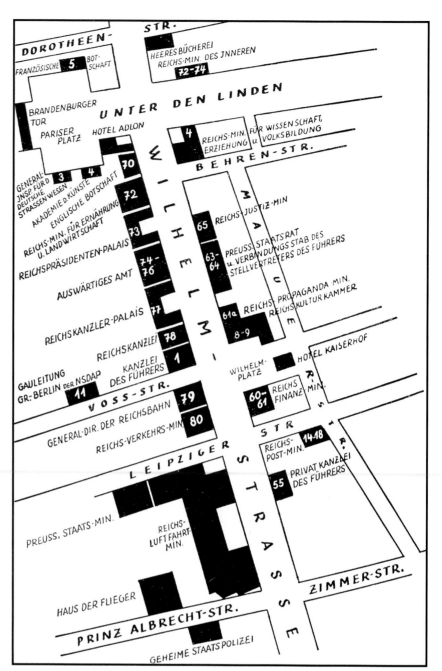

the livelihood and education of the rest of the survivors until they came of age. The effect of this was to bind the peasant to the soil, soothed with propaganda about being the salt of the earth under the slogan 'Blut und Boden', or 'Blood and Soil', and a fixed range of wholesale prices for agricultural products, which brought about an appreciable initial increase in income, later partially offset by the cost of fertilisers and machinery to meet the aim of self-sufficiency in food for Germany.

The press, radio and publishing houses, as well as the film industry, the theatre, fine arts and music, all came under separate divisions of Dr Joseph Goebbels's Reichs Chamber of Culture, which ensured the rapid demise of any opposition to the party line. Goebbels was to become famous for his development of propaganda, but the fact remained that the German public often found the end product to be boring. By controlling centrally what was said in the media, the choice of newspapers remaining after the opposition had been removed offered no real competition with each other, and even the official Party newspaper, the Völkischer Beobachter, lost sales. Similarly, by laying down strict guidelines for radio and films, the general effect was stifling.

This photographic comparison (taken, like all our present-day aerial shots, from a Gazelle by kind permission of the Army Air Corps at Gatow) shows the same view of the street looking north in October 1991.

Putting affairs of State on one side for a moment, we now come to a high spot in the pre-war Third Reich era in Berlin. Back in 1931, the games of the XIth Olympiad, to be held five years hence, were awarded to Berlin, little knowing how Germany would change during the intervening period. Coming as they did after Hitler had consolidated his position, they were a heaven-sent opportunity for him to portray the new Deutschland to the world. *Above:* The Haus des Deutschen Sports (at the top of the plan) under construction as part of the Olympic Games complex. This was intended for the training of the German team and contained outdoor and indoor Olympic-standard swimming pools, gymnasia and a special boxing arena. It also housed the offices of the Reichssportführer, Hans von Tschammer und Osten *(right)*, from where the 1936 Olympic Games were administered. *Far right:* The Olympic complex was designed by Professor Werner March on a site five miles west of the city centre where his father, Otto, had built the Deutsche Stadion in 1913.

REICHSSPORTFE

Badly damaged in the Second World War, during which it was bombed, shelled and fought through, the building first served the Soviets as a barracks and was then later repaired to accommodate the British Sector Headquarters, the British Military Government and the headquarters of the British Berlin Infantry Brigade.

The 1936 Olympics had been allocated to Berlin by the International Olympic Committee in 1931, and by the time Hitler came to power the plans for the provision of facilities were so far advanced that they could not be changed to any great extent. The selected main location on a small plateau had originally been a racecourse and was already well-served by public transport with its own S- and U-Bahn stations. It even had a stadium, the Deutsche Stadion, built by architect Otto March for the 1916 Olympics, prevented from taking place by the First World War, but this no longer met the 1936 standards. His son, Werner, designed a new stadium, oval in shape, with a sunken central arena, providing seating for 65,000 spectators and standing room for a further 35,000. Hitler inspected the Olympic Stadium while it was still under construction but did not like Werner March's idea of using

The new stadium takes shape. This picture was taken from the top of the bell tower overlooking the Maifeld.

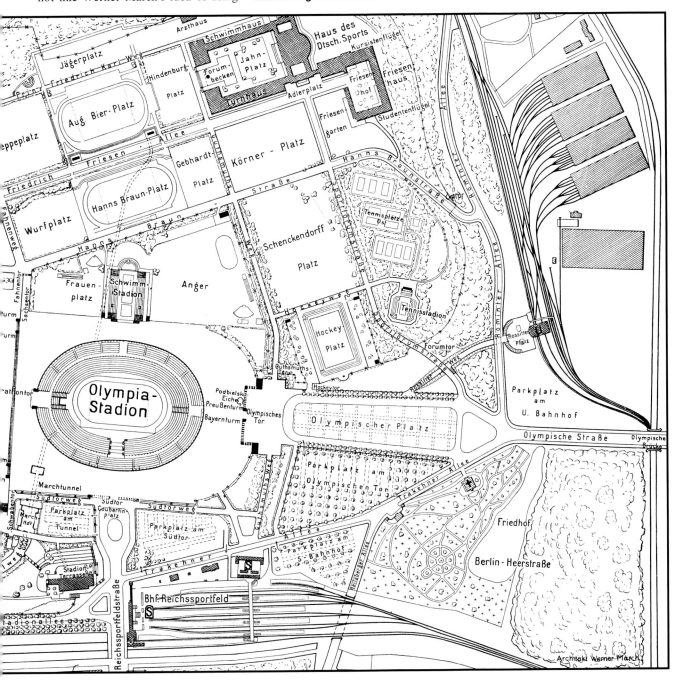

glass screens, so seized on Speer's suggestion to clad the steel framework with natural stone, thus providing it with a durability that was to prove valuable towards the end of the Second World War, when it housed both a field hospital and a factory manufacturing aircraft parts for Blaupunkt.

The complex included the numerous sports facilities of the National College of Physical Education, later to become the headquarters of the British Sector in the post-war period. The adjacent swimming pool had permanent seats for 7,600 and could be expanded to take 16,000 in all. Other facilities included tennis, hockey and riding stadiums, and an open air amphitheatre, then known as the Diedrich-Eckart-Freilichtbühne and later as the Waldbühne, with seating for 20,000 spectators. The largest spectator area, with room for 250,000 people, was provided by the Maifeld immediately behind the Olympic Stadium and dominated by the Glocken-turm bell tower, which also contained the Langemarckhalle war memorial to the reserve units formed of students that fought in the battle of Langemarck on November 10, 1914.

The Olympic village was built and administered by the Wehrmacht some

Surrounding the main stadium were several other purpose-built arenas for spectator sports. These included the amphitheatre which was the venue of the gymnastic competitions, named after Dietrich Eckart, Hitler's anti-Semitic mentor-poet who had dreamed up the Nazi slogan 'Deutschland Erwache' (which might well be loosely translated as 'Wake up Germany'!). He had died in 1923 while Hitler was in prison but was subsequently 'canonised' by the party.

Today, renamed the Waldbühne (Forest Arena), it has found a new lease of life as an outdoor location for Berlin's 'pop' concerts.

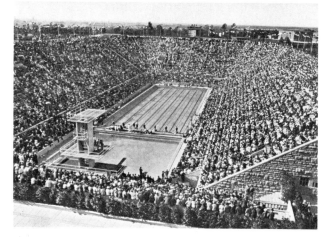

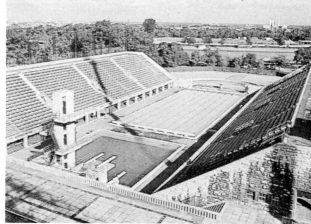

Left: **The swimming bath north of the Olympia Stadion provided for eight 50-metre lanes and a separate 20-metre-square diving pool. A temporary stand could encompass the** northern end so as to more than double spectator capacity. *Right:* **Today this is used for sunbathing and as a play area for toddlers with a sand-pit.**

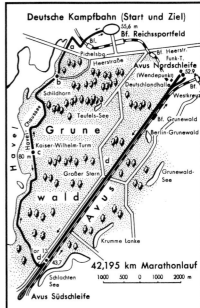

Several other locations, away from the main stadium complex, had to be used for the games. Sailing took place on the open sea at Kiel, although the rowing was somewhat nearer to hand on the Langer See, a lake south-east of Berlin. *Above:* The banked cycle track lay next to the Deutschlandhalle which had recently been built alongside the northern end of the AVUS (in the left of the photo — see also page 32). *Above right:* The motor track was also brought into play as part of the marathon course.

distance outside the city to the west at Döberitz, close to the big military training complex, and provided a choice of either rail or road connections, the latter being via the Heerstrasse, part of the East-West-Axis. It had a capacity for 4,500 athletes and was staffed by 300 stewards provided by Lloyds Shipping Company from Bremen. After the Second World War the village and its exercise facilities were used by the Soviet forces as a special training centre for their own athletes.

The Berlin Olympic Games lasted from August 1 to 16, and proved a

Left: The Olympic bell with its inscription 'I call the youth of the world' which rang out the opening of the games. *Right:* At the end of the war, it was buried under the Glockenturmplatz by a friend of the author, Major Freddie Newton, and not recovered until several years later. Today it is set up at ground level to the south of the stadium but therein lies a fascinating tale . . . one we shall recount in its rightful place in Part III.

Saturday, August 1, and the crowds gather. *Left:* The U-Bahn station at Reichssportfeld was above ground on the western side, some five minutes walk from the entrance. *Right:* It remains virtually unchanged today, except in name.

Left: **From the Temple of Zeus at Olympia to the Royal Palace in Berlin. The Olympic Flame, kindled by thirteen Greek maidens from the rays of the sun, is borne by the last of over 2,900 relay runners from Greece to the Lustgarten. At midday the flame** was lit to the roar of a crowd estimated at over a hundred thousand. *Right:* **The flaming urn stood directly in front of Karl Liebknecht's balcony. In the line-up of flags, Greece comes first and Germany last.**

major propaganda success. They were opened by Hitler at the head of the International Olympic Committee with a spectacular ceremony. Not only did numerous radio stations broadcast the news of the events to the rest of Europe and around the world, but television was also used seriously as a news media for the first time, and Leni Riefenstahl

Left: **Der Führer leads members of the International Olympic Committee across the Maifeld, having arrived at the stadium at the bell tower entrance. Note the camera track laid out on the left — Leni Riefenstahl's renowned film *Olympia* would be** released two years later. *Right:* **Today the Maifeld is part of the British military headquarters complex and a wire fence separates it from the main stadium. This is the Queen's Birthday Parade held before the Prince of Wales on June 7, 1985.**

Left: **Hitler, the patron of the games, enters the Olympia Stadion. The urn for the flame, as yet unlit, can be seen on top of the steps above the marathon tunnel in the background.** *Right:* **July 17, 1946 — ten years later almost to the day. The crowd is a bit thin on the ground for the British Athletic** Championships as Sergeant Roberts breaks the finishing tape in the 5000 metres. The winner of this race at the 1936 Olympics had been Gunnar Höckert of Finland in 14 minutes 22.2 seconds, but today the world record is nearly a minute and a half faster.

Left: **Meanwhile, the Olympic Flame was being brought on the final leg from the Lustgarten along the Charlottenburger Chaussee.** *Above:* **Television rears its ubiquitous head, having had its début in Berlin in March 1935.**

made a two-part documentary film that received world-wide acclaim. Hitler followed the games with great interest. However, as a result of missing the end of a late event for which he should have presented the medals, the Olympic Committee warned him that he should present all the awards or none at all. Hitler elected for the latter, consequently failing to shake hands in particular with the fabulous American athlete, Jesse Owens, who won four gold medals, giving birth to the story that he had refused to do so. Although the successes of some of the non-Aryan competitors caused a certain amount of heartache among the Nazi leadership, the overall results were a triumph for the German national team, which won the most of all categories of medals, including 33 gold, and came well ahead of the Americans in second place.

The flame enters the stadium before the assembled competitors from the 51 nations taking part. (In post-war games, up to 159 countries have competed.)

Herr Hitler spricht: 'Ich erkläre die Spiele in Berlin zur Feier der XI. Olympiade neuer Zeitrechnung als eröffnet.'

Ten years later, Marshal of the RAF Sir Sholto Douglas, the C-in-C, British Forces, Germany, occupies the same beflagged tribune for the Allied Forces European Association Football final. Result: Britain 6, Czechoslovakia 3.

The word 'race' in German is 'Lauf', pronounced very much like 'laugh'. Well, the last laugh of the 1936 Games came on the final day when, in the traditional way, the competing nations agreed to meet four years hence — in 1940 — in Tokyo! *Left:* The classic race — the Marathon — took place on the afternoon of August 9 with 56 runners. Here they leave the stadium via the tunnel. Ironically, the winner was Kitei Son of Japan. *Centre:* All the facilities came into use later on — this is a Hitler Youth rally with Baldur von Schirach, the organisation's leader, taking the salute. *Above right:* The marathon tunnel still remains, although it is somewhat difficult to get to this vantage point today due to fences and locked gates. *Right:* The Deutschlandhalle, at the other Olympic site near the AVUS, had been opened on November 29 the previous year. It had also been put up in record time for a building of its size which had a floor area of 35,000 square metres (over 375,000 square feet). It was used for the boxing and wrestling, but Hitler saw the hall as having a long-term use for party rallies.

Left: It was used, for example, before the Games for the Heldengedenktag remembrance service in March, and later in February 1938, the test pilot, Hanna Reitsch, actually flew a helicopter inside *(right)* in a remarkable publicity stunt for the new machine. As we shall see, the Deutschlandhalle came to a sticky end in January 1943.

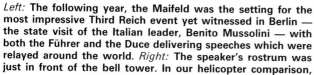

Left: The following year, the Maifeld was the setting for the most impressive Third Reich event yet witnessed in Berlin — the state visit of the Italian leader, Benito Mussolini — with both the Führer and the Duce delivering speeches which were relayed around the world. *Right:* The speaker's rostrum was just in front of the bell tower. In our helicopter comparison, a circle of grass has been removed near the stadium for a huge bonfire as part of a firework and laser display to celebrate Britain's traditional Guy Fawkes night in November 1991. It was a unique occasion as musicians of all the former occupying powers, including the Soviet Union, were on parade together for the first time.

With the Olympic Games over Hitler could now concentrate on other matters. His eyes were on expansion to the East and the means of achieving this. At the 1936 Party Rally at Nuremberg in the September of that year, at which the former British Prime Minister David Lloyd George was present as a guest, he launched an anti-Bolshevik campaign and announced the Four Year Plan to make Germany economically independent. Göring was placed in charge of

Goebbels claimed that three million people had taken part in the ceremony, either along the route, in the Olympic Stadium, or on the Maifeld. The speeches were carried on all Germany's wireless stations and those in twenty other countries in Europe, North and South America — excluding Great Britain and the Soviet Union. Even so, when he introduced the speakers, Goebbels could rightfully claim that the whole world was listening to them. *Left:* Hitler spoke first: 'We have just witnessed a historic event, the significance of which has no parallel. More than a million people have gathered here, participating in a demonstration which is being closely followed by the national communities of two countries, numbering one hundred and fifteen millions, besides hundreds of millions more in other parts of the world who are following the proceedings over the radio as more or less interested listeners. What moves us the most is the deep-rooted joy to see in our midst a guest who is one of the lonely men in history who are not put on trial by historic events but determine the history of their country themselves.' *Right:* The podium used by Hitler and Mussolini has been removed and the structure above the entrance tunnel simplified into two platforms, the lower of which serves as the VIP spectator box for the Queen's Birthday Parades which have been held annually by the British garrison since the end of the war.

Mussolini's visit to Berlin had begun the previous day — Monday, September 27 — when he arrived by train at Heerstrasse Station, just west of the Adolf-Hitler-Platz, from where Hitler escorted the Duce into the city centre. *Left:* This picture shows the square as it was decorated for the Games the previous year. *Right:* The building in the background was later to house the British Military Government in the immediate post-war period.

the latter, despite his total ignorance of the subjects, and immediately placed industry on a war-footing. His pronouncements and measures soon caused Dr Schacht to resign as Minister of Economics in protest.

Meanwhile, against a background of rising employment and growing prosperity, the Nazification of Germany continued apace. The concentration camps, although probably with a total of no more than 20,000 inmates, served as a constant background threat to enforce conformity.

The greatest spectaculars continued to be party events, in particular the annual rallies held at Nuremberg every September. The 700th anniversary of Berlin in 1937 failed to interest Hitler, and he left it to the local party officials under their Gauleiter, Dr Joseph Goebbels, to celebrate as they thought fit.

Hitler maintained a reasonably subdued tone at the 1937 Party Rally, comparing developments in Germany with the upheaval that was going on in the countries around them. He was not yet ready to work his followers up into a war fever.

Immediately afterwards his closest ally, the Italian dictator, Benito Mussolini, made a state visit to him in Munich. The two men got on very well together. Mussolini was entertained with a series

The Adolf-Hitler-Platz in 1932 when it was still called the Reichskanzlerplatz. The picture was taken looking east with the Kaiserdamm, down which Hitler and Mussolini drove to central Berlin, leading off top left, and Masurenallee top right. Top centre is the curved exterior of the Funkhaus, the radio broadcasting centre, with part of the exhibition grounds top right. The British Military Government building can be seen on the right next to the Amerika Haus, bottom right, which became the British amenities centre, housing a Servicemen's club, the Jerboa Cinema and the main NAAFI shop until the demolition of Spandau Allied Prison enabled a move to the purpose-built Britannia Centre in 1990. (We shall see this in more detail later on.)

A really full programme had been mapped out for Mussolini on Tuesday the 28th. The day began with a quick visit to the Zeughaus before he motored right out to Potsdam to place a wreath on Frederick the Great's tomb in the Garrison Church.

Then back to the centre for a visit to the Italian Embassy *(left)*. Today the building is a sorry sight with crumbling walls and bricked-up windows. It stands on the corner of Hildebrandtstrasse in the Tiergarten *(right)*.

At noon, he then drove with his son-in-law, Count Ciano, and his ambassador in Berlin, Bernardo Attolico, the forty-odd miles to Göring's recently extended home at Carinhall for lunch and to be presented with the Luftwaffe's highest award — the Pilot-

Observer badge in gold with diamonds. *Left:* Here we see Emmy and the Duce with the award pinned to his left breast pocket. *Right:* Little remains at Carinhall today, but readers inquisitive to know more are referred to *After the Battle* No. 71.

of parades and appearances at which he was received with great acclaim. He went on to see some army manouevres and visit the Krupp armament works in Essen, then on to Berlin, where again he was greeted by tumultous cheering crowds. Hitler had organised a vast torchlight parade for him on the Maifeld, where Mussolini, who spoke German, could address the assembled multitude. In his speech Mussolini declared, 'I have a friend; I go with him through thick and thin to the very end'. In the middle of his speech a sudden cloudburst threatened to bring matters to an abrupt end, drenching them all, but Mussolini went on to finish his speech to the disciplined audience, and then had to drive back through the rain in an open car. Hitler had further plans to honour his Italian friend with the renaming of Adolf-Hitler-Platz as Mussoliniplatz and the erection of a statue of him there, but these plans failed to materialise.

With little time to spare in his hectic schedule, the visit must have been very frustrating for Mussolini, as Göring kept his visitor hanging around till the last moment while he showed off his elaborate model railway layout and pet lion cub. The Duce then had to rush back to Berlin for afternoon tea with Goebbels, then on to the Reichspresident's Palace, where he was staying, for something to eat before getting ready to leave at six o'clock for the ceremonial drive to the Maifeld. To crown it all, right in the middle of his address, the heavens opened up and a torrential downpour turned his script to pulp and drowned out his speech over the waterlogged microphones and distorted loudspeakers. Soaked, he then had to travel back to the Wilhelmstrasse in an open car for the benefit of the crowds and, so we are told, there was no hot water for a relaxing bath once he finally reached his quarters. Next morning, a somewhat depressed Duce completed his Berlin visit with a wreath-laying at the War Memorial *(right)*, taking the salute at the march past that followed.

Germania

Hitler had not been greatly impressed with the efforts of the Berlin authorities in improving the appearance of the city during this period. He had his own grand concepts for converting it into a capital befitting his thousand-year Reich. Everything would eventually be bigger and better, wider or taller than its equivalent in any other capital city. Architecture was Hitler's private passion, his hobby as a relief from his political work, and in Albert Speer he found a kindred spirit and a means of implementing his ideas in this field.

Albert Speer, a struggling young architect, had come to Hitler's attention through his work on the refurbishing of the district offices in Berlin in 1933. He had then been given a commission to refurbish Goebbels's residence, which had been accomplished in record time. In this Speer had displayed a flair for coordinating the various aspects of the building industry in both the construction aspects and the furbishing of the completed object, a talent that Hitler was later to exploit more fully. A chance opportunity to re-design the setting for a local party rally had then led to Speer's work in the staging of the party rallies at Nuremberg from 1934 onwards.

In January 1937, Hitler decided to entrust Speer with the execution of his grand ideas. Speer was given the title of

'Give me ten years and you will not recognise the face of Germany.' Adolf Hitler's promise to transform the country, and in particular Berlin, was a result of his abiding interest in art and design. Architecture as a hobby can hardly be viewed as harmful, but as a rich man's passion it could easily become an extreme indulgence. If, at the same time, that person was a head of state with dictatorial powers, the result was liable to be megalomania on a grand scale. No more dramatic 'memorial' of Hitler's decade of change can be found in Berlin than the remains of the Anhalter Bahnhof — once a thriving hub of activity; now a stark ruin.

Hitler's cohort on the architectural front was Albert Speer, 31 years of age when he was created Inspector General of Buildings in Berlin in 1937. One of his first jobs for Hitler had been to add a balcony to the Reichs Chancellery in Wilhelm-strasse on which Hitler could stand and be seen at parades rather than just appear at one of the windows (as on page 42). Speer also had to convert the Borsig Palace (the ornate building on the corner of Voss-strasse where the flag is flying) into the SA headquarters immediately after the purge of that organisation in June 1934 (see page 62) so that Hitler could have the Brownshirt leadership close at hand. This resulted in the unceremonious displacement of the Vice Chancellor, Franz von Papen, who was forced to vacate his offices in the building within 24 hours.

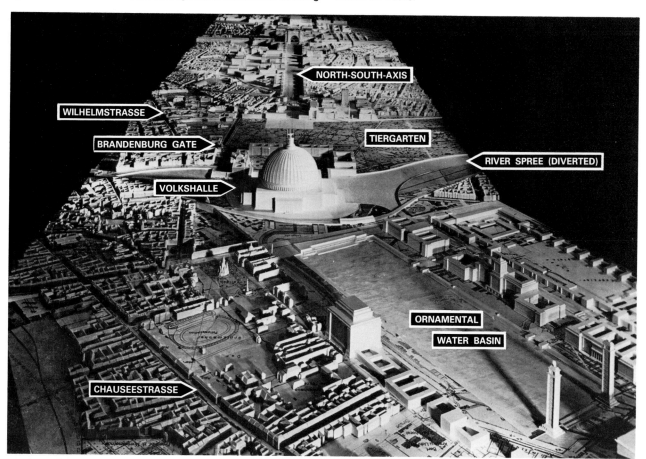

Hitler's dream was to rebuild Berlin according to his master plan based on two wide intersecting boulevards. The Unter den Linden was to be extended to the east and west where the road would be widened to 200 feet and renamed the East-West-Axis (Ost-West-Asche). At the same time, a new Nord-Süd-Asche would bisect it along the line of the Siegesallee. This North-South-Axis was inspired by the Champs Elysées in Paris, although Hitler's triumphal avenue was to be 70-odd feet wider at 400 feet. Just to the north of the intersection — on the Königsplatz — was to be erected the massive Volkshalle. In this view of Speer's incomplete 1:1000 scale model, we are looking in a southerly direction down the North-South-Axis.

Hitler had been busy sketching his ideas for rebuilding Berlin as long ago as 1925. As he handed over these two drawings to Speer for the Volkshalle *(right)* and Arch of Triumph *(bottom)*, Hitler told him that 'I saved them because I never doubted that some day I would build these two edifices.'

Inspector General of Buildings in Berlin, a position which gave him the status of a State Secretary and made him virtually independent within the system. He was given the Academy of Arts building on Pariser Platz as an office that Hitler could visit by traversing the back gardens of the Wilhelmstrasse without attracting public attention. One of Speer's earliest tasks was to provide a balcony for the Reichs Chancellery building from which Hitler could take the salute from passing processions.

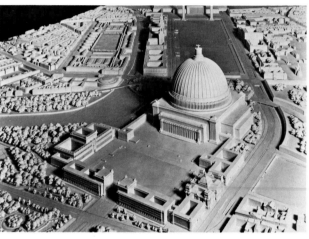

The Volkshalle, or People's Hall, was to be the centrepiece of the new Berlin which Speer advised could be finished by 1950. Completely dwarfing the Reichstag, it was to be larger than St Peter's in Rome and as tall as the Eiffel Tower, and was designed to provide standing room for 150,000 people. The River Spree was to be diverted to permit the Humboldt Hafen on the northern side to be replaced by a huge ornamental water basin 350 metres wide and a kilometre in length. Facing the Reichstag, more or less on the site of the Krolloper, was the new Palace of the Führer. The Siegessäule was to be dismantled and re-erected on the East-West-Axis to make way for a large parade square: the Aufmarschplatz der Nation.

Hitler's basic ideas called for the enhancement of the so-called East-West-Axis through Berlin and the construction of a shorter North-South-Axis to become the core of the city, a grand centrepiece carrying the main administrative buildings of the Third Reich.

The North-South-Axis would start from a central railway station replacing the Potsdamer and Anhalter stations just south of the S-Bahn ring and would pass under a triumphal arch, on which the names of all the German dead of the Great War would be inscribed, and end at the entrance to the Great Hall of the People on the River Spree.

Hitler was dissatisfied with the war memorial (see page 38) provided by the Weimar Republic on the Unter den Linden, which he described as paltry and undignified for a great nation. Obviously greatly impressed by Napoleon's Arc de Triomphe, Hitler designed a huge triumphal arch, twice as high as the Paris monument, on which the names of Germany's 1,800,000 dead would be inscribed. 'At least that will be a worthy monument to our dead of the world war,' he told Speer.

Speer saw the Reichstag as minuscule in contrast to the Great Hall of the People, which would dominate the northern side of Königsplatz (now Platz der Republik) and necessitate a change in course of the River Spree. A start was made with the demolition of that section of the area known as the Diplomatic Quarter between the Reichstag and the Kronprinzen Bridge, and the foundation pit for the entrance to the Great Hall of the People was dug across the northern part of Königsplatz. As the whole of this particular area was intended to be a motor traffic-free zone, connecting underpass tunnels were dug under the Charlottenburger Chaussee at the point where the North-South-Axis would form a T-junction. Another tunnel, this time for an S-Bahn connection from Potsdamer Platz to a station to serve the Great Hall of the People from Moltkestrasse was also begun, curving round the base where the Siegessäule had stood. The outbreak of war interrupted these preparations, and this abandoned worksite was eventually to provide the setting for the battle for the Reichstag.

June 1939. Demolition work begins on the Diplomatic Quarter along Krönprinzenufer bordering the Spree (see map overleaf).

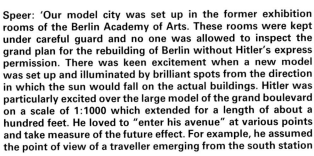

Speer: 'Our model city was set up in the former exhibition rooms of the Berlin Academy of Arts. These rooms were kept under careful guard and no one was allowed to inspect the grand plan for the rebuilding of Berlin without Hitler's express permission. There was keen excitement when a new model was set up and illuminated by brilliant spots from the direction in which the sun would fall on the actual buildings. Hitler was particularly excited over the large model of the grand boulevard on a scale of 1:1000 which extended for a length of about a hundred feet. He loved to "enter his avenue" at various points and take measure of the future effect. For example, he assumed the point of view of a traveller emerging from the south station [in the foreground in this view *left*], or admired the great hall as it looked from the heart of the avenue. To do so, he bent down, almost kneeling, his eye an inch or so above the level of the model, in order to have the right perspective.' *Right:* The North-South-Axis in reality. This late-war reconnaissance photograph taken by No. 138 Squadron, RAF, clearly shows the huge pit dug on the Königsplatz for the foundations of the Volkshalle. The Siegessäule has been removed, the curved water-filled excavation being the trench cut to extend the S-Bahn to the hall. The course of the new extension can be followed across the East-West-Axis and alongside the Siegesallee down through the Tiergarten.

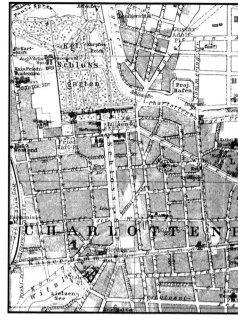

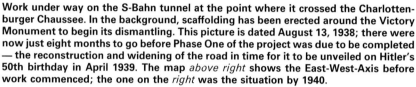

Work under way on the S-Bahn tunnel at the point where it crossed the Charlottenburger Chaussee. In the background, scaffolding has been erected around the Victory Monument to begin its dismantling. This picture is dated August 13, 1938; there were now just eight months to go before Phase One of the project was due to be completed — the reconstruction and widening of the road in time for it to be unveiled on Hitler's 50th birthday in April 1939. The map *above right* shows the East-West-Axis before work commenced; the one on the *right* was the situation by 1940.

The first practical work began on the western half of the East-West-Axis, which Hitler wanted widening for his parades. Extending in a straight line for ten kilometres out of the Brandenburg Gate from the Unter den Linden, the Charlottenburger Chaussee (now the Strasse des 17. Juni) led to the Knie, or Knee (today Ernst-Reuter-Platz), from where the original highway had turned half right towards Schloss Charlottenburg, then continued relatively flat along Bismarckstrasse as far as Sophie-Charlotte-Platz, in line with Schloss Charlottenburg, before beginning to climb the hill as the Kaiserdamm to Adolf-Hitler-Platz (now Theodor-Heuss-Platz). From there the road continued in the same straight line but downhill as the Heerstrasse to Scholzplatz, where it took a fifteen degree turn to cross the river Havel by the Frey Bridge and straight on out through Spandau to the city boundary at Staaken for another six kilometres. The Heerstrasse was the route the parading troops would use to enter the city from their training grounds at Döberitz.

The stretch selected for the saluting base and tribunes was along the Charlottenburger Chaussee between the Knie and the Charlottenburg Gate. The latter, which consists of a screen on either side of the road, was easily widened. The buildings of the Technical High School (now part of the Technical University) on the south side of the road formed an effective backdrop for the spectator tribunes, but all the existing buildings on the far side had to be removed to provide more space, except the one at the eastern end next to the Landwehr Canal that still stands.

Then Speer had the Siegessäule (Victory Column) and its flanking statues of Bismarck, Moltke and Roon transferred from its central site on Königsplatz opposite the Reichstag to their present location on the Grosser Stern in the middle of the Tiergarten. The Siegessäule had stood at the northern tip of the Siegesallee along either side of which were ranged groups of statues in white marble of heroes of German history commissioned by Kaiser Wilhelm I. These too had to be moved

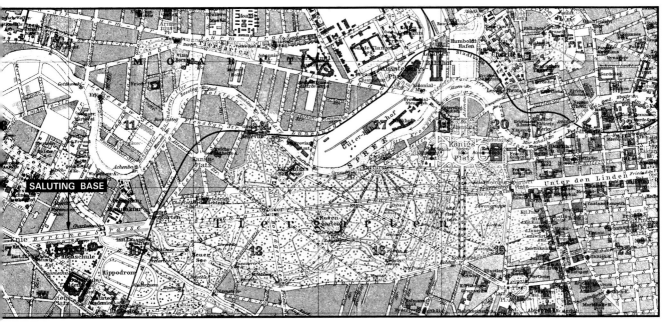

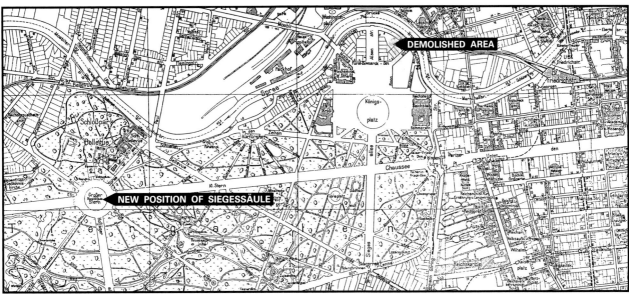

Four phases in the life of the Technical High School on Berliner Strasse (see map page 91), the forecourt of which was the location of the VIP stand for parades on the East-West-Axis.

Left: The building was erected between 1878–84 and was embellished with numerous sculptures. *Right:* The stand built for Mussolini's visit — before the reconstruction of the road.

Left: Rather the worse for wear, pictured by Clifforde Mark when he entered Berlin with the Army of Occupation in 1945.

Right: One might say that even more destruction was wrought on the classical building by the tasteless post-war repairs.

to make way for the North-South-Axis, so the radial path running south-east from the Grosser Stern was dubbed Neue-Siegesallee to take them. Some of these statues were damaged during the course of the war and then they were all buried in the grounds of Schloss Bellevue on the orders of the British authorities for a few years before being resurrected.

The lampposts that Speer used to line the route between the Brandenburg Gate and Adolf-Hitler-Platz still exist

except for the Tiergarten stretch, where they were removed during the last days of the war in a further widening effort in order to make a landing strip.

Hitler's 50th birthday on April 20, 1939, was celebrated with a massive display of military might parading through Berlin as the Luftwaffe thundered overhead. The previous evening he had opened the reconstructed East-West-Axis which had been completed as far as the Adolf-Hitler-Platz. Soon after 9.00 p.m., a motorcade, led by

Hitler in the front seat of the leading Mercedes, emerged from the Wilhelm-strasse and passed slowly through the Brandenburg Gate. Speer had lined the new road with white-painted plywood pillars alternately mounted with gilded eagles and swastikas. Each pillar was lit from within so that the tin symbols of German might glinted and shone against the night sky. Thousands of Berliners lined the route as the procession proceeded westwards along the five-mile completed section.

Before and after. The first picture was taken of the parade held on August 24, 1938, in honour of the visit to Germany of the Hungarian Regent, Admiral Miklós Horthy de Nagybánya. The picture on the right of Hitler's 50th birthday parade on April 20, 1939, shows how the Charlottenburg Gate on the left has been

moved outwards following the reconstruction. Speer's characteristic double-headed bronze lamp-posts now line the road, although he omitted them in front of the stand. This gap has since been filled in — probably by using some of those removed from near the Brandenburg Gate in 1945.

The East-West-Axis was opened on the evening prior to Hitler's birthday when he drove along the completed section. The repositioned Siegessäule was floodlit as were the decorative plywood pillars which lined the route as far as the Adolf-Hitler-Platz. *Left:* This picture, like our comparison *(right)*, was taken from the Tiergarten S-Bahn bridge.

The actual parade to mark his '50th' took four hours to pass the saluting base. April 20 had been declared a national holiday and thousands of Berliners lined the route to watch some 50,000 troops, either marching or riding on guns, trucks and tanks. In the picture *above* of the reviewing stand can be seen a rather surprising 'guest', bearing in mind the despicable treatment meted out to him by Hitler just a month earlier. The diminutive figure on the right, looking rather incongruous in his top hat, is the Czech President, Dr Emil Hácha, whose country had been taken over by Germany on March 15.

The war, or rather the German reverses in the war, finally put paid to Hitler's grandiose plan. Speer was also diverted to other duties when he took over the position of Minister of Armaments and Munitions on the death of Dr Fritz Todt in February 1942, an appointment which was to lead to Speer's indictment and subsequent imprisonment for 20 years for war crimes. While in prison, Speer drafted his memoirs which were published in 1969, three years after his release from Spandau. 'When on the morning after my release from imprisonment I passed one of these buildings on my way to the airport [the tourism building at the intersection of the grand avenue and Potsdamer Strasse], I saw in a few seconds what I had been blind to for years: our plan completely lacked a sense of proportion.' *Left:* The Haus des Fremdenverkehrs stood just north of the Viktoria (Potsdamer) Bridge. The ruin was later demolished, to be replaced by the Nationalgalerie *(above right)*. The only visible sign of the North-South-Axis today is this circular structure *(right)* beside the railway bridge on Dudenstrasse. Locals refer to it as an air raid bunker but it is in fact one of the first trial footings for the Triumphal Arch.

Only one of the projected buildings for the North-South-Axis was completed, the Haus des Fremdenverkehrs, a vast travel agency-cum-travel business centre, on the south-west corner of what was to be the Rundeplatz (where the Philharmonie now stands) immediately to the north of the Potsdamer Bridge. However, this building was badly damaged during the war and its site is now occupied by the Nationalgalerie.

Another part of Hitler's plan for Berlin was the development of a university city astride the Heerstrasse, south of the Olympic Stadium. Again work was commenced on only one of the proposed buildings, the Wehrtechnischen Fakultät or War Studies Faculty of the Technical High School, but this was never completed. The site served as one of the city's three main ammunition dumps at the end of the war and then was buried under the Teufelsberg, the 111-metre-high mountain of rubble extracted from the ruined city.

So, what else now remains? The most striking legacy still to be seen today of Speer's hand on the face of Berlin is the widened East-West-Axis with its repositioned Victory Monument which he increased in height with an additional row of cannon. In this early post-war shot, the Tiergarten S-Bahn bridge can be seen with the saluting base beyond. This section is now called the Strasse des 17. Juni as far as the Knie (now Ernst-Reuter-Platz) at which point it then changes to Bismarckstrasse. At Sophie-Charlotte-Platz it becomes the Kaiserdamm up to the Theodor-Heuss-Platz (the former Adolf-Hitler-Platz) where the name changes yet again to the Heerstrasse. The road on this side of the monument became the last-ditch airstrip.

We have already seen that street name changes in Berlin are part and parcel of its history. *Right:* The road bisecting the East-West-Axis right in front of the Brandenburg Gate had been renamed in September 1933 when the former Friedrich-Ebert-Strasse became the Hermann-Göring-Strasse. The two pictures *above* were taken over fifty years apart — 1938 and 1991 — and show surprisingly little change. (The street running from left to right, along the southern edge of the Reichstag, was then called Simonstrasse but now it has been changed to Scheidemannstrasse.) However, for the greater proportion of that period, the Hermann-Göring-Strasse lay in the so-called 'death' strip behind the Berlin Wall which ran the entire length of it. We shall see it again in Part IV. Now its name has reverted to Ebertstrasse. At its southern end it meets the Voss-strasse, the location of one of Speer's greatest achievements: the building of the New Reichs Chancellery in less than a year.

Left: This was the accommodation block for the Chancellery security guard (see plan overleaf) facing Lennéstrasse. *Right:* Although the Wall has been removed, the area remains a scene of desolation with the original cobblestones and tram lines of the old Hermann-Göring-Strasse still in situ. Thus, the drain gulley enabled us to pinpoint the exact spot.

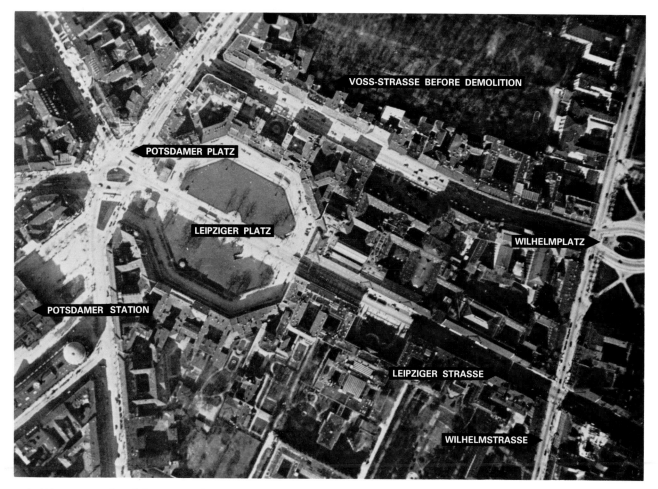

POTSDAMER PLATZ

VOSS-STRASSE BEFORE DEMOLITION

LEIPZIGER PLATZ

WILHELMPLATZ

POTSDAMER STATION

LEIPZIGER STRASSE

WILHELMSTRASSE

As if he was not already busy enough, at the end of January 1938, Speer was summoned by Hitler and abruptly given the task of producing a new Reichs Chancellery by January 10, 1939, the day when Hitler would give his next New Year reception for the Diplomatic Corps. Given the immense scale of the proposed building — some 1,400 feet long — and the almost impossible time-table, this was to prove Speer's greatest architectural challenge.

The Chancellery that Hitler had inherited upon becoming Reichs Chancellor was fairly new, having been erected in 1928-30, but Hitler described it as being only 'fit for a soap company', and Speer had already had to add a balcony to the structure. This building stood on the Wilhelmstrasse, sandwiched between the Presidential Palace and the Borsig Palace, which formed the corner with Voss-strasse, and which had previously been used by Vice-Chancellor Franz von Papen and was now occupied by Hitler's deputy, Rudolf Hess. Speer decided to incorporate the old Chancellery building and Borsig Palace into the new structure, which would replace the miscellany of buildings extending the length of the northern side of Voss-strasse.

By the evening of the first day Speer produced a list of deadlines for Hitler's approval. Work began immediately on clearing the site. The complexity of the task before him can be imagined, for not only had the structural and interior aspects of the design to be worked out in detail to Hitler's satisfac-

The Voss-strasse was a fairly minor side road running parallel to the fashionable Leipziger Strasse which terminated at its western end with the octagon-shaped Leipziger Platz. Hitler gave Speer carte blanche to use the whole of the Voss-strasse, but with an impossible time-table for the size of the project. His first step, even before any plans were drawn up, was to raze the whole of the northern side of the street.

tion, but the materials, fittings and furnishings had to be ordered so that their delivery dates fitted precisely into the completion programme. Speer himself said of this: 'Even at a later stage of the work I had to order many components before the architectural data had

been definitely settled. For example, the longest delivery times were required for the enormous hand-knotted rugs which were to be used in several large salons. I decided their sizes and colours before I knew what the rooms they were meant for would look like. In fact the

Fifty years later the same area undergoes yet another transformation after the demolition of the Berlin Wall. Having been razed a second time by the Communist authorities, this part of the city has now been zoned for commercial re-development. The outline of the Leipziger Platz is just visible within the new building site.

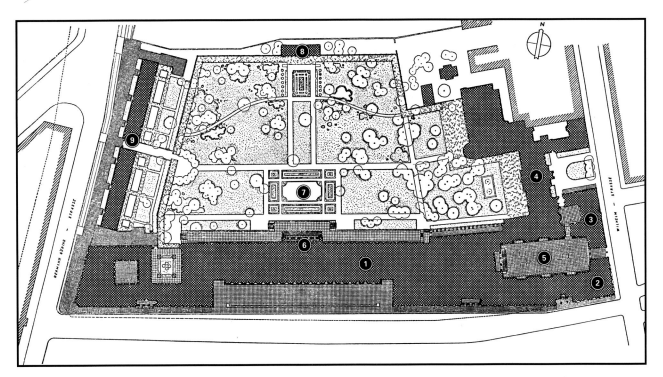

The New Chancellery (1) stretched right along the Voss-strasse from the Wilhelmstrasse in the east to the Hermann-Göring-Strasse in the west. The façade of the Borsig Palace (2) was retained on the corner, as was the 1929-30 extension (3) to the old Reichs Chancellery (4). The existing balcony was retained.

The usual entrance for visitors arriving by automobile was via an inner courtyard (5) called the Ehrenhof, Hitler's study was at (6) overlooking the garden with its ornamental pond (7) and conservatory (8). The guard barracks we saw on page 95 are the two blocks at (9).

rooms were more or less designed around these rugs. I decided to forgo any complicated organisational plan and schedule, since these would only have revealed that the project could not possibly be carried out within the time limit.'

The first part of the new building to be completed were the air raid shelters beneath. Whether this was the full complement that existed at the end of the war — less of course the Führer-bunker which was not built until 1944 — is not clear, but even at this stage the requirement was foreseen. The complex also included two barrack blocks at the rear aligning Hermann-Göring-Strasse for the SS guards.

The aim was to impress and awe distinguished visitors with the power and might of the Third Reich. Speer's plan was therefore to use this elongated site to produce a series of imposing halls and galleries through which the visitor would have to pass before being admitted to the Führer — a walk of nearly 250 yards.

The NSDAP publishers, Franz Eher Nache, produced a souvenir book which included this aquarelle by Paul Herrmann.

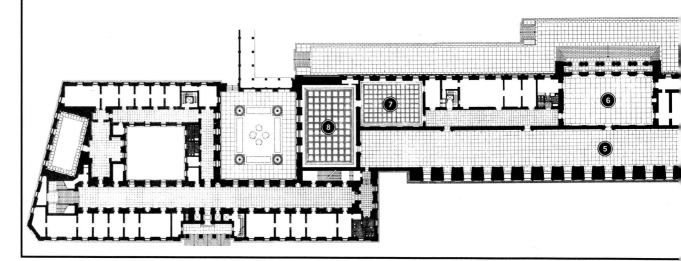

1. Ehrenhof (Courtyard of Honour)
2. Vorhalle (Ante-room)
3. Mosaiksaal (Hall of Mosaics)
4. Runder Saal (Round Salon)
5. Marmorgalerie (Marble Gallery)
6. Arbeitzimmer des Führers (Hitler's Office)
7. Reichskabinettssaal (State Cabinet Office)
8. Grosser Emfangssaal (Reception Hall)
9. Speisesaal (Dining Room)

Speer started by creating the Ehrenhof (Court of Honour). An entry passage was knocked through the left-hand end of the old Chancellery building next to the Borsig Palace and masked with two tall portals, through which the visitors would be driven. An outdoor staircase then led into a medium-sized lobby, from which seventeen feet-high double doors led into the Mosaiksaal, a large hall lined in red marble inlaid with double-eagle motive mosaics and illuminated from above by a large skylight. At the far end another massive door led into the circular Runder Saal, similarly decorated to the Mosaiksaal, but a necessary device to connect it with the slightly different alignment of the rest of the building. Next came the Marmorgalerie (Marble Gallery), nearly 500 feet long and twice as long as the Hall of Mirrors at Versailles. This was illuminated by tall, deeply inset windows overlooking the Voss-strasse on the left. A door at the far end led to the Grosser Empfangssaal (Reception Hall), and five doors were

Left: Hitler described the utilitarian office block extension constructed on the Wilhelmplatz side of the old Reichs Chancellery as giving one 'the impression of a warehouse or of the city fire brigade building' from the outside, while the interior was akin to 'a TB sanitorium'. One of his first moves was to switch the accommodation and reception rooms as far as possible to the ground floor and convert to offices the rooms on the first floor. The Chancellor's office which he inherited overlooked the street and was very noisy, and it quickly overheated if the windows were kept shut. He therefore had his room moved to the rear to overlook the garden. Thus the balcony that Speer added facing the street did not actually lead from Hitler's office. *Right:* When the new Chancellery building was proposed, Speer retained the old extension but cut a large double doorway, wide enough for vehicles, as the entrance to the Ehrenhof.

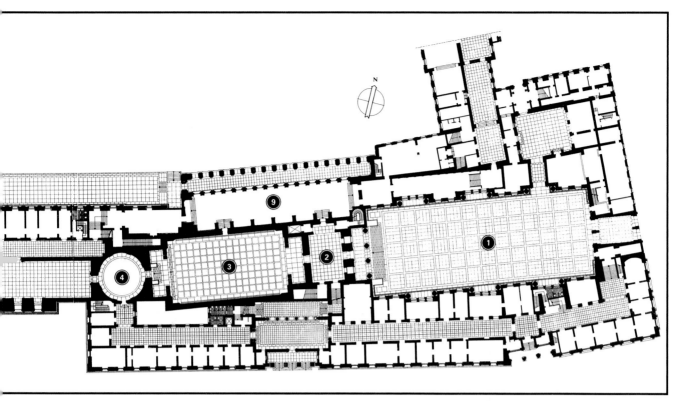

set at regular intervals in the right-hand wall, the second leading to an ante room and the third directly into Hitler's office. This was about 90 feet long by 50 feet wide and was illuminated by five French windows leading out through a pillared portico on to a long terrace overlooking the garden. Hitler's desk and a large map table were designed by Speer himself.

Only by having work going on round the clock, with 4,500 workers operating in two shifts, was it possible to meet the deadline, and on August 1, 1938, the topping out ceremony was held as planned, after only four months of construction work. Next day Hitler addressed the assembled staff and workforce in the Deutschlandhalle, praising their efforts and those of Albert Speer in particular.

The task was actually completed 48 hours ahead of schedule. The whole workforce, including all those that had contributed their efforts from all over the country, were invited to inspect the finished result. Afterwards Hitler addressed them in the Sportpalast:

'I stand here as a representative of the German people. And whenever I receive anyone in the Chancellery, it is not the private individual Adolf Hitler who receives him, but the Leader of the German nation — and therefore it is not I who receive him, but Germany through me. For that reason I want these rooms to be in keeping with their high mission. Every individual has contributed to a structure that will outlast the centuries and will speak to posterity of our times. This is the first architectural creation of the new, great German Reich!'

Hitler rewarded Speer with the Golden Party Badge for this achievement, and took a great delight in showing guests round his new establishment.

All the might of the new Germania was portrayed in the finished Chancellery. Not only through its typical 'Third Reich' style of architecture, but also in the ability to complete such an elaborate undertaking within a year — by January 7, 1939 — two days ahead of schedule. Hitler had already complimented his architect publicly at the topping out ceremony held the previous August: 'I myself have been in the business, in building, and know what a schedule means. This has never happened before. It is a unique achievement.'

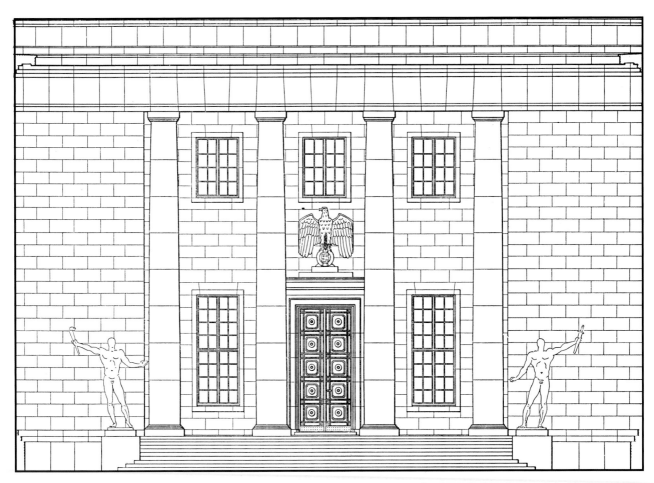

From paper to finished product — the Ehrenhof. This is the view a visitor would have had as he arrived at the inner doorway.

The two statues by Arno Breker denote, left, Die Partei (The Party) and, right, Die Wehrmacht (The Armed Forces).

The Mosaiksaal — predominantly red marble with inlays featuring a double eagle motif by Hermann Kaspar. One can almost hear the echoing footsteps and feel the trepidation of a visitor as he crossed the 150 feet of the Hall of Mosaics. Speer was concerned about the amount of dangerously slippery, highly polished marble on the floors, which he was reluctant to cover with carpets, but Hitler delighted in the thought that his visitors would have to negotiate this hazardous distance, passing comments like: 'On the long walk from the entrance to the reception hall they'll get a taste of the power and grandeur of the Third Reich!' and 'That's exactly right; diplomats should have practice in moving on a slippery surface.'

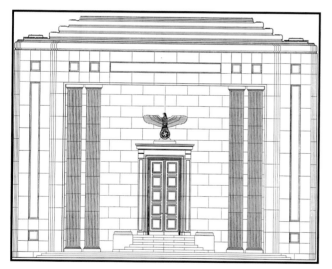

At the far end, a series of steps led up to the Runder Saal. The bronze eagle above the doorway was by Kurt Schmid-Ehmen, who was responsible for the many eagle sculptures throughout the building, including those in stone (see page 99). The eagle had been the national emblem of Germany ever since Charlemagne, King of the Franks, was crowned in Rome in AD 800 when he claimed direct succession to the Roman emperors. He adopted the Roman eagle for his coat-of-arms and, in various forms and attitudes, it was borne by successive German emperors. The Second Reich of 1871-1918 and the Weimar Republic both used the single-headed spread eagle, and Hitler continued the tradition with the addition of the swastika wreath held in its talons.

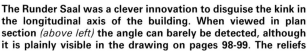

The Runder Saal was a clever innovation to disguise the kink in the longitudinal axis of the building. When viewed in plan section *(above left)* the angle can barely be detected, although it is plainly visible in the drawing on pages 98-99. The reliefs above the doorways were also by Arno Breker and depicted 'Genius' *(below left)* over the door from the Mosaiksaal, and 'Kämpfer' *(below right)* over the door leading to the Marmorgalerie *(above right)*.

Speer commissioned a special publication to commemorate the completion of the building, in which Wilhelm Lotz wrote in contemporary style:

'The big effect of the interior rooms, which Hermann Giesler has described as "obliging the visitor to traverse a secret wonderland at a calm and measured pace", makes its impact with practically no connection with the world outside. This seclusion, which makes itself felt through denying the Mosaiksaal and Runder Saal of any lighting except from above, is also achieved on the street side by the projecting western section, which contains only offices. On the garden side prominence is given to the dining room, the area containing the Führer's adjutants and his own office. This sequence thus runs in a straight line till it reaches the Ehrenhof, where the seclusion and powerful surroundings prepare the way to the inner rooms. The high windows of the Marmorgalerie provide a link with the outside world, but this does not impair the effect since the windows with their deep soffits give this gallery its own restrained rhythm.

'From the double doors on the Wilhelmplatz to the western end of the Marmorgalerie, the building covers a length of more than 300 metres, nearly half taken up by the Marmorgalerie itself. This is the route that official visitors have to follow if they wish to reach the Grosser Empfangssaal after entering the Ehrenhof. The enduring impression left by the rich and varied design of the rooms ranks among the finest that German interior decoration has ever produced. It is not so much the unusual dimensions and the richness of the very fine and rare materials used which evoke this impression, but the development of the elements deriving from the purpose and nature of each particular room. The high standard that Albert Speer set himself in fulfilling his task called for the use of very special materials which, in turn, demand the best design if their nature is to be fully expressed.

'A very successful feature of the design of the Chancellery is the insertion of a round, domed room — the Runder Saal — which invites the visitor to pause and collect his thoughts. The walls are inlaid with marble up to a height of 10.5 metres. The dome is the work of Hermann Kaspar. It has a light-coloured coating making it so light and free that we are scarcely aware that it is a dome as it rises above the marble walls. The skylight, at a height of 16 metres, consists of a broad bronze ring. The artificial lighting is provided indirectly through fittings inserted into recesses above the walls to illuminate the light-coloured vaulting of the dome. In addition, there are lights above the skylight so that light comes from the same direction as the natural light. The effect of the architecture at night is therefore the same as during the day. This avoids the contrast that we often encounter if a room has a quite different artificial lighting compared with daylight.

'The walls are divided into eight sections, in two of which are located the doors on the longitudinal axis. A further section contains a smaller door leading to the administrative wing. Statues by Arno Breker stand in front of the five remaining sections. The marble used in this room consists of two types of different colours, with the dark red and the lighter stone quarried at Adnet in Austria in juxtaposition. This involves a special technique known as incrustation. The floor of this room, 14.25 metres in diameter, consists of a mosaic designed by Hermann Kaspar.

More slippery surfaces in the Marmorgalerie — Speer's attempt to upstage the Hall of Mirrors at Versailles.

'We now enter the Marmorgalerie, which continues the east-west sequence. Here Albert Speer resurrected and gave a new meaning to a form of architecture for which there no longer appeared to be any place. Although this is basically a communicating area it is, above all, the climax of the room sequence — the area in front of the Führer's office.

'In those days when there was a feeling for lavish room layouts, special attention was always given to the contribution made by staircases, corridors and galleries. Wherever men appeared as representatives of the state and its power, the scope of the buildings concerned was widely extended, and the salons and halls became more important than the rooms and chambers themselves.

'The Marmorgalerie of the new Reichs Chancellery is its most impressive room as regards constructional lavishness. It covers 146 metres in length, has a breadth of 12 metres and a height of 9.5 metres, and runs behind the whole length of the middle section. A mirror-bright floor made of Saalburg Altrot marble extends over the whole surface. The walls consist of light-coloured marble slabs, giving the gallery an unrestricted and splendid lightness, and providing a most effective background for the colours of the furnishings and tapestries.

'On the street side the room is divided by nineteen high windows, strongly profiled, and constructed of a dark red marble known as Deutschrot. The soffit depth of each window is 2.1 metres, so that the deep window recesses making a striking accompaniment to the surrounding frames along the whole length of the gallery. The windows, which are 6 metres high and 2.35 metres wide, consist of frosted panes fitted into wooden frames with bronze glazing bars. Opposite stand five doors with borders of the same marble. The middle one leads into the Führer's office and is crowned with a monogrammed shield; the other doors, which lead to the areas in front of the adjutants' rooms, carry similar shields decorated with coats of arms, all being the work of the sculptor Hans Vogel. Above the doors which lead to the Runder Saal and the Grosser Empfangssaal are national emblems by Kurt Schmid-Ehmen. Wall lamps with gilded bronze fittings give the room a festive character, while lights built into the windows radiate additional light into the room from the same direction from which the daylight enters.

'The Marmorgalerie presents a picture of lively and beautiful colours as a result of the groups of furniture that are arranged on carpets between the doors in the long wall. Tapestries hang between the doors. The furniture, designed by Albert Speer, comprises brilliant examples of German furniture-making with beautiful marquetry and costly coverings. The room's splendid colour effects are further intensified by the choice flowers and plants.

And so to the holy of holies: the inner sanctum of the Führer, protected by his personal Leibstandarte bodyguard.

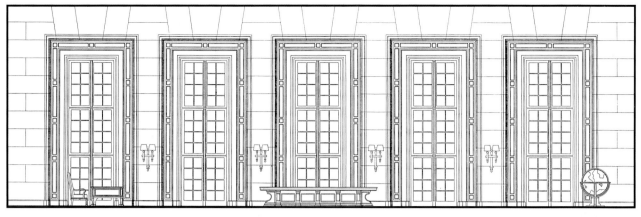

'The Führer's office looks out to the garden terrace through five French windows 6 metres high and 2 metres wide. Five similar bays to those formed by the French windows are repeated on the opposite wall, constructed with fine, inlaid panels. In the middle bay on this side is the entrance door leading in from the Marmorgalerie. (There are two more doors on each of the narrow sides leading to the State Cabinet Room and to the areas where the adjutants' room are located.) The office, which is 27 metres long and 14.5 metres wide, has walls consisting of a dark red marble from Austria known as Limbacher. With a height of 9.75 metres, the room has a panelled ceiling with beams of darker wood that is a splendid feat of joinery. On the floor made of Ruhpolding marble lies a single large carpet.

'The furnishings and layout are designed to be completely subordinate to the main spacial effects. On the narrow eastern side a marble fireplace measuring 2.7 metres high and 3.25 metres wide has been built of the same marble as the walls, for which Richard Klein has devised fine panels made of cast iron with figurative reliefs. The shields above the side doors are also the work of Richard Klein, while the national emblem above the entrance door, which is made of carved and guilded wood, was devised by Kurt Schmid-Ehmen. Albert Speer has designed the new furniture for this room: the Führer's big writing desk, the credenza unit on the west wall, and the large map table in

Speer: 'His study met with his undivided approval. He was particularly pleased by the inlay on his desk representing a sword half drawn from its sheath. "Good, good. When the diplomats sitting in front of me at this desk see that, they'll learn to shiver and shake".'

front of the centre of the window, which consists of an especially fine piece of marble from Austria quarried and dressed from a single slab measuring 5 by 1.6 metres. The pattern for the inlay work was designed by Hermann Kaspar.

'Over the fireplace hangs Lenbach's famous portrait of Bismarck. The basic colours of this room come from a combination of the beautiful brown shades of wood and the red-brown of the marble, the fine materials used creating a colour synthesis that is severe but filled with restrained strength, such as the Führer loves when at work. Great thoughts are born here, decisive decisions are made in the closest of circles, and we enter this room with a feeling of reverence, since the great creative spirit of the man who works here consecrates the surroundings.'

The Road to War

Germany's military might portrayed in all its glory before the Führer on Army Day, Monday, September 12, at Nuremberg. Earlier in the year, German troops had entered Austria and marched on Vienna — the first acquisition of territory outside Germany. Now the focus of attention was on the German-speaking areas of Czechoslovakia — a country which included large German, Polish, Hungarian and Ukrainian minorities.

Meanwhile, Hitler was bringing Germany inexorably towards war, his eyes on expansion to the east. However, at the beginning of 1938 Hitler encountered problems with his Minister of Defence, Generalfeldmarschall Werner von Blomberg, and Generaloberst Werner Freiherr von Fritsch, Commander-in-Chief of the Wehrmacht. Shortly after attending the marriage of Blomberg, ten years a widower, it was discovered that his bride had once been a prostitute. Hitler was furious and said that either Blomberg renounce his marriage or be fired. Blomberg refused to comply, leaving von Fritsch, who was

even more opposed to Hitler's policies, as the obvious candidate for this ministerial post. But Göring produced police evidence that Fritsch had been engaged in homosexual activites, which eventually proved to be false because of confusion with a retired old cavalry captain named Frisch. Von Fritsch too was dismissed and although exonerated by a court-martial later that year, never regained a position of prominence. (As honorary colonel of his old regiment, the 12. Artillerie, he went into the

Polish campaign with them only to meet his death in battle.)

Few people knew of these scandals and Hitler was able to mask it all by convening an assembly of general officers on February 4, at which he told them of the necessity to discharge Blomberg because of his unfortunate marriage and of the criminal charges pending against von Fritsch. He then announced the reorganisation of the Wehrmacht with himself as Commander-in-Chief of the Wehrmacht and

---

Soldiers of the German Army! Once again, as in past years, you stand here in Nuremberg on the occasion of the Reichsparteitag, but this year for the first time as soldiers of the Greater German Reich. That this dream of centuries could become a reality, we owe to two facts; first, the successful creation of a real community of the German people, and thereby of the conditions necessary for the fulfilment of this dream, secondly, the establishment of Germany's new armed forces, whose soldiers finally realised this dream by their march [into Austria].

From this two conclusions may be drawn. First, the necessity for the existence of the Movement which in less than two decades has succeeded in bringing the German people out of a condition of extreme internal chaos into the unity which we see today. The National Socialist teaching and Party are the guarantors of this community of the German people at home. Secondly, we may learn how necessary it is that to this community of the people, with its ordered domestic life, we should give protection from the foreign foe.

No negotiation, no conference, no agreement gave to us Germans our natural right to unity. We had to take this right for ourselves, and that we could take it was due solely to you, my soldiers!

And so these two great institutions of our people have two like tasks to perform. National Socialism educates our people into the community of the people at home, and the Army educates this same people to defend this community against attack from abroad.

You, my soldiers, have already in this new Reich been entrusted with a task. Through your performance of that task you have won the affection of the German people. It has placed its confidence in you; it knows that it can trust its sons in arms. For you have the best weapons that there are today, you have the best training, and I know that you have also the highest character. You can take your places in the eternal and imperishable Front of the German soldiery!

ADOLF HITLER,
TAG DER WEHRMACHT, SEPTEMBER 12, 1938

General Wilhelm Keitel, Blomberg's former 'office manager' as he described him, as Wehrmacht Chief-of-Staff and General Walther von Brauchitsch as Commander-in-Chief of the Army. His over-promotion of Keitel, and a cash advance that von Brauchitsch needed in order to take over the new job, ensured that both were deeply indebted to him. The military were now firmly in his hands, bound not just by a personal oath but also by the chains of command.

Göring had hoped for the Ministry of War but was considered by Hitler as too lazy for such a rôle. As a sop, the Führer made him Commander-in-Chief of the Luftwaffe, with the rank of Generalfeldmarschall, which pleased him greatly. At the same time Baron Konstantin Neurath was replaced by Joachim von Ribbentrop as Foreign Minister.

Hitler's first objective now was the incorporation of Austria into a Greater German Reich. Through his Minister to Austria, von Papen, he peremptorily summoned the Austrian Chancellor Kurt von Schuschnigg to Berchtesgaden on February 12 and gave him three days in which to get Austria to accede to his preposterous demands. These included the release of Chancellor Dolfuss's assassins and all imprisoned Nazis, the reinstatement of all dismissed Nazi officials and officers, and the appointment of Artur Seyss-Inquart as Minister of

Hitler's speeches at the 1938 Party Rally at Nuremberg (in the event, the last one ever held) made his aims over the Sudetenland area of Czechoslovakia crystal clear: 'I believe that I shall serve peace best if I leave no doubt upon this point. I have not put forward the demand that Germany may oppress three and a half million Frenchmen or that, for instance, three and a half million of the English should be given up to us for oppression: my demand is that the oppression of three and a half million Germans in Czechoslovakia shall cease and that its place shall be taken by the free right of self-determination. We should be sorry if, through this, our relations to the other European states should be troubled or suffer damage. But in that case the fault would not lie with us.'

I believe that it cannot benefit the cause of European peace that anyone should be left in doubt on the point: the German Reich is not willing in general to express a lack of interest in all European questions and in particular it is not prepared to remain indifferent to the suffering and the life of a sum-total of three and a half million Germans or to take no further part in their misfortune. We understand it when England or France champion their interests throughout an entire world. But I would like to assure statesmen in Paris and London that there are also German interests which we are determined to safeguard and that, too, in all circumstances. I would like to remind them of a speech delivered before the Reichstag in the year 1933 in which for the first time I declared before the world that there can be national questions where our way is clearly marked out and that then I would rather take upon myself every distress, every danger, and every hardship rather than fail in the fulfilment of such steps as were necessary.

ADOLF HITLER,
NUREMBERG, SEPTEMBER 12, 1938

---

the Interior with full powers over the police.

Hitler then ordered his generals to conduct manouevres on the Austrian border as if in preparation for an invasion. Hitler's bluff succeeded in frightening the Austrians into compliance. He gambled that neither France nor Britain would, or could, come to Austria's aid, and the gamble paid off. Prime Minister Neville Chamberlain virtually condoned the move in his spirit of appeasement with Germany, while France was virulent but equally ineffective. Only three weeks later Hitler imposed new demands on Austria, which resulted on March 9 in Chancellor Schuschnigg defiantly calling for a plebiscite on the question of unification with a plea for a free and independent Austria. This was too much for Hitler, who ordered military preparations for an invasion. On March 12, German troops marched into Austria unopposed, the Austrian government having ordered their troops to withdraw. They made their way with the aid of tourist guidebooks, cheered on by enthusiastic crowds, and refuelling at commercial petrol pumps as they went. Hitler made

The Zeppelinwiese stadium was another of Albert Speer's spectacular creations. It remained intact until 1967 when the colonnade of the main grandstand was demolished. It was 'de-Nazified' by XV Corps engineers on April 25, 1945 when they blew the swastika emblem from its plinth behind the tribune.

The crisis over the future of Czechoslovakia held the world in its grip for the next eighteen days. Berlin was not a party to the events which followed, as these were centred on Berchtesgaden, where the British Prime Minister, Neville Chamberlain, met Hitler on September 15; Bad Godesberg where the two statesmen had a further meeting on September 22-23, and Munich. However, on Monday, September 26 — at the height of the crisis — Hitler fuelled the flames with a vitriolic speech at the Berlin Sportpalast. William Shirer was giving a running broadcast on the event to CBS in the States. Sitting in the balcony just above the rostrum, he witnessed one of the Führer's most virulent outbursts, with Hitler 'shouting and shrieking in the worst paroxysm I had ever seen him in. He venomously hurled personal insults at "Herr Beneš", and declared that the issue of war or peace was now up to the Czech President.' Hitler's deadline was October 1.

his own triumphant entry, stopping at Linz the first night and moving on to Vienna the next day.

Rudolf Hess quickly set about the Nazification of the country, which was renamed Ostmark, while Himmler and Heydrich purged the police and established their own controls. The persecution of the Jews began immediately.

A month later a nationwide plebiscite approved the Anschluss by 99.73 per cent in Austria and 99.02 per cent in the rest of Germany. It could not have been a more convincing victory for Hitler.

The next target was Czechoslovakia, the excuse being the German population in the Sudetenland on the German-Czech border. First the French had to

be held in check, so over half a million men were sent to begin work on the West Wall, the German counter to the Maginot Line, under the same Todt Organisation that had been responsible for the construction of the autobahns.

Hitler also used the 1938 Party Rally at Nuremberg, celebrated as the first of Greater Germany, to condemn the Czechs for their handling of the Sudetenland Germans.

The British Prime Minister was sufficiently alarmed to fly out for the day to see Hitler at Berchtesgaden on September 15. From their discussions it was clear that nothing would satisfy Hitler other than an immediate handover of the Sudetenland by the Czechs. The British Prime Minister flew back to

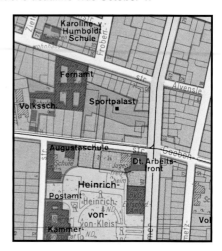

The central location of the Sportpalast on the Potsdamer Strasse made it an ideal venue for party events, and it was used frequently for public meetings by Hitler. After the war the hall experienced a different sort of sermon from the evangelist Billy Graham before it was demolished in 1974, to be replaced by blocks of apartments.

With tension in Europe at breaking point, at this point Benito Mussolini stepped in after responding to an official British request for an international conference to solve the crisis. When Mussolini said that he would represent Italy personally, Hitler agreed, inviting Britain and France to a Four Power meeting to be held in Munich. However, the country which was the centre of debate was not invited; only at the last moment was it agreed that the Czech President, Eduard Beneš, could send two 'observers' to Munich. France was represented by its Premier, Edouard Daladier. The conference convened on Thursday, September 29, and within twelve hours the fate of the Czechs had been sealed with an agreement signed over their heads. Hitler, Mussolini, Daladier and Chamberlain each returned to their capitals, claiming the outcome as a victory . . . though for entirely different reasons. *Right:* Hitler acknowledges the cheers of the crowds in the Wilhelmstrasse as he drives to the Chancellery from Anhalter station.

The Air Ministry building in the background is a common reference point — then and now. The comparison was taken right opposite the Voss-strasse.

consult with his Cabinet and the French, flying out again to see Hitler at Bad Godesberg on the Rhine on September 21, all to no avail. Hitler wanted the Czechs to evacuate by October 1 at the latest. If there was not to be war the British and French would have to persuade the Czechs to comply. The British Cabinet and people were alarmed at Hitler's ultimatum and began preparations for war, but Chamberlain knew how unprepared they were and was out for peace at any price. Between them the British and French persuaded the Czechs to comply on the basis of securing Hitler's guarantee of Czechoslovakia's new borders. As a safety precaution, the Czechs mobilised.

The French, British, Italian and German leaders then met for a conference in Munich on September 29, from which Chamberlain returned the next day to be received by cheering crowds as if he had been a conquering hero, waving his piece of paper guaranteeing 'peace for our time'.

A similar triumphal welcome greeted the British Prime Minister who waved a piece of paper aloft which he had asked Hitler to sign the following morning. The paper 'bears his name upon it as well as mine,' declared Chamberlain at Heston airport *(left)*, little realising the contempt with which Hitler viewed the whole matter. When Foreign Minister von Ribbentrop complained to Hitler about signing the document, Hitler replied scornfully: 'Don't take it so seriously. This paper has no importance at all!' *Right:* To Chamberlain, however, at the window of No. 10 Downing Street it was 'Peace for our time.'

The Munich Pact provided for the evacuation of the Czech Sudentenland in stages. Areas bordering Germany were to be taken over by the Germans between October 1 and 7, and further essentially Germanic areas three days later. Seven inner enclaves were to be occupied by international troops, whereupon plebiscites were to be held by the end of November.

Meanwhile Hitler was out on the streets of Berlin to celebrate his bloodless victory — a victory which we now know he could never have won had he resorted to arms. *Above:* Here he salutes the colours of an Honour Company drawn up on the Saarland Strasse on October 1. *Below:* Formerly Königgrätzer Strasse, today its name has changed to Stresemannstrasse.

The following month the true face of Nazism showed itself once again — but this time it was an evil portent of worse to come. The boycott against Jewish interests had begun in 1933, in the very first days of the new government (see page 60), but on November 9, 1938, this latent hostility against the Jews came out into the open. Overtly responding to the assassination of one of his diplomats in Paris by a 17-year-old Jewish immigrant, Herschel Grynszpan, Hitler declared that 'the SA should be allowed to have a fling'. Heydrich issued the orders detailing the measures to be taken against the Jews at 1.20 a.m. and by morning the deed was done. The *New York Times* described it as 'a wave of destruction unparalleled in Germany since the Thirty Years War'. *Above left:* In Berlin, one of the most famous German synagogues stood on the Oranienburger Strasse where it had been dedicated in September 1866. *Centre:* Burned out and further damaged by British bombing in 1943, it remained a gutted shell until restoration work began in the 1960s. *Right:* Now a museum of Jewish culture, its oriental façade still retains echoes of its former glory.

On November 7, 1938, a young Polish Jew shot a German diplomat in Paris. Two days later Counsellor Ernst von Rath died of his wounds, an excuse Goebbels used for launching a pogrom in Germany. The night of November 9, 1938, became known as 'Kristallnacht' from the broken glass that littered the streets as Nazi thugs went into action, smashing up over 7,500 Jewish-owned shops and over 170 houses. Throughout Germany 267 synagogues were destroyed, 236 Jews killed and more than 600 seriously injured. The world was outraged, but the persecution went on. Within the next few days an estimated 30,000 Jews were rounded up and put into concentration camps. The brunt of this action fell on Berlin where the two main synagogues in Fasanenstrasse and Oranienburger Strasse were totally destroyed, and 21 others damaged to varying degrees. Of the city's Jewish population, 12,000 were sent to camps. As Göring said: 'I would not like to be a Jew in Germany today.'

The sixth anniversary of the Nazis coming to power — January 30, 1939 — was marked by Hitler's speech to the Reichstag in which he declared war on world Jewry. On the same day he ordered the construction of a vast submarine fleet.

Left: In a small side street off the fashionable Kufürstendamm lay the Fasanenstrasse synagogue — even the Kaiser had attended its opening in 1912. It, too, was burned out on Kristallnacht — this photograph being taken 20 years after the event. *Above:* The old doorway was incorporated into the new Jewish community centre erected on the site in 1959.

Attention switched back to Czechoslovakia as Hitler ordered Goebbels to start a propaganda campaign against that country, accusing the Czechs of massing near the new border with the Sudetenland, of terrorising the German minority and of grossly mistreating the Slovak population, the latter point being aimed at splitting their fragile unity. When the Czechoslovakian President, Emil Hácha, called on Hitler to try and ameliorate the situation, he was told that plans were already advanced for the incorporation of his country into the Reich the next morning. A document was drafted placing the future of the country into Hitler's hands, which the shocked President and his Foreign Minister were bullied into signing in the early hours of March 15 just before the troops moved in. A triumphant Hitler went off to inspect his new territory.

This time the world took effective notice. Hitler had broken an international agreement less than a year old. The British and French governments countered by making pacts with Poland, Rumania, Greece and Turkey and even entered into discussions with the Soviet Union.

Hitler now turned his attention to Poland. On April 3 he issued a top secret directive to his senior commanders informing them that he intended to attack Poland on September 1. At the same time, in order to stop the Russians intervening on Poland's behalf, he started wooing the Soviet Union, at first with a trade treaty. Stalin's willingness to co-operate led to the signing of the German-Soviet Non-Aggression Pact on August 23 that wrote off Poland between them.

Then, on April 28, Hitler made a speech before a vast audience that was broadcast throughout Europe and even in the USA. In this he condemned the change in Great Britain's foreign policy, claiming that it negated the naval treaty between the two countries of 1935, and then attacked the Poles, declaring the non-aggression pact between Poland and Germany null and void as a result of Polish transgressions. Two international treaties were thus torn up in front of the world. The signal could not have been clearer.

On May 22 Italy and Germany signed the 'Pact of Steel' uniting their military efforts in case of war, and Hitler started working on Japan to join them.

'Beware the Ides of March . . .' The three crunch points in the countdown to the Second World War. March 1936: German troops re-enter the demilitarised Rhineland unopposed. March 1938: Austria incorporated into the German Third Reich. March 1939: Hitler breaks the Munich agreement and enters Prague. The year began with the spotlight falling on another item on Hitler's acquisition list: Germany's pre-1914 territory in the east. Its loss was aggravated by Article (ii) in the Versailles Treaty which not only ceded West Prussia to Poland but, at the same time, also provided her with access to the Baltic via a strip of land which cut Germany off from East Prussia. The Polish Corridor, and the creation of the Free City of Danzig under League of Nations jurisdiction, was a sore point with Hitler, especially as the population of the city was still 90 per cent German. The new word that Hitler began using more and more to justify German claims in the East was 'Lebensraum' — living space. On May 1, 1939, he drove to the Olympic stadium to deliver his May Day address to the nation. It was the clearest warning yet of what was about to come to pass.

By now a familiar scene: cheering crowds lining the streets; the whirring cameras; the 'Sieg Heils'; the open-top parade car flanked by security guards. *Top:* The procession passes the old Palace of the Crown Prince (see page 13) as it travels west along the Unter den Linden *(above)*.

Negotiations with the Soviets continued in competition with the British and French, suddenly coming to a conclusion on August 23 when Stalin agreed to a non-aggression pact with Germany, part of which was a secret protocol carving up eastern Europe:

'1. In the event of a territorial and political transformation of the territories belonging to the Baltic States (Finland, Estonia, Latvia, Lithuania), the northern frontier of Lithuania shall represent the frontier of the spheres of interest both of Germany and the USSR.

'2. In the event of a territorial and political transformation of the territories belonging to the Polish State, the spheres of interest of both Germany and the USSR shall be bounded approximately by the line of the rivers Narev, Vistula and San.'

The way was now clear for Hitler to act. The excuse was provided by Operation 'Himmler', a staged border incident in which a German radio station on the border would appear to have been attacked and taken over by a German-speaking Pole calling for conflict. Some dozen condemned convicts from a concentration camp were first dressed in Polish Army uniforms and then given lethal injections by an SS doctor before being given gunshot wounds and scattered around the area as if having been killed in the attack.

All went according to plan. The German attack commenced at dawn on September 1 with a Blitzkrieg war to smash the Polish forces. Two days later Great Britain and France honoured their commitments to Poland and were at war with Germany. The Second World War had begun.

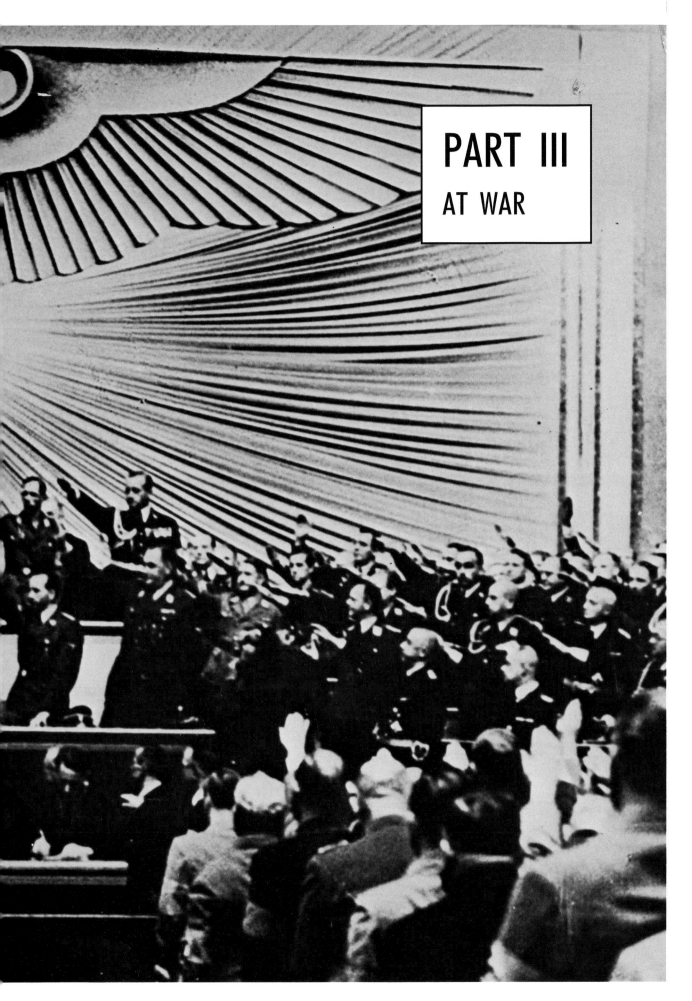

PART III
AT WAR

Friday, September 1, 1939, 4.47 a.m. A salvo from the German battleship *Schleswig-Holstein* begins the overture to the Second World War.

For months we have been suffering under the torture of a problem which the Versailles Diktat created — a problem which has deteriorated until it becomes intolerable for us. Danzig was and is a German city. The Corridor was and is German. Both these territories owe their cultural development exclusively to the German people. As in other German territories of the East, all German minorities living there have been ill-treated in the most distressing manner. More than 1,000,000 people of German blood had in the years 1919-20 to leave their homeland. . . .

You know the proposals that I have made to fulfil the necessity of restoring German sovereignty over German territories. You know the endless attempts I made for a peaceful clarification and understanding of the problem of Austria, and later of the problem of the Sudentenland, Bohemia, and Moravia. It was all in vain.

It is impossible to demand that an impossible position should be cleared up by peaceful revision, and at the same time constantly reject peaceful revision. It is also impossible to say that he who undertakes to carry out these revisions for himself transgresses a law, since the Versailles Diktat is not law to us. A signature was forced out of us with pistols at our head and with the threat of hunger for millions of people. And then this document, with our signature, obtained by force, was proclaimed as a solemn law. . . .

I am determined to solve (1) the Danzig question; (2) the question of the Corridor; and (3) to see to it that a change is made in the relationship between Germany and Poland that shall ensure a peaceful co-existence. In this I am resolved to continue the fight until either the present Polish government is willing to bring about this change or until another Polish government is ready to do so. I am resolved to remove from the German frontiers the element of uncertainty, the everlasting atmosphere of conditions resembling civil war. I will see to it that in the East there is, on the frontier, a peace precisely similar to that on our other frontiers.

In this I will take the necessary measures to see that they do not contradict the proposals I have already made known in the Reichstag itself to the rest of the world, that is to say, I will not war against women and children. I have ordered my air force to restrict itself to attacks on military objectives. If, however, the enemy thinks he can from that draw carte blanche on his side to fight by the other methods he will receive an answer that will deprive him of hearing and sight.

This night, for the first time, Polish regular soldiers fired on our own territory. Since 5.45 a.m. we have been returning the fire, and from now on bombs will be met with bombs. Whoever fights with poison gas will be fought with poison gas. Whoever departs from the rules of humane warfare can only expect that we shall do the same. I wiil continue this struggle, no matter against whom, until the safety of the Reich and its rights are secured.

For six years now I have been working on the building up of the German defences. Over 90 milliards have in that time been spent on the building up of these defence forces. They are now the best equipped and are above all comparison with what they were in 1914. My trust in them is unshakable. When I called up these forces and when I now ask sacrifices of the German people and if necessary every sacrifice, then I have a right to do so, for I also am today absolutely ready, just as we were formerly, to make every personal sacrifice.

I am asking of no German man more than I myself was ready throughout four years at any time to do. There will be no hardships for Germans to which I myself will not submit. My whole life henceforth belongs more than ever to my people. I am from now on just first soldier of the German Reich. I have once more put on that coat that was the most sacred and dear to me. I will not take it off again until victory is secured, or I will not survive the outcome.

Should anything happen to me in the struggle then my first sucessor is Party Comrade Göring; should anything happen to Party Comrade Göring my next successor is Party Comrade Hess. You would then be under obligation to give to them as Führer the same blind loyalty and obedience as to myself. Should anything happen to Party Comrade Hess, then by law the Senate will be called, and will choose from its midst the most worthy — that is to say the bravest — successor.

As a National Socialist and as German soldier I enter upon this struggle with a stout heart. My whole life has been nothing but one long struggle for my people, for its restoration, and for Germany. There was only one watchword for that struggle: faith in this people. One word I have never learned: that is, surrender.

If, however, anyone thinks that we are facing a hard time, I should ask him to remember that once a Prussian King, with a ridiculously small State, opposed a stronger coalition, and in three wars finally came out successful because that State had that stout heart that we need in these times. I would, therefore, like to assure all the world that a November 1918 will never be repeated in German history. Just as I myself am ready at any time to stake my life — any one can take it for my people and for Germany — so I ask the same of all others.

Whoever, however, thinks he can oppose this national command, whether directly or indirectly, shall fall. We have nothing to do with traitors. We are all faithful to our old principle. It is quite unimportant whether we ourselves live, but it is essential that our people shall live, that Germany shall live. The sacrifice that is demanded of us is not greater than the sacrifice that many generations have made. If we form a community closely bound together by vows, ready for anything, resolved never to surrender, then our will will master every hardship and difficulty. And I would like to close with the declaration that I once made when I began the struggle for power in the Reich. I then said: 'If our will is so strong that no hardship and suffering can subdue it, then our will and our German might shall prevail.'

ADOLF HITLER,
THE REICHSTAG, SEPTEMBER 1, 1939

Those first shots were fired at the Polish fortifications on Westerplatte from the Port Canal of the River Vistula . *(See also After the Battle No. 65.)*

Five hours after the *Schleswig-Holstein* opened fire at Danzig, Hitler addressed a special session of the Reichstag in Berlin. Forty-eight hours later Great Britain and France had declared war although neither country was in any position to counter the attack on Poland. That evening Hitler left Berlin aboard his personal train for the front which he toured extensively over the next two weeks. On September 17, the Germans demanded Poland's surrender. Two days later Hitler entered Danzig.

Victory

There followed three years of unqualified victory with very few setbacks; three years that swept the German population along with their Nazi leadership, turning many a 'doubting Thomas' into a fervent patriot. In Berlin, excited crowds lined the streets to cheer the victors, united in their enthusiasm and requiring no prompting from the Party organisations. With victory came its fruits: medals and awards for heroes, booty and loot from other lands, butter and other luxuries, silken stockings and underwear for the wives and girlfriends, and for avid collectors like Hermann Göring, art treasures beyond price. All in all, this was a time of celebration, great national pride in achievement, and confidence in the future under Hitler's leadership.

The campaign in Poland lasted only five weeks, the superior numbers, equipment and training of the German forces, helped by a 'stab in the back' Soviet invasion from the east on September 17, brought a speedy end to the spirited Polish resistance. For a loss of 10,000 dead and 30,000 wounded, the Germans inflicted severe casualties on the Poles and captured 700,000 prisoners, the Russians 200,000. During this time, the Western Allies were unable to bring any physical pressure to bear against the Germans, and the U-Boats out in the Atlantic sank 41 out of a total of 53 Allied ships lost for a loss of only two of their own in the first month. Moreover, one of these ships was indeed a prize, the British aircraft carrier HMS *Courageous* on September 17.

It's a 'counter-attack'! At dawn this morning Hitler moved against Poland. It's a flagrant, inexcusable, unprovoked act of aggression. But Hitler and the High Command call it a 'counter-attack'. A grey morning with overhanging clouds. The people in the street were apathetic when I drove to the Rundfunk for my first broadcast at 8.15 a.m. . . . Along the East-West-Axis the Luftwaffe were mounting five big anti-aircraft guns to protect Hitler when he addresses the Reichstag at 10.00 a.m. Throughout the speech, I thought as I listened, ran a curious strain, as though Hitler himself were dazed at the fix he had got himself into and felt a little desperate about it. Somehow he did not carry conviction and there was much less cheering in the Reichstag than on previous, less important occasions. . . .

Tomorrow Britain and France probably will come in and you have your second World War. The British and French tonight sent an ultimatum to Hitler to withdraw his troops from Poland . . .

WILLIAM SHIRER,
BERLIN, SEPTEMBER 1, 1939

Danzig is now almost exclusively referred to by its Polish name of Gdansk. This is the main street — Dluga — 50 years after Hitler rode along it as a conquering hero.

The Germans having seized the initiative, there was little the Allies could do to save Poland, and she was crushed between the German hammer and the Soviet anvil, Russia having invaded eastern Poland on September 17. The spoils were then divided up, Germany taking 73,000 square miles in the west containing the industrial sector with 22 million inhabitants, while the Soviets obtained the eastern oil fields, 77,000 square miles of land and 13 million people. On September 30, Hitler decorated the leaders of the air force, army and navy who had secured the victory with the Ritterkreuz (the Knight's Cross) in a ceremony held in his office in the New Chancellery. *Above left:* **Generalfeldmarschall Göring, Oberbefehlshaber der Luftwaffe.** *Above right:* **Generaloberst von Brauchitsch, Oberbefehlshaber des Heeres.** *Below left:* **Generaloberst Keitel, Chef des Oberkommandos der Werhrmacht,** and *below right* **Grossadmiral Raeder, Oberbefehlshaber der Kriegsmarine.**

The following month the British lost another capital ship when *U-47*, commanded by Kapitänleutnant Prien, sank the battleship *Royak Oak* at anchor in Scapa Flow on October 14.

On October 6, Hitler gave a major speech in the Reichstag offering peace to France and Great Britain, and three days later he issued a secret directive in which he stated his intent to attack England and France if they would not give up the war. The German General Staff produced the plans of Operation 'Gelb' (Yellow) within ten days, but the debate on how best to carry out this operation continued until mid-January 1940, when Hitler decided to postpone operations in the west until the spring. However, plans for the invasion of Norway were also under way.

Meanwhile, the real war continued at sea, where the German U-Boats and mines continued to exact their toll. The

> *In 1914, I believe, the excitement in Berlin on the first day of the World War was tremendous. Today, no excitement, no hurrahs, no cheering, no throwing of flowers, no war fever, no war hysteria. There is not even any hate for the French and British — despite Hitler's various proclamations to the people, the Party, the East Army, the West Army, accusing the 'English warmongers and capitalistic Jews' of starting this war. When I passed the French and British embassies this afternoon, the sidewalk in front of each of them was deserted. A lone Schupo paced up and down before each.*
>
> WILLIAM SHIRER,
> BERLIN, SEPTEMBER 3, 1939

German pocket battleships *Graf Spee* and *Deutschland* were also at large on the high seas, sinking and capturing Allied merchant shipping. However, on December 13, the *Graf Spee* was tracked down by three British cruisers off the River Plate estuary which then engaged her for two hours before her captain withdrew into neutral waters.

Three days later he scuttled his ship rather than enter into what he thought would be a hopeless contest.

On March 18, 1940, Hitler met Mussolini at the Brenner Pass, where the Duce stated his preparedness to join in the war against France and Great Britain, a gesture of bravado that was to cost Mussolini dear.

Just days later came news of another astounding German victory — this time by the U-Boat arm of the Kriegsmarine. In a daring operation on the night of October 13-14, Kapitänleutnant Günther Prien entered the main anchorage of the Royal Navy's Home Fleet at Scapa Flow in the Orkney Islands and torpedoed the battleship *Royal Oak*. Hitler had the entire crew flown to Berlin to be decorated. *Left:* Here Prien marches his men across the Wilhelmplatz from the Kaiserhof Hotel. *Right:* Today the massive bulk of the Czechoslovakian Embassy, built on the actual square itself, makes a comparison meaningless.

Then on April 8, 1940, the German warships and troop transports started moving towards Norway at the same time that British naval forces were also moving eastwards across the North Sea to try to prevent the Germans getting control of Norway's assets. Denmark was overrun and occupied without a fight. Despite landings by British and French troops leading to the first land battles involving the Western Allies against the Germans, by June 8 the whole of Norway was firmly under German occupation.

But this was now merely a side issue, for the attack in the west had been launched on May 10 with the invasion of Holland and Belgium. The highly-skilled airborne assault on the Eben-Emael fortress on the first day enabled a rapid crossing of the Albert Canal. The Dutch and Belgian Armies were unable to delay the German advance sufficiently to enable the British and French forces to redeploy effectively to their assistance. The Dutch Army surrendered on May 15, followed by the Belgian Army on May 28, by which time the remains of the British Expeditionary Force had been driven back on Dunkirk with some of their French Allies, and their evacuation to the United Kingdom, which was to continue until June 3, had begun. Nevertheless, the Germans had still captured 40,000 Allied troops and sank some 80 merchant and naval ships, as well as numerous smaller vessels.

The 'Blitzkrieg' pressed rapidly on through France, whose strategic reserves had already been used up. On June 11 Paris was declared an open city, and by June 14 was in German hands. The French government collapsed and was replaced by one that immediately started peace negotiations which Hitler, in his revenge for the humiliations of 1918, insisted on holding in the same historic railway carriage at Compiègne on exactly the same spot. On June 22 the armistice was signed. From then on France was split into a zone of occupation in the north and a subservient French-administered territory centred on Vichy in the south.

The question then arose, what to do about Great Britain? Air attacks on British targets, mainly shipping, started building up, and on July 13 Hitler issued a directive calling for an air war against Britain, which Göring eventually launched as 'Alder Tag' (Eagle Day) on August 15, while at the same time plans were in process for a possible cross-Channel invasion. By September 3 the plans were ready for implementation at ten days' notice, but a week later Hitler was still not satisfied that the Luftwaffe had gained sufficient air superiority and deferred his decision until, eventually, in October 1940, Operation 'Seelöwe' (Sealion) was postponed until the following spring, by which time it was well and truly forgotten.

With the Western Front secure on the line of the English Channel, the temptation was now to consider plans for the invasion of the Soviet Union, while diplomatic moves in the Balkans strove to secure Germany's vital connections with the Rumanian oilfields. The fiasco of the Italian invasion of Greece, which eventually involved British troops landing in that country, led to German plans to intervene. However, Yugoslavia resisted pressure to allow free movement of German troops across its territory, so on April 6, 1941, first Yugoslavia and then Greece were invaded under

Entering the Ehrenhof. In the front rank from left to right, Oberleutnant Hans Wessels, Oberleutnant Engelbert Endrass (Prien's second in command) and Oberleutnant Amelung von Varendorff.

Operation 'Maritha'. Belgrade was taken on the 12th and on the 17th Yugoslavia capitulated. By the end of

---

The place where the German U-Boat sank the British battleship Royal Oak was none other than the middle of Scapa Flow, Britain's greatest naval base! It sounds incredible. A World War submarine commander told me tonight that the Germans twice tried to get a U-Boat into Scapa Flow during the last war, but both attempts failed and the submarines were lost.

Captain Prien, commander of the submarine, came tripping into our afternoon press conference at the Propaganda Ministry this afternoon, followed by his crew — boys of eighteen, nineteen, twenty. Prien is thirty, clean-cut, cocky, a fanatical Nazi, and obviously capable. Introduced by Hitler's press chief, Dr Dietrich, who kept cursing the English and calling Churchill a liar, Prien told us little of how he did it. He said he had no trouble getting past the boom protecting the bay. I got the impression, though he said nothing to justify it, that he must have followed a British craft, perhaps a minesweeper, into the base. British negligence must have been something terrific.

WILLIAM SHIRER,
BERLIN, OCTOBER 18, 1939

the month all of Greece had been occupied and the British obliged to evacuate to Crete at considerable loss in ships, men and equipment. On May 20 the Germans went on to attack Crete in a combined air/sea operation. Although eventually successful, the heavy casualties suffered on this occasion resulted in the German decision not to use their airborne forces other than as ground troops for the rest of the war.

Meanwhile the Afrika Korps had been established under the command of General Rommel to put an end to the rout of Mussolini's desert armies by the British, and this proved so successful that by June 1941 Rommel was posing a serious threat to Cairo.

Then on June 22, 1941, Hitler launched his biggest gamble with Operation 'Barbarossa', the invasion of the Soviet Union with over 3,000,000 men. Surprise was complete and a series of staggering victories followed in rapid succession until the onset of the first Russian winter.

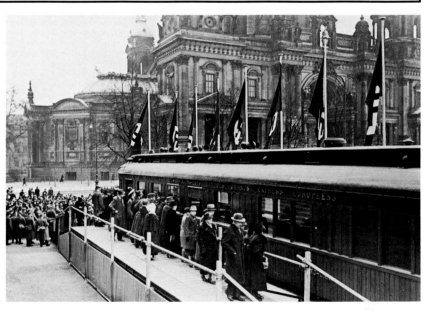

The French wagon-lits coach, scene of two surrenders, displayed on the Lustgarten.

The Führer's speaking style — captured here on film by a photographer of the Hoffmann organisation at a Reichstag sitting in 1939.

In the Reichstag tonight, Hitler 'offered' peace . . . very eloquently, at least for Germans. He said: 'In this hour I feel it is my duty before my own conscience to appeal once more to reason and common sense. I can see no reason why this war must go on.'

There was no applause, no cheering, no stamping of heavy boots. There was silence. And it was tense. For in their hearts the Germans long for peace now. Hitler went on in the silence: 'I am grieved to think of the sacrifices which it will claim. I should like to avert them, also for my own people.' The Hitler we saw in the Reichstag tonight was the conqueror, and conscious of it, and yet so wonderful an actor, so magnificent a handler of the German mind, that he mixed superbly the full confidence of the conqueror with the humbleness which always goes down so well with the masses when they know a man is on top. His voice was lower tonight; he rarely shouted as he usually does; and he did not once cry out hysterically as I've seen him do so often from this rostrum. His oratorial form was at its best.

I've often admired the way he uses his hands, which are somewhat feminine and quite artistic. Tonight he used those hands beautifully, seemed to express himself almost as much with his hands — and the sway of his body — as he did with his words and the use of his voice. I noticed too his gift for using his face and eyes (cocking his eyes) and the turn of his head for irony, of which there was considerable in tonight's speech, especially when he referred to Mr Churchill. I noticed again, too, that he can tell a lie with as straight a face as any man. Probably some of the lies are not lies to him because he believes fanatically the words he is saying, as for instance his false recapitulation of the last twenty-two years and his constant reiteration that Germany was never really defeated in the last war, only betrayed. But tonight he could also say with the ring of utter sincerity that all the night bombings of the British in recent weeks had caused no military damage whatsoever.

WILLIAM SHIRER,
BERLIN, JULY 19, 1940

'I wondered a little what answer the British would make,' wrote Shirer, 'and I had hardly arrived at the *Rundfunk* to prepare my talk when I picked up the BBC in German. And there was the answer already! It was a great big No. The more I thought of it, the less I was surprised. Peace for Britain with Germany absolute master of the Continent *is* impossible. Also: the British must have some reason to believe they can successfully defend their island and in the end bring Hitler down. For Hitler has given them an easy way out to save at least some pieces for themselves. . . . The BBC No was very emphatic. The announcer heaped ridicule on Hitler's every utterance.' That immediate, yet unofficial rejection, picked up by Shirer in Berlin, had been given by Sefton Delmer, then working in London at the BBC as a German-speaking news broadcaster. 'Herr Führer and Reichskanzler,' he retorted, 'We hurl it right back at you, right in your evil-smelling teeth . . . '

Berlin Under Attack

The first enemy aircraft over Berlin, despite Göring's boast that none would ever get through, were three Whitleys of No. 10 Squadron, Royal Air Force Bomber Command, which dropped leaflets on the night of October 1, 1939.

However, the first actual bombing

In August 1939, Göring boasted that 'The Ruhr will not be subjected to a single bomb. If an enemy bomber reaches the Ruhr, my name is not Hermann Göring: you can call me Meier.' (Meier is a very common name in Germany.) It was a wild claim that was to cause the Reichsmarschall acute embarrassment when the RAF attacked the Ruhr in May 1940. Hitler retaliated the following month, yet for the moment both sides shrank from bombing each other's capitals. However, all that changed on the night of August 24/25 when several Luftwaffe aircraft dropped bombs on the City in error as London was a forbidden target. *Above:* Flak gunners on the roof of the Reichsbank watch the skies over the city centre. In the background the Schloss, with the Dom beyond which was hit on December 20, 1940, causing damage estimated at £600,000.

Churchill had previously stated that if the centre of government in London was bombed 'it seems very important to be able to return the compliment the next day upon Berlin'. Thus the following night some 50 aircraft — Wellingtons and Hampdens — were detailed to bomb Berlin. Battling against strong headwinds, with little fuel to spare, the crews found the target covered in thick cloud and most bombs fell in open countryside to the south of the city. The only casualties occurred in the northern suburb of Rosenthal where two people were slightly injured and a garden chalet destroyed. Although the material damage was infinitesimal, the effect on morale was tremendous. William Shirer recorded that 'the Berliners are stunned. They did not think it could ever happen. When this war began Göring assured them it couldn't . . . they believed him. Their disillusionment today therefore is all the greater. You have to see their faces to measure it'. *Left:* We could not trace any pictures of the damage caused on that first raid, but this picture shows the results of another early raid (on October 18, 1940) in the southern borough of Steglitz when No. 33 Wundsiedeler Weg was hit.

raid on Berlin during the Second World War was conducted by the French Air Force and took place at about midnight on June 7, 1940, when a solitary Farman 223 bomber, with the name 'Jules Verne' and flown by Capitaine de Corvette Daillières and a four-man crew, approached the city from the north, having made a long circuitous flight over the North Sea and Denmark to the Baltic as far east as Stettin before turning south. Although it was a clear night, the pilot and navigator knew virtually nothing about Berlin and had no specific target, the aim of the mission being merely to avenge a 500-bomber German raid on Paris four days earlier. Their small load of incendiary bombs actually landed in Babelsberg, that is south of the city in a suburb of Potsdam, and proved completely ineffective. Their long, roundabout flight continued without incident until they landed in Paris at 0500 hours, having flown 5,000 kilometres in 13½ hours.

Following the bombing of London by the Luftwaffe during the Battle of Britain, the War Cabinet ordered a retaliation raid on Berlin but, of the 81 Hampden and Wellington bombers that took off from England on August 25, 1940, only 29 actually reached Berlin, dropping about 22 tons of incendiaries and high explosives on Reinickendorf in the face of heavy flak. Seven of these aircraft failed to return. Two days later there was another raid, this time on the city centre, killing twelve civilians and creating considerable damage. The following night it was the turn of parts of Neukölln, Siemensstadt and some other central areas to be attacked.

The city was then given a relative lull until the Royal Air Force resumed their bombing offensive in the autumn with a change of policy that involved launching all their available strength against one target at a time. On the night of September 23/24, a concentration of 112

The next night (August 26/27) the Luftwaffe struck back at London in a six-hour raid which the RAF returned on the night of August 28/29. On the previous British raids there were no deaths, but this time twelve civilians were killed, the news being telephoned to Hitler who was at his mountain retreat on the Obersalzberg. That afternoon he flew back to Berlin and announced that henceforth he would permit the Luftwaffe to retaliate in strength. Six days later, at the opening of the Winterhilfe (Winter Relief) campaign in the Sportpalast on September 4, he promised Berliners retribution: that he would respond a hundredfold and raze British cities to the ground.

I now want to take this opportunity of speaking to you, to say this moment is an historic one. As a result of the provocative British attacks on Berlin on recent nights, the Führer has decided to order a mighty blow to be struck in revenge against the capital of the British Empire. I personally have assumed the leadership of this attack, and today I have heard above me the roaring of the victorious German squadrons which now, for the first time, are driving towards the heart of the enemy in full daylight, accompanied by countless fighter squadrons. Enemy defences were, as we expected, beaten down and the target reached, and I am certain that our successes have been as massive as the boldness of our plan of attack and the fighting spirit of our crews deserve. In any event this is an historic hour, in which for the first time the German Luftwaffe has struck at the heart of the enemy.

REICHSMARSCHALL HERMANN GÖRING,
PAS DE CALAIS, SEPTEMBER 7, 1940

With the Luftwaffe ideally placed on forward airfields in the occupied countries, London was within easy reach, and the promised raid came three days later on the afternoon of Saturday, September 7. The military objectives singled out were the docks, warehouses and oil refineries bordering the Thames which were accurately hit. As bombing continued throughout the night, casualties among the civilian population increased, so that by morning 1,800 Londoners lay dead amidst the burning, shattered streets. To the East Enders it was a day to remember: Black Saturday.

The Führer's Wehrmacht Adjutant
Voss-strasse 4, Berlin W.8.
Tel: 11 61 91
Ref: 465 40 Secret
September 9, 1940

To: The Reichs Minister for Aviation and C-in-C of the Air Force:

The Führer has ordered the erection of Flak Towers in Berlin in several places in large parks and locations, such as the Tiergarten, Humboldthain, Friedrichshain, etc., on each of which fortifications are to be installed, light and heavy anti-aircraft guns, control equipment and searchlights.
Initially planned are:
in the Tiergarten 3 towers
in Humboldthain, Friedrichshain and near Tempelhof 1 tower each
On each tower there are to be 4 twin 10.5cm ships' anti-aircraft guns, as well as several 3.7cm and 2cm guns.
Furthermore the gun crews are to be provided with bomb-proof accommodation inside the towers.
The Führer has tasked Professor Speer with the architectural arrangements. The department of the Air Force responsible is to liaise with Professor Speer, who will carry out the construction in accordance with the Führer's orders.

von Below, Hauptmann

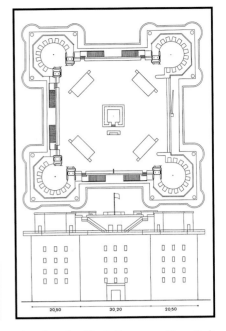

Free-fall bombing is rarely 100 per cent accurate, even in good visibility, and areas adjacent to the targets were bound to suffer. With Berlin at the extreme range of the RAF's existing bombers, night raids were the only option, so it was inevitable that residential areas would be hit as well as the intended targets. Whether Churchill and Hitler really believed that their air forces were capable of pin-point accuracy is academic; suffice it to say that when faced with civilian casualties, their rhetoric escalated the retaliation demanded on both sides. On the Monday, while the fires were still smouldering in Britain, Hitler issued immediate instructions *(left)* for the construction of six massive Flak-towers to protect his capital. *Right:* Each massive bomb-proof construction was to be 130 feet high and located in parks surrounding the government quarter.

In the event, only three of the towers planned for Berlin were actually built. The first, Flakturm I, located in the Tiergarten, was begun in October. Flakturm II *(above)* was started at Friedrichshain in April 1941, and Flakturm III at Humboldthain in October that year. Each took six months to construct, this picture having been taken as Flakturm II neared completion in October or early November. The towers were also used as public air raid shelters — they could hold up to 18,000 on the lower floors — and they proved ideal command posts during the ground battle in 1945. They also served as hospitals; depositories for art treasures; observation platforms and also for top secret research (for example, captured British radar equipment was tested on the Humboldthain tower). In this picture, the scaffolding on the left (eastern) side was needed to raise the six 70-tonne steel ammunition bunkers on to the roof to cover the internal shell hoists. The permanent crane was provided for lifting guns and replacement barrels. The zig-zag design painted on the concrete was so that the crews of the light flak guns positioned on the lower platforms could practise their traversing and aiming.

Left: Initially, the towers mounted four 10.5cm guns, later upgraded to twin-barrelled 12.8cm weapons. This picture taken on the roof of Flakturm I (Zoo) shows the ammunition bunker on the right, with a smaller one on the left over the shaft used for returning spent cases. *Right:* Light Flak, 20mm and 37mm, was mounted on the lower platforms.

aircraft out of the 129 that had been despatched reached the city to bomb specific targets, but the searchlights and ground mist obscured visibility. As the German records of this raid were deliberately expunged, the effects on the railway yards, power stations, gasworks and aero factories targeted remain unknown, except that the majority of bombs appear to have fallen on the district of Moabit, where one of the power stations was located, and that Schloss Charlottenburg was damaged. However, by the end of 1940, the civilian death toll had risen to over 200 and some 1,800 homes had been destroyed.

Left: Each Flak-tower was used in conjunction with a second smaller tower equipped with radar equipment and aerials on the roof. This picture was taken secretly in 1941 from the American Embassy (located beside the Brandenburg Gate) of the radar tower for the Zoo bunker on the far side of the Tiergarten. The aerial is a (Giant) Würzburg Riese which had a 7.5-metre paraboloid. *Right:* Flakturm I and its radar tower, at the western end of the Tiergarten near the Zoo Station as they appeared to the camera of a 542 Squadron Spitfire, surrounded by the burned-out ruins of central Berlin.

In the early period of the war the anti-aircraft defences of Berlin consisted of the 1. Flak-Division under Generalmajor Hoffmann with his headquarters in Dahlem (later the American HQ). The division consisted of Flak-Regiments 12 and 22, each of two battalions, a battalion each of the Flak-Regiments 32 and 52, Flak-Regiment GG (General Göring) of four battalions, and the 2. Luftsperrabteilung (balloon battery), giving a total of 45 heavy and 24 medium or light batteries of anti-aircraft guns and 18 searchlight batteries in and around the city. These resources were backed by four squadrons of night fighters. During 1940 some Messerschmitt Bf 110 fighters were specially equipped for night operations enabling them to fly blind. The first recorded success was the shooting down of a Whitley bomber on July 20, but it was not until the following year that the on-board 'Lichtenstein' SN-2 radar was introduced into service enabling an aircraft to home in on its victim.

In this case, the guns belonged to 3/662(o) Batterie located in the fields at Dahlem which fell within the American Sector. When we traced the location in 1990, we found it still occupied by the US forces who had erected a transmitting aerial on the site. The building in the background is the State Secret Archives.

In the early days, the RAF's raids were only of a pin-prick nature, and it was not until the heavy four-engined bombers arrived with their huge bomb loads that the picture changed. Berlin was largely left alone and had three years in which to build up its defences, learning from the experiences of towns and cities being hit further to the west. Beyond the inner zone of defences centred on the three Flak-towers, an outer ring was established in the suburbs and villages around Greater Berlin. These pictures taken at the end of the war by the US Signal Corps show the wrecked guns of a typical 88mm Flak battery. The white rings painted around the barrels would denote the number of aircraft brought down.

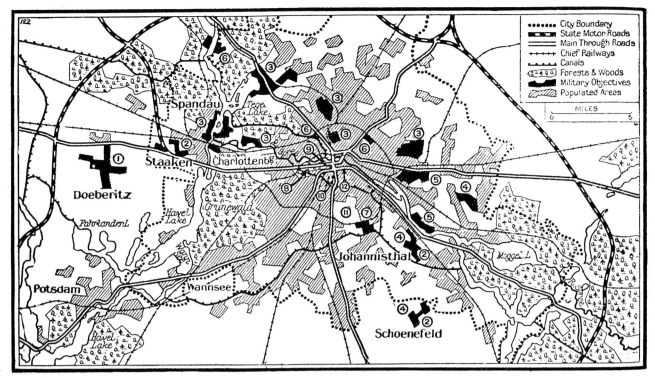

Meanwhile, in 1940, the British public was receiving geography lessons on the layout of Berlin. This contemporary map was published by courtesy of the *Evening Standard* with the rejoinder that 'when the RAF bomb Berlin, they do so not merely out of a determination to exact reprisals for the Nazi raids on London, but because there are many objectives which are ranked most definitely as military. Some of the most outstanding are indicated. 1. Troop Centre; 2. Air bases; 3. Small arms and munition works; 4. Aircraft Factories; 5. Electrical Plants, etc.; 6. Gas Works; 7. Telephone and wireless equipment works; 8. Tiergarten; 9. Reichstag; 10. Hitler's Chancellery; 11. Tempelhof (airport); 12. Unter den Linden.'

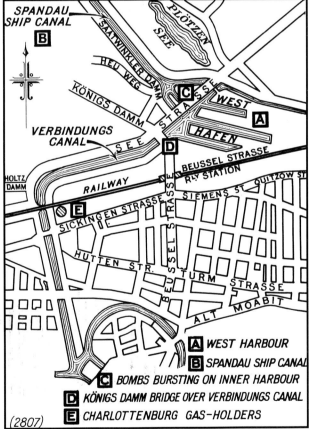

Left: The first picture released of an RAF attack on Berlin was this one of an unspecified raid early the following month. With the lengthening nights, which enabled the bombers to complete the round trip under cover of darkness, the city had been attacked more frequently. *Right:* This key was released with the picture — the area shown being some three kilometres north of the Zoo bunker. 'D' — the Königsdamm bridge no longer exists as the old Verbindungs Canal has been filled in and re-routed further to the north. The star at 'E' was caused by a reflection in the camera lens, while the broad streaks are searchlights.

And so the propaganda war continued, deteriorating into a mere slanging match. While the RAF tried to emphasise that it was hitting military (or industrial) targets, Dr Goebbels would be doing his best to illustrate that the attacks were entirely indiscriminate and really designed to terrorise the population. *Below:* This picture was transmitted by radio from Germany to New York showing the Opera House on Unter den Linden in flames after the RAF raid on the night of April 9/10, 1941.

In bombing terms, Berlin was always the big target, the 'Big B'. For most of the Second World War it was at the extreme range of Allied aircraft flying from their air bases in East Anglia and the Midlands, a distance of 600 miles in direct flight, which in itself was seldom either possible or feasible, and for the night bombers a return trip under cover of darkness reduced the operational possibilities to the winter months between November and March. A further natural operational difficulty lay in the city often being masked by ten-tenths cloud.

However, the city was recognised as one of the most important targets for various reasons. Apart from being the seat of government, it was Germany's largest industrial city and the communications hub of the Reich's rail, road and canal systems. Specific targets included the vast Siemens and AEG plants, the BMW, Dornier, Heinkel and Focke-Wulf aircraft factories, the Argus aero engine plant, the Deutsche Industrie Werke, Rheinmetal Borsig and Alkett ordnance factories, and so on.

Meanwhile the Luftwaffe General, Josef Kammhuber, was engaged establishing a line of 'Giant Würzburg' ground radar stations to screen Germany along a line that eventually extended right across northern France and into Denmark. Each station had a surveillance radius of 70 kilometres and was tied in with the fighter bases and searchlight organisations in a system designed to locate the incoming bombing fleets and to direct the waiting fighters to intercept them.

By the end of 1940, Berlin had received twelve of the new radar batteries. These had an immediate impact on the situation, resulting in seven out of 30 raiding aircraft being shot down on the night of November 14.

The Royal Air Force conducted only seventeen raids with its twin-engined bombers on Berlin in 1941, one of them being deliberately carried out during a visit by the Japanese Foreign Minister to the German capital. There were also two attacks by the Soviet Air Force just six weeks after Hitler invaded Russia. However, the Soviets, specialising in the tactical support of the Red Army, were not really equipped to conduct long distance raids, and so called on the Royal Air Force to conduct the strategic air campaign against Germany.

Left: **The Opera House, pictured by the Soviets in 1945, illustrating attempts to protect works of art, in this case the statue of Feldmarschall Gebhard von Blücher, revealed with his** foot on an enemy cannon. *Right:* **The front entrance was temporarily hidden behind hoardings in October 1990 following celebrations for the Unification of Germany.**

Although 1941 and 1942 brought little air activity over the city, Berlin prepared for the worst. Prominent landmarks were camouflaged to try to disorientate the attacking aircraft . . .

In the meantime, the British were developing a fleet of four-engined aircraft for this rôle but Air Marshal Sir Arthur Harris, who had taken over Bomber Command in February 1942, was not prepared to commit his resources against such a difficult target as Berlin at this stage when he had other priorities to deal with. The year was consequently another relatively quiet one for the city, there being only nine alerts over a period of twelve months, one being an incursion in the area by a few Soviet Ilyushin Il-2 aircraft, only one of which dropped some bombs on the city and was shot down for its pains.

. . . and air raid shelters constructed. *Left:* This one, virtually indestructible, is now incorporated into a block of apartments bridging Winterfeldstrasse. *Right:* Another bunker which provided shelter for travellers at the Anhalter Bahnhof.

By 1943, everything had changed and Hitler's star was firmly on the wane. Indeed, January 1943 can be regarded as the turning point of the whole war. In Africa, Rommel had fallen back over 1,000 miles in the face of the Eighth Army's breakthrough at El Alamein the previous November. In the Soviet Union, the fate of the 100,000 German troops besieged at Stalingrad was sealed by a massive Russian bombardment and call for surrender. At sea, the Battle of the Atlantic had been lost and Raeder sacked, with Hitler demanding that the High Seas Fleet be scrapped. As if all that was not bad enough, on the Home Front the Americans had finally entered the air war with their first raid against Germany. Finally, to round off Hitler's blackest month, Churchill and the American President, Franklin D. Roosevelt, issued a declaration that nothing less than the unconditional surrender of Germany, Italy and Japan would end the war.

That month Bomber Command returned to Berlin for the first time in 14 months with a double hit. The first attack on the night of January 16/17 caught the defences napping and the sirens sounded only when the bombers were over the city. Panic ensued when the first bombs caught people in the open. At the Deutschlandhalle, an audience of 10,000 was enjoying the annual Berlin circus. Police immediately began evacuating the building, managing to evacuate everyone, including the animals, just before the hall was struck by a shower of incendiaries.

The Berlin raid was a big show as heavy bomber operations go: it was also quite a long raid, and the Wing Commander who took me stayed over Berlin for half an hour. The flak was hot, but it has been hotter. For me it was a pretty hair-raising experience, and I was glad when it was over, though I wouldn't have missed it for the world. But we must all remember that these men do it as a regular routine job. The various crews who were flying last night from the Bomber Station where I'd been staying had flown on several of the Essen raids, and that means that night after night they've been out over one of the hottest parts of Germany, returning to eat, drink and sleep before going out again. That's their life, and I can promise you it's hard, tiring and dangerous.

Four-engined Lancasters, Halifaxes and Stirlings roared out over the North Sea. We flew among them, and turning back from the cockpit to look into the gorgeous sunset, I counted thirty or forty Lancasters seemingly suspended in the evening sky. They were there wherever you looked — in front, behind, above and below — each a separate monster; each separately navigated, but all bound by a co-ordinated plan of approach and attack. Up above the clouds, the dusk was short. The orange and crimson of sunset died back there where the coast of England lay, and ahead of us the brilliant moon hung with the stars around her; below us, the thick clouds hid the sea. We were climbing steadily, and as it grew dark we put on our oxygen masks when the air grew too rarified for normal breathing.

As we approached the enemy coast I saw the German Ack-Ack. It was bursting away from us and much lower. I didn't see any long streams of it soaring into the air, as the pictures suggest: it burst in little yellow, winking flashes, and you couldn't hear it above the roar of the engines. Sometimes it closes in on you, and the mid- or tail-gunner will call up calmly and report its position to the Captain so that he can dodge it. We dodged it last night, particularly over Berlin: literally jumped over it and nipped round, with the Wing Commander sitting up in his seat as cool as a cucumber, pushing and pulling his great bomber about as though it were a toy.

We knew well enough when we were approaching Berlin. There was a complete ring of powerful searchlights waving and crossing, though it seemed to me that most of our bombers were over the city. Many of the lights were doused: there was also intense flak. First of all they didn't seem to be aiming at us. It was bursting away to starboard and away to port in thick, yellow clusters and dark, smokey puffs. As we turned in for our first run across the city it closed right round us. For a moment it seemed impossible that we could miss it, and one burst lifted us in the air as though a giant hand had pushed up the belly of the machine; but we flew on, and just then another Lancaster dropped a load of incendiaries, and where, a moment before, there had been a dark patch of the city, a dazzling silver pattern spread itself — a rectangle of brilliant lights — hundreds, thousands of them — winking and gleaming and lighting the outlines of

JAN	17	,,	W	ι.	RICHARD DIMBLEBY F/O Russell Sub/Lt. Mulkins P/Lt Olive. P/O Mulligan F/O Wickens Sgt McGregor.	OPS. BERLIN. 1 X 8000 LB. A good trip and fairly successful. The residential quarters got it. / Dimbleby broadcasted next day. This is my 67th Bombing trip.	

To get maximum publicity for the opening shot in its forthcoming battle against Berlin, the RAF took along the media on the second raid the following night. Richard Dimbleby was flown by Wing Commander Guy Gibson although the Dams raid, which would make him a legend, was still four months in the future. This is how he recorded the flight in his log book. Gibson was flying with No. 106 Squadron at the time and he logged the round trip to Berlin as taking 9 hours 15 minutes.

Stewart Sale, Reuter's Special Correspondent, was in another Lancaster: 'For the first time on our flight the ground was clear, looking exactly as the big map in the briefing room had looked . . . Lying prone in the nose, the bomb-aimer was peering for his mark. At his direction the captain held the plane steady on the bombing course for two minutes . . . Then the plane was bucketing madly about the sky, plunging, turning, soaring, while flak burst all round. Our 4,000 lb. bomb had gone. Berlin was certainly getting it, and I wondered momentarily what the people of London and Coventry would have given to see it. The fires below spread and brightened. Incendiaries streamed across the city in glittering lanes. Looking down on this furnace, I remembered nights on Fleet Street roofs when the German bombers were over. By the time the bombers following us up were through with it, Berlin too would know what bombing means.'

The gutted Deutschlandhalle as photographed later by the RAF. The fact that so many people had been saved was seen by Berliners as a miracle.

the city around them. As though this unloading had been the signal, score after score of fire bombs went down, and all over the dark face of the German capital these great incandescent flower-beds spread themselves. It was a fascinating sight. As I watched and tried to photograph the flares with a cine-camera, I saw the pin-points merging, and the white glare turning to a dull, ugly red as the fires of bricks and mortar and wood spread from the chemical flares.

We flew over the city three times, for more than half an hour, while the guns sought us out and failed to hit us. At last our bomb-aimer sighted his objective below, and for one unpleasant minute we flew steady and straight. Then he pressed the button and the biggest bomb of the evening, our three-and-a-half-tonner, fell away and down. I didn't see it burst, but I know what a giant bomb does, and I couldn't help wondering whether, anywhere in the area of the devastation, such a man as Hitler, Göring, Himmler or Goebbels might be cowering in a shelter. It was engrossing to realise that the Nazi leaders and their Ministries were only a few thousand feet from us, and that this shimmering mass of flares and bombs and gun-flashes was their stronghold.

We turned away from Berlin at last — it seemed we were there for an age — and we came home. We saw no night fighter, to our amazement, nor did any of the flak on the homeward journey come very near us. We came back across the North Sea, exchanged greetings of the day with a

little coastwise convoy, and came in to England again, nine hours after we had flown out. There were so many machines circling impatiently round our aerodrome that we had to wait up above for an hour and twenty minutes before we could land, and it was two o'clock in the morning when the Wing Commander brought us down to the flarepath and taxied us in.

We climbed stiffly out, Johnny from the tail turret, Brian who used to be a policeman from the mid-upper, Hatch, the radio operator, Junior the navigator — by far the youngest of us all. Then the Scots co-pilot, a quiet calm sergeant, and last the short sturdy Wing-Co, who has flown in every major air raid of this war and been a night fighter pilot in between times. They were the crew — six brave, cool and exceedingly skilful men.

*Perhaps I **am** shooting a line for them, but I think somebody ought to. They and their magnificent Lancasters and all the others like them, are taking the war right into Germany. They have been attacking and giving their lives in attack since the first day of the war, and their squadron went on that show too. 'Per ardua ad astra' is the RAF motto. Perhaps I can translate it 'Through hardship to the stars'. I understand the hardship now, and I'm proud to have seen the stars with them.*

RICHARD DIMBLEBY,
7.00 and 8.00 a.m., JANUARY 18, 1943,
BROADCAST ON THE BBC HOME SERVICE

When it was opened in 1935, the Deutschlandhalle was hailed as the largest assembly hall in the world and its reconstruction after the war was deemed essential as 'a symbol of the divided city's vital energy'. (We saw it on page 82.) Rebuilt in a similar style to the original at a cost of DM25 million, it was reopened on October 19, 1957.

With his beleaguered army at Stalingrad in its final death throes, on January 30, the tenth anniversary of Nazi Germany, General Friedrich von Paulus sent his greetings to Hitler, then at his HQ in Prussia: 'On the anniversary of your assumption of power, the Sixth Army sends greetings to the Führer. The swastika still flutters over Stalingrad. May our struggle stand as an example to generations as yet unborn, never to surrender, however desperate the odds. Then Germany will be victorious.' Hitler responded by promoting von Paulus to Generalfeldmarschall — a rank he was to hold for barely a day. Back in Berlin, the RAF also wanted to help Hitler celebrate, and they planned their own special surprise. This was to be delivered to the Haus des Rundfunks — a distinctively-shaped building on Masurenallee — where both Göring and Goebbels were due to give laudatory speeches during the day.

However, 1943 brought devastating changes to the whole scene. On the night of January 16/17, 1943, Berlin experienced its first major air raid in 14 months when 190 Lancasters and 11 Halifaxes, all four-engined aircraft, attacked the city using proper 'target indicators' for the first time. The raid came as a complete surprise as the size of the force was not recognised until the bombs were actually falling, and opposition was slight as half of the Berlin Flak personnel were away on a course at the time. However, thick cloud on the way and then haze over the city seriously hindered navigation, so the raid was not as effective as it might have been, although about 370 tons of bombs were dropped, wrecking the Borsig factory and badly damaging the Lorenz works and many other concerns. Fortunately for the 10,000 Berliners attending the annual 'Mensch, Tiere, Sensationen' circus performance in the Deutschlandhalle when the raid began, were all safely evacuated before the building was devoured by incendiaries to become the first large ruin in the city. Elsewhere in Berlin, the raid resulted in 198 people killed, including 53 prisoners-of-war, one of them British, the rest French. Only one Lancaster was lost.

The next night 170 Lancasters and 17 Halifaxes returned under better weather conditions but again were unable to pin-point their targets and so once more no effective damage was created. Eight people were killed and 41 injured. Unfortunately, the aircraft followed the same route as the previous night so that the Luftwaffe fighters found them easily and 19 Lancasters and 3 Halifaxes were lost. The famous broadcaster, Richard Dimbleby, flew on this raid in the aircraft piloted by Wing Commander Guy Gibson, who only four months later was to win fame and be awarded the Victoria Cross for the attack on the Möhne Dam, and broadcast his impressions.

On February 2, Generalfeldmarschall von Paulus surrendered the German 6. Armee at Stalingrad, and on February 18 Goebbels called for 'total war' in his speech to an enthusiastic audience at the Sportspalast.

Preparations then began to counter the kind of aerial onslaught being dealt out to German cities closer to the British bases. The air war was now also being conducted by the American Eighth Army Air Force during daylight using B-17 Flying Fortresses and B-24 Liberators. Trenches were dug, air raid shelters improved and other measures taken to prepare the population for the worst.

Meanwhile a new kind of air attack was experienced with the appearance of the first de Havilland Mosquitos over Berlin on January 30, 1943, the tenth anniversary of the Nazi assumption of power. The target was the Haus des Rundfunks (Broadcasting House) in Masurenallee, where at specified times Göring was due to speak before a large audience in the morning and Goebbels in the afternoon. Three Mosquitos were despatched to attack each of these meetings, but Göring's speech had been postponed an hour and little damage was done. The second batch encountered a fully alerted German defence and one aircraft was shot down with the loss of its crew.

Various variants of this fast, two-engined, two-man aircraft of mainly wooden construction were developed for pathfinder, photo-reconnaissance, fighter and bomber functions, the latter versions eventually being able to carry a bomb load greater than that of a Fortress. The effectiveness of this aircraft and the difficulty combatting it can be seen from the fact that out of the 2,034 Mosquito sorties flown during the aerial 'Battle of Berlin', only ten aircraft were shot down and a further 89 damaged.

Three Mosquitos from No. 105 Squadron were to attack in the morning when Göring was scheduled to speak, and a similar number from No. 139 Squadron were to try to get Goebbels in the afternoon. These are the men who delivered the RAF's sermon. L–R: Pilot Officer R. G. Hayes; Flying Officer R. C. Morris; Flight Sergeant P. J. D. McGeehan; Flying Officer A. T. Wickham; Sergeant J. Massey; Flight Lieutenant J. Gordon; Squadron Leader R. W. Reynolds; Sergeant R. C. Fletcher; Pilot Officer B. Sismore; Air Vice Marshal N. H. Bottomley, Assistant Chief of Staff (Ops); and Pilot Officer W. E. D. Makin. Two men are missing: Squadron Leader D. F. Darling and his navigator, Flying Officer W. Wright, shot down and killed on the second sortie.

In all, Berlin suffered 170 Mosquito attacks, which, if inflicting less material damage than their four-engined brethren, brought all the physical and psychological wear and tear of full-scale alerts to the population of the city at odd hours of the day and night.

Then, in response to Soviet requests for stronger attacks by the Royal Air Force on Germany and its capital, Berlin suffered its heaviest raid to date on the night of March 1, 1943, when 257 out of the 302 aircraft despatched attacked, some dropping the new 4,000 lb Blockbuster blast bombs and equipped with the new, advanced H2S bombsights. One of the factories destroyed was the Telefunken concern, which had been in the process of analysing a captured sample of this bombsight although the Germans were able to resume their research with another example recovered from one of the 17 aircraft shot down that same night. In all, 191 civilians were killed and substantial damage inflicted on the railway repair workshops in Tempelhof, where 22 acres of buildings were burnt out and a further 20 factories badly damaged.

On February 18, Goebbels called for 'total' war and within two weeks the RAF had responded to his request. The attack on the night of March 1/2 was the heaviest yet, with the bombing scattered over 100 square miles of the city. Direct hits were scored on the marshalling yards at Tempelhof *(above)*, just to the west of the airfield.

I learned at Halle, on our trip to Berlin, that Berlin had undergone a bad air raid during the night [March 1-2]. From the first report which reached me I did not realise the seriousness of this attack, I became aware of it, however, when the train slowly pulled into Berlin. We were more than an hour late. The tracks were torn up. The report Schach gave me at the station indicated that it was the most serious air raid thus far experienced by the Reich capital.

A tremendous number of places have been damaged. Industrial plants and public buildings have been badly hit. St Hedwig's Church was burned to the ground, together with four other churches and a number of hospitals, homes for the aged, etc.

I am told that the morale of the population is exemplary, although the civilian anti-aircraft protection failed to some extent, in that the Berliners sat in their basements too long and let their houses burn meanwhile. The Party, too, failed in some respects. It is no longer fully conscious of its real task of leadership and no longer knows how to adjust itself to exceptional circumstances.

I immediately took the necessary measures. The population must in no circumstances be given the impression that the Party is not equal to the tasks imposed by such heavy air raids.

Things look pretty bad in the business sections of Berlin,

but in the suburbs they are even worse. The damage is extraordinarily heavy. We have registered about two hundred casualties, a number that is not very big compared with other raids, but which nevertheless is far from negligible.

A rumour went round Berlin that this attack was launched because of Air Force Day, which had been given some unfortunate publicity. On the whole it appears that the Luftwaffe has lost much of its popularity. Göring is quite unjustifiably blamed for it. The situation is aggravated by the unfortunate circumstance that he is neither in Berlin nor in his GHQ, but up on the Obersalzberg.

I immediately toured the city and viewed several damaged places. I began with St Hedwig's Church, which looks absolutely hopeless.

I also inspected a bombed-out hospital in Lützowstrasse. Several corpses were just being carried out — a touching picture. One of the nurses killed was an air raid warden. It drives one mad to think that some Canadian boor, who probably can't even find Europe on the globe, flies here from a country glutted with natural resources which his people don't know how to exploit, to bombard a continent with a crowded population. Let's hope we can soon deliver the proper reply . . .

JOSEPH GOEBBELS,
MARCH 3, 1943

Another casualty — visited by Goebbels on March 3 — was St Hedwig's Cathedral, built by Frederick II in the 1770s to the design, so the story goes, of an upturned coffee cup. It lies just behind the Opera, facing the square where the books were burned in 1933 (page 60). After some difficulty, the church was restored by the East Berlin authorities although the problems with re-creating the original dome were only solved by using self-supporting concrete segments, reinforced with steel.

The next big attack came at the end of March with two nights of bombing. The first on the night of March 27/28 with 396 aircraft taking part was somewhat of a failure, as the Pathfinders placed their aiming marks well clear of the centre of the city and about a quarter of the Blockbusters failed to explode. However, several Luftwaffe installations around the city were hit, including a technical store in Teltow, where a lot of valuable equipment was destroyed. The following night's raid with 329 aircraft was equally inaccurate, but in all over 300 people had been killed for a loss of 30 aircraft. At the end of March 1943 the death toll to date amounted to 1,700, of which over 500 had occurred in that month alone. Harris then broke off his attacks on Berlin until the end of the summer, turning to the Ruhr instead, although on the night of April 20 eleven Lancasters made a diversionary attack on Berlin from the main assault on Stettin.

The city's defensive measures were accelerated as a result of the devastating British and American air raids on Hamburg during the period July 24 to August 3, 1943, culminating in an horrendous firestorm with 50,000 civilian deaths and a further 800,000 made homeless *(See After the Battle No. 70)*. Goebbels ordered an immediate evacuation of as many 'useless mouths', as he called them, as possible, thereby reducing Berlin's population to 3,300,000. Despite all the measures taken, such as reinforcing all suitable cellars, masking their exits with brick walls and providing them with steel doors, preparing public shelters under gasometers and other large buildings with concrete foundations, and building 100 massive concrete shelters with roofs over a metre thick, there still were not enough shelters to accommodate everyone.

In the light of the unbelievable death toll in the firestorm at Hamburg in May 1943, Goebbels issued instructions for the evacuation of all children and young mothers from Berlin and, by the end of 1943, over three-quarters of a million women and children had left the city.

Before the two big attacks at the end of March, Bomber Command had pictures taken of various areas to show pre-strike damage. The characteristic honeycomb appearance of burned-out buildings was beginning to creep across the face of Berlin as the little incendiaries did their work, it being assessed that, ton for ton, fire was more than twice as destructive as the largest blast bombs. We have reproduced this picture of a section of the south side of the Unter den Linden upside down so that it relates more easily to the 1940 street map.

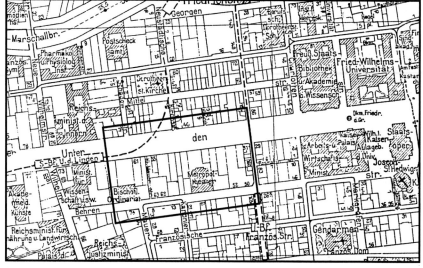

The ordeal by fire begins. August 1943. Bomber Command's first attack in what the RAF called the 'Battle of Berlin' took place on the night of August 23/24. By now there was no pretence of targetting military installations. The realisation of the futility of trying to hit individual buildings at night, through smoke, haze or cloud, had long been abandoned for a policy of carpet bombing whole areas, and even then the system was prone to failure. In the case of the first raid on the night of August 23/24, the Pathfinders, whose job it was to mark the targets with coloured flares (Target Indicators), were supposed to light the borough of Mitte, right in the city centre. However, the TIs were released some four miles south-east of the aiming point, causing the bomb loads to be scattered right across the south of the city, on the outskirts and in surrounding villages. Many people were caught in the open in the residential areas, resulting in a heavy death toll — the heaviest so far for a single raid — with 854 killed. As the compiler of the Operations Record Book for one of the Pathfinder Squadrons put it: 'The success of the attack was not due to our accurate bombing but to the Germans for building such a large city!'

There was also an increase in the night fighter strength allocated to the defence of the capital. One innovation was the adaptation of the Messerschmitt Bf 110 with upward firing cannon, which could thus engage the bombers from their blindest defensive angle rather than tackling them headon. Hauptmann Manfred Meurer was eventually to shoot down 52 aircraft with this device, being awarded the Oakleaves to his Knight's Cross in August 1943.

The flak and searchlights were now almost entirely manned by 15- to 17-year-old schoolboys and female auxiliaries in order to release the men for front line duties, but were no less effective as a result. In February 1944, the city's defences numbered a formidable 87 heavy flak batteries with 441 guns, 17 medium and light flak batteries with a further 445 guns, and 35 searchlight batteries with a total of 420 searchlights.

Under increasing pressure from the Soviets for the Western Allies to do something about the 'Second Front', Harris launched his aerial 'Battle of Berlin' with three raids during the period August 23 to September 4, 1943. Although the first raid with 727 aircraft was only partially successful, the Berlin authorities still reported it as the most serious so far with much damage to property and 854 people killed, the high count being attributed to people failing to take shelter as they should. The RAF lost 56 aircraft.

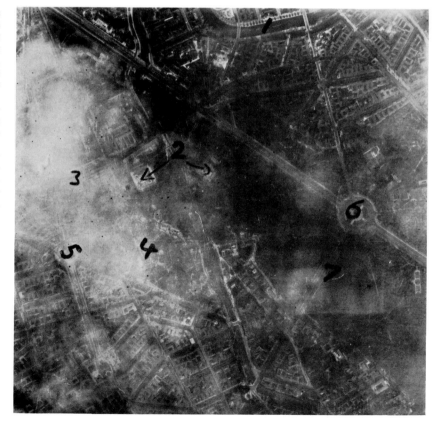

Eight hours after the raid, smoke still obscures the city centre from at least 100 fires still burning. The contemporary annotation identifies: 1. River Spree; 2. Flak towers; 3. Zoo Station; 4. Zoo; 5. Auguste-Viktoria-Platz; 6. Grosser Stern; 7. Tiergarten.

The next attack came a week later on the night of August 31/ September 1. It proved a lucky respite for Berlin as the bombs fell way off target in a long swathe up to 30 miles south of the city. As far as Bomber Command was concerned, it was an unmitigated disaster, with possibly only ten aircraft out of the 600-odd despatched actually hitting Berlin through the heavy cloud cover. With over 300 men lost (of whom 225 were killed), it was a heavy price to pay for the deaths of only 87 Germans on the ground. By the end of the war, over 2,500 crewmen had been killed during Bomber Command's attacks on Berlin. The majority lie here in the military cemetery established by the British occupation authorities and the Imperial War Graves Commission on the south side of the Heerstrasse in Charlottenburg. Graves were concentrated from many villages and towns in east Germany, including 88 from the civilian cemetery near the Olympic Stadium.

The second raid at the turn of the month was with 622 aircraft and as largely unsuccessful with 68 people killed and 47 aircraft lost. The third raid with 320 aircraft fell mainly on the Moabit, Charlottenburg and Siemensstadt areas, where several factories were hit as well as electricity and water works and a major brewery put out of action. Casualties were 422 people killed and 22 aircraft lost. These three raids had resulted in the loss of a disproportionately high number of aircraft and crew for the results achieved, so Air Chief Marshal Harris appears to have interrupted his campaign until an improved version of the H2S radar bombing aid became available.

The cemetery was subsequently landscaped with the traditional Cross of Sacrifice and permanent headstones. In the foreground, the collective graves of the crew of a Lancaster of No. 434 (RCAF) Squadron, who were brought down in the raid on January 20/21, 1944. (The establishment of a collective grave was necessary where the individual remains could not be positively indentified.) In the foreground, the headstone commemorating Sergeant Victor Baker, the Flight Engineer.

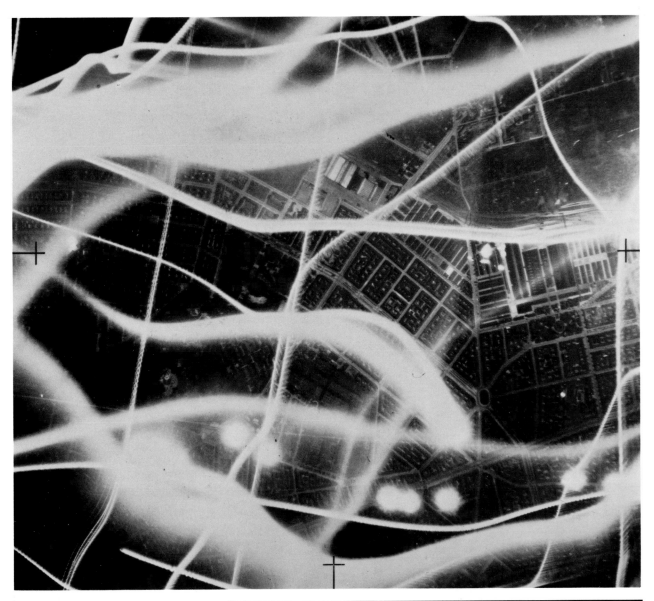

As far as the RAF was concerned, the third raid three nights later (September 3/4) was a little more successful. Bomber Command had deliberately made this an all-Lancaster attack because of heavy losses of Stirlings and Halifaxes on the previous raids, yet 22 Lancasters still failed to return out of the force of 316 which had set out. However, the city was free of cloud and clear photography was possible. This picture shows an area of about seven square miles just west of the centre, with bombs bursting along Frankfurter Allee. Also visible is the Flak-tower in Friedrichshain. The movement of the aircraft has smeared the image of the searchlights and tracer fire. Goebbels commented in his diary that 'During the last air raid on Berlin the Plötzensee prison was hit and a number of people condemned to death escaped. Thierack [Otto Thierack was presiding judge of the Nazi People's Court — the Volksgerichts-hof] therefore gave orders that clemency pleas were to be disposed of as quickly as possible and the executions to take place during the days immediately following. It would be beyond a joke if several hundred men condemned to death were let loose upon the population of the capital after every air raid!'

EUROPA HOUSE

POTSDAMER STATION

AIR MINISTRY

LEIPZIGER STRASSE

REICH CHANCERY

TIERGARTEN

WILHELM STRASSE

PROPAGANDA MINISTRY

AMERICAN EMBASSY

BRANDENBURG GATE

UNTER DEN LINDEN

RIVER SPREE

In the three attacks carried out against Berlin so far, Bomber Command had lost 125 four-engined bombers, one-third of its heavies, and about a quarter of the crews taking part had been lost. And all for poor results on the ground. Flak and night fighters had won the day, and during the week of September 10, Air Chief Marshal Sir Arthur Harris, the C-in-C of Bomber Command, called a temporary halt to further operations against the German capital. Target marking had been the major problem and the ground-scanning H2S radar mapping equipment had worked poorly against the sprawling city. A 'master bomber', whose job was to circle the target and direct the incoming bombers by radio, had been brought in to try to improve things on the second two raids, but this idea, too, had failed because the ground had not been visible through the cloud and smoke. This picture shows the government quarter at the end of the first phase with contemporary annotations.

The same area — approximately two-thirds of a mile wide and a mile deep — at the end of Phase Two. This picture was taken on March 8, 1944, following a further 16 operations. (1) Reichstag. (2) Ministry of Armaments gutted. (3) French Embassy gutted. (4) British Embassy gutted. (5) Ministry of Food severely damaged. (6) Dr Goebbels' private residence, top floors burned out. (7) Old President's Chancellery and Foreign Office, both damaged by fire. (8) Old Chancellery damaged by fire. (9) New Reichs Chancellery, undamaged. (10) Ministry of Transport, mostly gutted. (11) West wing of Göring's offices as President of Prussia damaged. (12) Forestry Office wrecked. (13) Potsdamer Station wrecked. (14) Treasury roof damaged. (15) Hotel Kaiserhof burned out. (16) Ministry of Fisheries mostly gutted. (17) Ministry of Education damaged by fire. (18) Ministry of the Interior partly destroyed. (19) Army Records Office severely damaged. (20) Post Office damaged.

Sir Arthur Harris *(below right)* had planned a prolonged campaign against Berlin to run throughout the winter with the intention of forcing the Germans to surrender by the following spring. He had knocked out Hamburg with three raids and 8,000 tons of bombs, and his prediction was that 40,000 tons — 25 attacks — would be necessary to destroy the German capital. On November 3 he wrote to Churchill: 'We can wreck Berlin from end to end if the USAAF will come in on it. It will cost between us 400–500 aircraft. It will cost Germany the war.' However, the US Eighth Army Air Force was putting its faith in a policy which suited daylight operations — accurate attacks against specific industrial targets and, as yet, it lacked long-range fighter cover to protect the bombers on the long flight to Berlin. Harris therefore had to put his faith in the Lancaster which he believed 'should be sufficient ... to produce in Germany by 1st April 1944 a state of devastation in which surrender is inevitable'. On January 20, 1944, at the height of the campaign against Berlin, the Press were invited to see and photograph the men and machines taking part. These are the crews of Nos. 12 and 626 Squadrons from RAF Wickenby.

The first raid of the renewed campaign took place on the night of November 18/19 and involved 444 aircraft, of which nine were lost. Berlin was completely covered in cloud but a considerable amount of damage was caused throughout the city and 131 people were killed. Four days later, on the night of November 22/23, the most effective bombing raid on the city occurred when 764 aircraft took part, of which 26 were lost. Bad weather caused many of the German fighters to be grounded but still 26 aircraft were lost. Again thick cloud obscured the target but the main area affected extended between Spandau through Charlottenburg to the Tiergarten district and several firestorms arose. About 2,000 people were killed, 500 of them in a large air raid shelter in Wilmersdorf and 105 in another shelter next to the Neukölln gasworks. Among the prominent buildings hit were the Kaiser-Wilhelm-Gedächtniskirche (the Memorial Church), Schloss Charlottenburg, the Zoo and several buildings on the Unter den Linden, as well as five factories in the Siemens group and the Alkett tank works, which had only recently been moved to Berlin from the Ruhr.

The following night 383 aircraft returned to bomb through the cloud at the fires still burning and a further 1,400 to 1,500 were killed. Twenty aircraft were lost. Some 450 aircraft took part in the next raid on the night of November 26/27, which was clear of cloud for a change, destroying 38 war industry factories, virtually eliminating the last of the livestock in the Zoo and bringing the death toll for these first three raids of the renewed campaign up to 4,330 for a loss of 28 aircraft that night.

Left: **The bomb load for 20 Lancasters was also put on display. A typical load used against Berlin would be four high explosive general purpose bombs used to block streets to hamper the work of the fire crews; a 4,000 lb 'Blockbuster' blast bomb to blow off roofs and smash windows, whereupon the little** four pound incendiaries (in the containers in the foreground) would be able to set fire to the open interiors. *Right:* **And these are the men (and women) behind the scenes; the armourers, mechanics, electricians, instrument fitters, airframe fitters, radio technicians, not forgetting the spark-plug testers!**

But the key to more cost-effective operations was new technology. By mid-November the first of an uprated H2S set (the Mark III) had been installed in six Pathfinder Lancasters, which were to be flown by hand-picked crews, and henceforth the navigator would operate the radar rather than the bomb-aimer. Electronic counter-measures had also been improved, with new equipment to jam and interfere with the German night fighters. Bomber losses had also been replenished and there were now around 475 Lancasters and 250 of the older Halifaxes available for operations. (The attrition rate on the Stirlings was so bad that they were withdrawn after the raid on November 22/23.) It was also planned to dramatically cut the time over the target from 16 aircraft per minute to 27 per minute by closing up the bomber stream. The first attack in the second phase found Berlin covered with cloud; many aircraft never even found the city, and the one aircraft carrying the new H2S Mark III turned back. Eight out of the 26 blind marking aircraft appear to have been sufficiently confident of their location to drop Target Indicators, but these were invisible through the murk. Skymarkers — flares on parachutes — were released although these were a crude device, completely at the mercy of wind. In the event, bombs were scattered right across the city. It was the next raid that marked the first real success for the RAF over Berlin. Although again totally covered by cloud on the night of November 22/23, the Pathfinders with the new Mark III equipment were able to accurately set down their Skymarkers just east of the city centre. This meant that the inevitable 'creep-back' in the bombing cut a four-mile swathe across the boroughs of Mitte and Tiergarten. With the intensity of the attack increased to 34 aircraft per minute, over 2,500 tons of mixed ordnance rained down in the short space of half an hour with disastrous results.

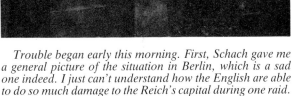

Trouble began early this morning. First, Schach gave me a general picture of the situation in Berlin, which is a sad one indeed. I just can't understand how the English are able to do so much damage to the Reich's capital during one raid.

The picture that greeted my eye in the Wilhelmplatz was one of utter desolation. Blazing fires everywhere. The Propaganda Ministry was spared, for the most part, chiefly because of the courageous fire fighting of our own air raid guards. Although damage in the Reichs Chancellery is quite heavy, it is nothing compared with other ministries. Schaub called on me and described the destruction in the Reichs Chancellery. Although he defended the private apartments of the Führer with the fury of a bear, he could not prevent their suffering some damage. From the outside the Chancellery looks almost unscathed. It is owing mainly to Schaub's intervention that it is standing at all.

In our home in Hermann-Göring-Strasse things are pretty desperate. The top floor is burned out completely. The whole house is filled with water. It is practically impossible to live there; there is no heat, no water, and all rooms are filled with pungent smoke. Magda has come to Berlin to salvage what she can. The impressions she gained on her trip, especially driving through the Wedding district, were terrible. The poor people, who are the victims of these low-down methods of English warfare, are really to be pitied. But it would be even worse if they fell into enemy hands, especially the Bolsheviks. In this case sufferings, which now can be limited to weeks or at least months, would continue indefinitely. . . .

In between I am able to sleep for half an hour. Then, however, duty again calls me. Large English formations are once more on their way, headed straight for the capital. It means we must stand a second blow. . . .

Meanwhile I learn that my mother and mother-in-law were bombed out completely in Moabit. Their homes have simply vanished. The house in which they lived was transformed into one vast shambles. But what is that at a time of universal misfortune which has now fallen upon this city of four and a half millions!

The attack began shortly after the alert sounded. This time more explosives than incendiary bombs were used. Again it was a major, grade-A attack. I was in the bunker on the Wilhelmplatz. It wasn't long before fires started all round. Large bombs and land mines were dropped over the whole government quarter. They destroyed everything around the Potsdamer Platz. The pressure was so strong that even our bunker, though constructed deep underground, began to shake. Unfortunately the fighter planes arrived twenty minutes late. This gave the English a big lead. During those twenty minutes the anti-aircraft guns were forbidden to shoot because it was believed our fighters had already arrived.

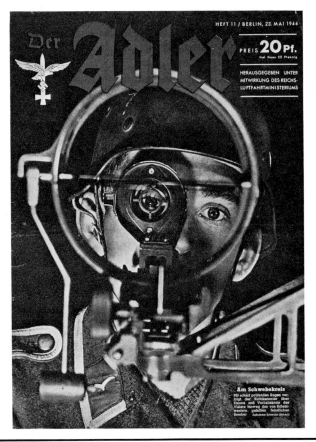

Devastation is again appalling in the government section as well as in the western and northern suburbs. The workers' quarters in Wedding and the region along Wolgaster Strasse are especially hard hit. The Schauspielhaus and the Reichstag are ablaze, but fortunately we can localise these fires. People keep coming and going in our bunker just as at a command point. Well, after all, we are living in a war and many a sector at the front would certainly not want to change places with us, so enormous is the strain. Hell itself seems to have broken loose over us. Mines and explosive bombs keep hurtling down upon the government quarter. One after another of the most important buildings begins to burn. As I look out on the Wilhelmplatz after the attack, the impression of the evening before becomes even more gruesome.

I went over to the Propaganda Ministry. It was burning at two points. The air raid wardens, under the leadership of Gutterer, are fighting these fires with the greatest energy, but sometimes things seem to hang by a silken thread. Only with the aid of large fire-fighting units were we able, after hours of fighting, to control the fire. Unfortunately I can't bother about these things myself as I am too busy worrying about the city as a whole.

Meanwhile Ley returned to offer his aid. It is most touching the way he is concerned about me and my Gau. But he can't help me very much. What I now need is not good advice but fire-fighting units. They are being requisitioned from nearby cities all the way to Hamburg. We must risk stripping other cities of their fire departments, as it can be taken for granted that Berlin will be the main target in future attacks. The enemy leaves no doubt on that score!

The Kaiserhof was hit by countless incendiary bombs and soon went up in flames. Although the largest fire-fighting units were put to work there, the edifice could not be saved; it burned to the ground. Nothing but the outer walls remain standing.

In the Reichs Chancellery, too, a big fire started in the Hall of Models, but we were able to contain it pretty well. Everything is at sixes and sevens in the Reichs Chancellery, but that is equally true of my own home, where almost all the windows and doors are gone because of the terrific blast from the explosive bombs and land mines. The government quarter is nothing short of an inferno.

It was 4 a.m. when I finally enjoyed a little rest. There are but few opportunities now to rest one's weary head. This time I slept in the shelter in Hermann-Göring-Strasse where Magda, too, took up quarters for the night. The house is a sad sight. I would far prefer to close my eyes and see nothing. This is one of the worst nights of my entire life. But I believe we got the upper hand. Although flames are still soaring sky-high, and in a part of Berlin large surface fires are still burning, we hope to overcome the worst difficulties by noon, and then to get ready for the next night. It would be a wonderful thing if we had one day's rest so that the fire department and the Party formations could for once get a little sleep.

Before taking my nap, I was able to read a few telegrams from abroad that I had neglected completely during the day. Naturally the raid on Berlin was the main theme of enemy propaganda. Cynical admission was made of the intention to ensure the same fate for Berlin as for Hamburg.

The initial communiqué issued by the Luftwaffe about the first air raid is very bad. Too much emphasis is laid on the damage done. That gave the enemy press the text for extensive comment. Malicious joy is expressed. But I'll stick to my course. I glanced only fleetingly at the telegrams. I have more important things to do than get angry with the English. The hatred of the English among the population of the Reich capital knows no bounds.

JOSEPH GOEBBELS,
NOVEMBER 24, 1943

The ruin of the once famous Kaiserhof, pictured in 1945. We also saw it on page 19.

Normally photographic evidence taken during a raid would confirm its success or otherwise. However, no photos could be taken this time because of the cloud, and a photo-reconnaissance Spitfire sent to the city early the following morning found Berlin still blanketed by cloud and smoke. Nevertheless, reports indicated that the attack had been very successful and Harris was anxious to take immediate advantage of the situation. Without waiting for further confirmation, he decided that another attack should go in that night, even though over a hundred of the Lancasters could not be made

ready in time. (The 'double hit' had been a very successful tactic used by the Luftwaffe against Britain in 1940-41 where the follow-up is intended to overwhelm the already hard-pressed fire and civil defence services.) The stress factor also came into play, and a larger-than-normal number of crews turned back — over 12 per cent of the 365 Lancasters despatched. Nevertheless, another 1,500 tons of bombs were delivered more or less in the same area as the night before, the glow of the old fires acting as additional aiming points. *Above:* Joachimstaler Strasse from Kantstrasse — then and now.

Left: **The view down Kantstrasse towards the Kaiser-Wilhelm-Gedächtniskirche — its 370-foot steeple making it one of the tallest buildings in Berlin.** *Right:* **The church still stands although masked by new buildings in this comparison.**

On the night of December 2/3 the bombers were back in strength, but nearly ten per cent of the 458 taking part failed to return. Inaccurate wind forecasts led to the Pathfinders having difficulty in placing their markers correctly and caused the bomber stream to scatter on the return flight and so facilitate the task of the German fighters. Nevertheless, much damage was caused and some 140 people killed. Two journalists, Captain Grieg of the *Daily Mail* and Norman Stockton of the *Sydney Sun* were killed in one of the five Royal Australian Air Force aircraft lost. Then on the night of December 16/17, 493 bombers attacked the city with some accuracy, inflicting damage

However, it stands now not as a church but as a memorial — and not to Kaiser Wilhelm I as originally dedicated in 1895, but, in the words of the new inscription, 'to remind us of the judgement that God passed on our people in the years of war'. *Left:* **The Gedächtniskirche ended the conflict a shattered ruin and it came very close to being demolished because it was** considered an obstacle to traffic, standing as it did right in the centre of Auguste-Viktoria-Platz (now Breitscheidplatz). However, in a straw poll in 1957, 90 per cent of Berliners wanted to keep the church, and it was retained while a new modernistic Gedächtniskirche was built alongside it. An exhibition in the old ruin was opened in 1987.

Nevertheless, the most unusual relic of the Berlin raids has to be that now on display at the Olympic Stadium. We explained on page 79 how a special bell to toll at the Games had been cast and installed in the tower (called the Glockenturm) in the centre of the grandstand facing the Maifeld. Günther Lincke was one of the many schoolboys who had been drafted in to ease the manpower shortage by helping out at night on the Flak guns. *Left:* His battery was located just beside the stadium — the Glockenturm is the tower on the right. *Right:* The tower was repaired after the war — minus the bell!

mainly on the railway system and housing. In this attack, 720 people were killed and 25 Lancasters lost.

On the night of December 23/24, 379 aircraft found the city covered in dense cloud. Trouble with some of the H2S bombsights resulted in the marking being much sparser than intended. The south-eastern districts of Köpenick and Treptow received the main blow and 178 people were killed for a loss of 16 aircraft. Again on the night of December 29/30, 712 bombers attacked the southern, south-eastern and eastern parts of the city, killing 182 people for a loss of 20 aircraft.

The New Year heralded no respite for the people of Berlin, with the first attack of 1944 coming on the night of January 1/2. This was conducted by 421 Lancasters but resulted in only scattered bombing through thick cloud. Bomber Command lost 28 aircraft but casualties on the ground were light at 79 people killed The following night brought another ineffective raid by 383 aircraft in conditions of dense cloud with insignificant damage caused and only 36 people killed to be set against the effective loss of over 160 crewmen in the 27 aircraft brought down.

Another 769 bombers returned to the charge on the night of January 20/21, again in conditions of dense cloud.

Although the marking and bombing appeared to go to plan, in this case no records of the results of the raid are available; 35 aircraft were lost. Similar conditions were encountered on the night of January 27/28 when 530 aircraft bombed through cloud killing 567 people for a loss of 33 Lancasters. On the following night 677 bombers found broken cloud over the city and bombed mainly the western and southern parts, although a high proportion of public and official buildings were hit, including Albert Speer's new Reichs Chancellery. More such buildings were hit on the night of January 30/31, including Goebbels's Propaganda Ministry, when

'We picked up a target coming in,' recounted Lincke to Martin Middlebrook, author of *The Berlin Raids*. 'Through my headphones, I was ordered to elevate the gun. The elevation was set electrically and my job was to keep the manual dial exactly on the electrical dial. My school friend had to do the same for the line of sight. Pjotr, our Russian loader, already had the shell in the breech, ready to fire. Unteroffizier Sturmegger, who came from Vienna, pulled the firing cord — one round every eight seconds. We kept on firing but then there was a dull clang.

What had happened? Someone had allowed a shell to hit the tower of the stadium and strike the bell which had called the youth of the world to the Olympic Games in 1936. That 'someone' was me! I had allowed the elevation of the gun to drop too low and the barrel had knocked away the wooden wall which would have stopped us firing in that direction. My battery commander was nearly disciplined for this mistake, but he was deemed not responsible for the error of a high-school boy who was a keener artilleryman than a Latin student!'

Following the big November raid on Berlin, Göring was under great pressure to retaliate against London. At a top secret meeting on November 28, the Reichsmarschall announced that he had told the Führer that 'we shall be ready in fourteen days'. Codename for the operation was 'Steinbock'. In the event, preparations took longer than envisaged and the first attack in what the British called The 'Baby' or 'Little' Blitz took place on the night of January 21/22, 1944, another 14 attacks taking place by the end of March. During the same period, Bomber Command mounted five operations against Berlin before the lighter evenings brought long-range operations to a halt. The final attack — the last major raid by the RAF on the city during the war — took place on March 24/25. This is Kantstrasse — a scene as familiar in London during the Blitz as in Berlin.

534 aircraft spread their loads over much of the city, killing an estimated 1,000 people and suffering the loss of 33 bombers.

Then there was a two week lull before 891 aircraft returned on the night of February 15/16 to inflict extensive damage all over the city, particularly to the war industries and killing 379 people for the loss of 43 aircraft.

> *Göring travelled west, on the Führer's orders, to prepare a retaliatory blow against England. We need about 200 heavy four-motored planes for it. They are to fly to England twice in the course of one night and strike a heavy blow against the British capital. Naturally we cannot repeat such an assault as often as we would like, but it will give the English something to think about. I expect great psychological results from it.*
>
> DR JOSEPH GOEBBELS, DECEMBER 7, 1943

In November and December the RAF had mounted nine attacks against Berlin, only half of which could really be called successful in that the correct target area was hit. At the same time, losses were frightening — up from 2 per cent on the first raid to 8.7 per cent on the night of December 2/3. The operation on December 16/17 was even worse, with 59 Lancasters lost out of the 483 taking part — over 12 per cent. This is Schubartstrasse, hit on January 28/29.

Hitler could not bring himself to personally visit the devastated areas — indeed, he was absent from Berlin on the Eastern Front throughout the period in question. It was left to Dr Goebbels to keep spirits up. 'I then took another trip through the damaged areas,' he wrote after the night of November 26/27. 'We also stopped at some soup kitchens. I inquired into even the smallest details. The people show a touching devotion. The misery that meets my eyes is indescribable. My heart is convulsed at the sights. But we must grit our teeth. The meals are everywhere praised as excellent. People without shelter are gradually being provided with quarters. They are weighed down with sorrow about loved ones who fell, but are getting over it. The attitude and morale of the population are exemplary. We shall never lose the war for reasons of morale.' *Right:* On February 7, 1944, he opened another feeding centre in Berlin to provide hot meals for those bombed out of their homes.

Another month was to pass before the final major raid by Bomber Command on Berlin took place on the night of March 24/25 under extremely windy conditions that caused difficulties flying to, over and back from the target, and many places lying outside the target area were hit as the markers drifted. The south-west districts were the worst affected and the Lichterfelde barracks of the Waffen-SS Division Leibstandarte 'Adolf Hitler' were hit. About 150 people were killed. Of the 811 bombers that took part, 72 were lost.

This air battle, lasting from August 1943 until the end of March 1944 and using only a third of Bomber Command's resources, is considered to have been a major 'Second Front' contribution to the Allied war effort. It involved 41 raids of various kinds on the capital, 16 of which were by the main British bomber fleet in which they dropped 45,000 tons of high explosive and incendiary bombs. The Americans too eventually joined in during the last month with six massive daylight raids. It resulted in Berlin's industrial capacity being wrecked with 326 factories completely destroyed. As Luftwaffe Generalfeldmarschall Erhard Milch told his staff on February 23, 1944: 'Everyone should pay a visit to Berlin. It would then be realised that experience such as we have undergone in the last few months cannot be endured indefinitely. That is impossible. When the big cities have been demolished it will be the turn of the smaller ones.'

The cost to the Royal Air Force had been 495 aircraft and 2,938 aircrew. Many of these airmen are buried in the British Commonwealth Cemetery on the Heerstrasse. This battle had seen the Luftwaffe night fighters in their ascendancy but for the Royal Air Force, which had improved its tactics so that it could now put 800 bombers over the target area in as little as 20 minutes from a bomber stream that had been condensed from 300 miles when it was first used in 1942 to only 70 miles long in 1944, there had been a steady decline in effectiveness as the costs mounted.

Although accurate figures are not available, one German report indicates that over 18 out of every hundred high explosive bombs dropped by the RAF failed to explode. (Later in the war, when the demand for bombs exceeded supply, old ones dating back to WWI had to be used, and of these it is believed that up to 60 per cent could have been duds.) Nevertheless, unexploded bombs still had to be dealt with, and prisoners were frequently employed on the work. *Above:* This incident was pictured in Schlegelstrasse — a back street in former East Berlin *(below)*.

The Americans maintained their daylight attacks right up to March 1945, while the British contribution switched to the Mosquito bombers, which continued to harass the city in growing numbers, anything from 30 to a 100 daily, making life a misery for the inhabitants with the irregular timing of their visits. The Americans also used a few Mosquitos and Spitfires but mainly for reconnaissance purposes.

After its six-month campaign, Bomber Command bowed out of the main battle. Opinions differ as to whether it was won or lost and comparisons are often invidious as no two sets of circumstances are alike. The Luftwaffe's night blitz on Britain in 1940-41 lasted eight weeks longer than the Battle of Berlin, but was infinitely more successful. German and British losses were roughly the same at 600 aircraft, yet the attrition rate per Bomber Command sortie was nearly four times that of the Luftwaffe. And the Luftwaffe killed three times more people: 40,000 to around 13,000. Martin Middlebrook, who has made the most detailed study of the Berlin air raids by the RAF, sums it up thus: 'The Luftwaffe hurt Bomber Command more than Bomber Command hurt Berlin.' Now it was America's turn and the US Eighth Army Air Force opened their daylight campaign with a massed attack on March 6.

 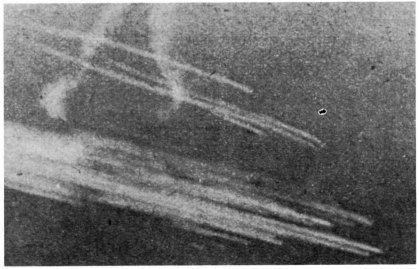

The serried formations trailing their condensation trails were a new sight in the sky over Berlin and *Der Adler*, the Luftwaffe's house magazine, included several pictures taken from the ground in its April 4 edition.

149

It was a beautiful sunny day and the photography from above was excellent. Although it was not a target, this was one familiar location spotted on the run in to the industrial areas to be attacked.

The first American aircraft over the German capital were P-38 Lightnings of Lieutenant Colonel Mark E. Hubbard's 20th Fighter Group on March 3, 1944, making a preliminary reconnaissance for the US Eighth Air Force's coming offensive. Next day the first American attack took place when 30 B-17 Flying Fortresses of the 3rd Bomb Division bombed Klein Machnow, just outside the city boundary, south of the Teltow Canal. Out of this division's 238 B-17s despatched in severe weather conditions, only 63 got anywhere near the target area and 11 were shot down. The 2nd Bomb Divison, equipped with B-24 Liberators, were obliged to turn back almost immediately after take-off. However, on March 6 in brilliant sunshine, 248 B-17s of the 1st Bomb Division dropped 459.5 tons of high explosives with a loss of 18 aircraft, and some B-24s of the 2nd Bomb Division, which lost 16 of the 198 aircraft despatched that day on various missions, dropped a further 165 tons of incendiaries in the city.

A major disaster for the 4th Combat Wing on this mission was the loss of their commanding officer, Brigadier General Russ Wilson, who was riding aboard *Chopstick*, a B-17 from the 482nd Bomb Group, which was acting as pathfinder for the 3rd Bombardment Division. Flak ignited the fuel tanks which exploded soon after the second picture was taken. The crippled aircraft can be seen descending over Moabit. (The West Hafen docks hit by the RAF on page 127 can be seen top left.) Of the twelve men aboard, only three survived, one being the pilot, Captain John C. Morgan, who managed to clip on his parachute as he fell. ('Red' Morgan had already been awarded the Medal of Honor in July 1943 when, as co-pilot, he continued with a mission after the aircraft had been hit and the pilot had been shot in the head.)

Two days later the Eighth Air Force was back in strength with a total of 310 B-17s of the 1st and 3rd Bomb Divisions and 150 B-24s of the 2nd Bomb Division, escorted by 170 fighters, to deliver 316 tons of high explosives and 665 tons of incendiaries on the eastern end of the city, where in Erkner they obliterated the vital ball-bearing factory of the Vereinigten Kugellagerfabriken company, for the loss of 28 B-17s, 9 B-24s and 17 fighters. The American airmen shot down 21 German fighters that day. Next day, the 1st and 3rd Bomb Divisions returned with 339 B-17s, losing 6 aircraft, and dropping 553 tons of high explosives and 242 tons of incendiaries.

There was a pause in the daytime bombing until March 22, when all three Bomb Divisions returned in poor visibility with 460 B-17s and 197 B-24s, of which 7 and 5 respectively were lost, all to ground fire as the German fighters did not engage that day. On this occasion, the primary objective of the aircraft factories in Oranienburg and Basdorf being shrouded with cloud, attention was diverted to Berlin as the secondary objective, which received 514.5 tons of high explosives from the B-17s and 957 tons of incendiaries from the B-24s, most of it missing the in-

On March 8 the target was the Vereinigten Kugellagerfabriken in the suburb of Erkner in eastern Berlin. This picture was taken from one of the departing Liberators from the 2nd Bomb Division. The aerodrome at Johannisthal lies in the foreground between the River Spree and the Teltow Canal.

tended industrial targets around Weissensee and falling on housing areas or open fields and garden plots. By the end of March 1944, about 1,500,000 people had been rendered homeless in Berlin, most having been bombed out during the previous winter.

Five weeks were to go by before the next big daylight raid on April 29, 1944, when 368 B-17s and 212 B-24s dropped 765 tons of high explosives and 733 tons of incendiaries between them in the Tempelhof and Kreuzberg areas, as well as on industrial plants in the north of the city. Losses numbered 38 B-17s and 25 B-24s, four of the B-17s falling to Oberleutnant Hans-Heinz König of Jägergruppe 11.

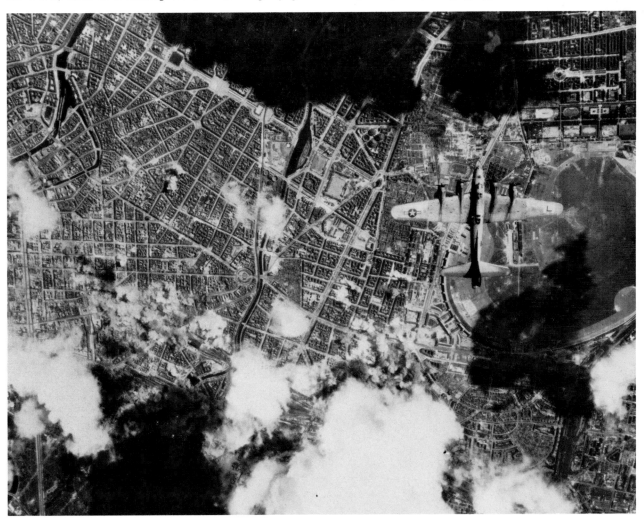

The primary targets for the big raid on April 29 were industrial areas in the suburbs. It was another clear day with scattered cumulus ideal for photography. Bombs can be seen bursting on the Tempelhof marshalling yards and also further north around the Anhalter station. The New Chancellery lies just clear of the bombing. The B-17 is from the 452nd Bomb Group.

One of the most famous pictures of the Berlin blitz — the flaming rotunda of the French Church on May 7.

May 1944 saw three major American air raids on the city, all by B-17s of the 1st and 3rd Bomb Divisions. On Sunday the 7th, 600 aircraft dropped 1,246.5 tons of high explosives and 98 tons of incendiaries, scoring a direct hit on the Französische Dom (French Cathedral) on the Gendarmenmarkt, whose upper part of the tower was burnt out. Eight aircraft were lost. Then on the 8th, 386 aircraft dropped a further 892 tons of

Right: **The Gendarmenmarkt with the ruins of the twin German and French Cathedrals and Schinkel's Schauspielhaus (Playhouse) in the centre. The latter has been fully restored as a concert hall, while the French Cathedral now contains the Huguenot Museum on the ground floor and an exclusive wine bar in its cupola. The German cathedral is now an art gallery.**

Left: **The Communists renamed the square 'Platz der Akademie' and took this symbolic photograph exactly 100 years after the** March Revolution of 1848. *Right:* **Upon restoration, the statue of Frederick Schiller, removed by the Nazis, was replaced.**

A lull was forced on both the Eighth Air Force and Bomber Command during the early summer as aircraft were diverted to support the invasion in France, but operations resumed in August — the B-17s and B-24s by day and the Mosquitos by night. This is the elevated section of U-Bahn between Nollendorfplatz and Bülowstrasse.

bombs through cloud, losing 25 of their number. Again on the 19th, 495 bombers dropped 1,075.5 tons in all for a loss of 16 aircraft. There was carpet bombing of Wedding and Pankow districts, and the Westhafen and Stettiner railway station was also hit. The Humboldthain Flakbunker was hit several times in this raid without suffering serious damage.

There was only one raid in June, on the 21st, when 590 B-17s and 103 B-24s dropped 1,302 tons of bombs on the city. Some 2,500 aircraft of all kinds had taken off for the two main target areas of the Ruhland synthetic oil plants and Berlin using deception tactics, and almost 200 German fighter aircraft waiting to intercept did not know where to concentrate to meet them. Part of the American force came in from the North Sea flying due east to Stettin and then turned south along the line of the Oder River to attack Berlin from the northeast, while the other part approached via Hannover to turn over the Spreewald and attack from the south-east. Bombs fell over the whole city; aircraft factories in the north, railway installations in the south, the governmental and newspaper districts in the city centre, including the Reichs Chancellery, were all badly hit, and much damage was done to housing areas by deep-penetration blockbusters which literally destroyed whole apartment blocks at a time. Half an hour after the raid had begun, a group of 114 B-17s of the 3rd Air Division suddenly swung away from the main force and headed south to attack the synthetic oil plant at Ruhland. A lone He 177 joined them unnoticed and reported their progress to the defences, thereby discovering that this group intended to fly on to Russia. That afternoon the American bombers landed at Poltava in the Ukraine, their escorting fighters at Mirgorod and Piryatin. That night the IV. Fliegerkorps, based in Poland, made a surprise attack on the Poltava airfield and destroyed 44 of the B-17s on the ground and damaged 26, a serious blow following the loss of 25 B-17s and 19 B-24s in the raid, 20 of them claimed by the Berlin Flak.

Support of the Normandy invasion was a priority task that year, so there

was another pause until August 6, when 128 B-17s of the 3rd Bomb Division made a 20-minute raid on the city, dropping 304 tons of bombs. The next big raid was on October 6, when concentrated bombing by 382 B-17s of the 3rd Bomb Division destroyed the Borsig factory in Tegel and tank engine factories and Wehrmacht depots in

Spandau with 922 tons of bombs. Seventeen aircraft were lost, four falling to the 4. Batterie, Flak-Abteilung 422. Next, on December 5, 404 B-17s attacked war industries and tank works in the Tegel, Spandau, Siemensstadt, Pankow and Weissensee areas, dropping 960 tons this time and losing 12 aircraft.

By now, there was hardly a street in Berlin that had not felt the effect of the Allied air bombardment. Gossowstrasse presented a sorry sight as seen from the corner with Winterfeldstrasse.

Then came the big one on February 3, 1945 — the heaviest raid of all against Berlin by the Eighth Air Force. The target centre was the circular Belle-Alliance-Platz which lay midway between the government buildings on Wilhelmstrasse and Tempelhof airfield. (It shows up quite clearly in the picture on page 151.)

Above: This picture was taken six months after the raid with the area plastered with Russian signs and slogans. *Bottom:* Today the whole layout of the traffic system in the area has been altered — only the overhead track of the U-Bahn remains the same.

Left: The ready-made bulls-eye of Belle-Alliance-Platz made a perfect aiming point. *Right:* After the war, advantage was taken of the wholesale destruction in the district to re-route traffic left and right of the circular 'square' which was reconstructed as a

largely pedestrianised area called the Mehringplatz. (These pictures make an interesting comparison as they show how Lindenstrasse on the right — the location of the *Vorwärts* office badly damaged in 1919 — has been diverted. See page 29.)

1945 brought the biggest American daylight raids yet, the worst that Berlin was to endure, and a change of title for the Bomb Divisions, which were now known as Air Divisions. On February 3, 950 B-17s, accompanied by 785 P-51 Mustangs, attacked in clear visibility, dropping 2,298 tons of bombs and using the unmistakeable roundel of the Belle-Alliance-Platz (Mehringplatz) as a reference point. Between 20,000 and 25,000 people lost their lives as a broad swathe of devastation swept across the city, with the Tempelhof and Schöne-berg railway junctions, the newspaper quarter and the government quarter in the city being the worst hit. The Anhalter railway station and Schloss Berlin (Royal Palace) were among the prominent buildings struck. Losses were 23 B-17s and seven P-51s.

'Bombs away!' Three sticks are dropping pretty much 'on target' which lies out of the picture to the right. Smoke markers are also falling.

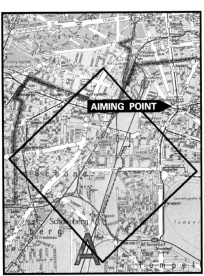

Left: **The sirens wail and Berliners rush to the shelters. Back in 1943, Goebbels had managed to convince Hitler to introduce two types of air alert for the city: 'One, a genuine alert, when bomber formations are on their way here, the other a mere warning in case of a few nuisance planes'. This was necessary, said Goebbels, 'for I don't want to throw a city of four-and-a-half millions into a panic merely because of two Mosquitos.' If we were to accept at face value the original caption on this picture, we would be calling it the 'Anhalter Station shelters'. However, it is in fact the Zoo bunker, the same entrance being photographed *right* in August 1946 when it was in use as the Robert Koch Hospital.**

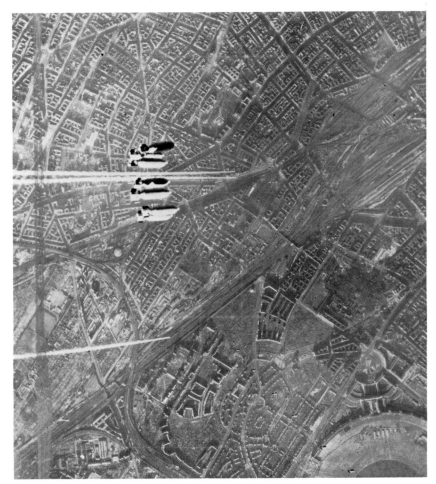

Europahaus on Saarland Strasse; pre-war, *left*, and post-attack, *above*. (The same building can also be identified in the background of the picture on page 110.)

Under attack on the morning of February 3, 1945. The picture was taken from Askanischer Platz with the Anhalter Bahnhof behind the photographer's right shoulder. Over 1,000 B-17s were despatched on this raid of which some 950 reached and bombed Berlin. Although the B-17 could carry only a fraction of the bomb-load of the Lancaster, this was by far the worst of any attack on the city as more than 2,000 tons of bombs landed on a concentrated area, killing over 20,000. And all for the loss of only 30 aircraft. Werner Girbig, writing in *Im Anflug auf die Reichshauptstadt*, states that 'The German people came to know about this heavy attack on Berlin only through eye-witnesses and those that had experienced it. Any disclosure in the press or on the radio about the extent and results of air attacks remained, as before, strictly forbidden.'

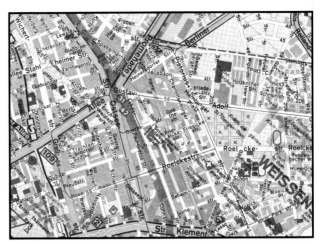

Above: One of the 381st Bomb Group's B-17s, streaming contrails, leaves the smoking city centre. Beneath is the northern suburb of Weissensee. *Below:* Post-strike cover of the government quarter shows severe damage to many of the buildings along the Wilhelmstrasse. Smoke is still rising from the Haus der Flieger and the Industrial Art Museum opposite. A section has been blown from the Air Ministry and the Prinz Albrecht Palais has been hit as well as the Gestapo headquarters round the corner. *Right:* This is the air raid shelter situated behind the building — some inmates were lucky enough to be taken to it during air raids. The Leipziger Platz can be seen lower right.

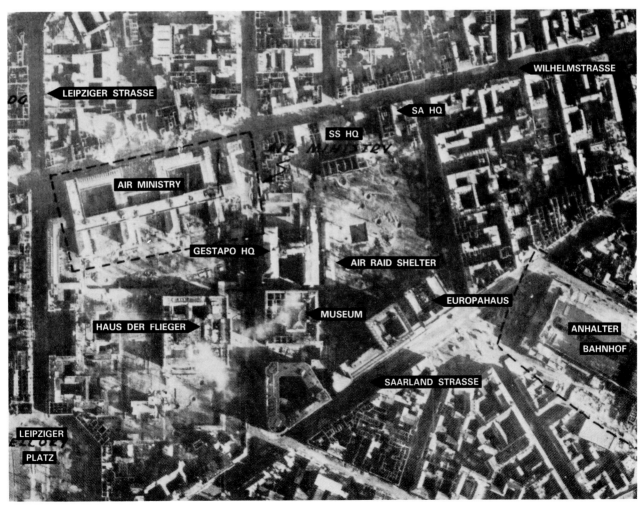

Left: 'Nach dem Alarm . . . verlassen die Berliner den Bunker in der Neuen Reichsbank.' Citizens leave the shelter beneath the Reichsbank. *Above:* It still stands between Kurstrasse and Unterwasserstrasse, although the surrounding buildings do not.

Mohrenstrasse runs eastwards from the Voss-strasse. One assumes that this is the sort of crater one gets from the

explosion of a 1,000-pounder as these were the main bombs used by the Eighth Air Force.

HAUSVOGTEIPLATZ

Left: Further down the road, another bomb has broken through the roadway, opening up the U-Bahn tunnel. *Above:* Fortunately one of the buildings in the background survives to link past with present.

Bomb damage to the west wing of the University on Dorotheenstrasse (now Clara-Zetkin-Strasse).

Then on Monday, February 26, 1945, for the first time over a thousand bombers, 781 B-17s and 285 B-24s, dropped a staggering 2,796.5 tons of bombs through thick cloud, but accurately guided by their H2S-equipped Pathfinders. Their goal was the railway complex in the eastern part of the city, centering on the Schlesischer station (Hauptbanhof), their carpet including Alexanderplatz, Frankfurter Allee and the Osthafen down to Rummelsburg in the east, and Museuminsel (Museum Island) and Prenzlauer Allee. The German defences were exhausted with many of their fighter pilots inexperienced and the Americans lost only three B-17s and three P-51s on this raid, Berlin's Flak defences having been severely reduced to provide artillery on the Oder front.

On March 18, 1945, the Eighth Air Force mustered 916 B-17s and 305 B-24s — over 1,200 bombers — for another massive strike at Berlin, dropping 3,276.6 tons of bombs in an hour-long attack that concentrated once more on the Schlesischer station, the government quarter and the city centre. Some 38 Me 262s of the III. Gruppe of Jagdgruppe 7, each equipped with twelve 5.5cm rockets, and commanded by Major Sinner, engaged the Americans over the city, shooting down eight of the thirteen bombers and five out of the six P-51s lost that day in conditions of poor visibility that allowed the German pilots to avoid the escorting American fighters to some extent.

Then on March 24 there was a surprise raid by the US Fifteenth Air Force with 150 B-24s, coming from Foggia in Italy, whose escorting P-51s shot down five Me 262s during the course of the action for the loss of only two bombers. There was another raid on the 28th of that month, when 383 B-17s of the 1st Air Division attacked Spandau and Falkensee on the western side of the city, dropping 1,038 tons of bombs for the loss of only two aircraft.

The final big American raid took place on Hitler's birthday, April 20, 1945, when 299 B-17s of the 3rd Air Division bombed rail targets just outside the city and were observed as if on parade by Keitel, Dönitz and their wives from a garden in Dahlem, keeping perfect formation above the reach of the Flak and dropping their bombs in unison. None of the aircraft were lost on this occasion.

The British and American air offensive was thus continued until the Soviet land battle for the city began and their own tactical aircraft took over the skies above Berlin.

It is impossible to draw a line between the amount of damage caused by aerial bombardment and the land battle that overlapped it, but some 6,427 acres of the city were reduced to a ruined waste, almost all of which can be attributed to the bombing, and of the 1,502,383 homes registered in 1939, only 976,500 remained intact at the end of the war. The number of war-related deaths totalled more than 49,000.

Goebbels: 'How beautiful Berlin was at one time and how run-down and woebegone it now looks.' *Above:* **The unsafe walls of his Reichspropagandaministerium are pulled down, March 13, 1945.** *Below:* **The enemy takes over, July 7, 1945.**

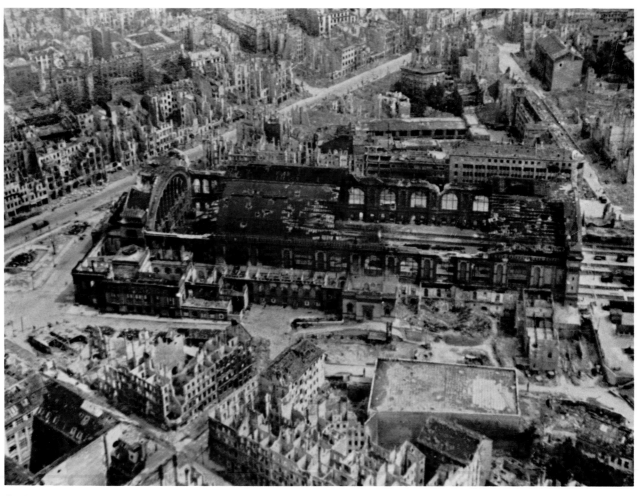

Göring: 'No enemy plane will ever fly over the German Reich . . . ' Anhalter Bahnhof, 1945-1991.

Hitler: 'Give me ten years and you will not recognise Germany.' Potsdamer Bahnhof, 1945-1990.

Our artist's impression of one of Hitler's daily conferences, normally held in the brick and concrete Lagebaracke which was situated within the innermost top security compound located in the 'Wolfschanze' Führerhauptquartier — the command post near Rastenburg in East Prussia from where Hitler conducted operations against the Red Army.

July 20, 1944

The assassination attempt on Hitler of July 20, 1944, was the high point of the resistance against Hitler, and yet failed abysmally, resulting in the imprisonment, torture and death of hundreds of opponents of the Nazi regime.

From the outset, the German Intelligence Service, known as the Abwehr, under Admiral Canaris proved a haven for opponents of the regime and from 1941 onwards Helmuth Graf von Moltke's Kreisau Circle (Kreisauer Kreis) provided a forum for discussion of a new Christian form of government for Germany with meetings on his Kreisau estate in Silesia and in Berlin. Seven of this group were later hanged for their complicity in the July 20 plot.

Co-ordination of resistance against Hitler was rendered impossible mainly by the disparity of political views, the apparent legality of the government's position, and close surveillance by the Gestapo. The only relatively safe area against infiltration by Gestapo agents was to be found within the closed ranks of the army's officer corps. (The air force was a child of the Nazi regime and the navy were anxious to live down their mutinous past.) However, even in the army, the traditions of military obedience and the oath of personal loyalty provided formidable barriers for individuals to overcome. Here the main turning point appears to have been the persecution of the Jews, especially when the horrors of the atrocities committed in the East became known, and then many were finally convinced in early 1943 by the wanton sacrifice of the German 6. Armee at Stalingrad, as a result of which a considerable number of senior army officers then started

actively conspiring to either assassinate or overthrow Hitler and replace the Nazi regime somehow or other.

Colonel Claus Schenk Graf von Stauffenberg had declared as early as September 1942 that he was prepared to assassinate Hitler, but his posting from a staff appointment to one in the field put Hitler beyond his reach. However, he was able to return to staff duties after having been severely wounded, losing an eye, a kneecap, his right hand and

two fingers on his left hand. A posting was arranged for him as chief-of-staff to General Friedrich Olbricht, also in the plot and commanding the Home Army from Berlin, and thus responsible for the training and supply of replacements to the operational armies. In this capacity von Stauffenberg was also able to revise the mobilisation orders for the Home Army units in the event of internal disorder, known as Operation 'Valkyrie', in such a manner as to deploy

The interior of the Lagebaracke following the explosion of the bomb on the morning of July 20, 1944. The device, carried into the conference room by Colonel Claus von Stauffenberg in his briefcase, contained just under a kilogramme of explosive, and it was amazing that, of the 24 people present, no one was killed outright. Dr Heinrich Berger, the shorthand writer who was standing right next to the bomb, lost both legs and died that afternoon. The Luftwaffe Chief-of-Staff, General Günther Korten, and Colonel Heinz Brandt, senior staff officer with the Army Operations Section, were both grievously injured and died in hospital two days later. General Rudolf Schmundt, the Führer's senior Wehrmacht aide (also head of the Army Personnel Office), who had been standing at the end of the table, died of his wounds three months later.

them conveniently for use against the government should the opportunity arise.

Meanwhile several plans for Hitler's assassination were evolved. One was for Hauptmann Axel Baron von dem Bussche to blow himself and Hitler up during a display of new uniforms and equipment at Hitler's headquarters. This fell through when the equipment was destroyed in an air raid. Before it could be replaced Bussche had to return to his front line unit and then lost a leg in combat. Another officer volunteered to replace him in this suicidal task but was unable to get the necessary assignment. Yet another attempt was made by Hauptmann Eberhard von Breitenbuch, who was prepared to shoot Hitler with his pistol while accompanying Generalfeldmarschall Ernst Busch to a conference on March 11, 1944, but at the last minute he was denied access to the room concerned.

Despite his severe handicap, von Stauffenberg was still determined to kill Hitler himself. His lack of fingers on the one remaining hand made it impossible for him to use a pistol, which would be of dubious value anyway, especially if Hitler wore a bullet proof vest. He first visited Hitler at Berchtesgaden early in June 1944, and on a subsequent visit the following month took a quantity of explosive with him in his briefcase, but had no opportunity of using it.

He then decided that he would have to both do the job himself and lead the coup, which meant he would have to survive the assassination and return to Berlin to direct operations. It also meant using enough explosive to kill everyone in the room in order to ensure that Hitler was eliminated. On July 15, von Stauffenberg reported to Hitler's Wolfschanze headquarters near Rastenburg in East Prussia all set to carry out the plan, but then found no opportunity of setting the fuse.

Then on July 20 von Stauffenberg flew out to Rastenburg from Berlin together with his aide, Oberleutnant Werner von Haeften, arriving at the Wolfschanze at about 1000 hours. They were given breakfast, then from 1100 hours von Stauffenberg was en-

Hitler, who had his chin in his cupped hand at the moment when the bomb went off, suffered a wound to his right elbow which had been resting on the table. There were superficial abrasions to the back of his other hand and he had burns on both legs. Both eardrums were pierced. The plan to kill Hitler had gone drastically wrong but, as von Stauffenberg drove from the compound after excusing himself from the briefing, he fully believed that the force of the explosion he had just heard must have killed everyone in the room, including Keitel and Jodl. Coincidentally, Mussolini was due to visit Hitler that same day, in fact the conference had been advanced by half an hour to get it out of the way before the Duce arrived. *Left:* After meeting Mussolini at the nearby railway station, Hitler took him to see the scene of his miraculous escape. *Right:* Having left the building (visible in the background), Mussolini is seen talking to Obergruppenführer Karl Wolff, Wehrmacht plenipotentiary in Italy. Martin Bormann stands between the Duce and Hitler, while Himmler is between Hitler and Göring. Luftwaffe General Lörzer is to the right of Göring, and SS-Obergruppenführer Julius Schaub is just visible on the extreme left.

gaged in conferences with members of Hitler's staff in preparation for the midday briefing. The last of these conferences was with Generalfeldmarschall Wilhelm Keitel and ended just as Hitler's briefing was due to begin in a building some distance away. On a pretext of wishing to change his shirt, von Stauffenberg had a few moments alone with his aide. There were two charges, each of two pounds of explosive, in von Haeften's briefcase and the

On the date of the attempted assassination, the Red Army had advanced to within 140 kilometres of the Wolfschanze HQ. Exactly four months later — on November 20, 1944 — Hitler finally quit Rastenburg for Berlin, leaving behind the elaborate complex of buildings and bunkers which had been his home for the larger part of the previous three years. In January 1945, with the Soviets only a few kilometres away, engineers of Kampfgruppe Hauser placed explosives in the bunkers and blew up the headquarters to deny it to the Russians. *Above:* Dr Richard Raiber, one of the world's leading authorities on the period, particularly on the construction and use of the various Führerhauptquartiere, photographed in November 1974 standing on the fallen roof slab of the conference building as it was left at the end of the war. *(For further details, see After the Battle No. 19.)*

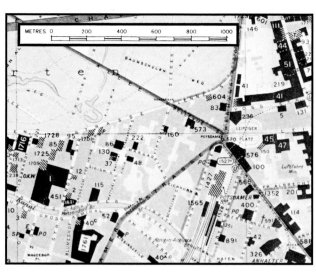

On that Thursday in July, the focus of attention in Berlin was on the General Army Office of the Wehrmacht High Command, headed by Generaloberst Friedrich Fromm, situated at No. 14 Bendlerstrasse (No. 1 on plan),

plan was for von Haeften to hold them up one at a time for von Stauffenberg to set the fuses and transfer them to his own briefcase. However, they were interrupted by a sergeant sent to hurry them up as Keitel was waiting impatiently outside. Von Stauffenberg was unable to set the second fuse with the sergeant watching. In the heat of the moment he therefore left with only one fused charge in his briefcase whereas, if he had taken both, the detonation of the first would have undoubtedly set off the second and killed everyone present.

On his way to the briefing room von Stauffenberg accepted an offer from Major John von Freyend (Keitel's adjutant) to carry his briefcase and, implying that he had become slightly deaf as a result of his injuries, asked him to place it and himself near Hitler so that he could hear what was being said. Hitler was standing as he usually did in the centre of the heavy map table listening to a briefing on the Eastern Front. The adjutant managed to place von Stauffenberg close to Hitler and put his briefcase on the floor under the end of the table. After a couple of minutes, von Stauffenberg signalled to the adjutant and said he needed to obtain some last-minute details from Berlin. The adjutant escorted him out and instructed the switchboard operator to make the requested connection. Before the call could be put through, von Stauffen-

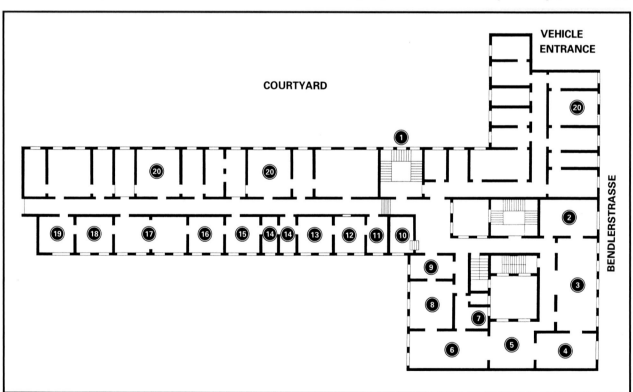

The suite of offices on the second floor at the Bendlerstrasse where the activity centred that evening. (1) Stairwell to courtyard. (2) Duty Officer. (3) Ante-room to Chief-of-Staff, Home Army (Allgemeine Army). (4) Chief-of-Staff, Home Army (Oberst Claus Schenk Graf von Stauffenberg). (5) Map Room. (6) Commander, Home Army (Generaloberst Friedrich Fromm). (7) Waiting Room. (8) ADC to Commander, Home Army (Rittmeister Heinz-Ludwig Bartram). (9) Chief Clerk. (10) Duty Clerks. (11) Ante-room to Staff Officer Ia, General Army Office. (12) Staff Officer Ia, General Army Office (Oberstleutnant Bolko von der Heyde). (13) Staff Officer Ia1, General Army Office (Oberstleutnant Karl Pridun). (14) Ante-rooms to Staff Officer Ia1. (15) Chief of Staff, General Army Office (Oberst Albrecht Ritter Mertz von Quirnheim — previously Oberst von Stauffenberg). (16) Secretaries (Anni Lerche and Delia Ziegler). (17) Chief, General Army Office (General Friedrich Olbricht). (18) ADC to Chief, General Army Office (Oberstleutnant Fritz von der Lancken). (19) Registry. (20) Offices of the General Army Office.

Having been ex-communicado for some two hours during the flight to Berlin, Oberleutnant Werner von Haeften, von Stauffenberg's aide, immediately telephoned the Bendlerstrasse on their arrival (the actual airfield where they landed has never been reliably determined), categorically telling their fellow conspirators that Hitler had been killed. Together they then drove to von Stauffenberg's office, arriving at about 4.30 p.m. *Left:* This picture is said to be of his office in 1944 although the features such as the radiators do not precisely match room '4' on the plan as it is today *(right)*.

berg hurried out and went directly to the parking area some 250 metres away. There he met General Fellgiebel, and the two walked to the Horch in which the conspirators had been transported from Rastenburg airfield earlier that day. Sitting in it, talking with Oberleutnant von Haeften, was their driver, Feldwebel Karl Fischer. Moments later they heard the explosion.

Von Stauffenberg and von Haeften jumped into the car and ordered the driver to take them to the airfield. As they drove to the first checkpoint they could see a great column of smoke rising from the building. However, Feldwebel Fischer was not alarmed as engineers had been using explosives to remove trees to expand the camp, so drove on unconcerned. They bluffed their way through the first and second checkpoints, but an NCO at the third insisted on verification, so von Stauffenberg telephoned an officer with whom he had had breakfast that morning and got him to clear them through. On their way through the woods, von Haeften threw out the second, unused explosive charge. This was observed by the driver and reported later to the Gestapo.

Von Stauffenberg and von Haeften then went to General Olbricht's office (17), only to be told that Generaloberst Fromm had refused to issue the vital orders to take over key positions in the city. Von Stauffenberg and Olbricht then went together down the corridor to Fromm's office (6), and it was in this room *(above right)* that the final drama was played out. With von Stauffenberg insisting that Hitler was dead, and Fromm equally adamant that he was alive, each declared that the other was under arrest. However, it was Fromm who, at pistol point, was marched into his adjutant's office (8) next door and placed under guard. It was now about 5.00 p.m. and several other high-ranking officers in the plot had arrived. *Right:* General Fromm's office today, looking from the map room (5).

Meanwhile General Fellgiebel was supposed to telephone the results of the attack through to Berlin, but to his amazement he saw Hitler, his clothes in tatters, walking out of the debris towards his bunker. He telephoned General Fritz Thiele in Berlin with the words: 'Something terrible has happened. The Führer is alive.' Then, hoping to protect the conspirators, he ordered an immediate communications blackout.

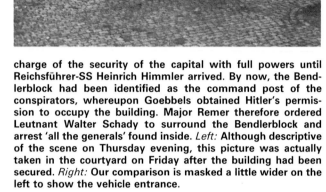

By late afternoon, the orders emanating from the conspirators at the Bendlerstrasse were beginning to have the desired effect, and the commanders of units sympathetic to the coup were co-operating, although the situation was still very confused. At the same time Keitel was endeavouring to counter the plotters through orders issued from Wolfschanze, though the regime was equally hamstrung with all its leaders, save Goebbels, out of Berlin. And it was around his house at No. 20 Hermann-Göring-Strasse that a move towards counter-action was established, with forces loyal to Hitler assembling in his garden under Major Otto Remer whom Hitler had personally put in charge of the security of the capital with full powers until Reichsführer-SS Heinrich Himmler arrived. By now, the Bend-lerblock had been identified as the command post of the conspirators, whereupon Goebbels obtained Hitler's permission to occupy the building. Major Remer therefore ordered Leutnant Walter Schady to surround the Bendlerblock and arrest 'all the generals' found inside. *Left:* Although descriptive of the scene on Thursday evening, this picture was actually taken in the courtyard on Friday after the building had been secured. *Right:* Our comparison is masked a little wider on the left to show the vehicle entrance.

General Thiele had no means of telling from this message whether or not the assassination attempt had gone ahead, or if the conspiracy had been compromised. He and General Olbricht therefore decided to take no action until they knew more. At about 1500 hours von Stauffenberg and von Haeften arrived back in Berlin, and von Haeften telephoned from the airfield to say that Hitler was dead. Meanwhile, at the army headquarters in the Bendler-strasse, Olbricht went to General Fried-rich Fromm's office to request the issue of the orders for the implementation of 'Valkyrie', but Fromm refused, so Olbricht and Colonel Albrecht Mertz von Quirnheim issued the orders on their own authority at 1600 hours. By the time von Stauffenberg appeared, Fromm had discovered from Keitel what had actually happened. Fromm suggested that von Stauffenberg had better shoot himself. Von Stauffenberg refused, so Fromm ordered his arrest, only to be arrested himself by the conspirators. Von Stauffenberg then took charge, issuing a proclamation signed by retired Generalfeldmarschall Erwin von Witzleben to the effect that

Since 5.00 p.m., the German Home Service had been repeatedly broadcasting the news of the failure of an attempt on Hitler's life and, in the face of this, the coup rapidly began to collapse. Before Remer's men had time to reach the building, half a dozen staff officers from within, seeing which way the wind was blowing, took matters into their own hands. Shots were fired, von Stauffenberg was wounded, General Fromm was freed from close custody, and the tables were turned. Fromm then told the conspirators that he was 'now going to do to you what you did to me this afternoon'. Holding an instant court-martial, he found the conspirators guilty. Generaloberst Ludwig Beck *(left)*, nominal leader of the conspiracy, was permitted to retain his pistol but was told by General Fromm to hurry up, whereupon Beck pointed the gun at his temple and pulled the trigger. However, he must have flinched, for he merely collapsed wounded in the arms of von Stauffenberg. He then fired again, only to botch the job a second time and fall to the floor. Fromm then ordered that the helpless Beck be given the coup de grâce. *Right:* The room where Beck died is now memorialised by a plaque on the wall.

After Beck's bungled suicide attempt, the other five leaders of the revolt were asked if they had any last wishes. One, Generaloberst Erich Hoepner, pleaded that he had nothing to do with the plot and that he wished to compose a defence. General Olbricht also asked to make a statement. This writing continued for some thirty minutes until it was reported that a detachment from the Grossdeutschland Guard Battalion (Leutnant Schady's men) had appeared in the Bendlerstrasse. Wasting no more time, General Fromm ordered the death

sentences to be carried out immediately. Fromm's adjutant, Hauptmann Bartram, was instructed to assemble a firing squad. Leutnant Schady, who had just arrived, was detailed to pick ten NCOs for the job and have them lined up in front of a pile of sand left over from construction work in the courtyard. *Left:* Although this picture was also taken the following day, it clearly shows the sand heap on the right. *Right:* The double doorway to the right of the tree is the one from which the condemned men emerged.

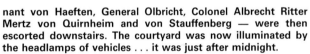

In the meantime, Hoepner had persuaded General Fromm to let him talk to him in private, and when the two men emerged from von Stauffenberg's office, Hoepner was split from the others and placed under arrest. The remaining four — Oberleut-

nant von Haeften, General Olbricht, Colonel Albrecht Ritter Mertz von Quirnheim and von Stauffenberg — were then escorted downstairs. The courtyard was now illuminated by the headlamps of vehicles . . . it was just after midnight.

Having been entrusted with putting down the coup and carrying out the investigation, Himmler had arrived at Goebbels' house about the time the executions were taking place at the Bendlerstrasse. Earlier that evening, SS-Sturmbannführer Otto Skorzeny, who had endeared himself to Hitler the previous September by audaciously freeing Mussolini from captivity on the Gran Sasso *(see After the Battle No. 22)*, had been summoned to Berlin, and he arrived at the Bendlerstrasse with an SS company at about 1.00 a.m. With the situation now under control, the arrests soon began. Goebbels planned show trials to be held by the People's Court — an instrument of the Nazi regime already long discredited as offering any measure of real justice. It was situated in the old Prussian Court of Appeal, built between 1909 and 1913. The building still stands in Heinrich-von-Kleist Park, whose entrance on the Potsdamer Strasse is flanked by the Königskolonnaden, the royal colonnades moved there in 1910 from the Königs Bridge at Alexanderplatz to allow for expansion.

the army had taken over the executive powers of the State and declaring martial law.

The orders for 'Valkyrie' arrived at the units concerned well after normal office hours. The duty officers then had to trace their commanding officers, and in many cases by the time these had checked back to their respective superior headquarters, the radio was already announcing the failure of an attempt on Hitler's life. Only a few units responded within reasonable time and arrested some Nazi officials. Some radio stations were seized but no use made of them to broadcast to the population.

In Berlin, the Guard Battalion secured the government quarter until Goebbels managed to convince the major in command that Hitler was still alive by getting them to speak to each other on the telephone. This officer was then promptly promoted and sent to the Bendlerstrasse to deal with the conspirators. By midnight the attempted coup was at an end and most of the conspirators in the Bendlerblock arrested. Fromm regained his liberty and ordered the immediate execution by firing squad of von Stauffenberg, von Haeften, Ollbricht and Mertz von Quirnheim. He was then summoned by Goebbels, who promptly had him arrested, suspecting that he too must have been involved in the plot. (Fromm was duly interrogated, tried and later executed.)

In Paris the whole army headquarters staff had committed themselves by having the local Gestapo organisation rounded up and preparations made for their execution.

The Gestapo investigation that followed involved hundreds of arrests, including relatives of the suspects under the Sippenhaft decree. Some of the wives and children were sent to concentration camps without trial. Those detained for investigation were held in various Berlin prisons, including the notorious 'Columbiahaus', a military prison off the Columbiadamm that has since been destroyed.

The trials of about two hundred persons took place before the so-called People's Court under the notorious President Roland Freisler. This was located in the main room of the Prussian Court of Appeal in the Heinrich-von-Kleist Park off Potsdamer Strasse. (The

The rôle of the building in the aftermath of July 20, 1944 is now recorded in this inscribed stone.

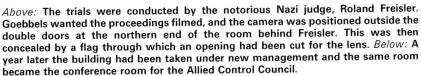

Above: The trials were conducted by the notorious Nazi judge, Roland Freisler. Goebbels wanted the proceedings filmed, and the camera was positioned outside the double doors at the northern end of the room behind Freisler. This was then concealed by a flag through which an opening had been cut for the lens. *Below:* A year later the building had been taken under new management and the same room became the conference room for the Allied Control Council.

building was later to become the home of the Allied Control Council and this room was to witness many more august events such as the signing of the Quadripartite Agreement.) The trials were filmed from the northern end of the room, where a hatch had been cut in the double doors to allow the camera lens to project discreetly through a masking flag as Freisler screamed his abuse at the battered defendants.

The first trial began on August 7. In the dock were General Helmuth Stieff *(above)*, Generalfeldmarschall Erwin von Witzleben *(below left)*, Generalleutnant Paul von Hase, Oberstleutnant Robert Bernardis, Hauptmann Karl Klausing, Oberleutnant Peter Graf Yorck von Wartenburg and Generaloberst Hoepner, the man who had tried so hard to save his life on the night of the coup. Initially, Hoepner appeared dressed in a cardigan *(below right)*, and von Witzleben was denied a belt to keep his trousers up. However, even Freisler saw that this belittling treatment might be counterproductive when the film was screened, and they both appeared after lunch more decently dressed. On the second day they were all adjudged guilty and taken away for immediate execution.

The eight men were taken across Berlin to Plötzensee Prison in the Königsdamm in Charlottenburg (right next to the West Hafen docks — see map on page 127). There, at the rear of the prison compound, stood the condemned cells and execution shed *(right)*.

Most of the latter were executed, some by garrotting, some by hanging. Of these, 89 were executed at Plötzensee Prison by being suspended from hooks set into an iron girder and left to slowly strangle to death, the so-called Austrian method where the executioner sometimes even had to hang on to the legs of the individual to hasten the end. Hitler had the executions filmed to savour his revenge in full.

The execution chamber at Plötzensee, where some 2,500 opponents of the Nazi regime were executed between 1933 and 1945, is now a public memorial, while the former Bendlerblock is now a museum and monument to the resistance against Hitler. Bendlerstrasse has also been renamed Stauffenbergstrasse in honour of the prime activist of the abortive coup.

The building, which had already been badly damaged in air raids, had undergone makeshift repairs. The room measured about eight metres by four and was divided in half by a black curtain. The only light was that which filtered through two small windows; directly before these windows there hung from the ceiling eight hooks on which the condemned men were to be hanged. There was also a guillotine in the room. The first victim was led through the black curtains between two executioners; in the ante-room on the other side of the curtain the Director of Public Prosecutions had again read out the death sentence to him: 'Accused, the People's Court has sentenced you to death by hanging. Hangman, do your duty.'

The condemned man walked forward with head held high; the executioners made him quicken his pace. At the end of the room he had to turn and the noose was placed around his neck, whereupon the hangman hoisted him up

and threw the upper noose of the hemp rope onto the hook, letting the victim fall sharply so that the noose immediately tightened around his neck. In my opinion death must have occurred very quickly.

After the first sentence had been carried out a smaller black curtain was drawn across to conceal the hanging body so that the next victim would not be aware of it. The second victim followed almost immediately. He, too, walked towards the rope with complete composure. After each execution a similar small black curtain was drawn across so that the last of the condemned could not see those who had gone before. The executions were carried out in rapid succession and all the victims met death with complete calm; they showed no fear and maintained their dignified bearing to the last.

HEINZ SASSE, 1961

The records are not clear as to whether Johann Reichhart, the principal German executioner from 1922 to 1945, was personally involved in the first hangings on August 8. His diary only details the years July 1924 to September 1942 and, with executions being carried out daily in the latter period, the entries are simply along the lines of 'Wien 11' without individual names being given. Prior to 1933, death sentences in Germany were carried out by beheading, but in Hitler's 'Enabling Act' of March 23 that year, hanging was introduced as an alternative method of execution. At Plötzensee, an iron girder fitted with eight hooks for multiple executions was installed at the far end above a raised platform. However, this Austrian method of hanging, without a measured drop, resulted more in the strangulation of the victim rather than the breaking of the neck as with a British scaffold with a trapdoor. When executions were carried out in rapid succession, black curtains shielded the hanging bodies from view. It has been estimated that upwards of 2,500 persons were either guillotined or hung at Plötzensee during the Nazi era, of whom 89 were conspirators of the July 20 plot.

The interior of the execution chamber. A wash basin was fitted to the wall on the left, just out of the picture. The guillotine disappeared at the end of the war after the prison was captured by Soviet forces.

Today the execution chamber has been walled off from the main prison buildings, which are still in use, and converted into a shrine. The porcelain tiles still remain where the wash basin once stood, but only five hooks have been fitted to the beam. The trials continued right up to the closing stages of the war, and even General Fromm, the man on the spot who had acted so decisively on the night of July 20, was brought to book in March 1945 accused of violating court-martial regulations. In the event, he was found guilty of cowardice and was shot in Brandenburg Prison on March 12.

There was also poetic justice for Roland Freisler who, while sheltering in the cellars of the People's Court during the American air raid on February 3, 1945, was struck on the head by falling debris when the building received a direct hit. He died later in hospital. It is difficult to accurately determine how many were implicated in the attempted coup and it is equally difficult to put a precise figure on the number who were found guilty. Published literature available in Berlin today tends to blur the difference between the military men directly involved in the attempted coup and those dissidents who were simply anti-Hitler. All are lumped together in the so-called 'German resistance movment' although the use of this description belies a direct comparison with the resistance organisations then active in the occupied countries. However, it would appear that around 600 were arrested in connection with the July Plot, of whom 200 were executed. This memorial wall at Plötzensee offers a general dedication to the victims of National Socialism during the years 1933-1945.

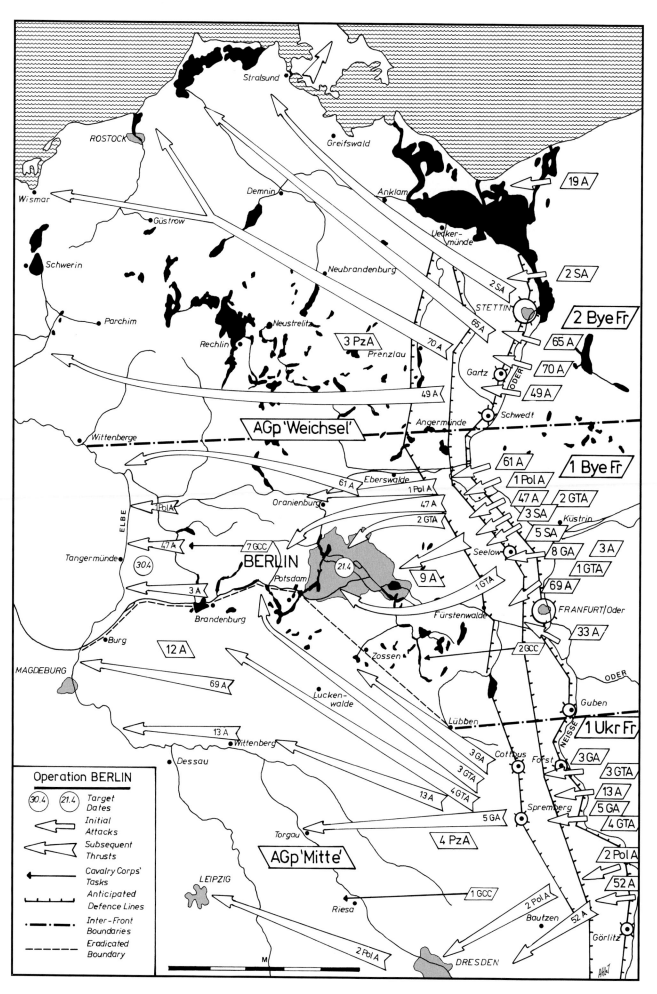

Operation BERLIN

30.4 21.4 Target Dates

Initial Attacks

Subsequent Thrusts

Cavalry Corps' Tasks

Anticipated Defence Lines

Inter-Front Boundaries

Eradicated Boundary

Rostock
Stralsund
Greifswald
Wismar
Demmin
Anklam
19 A
Güstrow
Uecker-münde
2 SA
Schwerin
Neubrandenburg
2 SA
STETTIN
2 Bye Fr
Parchim
Neustrelitz
65 A
65 A
Rechlin
Prenzlau
3 PzA
70 A
70 A
Gartz
49 A
49 A
Wittenberge
AGp 'Weichsel'
Angermünde
Schwedt
61 A
1 Bye Fr
61 A
Eberswalde
1 Pol A
1 Pol A
PolA
Oranienburg
47 A
47 A
2 GTA
2 GTA
3 SA
47 A
5 SA
Küstrin
Tangermünde
304
7 GCC
BERLIN
21.4
8 GA
3 A
Seelow
1 GTA
Potsdam
9 A
69 A
3 A
1 GTA
Brandenburg
Fürstenwalde
FRANFURT/Oder
Burg
33 A
12 A
Zossen
2 GCC
MAGDEBURG
69 A
Luckenwalde
Guben
13 A
Lübben
1 Ukr Fr
Wittenberg
3 GA
Cottbus
3 GA
Dessau
3 GTA
Forst
3 GTA
13 A
4 GTA
13 A
Spremberg
5 GA
Torgau
5 GA
4 PzA
4 GTA
AGp 'Mitte'
2 Pol A
LEIPZIG
1 GCC
52 A
Riesa
2 Pol A
Bautzen
52 A
2 Pol A
DRESDEN
Görlitz

ELBE
ODER
ODER
NEISSE

M

A Hilal

The Battle for Berlin

The battle that decided the fate of the city at the conclusion of the Second World War started forty miles to the east on April 16, 1945, on the Oder-Neisse river line. Roughly one million German soldiers of various units organised into three armies faced some two-and-a-half million Red Army soldiers in reciprocal army groups, the 2nd Byelorussian, the 1st Byelorussian and the 1st Ukrainian Fronts respectively.

Following a lightning strike out of their bridgeheads on the Vistula south of Warsaw, by the end of January 1945, elements of the 1st Byelorussian Front had reached the line of the Oder river, only forty miles from Berlin. Some even managed to cross the partially frozen river and established footholds on the west bank at a time when the Germans had yet to prepare their defences or bring regular forces into the area.

Marshal Zhukov, commanding the 1st Byelorussian Front, was prepared there and then to push straight on to Berlin with his existing supplies, which would have allowed only one ammunition and one fuel replenishment per tank, but the Supremo, Stalin, called him off to first help clear the Baltic provinces to their rear, where Reichsführer SS Heinrich Himmler's inept command of Army Group 'Vistula' nevertheless posed a serious threat to the extended flank in East Pomerania.

The scanty forces remaining on the Oder then had a difficult time retaining their bridgeheads against frantic German attempts to oust them with whatever forces they could muster. The Germans needed the security of a river boundary, whereas the Soviets fully appreciated the value of these bridgeheads as a springboard for their postponed offensive on the German capital.

All German attempts to dislodge them proved costly failures, and eventually the Germans had to turn their attention to preparing defences in depth to meet the inevitable major assault. The Soviets were eventually able to expand and develop their bridgeheads until they combined on March 29, cutting off the fortress of Küstrin and its large garrison, and providing an area great enough for their future needs. The successful conclusion of operations in East Pomerania at the end of March then enabled the release of the main body of the 1st Byelorussian Front to return to the Oder.

Simply 'on the road to Berlin' states the original Soviet caption to this picture. The plan for the Berlin operation that Stalin approved on April 3, 1945 is illustrated in Tony Le Tissier's map on the opposite page. Marshal Zhukov's 1st Byelorussian Front and Marshal Koniev's 1st Ukrainian Front were to launch their attacks on April 16, followed by Marshal Rokossovsky's 2nd Byelorussian Front as soon as possible thereafter. As Zhukov's troops on the direct route to Berlin could expect the most opposition, Stalin deliberately erased the inter-Front boundary beyond Lübben, implying that what happened beyond that point was up to the two rival Marshals. Note how the Soviets expected to take Berlin on the fifth day of the operation and to conclude the operation on the Elbe by the end of the month. Opposing these army groups was one German army each, plus a fourth guarding the line of the Elbe.

173

The rivals. Soviet staff were concerned at the likely strength of the opposition facing Marshal Georgi Zhukov *(left)* on the direct route, compared to that faced by Marshal Ivan. S. Koniev *(right)*. Stalin therefore silently erased the boundary beyond Lübben in the Spreewald, thereby implying that it was up to the rival marshals what happened beyond that point.

Meanwhile the Soviets had got wind of Montgomery's plan, subsequently turned down by Eisenhower, to head straight for Berlin. This Stalin could not tolerate and he hastily summoned a planning conference of Marshals Zhukov and Koniev, whose Fronts, or army groups, would be needed for the task of taking Berlin. The Soviets saw this as a race for glory, the prize being the German capital, and within that the Reichstag, albeit still a burned-out shell since the fire of 1933.

On April 1, 1945, G. K. Zhukov, Marshal of the Soviet Union and Commander of the 1st Byelorussian Front, and I were summoned to the General Headquarters of the Supreme High Command in Moscow. Stalin received us, as usual, in the Kremlin, in his large study with its long conference table. Also present were members of the State Defence Committee, Chief of the General Staff, A. I. Antonov, and Head of Chief Operations, S. M. Shtemenko.

No sooner had we exchanged greetings than Stalin asked: 'Are you aware how the situation is shaping up?'

Zhukov and I answered that, according to the information we had, we were. Stalin turned to Shtemenko and said: 'Read the telegram to them.'

Shtemenko read the telegram aloud. Its essence was briefly as follows. The U.S.–British Command was staging an operation to capture Berlin with the aim of taking the city before the Soviet Army could do it. The main forces were being organised under the command of Field-Marshal

Montgomery. The direction of the main attack was being planned north of the Ruhr, via the shortest road between Berlin and the main British forces. The telegram listed a series of preliminary measures taken by the Allied Command, including the organisation of an assault group and concentration of troops. The telegram ended with a statement that, according to all the available information, the plan to capture Berlin before the Soviet Army was regarded in the Allied headquarters as quite feasible, and the preparations to carry it out were proceeding apace.

As soon as Shtemenko finished reading the telegram, Stalin asked Zhukov and me: 'Well, then, who is going to take Berlin, us or the Allies?'

It happened that I had to answer the question first, and I said: 'It is we who will be taking Berlin, and we shall take it before the Allies.'

MARSHAL OF THE SOVIET UNION
I. KONIEV, 1966

On April 1, Stalin gave orders for Operation 'Berlin' to commence on April 16 with the aim of reaching the Elbe river in time for the May Day holiday. This gave the Fronts only two weeks in which to prepare for this major task, a drastic reduction on the two to three months normally considered necessary for such an enterprise. Apart from the redeployment of the main body over considerable distances from East Pomerania, the restocking of manpower, equipment and supplies involved routes extending some 2,000 miles back to the industries grouped in the Ural Mountains, some of the Lend-Lease supplies coming from ports the far side of Siberia.

By this time, mid-April, the German forces had been squeezed back into the area around their capital bounded in the east and west by the Oder and Elbe rivers, with the Western Allies closing up rapidly from the west.

The Soviet plan involved a massive assault on the German defences along the Oder-Neisse river line, using some two-and-a-half million Soviet troops against an estimated one million defenders. This was hardly the text book majority for such an operation but by this stage of the war the Soviets, like the Germans, had reached the end of their manpower resources.

On Sunday, March 3, Hitler visited his commanders on the Oder front but, unlike in his earlier days of glory, driving victorious in his open-top Mercedes, this time he was a broken man travelling in a tiny Kübelwagen along roads choked with dispirited troops. At the castle at Bad Freienwalde, 30 miles north-east of the city in Cl. Korps sector, he met with General Theodor Busse of the 9. Armee to discuss defence plans. It was the last time Hitler would leave Berlin — alive.

The Decisive Battle of the Seelow Heights

Facing them were three German armies of ad hoc composition despite their formal titles: the 3. Panzer-Armee in the north and the 9. Armee covering Berlin in the centre, together forming Army group 'Weichsel', and the 4. Panzer-Armee of Army Group 'Mitte' in the south.

The plan saw Zhukov's 1st Byelorussian Front taking the direct route to Berlin, while in the north, Rokossovsky's 2nd Byelorussian Front, and in the south, Koniev's 1st Ukrainian Front, would defeat the enemy forces opposing them and prevent them intervening in the attack on the capital.

However, circumstances dictated that the fate of Berlin would be decided on this Oder-Neisse river line. Not only were the Germans short of manpower, arms and equipment, but they were also desperately short of fuel for their few remaining tanks and aircraft, and consequently lacked the means for a more flexible defence. A defence system for Berlin had been worked out, and great efforts made to put it into effect, but there were insufficient resources available to man it properly.

The Germans also had a new 12. Armee forming from training establishments and the Reichsarbeitsdienst (labour service), to cover the fully exposed rear along the line of the Elbe river, which elements of the American Ninth Army were to reach on April 17.

Some American troops did get across the Elbe south of Magdeburg, but their orders prevented them from going further, and eventually they were withdrawn, leaving the field to the Russians.

Tony Le Tissier looks across the Oder River at Kienitz where the first Soviet crossing took place at the site of the ferry. The river was then frozen over and the Soviets followed the sleigh tracks of farmers that had been collecting firewood on the far side. The opposite bank is now Poland, the ferry has not operated since 1945 and the river has become unnavigable through disuse leading to silting up.

Although the 2nd Byelorussian and the 1st Ukrainian Fronts had initially to contend with river crossings, Zhukov's 1st Byelorussian Front in the centre opposite Berlin already had a sufficiently large bridgehead opposite Küstrin from which to launch its main assault with four combined-arms armies, each of three infantry and one armoured corps, while two armies tackled either flank. The two armies in the north were to help clear the way through the communications centre of Wriezen, and those in the south to secure the autobahn as a main supply route, bypassing the fortified town of Frankfurt-an-der-Oder, which could be expected to fall into their hands like a ripe fruit in due course. In reserve were his two tank armies, held back for the attack on the capital itself, and one infantry army.

The disused harbour at Kienitz gives a fair impression of how the whole area appeared in 1945 with inundations crossed only by the raised bund roads.

Waterways were still the main factor dominating the area of Marshal Zhukov's operations, forming either obstacles to be crossed, or natural boundaries, but generally channelling the course of action. From the sump of the Oderbruch valley bottom in the east, to the Elbe river in the west, the waterways framed this battlefield. At the top the Finow Canal formed the boundary of operations to the point where it connected with the north-south course of the Havel river on the far side of Berlin. Then in the south the Spree river narrowed the operational boundary to the point where it ended in Berlin at Spandau.

The main objective was the highway

Left: **Taken a little further back on the high ground looking out over the dykes and marshy terrain along the banks of the Oder.** *Right:* **The inscription on the unusual stainless steel monument erected on the dyke reads: 'The offensive demands a boundless mass of energy from us in order to bring the Fascist filth to an even quicker end. Extract from a letter by Konrad Wolf, Lieutenant in the Red Army, to his family in Moscow, 1945.' After the war, Konrad Wolf went on to become head of the GDR's intelligence service.**

from Küstrin to Berlin, with the Wriezen-Berlin road and the Frankfurt-Berlin autobahn as secondary objectives. However, with their dependence on the railways for their supply system — the vehicular establishment of a division was only 30 motor vehicles of all kinds — the three railway tracks leading towards Berlin were equally important.

The main problem, was the terrain. Deliberate flooding by the Germans had turned the marshy valley bottom of the Oderbruch, already criss-crossed with canals and irrigation ditches, into a soggy morass, restricting the lines of advance to the few causeways carrying tracks, roads and railways leading across it to the eroded escarpment of the 150-foot Seelow Heights.

In the centre of Kienitz, a T-34 stands proudly on a plinth erected by the German Democratic Government. The plaque below reads: '31 January 1945 — Kienitz, the first place in our country to have been liberated from Fascism. Glory and honour to the fighting soldiers of the 5th Shock Army and the 2nd Guards Tank Army.'

The plan was to take the Heights by nightfall. The time offered by daylight at that time of year was short, so it was decided that extra daylight hours could be added with the aid of searchlights taken from the Moscow anti-aircraft defences, where they were no longer needed.

For this task Zhukov had at his disposal 768,000 men and women combatants, 3,000 tanks and self-propelled guns, of which half were with the attacking formations and half in reserve with the tank armies, and 14,600 guns, his normal establishment having been augmented from the Stavka reserve, giving him a then unprecedented 295 guns to the kilometre at his breakthrough points. In addition, he had the aircraft of two air armies committed in support, which in Soviet philosophy were considered merely an extension of the artillery arm, and the gun boats of the Dnieper Flotilla, which had been especially brought all the way from the Soviet Union by canal and road.

Twenty-one bridges and forty ferries connected the east bank of the Oder with the Küstrin bridgehead, which was packed with men, equipment, ammunition and essential supplies. The phenomenal logistics the Soviet preparations involved are perhaps best demonstrated by the over 1,200,000 shells fired on the first day, weighing 98,000 tons and requiring 2,450 railway wagons to move them.

To face this formidable concentration General Theodor Busse, commanding the 9. Armee, is believed to have had 220,000 men, and 512 tanks and self-propelled guns. Later he was to be reinforced by three other panzergrenadier divisions from the last of the central reserves.

The main thrust was expected to come along the Küstrin-Seelow-Müncheberg highway to Berlin, so General Busse had the 'Müncheberg' Panzer-Division deployed there in immediate reserve with a final line of defence astride that town of anti-tank brigades under the title of the 541. Volksgrenadier-Division. In addition each of his three corps had a panzer-grenadier division in reserve.

On April 14 and 15 the Soviets used battle groups of up to regimental strength to conduct a reconnaissance in force along the whole length of the Küstrin bridgehead, thereby expanding it even further in preparation for their attack. Despite their deception plans, the Soviets were unable to disguise their intentions from the Germans, who prepared themselves as best as possible for what was to come.

Marshal Zhukov: 'The reconnaissance on April 14 and 15 was accompanied by strong artillery fire, including large-calibre guns. The enemy mistook the reconnaissance for the beginning of our offensive. Suffice it to say that some German units were dislodged from their forward positions as a result of action by our recon groups, and ... the aim we had pursued had been attained. The enemy rushed his reserves to the second positions. However, our troops stopped their advance and dug in. This was perplexing for the enemy command. As it was learned later, some of the German commanders decided that our offensive had failed.'

Above: The Reitwein Spur from where Zhukov watched the opening barrage for the Battle of the Seelow Heights.

The command post can still be identified a few hundred yards into the forest beside the track which leads past the Soviet cemetery which lies at the foot of the spur.

Late at night, a few hours before the artillery and air barrage, I set out for the observation post of the Eighth Guards Army Commander, General Chuikov. I arrived together with member of the Military Council, K. F. Telegin, and Front Artillery Commander, V. I. Kazakov. The member of the Army Military Council, the Army Chief-of-Staff, the Artillery Commander, and other army generals and senior officers were already there.

It was 3.00 a.m. Moscow time. Last-minute checks of combat readiness for the operation were being made in all the units. The artillery barrage was fixed for 5.00 a.m. Moscow time. The hands of the clock moved slowly as never before. In order to fill the remaining minutes, we decided to have some hot strong tea which was made for us in the dugout by a girl. I remember that she had a non-Russian name, Margot. We sipped tea in silence, each deep in his thoughts.

At exactly three minutes before the beginning of the artillery preparation we all went out of the dugout and took up positions at the observation post which had been built with particular care by Eighth Army engineers. The entire vicinity beyond the Oder could be seen from here in the daytime. Now there was a morning mist there. I looked at my watch: it was five o'clock sharp.

And at this moment, the vicinity was lit up by the fire of many thousands of guns, mortars and the legendary Katyusha rocket launchers followed by a tremendous din from the discharges and explosions of shells and aircraft bombs. The continuous roar of bombers was steadily growing louder.

Thousands of flares of different colours flew into the air. This was the signal for 140 searchlights placed at intervals of 200 metres to flash spotlights equalling more than 100,000 million candlepower, lighting up the battlefield and blinding the enemy, snatching objects for attack by our tanks and infantry from the darkness. It was a striking picture, and I remember never having seen anything like it during my whole lifetime!

MARSHAL OF THE SOVIET UNION G. ZHUKOV, 1974

Left: The author standing in front of one of the two entrances to General Chuikov's command bunker on the Reitwein Spur in 1991. The bunker was cut out of the clay, forming a rough 'H' of tunnels, the clay then being sealed with flame-throwers, thus avoiding the use of props and liners. *Right:* It remained to be seen for forty years until the structure became sufficiently dangerous for the entrances to be deliberately collapsed. Picture taken by Oberst Diebbert Lang in 1988.

Although the entrance to the tunnel beneath the hillside has been filled in, the actual observation post above remains to be seen almost as if it were yesterday. Communication trenches still wind up the steep slope to where the OP is perched on the edge of a crumbling cliff, held together only by the roots of the saplings that have grown up there since the battle. Although the view towards Seelow is now obscured, Tony looks out . . . and remembers.

At 0300 hours on April 16 Zhukov's massive array of artillery opened fire, and at 0330 hours the searchlights were switched on as the signal for the general advance. As in the Revolution in 1917, the troops advanced with banners flying, a ploy that the propaganda people hoped would boost their morale.

The effect of this barrage was cataclysmic. Not only was it heard in Berlin forty miles away, but it threw up such a cloud of muck and smoke, that when daylight came at 0530 hours, the supporting aircraft were unable to find their targets.

The searchlights proved utterly useless. Instead of copying the artificial moonlight technique developed by the British of reflecting light off the clouds, they were pointed straight ahead, illuminating nothing but the impenetrable murk raised by the bombardment and causing night blindness among the troops. Then came requests from the attacking units to switch off, and counter-orders from above to switch on again. The overall confusion was such

Marshal Georgi Zhukov with his staff in the observation post prepared for them at Colonel-General Chuikov's Eighth Guards Army's command post on the Reitwein Spur. However, they could see little from here due to the murk thrown up by the bombardments and the distances involved.

The forest is riddled with earthworks. *Left:* These two revetments probably accommodated tanks screening the approach to the CP further up the hill. *Right:* The remains of a Soviet dugout on the north-facing side of the spur.

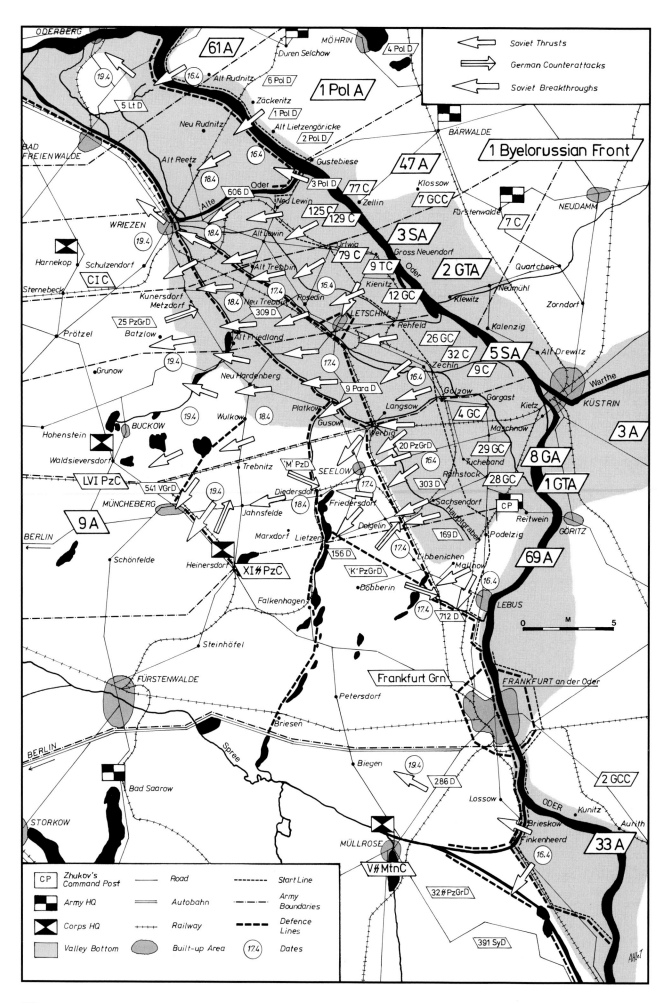

ODERBERG

61 A

MÖHRIN
Düren Selchow
4 Pol D

Soviet Thrusts

German Counterattacks

Soviet Breakthroughs

19.4

16.4
Alt Rudnitz
6 Pol D
Zäckeritz
1 Pol D
Neu Rudnitz
Alt Lietzengöricke
2 Pol D

1 Pol A

BÄRWALDE

1 Byelorussian Front

5 Lt D

BAD
FREIENWALDE

Alt Reetz
18.4
16.4
Gustebiese
3 Pol D
77 C

47 A
Klossow
7 GCC
7 C
NEUDAMM

606 D
Oder
Neu Lewin
Zellin
125 C
129 C
3 SA
Fürstenwalde
7 C

WRIEZEN
19.4
18.4
Alt Lewin
Ortwig
79 C
Gross Neuendorf
9 TC
Oder
2 GTA
Quartchen

Harnekop
Schulzendorf
CIC
Alt Trebbin
17.4
16.4
Rosedin
Kienitz
12 GC
Klewitz
Neumühl
Zorndorf

Sternebeck
Kunersdorf
Metzdorf
18.4
Neu Trebbin
309 D
LETSCHIN
Rehfeld
26 GC

25 PzGrD
Batzlow
Alt Friedland
17.4
Zechin
32 C
9 C
5 SA
Alt Drewitz

Prötzel
19.4
Neu Hardenberg
9 Para D
Golzow
Gorgast
Kielz
Warthe
KÜSTRIN

Grunow
Platkow
Langsow
Werbig
4 GC
Maschnow
3 A

Hohenstein
BUCKOW
19.4
Wulkow
18.4
Gusow
20 PzGrD
29 GC
Tucheband
8 GA

Waldsieversdorf
LVI PzC
541 VGrD
'M' PzD
SEELOW
17.4
16.4
303 D
Rathstock
28 GC
1 GTA
CP
Reitwein
GÖRITZ

MÜNCHEBERG
19.4
Diedersdorf
18.4
Friedersdorf
Sachsendorf
169 D
Podelzig

9 A
BERLIN
Jahnsfelde
Marxdorf
Lietzen
Dolgelin
17.4
69 A

Schönfelde
Heinersdorf
XI ⚡ PzC
156 D
'K' PzGrD
Libbenichen
Mallnow
16.4
LEBUS

Falkenhagen
Döbberin
17.4
712 D

Steinhöfel

FÜRSTENWALDE

Frankfurt Grn
FRANKFURT an der Oder

BERLIN
Spree
Briesen
Petersdorf

Biegen
19.4
286 D

Bad Saarow
ODER
Kunitz
2 GCC

STORKOW
Lossow
Brieskow
Finkenheerd
33 A

MÜLLROSE
V ⚡ MtnC
32 ⚡ PzGrD
391 SyD

0   M   5

CP   Zhukov's
     Command Post
     Army HQ
     Corps HQ
     Valley Bottom

───── Road
═════ Autobahn
+++++ Railway
     Built-up Area

----- Start Line
-·-·- Army
     Boundaries
━ ━ ━ Defence
     Lines
17.4 Dates

AHel

This map shows the decisive battle for the Seelow Heights upon which the fate of Berlin depended. Zhukov had four combined armies massed in the Oderbruch Valley (shaded area) for his main thrust, attention being concentrated on the Eighth Guards Army astride the main road to Berlin running through Seelow. Initially, his two tank armies and the Third Army were kept in reserve, while two other armies operated on either flank. The attacks on April 16 suffered tremendous casualties and failed to penetrate the main line of defence running along the Seelow Heights. Progress was so slow that during the course of the day, Zhukov committed his two tank armies, adding to the confusion on the already congested battlefield.

On the 17th and 18th, the Soviet armour eventually broke through and bypassed Seelow, which fell on the afternoon of the 18th. A German counter-attack at Diedersdorf that day caused further heavy casualties but could not prevent the much stronger Soviet forces breaking through. Finally, on April 19, the last of the German lines of defence was breached near Müncheberg and Batzlow, the German 9. Armee being split asunder and the remains of the LVI. Panzerkorps driven back on Berlin. *Above:* The sleepy town of Letschin which was taken by the 9th Tank Corps of the Third Shock Army. It could almost be a comparison for the picture on page 173 — typical of the positions bitterly fought for on April 16.

that many units decided to wait until daylight to continue.

As for the bombardment itself, most of the Germans had been evacuated from the first line of defence that night in anticipation of what was coming, so that the main weight of the barrage was wasted on already abandoned positions.

The battlefield split naturally into different sectors. In the north the Sixty-First Army and the First Polish Army had to mount river crossings against an immediate front line. Each of these armies had a battalion of amphibious vehicles driven by female Soviet soldiers to assist them. Although the Poles eventually managed to clear their area of the Oderbruch, they were unable to progress further across an arm of the Alte Oder until the capture of Wriezen by the Forty-Seventh Army gave them the leverage to do so.

In the Letschin sector the Forty-Seventh Army and the Third and Fifth Shock Armies had to contest with the main German line of defence along the railway embankment astride the little town. Their progress proved uneven against the determined resistance they encountered, but they gave the 9. Fallschirm-Jäger-Division a tremendous pounding, forcing them back several kilometres that first day.

In the centre on the main axis, Colonel-General Vassili Ivanovich Chuikov's Eighth Guards Army found that the Germans had almost entirely withdrawn to the Seelow Heights. We

will return to this sector, which was the main focus of attention, in a moment.

Further south the Sixty-Ninth and Thirty-Third Armies sought to bypass and cut off the corps-sized Frankfurt garrison from either side in order to seize the communication routes behind. However, they were held short of their objectives in some heavy fighting in which the counter-thrusts of the 'Kurmark'

Panzer-grenadier-Division successfully prevented the breach that would have enabled an alternative breakthrough point for the First Guards Tank Army as previously contemplated by Zhukov. Consequently the German defences in this area on the plateau held until it became necessary to conduct an orderly withdrawal to the south following the collapse of the main front further north.

All along the route to Berlin, small cemeteries spell out the tremendous price paid by the Red Army for the capture of Berlin. This 'corner of a foreign field' lies under the trees on the right of the picture at the top of the page.

Above: **The panoramic view from the 303rd Division's commanding positions on the Seelow Heights (looking north on this page and east opposite) overlooking the approach road from Sachsendorf in the middle distance. The trees marking this road form a dog's leg to run under the escarpment to the left. The Hauptgraben main drainage canal, which formed the forward obstacle denoting the leading edge of the defence's killing ground, is just visible running across the angle of the dog's leg leading from the clump of trees. The Küstrin-Seelow highway, Reichsstrasse 1, is marked by the line of dark trees across the left of the picture in the distance. The broken nature of the eroded escarpment is clearly shown, and traces of German entrenchments scar the foreground. The Reitwein Spur can be seen on the far right. German 88mm guns dug in and well concealed at the foot of the Heights were able to inflict enormous damage on the attackers.**

Progress proved so slow across the valley bottom that morning that, with Stalin urging him on, at 1100 hours Zhukov ordered in his armoured reserves from across the Oder to try to force the pace. This only made matters worse, for it brought even more congestion on the few causeways leading forward, and totally disrupted the deployment of the formations already engaged.

The routes forward were by narrow roads and tracks on causeways above the inundated morass of the Oderbruch, which then climbed up the re-entrants of the Heights to the plateau above. The sheer flat expanse of the Oderbruch gave the escarpment a deceptively innocent appearance in the distance. The elevation was only 150 feet, but had gradients of up to 45 degrees, thus limiting tank access, and gave full advantage to the defence. The German artillery and counter-attack resources were out of sight to the attacking

Soviets, whose opportunities for redeploying their own artillery were in any case extremely limited. These routes thus provided easy killing grounds for the defence. Mines and blown bridges hampered progress, then anti-tank and heavy machine-gun positions in the defiles slowed down the attacking forces, whose tanks were then exposed to the German armour as they emerged on the plateau. As Chuikov later argued in criticism of Zhukov, clearing the forward slopes of the Heights and the re-entrants leading up could only be effected by the infantry. No wonder the Soviets took such heavy casualties here.

Opposing them, Waffen-SS Obersturmführer Klust reported: 'At about 0600 hours six Tigers of the 1. Kompanie took up positions on the eastern edge of Dolgelin village. We could clearly make out huge masses of Russians heading west towards us. Near the Heights on which we were standing ran the Sachsendorf-Dolgelin road,

Left: **The well-tended Soviet cemetery in the village of Sachsendorf on the 29th Guards Corps' approach route to the Seelow Heights at Dolgelin. Sachsendorf was defended by the Germans as a delaying point in the main battle.** *Right:* **The road leading from Sachsendorf to the foot of the Seelow Heights below**

Dolgelin village. Parallel on the right is one of the large drainage canals that prevented the Soviets from deploying and made the road such a death trap. From here the 28th Guards Corps unsuccessfully launched their attack on the Germans emplaced on the Heights.

BIN HAUPTGRABEN REITWEIN SPUR

HAUPTGRABEN · REITWEIN SPUR

WARTHE ESTUARY ZHUKOV'S CP

DOGLEG SACHSENDORF REITWEIN

which was blocked in front of us by an anti-tank barrier. The Russians were in front of it with about twenty tanks, but they could not move the barrier, and we could not engage them as our gun barrels could not depress that far.

'Nevertheless our Tigers soon shot up eleven tanks opposite us. Two of our Tigers were hit but remained operational, despite hull and track damage. Then we engaged targets and columns moving up to the Seelow Heights. Everywhere vehicles were being hit and infantry blown apart by the high explosives, and the Russians were unable to gain the Heights for the time being. During the night we pulled back into the village as planned.'

The excellent quality and performance of the German armour and anti-tank weapons was clearly demonstrated in these counter-attacks. Skilfully handled, they often inflicted terrible punishment before withdrawing to fight again elsewhere, but wherever the Germans gained a tactical success the Soviets were eventually able to swamp them with sheer weight of numbers and so win the day.

The small country town of Seelow lay directly on the main axis of advance. Successive waves of Soviet armour and infantry failed to budge the defence on that first day, but by evening the 4th Guards Corps on the Eighth Guards Army's right flank managed to get a foothold on the Heights behind Werbig and take the railway station below Seelow. From these positions they gradually began prising the defence out of the town, although it was to take until the morning of April 18 before they had full possession.

The casualties in these frontal assaults on the Heights were such that Zhukov had to order forward as replacements every man and woman that could be spared from his rear services, and Chuikov was obliged to weaken his left flank in order to maintain pressure on the main axis.

The Soviet memorial to the battle for the Seelow Heights at Seelow. The inscription reads: 'Soviet soldiers, may you be remembered for ever! Chiselled in stone, your names endure, your memory inscribed, your deeds live on. You gave your lives to free us from Fascism and war. What burned in you will be a torch within us.' In the foreground lie the individual graves of those holders of the Hero of the Soviet Union award who fell in the fighting.

Lying in the shadow of the memorial is the Seelow Heights museum. *Below left:* Specific to the opening phase, the APM-90 searchlight. *Below right;* Lorry-mounted 'Katyusha' rocket-launcher, officially the BM-13, unofficially 'Stalin's Organ'!

Left: The 76mm ZIS-3, range 13,290 metres, capable of firing 25 rounds per minute. *Right:* The 152mm artillery piece had a similar range but a slower rate of fire at around four shells per minute and was most useful against hard targets like forts.

Above and right: German war graves in Seelow town cemetery. The granite cross in the background pre-dates the collapse of the German Democratic Republic, but the general layout of these graves within a civic cemetery shows how little regard was paid to the Wehrmacht dead during the Communist era. Some individual graves have an additional marker provided by relatives.

Below: Close by the crossroads at the north-eastern approach to Lietzen village lies the German military cemetery in its original hillside setting. This area became the northernmost point of the 9. Armee's defences after the Soviets had broken through at Müncheberg and the coherent remains of the 9. Armee began withdrawing south of the Spree river. Here on April 18 the Soviets first used the so-called 'Seydlitz' troops, mixed with their own men, against their former comrades.

The view from Reichsstrasse 1 looking east towards Diedersdorf at the point where the German counter-attack took place on April 18. Behind the trees in the dip are the fields which the Soviet armour had to cross in the face of German guns concealed in the woods to the left of this picture from what was known as the Stein position. The 'Müncheberg' Panzer-Division, supported by the Luftwaffe, counter-attacked up the valley from left to right. Although sheer weight of numbers won the day for the Soviets, their casualties were such that Marshal Zhukov issued orders belatedly combining the First Guards Tank Army with the Eighth Guards Army under the latter's commander, Colonel-General Chuikov.

Then on April 18, with the Soviet armour lined up nose to tail on the main road leading out to Müncheberg, the Germans caught them in a sharp counter-attack backed by the Luftwaffe as they crossed the north-south flaw in the terrain at Diedersdorf, inflicting severe casualties. However, this position could not be held as the Soviet armour was able to outflank it from the north.

Finally, it took Zhukov until the afternoon of April 19, three full days behind schedule, for his armour to break through the last of the German defences. By this time his troops were utterly exhausted. The Soviets had suffered some 33,000 killed and had also lost 743 tanks and self-propelled guns in this battle, but two large breaches had been opened in the German lines. There was now no way the defence could recover and the road to Berlin was clear for a Soviet advance.

The Germans had lost an estimated 12,000 men in the defence. Similarly exhausted, and with no reserves, motor fuel or other supplies to draw upon, the 9. Armee was now split asunder in two places just south of Wriezen and Müncheberg respectively. Its northern corps had to swing back across the Finow Canal, leaving the LVI. Panzerkorps isolated in the centre and driven back on Berlin — though always looking for an opportunity of rejoining the main body to the south. The rest of the army had to gradually shrink back across the Spree to regroup in the swampy, lake and river enclosed area of the Spreewald, where they were joined by many tens of thousands of refugees.

Right: **The road bridge across the Stolp Canal, which formed part of Berlin's forward defence line. This was the last obstacle to be overcome by Chuikov's forces in their advance to the outskirts of the city.**

Above: **West of Müncheberg, this is the bottleneck of woods that obliged Chuikov's Eighth Guards Army and First Guards Tank Army to keep to the narrow main road, where they were constantly harrassed and sniped at by the retreating LVI. Panzerkorps and Hitler Youth using Panzerfausts.**

At the beginning of the assault on Berlin, a special Victory Flag was prepared by the Third Shock Army, and a hand-picked squad was charged with the honour of raising the banner above the Reichstag — the building which, to the Soviets, epitomised imperial Germany. After several of the party had been killed, Sergeants M. A. Yegorov and M. V. Kantaria managed to fulfil Stalin's order by hoisting the flag on the rear parapet of the Reichstag just seventy minutes before May Day.

Closing in on the Capital

The original Soviet plan for the taking of the city had been for Zhukov's two tank armies to advance quickly on Berlin in a classic pincer movement. Three of the combined arms armies would then convert and mop up within the city, while the fourth, the Forty-Seventh Army, shielded the western flank. This plan carried the curious presumption that the tank armies would be able to operate ahead and independently of the rest of the Army Group.

However, apart from some hard lessons on infantry/tank co-operation just learnt, the condition of Zhukov's forces no longer permitted the execution of this plan. Instead, it was decided that the northern pincer, Second Guards Tank Army, would be temporarily split, one corps going to assist Forty-Seventh Army with its tasks on the west bank of the Havel, and one corps each to bring forward the remaining combined arms armies (Third and Fifth Shock) to their start-points on the Berlin perimeter. The Second Guards Tank Army would then take over the northern sector of the perimeter with just these last two corps. The First Guards Tank Army, which had been belatedly grouped with Eighth Guards Army during the course of the opening battle under Colonel-General Chuikov, would now be responsible for the investment of Berlin from the south.

Privates, sergeants, officers and generals of the First Byelorussian Front!

Comrades! The decisive hour of battle has come. In front of you lies Berlin, the capital of the Nazi state, and beyond Berlin, the meeting with the troops of our Allies, and complete victory over the enemy. Doomed to perish, the remnants of German units are still resisting. The Nazi Command is drawing on its last left-overs of Volkssturm reserves, sparing neither old men nor 15-year-olds to attempt to stem our offensive so as to delay the hour of its destruction.

Comrade officers, sergeants and Red Army men! Your units have covered themselves with unfading glory. Nothing could stop you — either at the walls of Stalingrad, or in the steppes of the Ukraine, or in the forests and swamps of Byelorussia. You were not stopped by the strong fortifications which you have overcome at the approaches to Berlin.

You are faced by Berlin, Soviet warriors. You must take Berlin, and take it as swiftly as possible so the enemy has no time to come to his senses. Let us then bring all the power of our military equipment to bear on the enemy. Let us rally all our will for victory and all our intelligence. Let us not disgrace our soldier's honour and the honour of our military colours.

On to the assault on Berlin, to the complete and final victory, comrades-in-arms! By daring and courage, good teamwork between all arms of the service, and good mutual support, sweep aside all obstacles and forge ahead, only forward, to the centre of the city, to its southern and western outskirts — to meet the Allied forces moving from the west. Forward to victory!

The Front Military Council is sure that the glorious soldiers of the First Byelorussian Front will fulfil the mission entrusted to them with honour, wipe off the face of the earth the last obstacles on the way to the new victory and raise their military colours over Berlin in glory.

Forward to the assault on Berlin!

MARSHAL OF THE SOVIET UNION, G. ZHUKOV
First Byelorussian Front
LIEUTENANT-GENERAL K. TELEGIN
Member of the Military Council
APRIL 1945

Above: **In a scene reminiscent of Britain's Home Guard (or Local Defence Volunteers as they were first called) back in 1940, drilling with broomsticks to repel the expected German invasion, Berlin's civilian home guard line up with a single Panzerfaust, the all-in-one anti-tank grenade and launcher.** Below: **These men are lucky as they are being shown the Mauser K98k, the standard German bolt action service rifle, a much better weapon than many of those that were issued to the Volkssturm.**

uniform that could be found or even their own civilian clothes. As a typical example, the commanding officer of the 42. Volkssturm-Bataillon reported: 'I had four hundred men in my battalion, and we were ordered to go into the line in civilian clothes. I told the local Party leader that I could not accept the responsibility of leading men into battle without uniforms. Just before commitment were given 180 Danish rifles, but no ammunition. We also had four machine guns and a hundred Panzerfausts. None of the men had received any training in firing a machine gun, and they were all afraid of handling the anti-tank weapons. Although my men were quite ready to help their country, they refused to go into battle without uniforms and without training. What can a Volkssturm man do with a rifle without ammunition? The men went home; that was the only thing we could do.'

The Volkssturm thus represented a most uncertain factor, and the Germans soon found the Soviets deliberately selecting Volkssturm positions for attack as an easy means of breaching the defences.

The exhausted Soviet forces moved forward slowly and cautiously, with LVI. Panzerkorps retiring before them in reasonably good order, always trying to side-step to rejoin the 9. Armee. Chuikov commented on the difficulties of the follow-up at this stage with the armour being constantly harassed by individual German soldiers hidden in the woods and hamlets equipped with the highly effective Panzerfaust short-range anti-tank weapon. Certainly the Germans, including Hitlerjugend units carrying their Panzerfausts on bicycles, exacted a heavy toll, and First Guards Tank Army had to be re-incorporated with his Eighth Guards Army to ensure adequate infantry protection.

Berlin's outer defence line, which ran along a geographical flaw involving a chain of small lakes extending north of Erkner, was to prove of little value, as the few improvised Volkssturm (Home Guard) units belatedly sent forward to man it as the Oder Front collapsed were easily overrun or bypassed.

The Berlin battalions of the Volkssturm had been raised under the aegis of Dr Joseph Goebbels in his capacity as Gauleiter of the city. Although originally intended purely for local defence and defence construction duties, and raised from men from the age of sixteen upwards capable of bearing arms in an emergency, but not normally considered fit enough for active service, these units soon found themselves committed to front line duties. There were no set establishments, so the Berlin battalions varied in size from 400 to 1,500 men, and, as a Party-sponsored organisation, they were meant to be armed, equipped and maintained purely from local resources. Consequently they often ended up with a miscellany of foreign weapons with ill-matching ammunition and few machine guns. Their only common item was an identifying arm-band worn over any kind of

German Counter-Attacks

Seeking a means of countering the Soviet breakthrough, on April 21, Hitler seized on the idea of nipping off the head of the Soviet offensive by simultaneous attacks from either flank. SS-Obergruppenführer Felix Steiner was responsible for covering the 3. Panzer-Armee's ever-extending southern flank along the line of the Finow Canal with the survivors of the 9. Armee's CI. Korps and the few reserve units of the 3. Panzer-Armee under his headquarters III. SS 'Germanic' Korps. Reinforced with all available manpower and, supported by the Luftwaffe, he was to strike southwards from the canal next day, while the 9. Armee was to strike northwards. Nobody dared gainsay the Führer and so frantic efforts were made to muster a force to despatch to Steiner in time. The Luftwaffe found some 12-15,000 ground staff from its installations behind the 3. Panzer-Armee, to which were added railway troops, cadets, policemen, firemen, Volkssturm and even some convicts from Berlin. Transport was found and precious aviation fuel commandeered to move them.

However, the whole idea was clearly nonsensical, for these reinforcements were ill-equipped and totally untrained and unsuited for the rôle required of them, and Steiner was appalled by the task and means assigned to him. He certainly could not meet the deadline set him but, under constant pressure and threats from above, on April 24 he managed to launch an attack from his two bridgeheads across the Finow Canal at Kreuzbruch and Zerpenschleuse with a force equivalent to seven battalions. This caught the Sixty-First Army by surprise and so achieved an initial success, advancing about seven kilometres before being turned and chased back to the canal.

The 9. Armee's southern group was by now firmly bottled up in the Spreewald, hemmed in by elements of the 1st Byelorussian and 1st Ukrainian Fronts, and being pounded remorselessly by artillery fire and air attack, and was thereby prevented from playing any part in this operation. With them were thousands of refugees.

Meanwhile, on April 22, Hitler decided that the 12. Armee on the Elbe no longer had to fear a possible attack from the Americans and could therefore be safely combined with the 9. Armee to breakthrough to Berlin from the south.

Within the city, civilians had also been impressed into the preparation of defences like pillboxes and anti-tank barriers. That *above* was constructed just alongside the S-Bahn station in Hermannstrasse. This was on one of the Eighth Guards Army's two main routes into Neukölln on April 25. *Below:* The bridge was rebuilt in 1974. *Bottom:* This pillbox is being built at the vital junction midway along the East-West-Axis called the Knie (now renamed Ernst-Reuter-Platz).

Generalfeldmarschall Wilhelm Keitel was therefore sent to brief General Walter Wenck on the new rôle for his 12. Armee.

Wenck went through the motions of accepting these new orders, but was keenly aware of the true nature of the situation and had no intention of complying in detail. He saw that the war was lost and that the only choice of action available to him and his men was between Soviet and western captivity. He was already aiding civilian evacuation to the west, and decided to use this opportunity to rescue as many of the 9. Armee and any others that could break through to him by advancing to a suitable point south of Potsdam where he could hold on for a few days before falling back again on the Elbe.

189

'Towards evening our battery reached the heights, and we saw an enormous city,' recalled Senior Sergeant Nikolai Vasilyev of the 832nd Artillery Regiment's 6th Battery of the 266th Rifle Division. 'We were overwhelmed by a feeling of joy and jubilation: it was the last enemy line and the hour of reckoning had come! We didn't even notice how a car drove up and our C-inC, General Berzarin, climbed out. Hailing us, he ordered our commander to open fire against the Nazis in Berlin!'

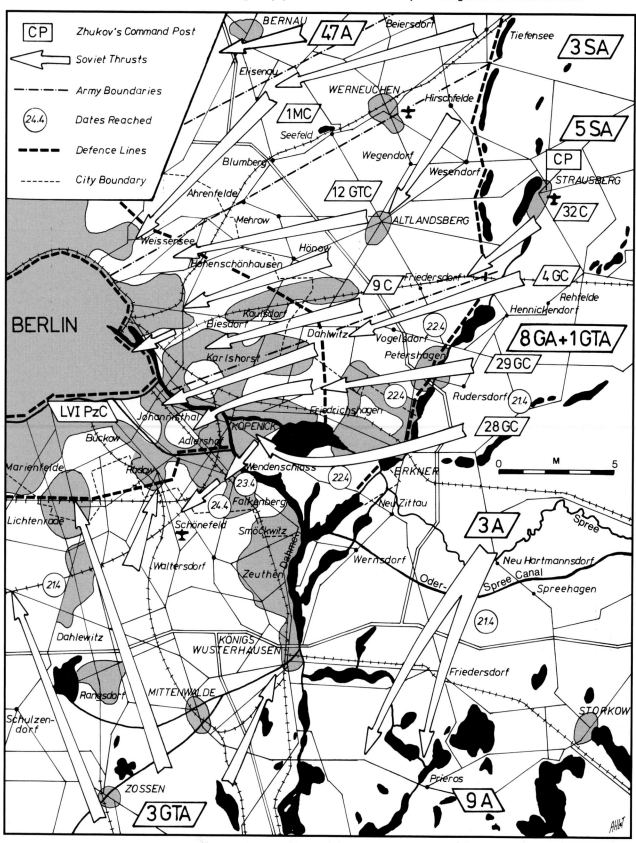

Soviet troops close in on Berlin. The First Guards Tank Army was combined with the Eighth Guards Army under Colonel-General Chuikov and expected to have to clear the whole of the southern suburbs, but were surprised to find elements of the 1st Ukrainian Front waiting for them on Schönefeld airfield when they arrived on the 24th. What had happened was that Marshal Koniev had succeeded in eliminating the German forces opposing him in rapid time and had then been given permission by Stalin to send his Third Guards Tank Army to Berlin although apparently Zhukov was not informed.

Into Berlin

The first Soviet artillery shells were fired into the city on April 20, heralding a new era of misery for the inhabitants, in which fires raged unchecked, smoke and fumes filled the air, and great risks had to be taken in the search for water.

The air raids had been terrifying enough but at least there had been some warning and time to prepare and take shelter. Now the shells arrived unheralded, creating havoc in the streets. Conditions were particularly bad in the central districts where people had to remain in their air raid shelters with shattered plumbing and sewage systems adding to the problems of survival. Only the Flak-towers had their own water supplies, but the tower at the Zoo was said to contain twice its designed capacity of 15,000 people.

The first Soviet troops across the city boundary were of the 1st Mechanised and 12th Guards Tank Corps of the Second Guards Tank Army spearheading elements of the Third and Fifth Shock Armies into the suburbs of Weissensee and Hohenschönhausen respectively on April 21, where they rested and prepared for the next phase of the battle. A witness described their arrival: 'Twelve assault tanks appeared, flanked left and right by infantry, approximately one company, armed with sub-machine guns and spraying the walls of the houses whilst moving from door to door at the double. They were followed by anti-aircraft guns. Behind these assault troops came carts drawn by two or four horses, containing food and ammunition as well as loot.'

Another witness reported: 'Rosenthal was taken after an artillery barrage, followed by an advance of tanks supported by helmetless infantry, excellent fighters. As soon as they arrived the men dug individual foxholes and took care of the wounded and their weapons. No uniforms to speak of. Then the

'Twelve assault tanks appeared . . . and . . . infantry . . . armed with sub-machine guns spraying the walls of the houses while moving from door to door at the double.' Well, the pictures certainly fit the action although it would be cheating to claim them as showing the entry into the city proper on April 20, nicely timed for Hitler's birthday.

looting and the rape. No discipline at all for most of the troops, as admitted by several Soviet officers, but this was only after the fighting was over.'

For the mainly primitive peasants forming the Red Army this was a time and opportunity for revenge on the Germans for all the atrocities and devastation that had been inflicted on their own country. They had behaved abominably to the civilian populations they had encountered ever since leaving Russia, raping, murdering and looting indiscriminately. At first this had been officially encouraged, seemingly to help distance the conquering have-nots from the conquered haves, whose lives had been so much richer in all respects, but now the need to woo the Germans to an

acceptance of communism had been recognised and the official policy had been changed. However, it was too late to change the minds of the troops, and the raping, looting and murdering were to continue for some time yet, particularly during the pauses in the fighting at night. Governing Mayor Ernst Reuter was later to quote the figure of 90,000 Berlin rape victims. Fear of the Russians, exacerbated by German propaganda, also led to numerous suicides, and the principal motive for maintaining a resistance against them by the German troops, regardless of the drastic measures used by the Nazis against suspected deserters and malingerers, was the fear of falling into Soviet captivity.

The difficulty of tracing the locations depicted in captionless Soviet photographs is compounded in that German shop names rarely state the owner but merely say 'bicycle shop' (top picture), or 'hardware goods', 'barber' and 'pet shop' (above).

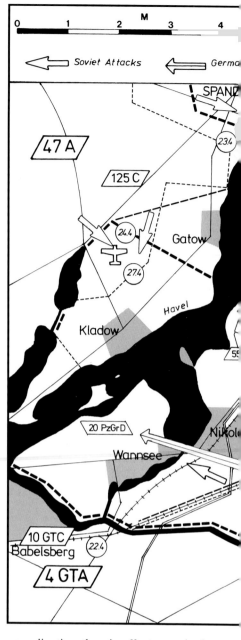

Sometimes, however, one strikes lucky — like this shot showing the Schöneberger Leihhaus at Hauptstrasse 20 with a branch of the Dresdner Bank next door. This is a still from Soviet film shot in Berlin — but is it genuine action? The artillery is firing westwards, away from the city centre. Tempelhof lies behind the cameraman.

Enter Koniev

The northern Soviet group encountered little resistance, and the Forty-Seventh Army was able to cross the Havel north of the city on the night of April 22/23 without difficulty. From there they spread out to clear the west bank of the river and to block possible relief attempts from the west.

Chuikov's southern group came through to the south-eastern suburbs and started swinging west across the water obstacles of the Spree and Dahme rivers to take up their position across the southern boundary. They were in for a big shock. On the morning of April 24, their leading elements bumped into a 1st Ukrainian Front unit awaiting their arrival on Schönefeld airfield.

Zhukov, shattered by the news, at first simply refused to believe it. However, Chuikov reacted promptly, quickly readjusting his deployment of the Eighth Guards and First Guards Armies under his command to meet the new situation.

While in the north Marshal Rokossovsky's 2nd Byelorussian Front, with a late start, were trying hard to catch up and pin down the 3. Panzer-Armee, in the south Koniev's opening battle had succeeded in smashing the enemy forces confronting them in just two days, releasing his two tanks armies for the push on Berlin, while the rest spread out as previously planned. This included the historic meeting of American and Soviet troops at Torgau on April 25.

The Fourth Guards Tank Army was committed to closing the ring around Berlin near Potsdam, but his Third Guards Tank Army was free, with Stalin's permission, to have a stab at beating Zhukov to the Reichstag.

This change of plan was all part of Stalin's plot to ensure that his popular and ambitious Marshals would be firmly reminded that he alone was the master of the newly-won Soviet empire and would brook no rivals. Zhukov had not been informed of this development and it seems that the air force commander

co-ordinating the air effort over both Fronts must also have been in on the plot, otherwise they would have been aware of each other's movements. The other extraordinary factor demonstrated here was the complete lack of communication between these neighbouring army groups, a factor that was to have devastating consequences four days later.

Consequently, the encounter at Schönefeld airfield on April 24 appears to have been Zhukov's first indication that Koniev was competing with him for the taking of the Reichstag. Stalin confirmed this with a new inter-Front boundary announced that night which followed the railway tracks running north to the Anhalter station, thus giving Koniev the opportunity of reaching the Reichstag from the south. However, Koniev's deployment of the Third Guards Tank Army along the line of the Teltow Canal indicates prior knowledge of this new inter-Front boundary, a further demonstration of Stalin's deviousness in this matter.

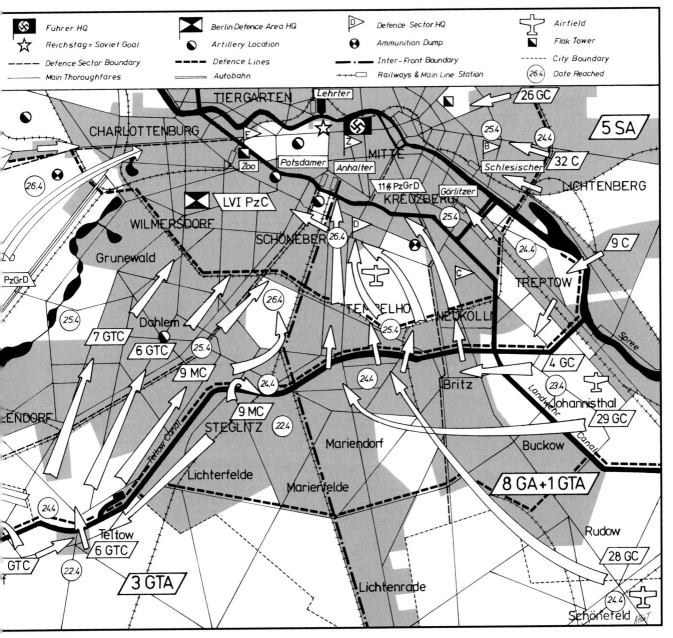

TIERGARTEN · Lehrter · CHARLOTTENBURG · 26 GC · 5 SA · Zoo · Potsdamer · MITTE · Anhalter · 25.4 · B · 24.4 · 32 C · LVI PzC · 11 SS PzGrD · KREUZBERG · Görlitzer · Schlesischer · LICHTENBERG · WILMERSDORF · D · 26.4 · SCHÖNEBERG · C · 9 C · Grunewald · TREPTOW · PzGrD · TEMPELHOF · NEUKÖLLN · 24.4 · Spree · 7 GTC · Dahlem · 25.4 · 25.4 · 4 GC · 6 GTC · 23.4 · Johannisthal · 9 MC · 24.4 · 24.4 · Britz · Landwehr Canal · 29 GC · ENDORF · 9 MC · STEGLITZ · 22.4 · Mariendorf · Buckow · Lichterfelde · Marienfelde · 8 GA + 1 GTA · Teltow · 6 GTC · 24.4 · Rudow · GTC · 22.4 · 3 GTA · Lichtenrade · 28 GC · Schönefeld · 24.4

Koniev was already attacking across the Teltow Canal on the morning of the 24th as Chuikov's troops deployed in accordance with the new inter-front boundary. This ended at the Anhalter railway station, thus giving Koniev the opportunity of competing against Zhukov for the Reichstag. Koniev took personal charge of the Third Guards Tank Army and aimed all but one brigade directly at his goal, but Chuikov's forces were slightly stronger and had less distance to go. Having taken Tempelhof airport *(right)* on the 26th, they cut across the boundary towards the Zoo stronghold, blocking Koniev's path without his knowledge.

To Koniev, the prize of the Reichstag was so important that he flung everything he could lay his hands on into the gamble. He took personal charge of the Third Guards Tank Army's operations, bringing in all his Front staff advisers on artillery, engineers, air support, etcetera, in the meantime leaving the supervision of the other eight armies to his chief-of-staff.

The German Defences

A lot of energy, not always wisely directed, had already been put into the preparation of the city's defences as a result of a plan produced by General-leutnant Helmuth Reymann when he had been appointed Defence Area Commander a month previously, but no provision had been made for troops to man these defences apart from a few Volkssturm battalions.

Again the waterways formed the dominant feature, the Spree and Dahme rivers joining at Köpenick in the east to run through the city centre and then join the north-south line of the Havel at Spandau in the west, the Teltow Canal skirting the southern suburbs, the Landwehr Canal making an island out of the city centre, and another canal separating the modern industrial centre of Siemensstadt from the north.

These waterways, together with the S-Bahn suburban railway loop, provided the obvious basis for the city defences. Trenches and gun emplacements had been dug, barricades erected and other preparations made for defence, including the digging in of immobile tanks, but the vast number of soldiers required to man them effectively was lacking.

Consequently the arrival of the LVI. Panzerkorps on the eastern outskirts of the city was regarded as a godsend by both Hitler and Goebbels; the latter as Gauleiter of Berlin being directly responsible for the defence measures in and around the city. Thus on April 23 Weidling found himself committed with his corps to the defence of the city, and on the following day, appointed Berlin Defence Area Commander but without the clear-cut mandate from Hitler that he wanted.

It was all too late for him to do anything other than improvise with the existing defence system. The city had been divided into ten Defence Sectors, nine designated 'A' to 'H' radiated

Last-minute preparations for the defence of the city centre. Volkssturm men pushing the wreck of a tram into position to form the framework of a barricade on Brunnenstrasse in Wedding. The tram would later be filled with rubble and cobblestones. This barricade was close to the Humboldthain Flak-tower, a defensive position that held out until the surrender. (No worthwhile comparison as virtually the whole of this stretch of the road has been redeveloped.)

outwards from the central hub of the ninth, known as 'Z' or 'Zitadelle'. The outer defence lines had already been overrun and the interior lines of defence were under attack in several places. Apart from changing some of the Defence Sector commanders, he left things much as they were but bolstered the

With the River Spree to the north and the Landwehr Canal to the south, attempts were made by German engineers to isolate the 'Zitadelle' by blowing all the bridges across the waterways. *Above:* Initially, road blocks were set up — this is Hansabrücke over the Spree on Levetzow Strasse. *Below:* The blown bridge was rebuilt in 1952–53.

defence with the LVI. Panzerkorps, using the remaining tanks from the 'Müncheberg' Panzer-Division as his 'fire brigade.' The 9. Fallschirm-Division was sent to hold the Defence Sector based on the Humboldthain Flak-tower, the 20. and SS 'Nordland' Panzergrenadier-Divisions to hold the line of the Teltow Canal, while the 18. Panzergrenadier and 'Müncheberg' Panzer-Divisions were kept in reserve near Tempelhof airport.

In all, it is reckoned that the defence consisted of about 60,000 men with 40 to 50 tanks, a few guns and a very limited amount of ammunition for all weapons, which became even more critical when the city's ammunition de-pots were quickly overrun. Included in these troop figures were odd Wehr-macht units, the Berlin Flak, Vlassov troops, Waffen and Allgemeine SS, Reichsarbeitsdienst (Labour Service), Police, Fire Brigade, Plant Protection Units, Volkssturm and Hitlerjugend.

Above: **Grossbeeren-Brücke across the canal beside the Mehringdamm. The railway is the elevated section of the U-Bahn. Some of Colonel-General Chuikov's troops and vehicles can be seen on the northern bank at the southern end of the Wilhelmstrasse, so this picture must have been taken during the last days of the fighting.** *Below:* **We took the comparison view from the same corner building on Grossbeerenstrasse.**

Left: **The ruins of the Schloss Bridge across the Spree in Charlottenburg, which the Second Guards Tank Army forced on April 29. Despite the damage, it was still possible to get their** tanks across. *Right:* **Electrical switchgear has now been installed on the exact spot where the photographer stood in 1945. We squeezed in between the cabinet and the railings.**

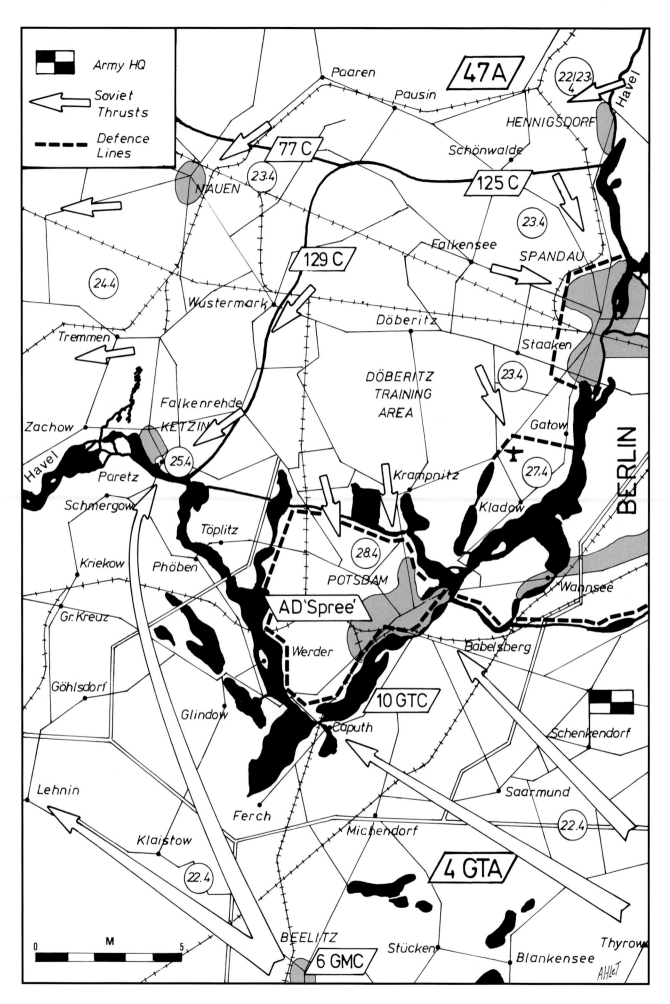

Army HQ

Soviet Thrusts

Defence Lines

47 A

22/23 4

HENNIGSDORF

77 C

23.4

Paaren

Pausin

Schönwalde

125 C

23.4

NAUEN

Falkensee

SPANDAU

24.4

129 C

Wustermark

Döberitz

Staaken

23.4

Tremmen

DÖBERITZ TRAINING AREA

Falkenrehde

KETZIN

Gatow

Zachow

25.4

Krampnitz

27.4

Havel

Paretz

Kladow

Schmergow

Töplitz

28.4

BERLIN

Kriekow

Phöben

POTSDAM

Wannsee

Gr. Kreuz

AD 'Spree'

Babelsberg

Göhlsdorf

Werder

10 GTC

Schenkendorf

Glindow

Caputh

Lehnin

Saarmund

Ferch

22.4

Klaistow

Michendorf

4 GTA

22.4

0 M 5

BEELITZ

Stücken

Blankensee

Thyrow

6 GMC

AHLeT

196

The encirclement of Berlin was completed on April 25 when elements of the Forty-Seventh Army sweeping down from Hennigsdorf met up with elements of the Fourth Guards Tank Army near Ketzin. Spandau and Gatow airfield were invested on the 23rd but did not fall until the 27th, after which it was Potsdam's turn to be attacked. The 20. Panzergrenadier Division held out on Wansee Island right up until May 1, as the Glienicker Bridge across the Spree at Potsdam had been blown. *Above:* In this picture Russian pioneers have constructed a timber-piled bridge alongside. *Below:* The bridge pictured from the 'Berlin' bank in July 1945.

three points, Stahnsdorf, Teltow and Lankwitz, each being supported by ground attack aircraft and a thousand guns (650 guns to the kilometre as compared with Zhukov's 295 on the Oder). The two flank attacks failed for various reasons, so he pumped all his resources through the successful central route. In so doing, he forced the newly-arrived 20. Panzergrenadier-Division off balance, and back on to Wannsee Island, where, down to only 92 effectives, it remained isolated, being easily bottled in for the remainder of the battle by elements of the 4th Guards Tank Army. From then on, his unremitting goal was the Reichstag. Detaching only one reinforced tank brigade to cover his exposed left flank, he concentrated everything else in a powerful thrust aimed directly at the Reichstag itself.

With the three armoured corps of the Third Guards Tank Army side by side on the main axis and supported by infantry elements of the Twenty-Eighth Army, Koniev thrust north-east from Zehlendorf through Dahlem and Lichterfelde, then Schmargendorf and Steglitz to reach the S-Bahn ring, which formed the next German line of defence. With all the resources at his disposal he smashed his way through and started occupying Schöneberg on April 27.

Rivalry in the Southern Sectors

On April 22, the leading elements of Koniev's Third Guards Tank Army had reached the line of the Teltow Canal from the south. He needed all of April 23 to bring up his forces and prepare his attack across the canal, but there was little to oppose him, as Volkssturm Leutnant von Reuss reported:

'Preparations for the defence of the Teltow Canal included the construction of works along the northern bank and the organisation of a bridge demolition team. A fire trench was laid out at a varying distance from the canal and machine gun emplacements were established 500-600 metres apart. Each emplacement was connected with a protected shelter by means of a communications trench.

'The trenches led partly through marshy terrain and interfered greatly with troop movements. A machine gun emplacement protected with concrete slabs was constructed in the grounds of an asbestos factory. There were no artillery emplacements to the rear, although two anti-aircraft guns had been brought into position. A rocket-launcher had also been set up.

'The only complete unit that figured in this sector was the Klein-Machnow Volkssturm-Kompanie, which was joined by a few stragglers from the Wehrmacht.

'The platoon was armed with only one machine gun of Czech manufacture, which went out of action after having been fired only once. In addition there were some rifles of various foreign makes, including even some Italian Balilla *(sic)* rifles.'

At dawn on April 24, Koniev launched a massive attack across the canal at

It was rebuilt in its original style and reopened on December 19, 1949.

Soviet Organisation and Tactics

The sudden change to a street fighting rôle caused not only extensive reorganisation within the Soviet ranks but also brought some expensive lessons with it. Tanks proceeding in column along a street would find the first and last vehicles knocked out by men or boys hidden with Panzerfausts among the rubble and then be eliminated one by one. The casualties within the Third Guards Tank Army were particularly heavy. As Chuikov later wrote: 'In street fighting, when squares and streets are empty and the enemy is defending himself in buildings, attics and cellars, the tank crews cannot see the opposing troops. Neither can they drive their tanks into buildings, let alone cellars or attics. At the same time, they are an excellent target for enemy tank hunters armed with incendiary bottles or, worse still, with Panzerfausts. This is not to say, of course, that tanks are not usable in street fighting. Far from it. They are needed, but only if they co-operate closely with the other arms in assault groups.

'It is only by co-operating with the infantry, artillery, sappers and chemical support troops that tank crews can know in what buildings, on what floor, in what attic or cellar the enemy has established himself and they can then join efforts to destroy him. In street fighting, tanks should be used principally as artillery on tracks and their crews as armour-protected gunners.'

The various combat arms of the service were combined into combat teams generally consisting of a platoon of infantry, one or two tanks or self-propelled guns, some sappers, some man-pack flame-throwers, a section of anti-tank guns, and two or three field guns. Usually 76mm, but sometimes even 150mm guns or 203mm howitzers were used. In this direct support rôle, the guns advanced with the combat teams, firing along the streets over open sights. The gun crews were vulnerable to infantry fire and their forward observers had an extremely stressful time.

The heavier artillery were crammed into every available open space, pounding the avenues of advance for the combat teams. Heavy mortars were extremely useful in this kind of fighting as they could be deployed almost anywhere. Rocket-launchers were often

Above: **At point-blank range, an SU-76 self-propelled gun wreaks havoc with a block of flats. More stills from the cine.**

As the designation implies, the gun on the SU-76 had a calibre of 76mm. Sixty rounds could be carried on board and available for use.

The 152mm ML-20 gun-howitzer lets fly a 44kg high-explosive shell.

dismantled from their truckbeds and manhandled into the upper storeys of buildings. A pattern gradually emerged whereby the day would begin with an hour's bombardment of that day's objectives. At night the artillery fire diminished considerably, but Colonel-General Nikolai Erastovitch Berzarin of the Fifth Shock Army could later boast: 'The Allies dropped 65,000 tons of bombs — we fired 40,000 tons of shells in two weeks!'

The techniques used were based on the principle that each street should be tackled by a regiment, one battalion working down each side of the street and a third in reserve bringing up the rear. Usually the troops did not advance down the streets themselves but mouseholed their way through the buildings at the various levels, while the supporting artillery worked their way down the back yards and alleys with engineer assistance. In attacking a heavily defended building the assault group would split in two, one part concentrating on bottling up the enemy in the cellars, where they would normally have taken shelter during the preliminary bombardment, and the other clearing the upper storeys.

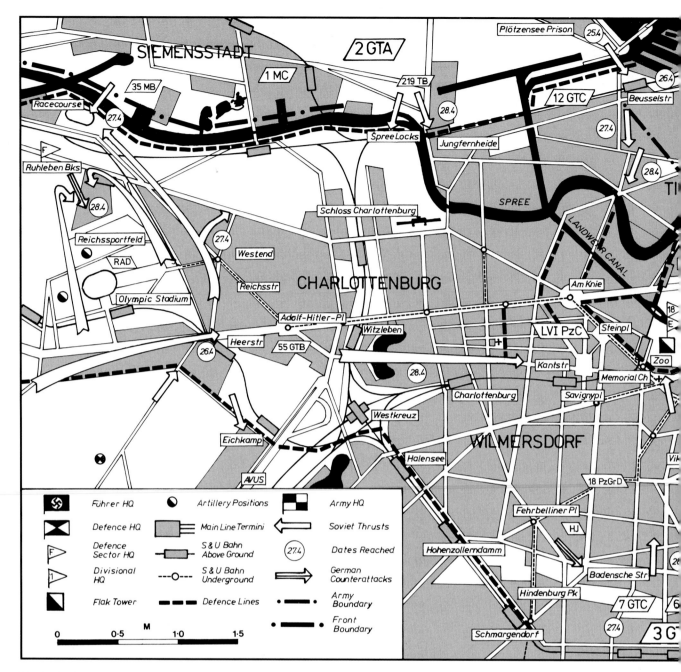

Koniev's Western Flank

In the meantime, to cover his exposed left flank Koniev had detached the reinforced 55th Guards Tank Brigade, first to clear the rear in Zehlendorf, then to move up through the Grunewald and hook round on to the Heerstrasse part of the East-West-Axis with a view to forming a blocking position on the line Preussenallee/Reichsstrasse in Westend.

The 18. Panzergrenadier-Division, which had been brought out of reserve to replace the lost 20. Panzergrenadier-Division, and deployed along the eastern edge of the Grunewald behind the chain of small lakes, now found itself outflanked by these manoeuvres and so pulled back into Wilmersdorf to face the main threat from the Third Guards Tank Army.

By the evening of April 26, the head of the 55th Guards Tank Brigade had reached the vicinity of Heerstrasse S-Bahn Station. Next day they wheeled

On April 28, by which time the inter-front boundary had been changed to end at the Potsdamer railway station, Koniev launched a major attack with the Third Guards Tank Army, aiming to reach the Tiergarten by nightfall. This attack was supported by his flank guard, the 55th Guards Tank Brigade, which thrust down Kanstrasse while a rearguard pinned down the Ruhleben garrison with an attack over the Olympic Stadium area. It was not long before Koniev discovered that he was in fact attacking the rear of Chuikov's troops. Humiliated, he returned to his Front headquarters, leaving the Third Guards to switch its line of advance towards the Kurfürstendamm.

north and by noon reached Ruhleben U-Bahn Station, where they came across elements of the 35th Guards Mechanised Brigade of the Second Guards Tank Army that had just crossed the Spree from the north. The latter was persuaded to withdraw back across the river and the 55th Guards Tank Brigade then turned to its blocking rôle astride Westend. Behind it was still a considerable element of the German defence based on Ruhleben Barracks, with mixed anti-aircraft and field artillery positions in the Olympic Stadium area guarded by Reichsarbeitsdienst, the Hitlerjugend Regi-

ment guarding the still intact Havel bridges, Volkssturm units along the southern bank of the Spree, and Wehrmacht troops in reserve.

Chuikov's Ploy

However, Zhukov's southern grouping of Chuikov's combined Eighth Guards and First Guards Tank Armies was even stronger than Koniev's reinforced Third Guards Tank Army. Consequently Chuikov was able to clear his side of the boundary, including the strongly defended Tempelhof airport, and close up to the next major obstacle of the Landwehr Canal in good time.

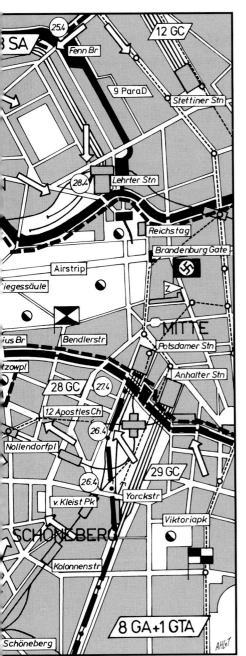

Battered and bombed, the Olympic Stadium fell to the Russians on April 28. *Above:* However, they missed this fine eagle trophy, seen here being purloined two months later by two American GIs of the 3264th Signal Service Company. *Below:* Seventeen years on . . . and the torches are back in an evening spectacle in September 1962.

At dawn on April 25, Chuikov's forces, a total of three infantry and four armoured corps, attacked across the Teltow Canal from Tempelhof to Neukölln with the seizure of the strongly defended airfield as their immediate objective. The airfield was tackled by the 28th Guards Corps with one division hooking round either side and the third coming up the centre with special tank groups detailed to prevent any aircraft taking off, as the airfield was known to have underground hangars and it was expected that some of the Nazi leaders would attempt to escape this way.

It took until noon the following day to overcome the airfield defences, but by that evening the Soviets had not only pushed the SS 'Nordland' Panzergrenadier-Division back to the Landwehr Canal, but their main weight was now shifted to their left flank and reached as far as Potsdamer Strasse. Significantly, and presumably with no lack of prompting by Zhukov, Chuikov ignored the Moscow-imposed boundary, and on April 27 he pushed right across as far west as the Zoo, where the massive Flak-tower formed a defensive nucleus, and also closed up to the Landwehr Canal from the Hallesches Tor to the vicinity of Lützowplatz.

However, Chuikov had then to allow time to prepare for the crossing of the Landwehr Canal, the last formidable obstacle in his path, his attack being scheduled for April 29.

Koniev's Humiliation

It was Koniev's turn to be humiliated. Having concentrated his main force along the line of Badensche Strasse between the Potsdamer Strasse and Kaiserallee (Bundesallee), and apparently totally unaware of the presence of Chuikov's troops across his front, on the morning of April 28 he launched an all-out attack with the aim of getting across the Landwehr Canal into the Tiergarten by evening. What happened then, daunts the imagination, with all that artillery hammering into the area occupied by Chuikov's troops, but by 1100 hours that same morning the truth must have percolated through, for the right-hand corps was abruptly switched to the left flank, and the whole direction of attack turned north-west towards the Kurfürstendamm.

In support of this operation and in order to distract the German forces on his left flank, Koniev had ordered the 55th Guards Tank Brigade out of Westend to attack down Kantstrasse. They in turn used their reserves to distract the Ruhleben group with subsidiary attacks that initially overran the Olympic Stadium area but were eventually driven back. Now orders had to be sent to the 55th Guards Tank Brigade to return to their blocking rôle in Westend, but they had meanwhile become so involved in street fighting on the Kantstrasse axis that it was to take them until the following evening to comply.

The Western Sectors

Soundly humiliated, Koniev quit Berlin with his entourage to return to his Front headquarters, leaving the Third Guards Tank Army to its own devices.

Stalin again re-drew the inter-Front boundary, restricting the Third Guards Tank Army to south of the elevated S-Bahn tracks running through the Savignyplatz and Charlottenburg Stations, and left the now greatly reduced glory of conquest to the already chastened Zhukov.

On the night of April 22/23, the reinforced Forty-Seventh Army crossed the Havel immediately north of the city boundary at Hennigsdorf and began its multiple rôle of securing the western approaches to the city, clearing the west bank of the river and completing the encirclement with the Fourth Guards Tank Army to the west of Potsdam.

The old town of Spandau, which had been incorporated into Greater Berlin in 1920, and Gatow airfield, were attacked on April 24. The fighting in Spandau was so confused that the

Soviets withdrew at night to consolidate, and the defence was subsequently able to hold out until the night of April 25 before retiring back across the Havel into Stresow.

Gatow airfield housed the Luftwaffe's main academies and was strongly defended. It even managed to remain operational until almost the last minute, being finally overrun on April 27. Major Komorowski, who commanded an ad hoc battalion on the outer defence ring there later recorded: 'The battalion, as part of a regiment, defended a section of the first position located along the western perimeter of Gatow airfield, which was to be protected from attack from the west. If the first position were lost, the troops were to cross the Havel in boats lying in readiness, in order to occupy the second position on the east side of the lake.

'The position consisted of a well-built, continuous trench. The battalion was composed of construction and Volkssturm troops, none of whom had any combat experience. They were armed with captured rifles and a few

machine guns, and only had a limited supply of ammunition. The infantry were supported by an 88mm anti-aircraft battery and a heavy infantry gun platoon, although the latter had never fired its weapons. Support was also received from the Zoo Flak-tower. On the evening of the first day of battle all the Volkssturm troops deserted, and the gaps were filled by recruiting stragglers. In two days of fighting all the defenders were either killed or captured.'

Somehow during a lull in the fighting on April 24, SS-Brigadeführer Dr Gustav Krukenberg, while on his way to reinforce the garrison, managed to bring some 350 volunteers, mainly from his old command, the SS 'Charlemagne' Panzergrenadier-Division, on foot right past the airfield without noticing anything unusual.

One of the last aircraft to land at Gatow was a Focke-Wulf FW 190 carrying Generaloberst Robert Ritter von Greim, the commander of Luftflotte 6, and his girl friend, the famous aviatrice Hanna Reitsch, who was small

In the earlier battles for Breslau and Königsberg, the airfields on the outskirts had been seized almost immediately by Soviet forces. The same was foreseen when it became the turn of Berlin, and the idea had been advanced back in March to utilise the widened East-West-Axis as an emergency runway, right in the city centre. In spite of Speer's protests, his treasured lamp-posts were removed and the strip marked with red lamps. However, there was only an available length of 1700 metres (1,800 yards) — nowhere near the two miles claimed by Hitler in his conversation with General Wilhelm Burgdorf on March 23! Added to that, at one end was the 85-foot Brandenburg Gate and at the other the 200-foot Siegessäule.

and determined enough to travel stuffed into the storage compartment in the tail. Von Greim had been summoned by Hitler and arrived with an escort of twenty aircraft, seven of which were shot down en route. They flew on to an improvised airstrip on the East-West-Axis between the Victory Column and the Brandenburg Gate in a Fieseler Storch with von Greim at the controls and Hanna in the passenger seat behind him. On the way, von Greim was badly wounded in the leg and Hanna had to lean over him to take the controls, eventually landing them safely at their destination. They then obtained a ride to the Führerbunker, where Hitler announced von Greim's promotion to Generalfeldmarschall and Commander of the Luftwaffe in succession to Göring, something he could have done just as well by radio or teleprinter. Von Greim and Hanna took off again on April 30, flying direct to Rechlin in an Arado 96 that had come especially for them, their Storch having meanwhile been wrecked by shell-fire.

The airstrip on the East-West-Axis had been opened on April 24 with a view to providing a supply route for desperately needed ammunition now that the ammunition dumps on the city's outskirts had been overrun. Supply by

The available distance would be safe enough for the Arado 96 and Fieseler Storch (which was specifically designed for short take-offs and landings), but with the Ju 52 it was another matter. The aircraft normally required around 1,200 yards to unstick with 25 degrees of flap (more flap would increase the payload but lengthen the take-off). If it was fully loaded, one must add at least 300 yards, making a run of 1,500 yards in all. However, 300 yards ahead would be the 200-foot Victory Monument and, with lift-off coming at 115 kph, the pilot would have had little speed in hand to bank the aircraft in a climbing turn and would risk stalling into the ground. *Left:* **From the position of the wreckage, this would appear to be exactly what happened on April 26.**

air drop proved a failure, so on the morning of April 26 two Ju 52s landed with tank ammunition, but as they were taking off again with wounded aboard one of them hit an obstruction and crashed, killing all aboard, so this method of delivery was also abandoned.

The difficulty pilots experienced in trying to get into Berlin was described by the 'Stuka' ace. Oberstleutnant Hans-Ulrich Rudel, who had been summoned by Hitler and proposed landing on the airstrip: 'Upon arriving near Berlin we were picked up by the Russian detectors and the anti-aircraft artillery opened fire on us. It was very difficult to recognise the features of the capital because of enormous clouds of smoke and a thin layer of mist. the fires were so fierce in some places we were dazzled by them and prevented from seeing anything. I had to concentrate on the shadows in order to see anything

and was unable to pick out the East-West-Axis. There were flames and cannon fire everywhere. The spectacle was fantastic. We then received a message saying that landing was impossible as the East-West-Axis was under heavy artillery fire and the Russians had already taken Potsdamer Platz.'

The encirclement of Berlin was completed on April 25 when troops of the Forty-Seventh Army's 328th Division and 65th Guards Tank Brigade met up with the elements of the Fourth Guards Tank Army's 6th Guards Mechanised Corps near Ketzin, north-west of Potsdam. The Forty-Seventh Army then went on to establish a west-facing front immediately west of Nauen.

Eventually the Forty-Seventh Army attacked and entered Potsdam from the north on April 28, by which time most of the garrison had already escaped to the south.

Nearby lay the remains of a Storch — one wonders if this was the actual machine in which Generaloberst Robert Ritter von

Greim and his girl friend, Hanna Reitsch, made their precarious flight to the capital at low level while under fire.

The Northern Sectors

On the night of April 22/23, the Second Guards Tank Army's two remaining corps swept round in an arc to the north to commence converging on the city from that direction. Clearing Reinickendorf and the Jungfernheide, they had two small bridgeheads across the Hohenzollern Canal into Siemensstadt by the evening of the following day. There then followed a period of intense fighting in that heavily built-up industrial and housing area and it was not until the evening of April 26 that they were able to close up to the line of the Spree.

On their left flank the 79th Corps of the Third Shock Army also wheeled through Reinickendorf and took the Hermann-Göring-Kaserne (Quartier Napoléon) on April 24, ending the day at Plötzensee. Next morning they attacked across the canal locks towards the strongly defended prison area, which they had to spend the whole day clearing before turning to face the next obstacle, the badly damaged bridge leading to the Westhafen and Moabit.

On April 26 the 79th Corps succeeded in crossing the bridge at Westhafen after a costly battle against Vlassov and German troops, and turned south-eastwards into Moabit. That day and the next they were able to release several hundred of their own prisoners-of-war, who were promptly fed, armed and thrust back into action to make up for their casualties.

The 12th Guards Corps advanced from the north-west, approaching the Flak-tower in Humboldthain park on April 26. The railway tracks lay between them and the tower which resisted everything the Soviets could throw at it. Below it on the far side of the park is the radar tower.

The northern face of Flakturm III bearing numerous pock-marks from Soviet artillery fire. The towers were formidable strong-points and impervious to shot and shell, one bomb actually bouncing off the roof before it exploded on the ground.

The Potsdam Declaration signed on August 2, 1945 by Generallissimo Stalin, President Truman and Prime Minister Attlee, stated that the main purpose of the occupation of Germany was: '(i) The complete disarmament and demilitarization of Germany and the elimination or control of all German industry that could be used for military production. (ii) To convince the German people that they have suffered a total military defeat and that they cannot escape responsibility for what they have brought on themselves, since their own ruthless warfare and the fanatical Nazi resistance have destroyed the German economy and made chaos and suffering inevitable. (iii) To destroy the National Socialist Party and its affiliated and supervised organisations; to ensure that they are not revived in any form. (iv) To prepare for the eventual reconstruction of German political life on a democratic basis.' To this end, the Flaktowers were deemed military installations requiring demolition, the one in the Humboldthain park falling within the French Sector.

Attempts were made to demolish it with explosives on October 25, 1947, February 28 and March 14, 1948 (top), but French engineers had to go very carefully because of the close proximity of the railway. In the end, only the rear portion could be destroyed, the remainder being infilled with rubble and landscaped into an observation platform. Left: This picture was taken in 1950, and the second one (right) in July the following year as sunbathers enjoy a brief respite from war-torn Berlin.

Meanwhile the 12th Guards Corps in the centre of the Third Shock Army had come up against the formidable defences around the Humboldthain Flaktower, which held them in check, but they were able to take the strong point at Wedding S-Bahn Station covering the approaches from the north and also secured the Fenn Bridge leading into Moabit. From then on they were to push down Chausseestrasse towards the Charité Hospital and raid the area defended by the 9. Fallschirm-Jäger-Division from a secure base held along the line of the S-Bahn ring, although they were unable to dominate it.

Further east the 7th Corps of the same army quickly pushed through to the Alexanderplatz defences by the evening of April 24. But these were robustly held under the direction of the recently-promoted Generalmajor Erich Bärenfänger, and the 7th Corps soon became entangled in the confused fighting for that part of the city, so that it was not until April 30 that they were able to join in the attack across the Spree on to 'Museum Island'.

The view from the top taken by Elmar Widmann in 1983. This is one of the two remaining twin 12.8cm gun positions, the other two having disappeared.

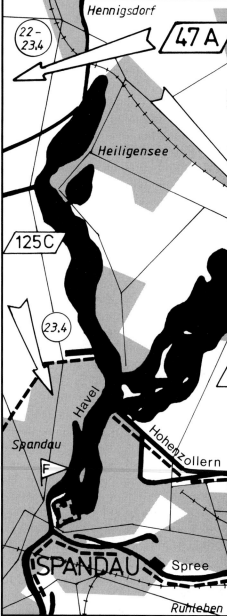

Two versions of the same attack, but is it action . . . or re-creation?

Although we obtained the originals from different sources in East Berlin and Moscow, the name of the photographer is not given, nor the location. Something about them says that they have been staged, although the clip *(above)* looks a little more realistic having an air of unrehearsed immediacy.

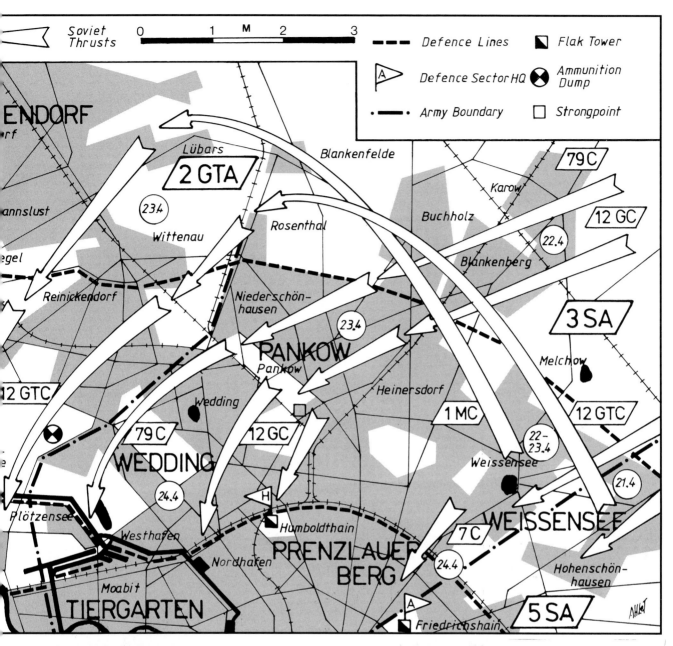

ENDORF

rf

Lübars

2 GTA

(234)

annslust

Wittenau

egel

Reinickendorf

Blankenfelde

Karow

Buchholz

(22.4)

Blankenberg

Rosenthal

Niederschön-
hausen

(23.4)

PANKOW

Pankow

Wedding

79C

3 SA

Melchow

12 GTC

79 C

12 GC

Heinersdorf

1 MC

12 GC

(22-23.4)

Weissensee

(21.4)

WEDDING

(24.4)

H

Plötzensee

Westhafen

Humboldthain

7 C

12 GTC

WEISSENSEE

Nordhafen

PRENZLAUER BERG

(24.4)

Hohenschön-
hausen

Moabit

TIERGARTEN

A

Friedrichshain

5 SA

AH⟨et⟩

We found that the troops were pictured running eastwards on Turmstrasse, the church being the Heilandskirche on Berlin's shortest street, the Thusnelda-Allee in Moabit. Once having established the location, we confirmed that the infantrymen lying on the rubble are at least facing the correct way — due south.

The first Soviet troops into Berlin were the vanguards of the Third and Fifth Shock Armies led in by two corps of the Second Guards Tank Army into Weissensee and Hohenschönhausen respectively on April 21. On the night of the 22nd/23rd, the armoured corps of the Second Guards Tank Army swung round to sweep through the northern suburbs, clearing the site of today's Tegel airport on the Jungfernheide on the 26th and then crossing into the industrial suburb of Siemensstadt. The central 12th Guards Corps of the Third Shock Army was baulked by the Humboldthain Flak-tower position, so established itself along the line of the S-Bahn ring, from where it conducted raids into the 9. Fallschirm-Jäger-Division's territory. The 79th Corps on the right flank began a series of opposed water-crossing operations over the Plötzensee Locks and the Westhafen that eventually brought it into Moabit, where they were able to restock their ranks with released Soviet prisoners of war, while the 7th Corps on the left flank advanced rapidly to Alexanderplatz.

The Eastern Sectors

The Fifth Shock Army had one corps astride Frankfurter Allee, one working along the east bank of the Spree and one on the west.

The 26th Guards Corps had to bypass the Friedrichshain Flak-tower position, which was simply too strong to be tackled head-on, but progress down Frankfurter Allee on the East-West-Axis was marked by deliberate, obliterating bombardments. The Stavka artillery reserves, originally allocated to the Front for the battle of the Seelow Heights, had rejoined them and, with the main railway system coming in behind, there was no shortage of ammunition for the guns.

Dieter Borkowski, a sixteen year-old schoolboy and member of the Hitler-jugend, like many of his age group, was a Luftwaffe auxiliary serving as an anti-aircraft gunner in the Home Defence, stationed at the Friedrichshain Flak-tower. In his diary he wrote of April 29: 'We could already hear the "Hurrahs!" from the attacking Soviet troops in Kniprodestrasse. There were dead and wounded lying everywhere in the five stories of the Flak-tower, and an unpleasant sweet smell permeated the tower. We received the order to occupy the new front line in Höchstestrasse. The two Flak-towers now stand like islands in the sea, for the Russians have long since forced their way past these

The Nazis had renamed the borough of Friedrichshain 'Horst Wessel' as this had been their martyr's stamping ground. How painful it must have been, therefore, to see this, the sacred battleground of the 1920s, turned once again into a killing ground by Communist forces in the 1940s. *Top:* This is Landsberger Allee, close to the S-Bahn station. *Above:* The road was subsequently renamed Leninallee and a suitable statue of some stature erected a few hundred yards along the road in his honour.

Öffentliche Luftschutzräume
befinden sich:
Frankfurter Allee 113

fortresses, so the enemy can make a surprise attack from any direction, which is not a good feeling. The provision of supplies and ammunition has become very bad. We are lying upstairs in old housing blocks from which the workers' wives would rather see us go.'

The 32nd Corps was to experience

Just to the south, on the converging Frankfurter Allee, more troops of the Fifth Shock Army were fighting their way westwards towards the Alexanderplatz. This is the U-Bahn station near the junction with Möllendorff Strasse (now Jacques Duclos Strasse). Frankfurter Strasse then became Stalinallee (we shall see his statue in a later chapter) until 1961 when it was belatedly renamed Karl-Marx-Allee.

some difficulty in its push along the east bank of the Spree through some

densely populated and industrial districts when it ran up against the defence

As the map shows, the Fifth Shock Army's advance through the eastern suburbs included a water-crossing by the 9th Corps to Treptow Park, assisted by the boats of the Dnieper Flotilla. Although progress was held up by the strong points formed by the Schlesischer and Görlitzer railway stations, the advance along Frankfurter Allee was given massive artillery support, smashing everything in its path. By the 29th, the 9th Corps was fighting its way westwards astride Leipziger Strasse. *Above and opposite:* It would take a brave man to hazard a guess as to the exact locations depicted on Frankfurter Allee as the whole street was redeveloped after the war.

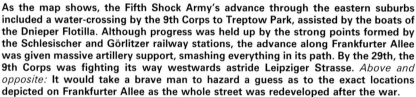

The 286th Guards Rifle Regiment of the 94th Guards Division (commander Lieutenant-Colonel A. N. Kravchenko) and the 283rd Guards Rifle Regiment of the same division, commanded by Lieutenant-Colonel A. A. Ignatyev, won particular distinction in the fighting during the storming of Berlin's eastern part.

The soldiers sought to advance and showed mass heroism. Seeing that it was difficult to capture by means of a frontal attack the strongly fortified corner building that prevented the regiment from moving on, Company Party Organiser of the 283rd Guards Regiment, Alexei Kuznetsov, with a group of soldiers, sneaked round the building and attacked from the rear. The enemy strong point was captured.

Unparalleled valour was displayed by Senior Lieutenant I. P. Ukraintsev of the 283rd Guards Regiment. During the attack on a house, hand-to-hand fighting broke out and he rushed at the enemy. The brave officer knifed nine Nazis to death. Following his example, Guards Sergeant Stepan Grobazai and his section killed several dozen more Nazis.

The remarkable Komsomol leader of the 94th Guards Division, Captain Nikolai Gorshelev, deputy chief of the division's political department, died the death of a hero in this fighting. He inspired the soldiers by his own example in combat, always being everywhere where the battle was decided. He was respected and loved by the division's men for valour and the concern he showed for the rank and file and officers.

The 9th Rifle Corps commanded by Hero of the Soviet Union Major-General I. P. Rosly achieved the greatest success in storming Berlin on April 23. The soldiers of the corps seized Karlshorst and part of Köpenick by a resolute storm and forced the Spree on the march.

Brave actions were undertaken in forcing the Spree by the 1st River Boat Brigade of the Dnieper Flotilla, particularly by the brigade's motor-boat unit commanded by Lieutenant M. M. Kalinin. Despite strong enemy fire, Petty Officer G. Dudnik ferried several rifle companies of the 301st Rifle Division to the enemy bank.

Lieutenant Kalinin, Petty Officers Dudnik, G. P. Kazakov and A. P. Pashkov; sailors N. A. Baranov, A. Ye. Samokhvalov, M. T. Sotnikov, N. A. Filippov and V. V. Cherinov, were bestowed the title of Hero of the Soviet Union by a decree of the USSR Supreme Soviet on May 31, 1945, for military valour and heroism displayed by the seamen of the 1st Bobruisk Brigade of the Dnieper Flotilla. The flotilla itself received the Order of Ushakov 1st Class.

MARSHAL OF THE SOVIET UNION G. ZHUKOV, 1974

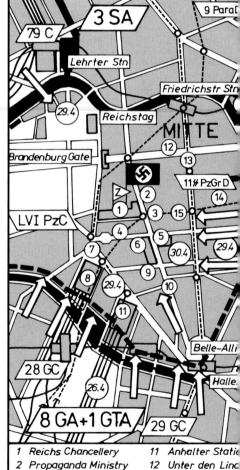

1 Reichs Chancellery
2 Propaganda Ministry
3 Kaiserhof Hotel
4 Leipziger Strasse
5 Post Office
6 Air Ministry
7 Potsdamer Platz
8 Potsdamer Station
9 RHSA & Gestapo HQ
10 Wilhelmstrasse
11 Anhalter Statio
12 Unter den Linc
13 Friedrichstrass
14 Gendarmenmar
15 'Mitte' U-Bahn
16 Museum Islan
17 Schloss Berlin
18 Fischerinsel
19 Spittalmarkt
20 Stock Exchang

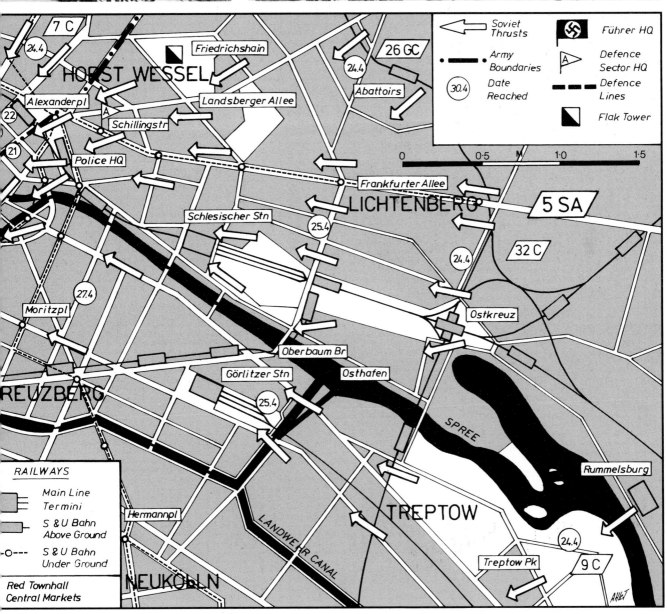

Above: On reaching the Strausberger Platz, the Frankfurter Allee kinked a few degrees to the north (towards the bottom left-hand corner in the picture *above*), the remainder of the street as far as the Alexanderplatz then being called Grosse Frankfurter Strasse (the street where young Wessel was shot). *Below:* The reconstruction of this avenue in the 1950s was regarded as a symbolic laying of the foundations of the newly-created GDR as a socialist nation.

GROSSE FRANKFURTER STRASSE

ALEXANDER STRASSE

POLICE HEADQUARTERS

HERTIE STORE

LOOKING SOUTH-EAST

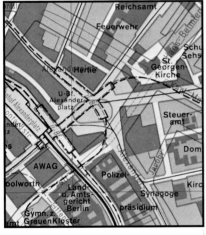

After another turn at the junction with Landsberger Allee, Grosse Frankfurter Strasse reached Alexanderplatz — the focus of city life in eastern Berlin. Here, too, the GDR made more bold statements, cutting out the dog-leg, dramatically re-aligning roads and streets, and cutting through a wide new dual-carriageway.

based in the strong buildings of the Schlesischer railway station (Hauptbahnhof), whose railway tracks provided ample fields of fire to keep the attackers at bay.

The 9th Corps, supported by the gun boats of the Dnieper Flotilla made an assault river crossing across the Spree to Teltow Park on April 24. They were opposed by the engineer battalion of the SS 'Nordland' Panzergrenadier-Division and some local Volkssturm, but soon had 16,000 men and 100 guns and mortars, as well as 27 tanks and 700 trucks across. They went on to clear the area between the river and the Landwehr Canal leading up into Kreuzberg. Again they too had difficulty with the defence based on the Görlitzer railway station.

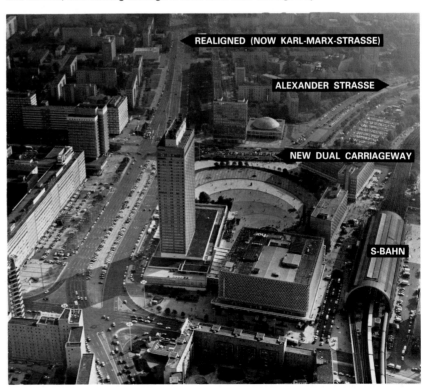

REALIGNED (NOW KARL-MARX-STRASSE)

ALEXANDER STRASSE

NEW DUAL CARRIAGEWAY

S-BAHN

Unfortunately the wartime photographer just missed out the S-Bahn station to the south-west of the Platz which remains in its original position and would have helped orientate the two pictures.

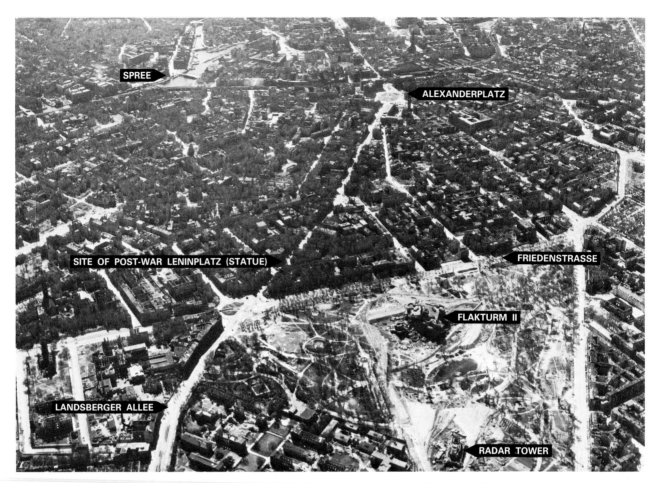

A wider view of the battle zone fought over by the 26th Guards Corps. In the foreground the Friedrichshain park with the Flak-tower which was bypassed in the drive down Landsberger Allee towards Alexanderplatz in the distance. The roundabout junction with Friedenstrasse (crossing from left to right) is the Landsberger Platz. Although dated 1945, this picture must have been taken after August 1946 as the towers have been split asunder by the post-war demolitions.

Not much detail is known about the Russian demolitions (Friedrichshain fell in the Soviet Sector of Berlin), save that the first attempt to demolish the Flak-tower was made by its garrison on May 2 and the job completed three months later by the Soviets. By the look of it after the big blow, they were somewhat generous with the use of their explosives.

Above: The Soviets had reduced the tower sufficiently in height for the remains to be left in situ. *Below:* Over the next thirty years, as debris was cleared from the demolition of bombed buildings, a 'rubble mountain' was slowly built up around the tower. These two pictures of the so-called Trümmerfrauen (rubble women) were taken in August 1947.

Today, landscaped and planted with trees, Flakturm II is virtually covered over. All that shows is the topmost rim of one of the gun positions (the one on the left of the picture on the opposite page).

Important landmarks not so far illustrated on the East-West-Axis, which was crossed by the Second Guards Tank Army on April 29, include the Schiller Theatre on the corner of Bismarckstrasse and Grolman Strasse, just yards from the vital junction of the Knie. *Left:* It finished the war a burnt-out pock-marked shell, this picture being taken in October 1949 shortly before work began on its restoration. *Right:* It had been rebuilt by 1951.

Charlottenburg

On the morning of April 28, the Second Guards Tank Army joined in from Siemensstadt with the 12th Guards Tank Corps, taking the 79th Corps's route into Moabit to drive towards the Knie (Ernst-Reuter-Platz), while the 1st Mechanised Corps attacked the river locks and Jungfernheide S-Bahn Station just north of Schloss Charlottenburg. The latter corps had no success that day, but next day broke through at both points and fought its way through the Schloss gardens and the palace itself with infantry, while the tanks negotiated the remains of the Schlossbrücke. The corps then headed due south with two brigades to the Lietzensee Lake, from where they turned east to clear the area either side of Bismarckstrasse and Kantstrasse (from which the 55th Guards Tank Brigade had since withdrawn), while the third brigade headed down Berliner Strasse (Otto-Suhr-Allee) for the Knie.

However, this army, mainly equipped with American Sherman tanks, had suffered such severe casualties among its supporting infantry that on the evening of April 29 they were obliged to call for reinforcements. The Soviets had none of their own left to offer so it was decided to call in the 1st Polish Infantry Division from the First Polish Army on the northern flank near Oranienburg. It took all day to move the division to its new location, which meant that the Poles could not take up their new rôle until early on May 1, when they were horrified to discover that the Soviet infantry units they were nominally supporting, had lost up to 95 per cent of their effective strength, and that one tank brigade was down to 15 tanks, having already lost 82 since the operation began, mostly within the city.

The Polish Divisional Commander, General Wojciech Bewziuk, split his forces into three groups in support of the component brigades of the Second Guards Tank Army, and although nominally subordinate, it was in fact the Poles who led the fighting in this sector from now on.

Three principal actions occurred, involving the defences at Karl-August-

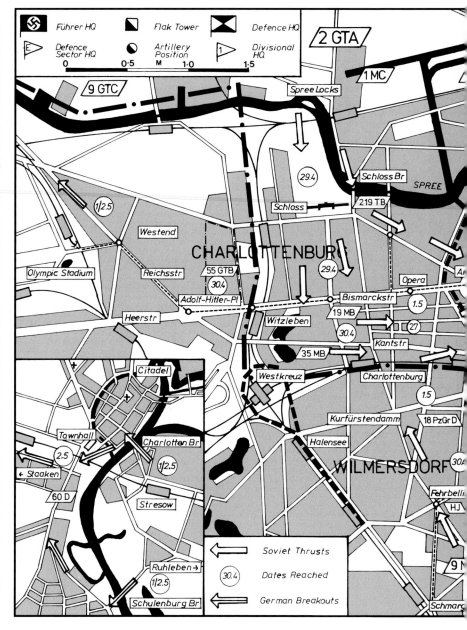

April 29 saw the Second Guards Tank Army fight its way across the Spree and into Charlottenburg, while Chuikov launched a major attack across the Landwehr Canal towards the Reichs Chancellery. This map also shows the break-out routes used by the defence on the night of May 1/2 from the Reichs Chancellery and Mitte over the

Left: **A little further to the west lay the German Opera House (not to be confused with the State Opera on Unter den Linden).** *Right:* **Burned out during the bombing and subsequent battle, the Charlottenburg opera was rebuilt as the Deutsche Oper in**

1961, retaining some parts of the original 1912 structure. The windowless frontage is designed to keep out the noise of traffic and the abstract sculptures are known as the 'Seed-Cake' and 'Schashkik' respectively by Berliners.

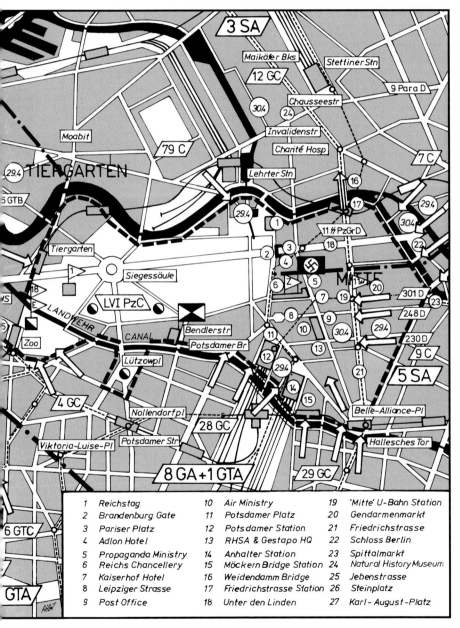

1	Reichstag	10	Air Ministry	19	'Mitte' U-Bahn Station
2	Brandenburg Gate	11	Potsdamer Platz	20	Gendarmenmarkt
3	Pariser Platz	12	Potsdamer Station	21	Friedrichstrasse
4	Adlon Hotel	13	RHSA & Gestapo HQ	22	Schloss Berlin
5	Propaganda Ministry	14	Anhalter Station	23	Spittalmarkt
6	Reichs Chancellery	15	Möckern Bridge Station	24	Natural History Museum
7	Kaiserhof Hotel	16	Weidendamm Bridge	25	Jebenstrasse
8	Leipziger Strasse	17	Friedrichstrasse Station	26	Steinplatz
9	Post Office	18	Unter den Linden	27	Karl-August-Platz

Weidendamm Bridge, and from the Zoo position on foot up the U-Bahn tunnels towards Ruhleben, while the remaining armour and vehicles made a clean run up Kantstrasse to join them in the break-out over the Spandau bridges (see insert). In the end, very few German troops were to evade either death or capture by the Soviets.

Platz, where the 55th Guards Tank Brigade had been engaged two days previously in their Kantstrasse probe, and the assaults on the Technical High School (Technical University) and the 'Tiergarten' S-Bahn Station. That on the Technical High School involved a frontal assualt across the very spot where Hitler had taken the salute at the parade in honour of his 50th birthday. This assault was supported by the fire of artillery pieces dismantled and placed in the upper storeys of the sole surviving building opposite. However, success was not achieved until the divisional reconnaissance company made a flanking attack across Hardenberg-strasse.

The assault on the 'Tiergarten' S-Bahn Station was the final action by the Poles and enabled them to push forwards and raise their national flag in triumph on the Victory Column.

The 55th Guards Tank Brigade was now back in its blocking position in Westend, the inter-Front boundary, as previously mentioned, having been re-drawn to keep the Third Guards Tank Army south of the railway embankment from Savignyplatz to Westkreuz and then west of the Witzleben cutting. However, the brigade was inadequate in size to prevent determined troops breaking through westwards to Ruhleben and seems to have gone to ground in the barracks and tram sheds off Königin-Elisabeth-Strasse, thus leaving the German defenders of the Ruhleben/ Olympic Stadium/Havel bridges area undisturbed except for artillery and air attack until the end of the battle.

Under these conditions, when General Weidling was eventually able to authorise a breakout on the night of May 1/2 before surrendering the Berlin garrison, it is hardly surprising that vast numbers were able to escape on foot through the U-Bahn tunnels, right under the centre of the 1st Mechanised Corps' area, and that the remaining armour and vehicles were able to drive out through Kantstrasse unscathed. The latter route was also taken by those being squeezed out of Third Guards Tank Army's area around the Kurfür-stendamm.

The fiercest fighting broke out in the city's centre on April 29. The Town Hall was assaulted by the 1008th Rifle Regiment (commander Colonel V. N. Borisov) and the 1010th Regiment (commander Colonel M. F. Zagorodsky) of the 266th Rifle Division.

Captain N. V. Bobylev's battalion was set the mission of breaking through to the Town Hall and capturing it jointly with Major M. A. Alexeyev's battalion supported by tanks and self-propelled artillery. Our men were met by such a strong avalanche of fire that further advance along the street was simply impossible.

It was decided then to break into the Town Hall through the walls by breaching them with explosives. Under enemy fire, the sappers blew in the walls one by one. The smoke had not had time to disperse before assault groups rushed through the breaches and cleared the building adjacent to the Town Hall from the enemy after hand-to-hand fighting.

Tanks and self-propelled guns were committed to battle. Firing a few shots they smashed the heavy wrought-iron gates of the Town Hall, breaching the walls while setting up a smokescreen. The whole building was engulfed in thick smoke.

Lieutenant K. Madenov's platoon was the first to break in. Privates N. P. Kondrashev, K. Ye. Kryutchenko, I. F. Kashpurovsky and others acted bravely together with the daring lieutenant. They used hand-grenades to clear the lobby and halls. Every room was fought for.

Komsomol organiser of the 1008th Rifle Regiment's 1st Battalion, Junior Lieutenant K. G. Gromov, climbed up on the roof and, having thrown down the Nazi flag on the pavement, hoisted the Red Banner. Konstantin Gromov was granted the title of Hero of the Soviet Union for heroism and courage displayed in these battles.

MARSHAL G. ZHUKOV, 1974

Left: The battle for the town hall absorbed two regiments of infantry plus supporting armour: this view of the shattered Rotes Rathaus being taken in 1947. *Right:* Our comparison is from Jüdenstrasse, virtually from the site of No. 51 which had been Horst Wessel's boyhood home. It, too, had been turned into a shrine in 1933 emblazoned with the inscription: 'In this house lived Horst and Werner Wessel who fought for Germany's honour and freedom.' Today all the old buildings have gone, replaced by the massive eastern extension of the Leipziger Strasse (called Grunerstrasse at this point).

The ruins of the Molkenmarkt area of central Berlin. A temporary bridge spans the Spree on the site of the Mühlendamm Bridge.

The Central Area

The hard core of the defence, the central sector known as 'Zitadelle', was within the area bounded by the Spree and the Landwehr Canal with external bastions as far as Alexanderplatz in the east and the Knie in the west. This contained the government quarter, including Hitler's bunker, the Reichstag and the Defence Headquarters at Bendlerstrasse (now Stauffenbergstrasse), and was commanded by SS-Brigadeführer Wilhelm Mohnke, who had the equivalent of half a division of Waffen and Allgemeine SS under his direct command.

In the city centre the area of mainly public buildings backing on to the Spree within the Alexanderplatz S-Bahn loop was the scene of intense house-to-house fighting. The town hall (Rotes Rathaus) for instance, was attacked on April 29 by two regiments of infantry supported by tanks and self-propelled guns, and was eventually only penetrated after holes had been blasted through from adjacent buildings.

The previous day, while the 26th Guards Corps were still engaged east of the river, the 32nd Corps, who themselves had pockets of resistance still holding out in their rear, launched an attack across the Spree on to the central island. Marshal Zhukov described this as one of their most difficult operations of the war. They were assisted by the boats of the Dnieper River Flotilla and barges taken from the Osthafen upstream. The 9th Corps, swinging round through Kreuzberg, cleared the Spittelmarkt area, which had already been pulverised by artillery, and started pushing westwards down Leipziger Strasse with one division on either side, and the third operating parallel further south along the line of Kochstrasse.

Opposing them, the defence was centred on SS-Brigadeführer Krukenberg's 11th SS 'Nordland' Panzergrenadier-Division, its basic Danish and Norwegian regiments reinforced by French volunteers. Krukenberg's command post was in a railway carriage in the Stadtmitte U-Bahn Station under the junction of Friedrichstrasse and Leipziger Strasse (see page 250). Among the miscellany of army, navy, air force, Reichsarbeitsdienst and Volkssturm units now concentrated in the eastern end of 'Zitadelle', was the 15. lettischen (Latvian) Fusilier-Bataillon defending the Air Ministry building and, closer in around the Reichs Chancellery, were the volunteer SS fanatics under SS-Brigadeführer Mohnke as well as his 'Liebstandarte Adolf Hitler' veterans. Of particular value to the defence were some 'Tigers' of the schwere Panzer Abteilung 503.

The pressure on 'Zitadelle' from north and south became even more acute on April 29 when Chuikov's combined Eighth Guards and First Guards Tank Armies attacked across the Landwehr Canal between the Potsdamer Bridge and the Hallesches Tor, as described below.

As could be expected, the fighting in this area was particularly bitter. The converging Soviet lines were now too close for ground-attack aircraft to be used, but there was no lack of artillery to hammer away at this last bastion as May Day approached.

At first glance, this Tass agency picture, printed exactly as received, conveys all the immediacy of the final assault on the city centre. However, seeing is not always believing. We recognised the statue as the central part of the monument to Wilhelm I erected beside the Schloss in 1897. The pedestal is (or rather was) over 60 ft high topped with a colossal 30 ft equestrian figure of the Emperor attired in a field cloak being led by a graceful figure symbolising Peace. However, something was wrong. First, the picture has been reversed — a subterfuge often adopted by picture editors as running figures always look more dramatic if they are moving from left to right. But, if the picture *is* turned the right way round (you can check this in a mirror), the Dom in the background cannot possibly appear from this angle!

Left: To prove the point, this shot was taken by a French Army photographer soon after the quadripartite occupation began. A Soviet traffic policewoman stands on the left. The angle of the statue is approximately that of the Tass picture, but no cathedral for it lies right on the opposite side of the Lustgarten; proving that the photo has been made up as a composite in the studio! *Right:* Present-day comparison: Kaiser Wilhelm was another casualty of the communist order although the base with its steps still remains. In the background the former GDR Foreign Ministry.

Above: **The ruins of the Schloss pictured from outside the burning shops in Brüderstrasse. As we have already seen in Part I, the palace was demolished after the war so one now looks out across open ground** *(right)* **now used for parking towards the Altes (Old) Museum at the rear of the Lustgarten.** *Below left:* **One is not suggesting that the desperate German defenders in the area used these trophies from the First World War to try to resist the Soviet attack, but no doubt the Russians still shot them up for good measure. Between the square, where several guns and tanks were displayed, and the Zeughaus (in the background on the right) is the stone-lined channel of the Kupfergraben Canal with the Krönprinzen Palais visible beyond the Schloss Bridge.** *Below right:* **The former GDR Foreign Ministry now fills the little park next to the Kronprinzen Palais.**

With the third of the three massive Flak-towers — the one at the Zoo — also holding out while the battle surged all around it, this picture of the Tiergarten 'under attack' is appropriate at this point in our story. However, it was taken on January 20, 1947 and it actually shows the demolition process under way in the British Sector. Flakturm I can be seen on the left.

At the western end of 'Zitadelle' the Zoo Flak-tower defences were under attack across Budapester Strasse from the evening of April 27. Like its sister towers at Humboldthain and Friedrichshain, each Flak-tower had a garrison of one hundred, mainly schoolboys under experienced Luftwaffe officers and

Its associated radar control tower was even more important at this late stage in the battle, as it was serving as a communications centre linking the Führerbunker under the Chancellery garden with the outside world. Smaller than the gun tower, it was successfully blown up *(right)* by the Royal Engineers on June 28, 1947. The method used was to detonate a large 'concussion' charge of ammonal inside after all the entrances and windows had been sealed, thereby allowing a pressure wave to build-up within the structure to burst the building.

Having achieved success with the radar tower, the REs turned their attention to the nearby gun tower. However, further supplies of British ammonal were not available in sufficient quantities, and TNT had to be used instead. Although over 20 tons were employed, the concussive effect of the weaker explosive failed to shatter the building and it emerged from the smoke, to all outward appearances, unscathed. However, it had been badly damaged internally, so badly in fact that it was no longer possible to seal all the openings for a second attempt. It was therefore decided to try an experimental blow on the north-west corner, the one furthest from the railway line, using Beehive charges placed both inside and outside in an endeavour to 'fold' the wall outwards. These charges were fired on September 27 *(above)*.

Left: **The Press and the BBC misinterpreted the experimental nature of the blow and, when the tower emerged unscathed from the smoke, announcements were made that gave the** impression of another Sapper failure. *Right:* **We found the self-same vantage point overlooking the Zoologischer-Garten S-Bahn Station on the fifth floor of the office at Jebenstrasse 1.**

Although the tower had been badly cracked at third floor level, at least the experiment had proved that it was not possible to create the outward 'turning' effect to collapse the wall as had been hoped. Meanwhile some wag had breached security and painted 'Made in Germany' on the bunker. Rising to the bait, the REs were determined to make a good job of it next time. They brought in the very first type of thermic lance, in which oxygen is forced under pressure through a pipe filled with steel wire to produce a white-hot flame capable of melting concrete. Using this method, some 435 holes were bored through the 8-foot walls and plugged with explosives. Further demolition charges were placed against internal walls, pillars and staircases. This time there was no mistake and, after four months preparation, the button was pressed at noon on July 30, 1948.

NCOs, and mounted an eight-gun battery of 128mm anti-aircraft guns and twelve multi-barrelled 'pom-poms.'

The massive structure proved impervious to Soviet shellfire, although many of the young gunners were killed by shrapnel while serving their guns, whose elevation and range enabled them to provide support as far afield as Gatow, which being a Luftwaffe base naturally received priority. The Zoo bunker continued to hold out as a hard core of resistance against the left wing of Chuikov's combined First Guards Tank and Eighth Guards Armies, while the Third Guards Tank Army converged on the Kurfürstendamm and Savignyplatz S-Bahn Station from the south, and the Second Guards Tank Army and the 1st Polish Infantry Division closed in from the west and north.

The ruin remained until 1955 when it was decided to clear the site completely, partly because the foundations were in the way of an extension required to the U-Bahn.

223

Above: The shattered Elephant Gate to the Zoo, itself almost totally destroyed, bears witness to the intensity of the fighting, as the 4th Guards Corps sought to take the Flak-tower. *Right:* Dumb friends suffered alongside Homo sapiens. Pongo, the gorilla, was killed, his grave not being rediscovered until November 1952.

On the right flank, armour was also closing on the 'Zitadelle'. This cine shot shows self-propelled guns thundering through Mariannenplatz. This church also suffered greatly during the war and the ruin was still undergoing reconstruction work in 1992 when Jan Heitmann took the comparison. Jan comments that 'The street on the left was once divided by the Wall. Today this area and the former death strip is occupied by so-called "autonomous" young people who are living in caravans and self-built wooden huts. The many burnt-out cars which litter the area are the evidence of today's street fighting!'

By evening on April 26, the 34th Heavy Tank Regiment *(left)* had negotiated the Yorckstrasse complex of railway tracks and closed up to the line of the Landwehr Canal, preparatory to their assault on the Tiergarten on the 29th. *Right:* Dr Peter Schenk sent us his comparison with St Bonifatius Church in the background, this picture being of particular interest to him as the tanks are passing his own front door!

The Landwehr Canal

Colonel-General Chuikov launched his assault across the Landwehr Canal on April 29 with his combined Eighth Guards and First Guards Tank Armies. This was a unique situation with everyone converging on a central point: the 79th Corps was attacking across the Spree to the Reichstag in the north, while the Third and Fifth Shock Armies were closing in from the right. Consequently Chuikov's operational area was limited to the East-West-Axis in the north and Wilhelmstrasse in the east, and the overall combat area was now so narrow that air support could no longer be used.

While one corps engaged the enemy concentration based on the Zoo Flaktower and sealed off the bridgehead at Lützowplatz, Chuikov concentrated his attack on a fairly limited stretch of the canal, less than two kilometres long, pushing his armour across on both flanks, where the bridges on Potsdamer Strasse and at the Hallesches Tor were still intact or traversable with engineer assistance.

In planning the attack he realised how difficult it was to command such an operation with no overseeing observation post in the confusing ruins of this heavily built-up area, so he turned to the Party apparatus, ensuring that there

Post-war evidence of the SS demolition below the bunker-like sluice gates control chamber for the S-Bahn tunnel on the Hallesches Ufer of the Landwehr Canal east of the Schöneberger Bridge. According to Rittmeister Gerhard Boldt, the canal was blown on the orders of Hitler as a result of reports of the Russians using the tunnels to infiltrate German lines. Suction pumps have been inserted into the hole caused by the demolition to remove the water in the tunnel below.

Left: The Schöneberger Bridge (in the left background of the top picture) which lies between the Anhalter and Potsdamer Bridges, being rebuilt in 1947. Right: After the war, the canal harbour at this spot was infilled with rubble from the ruins.

225

The Anhalter underground S-Bahn Station flooded to platform level as a result of the SS handiwork. The S-Bahn tunnel leading to the Unter den Linden held four trains full of wounded. Although rumours persist that many people died as a result of this flooding, contemporary evidence indicates that only those below carriage/platform level could have been affected by the water, some perhaps from the panic to escape the flooding. The official railway appreciation of the proposal to flood the tunnels before the SS put it into effect was that the sandy base would restrict the flooding level to about one metre.

was an even distribution of Party and Komsomol members among the units to ensure that his orders were carried out.

Shortly before the opening barrage was due to commence, Colour Sergeant Nikolai Masalov of the 220th Guards Rifle Regiment won undying fame by crossing the canal to rescue a child he could hear crying besides its dead mother. [The statue, depicting him holding the child in his arms as he symbolically smashes a swastika with a sword, now forms the focal point of the Soviet cemetery in Treptow Park.]

The Soviets managed to take the mined Potsdamer Bridge by means of a trick. By this stage of the battle they had learned to protect their tanks against Panzerfausts by covering them with sandbags, spring mattresses, and the like, to cause these missiles to explode before they could penetrate the armour. By soaking these additives with inflammable liquid and then bursting into flames as it crossed the bridge, one of their tanks was able to get behind the enemy forward positions unscathed and turn against them.

Chuikov left the actual means of crossing the canal to the local commanders to decide, so tunnels, a ruined footbridge, swimming, improvised boats, floats and rafts were all used to get the men across. Direct artillery fire was relatively ineffective as the German were in enfilade positions, so he 'used a wedge to knock out a wedge' technique as he described it, using the curves of the canal to fire obliquely into the defences opposite.

Nevertheless, it was no easy operation and, despite the short distances involved, it was not until May 1 that the 79th Guards Division reached Potsdamer Platz after taking the railway station and then had a bitter struggle for the U-Bahn station there.

The scene in the S-Bahn tunnel as depicted by Soviet producer/director Yuri Ozerov in his film series *Liberation: The Battle for Berlin*.

> *The new command post is in the S-Bahn tunnels under Anhalter railway station. The station looks like an armed camp. Women and children huddle in niches, some sitting on folding chairs, listening to the sounds of the battle. Shells hit the roof, cement crumbles from the ceiling. Smells of powder and smoke in the tunnels. S-Bahn hospital trains trundle slowly by.*
>
> *Suddenly a surprise. Water splashes into our command post. Shrieks, cries and curses. People are struggling around the ladders leading up the ventilation shafts to the street above. Gurgling water floods through the tunnels, The crowds are panicky, pushing though the rising water, leaving children and wounded behind. People are being trampled underfoot, the water covering them. It rises a metre or more, then slowly runs away. The panic lasts for hours. Many drowned. Reason: on somebody's orders, engineers have blown up the safety bulkhead control chamber on the Landwehr Canal between the Schöneberger and Möckern Bridges to flood the tunnels against the Russians. The whole time heavy fighting continues above ground.*
>
> *Late afternoon command post moved to Potsdamer Platz station first level, the lower tunnel being flooded. Direct hit through the roof. Heavy losses among wounded and civilians. Smoke drifts through the hole. Outside stocks of Panzerfausts explode under heavy Russian fire. Terrible sight at the station entrance, one flight of stairs down where a heavy shell has penetrated and people, soldiers, women and children are literally stuck to the walls. At dusk a short pause in the firing.*

'MÜNCHEBERG' PANZER DIVISION DIARY

Soviet film-makers in action — then and now. *Right:* Yuri Ozerov's project to depict the Great Patriotic War in colour has spanned 25 years. Under the Russian title *Osvobozhdenie*, the series comprises separate films dealing with Soviet military achievements from the German invasion in June 1941 through to the storming of the Reichstag in April 1945. *The Flaming Bulge* and *The Breakthrough* which dealt with the Battle of Kursk were both released in 1971; *The Direction of the Main Blow* in 1971, *The Battle for Berlin* and *The Last Storm* in 1972. *Soldiers of Freedom* came out in 1977, *The Battle for Moscow* in 1985, and *Stalingrad* four years later. Although the films were not made in chronological order, to date the series runs to 24 hours overall. Both Marshal Zhukov and Marshal Koniev assisted Ozerov with technical advice and took an active interest in casting their screen counterparts. In this still from *The Battle for Berlin*, German and Soviet infantry battle it out in the tunnels.

The battle in reality. More shots from Soviet cameramen in 1945. The diarist of the 'Müncheberg' Panzer Division described those last hours in Berlin: 'Continuous attacks throughout the night. The Russians are trying to break through in Leipziger Strasse. Prinz-Albrecht-Strasse has been retaken, as has Köthener Strasse. Increasing signs of disintegration and despair, but it makes no sense surrendering at the last moment and then spending the rest of your life regretting not having held on to the end. Hardly any communications among the combat groups, inasmuch as none of the active battalions have radio communications any more. Telephone cables are shot through in no time at all. Physical conditions are indescribable. No relief or respite, no regular food and hardly any bread.

Nervous breakdowns from the continuous artillery fire. The not-too-seriously wounded are hardly taken in anywhere, the civilians being afraid to accept wounded soldiers and officers into their cellars when so many are being hanged as real or presumed deserters and the occupants of the cellars concerned being ruthlessly turfed out as accomplices by the members of the flying courts-martial. These flying courts-martial appear particularly often in our sector today. Most of them are very young SS officers with hardly a decoration between them, blind and fanatical. Hope of relief and fear of the courts-martial keep our men going.' *Above:* Victim of friend ... or foe? A Reichsarbeitsdienst labour corpsman lies in the dirt, his battle over. *Below:* A wounded Russian tanker is given first aid.

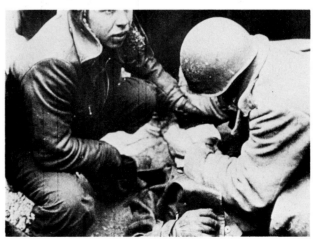

Potsdamer Platz: once the heart and soul of commercial life in Berlin. *Above left:* Looking from Leipziger Platz towards the Columbushaus on the corner of Hermann-Göring-Strasse. The

S-Bahn entrances were either side of the twin Grecian-like temples. *Above right:* The scene before the final battle started. Tank barricades attempt to seal off Leipziger Strasse.

After the battle. Taken nearer the station forecourt, a King Tiger stands disabled. The contemporary diary of the 'Müncheberg' Division continues the story: 'Potsdamer Platz is a ruined waste. Masses of wrecked vehicles and shot-up ambulances with the wounded still inside them. Dead everywhere, many of them frightfully mangled by tanks and trucks. Violent shelling of the city centre at dusk with simultaneous attacks on our positions. We cannot hold on to Potsdamer Platz any longer and at about 0400 hours make for Nollendorfplatz as Russians heading for Potsdamer Platz pass us in the parallel tunnel.'

The barren wasteland of Potsdamer Platz in 1991. The road is new, having been cut through when the Wall was demolished.

An entrance (formerly sealed) to the S-Bahn can be seen fenced off near the corner of Hermann-Göring-Strasse.

All the buildings on Potsdamer Platz (and the adjoining Leipziger Platz) were demolished by the East Berlin authorities in the 1960s and '70s as a security measure to create a free fire zone when the city was divided by the Wall. *Above:* Fortunately, however, part of one block with a characteristic dome survives, appropriately linking past with present.

Above: Looking straight across at the main railway station. *Left:* Both the S-Bahn and U-Bahn station entrances in the former death strip had to be sealed up to prevent potential escapers jumping trains as the lines still operated between East and West. *Right:* This is the former 'Müncheberg' Division command post described on page 226.

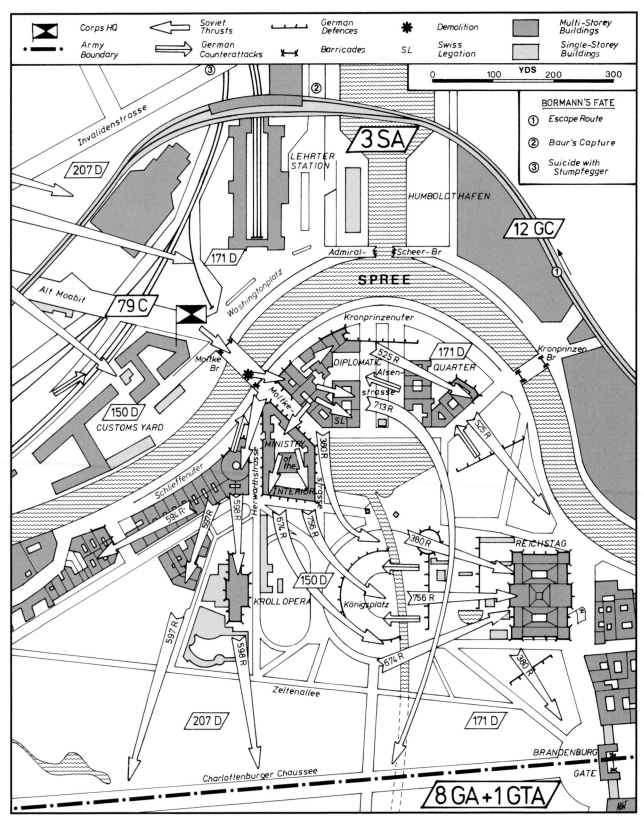

Legend

Corps HQ	
Army Boundary	
Soviet Thrusts	
German Counterattacks	
German Defences	
Barricades	
Demolition	
SL	Swiss Legation
Multi-Storey Buildings	
Single-Storey Buildings	

BORMANN'S FATE
1. Escape Route
2. Baur's Capture
3. Suicide with Stumpfegger

Map labels: Invalidenstrasse, 207 D, LEHRTER STATION, 3 SA, HUMBOLDTHAFEN, 12 GC, 171 D, Washingtonplatz, Admiral- Scheer-Br, SPREE, Alt Moabit, 79 C, Kronprinzenufer, 525 R, 171 D QUARTER, Kronprinzen Br, Moltke Br, DIPLOMATIC, Alsen-strasse, 713 R, 150 D, CUSTOMS YARD, SL, Moltke-strasse, 380 R, 525 R, MINISTRY of the INTERIOR, Schlieffenufer, 594 R, 597 R, 598 R, Herwarthstrasse, 674 R, 756 R, 380 R, REICHSTAG, 597 R, 598 R, KROLL OPERA, 150 D, Königsplatz, 756 R, 674 R, 380 R, Zeltenallee, 207 D, 171 D, BRANDENBURG GATE, Charlottenburger Chaussee, 8 GA + 1 GTA

The battle for the Reichstag was like a play within a play, for it was fought within an area barely 700 metres square in virtual isolation from what was going on around it. A special feature of this battlefield was the centrally located abandoned worksite for Albert Speer's Volkshalle, with its flooded tunnel. The 79th Corps attacked across the Moltke Bridge at about midnight on April 28 and by daybreak the remains of the leading two divisions were safely installed in the western segment of the Diplomatic Quarter. At 0700 hours the 150th Division then attacked across Moltkestrasse and started a bitter fight, room by room, for the Ministry of the Interior opposite. When they finished clearing this building at 0400 hours next morning, they were promptly ordered to attack the Reichstag, but then came under fire from the Kroll Opera behind them as soon as they emerged into the open. The 207th Division then had to be brought out of reserve to clear the Schlieffenufer and Kroll Opera areas, which took until 1130 hours, during which time the Soviets were able to bring tanks and artillery across the partially blown bridge to support their next attack. Frontal attacks at 1130 and 1300 failed for various reasons, so it was decided to wait until nightfall to continue, during which time the 171st Division on the left flank managed to take the eastern segment of the Diplomatic Quarter, to provide enfilade fire for the final assault at 1800 hours.

The Reichstag

Soviet attention was now, however, focused on the northern edge of 'Zitadelle', where a reconnaissance group of the 79th Corps advancing through Moabit on April 28 had first spotted the Reichstag through the smoky murk that overhung the city.

The focal point for the whole Soviet operation was the Reichstag itself, to them the symbolic, if not the actual, seat of German power and might. As a military goal it also made sense as an

The last battle. Having forced the Germans back over 1,000 miles from the gates of Moscow, the Red Army now had barely 1,000 yards to go to fulfil their final task. The journey had taken them four years, but there were now less than four days left before the dawning of May Day. General Perevertkin set up his command post in the customs building just this side of the Moltke Bridge.

easily identifiable building, standing apart from the mass of the built-up area behind it.

However the whole area had by now been turned into a vast construction site in accordance with Albert Speer's grandiose scheme for the building of the

Great Hall. The Victory Column had been removed in 1937 but by 1945 this project had long since given way to other priorities, and ground water had flooded the enormous foundation pit excavated for the entrance to the Great Hall and the cutting for an S-Bahn

The other bridge — the Krönprinzen Brücke — in the background of the top picture did not feature in the assault. It had been barricaded at both ends and was no doubt considered to be too close and under direct fire from the Reichstag. *Left:* This picture from German sources is described as being taken some

time during the fighting for the Reichstag. The Russians are on the far bank with the Reichstag behind the photographer. *Right:* The bridge was dismantled after the war by the East Germans as part of their severance of the Western Sectors from the rest of the city and its hinterland.

Left: In happier days, this would have been General Perevert-kin's view of the Reichstag down Moltkestrasse looking from his CP. Part of one of the dragons adorning the bridge can be seen intruding into the picture on the right. His plan was to send across two battalions of the 79th Corps under cover of darkness to capture the corner house. Although the Germans tried to demolish the bridge, the explosion only blew a piece out of one of the spans, leaving the other half of the roadway still passable. By 0200 hours on the morning of Sunday, April 29, the building had been taken. Reinforcements from the 150th Infantry Division were brought across, and at 0700 they emerged from the adjacent doorways to attack the Ministry of the Interior directly opposite. *Right:* Rush-hour traffic 1990 — the advance across the bridge continues.

tunnel leading into the site from the Tiergarten just to the south. These two flooded features (which the Soviets thought were anti-tank ditches) were to form significant obstacles to the course of battle.

The taking of the Reichstag turned out to be a battle within a battle, a play within a play, set on a stage barely 700 metres square. The battleground was limited to the area south of the Spree river as far as the East-West-Axis, here known as the Charlottenburger Chaussee, running up to the Brandenburg Gate. The Tiergarten on the other side of the road belonged to Chuikov's forces. The converging Soviet forces were now too close to allow air support, but there was no lack of artillery fire smashing into this last bastion of the German defence from every direction.

In order to get his troops over the Spree, General S. N. Perevertkin had no choice but to use the Moltke Bridge, which was barricaded, mined and covered by defensive positions in depth as the river's stone-covered embankments were too high and steep to attempt a crossing elsewhere.

His overriding instructions were to capture the Reichstag by May 1, and so provide a victorious theme for the public holiday celebrations.

Under cover of darkness the corps's artillery was brought forward to the very edge of the Spree to fire over open sights at the enemy positions across the river.

The bridge was stormed at about midnight, the assault being led by one battalion each from the two leading divisions. Despite the daunting fire provided by the Soviet artillery, the Germans were able to sweep the bridge with cross-fire from their well enfiladed positions on the southern bank. They mounted counter-attacks on either side of the river and also blew the previously set demolition charges on the bridge. However, the counter-attacks were driven back and the bridge proved stronger than expected, for only half of one of the three spans over the water collapsed, leaving just sufficient room for vehicles to pass.

By 0200 hours the survivors of the leading battalions had secured their first objective, the corner house of the diplomatic quarter. They then began expanding outwards by the usual technique of mouseholing from house to house and floor to floor. Behind them reinforcements were rushed across the bridge, pouring into the corner house at such a rate that by daybreak the whole of the first echelons of the two leading divisions were inside.

While the 150th Division concentrated on securing the buildings facing the Ministry of the Interior across Moltkestrasse, the 171st Division covered their rear by working through the buildings along the embankment and through the centre of the block. Meanwhile the corps engineers worked desperately under a hail of fire to clear a way across the bridge for the supporting armour.

Left: The Ministry of the Interior, pristine in 1935. Ten years later it became the focus of much bloodshed when the 150th Infantry battled from room to room and from floor to floor, losing half their strength in the process. It was not finally cleared until 0400 hours on Monday morning after 21 hours of bitter and bloody hand-to-hand fighting. *Right:* After standing empty for over 40 years, the site was earmarked by the Federal Republic in 1987 (Berlin's 750th anniversary) for the German Historical Museum, but the unification of Germany has brought a change in plans and the future of this historic spot is uncertain.

At 0700 hours, following a ten minute bombardment, the 150th Division attacked the Interior Ministry across the street. Fighting rapidly spread up the main staircase and along the various floors in a savage hand-to-hand struggle, in which possession of every room was bitterly contested. Fires broke out creating clouds of choking smoke and the SS defenders put up such a stiff fight that eventually the divisional reserve regiment had to be called in.

It was not until 0400 hours the following morning (April 30) — 21 hours later — that the 150th Division was able to report the building clear of enemy. During this time it had lost a quarter of its strength.

With only twenty hours left in which to get the Red Flag flying atop the Reichstag, time was pressing. Orders were given for the assault on that building to commence within half an hour, allowing no time for rest, preparation or reconnaissance.

The Soviet artillery had failed to subdue the defence, and as the remains of the 150th Division left the cover of the building it had just cleared, the

There were now less than 20 hours left to fulfil Stalin's command: to raise the Red Flag over the Reichstag by May Day. However, the troops were now coming under fire from three directions: the Reichstag in front; the Krolloper from behind, and from the Flak guns on top of the Zoo tower. General Perevertkin therefore called up guns, rocket-launchers and tanks to reinforce the men on the ground. *Above:* The shattered corner of the Ministry building — which the Russians called 'Himmler's House' — can be seen on the left as the armour debouches from the bridge.

With their backs to the Krolloper (see pages 56-58), artillery engages the Reichstag over open sights.

exhausted troops came under such a deadly hail of fire that the attack quickly fizzled out. Not only had this fire come from ahead as they swung round to face the Reichstag but also from the rear. Unknown to them, the Germans had heavily fortified the ruins of the Kroll Opera House facing the Reichstag across Königsplatz, and had placed light artillery and machine guns high up in the building to dominate the open ground.

It was now clear that until the Opera House had been secured there would be little chance of the attack succeeding. The Reserve Division was hastily brought across the river to deal with this problem, but first had to clear the buildings on the river bank in order to get at their objective.

This delay also enabled the Soviets to bring forward more guns, rocket-launchers and tanks to reinforce the main assault force. Some ninety guns,

including tanks, were brought across the river and several guns and rocket-launchers were manhandled into the upper stories of the Ministry of the Interior.

The main attack was resumed at 1130 hours after the usual heavy artillery bombardment, and this time the infantry reached as far as the flooded cutting forming an anti-tank ditch before being pinned down by the weight of enemy fire.

Only one original building from the entire Diplomatic Quarter survives — the Swiss Legation (see map page 230) — tucked away amidst the trees. Its scars of battle are still evident in the patched stonework. The Reichstag is on the far right.

There is no doubt that these shots are re-enactments as the final assault on the building took place after dark.

With the Flag of Victory unfurled, the colour party advances on the battered building, still bricked up following the 1933 fire.

After the fire, Hitler had had no interest in repairing the Reichstag, which he called 'a trashy old shack', and the interior was left as it was. The Russian shelling had not improved matters, and by the time the building was stormed, the floors were covered with a tangled mass of debris and stonework.

The inside was pitch black, lit only by the flashes of gunfire and grenades. The noise in the empty corridors and landings must have been deafening as the battle reached its climax. This is the Wandelhalle in 1924 and 1945 (see plan page 25) which led to the Octagon with its marble monument to Wilhelm I.

The Germans then mounted several counter-attacks, but all were held and driven back.

The Soviets tried again at 1300 hours, this time using even more artillery for the thirty-minute opening barrage, in which tanks and even infantry using captured Panzerfausts joined in. But when the infantry scrambled to their feet at 1330 hours there was yet another unpleasant surprise awaiting them. This time it was the anti-aircraft artillery firing at them from the Zoo Flak-tower some 3,000 metres away across the Tiergarten.

It was then realised that they would have to await the cover of darkness for the final assault. Meanwhile the 171st Division was able to clear the eastern part of the diplomatic quarter, thus enabling tanks and self-propelled guns to be brought well forward on the flank to provide enfilade fire.

It was 1800 hours before the attack

The close combat boys went into action. Their leader was SS-Obersturmführer Babick, battle commandant of the Reichstag. I was acting as runner between the AA gunners and the SS battle group, a part of the SS 'Nordland' Division. Its headquarters were in the Europahaus near the Anhalter Bahnhof. Babick now waged the kind of war he had always dreamed of. Our two battery commanders, Radloff and Richter, were reduced to taking orders from him. Babick's command post was not in the Reichstag itself but in the cellar of the house on the corner of Dorotheenstrasse and the Hermann-Göring-Strasse, on the side nearer the Spree. There he ruled from an air raid shelter measuring some 250 feet square.

Against the wall stood an old sofa and in front of it a dining table on which a map of the centre of Berlin was spread out. Sitting on the sofa was an elderly naval commander and next to him two petty officers. There were also a few SS men and, of course, SS-Obersturmführer Babick bending over the map. He played the great general and treated everyone present in the dim candle-lit room to great pearls of military wisdom. He kept talking of final victory, cursed all cowards and traitors and left no one in any doubt that he would summarily shoot anyone who abandoned the Führer.

I had no difficulty in reaching this 'battle station' through an underground passage beneath Hermann-Göring-Strasse. As I remember, there was a thick central-heating pipe which presumably ended in the Prussian Landtag. It was my job to carry Babick's orders to my unit. The shelling of the Reichstag never stopped for a moment. During the short periods I spent in Babick's headquarters, I always heard what the latest position was. I was told yet another Russian shock detachment had tried to enter the upper storeys of the Reichstag but had been wiped out. Babick was tremendously proud of his successes. He was hoping for reinforcements. From somewhere or other, sailors had come to Berlin on the night of April 28, led by the very Lieutenant-Commander who was now hanging about the cellar with nothing to say for himself. Babick never moved from his map, plotting the areas from which he expected reinforcements and even the arrival of King Tigers.

Then an SS ensign, aged about nineteen, came to Babick with the report that Undermann and his men had come across some alcohol and that they had got roaring drunk. As a precaution he had brought Undermann along; he was waiting outside. Babick roared out the order: 'Have him shot on the spot.' The ensign clicked his heels and ran out. Seconds later we heard a burst of fire from a sub-machine gun. The boy reappeared and reported: 'Orders carried out.' Babick put him in charge of Undermann's unit.

Our ranks in the Reichstag got thinner and thinner. Part of our battery gradually dispersed, and by the night of April 30, no more than forty to fifty people, soldiers and civilians, were left in the cellar. This remnant was now looking for the safest possible hiding places. There we intended to sit tight until the Russians came. But they kept us waiting for another twenty-four hours.

GERHARD ZILCH, 1965

William, minus his head, still remained to be seen in 1945 in one corner of the Octagon *(left)*, and even by 1951 *(right)*, when the second picture was taken, he had merely lost his balance. The hundreds of Cyrillic inscriptions which covered the walls and pillars mainly gave the names and home towns of the soldiers concerned.

could be resumed, but this time the cover of darkness — earlier than usual with the smoke-filled sky — and with the armour and self-propelled assault artillery providing close support, the infantry was able to break through to the steps of the building.

There they found their way barred by the still intact bricked-up doorways. Fortunately they had two light mortars with them, and by firing them horizontally at point-blank range they were able to blast a hole just large enough for them to pass through one at a time into the main hall.

Vicious hand-to-hand fighting then spread further into the building. The Germans put up a vigorous defence, and the Soviets experienced great difficulty making their way through the unfamiliar surroundings in almost total darkness.

In front of the stone columns of the South Vestibule stood eight magnificent bronze statues of early emperors: Charlemagne by Breuer, Henry I by Brütt, Otho I by Maison, Henry III by Manzel, Frederick Barbarossa by Baumbach, Rudolf of Hapsburg by Vogel, Charles IV by Diez, and Maximilian I by Widemann. These were grand prizes and no doubt soon found their way into some Russian melting pot. *Right:* The empty lobby photographed in 1951.

At last the Victory Banner is raised . . . but, the question is, which is the correct one?

We are told that, in spite of the battle still going on in the building, the banner was carried through to the roof by 10.50 p.m. on April 30 — just 70 minutes before the deadline expired. Naturally it was essential that pictures were available for propaganda purposes, and enthusiastic flag-waving scenes were later photographed on the roof. As the whole building was not in Russian hands until after midday on May 2, possibly the pictures were not taken until Wednesday afternoon.

The final stages of the operation called for the 171st Division to defend the exterior of the building while the 150th finished mopping up inside. That same evening various elements closed up to the Charlottenburger Chaussee to await Eighth Guards Army's arrival from the south.

The fighting had reached as far as the second floor before contact could be established with the rear to report their success. This had to be done by field telephone, as their radios failed to function indoors.

One unusual aspect of the fighting previously mentioned was that for Operation 'Berlin' the Soviets had re-introduced the carrying of regimental and battalion banners into action as a morale-boosting measure. Whether this was a popular assignment for the standard bearers or not, the attacking units were proud to hoist their banners at the entrance to the Reichstag.

Left: **The honour of placing the special official Red Banner No. 5 went to Sergeant Militon Kantaria (holding the flag), supported by Sergeants M. A. Yegorov and K. Samsonov but, as we can see from the street scene down below, the battle must have been over as people are standing around in the open. The photographer has picked a spot on the rear of the building overlooking Hermann-Göring-Strasse to get the Brandenburg** Gate in the background. *Right:* **A day after German re-unification in October 1990, we attempted to duplicate the well-known picture but only then did we discover the precarious-ness of the situation. The Soviet cameraman (stated on one of the pictures in the series as Chaldej) had edged out on a narrow ledge over a 100-foot sheer drop. Regrettably, your Editor felt that, in this case, discretion was the better part of valour!**

However, the Military Council of the parent Third Shock Army had previously prepared a special 'Red Banner No. 5' for the hoisting ceremony on the Reichstag. This special banner was now sent forward under a picked escort of Communist Party and Komsomol members, with instructions to hoist it on the roof of the building without delay. May Day was almost upon them.

When the groups with the special banner arrived within the Reichstag, other assault groups were given the task of diverting the enemy's attention, while the banner party fought its way through to the roof.

Eventually the flag was triumphantly wedged into position on the rear parapet of the building just seventy minutes before the deadline of midnight. The ruined dome above was still manned by German machine-gunners.

The battle was by no means over. Fighting continued in the same ferocious manner within the building for another day and a half. It was not until General Weidling's orders to surrender that the survivors of the Reichstag garrison eventually yielded at 1300 hours on May 2, 1945.

In accomplishing this particular mission, the 79th Corps took some 2,600 prisoners and counted 2,500 enemy dead. Their own casualties have not been published as a separate figure, but the nearby Soviet War Memorial plot significantly contains 2,200 of their dead.

The banner was later adorned with the words: '150th (Idrisk) Rifle Division, Order of Kutuzov (2nd Class)' followed by abbreviation for the '79th Rifle Corps', the 'Third Shock Army', and the '1st Byelorussian Front'. Today it is on display in the Central Museum of the Soviet Armed Forces in Moscow.

Above left: This flag, on the other hand, is definitely false, having been painted on by an artist. The inscription on the KV-85 tank reads: 'Fighting girlfriend'. *Above right:* The ornamental statues which appear in the Kantaria picture can be seen on the rear of the building. *Right:* Stated as being one of the first tanks to reach the Reichstag, another KV-85 commanded by George Garbus. *Below:* Wednesday, May 2. 'Between 4.00 and 5.00 a.m. we heard Russian voices,' recounted Gerhard Zilch to Erich Kuby. 'There were no more shots. Two young Russian soldiers came into our room and called out: "Krieg kaputt! Gitler kaputt!" The next question was: "Du Uri?" [You watch?] Then we were taken to the Debating Chamber where we saw daylight for the first time in five days. The square was full of smashed German guns and dead German soldiers. The Russians pointed to the Swiss Embassy and said: "You, over there." '

Victory! 'How many thoughts swept through our minds in those joyful minutes!' wrote Marshal Zhukov later. 'We recalled the hardest Battle of Moscow where our troops stood firm to the death not letting the enemy reach the capital; Stalingrad in ruins but unvanquished; glorious Leningrad which withstood the fiercest blockade; Sevastopol which fought so valiantly

Every victory has its price, in this case some 2,500 German and 2,200 Red Army soldiers fell in the final battle for the Reichstag. To mark the sacrifice of their troops, the Russians chose the actual battlefield as the location for their first war cemetery in Berlin and, just to rub salt in the wound, they positioned it directly on the old Prussian Siegesallee. Working night and day, within six months the monument had been completed in its enclosure in the British Sector.

against picked Nazi troops; the triumph on the Kursk Bulge, and thousands of destroyed towns and villages and the millions of lives the Soviet people lost, the people who endured and

won . . . And at last the most important moment for which our people suffered immensely had come: the complete defeat of Nazi Germany and the triumph of our just cause.'

This picture was taken in 1991, shortly after the Soviet guard was withdrawn. With the re-unification of Germany, the occupation of the city came to an end, and the safekeeping of the memorial was handed over to the local Berlin authorities.

Now visitors can walk right up to the monument where formerly they were restricted by the barrier on the pavement. The Siegesallee has shrunk to a mere forest path hidden within the woodland of the Tiergarten.

The Führerbunker

Hitler's first air raid shelter had been constructed in 1936 thirty feet below the large hall to the rear of the old Reichs Chancellery. In keeping with the spirit of the times, when Albert Speer built the new Reichs Chancellery he planned the cellars as capable of being also used as air raid shelters. Consequently, as the war progressed it was relatively simple to connect these two installations and link them by tunnels to the shelters of the Foreign Ministry next door and Goebbels's Propaganda Ministry across the street. However, the connecting tunnel from the new Reichs Chancellery, passing under the garden at the rear of the old Reichs Chancellery, was quite shallow and proved vulnerable to shelling in the last days of its use.

As far as the general public was concerned, the only clues that a subterranean warren of tunnels and air raid shelters existed beneath the new Reichs Chancellery were the tops of the emergency exits in Voss-strasse. They can just be seen as dark shadows on the forecourt of the centre section. The vehicle lift lies in deep shadow at the far end. (These particular exits are significant as we shall see a little later on.)

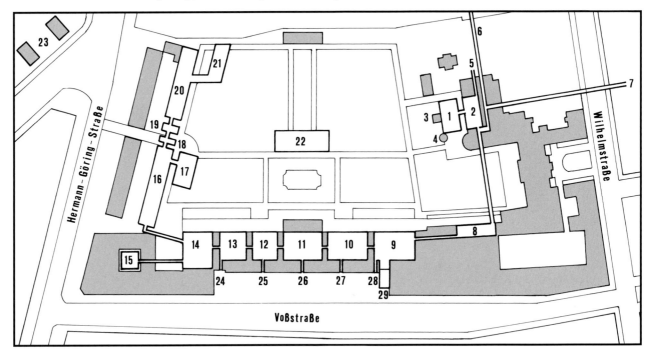

The underground world of the Reichs Chancellery. (1) Führerbunker. (2) Vorbunker. (3) Emergency exit to Chancellery garden. (4) Observation tower. (5) Emergency exit to Foreign Office garden. (6) Tunnel to various ministries. (7) Tunnel to Propaganda Ministry. (8) and (9) Aides and military staff. (10), (12) and (13) Civilian staff. (11) Field hospital. (14) Canteen. (15) and (16) Garage. (17) Accommodation for drivers. (18) and (19) MT offices. (20) Garage. (21) Workshop. (22) Garage. (23) Above-ground bomb-proof garages with fuel reserve. (24) to (28) Emergency exits. (29) Vehicle lift.

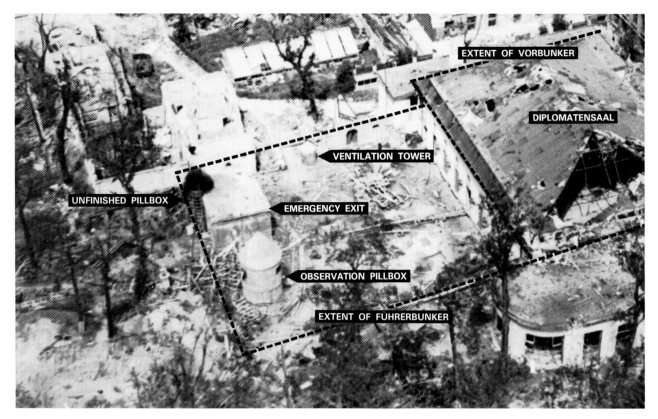

EXTENT OF VORBUNKER

DIPLOMATENSAAL

VENTILATION TOWER

UNFINISHED PILLBOX

EMERGENCY EXIT

OBSERVATION PILLBOX

EXTENT OF FÜHRERBUNKER

In 1935-36, an opportunity was taken to construct a reinforced cellar beneath the new Diplomatensaal (Diplomats' Hall) which was then being erected at the rear of the Reichskanzlerpalais. This shelter measured 25,50m by 21,50m overall, covering an area of 548m² (nearly 6,000 square feet). However, allowing for the 3,30-metre thick walls, the internal usable area was only 208m² (2,230 square feet). The inner walls were 0,50m (18 inches) thick, with a room height of 3,05 metres (10ft). When the RAF attacks increased in severity during the winter of 1943-44, Hitler ordered that a stronger bunker, deeper and with a thicker roof, should be constructed alongside. It was to cover an area of 26 metres by 24,5 metres which would give a slightly larger working area than the old shelter at 312m² (3,350 square feet). As it was to lie at a lower level, an angled stairway was to be constructed linking the 'Vor' (or Front) bunker with the lower 'Führer' bunker. In all, the roof protection to the new bunker would be over 3 metres (10 feet). It is believed that Hitler also ordered that the Führerbunker be overlaid with a buried steel wire mesh and granite slabs supposedly to detonate bombs at surface level.

The cellars under the central section of the new Reichs Chancellery were divided into six main shelters and some smaller ones, the large one under Hitler's study being used on Hitler's instructions as a field hospital for some five to seven hundred wounded military and civilians alike. Linked by the tunnel system under the western end of the Chancellery was a small underground garage for two staff cars and two half-tracks. Then behind the barrack blocks on Hermann-Göring-Strasse there were further underground garages, workshops and drivers' accommodation for the Chancellery motor transport pool, plus another underground garage for ten cars to the north of the ornamental pond in the Chancellery garden, all under the care of Hitler's chauffeur, SS-Obersturmbannführer Erich Kempka. There were also two more garages for another twelve vehicles across the road in the Tiergarten, where Kempka had a secret reserve of petrol.

By 1943 the situation had become sufficiently serious — the hall above had collapsed from bomb damage — for the firm of Hochtief to be called in to reinforce the original air raid shelter and then in 1944 to begin constructing an even deeper and stronger command bunker for the Führer beneath the Chancellery garden that would be, hopefully, proof against the Allies' most powerful penetrating bombs. The working area of the Führerbunker would be some 10 metres (over 30 feet) below ground level with a roof 2.8 metres (9 feet) thick. It had its own emergency exit direct to the garden but was normally entered through the tunnel system via the original shelter, now known as the Vorbunker, from which a concrete staircase descended in right-angle turns to an entry passage leading into the Führerbunker itself.

An emergency exit with a door facing west was provided leading directly to the garden of the new Reichs Chancellery. Five flights of concrete stairs led to a blockhouse-like structure fitted with a recessed, gas-tight, armoured door to protect the stairwell. Work on the new bunker does not appear to have started in the aerial shot on page 139 taken in March 1944, and it was still not finished when captured by the Russians in April 1945 with shuttering and cement mixers still on site.

245

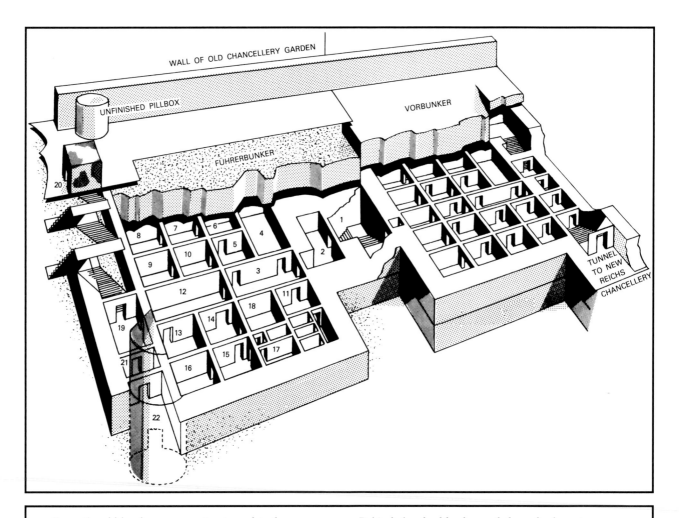

From the old bunker a connecting tunnel to the new was broken through with a staircase [1], which ended in a small chamber [2] with an armoured door. Behind this door began the broad, two-part passageway of the Führerbunker.

In the near half of the passageway [3] stood, on the right wall, cabinets with air raid equipment (gas masks, fire equipment, etc.). A door on this wall led to the machinery room [4] and air-conditioning plant. The second armoured door led into six adjoining rooms. Here was a telephone station [5] operated by an officer of Hitler's bodyguard, a telephone switchboard and a telegraph [6], Dr Morell's room [7], a first-aid station [8], where also there was a bed for Dr Ludwig Stumpfegger, the emergency physician; a sleeping room [9] for Heinz Linge [Hitler's valet] and orderly officers as well as a social room [10].

On the left wall in the first half of the corridor stood a four-cornered table and an armchair. A wall clock hung over the table. Nearby was a telephone station, from which the watch sergeant of the telephone service announced trunk calls to the participants in the situation conferences. A door on the left side led to washrooms [11]. There Hitler's Alsatian Blondi had her place.

An armoured door separated the first part of the passageway from the second, the reception room [12]. At the entrance to the reception section stood an officer of the bodyguard. In the reception section, the participants assembled before the situation conferences and waited for Hitler. On the wall hung large paintings, above all of landscapes. On the right wall stood 12 to 16 armchairs. On the opposite wall was a cushioned bench, in front of which stood a four-cornered table with cushioned chairs. To the right and left of the cushioned bench were two armoured doors. The left led into the rooms of Hitler and Eva Braun, the right into the situation conference room [13].

In front of Hitler's apartment was a little refreshment room [14]. In front of its door stood a screen which blocked the view into the rooms of Hitler and Eva Braun from those in the passageway.

Behind the double door of the refreshment room was Hitler's office [15], laid with a thick, soft carpet. On the table was a bronze lamp, ink stand, telephone, world atlas, and a magnifying glass and usually the eyeglasses of the Führer. Over the table hung one of Menzel's paintings, a half-length portrait of Frederick II in an oval frame. On the opposite wall stood a sofa, and in front of it there was a table and three coloured silk-covered chairs. A still life hung over the sofa. To the right of that stood a tea table, to the left a radio receiver. On the right wall hung a painting by Lucas Cranach.

A door on the same wall led to Hitler's bedroom [16], whose flooring was likewise laid with a carpet. Here was a bed with a night table, a clothes cabinet, a mobile tea table on castors, a safe in which he kept secret papers, book shelves, and oxygen apparatus. To the left in Hitler's office was a door to Hitler and Eva Braun's bathroom [17]. From the bathroom a door led to Eva Braun's toilet and bedroom [18]. Here stood at the right of the door a dark couch, a small round table and an armchair. Opposite the couch on the opposite wall stood Eva Braun's bed, a clothes cabinet, and a box for her dog. On the floor was a dark, fancy-flowered carpet. The walls were decorated with flower paintings. The second door from Eva Braun's room led into the refreshment room.

At the end of the reception section was the so-called 'air lock' [19] with armoured door. In the air lock there were to the right and left emergency exits to the park behind the Reichskanzlei. From the right exit [20] led a winding stairway. A steel staircase, like a fireman's ladder, led to the left emergency exit [21]. This exit likewise was roofed with a dome-shaped tower with machine gun ports, in which was an observation post [22]. SS personnel from the bodyguard manned the watch in this tower. The tower had telephone communication with the Führerbunker.

SOVIET INTERROGATION REPORT,
REICHS CHANCELLERY GROUP

A steel door permanently guarded by two sentries of the Führer-Begleit-Kommando, the personal bodyguard detachment of the Waffen-SS Leibstandarte 'Adolf Hitler' Regiment, led to a narrow central corridor divided by a door halfway along. The first half of this corridor served as a lounge or anteroom, with toilet and washing facilities off to one side, while the second half was used as a reception room. Hitler's suite occupied most of the left-hand side of the bunker, consisting of a conference room, office, bedroom, bathroom-cum-dressing room, with a separate bed-sit for Eva Braun.

On the opposite side of the corridor were two bedrooms, one used by Hitler's physicians of this late time, SS-Standartenführer Ludwig Stumpfegger and Professor Werner Haase, and the other taken over by Goebbels, leading off a room shared by them as an office and surgery. Another room combined an office for Reichsleiter Martin Bormann, Hitler's all-powerful private secretary, with the telephone switchboard operated by SS-Oberscharführer Rochus Misch. Lastly there was the room containing the generator and ventilation plant tended by Johannes Hentschel. This plant also served as a pump for the water supply to the bunker and also the field hospital, the water being drawn from an artesian well below the Führerbunker.

At the far end of the central corridor, beyond the armoured gas lock, was a guardroom and a small passage occupied by other members of the Führer-Begleit-Kommando leading to five steep flights of stairs to the emergency exit. Above ground, the exit was flanked by one complete, and one partially completed, cone-topped observation pillbox which could also double as a secondary emergency exit.

The Vorbunker consisted of a series of narrow rooms with a central line of connecting doors, starting with a hall-way and stores area, going on to a central dining room and then to a passage leading to the lower bunker. On one side were located the showers and toilets, a kitchen and a suite of three rooms occupied by Frau Goebbels and her children, and on the other side a guardroom for members of the Führer-Begleit-Kommando and the policemen of the Reichssicherheitsdienst (Reich Security Service) that carried out the actual bodyguard duties, and an office for the secretaries.

The accommodation in both of these bunkers was extremely cramped and the ventilation poor. The noise of the diesel machinery necessary to run the ventilation and pumping systems was such that Hitler would order it switched off during conferences, but participants would then suffer from the stuffiness and complain of headaches.

Hitler returned unannounced to Berlin on January 15, 1945, after the failure of the Ardennes offensive (otherwise known as the Battle of the Bulge), and occupied his private quarters in the old Reichs Chancellery, his presence remaining a secret. However, the air raids repeatedly disrupted his own erratic

Photographs taken in the Führerbunker prior to May 1, 1945, are virtually non-existent. This picture was supplied by Admiral Karl-Jesko von Puttkamer, Hitler's naval adjutant (who quit the bunker for the last time on the night of April 22-23) to American author John Toland for his *Pictorial Documentation of Hitler's Life*. It is described as being taken in the waiting room but, with the right-angle in the wall, it is more likely to be the corridor (2 on plan) outside the Führerbunker itself.

schedule and in the middle of March he decided to move down into the underground command post prepared for him, even though it was not fully ready; problems with the ventilation system had not yet been resolved and there was also some flooding in the Vorbunker from the high water table. He was to remain there isolated and remote from reality almost continually until his death. Eva Braun, who had determinedly come to join him in Berlin in mid-March, moved down into the bunker on April 15. This was taken as a serious omen by the staff, one of whom dubbed her the 'Angel of Death'.

As a command post for the Führer of the Third Reich and Supreme Commander of the German Armed Forces, the Führerbunker had some serious drawbacks, apart from the atmospheric conditions already mentioned. Telephonic communications were dependent upon a small, one-man switchboard such as one would find in a medium-sized hotel, the only addition being a scrambler device for highly classified exchanges. The Armed Forces communications network was not centred on Berlin but on Zentrale 500 at the Armed Forces High Command, the Oberkommando der Wehrmacht (OKW) and Oberkom-

This picture could be more helpful — most likely taken in the reception room (12). On the left Generalfeldmarschall Ferdinand Schörner (promoted on April 5, 1945). Schörner had already been decorated with the Oakleaves to his Ritterkreuz in August 1944 when commanding Heeresgruppe-Nord, and the Diamonds were awarded to him on New Year's Day 1945. One of Hitler's faithfuls, the Generalfeldmarschall came to Berlin for the afternoon war conference in the bunker on April 21 and, as a final act on April 30, Hitler appointed him head of the Wehrmacht, by then non-existent! On the right, SS-Obergruppenführer Julius Schaub, Hitler's personal adjutant.

During his last eight weeks of life, Hitler left the Chancellery and bunker complex only once — to visit the Oder front (page 174). His only relaxation would be a walk outside with his dog through an area which looked more like a construction site than the immaculate garden it once was. In this view we are looking from the observation tower-cum-pillbox towards his office (behind the central pillars) in the Chancellery.

mando des Heeres (OKH), located in the vast Maybach I and II bunkers at Zossen-Wünsdorf some 15 miles south of Berlin (which became the Soviet Forces Headquarters in Germany after the war). As no direct line had been provided from the Führerbunker, although there were such facilities above ground from the Reichs Chancellery, the Führerbunker exchange had to operate via the busy switchboard (Zentrale 200) at the Flak control tower in the Tiergarten opposite the Zoo Flaktower. Alongside the Führerbunker switchboard there was a single medium- and long-range Army radio transmitter, whose aerial was suspended from a vulnerable balloon outside, and which provided a radio-telephonic capability. The only other means of communication was by messenger.

Apart from evening strolls in the garden with his Alsatian, and the occasional visit to his new Reichs Chancellery building in the gaps between the American daylight and British nighttime air raids, Hitler only left his bunker on two occasions before his death. The first was to attend a secret meeting of Gauleiters on the outskirts of Berlin on February 25, the second a highly unusual visit to General Busse of 9. Armee to discuss the plan of defence at CI. Korps headquarters on the Oder front on March 3. Two weeks later, he went up into the garden to congratulate some boys of the Hitlerjugend assembled there by Artur Axmann on their award of the Iron Cross, his last appearance before the cameras.

Despite the general situation, the formalities of Hitler's 56th birthday were still observed. On the evening of

April 19, Goebbels delivered his customary eulogy of the Führer to the nation over the radio, and on the afternoon of the 20th Hitler received the congratulations of the assembled leadership of the Third Reich — Goebbels, Himmler, Göring, Bormann, Speer, Ribbentrop, Keitel, Jodl, Krebs and a few others — in a brief ceremony, at which no champagne was served. Some tried to persuade him to leave for

Berchtesgaden before it was too late, but in vain: he was determined to stay on in Berlin. He even ventured up into the garden to congratulate some uniformed children on their decorations for bravery, which his staff handed out on his behalf. (This was not, however, the group filmed in similar circumstances exactly a month previously, and which has often mistakenly been associated with his birthday.)

So many of those now fighting for the defence of the city were youngsters and, on at least two occasions, Reichsjugendführer Artur Axmann (right) brought boys who had particularly distinguished themselves to the Chancellery to meet their Führer. Here, on March 20, Hitler Youth members who have been awarded the Iron Cross are lined up in front of the wall below Hitler's office.

These two oblique views taken in 1945 show the relationship of the emergency exit to its surroundings. *Above:* Both the Chancellery on the right and the Propaganda Ministry in the background were linked by tunnels to the bunker complex. In the foreground lies the ornamental pool outside Hitler's office with an emergency water supply tank between it and the exit.

papers. Those items he wished to preserved were packed in metal boxes and the rest destroyed by his aides by burning up in the garden. Meanwhile Goebbels and his family arrived to take up residence in the bunker at Hitler's invitation. The relationship between Goebbels and his wife was at best a strained one, despite their large family. Magda already had one son by a previous marriage, then had produced a further six children for Goebbels, but the last was commonly known to be the result of a reconciliation forced on them by Hitler, who could not allow their individual love affairs to result in the scandal of divorce. Goebbels moved into a room opposite Hitler's suite in the Führerbunker, while Magda had three rooms for herself and the children in the Vorbunker.

That evening some forty members of the Chancellery staff took advantage of an evacuation plan organised by Hitler's personal pilot, SS-Gruppenführer Hans Baur, under the code-name Operation 'Seraglio' to fly out of Gatow airfield in ten aircraft. Nine arrived safely and their passengers were driven on to Berchtesgaden, but the tenth, which was also carrying Hitler's documents, crashed in Bavaria killing all but the rear gunner. (This incident was later used as background in the elaborate 'Hitler Diaries' hoax of the 1980s.)

Also that evening Hitler informed Keitel and Jodl that he proposed committing suicide rather than let himself fall into the hands of the enemy. When they asked for their final orders, he referred them to the Reichsmarschall. This came as a shock, for it meant that he was abdicating his command of the Armed Forces still fighting for him,

Hitler's decision to remain in the Führerbunker and not move to the OKW facility at Zossen, from where he could far easier have conducted his command function, signalled his growing lack of interest in the overall scene and a shift to a realm of fantasy that was to become increasingly more apparent as time went by. It also meant that the Chief of the General Staff had to spend a considerable amount of time travelling twice a day from his base in Zossen in order to attend Hitler's briefings and war conferences, a serious handicap to the conduct of the war.

The failure of SS-Obergruppenführer Steiner to carry out on schedule an attack from the line of the Finow Canal for the relief of Berlin as ordered reduced Hitler to a paroxysm of rage during the evening conference of April 22, raving about betrayal, cowardice and corruption. Eventually he declared that he would remain in Berlin until the bitter end. All attempts to dissuade him failed. Then he said he would remain with Goebbels and take personal charge of the defence of the city, ordering a radio announcement to this effect.

Hitler withdrew into his private quarters and started going through his

Taken looking almost due west towards the conservatory situated midway along the wall at the bottom of the garden.

none of whom would follow Göring, now generally regarded as a buffoon. But Hitler went on to say that it was no longer a question of fighting but for negotiating, and Göring was the best suited for that.

Hitler then turned to the maps and suggested that the 12. Armee facing the Americans on the line of the Elbe, which the latter appeared to have no serious intention of crossing, could be turned about to come to the relief of Berlin in conjunction with the remains of the 9. Armee. It was decided that Keitel would organise this in person, while Jodl would take the OKW staff north to Plön, and Krebs would remain as Hitler's military adviser.

On April 23, SS-Brigadeführer Mohnke brought the Leibstandarte 'Adolf Hitler' depot unit of 2,000 combat veterans from their Lichterfelde barracks to defend the Reichs Chancellery complex. These were men on rotation from the front-line division, usually as a result of wounds, from whom the 40-strong Fuhrer-Begleit-Kommando under SS-Hauptsturmführer Franz Schädle was also drawn. This latter group also provided waiters, valets and servants for Hitler's court when necessary.

SS-Brigadeführer Wilhelm Mohnke *(left)* was responsible for the security of the 'Zitadelle' and on April 23 he drafted in 2,000 Leibstandarte for the close defence of the Chancellery area. *Right:* Even Hitler's famous balcony was converted into an improvised fire position to cover the Wilhelmplatz. *Below:* The actual map of central Berlin used in the Führerbunker, possibly by Hitler himself, for the defence of the capital, is now a prize exhibit at the Red Army Museum at Karlshorst.

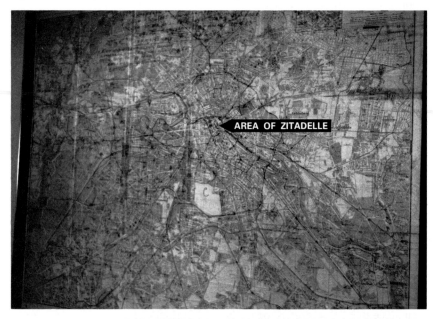

AREA OF ZITADELLE

The nearby Kaiserhof U-Bahn Station was still in German hands and it remained so right up until May 1, as did the next station up the line: Stadtmitte. *Left:* Here SS-Brigadeführer Krukenberg had set up his command post in a railway carriage beside the platform. *Right:* When the Wall divided Berlin, Stadtmitte was one of those stations sealed up as a security measure and no longer used. Our picture was taken in 1991 soon after its reopening and refurbishment.

Had Hitler decided on a last-minute attempt to escape, no doubt these armoured cars parked in the Ehrenhof would have been useful. The large four-wheeler on solid rubber tyres was a Daimler DZVR Schupo-Sonderwagen, 1921 model, and one of 31 built for police use in the early 1920s. The six-wheeler was one of only three constructed by the Dutch shipbuilding firm 'Wilton-Fijenoord' on a Krupp L2H143 6×4 truck chassis in 1933-34. It had been captured in Holland in 1940.

When later that day General Weidling contacted Krebs from his command post in Rudow to try to discover why he was supposed to be under arrest, he was ordered to report to the Führerbunker at 1800 hours. After an initially cool reception by Krebs and Burgdorf his explanations were accepted and he was taken to see Hitler. Weidling was shocked by Hitler's obvious deterioration. Shortly afterwards he was told that he was to take over the defence of the city's south-eastern and southern defence sectors with his LVI. Panzerkorps, and then next morning was summoned back to the Führerbunker to be appointed overall Commandant of the Berlin Defence Sector, directly responsible to the Führer. His request for having sole authority for the issue of orders for the defence was ignored.

Meanwhile news of the dramatic events in the Führerbunker on the evening of April 22 had been relayed to Göring by General Karl Koller, who had travelled down from Berlin for this purpose, resulting in Göring then reluctantly signalling Hitler:

'Führer!

'In view of your decision to remain at your post in the fortress of Berlin, do you agree that I take over, at once, the total leadership of the Reich, with full freedom of action at home and abroad, as your deputy, in accordance with the decree of June 29, 1941? If no reply is received by 2200 hours I shall assume that you have lost your freedom of action, consider the conditions of your decree as fulfilled and act for the best interests of our country and our people. You know what I feel for you in this gravest hour of my life. Words fail me to express myself. May God protect you and speed you here quickly in spite of all. Your loyal,

Hermann Göring'

Bormann deliberately held this signal back until he could catch Hitler in a nervous, irritable mood before presenting it with the suggestion that Göring was trying to seize power for himself. Predictably Hitler flew into a rage,

denouncing Göring as a traitor, and then despatched two signals, one forbidding him to take action and the second ordering his resignation from all official posts if he wished to avoid being charged with treason. Bormann then sent off a third signal on his own initiative ordering the house arrest of Göring and his entourage.

This episode was witnessed by Albert Speer, who had flown back into Berlin at considerable risk to himself and others flying and escorting him, for the curious purpose of confessing to Hitler his obstructive action towards Hitler's 'scorched earth' policy. Fortunately for him, Hitler chose to ignore this disloyalty and Speer was able to fly out again in the early hours of April 24. The purpose of this visit is doubly peculiar when one considers Speer's claim that he had previously planned to murder Hitler and other occupants of the Führerbunker by the introduction of poison gas into the ventilation system from the vents in the garden. However by the time he had obtained the gas, Hitler had noticed the weakness in the system from his experience of mustard gas in the First World War and ordered the construction of the ventilation towers to mask the vents.

Curiously enough, most of the people now living or working in the Führerbunker were those who had been closely associated with Hitler pre-war at Berchtesgaden. They looked upon themselves as 'the mountain people' and reminisced endlessly of their time together there as they awaited developments in the bunker. The female contingent included Hitler's four remaining secretaries — Fräulein Johanna Wolf, Fräulein Christa Schroeder, Frau Gerda Christian and Frau Gertrud Junge, and his Austrian vegetarian cook, Fräulein Konstanze Manzialy. Frau Junge was the widow of one of Hitler's bodyguards killed on the Eastern Front, and Frau Christian was married to a Luftwaffe Generalmajor whom she divorced after the war.

On the evening of April 24, Hitler issued a new directive terminating the former OKW/OKH division of oper-

ational responsibilities and uniting them under the OKW with himself as the Supreme Commander. He then ordered Generaloberst Ritter von Greim, commander of Luftflotte 6, to report to him in person. Von Greim was prevented by air raids from leaving his base in Munich straight away, so he called on General Koller at Berchtesgaden to find out what was going on and there learnt of Göring's disgrace, reluctantly promising to convey Koller's plea of Göring's innocence to the Führer. He then returned to Munich and was joined by his mistress, the famous female test pilot, Hanna Reitsch, for the hazardous flight to Berlin. Gatow was under ground attack, so they flew on to Rechlin with the intention of flying into Berlin from there by helicopter under cover of darkness, but the last remaining helicopter had been badly damaged and they had to wait until daylight for an aircraft and escort to be prepared for them. The daring pilot who had previously flown Speer in and out of Berlin

Formerly at ground level, the air intake for the ventilation plant was modified and raised on Hitler's orders to avoid the risk of a heavier-than-air poison gas entering the system.

251

then took von Greim in a Focke-Wulf 190, which had only one passenger seat, so the diminutive but determined Hanna climbed into the baggage locker. Seven out of the escort of twenty fighters were lost on the flight to Gatow, and their own aircraft suffered some minor damage. From there, as previously recounted, they took a two-seater Fieseler Storch with von Greim at the controls, but on the way they were hit by ground fire and von Greim badly injured. He was not yet fit to travel so they remained in the bunkers with Hanna helping to entertain the Goebbels' children.

That day, April 26, Berlin's last telephonic links with the outside world, which had been operating only intermittently over the previous two days, were finally severed.

At the following evening's conference Hitler suddenly noticed the absence of SS-Gruppenführer Hermann Fegelein, Himmler's liaison officer and brother-in-law to Eva Braun, who had in fact been absent for the last three days. Suspecting desertion, Hitler ordered a search, and he was eventually traced to an apartment in Bleibtreustrasse. Telephoned instructions failed to get him to report back so an escort was sent to get him, which found him drunk and unshaven. He promised to return once he had cleaned himself up but again he failed to do so, so a second escort was sent to collect him. The escort found him still very drunk but shaved and properly dressed in uniform, apparently in the process of packing a suitcase in company with a young woman. The latter left the room on a pretext and escaped through a kitchen window, so the escort returned with Fegelein and the suitcase, which was found to contain passports, valuables and money suitable for an escape attempt. Upon arrival at the Chancellery Fegelein was stripped of his rank and sent to Mohnke for immediate court-martial but proved to be too drunk to stand trial.

Meanwhile, Bormann, from what he had been told by the SS officer commanding the escort, deduced that they

Left: **This picture is claimed to have been taken ten days before Hitler's death when Arthur Axmann (left) brought another party of Hitler Youth to be inspected by Hitler on his birthday. Also in the picture is General Krebs (second from right), the Chief of the Army General Staff, and also Hitler's valet, Heinz Linge (extreme right). More interesting, though, is the presence of the man second from the left — Hermann Fegelein. He was Himmler's liaison officer at the Führer's headquarters but, more important, he was part of Hitler's close family circle, having married Eva Braun's sister, Gretl, in June 1944. He was injured alongside Hitler the following month when the bomb exploded at Rastenberg (page 162), but three days before Hitler's suicide he fell out of favour when he was found to have absented himself without leave from the bunker. He was traced rather the worse for drink at his flat in Bleibtreustrasse and brought back to face the music. As Gretl was pregnant, at first Hitler acceded to Eva's plea but, when news arrived of Himmler's defection, Hitler suspected a plot. Fegelein was interrogated by the Gestapo and then taken to the garden for summary execution late on the evening of Saturday, April 28.**

had uncovered the source of the security leak at the Führer's headquarters that had been the cause of considerable concern over the past few months, and that the woman was probably a British agent with whom Fegelein had been about to flee. He therefore had Fegelein handed over for interrogation to the Gestapo chief, Heinrich Müller. Fegelein was eventually shot in the Chancellery garden late on April 28. No further trace was ever found of the woman, and the veracity of those aspects of the story with regard to the

woman and a security leak remains suspect.

Late on April 28 news of Himmler's secret negotiations with Count Bernadotte of Sweden were picked up by the Propaganda Ministry. Hitler was profoundly shocked at this betrayal and ordered von Greim to seek out Himmler and bring him to justice. The same pilot that had flown Speer in and out of Berlin and brought them down to Gatow from Rechlin air base returned in an Arado 96 to fly von Greim and Hanna Reitsch out at midnight.

When we visited Bleibtreustrasse, which lies just off the Kurfürstendamm, to seek out No. 10–11 where Fegelein had been arrested, we found that we had been beaten to it. The street was in chaos and tempers were flaring as the whole gamut of the German television industry was present, filming outside the house!

By the evening of April 29 the Russians had occupied all of Saarland Strasse (Stresemannstrasse) and almost reached the Air Ministry on Wilhelmstrasse from the south. General Weidling called on Hitler and managed to persuade him to allow a break-out now that the defence's ammunition was virtually exhausted. Hitler then consulted with SS-Brigadeführer Mohnke and was told that the Russians were indeed at the Air Ministry, as well as in the Lustgarten to the east, at the Weidendammer Bridge in the north and only 300 to 400 yards away in the Tiergarten. In desperation he signalled the OKW: 'I am to be informed immediately:

1. Where are Wenck's spearheads?
2. When will they resume the attack?
3. Where is the 9. Armee?
4. Where is it breaking through?
5. Where are Holste's XXXXI. Panzerkorps' spearheads?

The reply from Keitel, surprising in its honesty, was received at 0100 hours on April 30 and read:

'1. Wenck's point is stopped south of the Schwielowsee.

Strong Soviet attacks along the whole east flank.

2. Consequently the 12. Armee cannot continue their attack towards Berlin.

3 & 4. The 9. Armee is surrounded. An armoured group has broken out to the west; location unknown.

5. Corps Holste is forced on the defensive from Brandenburg via Rathenau to Kremmen.

'The attack towards Berlin has not developed at any point since Army Group 'Weichsel' was also forced on the defensive on the whole front from north of Brandenburg via Neubrandenburg to Anklam.'

By Sunday evening (the 29th), Soviet forces were virtually knocking at the door of the Chancellery. They had almost reached the Air Ministry . . .

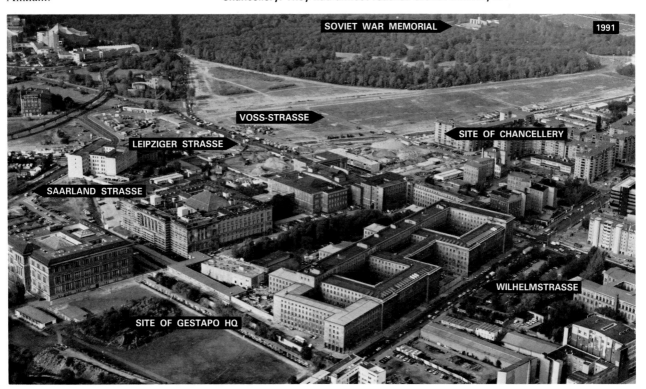

. . . and Saarland Strasse, further to the west. It was now 'five minutes to midnight' . . . and the final drama was about to begin.

By 1945 Hitler had known Eva Braun for some fifteen years, having first met her in Heinrich Hoffmann's photographic shop in Munich where she was working as a sales assistant. She became his mistress, yet the German people knew little of her existence as she was never seen in public with Hitler. She had little influence on his political life, yet remained the faithful woman behind the scenes, her final act of devotion being to meet death at his side. Normally she was never permitted by Hitler at his various headquarters, but she arrived in Berlin on April 15 to share her last days with him, even though Hitler tried hard to persuade her to leave. He had always believed that his appeal as a strong leader would be diminished were he to marry but, in an attempt to repay Eva's unswerving love and loyalty, on Sunday evening he decided to take her as his wife. Yet the honeymoon between the 56-year-old Führer and his 33-year-old bride was to last a little over thirty hours with precious little privacy in the cramped, oppressive conditions.

At dawn on April 26, the 12. Armee had launched its operation towards Berlin attended by much propaganda publicity to inspire the garrison to fight on in hope of relief. However, as we know, General Wenck had no intention of becoming embroiled in that hopeless situation and wanted simply to offer an avenue of escape to those who could break through to him. The attack had been led by the XX. Korps, whose youngsters showed all the élan of the Wehrmacht in the early years of the war, while the other corps protected the flanks of the operational area. Going cross-country to avoid the roads blocked by refugees, it had made rapid progress, catching the 6th Guards Mechanised Corps of the Fourth Guards Tank Army on an exposed flank and capturing a number of Soviet units intact. At Beelitz they recaptured a German field hospital and immediately started shipping the wounded and some refugees back in a commandeered train by shuttle service to their evacuation assembly area opposite Tangermünde.

By the evening of April 27, the XX. Korps had reached the village of Ferch at the southern tip of the Schwielowsee lake, about six miles south of Potsdam. To have gone any further would have been suicidal, but by remaining in that position it offered and held open an escape route, an opportunity for the remains of the 9. Armee, still trapped in the Spreewald, as well as for the Berlin and Potsdam garrisons, to break through to them.

This was in concert with the ideas of the other German Army commanders in this battle. Having fought their fight to the best of their ability, and lost, their sole aim was now to spare their men from Soviet captivity.

Wenck was in radio contact with General Busse of the 9. Armee, who started his break-out from the Spreewald, where he was being pounded day and night by elements of both the 1st Byelorussian and 1st Ukrainian Fronts and their air forces. That same night some 20,000 troops of the Potsdam

The ceremony was held in the conference room (13 on plan on page 246). This is how it looked under new management three months later.

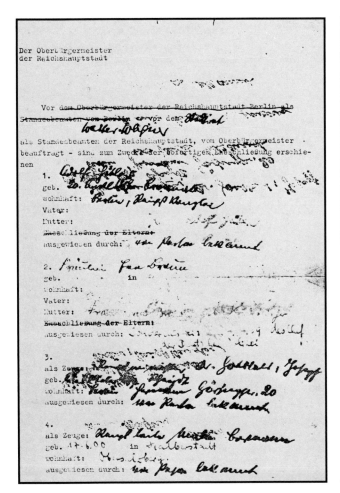

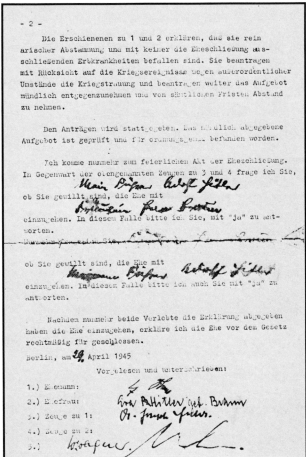

Der Oberbürgermeister
der Reichshauptstadt

Vor dem Oberbürgermeister der Reichshauptstadt Berlin als
Standesbeamten von Berlin vor dem Stadtrat
Walter Wagner
als Standesbeamten der Reichshauptstadt, vom Oberbürgermeister
beauftragt - sind zum Zwecke der sofortigen Eheschliessung erschie-
nen

1. Adolf Hitler
geb. 20. April
wohnhaft: Berlin, Reichskanzlei
Vater:
Mutter:
Eheschliessung der Eltern:
ausgewiesen durch: vom Pastor bekannt

2. Fräulein Eva Braun
geb.   in
wohnhaft:
Vater:
Mutter: Frau
Eheschliessung der Eltern:
ausgewiesen durch:

3.
als Zeuge Dr. Joseph Goebbels, Joseph
geb.
wohnhaft: Berlin Göbbelstr. 20
ausgewiesen durch: vom Pastor bekannt

4.
als Zeuge
geb. 17.6.00 in Halberstadt
wohnhaft:
ausgewiesen durch: vom Pastor bekannt

- 2 -

Die Erschienenen zu 1 und 2 erklären, daß sie rein
arischer Abstammung und mit keiner die Eheschliessung aus-
schließenden Erbkrankheiten befallen sind. Sie beantragen
mit Rücksicht auf die Kriegsereignisse wegen außerordentlicher
Umstände die Kriegstrauung und beantragen weiter das Aufgebot
mündlich entgegenzunehmen und von sämtlichen Fristen Abstand
zu nehmen.

Den Anträgen wird stattgegeben. Das mündlich abgegebene
Aufgebot ist geprüft und für ordnungsgemäß befunden worden.

Ich komme nunmehr zum feierlichen Akt der Eheschliessung.
In Gegenwart der obengenannten Zeugen zu 3 und 4 frage ich Sie,
ob Sie gewillt sind, die Ehe mit
einzugehen. In diesem Falle bitte ich Sie, mit "ja" zu antworten.

ob Sie gewillt sind, die Ehe mit
einzugehen. In diesem Falle bitte ich auch Sie mit "ja" zu
antworten.

Nachdem nunmehr beide Verlobte die Erklärung abgegeben
haben die Ehe einzugehen, erkläre ich die Ehe vor dem Gesetz
rechtmäßig für geschlossen.
Berlin, am 29. April 1945
Vorgelesen und unterschrieben:

1.) Ehemann:
2.) Ehefrau: Eva Hitler geb. Braun
3.) Zeuge zu 1:   Dr. Joseph Goebbels.
4.) Zeuge zu 2:
5.) Wagner   als Standesbeamter

Having sworn that they were both of pure Aryan descent, the bride and groom added their signatures — Eva in her obvious excitement beginning to use her maiden name before crossing out the 'B'. She then added the words 'born Braun'. The witnesses are (1) Dr Joseph Goebbels and (2) Martin Bormann. The original copy of the document is now in the National Archives in Washington. The actual ceremony may have taken place just before midnight (i.e. on the 28th) as a revision is evident in the original which was smudged when Wagner folded the document before the ink was dry.

garrison broke out to the south and joined up with 12. Armee, but it was to take until the morning of May 1 for an estimated 40,000 exhausted survivors of the 9. Armee, accompanied by thousands of civilians, to break through to them. The Soviets did everything they could to stop them and Koniev was later to deny that any significant numbers got through. Certainly the cost in human lives was horrendous and the cemetery at Halbe, where the operation started, contains thousands of German dead, both military and civilian.

Wenck then withdrew his forces methodically to the area bounded by the lower Havel and the Mittelland Canal opposite Tangermünde. The Americans on the far bank of the Elbe already held more prisoners than they could cope with, and so tried to prevent the German evacuation. However, the Soviet Air Force attacked the crossing points, which caused the Americans to

The same map table that had been used over the past weeks in the defence of Berlin was now used by a local municipal official, Walter Wagner, to complete the marriage certificate. Another picture taken in July 1945.

Just before the ceremony began, Hitler called for his secretary, Gertrud 'Traudl' Junge, and led the way through the reception area (12) to the conference room (the door on the left). She noted that a table had already been laid with silver service and champagne glasses. Hitler then began dictating a final statement setting out his justification for the war and naming his successors: Admiral Dönitz as President and head of the armed forces, with Goebbels as Chancellor. Bormann was to be Party Minister. Hitler then dictated his last will and testament. This picture has been taken looking towards the emergency exit through which the bodies of both bride and groom would be carried a few hours later.

withdraw to a safe distance, and Wenck was able to continue his desperate evacuation. The operation continued until May 8 and, in the end, he got an estimated 100,000 troops and 300,000 civilians across — no mean feat. Unfortunately some of the German troops ended up in Soviet captivity after all when the Americans handed them over in sheer desperation at coping with the numbers involved.

Back in the bunker, on the evening of the 28th Hitler suddenly announced his intention of marrying Eva Braun. A suitably qualified official was found among the Volkssturm fighting in the area, a Gauamtsleiter Walter Wagner, and he performed the ceremony at about 0130 hours on April 29.

Hitler had already dictated his personal and political testaments to one of his secretaries. Grossadmiral Dönitz was named as his successor as President and Goebbels as Chancellor. Two copies of these testaments were to be sent to Dönitz by separate couriers to ensure delivery, one courier being SS-Standartenführer Wilhelm Zander, Bormann's aide, and the other Oberbereischleiter Heinz Lorenz from the Propaganda Ministry, while a third copy

> *Although during the years of struggle I believed that I could not undertake the responsibility of marriage, now, before the end of my life, I have decided to take as my wife the woman who, after many years of true friendship, came to this town, already almost besieged, of her own free will, in order to share my fate. She will go to her death with me at her own wish, as my wife. This will compensate us for what we both lost through my work in the service of my people.*
>
> *My possessions, in so far as they are worth anything, belong to the Party, or if this no longer exists, to the State. If the State too is destroyed, there is no need for any further instruction on my part.*
>
> *The paintings in the collections bought by me during the course of the years were never assembled for private purposes, but solely for the establishment of a picture gallery in my home town of Linz on the Danube. It is my most heartfelt wish that this will should be duly executed.*
>
> *As executor, I appoint my most faithful Party comrade, Martin Bormann. He is given full legal authority to make all decisions. He is permitted to hand over to my relatives everything which is of worth as a personal memento, or is necessary to maintain a petty-bourgeois standard of living; especially to my wife's mother and my faithful fellow workers of both sexes who are well known to him. The chief of these are my former secretaries, Frau Winter, etc., who helped me for many years by their work.*
>
> *My wife and I choose to die in order to escape the shame of overthrow or capitulation. It is our wish that our bodies be burned immediately in the place where I have performed the greater part of my daily work during the course of my twelve years' service to my people.*
>
> ADOLF HITLER,
> LAST WILL AND TESTAMENT,
> APRIL 29, 1945

was to be taken by Major Willi Johann-meyer, Hitler's army adjutant, to give to Generalfeldmarschall Ferdinand Schörner.

These emissaries set off at midday on April 29, making their way via the Tiergarten, Zoo position, Kantstrasse and the Olympic Stadium to the Hitler-jugend Regiment's position on the Havel, where they rested until midnight before continuing down river by boat. Three of the now unemployed aides, Oberstleutnant Rudolf Weiss, Major Bernt Freiherr Freytag von Loring-hoven and Rittmeister Gerhard Boldt, then obtained permission to try and break out to Wenck's 12. Armee, and left by the same route that afternoon. At midnight they were followed by Oberst von Below, his adjutant and their two orderlies, taking with them a missive to Keitel concerning the appointment of Dönitz as Hitler's suc-cessor as head of state. These last two groups met near the Olympic Stadium and then had to wait until the following night with the Hitlerjugend for a chance to slip down the Havel.

Meanwhile Hitler's emissaries had reached the remains of the 20. Panzergrenadier-Division bottled up on Wannsee Island and managed to get a radio message out asking Dönitz to retrieve them by flying boat. They then moved to Pfaueninsel (Peacock Island) where they were join by Weiss's party, but von Below's group had landed on the west bank of the Havel and was already heading west. A three-engined Dornier flying boat duly landed close to Pfaueninsel on the night of May 1 and established contact with the party wait-ing to be taken off. Unfortunately the 20. Panzergrenadier-Division were making a desperate bid to break out over the Wannsee Bridge and attracted so much Soviet artillery fire on their old locations that the pilot took off again without them. Although they all eventually reached safety, none accom-plished their mission and all the docu-

Eva did not appear from her combined sitting room and bedroom (18 on plan) until after midday on Sunday. By this time, copies of Hitler's will had already been despatched through enemy lines by courier. The senior military man present, General Hans Krebs, the Chief of the Army General Staff, realised that those left in the bunker had only another day left at most, as Marshal Zhukov undoubtedly intended to present the capture of Berlin to Stalin on May 1. For Eva, alone in her room, her happiness must have been tinged with melancholy, for fresh in her memory must have been the thought that her sister had just been widowed when Hitler ordered her brother-in-law shot. Some even believe that Fegelein was her lover and that another reason for his death could be that he had tried to persuade Eva to escape from Berlin with him.

ments, except those carried by von Below, which he destroyed once he realised the futility of his task, were recovered during the course of the subsequent Allied investigation.

During the early hours of April 30,

General Weidling received a letter from Hitler authorising a break-out in small combat groups, as a result of which Weidling conferred with his defence sector commanders and told them to prepare to leave at 2200 hours.

Little more than a plain concrete cell, she had tried to add her personal touch to the room by having pieces of her own furniture (which had been designed by Speer specially for her)

brought down from the Chancellery. Was the champagne bottle being used as a flower vase a keepsake from her wedding breakfast, one wonders?

Hitler's bedroom, which contained a bed with a night table, a wardrobe, a mobile tea trolley on castors, and a safe in which he kept his personal files. The safe has been cut open by the Russians although most of its contents had already been burned in the garden. Unfortunately the picture is just not clear enough to read the title of the book on the bedside table.

Suicide was now Hitler's only option. After a restless Sunday night, he summoned Mohnke again early on Monday morning for a report on the situation and was told that the Russians had now closed in as near as the Adlon Hotel to the north and in the U-Bahn tunnels in Friedrichstrasse to the east, while some forces were even in the Voss-strasse right alongside the Reichs Chancellery. Mohnke warned that his troops were close to exhaustion and could not be expected to fight on much longer. He anticipated a major assault on the Chancellery to begin at dawn next morning, this being May Day. Hitler took this all calmly and gave him copies of his testaments for conveyance to Dönitz who had established his headquarters at Plön, north of Lübeck.

Hitler had already had the poison capsules tested on his German Shepherd dog, Blondi. Then, after saying goodbye to the remainder of his staff, Hitler and his wife withdrew into their private apartment, where they committed suicide at 1530 hours on April 30 by taking cyanide, Hitler also shooting himself in the head. Their bodies were wrapped in blankets and then taken up the emergency exit staircase into the Chancellery garden and laid in a trench. With the aid of petrol taken from Kempka's secret reserve in the Tiergarten the corpses were set alight and some time later the charred remains were buried in a nearby shell-hole.

Bearing several wound stripes on his right breast, this young Soviet senior NCO is stated in the July 1945 caption to be standing 'where Hitler and Eva Braun are alleged to have poisoned themselves'. At the time, no one really knew what had happened in the last hours in the bunker so in September 1945 British Intelligence appointed Hugh Trevor-Roper to investigate the facts. Although hampered by non-access to crucial witnesses held in Soviet prison camps, his report appeared in 1947 as *The Last Days of Adolf Hitler*. Over the years, the miscaptioning of photographs taken inside the bunker complex has only helped to confuse the issue. We are now confident that we have correctly identified the layout and pictorial record once and for all.

The actual room where the suicides took place was Hitler's office (15). By midday on Monday, Soviet troops were reported right outside in the Voss-strasse and it was obvious that the Chancellery might be overrun at any moment. After taking their formal leave of those remaining in the bunker in the reception room, Eva led the way through the refreshment room (14) to her husband's study. The armoured door was closed and Günsche took up station to prevent anyone entering. After an interval of ten minutes or so no sound had been heard and eventually Linge opened the door but, when assailed by the strong smell of cordite and bitter almonds, called for Bormann to lead the way. Günsche, Goebbels and Axmann followed. They found Hitler lying on the sofa with blood dripping from a head wound. Eva was sitting beside him, her feet tucked up beneath her. She had taken poison. 'I then went into the antechamber of the briefing-room,' said Erich Kempka, Hitler's chauffeur, when interrogated later. 'Günsche told me that the Führer was dead. A short time after that Linge, and an orderly whom I do not remember, came from the private room of the Führer carrying a corpse wrapped in an ordinary field-grey blanket. One could only see the long black trousers and black shoes which the Führer usually wore with his field-grey uniform jacket. I could not observe any spots of blood on the body wrapped in the blanket. Thereupon Martin Bormann came from the Führer's living-room, carrying the corpse of Mrs Eva Hitler in his arms. He turned the corpse over to me. Mrs Hitler wore a dark dress. I did not have the feeling that the corpse was still warm. I could not recognise any injuries on the body. The dress was slightly damp only in the region of the heart. The orderly now went upstairs with the corpse of the Führer to the bunker exit towards the garden of the Reichs Chancellery . . . I followed with the corpse of Mrs Hitler.'

Hitler had given implicit orders that after his death his body was to be completely destroyed, possibly only too aware of the fate of Mussolini who had been publicly displayed hanging alongside his mistress on a garage forecourt in Milan only the day before. Günsche had instructed Kempka to supply 200 litres of petrol (i.e 10 jerrycans of 20 litres each although Kempka confuses the point in his interrogation report by stating that he brought five cans) and have it brought to the garden exit. The bodies were then manhandled up the narrow stairway, and placed in a convenient trench a few metres from the doorway. Here, using a fairly accurate stage set, Yuri Ozerov re-creates the scene for *The Last Storm*.

Even as the garden was being swept by shell-fire, the contents of several cans was poured over the bodies and a lighted taper tossed from the cover of the entrance. Although the blaze was replenished over the next few hours, it failed to totally consume the corpses which were later buried close to the unfinished watch tower.

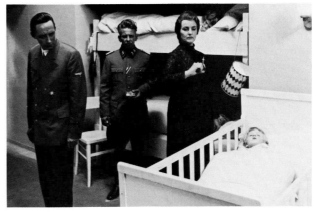

Although Hitler's death was meant to be kept secret, the word soon spread through the Chancellery bunker complex, leading to a growing breakdown of discipline. His demise left Goebbels in the rôle of Chancellor and anxious to secure Soviet recognition of his government, as nominated by Hitler, before Himmler could take similar action with the Western Allies. He summoned General Weidling and swore him to secrecy about Hitler's death, withdrew permission for the break-out and told him that General Krebs would attempt to establish negotiations with the Russians. Meanwhile Bormann had sent a signal to Dönitz informing him of his nomination as Hitler's successor as President but omitting the essential information that Hitler was dead.

Krebs' negotiations with Colonel-General Chuikov failed to achieve the desired result. Goebbels now had no choice but to commit suicide. Magda Goebbels, in collusion with her husband, gave their children chocolates drugged with a soporific before they went to bed. Once they were asleep she fed them each a cyanide capsule. The eldest child resisted and had to be forced to take the poison. Then she went below to the Führerbunker and sat quietly sipping champagne and playing patience in her husband's study until she was joined by him some time later. Nothing was said about the children, although everyone suspected that they were already dead. A little later on both went back briefly to the Goebbels' rooms in the Vorbunker before returning to the Führerbunker. They then climbed up through the emergency exit to the garden, where Goebbels first shot his wife, then himself, both simultaneously taking poison. Petrol was poured over them and their bodies set alight.

The break-out from the Reichs Chancellery originally planned for the night of April 30 had been delayed for 24 hours, mainly because the guards were so exhausted they needed a day's rest and also because the Soviets had cut the East-West-Axis, obliging the planning of a new route. Generals Krebs and Burgdorf declined to join in, choosing suicide instead.

Those in the break-out party were divided into ten groups, the first, led by Mohnke, leaving at 2300 hours on May 1, the others to follow at ten-minute intervals.

Now it was the turn of Goebbels and his family. *Left:* His wife, Magda, had already planned the deaths of their six children who were drugged and then poisoned while they slept in the Vorbunker. *Right:* The act as depicted by Yuri Ozerov, although we are told that Goebbels was not present at the deaths. Dr Stumpfegger is believed to have prepared doped chocolate to put the children to sleep before Magda alone administered the poison, though there is reason to believe that the eldest girl, Helga, woke up and had to be forcibly held down. Then, in order to save the trouble of having their dead bodies carried up the long flight of stairs, Goebbels and Magda went up arm in arm to the garden. Night had fallen — the last night of the Third Reich. Just outside the entrance, Joseph shot his wife as she bit on a poison capsule before turning the pistol on himself as he, too, took poison. Their bodies were laid in the trench and set alight.

On Tuesday (May 1) the Russians began their assault on what they called the 'Imperial' Chancellery with an attack by the 248th Rifle Division under General N. Z. Galai and the 230th Rifle Division under Colonel D. K. Shiskov with an attack on the buildings facing the Chancellery. As the bitter, last-ditch battle was fought out over their heads, the survivors in the bunker prepared to try to escape. Waiting until nightfall, SS-Brigadeführer Mohnke led the first party out an hour before midnight. One of the last to leave was SS-Hauptsturmführer Günther Schwägermann, Goebbels' adjutant. Taking the last jerrycan, he doused the refreshment room (14) with petrol, tossed a flaming rag inside and quickly shut the door. In this picture we can see that the screen which hid the door to Hitler's study has been pulled aside — leaving the suicide couch visible through the open doorway on the left.

261

Breakout or Surrender

Although General Weidling had prepared a plan for an operational breakout to the west, taking Hitler with him, when it was discussed on the evening of the 28th, Hitler decided that he could not risk exposing himself to the possibility of being captured alive and he then announced his decision to fight on in Berlin. Nevertheless, on April 29 Weidling obtained Hitler's grudging consent to an attempt to escape in small groups the following evening.

Preparations were well under way when Weidling was summoned to the

The carnage outside Friedrichstrasse railway station short of the Weidendamm Bridge following SS-Brigadeführer Dr Gustav Krukenberg's break-out attempt with some of his SS 'Nordland' Panzergrenadier-Division on the night of May 1/2. This photograph was taken by a US Army Signal Corps photographer, Tech/5 Jas F. Kilian, on May 4, one of an enterprising group of six correspondents from the US Ninth Army's XIXth Corps that managed to get through the Soviet lines in jeeps and reach the city. It was an amazing feat, for American forces were not to officially enter the city for another two months.

Führerbunker at 1900 hours on April 30 to learn of Hitler's death and to receive Goebbels' countermanding instructions. Consequently, by the time Weidling was free to proceed with his plan, the situation had worsened to the extent

that surrender was the only feasible solution, although he gave those who wished to do so a chance to break-out during the final hours of darkness before calling for a cease-fire at dawn on May 2.

The captioning of the photographs Kilian took is abysmal, but we can surely forgive him in the circumstances. This was described as the burning Kaiser Frederick Museum — it is of course merely the right-hand continuation of the Friedrichstrasse S-Bahn Station. Bormann and Co. had passed this spot in their escape bid just three days earlier.

Several groups took advantage of this opportunity, and there was a mass break-out from the Zoo, including civilians. Those on foot went through the U-Bahn tunnels, while the remaining armour went up Kantstrasse, successfully joining up with troops from the Kurfürstendamm area on the way. They continued via Ruhleben to Stresow, where the Schulenburg and Charlotten bridges had to be fought over several times, and many were killed in the artillery fire that this action attracted. The survivors then had to run a gauntlet of fire out through Staaken into the Döberitz military training area. Led by a few tanks until they ran out of fuel, one party reached a point half-way between Brandenburg and Nauen before being caught. Nearly all were rounded up by the Forty-Seventh Army before they could reach the safety of the German lines near the Elbe.

Another group smashed their way north across the Spree from the city centre. This was a precipitate move led by five tanks under SS-Brigadeführer Krukenberg, whose foreign volunteers were defending that sector. Mohnke's break-out teams from the Führerbunker had attracted enemy fire on the only exit over the Weidendamm Bridge before Krukenberg had had time to organise his own men properly, and he saw this as a last chance to escape. His tanks were immediately engaged by the Soviet tanks in the area and destroyed, but Krukenberg and a few men got away to a goods yard near the Stettiner railway station, where they were later joined by Mohnke's group and stragglers from the immediate area. They set off again about 200 strong in daylight and came to the Humboldthain Flak-tower, where, to their astonishment, they found flags flying and troops parading as normal under a recently-appointed Generalmajor Erich Bärenfänger, unaware of General Weidling's message. While they were there Weidling's order to surrender was picked up by radio and Bärenfänger's troops prepared to comply, but Mohnke's group continued on its way to the Schultheiss Brewery in Pankow, where they were trapped and obliged to surrender.

However, part of the famous 'Grossdeutschland' Regiment, that had been fighting along with the 7. Fallschirm-Jäger-Division in that area, managed to break out of Prenzlauer Berg with five tanks and 68 men and reach the vicinity of Oranienberg, where the tanks had to be blown up. The men then split up into four groups to continue on foot, most of them getting through safely to the west.

Of this break-out on May 2 Borkowski wrote: 'At the break of day we were taken from our position by a runner. In front of the Flak-towers, from which the soldiers and the men of our battery were streaming, came the word: "Rendezvous at Schönhauser Allee. Break-out to the north."

'The remains of the German Army broke out of the rubble-strewn streets, at first in small groups, constantly growing, finally as a wide, endlessly long column going down Lothringer Strasse to reach Senefelderplatz. There there was an odd silence; hardly a soldier whispered; an unusual tension lay over this march into the unknown. It was quickly becoming light. There where Pappelallee and Schönhauser Allee cross seemed to be the command post, as the procession was being formed up directly under the Danziger Strasse elevated station. Restrained orders could be heard: "Form up for a break-out to Mühlenbeck-Prenzlau." Suddenly I made out the man giving the orders. He was the commander of the three Flak-towers at the Friedrichshain, Humboldthain and the Zoo, Oberstleutnant Hoffmann, sitting in a jeep and looking as elegantly smart as ever.

'The Army tried to break through at about six o'clock in the morning. The

'The Russians broke the bank at Berlin' is the humorous rejoinder to this close-up shot taken by Kilian of the burning building. The fire appears to have now been extinguished.

Kurz vor Beendigung des verbrecherischen Hitlerkrieges wurden hier zwei junge deutsche Soldaten von entmenschten SS-Banditen erhängt.

Das Original - eine der ersten Gedenktafeln Berlins nach dem Krieg - wurde 1990 gewaltsam entfernt.

Today, under the station arches, a plaque records one of the incidents we have already recounted — the summary execution of waverers by the flying court-martial squads.

263

Further up the street, close to Oranienburger-Tor U-Bahn Station, a Soviet picture of a dead Waffen-SS officer. He could well be one of Krukenberg's men or even a straggler from Mohnke's Chancellery escapees as they, too, passed this way.

tracks of German Königstiger tanks rattled, and behind them we were formed up in a long column. Behind us marched SS officers with sub-machine guns held high behind our backs. The astonishing thing is that still no sound of a shot was to be heard. Did the Russians want to spare us, or was the war already over? Then at the Schönhauser Allee S-Bahn Station in front of us I could see Soviet soldiers bringing an anti-tank gun into position. A lanky grenadier from the Grossdeutschland Regiment (he was still wearing the title armband) bellowed: "Long live the Führer, long live Germany!" His words vanished in the thunder of the Russian guns, he was hit and gurgled unintelligibly as he collapsed. A hellish concert began after the Russians had let the tanks drive through, with machine guns, anti-tank guns, bursting shells, as well as the cries of the wounded and dying. I stood in an entrance, while behind me lay Karl-Heinz wounded. Manfred and Peter helped me to carry him over to the S-Bahn station, where we were a little safer from the gun-fire. Bright blood bubbled from his chest, and he was no longer conscious. It was only a few weeks since we had celebrated his sixteenth birthday.

'Up above on Schönhauser Allee the troops were streaming back. The Russians were no longer firing. At Stargarder Strasse the SS officers formed a loose chain with brown-uniformed party members and threatened those going back with sub-machine guns.

This 'Nordland' SdKfz 250/1 from its 3. Kompanie under SS-Obersturmführer Hans-Gösta Pehrsson has been abandoned by its Swedish crew who appear to have been cut down as they emerged. This picture was most probably taken in the Chausseestrasse which continues northwards from Friedrichstrasse. However, nearly all of the street has been rebuilt making any comparison pure guesswork.

"Forwards, comrades, have no fear of those Bolshevist rabble. Grossadmiral Dönitz is coming towards us!" stuttered a drunken officer with SS runes on his collar patches. No one said anything when an Unteroffizier knocked the SS officer down with a pistol shot.'

The remains of the 20. Panzergrenadier-Division tried to break out of Wannsee Island on the same night over the broad bridge leading to Wannsee itself and came under heavy fire from the Soviet troops waiting for them along the line of the railway embankment, where they had barricaded the Potsdamer Chaussee underpass. However, 56 survivors attacked the headquarters of the Fourth Guards Tank Army in the village of Schenkenhorst on May 2. The Russians had to call for help and took two hours of hard fighting to subdue their attackers.

A little later the same spot is crammed with those on their long journey to captivity in the Soviet Union. Tens of thousands of German prisoners were held in Russia right into the 1950s, long after those held in the West had been repatriated. This soured relations between West Germany and the Soviet Union for a decade during which time many prisoners perished.

265

When Bormann's party found Friedrichstrasse blocked where the Weidendamm Bridge *(left)* crosses the Spree, they retraced their steps to the station. From there they moved westwards along the S-Bahn tracks towards Lehrter Stadtbahn Station, crossing this bridge *(right)* where the lines span the Humboldt-haven. As they dropped down to the Friedrich-List-Ufer (in the foreground), they landed right in the middle of a group of Russians under the bridge. Bormann and Dr Stumpfegger managed to break away, running out of the picture to the right towards the Invalidenstrasse.

The escape route that Mohnke had chosen was via the U- and S-Bahn tunnels as far as the Stettiner railway station, at which point he hoped to emerge behind the enemy lines. The party was then to proceed above ground to the Humboldthain Flak-tower, from where each group would have to find its own way to the west via Neuruppin.

First each person had to sprint across Wilhelmplatz to the Kaiserhof U-Bahn Station. This was accomplished in good order and they travelled as far as the part of the tunnel running under the River Spree before they encountered any difficulty. This came from two railway employees who had firm instructions to close the watertight bulkheads once the trains stopped running at night. Although no trains had come through for a week, the doors were still closed and they were not prepared to open them. Surprisingly, Mohnke, who was renowned for his ruthlessness, accepted this situation and they made their way back to Friedrichstrasse railway station, from where they used the footbridge leading across the river, the Weidendamm Bridge being blocked by a German barricade and under Soviet artillery fire. They then worked their way northwards through the devastation until they recognised the ruins of the Natural History Museum on Invalidenstrasse.

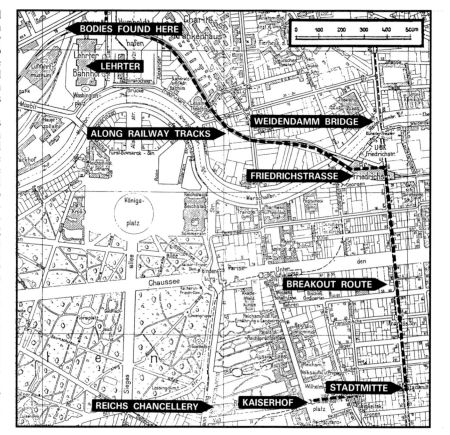

Left: Turning the corner on the far side into Invalidenstrasse, a main thoroughfare most probably crawling with Soviet troops, they must have realised that there was no real hope of escape.

Right: A few yards further on, having reached the bridge over the railway lines, both took poison. Axmann came across the two bodies later that night.

Meanwhile the artillery fire, which had died down at 0130 hours, intensified at 0230 hours and they saw that the Weidendamm Bridge area was being heavily shelled and also illuminated by Russian searchlights. This had happened as a result of subsequent groups from the Reichs Chancellery attempting to make their way above ground, thus attracting Soviet attention. SS-Brigadeführer Krukenberg, commanding the foreign volunteers holding this area, was also obliged to make an impromptu break-out attempt with his last five tanks across the bridge, losing them all in the melée and sustaining heavy casualties. Only a few survivors managed to get through Soviet lines with their general.

Mohnke used this distraction to try and make his way up Chausseestrasse but found his way blocked and was obliged to return to Invalidenstrasse. Eventually his group and Krukenberg's survivors, together with other parties, met in a goods yard near the Stettiner railway station and rested before pushing on to the Humboldthain Flaktower position after daylight. Ninety per cent of the members of these Reichs Chancellery break-out groups are believed to have made a successful escape from the city centre, of which about ten per cent avoided capture by the Russians.

However, one group of five Reichs Chancellery survivors, Bormann, Stumpfegger, Baur, Axmann and Major Wetzen, his aide, had turned left off the footbridge and continued on the railway tracks running along the Schiffbauerdamm towards Moabit. Opposite the Reichstag they came under sniper fire and Baur was somehow left behind when the others continued. They crossed over the Humboldthafen by the railway bridge and then dropped down to the roadway beside the Lehrter railway station right into the middle of a Soviet bivouac. The Soviets took them for relatively harmless Volkssturm making their way home and allowed them through unmolested until Bormann and Stumpfegger made a break for it. They all got away safely but Baur following them was shot and badly injured.

Soon afterwards Bormann and Stumpfegger appear to have considered the situation hopeless and they both committed suicide by taking poison near the railway bridge on Invalidenstrasse, where their bodies were seen shortly afterwards by Axmann and Wetzen. The latter split up shortly afterwards, Axmann finding temporary refuge with an old girlfriend before escaping safely to the west, while Wetzen was caught that same morning.

After the battle, the bodies of Bormann and Stumpfegger were cursorily buried like so many others lying around. All kinds of wild stories circulated about Bormann's fate, and it was not until 1965 that a shallow grave was discovered beside the road barely a hundred yards from the police forensic laboratory. Stumpfegger's unusual size gave the first clue to their identities, which were later substantiated from the dental evidence.

Bormann's body was never recovered, and after the war rumours were rife about his possible escape to South America. The mystery remained unsolved for twenty years until the land between the road and the S-Bahn *(above)* was being excavated for redevelopment. Two skeletons were uncovered — one tall, the other short — which, after forensic examination, proved to be Bormann and the doctor. *Below:* As the burial site is now occupied by the Landesuntersuchungsinstitut für Lebensmittel, our comparison of the police investigation in July 1965 is taken looking back at the elevated S-Bahn, whose arches are now used for workshops.

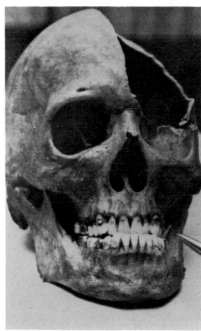

Left: **Bormann's skull as found;** *right* **Stumpfegger after cleaning.**

267

Surrender

Precise date and place unknown, a unit of the Berlin garrison surrenders to the all-victorious Red Army. The war for you is over.

The first negotiations with the Russians had been conducted on April 30 by General Hans Krebs, Chief-of-Staff of the OKH, accompanied by Oberst Theodor von Dufving who had previously been Weidling's chief-of-staff. This was on orders from Goebbels following the death of Hitler. Krebs had been the last military attaché in Moscow, spoke Russian well, and so was a good choice. Krebs's task was to try to obtain Soviet recognition of Goebbels's government (as dictated by Hitler) and a chance of assembling it in Berlin, but he had no authority to negotiate an unconditional surrender, which was all that the Soviets were interested in.

Having been passed safely through the lines with Mohnke's assistance, Krebs was taken to Chuikov's command post in Tempelhof. Krebs started by announcing Hitler's death the day before. Chuikov pretended that he knew already. Krebs then produced a letter from Goebbels giving him the authority to make this statement, his authority to negotiate a cease-fire signed by Bormann, and the proposed Cabinet list drawn up and signed by Hitler the previous day.

Chuikov passed on the contents by telephone to Zhukov at Strausberg, who in turn passed them on to Moscow. A little later, attempts by Oberst von Dufving to establish direct communication with the Führerbunker by field telephone failed, the Soviet signals major accompanying him being shot by German troops and the line repeatedly severed by shell-fire. When von Dufving reported to Goebbels and Bor-

mann that Krebs was making no progress, Goebbels told him to recall Krebs, but by the time he could contact Krebs, sometime after 1100 hours, the latter was about to return anyway, a reply having come through from Moscow.

While all this had been going on, Zhukov had first called upon Chuikov to tell him to get a move on, only to be told that resistance was still as severe as ever and no one was keen to get killed at this point when victory was so near.

---

1. The Reichstag district in the city of Berlin was defended by crack SS units. In the early hours on April 28, 1945, the enemy parachuted in a battalion of marines [sailors] to reinforce the defences of the district. In the Reichstag district the enemy resisted our advancing troops desperately, having turned every building, stairway, room, cellar into strong points and defensive positions. The fighting within the main building of the Reichstag repeatedly took the form of hand-to-hand combat.

2. Continuing the offensive the troops of Colonel-General Kuznetsov's Third Shock Army overcame enemy resistance, took the main building of the Reichstag and today, on April 30, 1945, raised our Soviet Flag above it. Major-General Perevertkin's 79th Rifle Corps and Colonel Negoda's 171st Rifle Division and Major-General Shatilov's 150th Rifle Division won particular distinction in the fighting for the district and the main building of the Reichstag.

3. Congratulating with the victory won, I commend all the men, sergeants, officers and generals of the 171st and 150th Rifle Divisions and the Commander of the 79th Rifle Corps, Major-General Perevertkin, who personally directed the fighting, for the daring they displayed, and skilful and successful fulfilment of the combat mission. The privates, sergeants, officers and generals who won particular distinction in the fighting for the Reichstag will be selected for government awards by the Military Council of the Third Shock Army.

4. The hour of the final victory over the enemy is nearing. The Soviet Flag is already flying over the main building of the Reichstag in the centre of Berlin.

Comrade soldiers, sergeants, officers and generals of the First Byelorussian Front! Forward against the enemy — with our last swift blow let us finish off the Nazi beast in its lair and bring the hour nearer of final and complete victory over Nazi Germany.

This order is to be read in all companies, squadrons and batteries of the front.

CHIEF-OF-STAFF OF THE FIRST BYELORUSSIAN FRONT,
COLONEL-GENERAL M. MALININ

Left: General Krebs arrives at General Chuikov's command post on May 1 which had been set up on the first floor in an ordinary house in a side street near Tempelhof airport. The precise location of Chuikov's CP was not known until the Soviet war poet, Jevgeny Dolmatovsky, returned to Berlin 30 years later. Together with Vsevolod Vishnevsky, a distinguished writer, he had been at the house at the beginning of May 1945, when they had both been witnesses to the surrender negotiations, although the Germans present had been unaware of their identities. Meanwhile, one storey above General Katukov continued to conduct their combined armies' operations. Now the surrender house — No. 2 Schulenburgring — has its place in the battle recorded by a plaque *(left)* beside the front door of a 'house where history was made' *(right)*.

It was a particular feature of Soviet war operations that Russian poets and writers, equipped with honorary officers' ranks, as well as political commissars, went along with the troops to boost their morale with speeches, pep talks and readings from their works. Here Dolmatovsky is seen spreading the word at the midday lesson on May 2. His pulpit is the Pariser Platz.

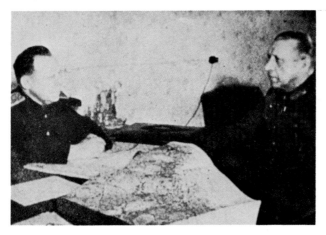

Left: **General Weidling (right) in consultation with General Chuikov after his arrival at the latter's command post early on Wednesday morning. Chuikov told Weidling to write out his** own capitulation order to those of his men who were still resisting. *Right:* **The table at which he signed the surrender note is now at the local history museum in Tempelhof.**

Now Stalin called for a renewed offensive during the afternoon of May 1, interrupting the impromptu celebrations that the Red Army soldiers were indulging in wherever they could. In a late afternoon attack further progress was made, such as the 29th Guards Corps penetrating the Zoo gardens and occupying the Memorial Church overlooking the area, but as soon as night fell the troops inevitably returned to their May Day carousing once more.

Meanwhile General Weidling and his staff were preparing to surrender the Berlin garrison. Late on May 1 the 79th Guards Division picked up a radio message transmitted in Russian: 'Hello, Hello. This is the LVI. German Panzer-

> *On April 30 the Führer, to whom we had all sworn an oath of allegiance, forsook us by committing suicide. Faithful to the Führer, you German soldiers were prepared to continue the battle for Berlin even though your ammunition was running out and the general situation made further resistance senseless.*
>
> *I now order all resistance to cease immediately. Every hour you go on fighting adds to the terrible suffering of the Berlin population and our wounded. In agreement with the Soviet High Command of the Soviet Forces, I call on you to stop fighting forthwith.*
>
> WEIDLING
> GENERAL OF ARTILLERY
> FORMER COMMANDER, BERLIN DEFENCE AREA

korps. We ask you to cease fire. At 0050 hours Berlin time we are sending envoys to parley at the Potsdamer Bridge. The recognition sign is a white square with a red light. We await your reply.'

Colonel-General Chuikov agreed to a temporary cease-fire. Oberst von Dufving, accompanied by two majors, then

The final battle for the Chancellery had been carried out by the 248th and 301st Rifle Divisions, fighting a bitter hand-to-hand battle on the approaches to and inside the building. The courage of Major Anna Nikulina (the instructor of the political department of the 9th Rifle Corps) was singled out by Marshal Zhukov for special praise as she made her way to the roof with a Red Flag under her jacket which she tied to the flag-pole with a piece of telephone wire.

brought the message that General Weidling wished to surrender. The Germans asked for three or four hours in which to prepare as they needed daylight to ensure that their surrender instructions would be complied with, in view of the problem posed by fanatical Nazis still trying to hold out. Chuikov passed a message back to von Dufving that he could inform General Weidling that his offer to surrender was accepted. He added that honourable terms were guaranteed, officers would be allowed to keep their side-arms and take as much hand luggage as they could carry, and that the Soviet High Command would ensure the protection of the civilian population and care for the wounded.

Meanwhile Dr Hans Fritzsche, Permanent Under-Secretary in the Propaganda Ministry, finding that he was the senior civil servant left following Goebbels's suicide, had decided that he should act on behalf of the civilian population and seek Soviet protection for them. He sent a delegation to Chuikov's headquarters during the early hours of May 2 with a letter asking him to be allowed to broadcast to the people and the garrison. Although negotiations with Weidling's envoys were still in progress, Chuikov saw the value of this latest proposal, and ordered its implementation.

General Weidling crossed the Landwehr Canal by means of an improvised suspension bridge near the Potsdamer railway station and was escorted to Chuikov's command post, arriving at about 0400 hours.

'May 2, 1945', wrote Zhukov, 'was a day of great jubilation for the Soviet people, the Soviet Armed Forces, our Allies and the peoples of the whole world.' With over 130,000 men surrendering in Berlin, later that day General Weidling was taken, together with Mohnke, Günsche and other survivors from the bunker, to the airfield at Strausberg (where Zhukov had his HQ), about 35 kilometres east of the city, where the Russians had established a special holding camp for VIP prisoners. Mohnke has told us that the next day (May 4) Weidling and his staff had to leave the camp in the morning, returning that night. Weidling told him that he had been taken to the Reichskanzlei where he was filmed coming out of one of the exits to the Voss-strasse from the cellars beneath the Chancellery. Later the Russians were to use this piece of film, saying that it had been taken at Weidling's headquarters (he had actually fought the battle from the Bendlerblock) after he had signed the surrender document. This would appear to be exit (28) on the plan on page 244, right next to the vehicle lift in the corner.

Voss-strasse today — 45 years on — with the original wartime road surface still to be seen. The Chancellery was stripped of its fittings and fixtures and demolished in 1949; we will show the work under way on a later page. When the Berlin Wall was erected, the street lay right in the middle of the prohibited zone, accessible to no one save the Volkspolizei and Grenztruppen patrols. According to the Communists, one was told that all that remained of the Führerbunker was a mound of earth.

Bearing white air recognition stripes, Soviet armour rolls down the East-West-Axis. Now the rejoicing begins.

'The troops of the First Byelorussian Front, supported by the troops of the First Ukrainian Front, after stubborn street fighting, have completed the routing of the Berlin group of the German forces and today, on May 1, have gained full control of Berlin, the capital of Germany, the centre of German imperialism, and the hotbed of German aggression.' Joseph Stalin.

The surrender was due for implementation at 1300 hours on May 2, but it was nearer 1700 hours before the firing eventually ceased. Long columns of prisoners then started making their slow and painful progress to the assembly point in the chalk mines on the city's edge at Rüdersdorf in the first stage of a process that would keep those that survived the dreaded ordeals of Soviet captivity away for up to ten years.

The fighting within the city had cost the Soviets some 20,000 dead. The German losses are estimated at about 22,500 military and about the same number of civilian casualties.

Aerial bombardment and the land battle had left the city completely de-

Plans for the occupation of the city were already well in hand. Order No. 5 had been issued by the Military Council of the First Byelorussion Front on April 23, and specified that 'All administrative power on the territory of Germany occupied by the Red Army is to be exercised by the military command acting through the military commandants of towns and districts. Military commandants are to be appointed in each city. Executive power is to be exercised by local citizens: burgomasters in the cities and aldermen in towns and villages. They are responsible to the military command for the observance by the population of all orders and ordinances.' The first commandant of Berlin was appointed the following day, a full week before the city was in Soviet hands. Colonel-General N. E. Berzarin who was already a Hero of the Soviet Union, having earned his reputation in the battles of Yassy-Kishinev and Vistula-Oder, was commander of the Fifth Shock Army and a staunch Communist Party member. Here Berzarin (with the cigarette) is seen with Vsevolod Vishnevsky on May 2.

vastated. Much of it looked like a vast wasteland of ruins and rubble-choked streets, littered with burnt-out vehicles and the remains of barricades. Over one fifth of all the buildings in Berlin had been completely destroyed or damaged beyond repair, including 90 per cent of the city centre.

Left: Berzarin (right) begins to cope with his first problem — the thousands of German prisoners now emerging from the ruins. The new Town Commandant had already established his headquarters on Frankfurter Allee in a building far enough from the city centre to have survived the intense shelling. *Right:* The historic house still survives on what was renamed 'Strasse der Befreiung' (Liberation Street) but now changed to Alt Friedrichsfelde. No. 1 lies on the corner of Rosenfelde Strasse.

Their fighting days over, troops are disarmed as they emerge from the subway tunnels. This is the entrance at the northern end of Friedrichstrasse — then and now.

The victors and the vanquished. These dejected prisoners are passing the ornate façade of the Wertheim store on Leipziger Platz.

Some of the 130,000-odd German prisoners taken during the battle being marched away on May 3 past the Schlesisches Tor U-Bahn Station in Kreuzberg. While officers were taken to the camp at Strausberg, other ranks were marched to the mass collecting point in the Rüdersdorf chalk pits to the east of the city to await trans-shipment to the Soviet Union.

As early as the end of March, it was seen that there was a danger that the forces of the Western powers might drive headlong into Soviet troops. By now the advance eastwards had reached a point at which divisional commanders were not always sure just how far their leading elements had travelled, and a clash between friendly ground forces had to be avoided. There was no direct communication with the Russians, but the line of the Rivers Elbe and Mulde was deemed a suitable natural feature at which Western forces could be halted. It was also felt that there would be no advantage in capturing territory which would subsequently have to be handed over to the Soviets as part of their previously agreed Zone of Occupation. The US Ninth Army held its position some 50 miles west of Berlin near Magdeburg and between 70,000 and 100,000 Germans had surrendered to the Americans by May 8. Meanwhile, our intrepid band of Ninth Army correspondents had reached Berlin on Friday, May 4 — we saw some of the pictures Tech/5 Jas F. Kilian took on pages 262–263. *Above:* He described this shot as the 'Berlin Art Institute still burning from the fury of Russian shelling with no attempt to put out the blaze.' *Below:* It is in fact the Altes Museum on the Lustgarten — favoured venue for festivities both before and after the war.

Jas Kilian appears to have carried out a whistle stop tour of the Unter den Linden area, hurriedly banging off shots with his

Speed Graphic plate camera with little thought of framing or whether the subject matter was really worth it.

Left: This photo is more interesting as it shows the barricade at the Brandenburg Gate which was said to be a model of its kind. These civilians appear to be about to start work on clearing it, supervised by a Soviet officer. Right: This undated picture from

East German archives was a remarkable find as the Jeep is described as carrying Soviet and American soldiers. It must be an early picture as the barricade is still in the process of being dismantled; surely this *has* to be Kilian!

Skateboards at the Gate and roving beer wagons outside the site of the Adlon (see plan page 74) — how things have changed in the Berlin of 1990. As Kilian toured Berlin that Friday in May 1945, events 130 miles to the west at Lüneburg were sealing the fate of the German armies in the west. Those forces remaining in north-west Germany and Denmark were facing the British 21st Army Group under Field-Marshal Sir Bernard

Montgomery, and a delegation led by Generaladmiral Hans Georg von Friedeburg, acting on behalf of the new German leader, Grossadmiral Karl Dönitz (now at Flensburg near the Danish border), had arrived at Montgomery's tactical headquarters the previous day. After initial prevarication and attempts to negotiate a settlement, the German party signed unconditionally just before 7.00 p.m. that Friday evening.

Meanwhile Marshal Zhukov, walking in Kilian's footsteps, was making his own tour of the city centre. In this shot, the barricade has been cleared, so the undated picture (from Soviet archives) must have been taken sometime after May 4, although Zhukov describes his visit to the Reichstag and surrounding battlefield as having taken place on May 3.

Left: The Marshal also visited the Bendlerstrasse though no doubt unaware that he was standing on the stage of an even greater drama less than a year before. It appears that the pile of sand, against which the four bomb plotters had been shot, still remains in situ in the background. *Right:* The pillbox covering the vehicle entrance no longer exists.

As described earlier, the Bendlerblock was used by General Weidling as his HQ for the defence of Berlin. This is the front of the building facing the Landwehr Canal, photographed *(left)* in July 1945 and *(right)*, repaired and restored, in 1990.

'After the seizure of the Imperial Chancellery', wrote Marshal Zhukov in his memoirs, 'I went there with Colonel-General Berzarin, Lieutenant-General Bokov, member of the Military Council of the Army, and some other officers who had taken part in the assault in order to make certain of the suicide of Hitler, Goebbels and other Nazi leaders.'

Top: Zhukov and Co. are filmed crossing the Ehrenhof. *Above left:* The symbol of the Nazi defeat. *Above right:* The Marble Gallery, 500 feet long, with Hitler's door on the right. Zhukov: 'On our arrival we found ourselves in an embarrassing situation. We were told that the bodies of the suicides had allegedly been buried by the Germans, but no one knew who exactly had done it or where. Different hypotheses were put forth. The PoWs, mostly wounded, knew nothing about Hitler and his entourage. In the Chancellery only a few dozen people were found. Apparently, at the last moment, the high-ranking officers and the SS men had left the building by secret tunnels and gone into hiding in the city. We looked for a place where the bodies of Hitler and Goebbels were burned, but could not find it. Admittedly, we saw the ashes of some fires but they were obviously too small. Most likely German soldiers had used them to boil water.'

'When we had almost finished inspecting the Imperial Chancellery, it was reported to us that the bodies of Goebbels' six children had been found in an underground room. I must admit I had not the heart to go down and look at the children killed by their own mother and father. Shortly afterwards the bodies of Goebbels and his wife were found close to the bunker. Dr Fritsche, who was brought to identify the bodies, testified that they were those of Goebbels and his wife.' Marshal Zhukov, writing in 1974. According to the account published four years earlier by an interpreter on his staff, Lev Bezymenski, a Counter-Intelligence Section of SMERSH had been formed to search for 'important documents, capture of war criminals, etc.', and a detachment under Lieutenant-Colonel Klimenko was sent to the Chancellery on the afternoon of May 2. *Above left:* The bodies of Goebbels and Magda were taken to Plötzensee Prison, where the unit was stationed. Various Germans who had been captured were brought in to identify the bodies, including Vizeadmiral Hans-Erich Voss *(above right)*, Dönitz's liaison officer in the bunker.

According to Bezymenski, the children were not discovered in the Vorbunker until the following day (May 3) by Senior Lieutenant Ilyin. Their bodies were taken to Plötzensee together with that of General Krebs who had also committed suicide in the bunker. As these bodies had not been damaged by fire, indentification was easier.

Now the search was on for Hitler. Voss told Klimenko that although he had not witnessed it himself, he had been told that Hitler's body had been burned in the garden. In spite of the fact that it was now evening, Klimenko took Voss back to the Chancellery where they poked about in the bunker and looked around the garden. Although not fire damaged, one corpse discovered in the pond bore a remarkable likeness to Hitler, but in daylight the following day it was rejected. Klimenko then began searching again in the area close to the bunker exit where Goebbels had been found, and where one of his men had come across human remains the previous day. On May 5, two soldiers, Deryabin and Tsybochin, were set to work to disinter two bodies *(left)* which were recovered together with that of a German Shepherd dog *(right)*.

The badly burned corpses were put in two wooden crates and taken, together with the bodies of two dogs (a second had been found nearby), to the headquarters of the Third Shock Army which had been established in the northern suburb of Buch.

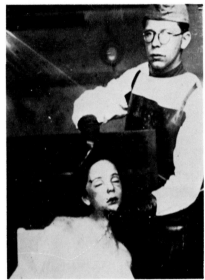

Buch was and still is a centre of medical facilities which the Russians had taken over to establish field hospitals. The nine bodies previously discovered had already been taken to the hospital mortuary where a team of pathologists under Professor N. A. Krayevski, the chief anatomical pathologist of the Red Army, performed the autopsies on May 8. *Left:* In this picture, the body of General Krebs is on the dissecting table. The woman pathologist is Dr Anna Yakovlevna Marents, the chief pathologist with the First Byelorussian Front. *Right:* Helga Goebbels — the eldest of the six children.

The mortuary *(left)* lay at the rear of the main hospital (now the Stadt Klinikum *right*) near the S-Bahn station. During the post-mortem, the jaw from the male corpse was removed complete with the teeth and an associated dental bridge which was subsequently identified by Hitler's dental assistant, Fräulein Käthe Heusermann, as belonging to Hitler. Cyanide compounds were detected in the internal organs and fragments of glass in the mouth indicated death by poisoning. Much has since been made of the fact that no direct evidence was offered in the Soviet report of bullet wounds in the head, conflicting with descriptions by bunker survivors who state that Hitler had shot himself. The autopsy noted that part of the cranium was missing and that the right side of the head — the side through which Hitler is supposed to have shot himself — was more badly burned. Other commentators on Hitler's suicide find the omission of gunshot evidence, or the description of it, suspicious, and believe that it was suppressed deliberately by the Russians in order to discredit the manner of Hitler's death assuming, one supposes, that it is more cowardly and less soldierly to take poison than a bullet.

While these macabre events were taking place at Buch, elsewhere affairs of state were occupying the minds at the top. The surrender signed at Field-Marshal Montgomery's headquarters on the evening of May 4 had been followed up the next day by individual capitulations at Innsbruck, Austria; Baldham, Germany, and Wageningen in the Netherlands. Later that afternoon, von Friedeburg (right) was despatched to SHAEF headquarters at Reims to prepare the way for an overall German surrender. The Chief of the OKW Operations Staff, Generaloberst Alfred Jodl (centre) arrived in Reims on the evening of May 6 and the document was signed just after midnight. (On the left Major Wilhelm Oxenius, ADC to Jodl.)

Karlshorst

Following the surrender of the German Armed Forces in the Netherlands, north-western Germany and Denmark to Field-Marshal Montgomery on the Lüneberger Heide on May 4, General-admiral von Friedeburg was sent on to the Supreme Headquarters Allied Expeditionary Force (SHAEF) at Reims to implement an overall German capitulation. Von Friedeburg attempted to do a deal for a partial surrender that would enable the Germans to evacuate 50,000 troops from Courland and 100,000 from East Prussia, for which he needed at least another ten days. Eisenhower would not agree to this and demanded an immediate unconditional surrender to be effective at midnight on May 8. A message to this effect was sent to Dönitz who had no option but to agree. Dönitz then ordered his commanders on the Eastern Front to break out to the west with their troops as fast as possible and fight their way through the Russians if they had to. All hostilities against the Western Allies were to cease immediately.

Consequently, Generaloberst Alfred Jodl, in his capacity of Chief of OKW operations staff, arrived in Rheims and signed an act of surrender at 1245 hours (2.41 a.m. BST) on May 7. It was countersigned by Lieutenant General Walter Bedell Smith, Chief-of-Staff Supreme Headquarters Allied Expeditionary Force, on behalf of the Supreme Commander; by Major-General Ivan Susloparoff on behalf of the Soviet Supreme Command, and by General François Sevez on behalf of the French

However, Joe Stalin was not amused. Not only had the ceremony been held in a French town, using a document other than the one that had already been agreed, but he had not even authorised the Soviet representative to sign anything at all! Furious, he called Zhukov in Berlin: 'Today, in the town of Reims, the Germans signed an act of unconditional surrender. It was the Soviet people who bore the main brunt of the war, not the Allies. Therefore the Germans should sign the surrender before the Supreme Command of all the countries of the anti-Hitler coalition, and not just before the Supreme Command of the Allied Forces.' Stalin went on to say that 'I also did not agree to the unconditional surrender not being signed in Berlin, the centre of Nazi aggression. We reached an understanding with the Allies that the surrender act signed at Reims should be considered a preliminary protocol of surrender. Tomorrow, representatives of the German High Command and representatives of the Supreme Command of the Allied Forces will arrive in Berlin. You are appointed representative of the Supreme Command of the Soviet Forces. Vyshinsky will join you tomorrow. After the act is signed he will remain in Berlin as your assistant in charge of political affairs.' This is the German engineering school at Karlshorst in south-east Berlin which the Red Army had taken over for their military headquarters.

The representatives of Britain, France and the United States arrived at Tempelhof at midday on May 8 to receive a warm welcome from Colonel-General Berzarin and other high-ranking members of the Red Army. After inspecting the Soviet guard of honour drawn up on the tarmac, and watching a march past, the Allied delegation was then driven at high speed to Karlshorst. The Western Press was now in Berlin for the first time: this is the scene outside the officers' mess where the ceremony was scheduled to take place, pictured by a photographer of the US Signal Corps.

chief-of-staff. However, the document which had been used was a last-minute draft by Smith, who had forgotten that he already held the text of the official surrender document that had taken the diplomats of the European Advisory Council six months to prepare. This whole business greatly upset Stalin as he wanted the surrender to be effected on his own ground and, with the questionable validity of the document signed at Reims, the Allies were obliged to agree to the whole process being repeated in Berlin the next day. Major-General Susloparoff was promptly ordered to return to Moscow in disgrace and was never heard of again.

Stalin therefore sent to Berlin Andrei Vyshinsky, his First Deputy Commissar of Foreign Affairs, to organise the event which would be presided over by Marshal Zhukov. Representing General Eisenhower would be Air Chief Marshal Sir Arthur Tedder accompanied by General Carl Spaatz, commanding the US Strategic Air Force in Europe, and Général Jean de Lattre de Tassigny, commanding the First French Army. They were met on landing at Tempelhof airport by Colonel-General Vassili Sokolovsky, Zhukov's deputy, a large Soviet guard of honour bearing hastily improvised flags of the victorious nations, and a band to play

the national anthems. They were then driven through the ruined city to Karlshorst, where the officers' mess building of the former Germany Army engineer training centre had been selected as a suitable location for the forthcoming ceremony.

Behind the official Allied delegation, in a separate C-47 provided by the Royal Air Force, came the German delegation headed by Generalfeldmarschall Wilhelm Keitel with General-admiral Hans-Georg von Friedeburg and Luftwaffe chief Hans-Jürgen Stumpff, attended by half a dozen aides, who had been authorised by Dönitz to sign the capitulation. They

Now part of the main Soviet military headquarters in Berlin, the building in which the surrender was signed was opened in 1967, as a combined museum and memorial to the Red Army's exploits in the capture of Berlin. Now its long-term future is in the balance as the withdrawal of all Russian forces from the city is due to be completed by 1994.

Protocol again dictated events as General Eisenhower prepared to fly to Berlin when it was pointed out that, as Allied Supreme Commander, he would way outrank Marshal Zhukov who was nominally only an army group commander. Ike's place was therefore taken by his deputy, Air Chief Marshal Sir Arthur Tedder, seen here entering the Soviet headquarters, a hundred yards or so from the mess. The building is still in use and subject to strict security — hence no comparison.

too were driven from Tempelhof to Karlshorst, where they were accommodated in a separate building pending a summons to the ceremony.

The Allied delegates, after a luncheon break provided by the Russians in some houses across the road from the building in which the ceremony was to be held, went to the main building to discuss the procedures to be followed in the surrender ceremony with Zhukov, but first there was a short session with the representatives of the news media in attendance.

There were some problems to be resolved. The ceremony had originally been scheduled for 1400 hours but they had to wait for Vyshinsky to arrive from Moscow with all the necessary documents for signature in order to begin. The Russians had failed to provide a French flag among those displayed in the hall where the ceremony was to take place, and de Lattre insisted there be one, so the Russians agreed to make one, but the first attempt came up with the colours shown horizontally as opposed to vertically. Then there was a dispute with Vyshinsky about who should sign. Zhukov and Tedder had agreed to sign as principals with the others as witnesses, but Vishinsky at first argued that although de Lattre might sign on behalf of his country, Spaatz could not as Tedder was already representing both the British and American forces. It was nearly 2300 hours before agreement was finally reached that all four would sign.

At 2345 hours Moscow time (2145 hours Central European Time) the Allied representatives assembled with Vyshinsky, Generals Telegin and Soko-

lovsky in Marshal Zhukov's panelled office so that they could move into the main hall promptly on the hour. The four senior representatives sat down at the green baize-covered top table, behind which the flags of the four victorious nations were displayed on the wall. Before them at right angles three other green baize-topped tables were

crowded with the Soviet generals of Zhukov's 1st Byelorussian Front that had taken part in the capture of Berlin and the staff officers accompanying the Allied delegation, while representatives of the news media crowded round under a blaze of arc lights.

Marshal Zhukov opened the ceremony by declaring: 'We, representatives of the Supreme Command of the Soviet Armed Forces and the Supreme Command of the Allied Forces, have been authorised by the governments of the anti-Hitler coalition to accept the unconditional surrender of Germany from the German Military Command. Bring in the representatives of the German High Command.'

Generalfeldmarschall Keitel came in first and saluted the top table with his raised baton. He was followed by von Friedeburg and Stumpff. They were asked to seat themselves at a small table prepared for them by the door through which they had come. Their aides stood behind them.

Zhukov asked them: 'Do you have the instrument of unconditional surrender of Germany? Have you studied it and are you authorised to sign this document?'

Air Chief Marshal Tedder repeated these questions in English.

Keitel replied: 'Yes, we have studied it and are ready to sign.' he then handed over a document signed by Dönitz authorising Keitel, von Friedeburg and Stumpff to sign the instrument of unconditional surrender.

Zhukov stood up and said: 'I ask the German delegation to come over to this table. Here you will sign the instrument of Germany's unconditional surrender.'

Keitel walked across, sat down on the edge of a chair and started signing five copies of the document. Next came von

Generalfeldmarschall Keitel (left), the senior German Army officer present, arrives with von Friedeburg representing the German Navy. The third German delegate, not visible, Generaloberst Hans-Jürgen Stumpff, was head of the Luftwaffe.

Marshal Zhukov: 'The first to enter, slowly and feigning composure, was Generalfeldmarschall Keitel, Hitler's closest associate. Keitel was followed by Generaloberst Stumpff. He was a short man whose eyes were full of impotent rage. With him entered Generaladmiral von Friedeburg who looked prematurely old. The Germans were asked to take their seats at a separate table close to the door through which they entered. The Generalfeldmarschall slowly sat down and pinned his eyes on us, sitting at the Presædium table. Stumpff and von Friedeburg sat down beside Keitel. The officers who accompanied them stood behind their chairs. Rising, I said: "I ask the German delegation to come over to this table. Here you will sign the instrument of Germany's unconditional surrender." Keitel quickly rose, shooting a malign glance at us. Then he lowered his gaze . . . and walked unsteadily to our table. His face was covered with red blotches. . . . Putting his monocle in place, Keitel sat down on the edge of the chair . . . His hand was shaking slightly.'

Friedeburg, followed by Stumpff. By 0043 hours on May 9 Moscow time (2243 hours on May 8 Central European Time) the signing ceremony had been completed by all the signatories and Zhukov asked the German delegation to leave.

As soon as the German delegation had gone, Zhukov stood up and cordially congratulated everyone present on behalf of the Soviet High Command on their long-awaited victory. There was uproar as everyone started congratulating everyone else. Then followed a vast banquet at which many toasts were drunk and many speeches given. It ended in the small hours of the morning with singing and dancing, even by Zhukov himself. As the participants left the premises the Red Army guards outside fired their weapons into the air in jubilation.

The Second World War in Europe, which the Russians called the Great Patriotic War, had at last officially come to an end.

The room used for the signing is now the centrepiece of the Karlshorst museum. It remains exactly as it was on May 8, 1945, save for the addition of a large green carpet which, it is claimed, was booty removed from the Reich Chancellery.

One of the reporters present was Clifford Webb of the *Daily Herald*: 'And then an astonishing thing happened. The eager crowd of Russian photographers could contain their enthusiasm no longer. They surged forward until they all but engulfed the top table, pushing and struggling among themselves to thrust their cameras within inches of Keitel's furious face while he signed. Reporters stood on chairs until other reporters pushed them off. It was probably the most uproarious surrender scene in history, and yet the top table somehow managed to retain a calm dignity and the signings proceeded as arranged. The signings complete, the documents were carefully stored away in blue folders, and everybody repaired to the largest ante-room for conversation and beer, Marshal Zhukov among them.'

PART IV
OCCUPATION

Military Government

The East-West-Axis (which from now on we should more properly call the Charlottenburger Chaussee) being given the once-over in the aftermath of battle.

Colonel-General Nikolai Erastovitch Berzarin, Commander of the Fifth Shock Army, was appointed Soviet Commandant of Berlin and Commander of the Berlin Garrison on April 24, while the fighting for the city was still in progress. He issued his first orders to the populace on April 28, banning all organs of the Nazi Party and encouraging the reopening of businesses, shops, bakeries, cinemas, theatres and restaurants. The Soviets immediately began re-establishing the local administrations under their control, that for the Borough of Reinickendorf being pro-visionally established on April 29, and arrangements were made for the distribution of food, the military themselves handing out some of their rations.

On April 30 the first group of German Communists, led by Walter Ulbricht, were flown from Moscow to start work on forming a Communist-guided administration for the whole of the future Soviet Zone of Occupation in accordance with plans they had been working on for the past two years.

However, for most of the civilian population their first encounter with the occupying troops involved arbitrary looting, rape and sometimes even summary execution. Although the official policy of revenge had been revoked, this as yet had had little effect on the troops, and those who had experienced German atrocities at first hand were the worst offenders. Later the governing mayor, Ernst Reuter, quoted the figure of 90,000 victims of rape within the city. This state of lawlessness was to continue for about two months until the Soviets could impose proper disciplinary measures, and the arrival of the Western Allies brought about more effective control of their sectors.

Left: **Travelling westwards, these refugees have just crossed the Charlottenburg Bridge on the approach to Hitler's old** saluting base. *Right:* **Save for the high-rise blocks, the lamp-posts, the stonework and the Ernst-Reuter-Haus still stand.**

Above left: **The Russians chose a new location for their saluting base, midway between the Brandenburg Gate and the Grosser Stern, close to where the Siegesallee crossed the road. In typical Soviet style, the tribune included portraits of Roosevelt, Stalin and Churchill, a noble gesture on behalf of the Soviets because Harry Truman had now replaced the former President who had died on April 12.** *Above right:* **Later that year, the permanent Soviet war memorial replaced the tribune.** *Right:* **On the opposite side of the road stood this stylised painting of the Big Three at Yalta, seen here being photographed by an American soldier and his buddy in July. As far as Stalin was concerned, he intended to hold his main victory parade on his home ground in Moscow on June 24, at which he intended to give Marshal Zhukov, to whom he had awarded a third Gold Star for his Hero of the Soviet Union decoration, the honour of taking the salute. The Red Banner of Victory was to be brought from Berlin together with the flags and standards of 200 German units which were to be cast down on the steps of the Lenin Mausoleum in a dramatic, symbolic act of finality.** *Below:* **Meanwhile the Russian victory was being celebrated in Berlin.**

Bells are ringing over Berlin in celebration of the Allied victory. Somewhere at this hour the famous parade is taking place — it doesn't concern us. We've heard that for the Russians today has been made a special holiday, that the troops have been issued vodka to celebrate the victory. At the pump we were told that women should keep to their houses. We don't know whether to believe this. I decide to wait and see.

Meanwhile we discuss the subject of alcohol. Herr Pauli says he had once been told that German troops had been given orders never to destroy stores of alcohol, but to leave them to the advancing enemy since experience had shown that alcohol delays him and diminishes his ability to fight. This is so much male twaddle, invented by men for men. Two minutes' thought should be sufficient to make them realise that alcohol makes men lecherous and increases considerably their sexual drive (although not their potency, as it has been my lot to learn). I'm convinced that had the Russians not found so much alcohol here, there wouldn't have been half the number of rapes. These Ivans are no Casanovas. To commit their acts of sexual aggression they first have to work themselves up artificially, drown their inhibitions. I'm sure they know this, or at least guess it, otherwise they wouldn't be so crazy for anything even smelling of alcohol. . . .

Thursday, May 10

Gisela was not alone. She had taken in two young girls, sent to her by some acquaintances — two students, refugees from Breslau. They sat there in silence, in the almost empty but clean room. After the first excited exchange of words, a silence fell over us all. I sensed some tragedy in the air. The two young girls had deep black rings under their eyes. The few words they spoke sounded hopeless and bitter. Gisela took me out on to the balcony where she whispered that both girls had lost their virginity to the Russians and that they'd had to take it many times. Hertha, the twenty-year-old blonde one, has been in great pain ever since and doesn't know what to do. She cries a great deal, Gisela says. The other, Brigitte, nineteen and finely made, covers up her psychological shock with angry cynicism. She overflows with hatred and bile.

Gisela herself managed to get off unharmed, with the help of a trick I wish I had known before: before becoming an able editor Gisela had had some ambitions for the stage and among other things had taken a class in make-up in her dramatic school. She used this knowledge to transform her face into that of an old woman, covering her hair with a scarf. On arriving in the cellar with their flashlights, the Russians immediately picked out the two girls but pushed Gisela, with all her wrinkles of charcoal, back in her chair: 'You Babuschka, no good!' . . .

Monday, May 21

Ilse and I quickly exchange the inevitable first question: 'How often, Ilse?' — 'Four times. And you?' — 'No idea. I had to work my way up through the ranks as far as a major.'

We sit together in the kitchen, drinking real tea produced to celebrate the occasion, eating bread and jam and telling our stories . . . Yes, we've all had our share. Ilse had had to take it first in the cellar, then in an empty flat on the first floor into which she had been shoved with rifle-butts. One of them, she says, had tried it with his rifle over his shoulder. At this she got really scared and with gestures tried to tell the man to put his weapon away — which he actually did. Before Ilse had come to the end of her story her husband excused himself, ostensibly to get some news from his neighbour's crystal set. As he went out, Ilse made a grimace. 'Tcha, he can't take that.' It seems he torments himself with reproaches for having remained passive in the cellar while the Ivans were raping his wife. The first time, in the cellar, he was even within earshot. Must have been a strange experience for him. . . .

Thursday, May 24

Woke up early. This time I put on my blue overalls and an apron. The sky was cloudy again, and by the time we lined up it had begun to drizzle. We worked hard; there were even two men shovelling with us — though they worked only when they felt the supervisor's eye on them. Suddenly at about ten o'clock we heard a shout. A Russian voice: 'Woman, come! Woman, come!' — words only too familiar to us. In an instant the women had scattered in all directions. They crept into doorways, cowered behind tubs and hills of rubble. But before long some of them, myself included, came out again into the open. 'They wouldn't dare! — Here, on the open street! Anyway, there's only one of them . . .'

This one, however, proceeded to act. He was a lieutenant, and with his rifle gripped in both hands he drove the rest of the women out of their hiding places and into a group. Having rounded us up as though we were a flock of sheep and he a dog, the lieutenant herded us across the allotment gardens and into the grounds of a tool factory. In the huge halls hundreds of work benches stood deserted. The walls, however, resounded with the shouts of Heave-ho! — for German men under Russian supervision were loading the gigantic parts of a power press on to trucks, while more men were unscrewing and dismantling the machines, lubricating them and dragging them away. Outside on the factory tracks stood a long line of trucks, some of them already loaded high with machinery. . . .

Monday, May 28

Today our Ivans were especially gay. They patted and pinched us and repeated their favourite bit of German: 'Bacon, eggs, sleep at your home.' And in order to make their meaning quite clear they laid their heads in the crook of their right arms, like Raphael's angels.

Bacon, eggs — we certainly could do with some. So far as I could see, however, there were no customers for the tempting offer. I dare say that rape in the open, in broad daylight, with so many people about, would be rather difficult. Hence the 'sleep at your home'. What they want is a willing girl in need of bacon to take them to her flat. I'm sure there are any number of girls who would be willing, but none of them dares.

Again we wash shirts, underwear, and handkerchiefs. By now I've come to know my two companions quite well. Little Gerti, nineteen, delicate and thoughtful, told me in an undertone several stories about her love troubles, of one friend who left and of another who was killed in the war. . . . I steered the conversation toward the last days of April. After some time she told me with lowered eyes that one night three Russians had dragged her out of the cellar and raped her, one after the other, on the couch in someone else's flat. After they had had their way the three young men had revealed a strange sense of humour. While rummaging through the kitchen cupboard they had found nothing but some jam and ersatz coffee. Amidst loud peals of laughter they had slowly spooned out the jam on to little Gertie's head and then sprinkled the jam with ersatz coffee. . . .

One real problem for us washerwomen is the toilet. The only place at our disposal is enough to make one shudder; there isn't a spot less than an inch high in filth. During the first days we tried to clean it up a bit with our slop water, but the pipes are completely blocked. The worst of all is that the Russians waylay us there. . . .

Incidentally, by now an official expression has been coined for the whole business of rape: 'Compulsory intercourse' — a phrase that might be included in the new edition of the soldiers' dictionary.

A WOMAN IN BERLIN

For two months, Berlin was in the exclusive control of the Russians who made few bones about taking what they considered were their rightful spoils of war; either at an official level or by the soldiery themselves. At the same time came the import of the political aspect of a communist state: the slogans and the portraits. The banner reads: 'Long live the Soviet soldiers who hoisted the Flag of Victory over Berlin.'

In the meantime the official Soviet looting to meet reparations had begun. Special units were deployed throughout the city for the systematic stripping of industrial assets and anything that might help in the reconstruction of the devastated Soviet Union. Some 80 per cent of Berlin's industrial machinery was removed in this manner, much of it being damaged in the process through ignorance on the part of the work-force. One special item was three million dollars worth of gold found in the vaults of the ruined Reichsbank.

On May 29 a recommendation was made in the European Advisory Council whereby the Commanders-in-Chief of the Four Powers should meet in Berlin on June 1 to sign the 'Declaration Regarding the Defeat of Germany and the Assumption of Supreme Authority by the Allied Powers', which read:

'The Governments of the United States of America, the Union of Soviet Socialist Republics and the United Kingdom, and the Provisional Government of the French Republic, hereby assume supreme authority with respect to Germany, including all the powers possessed by the German Government, the High Command and any state, municipal, or local government or authority. The assumption for the purposes stated above, of the said authority and powers does not affect the annexation of Germany.'

The importance of the second sentence was that it avoided the permanent extinction of Germany as a country, although it was to be another 45 years, in fact not until March 15, 1991, before Germany was actually to regain its full

However, it was not all bad. Policewoman Katya Spivak demonstrates her attributes on Hindenburgplatz directing traffic to (left) Potsdamer Railway Station, Steglitz, Leipziger Platz; (right) Lehrter Railway Station, Reichstag, Ministry of the Interior.

From occupation . . . to re-unification. We grabbed this appropriate matching shot of two young revellers on the eve of German unification in October 1990.

Left: **The text beneath the huge portrait at the top of Unter den Linden simply stated 'Marshal of the Soviet Union, J. V. Stalin.' In the background the ruined French Embassy.** *Right:* **A group of visitors on a whistle-stop tour of the city are given the local spiel but, without photographs to compare, how can they** conjure up the sights of yesteryear? The S-Bahn entrance, just visible behind Joe Stalin, was being broken open when we took our comparison, as part of the removal of the security restrictions imposed by the 40-year rule of the GDR which led to the stations near the Wall being sealed.

sovereignty with the Soviet government's ratification of the Four-plus-Two Agreement.

The meeting was eventually agreed and, on the morning of June 5, General Dwight D. Eisenhower, Field-Marshal Sir Bernard Montgomery and Général Jean de Lattre de Tassigny flew in their own individual aircraft to Berlin with the basic staff to establish the Allied Control Council (also referred to as Commission), which they anticipated would come into being as soon as the 'Declaration' was signed. They were driven in separate convoys to the suburb of Wendenschloss, where Marshal Zhukov was occupying a villa alongside the Dahme river. They too were allocated riverside villas, where, after Eisenhower had presented Zhukov with the American Legion of Merit, they were made to wait, and it was only when they threatened to leave that they were summoned to the yacht club. There the signing ceremony eventually took place at 1700 hours.

Eisenhower then asked Zhukov when the Control Commission staff could begin work, but Zhukov said that the troops would first have to be established in their proper zones, the Americans and British having to withdraw to the agreed zonal boundaries from the temporary boundary on the Elbe. Montgomery gave an estimate of three weeks to achieve this, with which Zhukov agreed. As the Russians had clearly made no provision for overnight accommodation and had been so aggressively discourteous to their guests, the Western Allies declined an invitation to a lavish banquet prepared for them.

Truman told Stalin that he was prepared to order the American withdrawal to commence on June 21 'in accordance with arrangements between the respective commanders, including in these arrangements simultaneous movement of the national garrisons into Greater Berlin and provision of free access by air, road and rail from Frankfurt and Bremen to Berlin for US forces.' However, Stalin asked for a postponement, saying that Marshal Zhukov was needed back in Moscow for

On June 5, 1945, the first glimmer of the problems to come between 'East' and 'West' was made apparent at the initial meeting between the military leaders of the four Allies to set up the Allied Control Council which was to be the organisation responsible for the governing of Germany. Ike and Monty fume as they are kept waiting by Zhukov for the conference to start at Wendenschloss — a suburb on the south-eastern outskirts of the city at Köpenick.

Although an advance party under Colonel Frank Howley had reached the city on June 17 after considerable difficulty with the Russians, the appearance of the US 2nd Armored Division on July 4 signified the official entry of the Western Allies into Berlin. July 1 had been the chosen date for the occupation to begin, but delaying tactics by the Soviets had squeezed another four days' grace. As it happened, the new date was more historic — American Independence Day. This 'Hell on Wheels' Sherman has halted for a moment on the Hauptstrasse at Innsbrücker Platz near Rathaus Schöneberg.

a meeting of the Supreme Soviet and for the Victory Parade scheduled for June 24, suggesting instead July 1 as a suitable date. Truman agreed, providing sufficient troops could arrive before then to start preparing for the Big Three conference due to commence in Berlin in mid-July.

Major-General Floyd L. Parks, the nominated Commanding General, Headquarters Berlin District (US Sector), obtained grudging Soviet permission to fly into Berlin on June 22, and was taken to Babelsberg, where he was met by Colonel-General Sergei Kruglov, Stalin's security chief, and shown the areas reserved for the various delegations and the Cecilienhof, where the meeting was to take place.

The Americans then despatched a large reconnaissance party under the

The Americans had used Reichsstrasse 1, the main road from the south-west, which joined the Berlin autobahn beyond Potsdam. However, a visible reminder of just who had got to Berlin first greeted the Yanks at the beginning of the Potsdamer Strasse at Zehlendorf where the Russians had constructed a monument on which sat the first Soviet tank to have entered Berlin.

Even during the early occupation years, the tank was defaced by Berlin youths, causing its subsequent removal to a new, more inaccessible location beside the autobahn. (We will show it in its new position later on.) We sought out the original spot, virtually unchanged save for the growth of the trees. The house visible in the 1945 photo still remains.

Potsdamer Strasse changes its name several times on its ten-mile run to the city centre where it ends at the Potsdamer Platz. *Above:* At the same time that the Americans were entering their designated sector, Russian troops were leaving it, taking with them as much loot as they could carry. The Soviets had already removed vast quantities of property, livestock and industrial machinery as reparations during the two-month interregnum. Sergeant Bonwitt of the Signal Corps pictures the scene as a colleague on the left films the Russian convoy proceeding south.

command of Colonel Frank L. Howley on June 17, but they were so harrassed and obstructed en route by the Russians that only a limited number of them got through as far as Babelsberg, where they were penned into the UFA film compound by Red Army sentries. However, Howley and his deputy managed to get permission to drive to Tempelhof with an NKVD escort in order to confer with an American aircrew due to fly in, and, as their escort did not know his way through Berlin, they were able to arrange a route that took them through five of the six boroughs which had been allotted to the American Sector.

On June 29, Lieutenant General Lucius D. Clay and Sir Ronald Weeks, the US and British Deputy Military Governors, flew to Berlin to confer with Marshal Zhukov. It transpired that the

The former Deutsche Bank on the right is the only building still standing at the very top of Potsdamer Strasse as the street at the northern end has since been realigned a little further to the west. We have already seen the same domed building looking from the opposite direction on page 229.

The Red Army had captured the Leibstandarte 'Adolf Hitler' barracks at Lichterfelde on April 24; now they were forced to vacate and let the Americans take charge. *Right:* The Stars and Stripes is raised to fly alongside the Hammer and Sickle. Note that the Nazi eagle has been removed from its plinth.

latter was not prepared to allow the Allied garrisons into Berlin until the remainder of the Soviet Zone had been vacated, but was prepared to allow reconnaissance parties into Berlin on July 1 with the main bodies arriving on July 4, using the Helmstedt-Berlin autobahn, the adjacent railway line and one air corridor splitting over Magdeburg to allow access from Frankfurt and Hannover.

On July 2 the American and British divisional commanders, Major-Generals Parks and Lewis Lyne, accompanied by Colonel Howley, went to meet the Soviet City Commandant, Colonel-General Aleksandr Gorbatov, with whom it was agreed that the Americans and British would take over control of their sectors at midnight on July 4.

Consequently, the advance parties of the British and Americans arrived in Berlin on July 1 and began taking stock of the situation, earmarking accommodation for the main bodies of about 20-25,000 troops each due to arrive on July 4. These parties, consisting mainly of officers assigned to military government duties, were totally unprepared for the extent of devastation that greeted them in Berlin, which was far greater than anything they had experienced in Germany so far.

The US 2nd Armored Division and the British 7th Armoured Division started off for Berlin on July 4 only to find themselves held up by the Russians at the Elbe and obliged to make lengthy detours, which eventually had them both converging on the Helmstedt-Berlin autobahn in some confusion and arriving in the city tired and late. The American troops were even more annoyed to find themselves involved in a previously-agreed handover ceremony with the Russians at the Lichterfelde Barracks before belatedly having to bivouac in the Grunewald, events hardly in keeping with their idea of how to celebrate Independence Day.

General Omar N. Bradley, First Army Group Commander during the invasion of Europe, but present here in his capacity as Acting Commander of US Forces in Europe during the absence of General of the Army Dwight D. Eisenhower. Handing over is Major-General Baranov, the Soviet representative. Also present are Major General Floyd L. Parks, the new commandant of the US Sector of Berlin, and Général Jeoffroy de Beauchêne, the first French Commandant.

First German, then Russian, now American. Andrews Barracks: we saw its early history on pages 15, 62 and 63.

After taking over the American Sector of Berlin, General Bradley and his staff toured the Reichstag. The hole blasted by mortars firing horizontally, through which the Soviet troops gained entrance, can be seen behind the central left pillar.

British troops also entered Berlin on July 4 along their own route — Reichsstrasse 2 — west of the Havel River. Major-General Lewis Lyne took the salute as his 7th Armoured Division, the 'Desert Rats' of El Alamein fame, led by the 11th Armoured Brigade, drove up Pichelsdorfer Strasse in Spandau to cross the Havel by the Schulenburg Bridge.

The British 7th Armoured Division, the famous 'Desert Rats', entered their sector from the west along Heerstrasse. They could now proudly boast that they had advanced all the way from their famous victory at El Alamein to Berlin. The war had been over for a month and so they had had plenty of time to smarten up their vehicles and themselves for this triumphant entry into the enemy capital. As the Frey Bridge over the Havel had been blown by a chance Russian shell hitting the demolition chamber on May 1, they turned north into Pichelsdorfer Strasse, where their commander, General Lyne, took the salute on a dias erected outside a tram depot. They then swung east across the Schulenburg Bridge and so on towards the city centre. The Berliners watching were suitably impressed and some even applauded, as others did the Americans, welcoming the arrival of the Western Allies as a relief from their treatment under the Russians.

The tram depot, in front of which the saluting dias was located, has since been replaced by a block of apartments.

A Bren-gun carrier turns off Pichelsdorfer Strasse into Weissenburger Strasse, heading for the bridge. The sign says 'Berlin Centre'.

Skirting Wannsee and following the left bank of the Havel, we drive towards Spandau, through green woods where the birds are singing, and where flowers have sprung up round a few graves by the roadside, mostly German, with curved steel helmets stuck awkwardly on rough wooden crosses; though Berlin is so close we are in the country again, till a dead-tank park looms up, crowded with buckled, broken, twisted wreckage and black and grey monsters of every kind, their caterpillar tracks sprawled out or looped up or broken into chunks, as though it were some ghastly workshop where Vulcan had indulged a whim to play with mechanical toys, until one day he became cross and in a fit of ungovernable rage smashed them all.

Just after four o'clock the column draws to a standstill on the Pichelsdorferstrasse, some half a mile away from the saluting base where the General, our own Divisional Commander, is waiting for us. Everyone is tired and dusty, but in good heart. We decide there is time (as there always is for the British soldier) for a quick cup of tea, and after that and a brisk check over the cars we are off again in a few minutes.

It is exactly 1625 hours Russian time when the leading armoured car comes in sight of the saluting base where Major-General Lyne stands, flanked by motion-picture cameras and military police. Even if we are not the first Allied armour to reach Berlin — earlier today tanks of the US 2nd Armoured Division (a formation whose nickname is that unforgettable piece of Americana, 'Hell on Wheels') rolled in from Halle — this is still in its way a big moment. Tomorrow's papers will be full of references to Journey's End for the Desert Rats and A Trail Blazed from El Alamein to Berlin, but there are few soldiers among us who think of it in that way; for it does not seem like the end of a journey, only another stage. Yet Berlin has been for so long the hub around which so many hopes and fears and jokes

and allusions revolved, that only by reaching the city can we really seem to have won the war. Twelve months ago the armoured cars began to carry the chalked inscription 'à Berlin' which pretty French and Belgian girls scrawled on their plating (besides their addresses and telephone numbers), and today, unreal as it seems, this has come true.

The cars shine brilliantly in the late afternoon sun, for they have been painted and varnished and repainted and polished over the last weeks. They are medium green, with their squadron and divisional signs picked out in red and yellow, and wherever webbing appears it is a glossy white. The little scarlet jerboas, or desert rats, with their looped tails, looked especially fine. All this contrasts with the drab ruins of Pichelsdorfer Strasse and the dark crowd of Germans which lines the pavements and clusters in knots on the uneven rubble. These hundreds of Germans are by no means sullen or resentful, as some of the papers will report them tomorrow for greater effect: they gaze fixedly, but many smile and some wave, a few almost cheer. It is indeed more like a sober liberation welcome than a triumphant entry into a conquered city, and for that, without doubt, we have the Russians to thank. Who could ever have foretold this, the most amazing irony of all, that when we entered Berlin we would come as liberators, not as tyrants, for the Germans?

The cars sweep by, the cameras whirr, the General stands stiffly to attention and salutes; our yellow pennants flutter from the wireless aerials: they have been made, with a certain relish, out of captured Nazi flags, dyed and stitched by the womenfolk of Schleswig-Holstein. In a few moments our last car has gone by, and the infantry, led by the 1st Battalion Grenadier Guards and the Devonshire Regiment, have their turn.

RICHARD BRETT-SMITH, *BERLIN '45*

This was one of the two bridges over which part of the Berlin garrison had fought to break out on the night of May 1/2.

At first, whatever the differences brewing at top level, it was all 'comrades in arms' to the infantrymen on the ground. *Left:* Clifforde Mark, a keen amateur photographer, was one of the first in the city with the Signals section preparing communications for the Potsdam Conference. He took this picture overlooking the River Spree which formed the boundary between the British and Soviet Sectors just north of the Reichstag. *Right:* Lazy days and holidays 45 years later. The open ground on the far side of the river was the scene of several escape attempts after the Wall was erected along the line of the S-Bahn embankment — the one along which Bormann had tried to make his own escape to the west.

The barracks taken over by the Allies had been stripped by the Russians of everything removable, including electric power plugs, door handles and even water taps. All that was left were piles of rotting potatoes and excreta, for even the toilets, which many of the simple Red Army soldiery did not know how to use anyway, had gone. Consequently the local housewives were rounded up and set to cleaning out the premises, as Richard Brett-Smith recalled in his book *Berlin '45 — The Grey City:*

'These Hausfrauen, indignant at first, soon found that there was no escape, and sensibly concluded that it would be wisest to work with a will and finish their unpleasant task as soon as possible . . . They were "commanded" by one of our captains with a staff of interpreters, and he worked with such tireless equanimity, directing, chasing, encouraging, and jockeying his Amazonian horde, that very soon he was the most popular man in Spandau. Considering the disgusting nature of the work this would have been extraordinary, were it not that the British were confirmed in their character of bulwark against Russian oppression, and these Berliners, who were in any case only too eager to make friends, demonstrated the truth of the assertion, "The more you organise a German, the more he looks up to you".'

The attitude of the citizens at that time was described by Major J. Butlin, who was on the advance party and became the first Town Major of Charlottenburg.

'Among the Berliners I met, I found little or no sense of guilt for initiating a world cataclysm, accompanied by brutalities and bestialities which are now known all over the world. Such an attitude was regrettable but, to me at

The sector boundary ran close by the eastern side of the Reichstag along the western curb line of the Hermann-Göring-Strasse. These trams — the same ones visible in the flag-raising picture on page 240 — lie in the Soviet Sector.

Our comparison looks directly along the line of the Wall a few months after it had been dismantled. (The sector boundary actually ran through the centre of the lamp posts.)

The dead had been buried where they fought their last battle. These German graves lie in the borough of Schöneberg beside Nollendorfplatz U-Bahn Station, just inside the American Sector.

'To nationals other than our own, we are an incomprehensible race and it must be admitted that at times we have done little to dispel that idea and not perhaps least when we assumed the occupation of the British Sector of Berlin. The inhabitants greeted us with servility and wondered what was going to happen next. But to their astonishment this small though powerful force, having rumbled its way through their streets in every form of warlike vehicle from Churchill tank to Jeep, tucked itself modestly away among the ruins and forthwith began to take a frenzied interest in such prosaic matters as drainage and water-supply, trams and buses, lighting and heating, hospitals and feeding for the civilian population, and all those thousand and one domestic details so dear to the British heart.

'To the Germans all this just didn't make sense. To many of them this lack of initiative on our part was a matter of considerable disappointment. Especially to some of the ladies. No sacking of the city. No fate worse than death.

any rate, partly understandable. The non-Nazi element of the German people feel, rightly or wrongly, that they have already suffered enough and are convinced they were powerless to overthrow the Nazi regime once it had got into its stride.'

His own attitude effectively reflects his reaction to the problems that confronted him: 'Whatever conflict of views there may be among the four occupying powers, the British name will go down to posterity with enhanced glory if, in the aftermath of victory, we never lose sight of the principle that "Unconditional surrender demands unconditional responsibility".'

In the British sector alone, only 28,000 homes had survived undamaged out of 300,000, with about 900,000 inhabitants living somehow in the ruins out of a total remaining population of 2,500,000. At the same time, thousands of dispossessed refugees from the eastern provinces were passing through the shattered city every day. Apart from the prevailing hunger, there was a constant threat of epidemics and disease arising from these circumstances. Unconditional responsibility meant a lot of hard work for the victors, as Major-General E. P. Nares, the second British Com-

mandant, wrote a year later in a brochure for British troops visiting the city:

'For many of us July 1945 marked the end of a long journey, when as victors in a desperate war on the result of which our future existence depended, we entered the enemy capital.

No executions. All quite astonishing and unprofessional. And so the occupation continued to unfold as it had begun. Churchill's "Blood and tears, toil and sweat" took on a new meaning. Few of us have worked harder, even in war, than we did then to save our recent enemies from pestilence and famine.'

With hundreds of eager, souvenir-hunting British and American soldiers suddenly let loose in the capital, the Number One target was the Chancellery and Hitler's bunker. *Above:* The Russians may have had their pick of the souvenirs, yet this series of pictures taken outside the main entrance would appear to have been specially set up with the dead German deliberately positioned on the steps surrounded by dozens of NSDAP insignia. *Left:* More substantial souvenirs. The eagle is the one from over the Ehrenhof doorway (see page 100) and is now on display in the Central Museum of the Soviet Armed Forces in Moscow *(below left)* along with the banners gathered together for the Moscow victory parade (page 289). No sooner had the troops arrived on the 4th than dozens made a bee-line for the Wilhelmplatz. The Chancellery was guarded by Russian soldiers, its vast halls and corridors a shambles. *Below:* A direct hit had made a mess of the Runder Saal on the direct route to Hitler's office.

Above left: **In the hall of the mountain king — the Marmorgalerie leading to the Führer's lair.** *Above right:* **At the far end the doorway led to the Grosser Emfangsaal — the large reception room (the plan is on pages 98-99). Richard Dimbleby** (second from left), **now with his feet planted firmly on terra firma, made his first broadcast from occupied Berlin on the first day while sitting in Hitler's office** *(below).* **The broadcast went out at 9.00 p.m. that evening.**

In this room were hatched many of the major plots of National Socialism. It was, in its time, a grand — almost overbearingly grand apartment; a huge, high chamber with brown marble walls on which great tapestries were hung. Those tapestries now have disappeared into the rubble and the chaos that lie along the marble floor, making it with the dust that lies powdered on it so slippery that you have to pick your way across. Here by the window where Hitler sat and Hitler worked, I found his chair and I am sitting in that chair now. What's left of it is just the back, which has been ripped up; it looks as though it was done by bayonets. The tapestried seat and one broken arm. And by its side, turned upside down and crashed on to the floor, is his great marble desk, fifteen feet long and five feet wide.

That is where Hitler worked. Today it lies in the filth and the rubble that are found in every corner of this huge building in Berlin.

RICHARD DIMBLEBY,
BBC BROADCAST, JULY 4, 1945

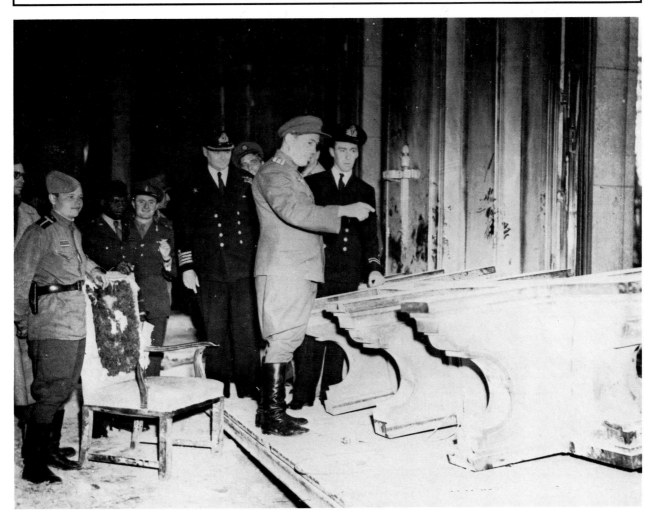

One of the first pressmen on the scene was Jim O'Donnell of *Newsweek* who was also at the Chancellery on the 4th: 'In the long Parian marble halls of the New Reich Chancellery itself, most of which, to my surprise, was still defiantly standing, I met perhaps a dozen uniformed soldiers, Russian, British, American — and one Frenchman, a liaison officer. Nobody seemed to know for sure just where the already half-legendary Führerbunker was.

'I went outside into the Chancellery garden which looked as if it had been churned up by giant moles. What had once been trees were now blasted, uprooted stumps. The rusty tail of a dud bomb poked up from a crater. I trod warily. In the far corner of the garden, I came across a rectangular, tawny-coloured cement block, perhaps twenty feet high, with a narrow oblong entrance and indented vestibule. This was the obscure entry to the bunker, yet it resembled nothing so much as an old weathered pillbox in the Maginot or the Siegfried Line. A single Russian soldier, armed but pleasant enough, stood on sentry duty. At first I feared he might have orders to turn sightseers away. No, he simply wanted to show me a snapshot of his Natasha far away, back in Russia. He was only a private first class, but he was proudly wearing his Stalingrad medal. I saluted him in the name of the common victory, and offered him a pack of Camels. He accepted and in return handed me a yellow kerosene lantern. . . .

'Worse than the darkness and the dankness was the odour. The ventilation system had long since been closed down, but from the sickening sweetness of the stench coming from it, I guessed that a rat must have got trapped inside and

died. The untended latrines, although still in use, were clogged. There had been suicides down here, but the smell was not the sweet-sour smell of decaying human flesh; it was the distinct malodour of the rubble of war.

'I had now been underground perhaps twenty minutes. I noticed that one of the visiting Red Army officers, less booby-trap-conscious than I, had donned an old German gas mask. That had solved for him the problem of the smell. As he left, he handed the mask to me. I, too, had been about to flee up those steep concrete stairs gasping for fresh air. Now I could move about, room by room. I counted more than thirty cubicles, and was astonished by how cramped they were — three by four metres, at most; many even smaller. Obviously the origi-

nal German occupants had fled in a hurry, for they had left behind a mass of military impedimenta. It was equally obvious that victorious Russian soldiers had ransacked the place. There was nothing much of any intrinsic value left, no full liquor bottles, no usable weapons, no blankets or articles of clothing, no dress-daggers, radios or cameras. Everywhere the floors, corridors, and duckboards were littered with glass shards, bottles, rusty picture frames, German Army cheesecake photos, warped gramophone records, scattered sheet-music, dented air raid warden helmets, empty first-aid kits, bloodied bandages, old knapsacks, tin cans, ammunition drums, empty pistol clips, scattered playing cards, film magazines, cigar and cigarette butts, slimy condoms . . . '

Richard Brett-Smith: 'On 6th July I watched the Union Jack run up a flagstaff at the foot of the Siegessaüle, the memorial of the German victory in the Franco-Prussian war. The ceremony in the Grosser Stern took place in a drizzle of rain, was simple and impressive, and seemed to awe the watching Germans. Richard Dimbleby broadcast it expertly and quietly from the monument itself for the BBC. The flag would fly, it was said, as long as British troops remained in Berlin. Whether or not the same promise was made about the French tricolour, which waved on high from the gilded figures of victory above the four rows of cannon which the Germans had filched from Paris in 1871, the subject was an unfortunate one and stupidly brought up: for by 1949, and perhaps before that, neither British nor French flag could be seen in the Grosser Stern'. The 7th Armoured Division parade at the Victory Column, held two days after the occupation of the British Sector began, including a composite Canadian infantry battalion headed by the pipes and drums of the Argyll and Sutherland Highlanders of Canada.

In 1943 when the cross-Channel invasion of France was being planned, due regard was given to the end product — the occupation of Germany. The staff of COSSAC (Chief-of-Staff to the Supreme Allied Commander), meeting in London under the chairmanship of the Deputy Prime Minister, Clement Attlee, put forward their plan for the division of Germany between Britain, the United States and the Soviet Union. Germany proper would be divided into three 'Zones', while Berlin would be sub-divided into three further areas to be called 'Sectors'. The Attlee plan used the existing boundaries of the various German Länder (or states) and gave the Soviet Union Mecklenburg, Pomerania, Brandenburg (the state surrounding Berlin), Saxony-Anhalt, Thuringia, Saxony, Silesia and East Prussia. Because US forces were to be assigned the western landing beaches in France, American forces would therefore be obliged to advance to Germany on a southern axis with the British to the north. This determined that the United States would end up occupying southern Germany — the states of Bavaria, Baden-Würtemberg, Hesse, and the Rhine Palatinate, while Great Britain would be in possession of the north-west: Schleswig-Holstein, Lower Saxony, the Ruhr, North Rhine-Westphalia. The European Advisory Commission, set up to define the terms of the post-war government of Germany, agreed the Attlee proposals in September 1944.

Two days after their arrival, on July 6, the American and British Deputy Military Governors, Generals Clay and Weeks, went to see Marshal Zhukov at his headquarters in Pankow to determine the procedures for the four-power administration of Berlin. The Russians showed themselves far from friendly and the atmosphere deteriorated even further as the meeting progressed. Zhukov and his staff were clearly reluctant to give up control of any part of the city. When Clay put forward the proposal the city be run as a whole by one central administration, Zhukov agreed to having a central policy-making body but insisted that each nation have full and exclusive control of its own sector. To their surprise and dismay he also told them that they would have to assume responsibility for providing their own sectors with food and coal, claiming that the system in the hinterland from which Berlin normally drew its food supplies had completely broken down and that the coal sources in Upper Silesia were now in Polish hands. However, they could have a single distribution and ration system for the whole city, providing the British and Americans produced their due quotas. With an estimated 900,000 inhabitants in the British Sector and 800,000 in the American, this would mean about 40,000 tons of food per month according to his calculations. The British and Americans had naturally expected Berlin to be fed from its hinterland and their governments had not yet recognised the transfer of Upper Silesia to Poland, so this all came as a nasty shock.

The western zones were incapable of providing sufficient food, as was the United Kingdom, so eventually Washington agreed to provide the necessary foodstuffs, while the British organised coal supplies from the Ruhr. The Allied Kommandatura was established in an insurance company's offices off Thielallee on Kaiserwerther Strasse in the American Sector. The first meeting took place on July 11 with General Gorbatov, Major-General Parks, Major General Lyne and Général Jeoffroy de Beauchêne as the representatives of the

The protocol provided for Berlin to be controlled by an 'Inter-Allied Governing Authority' consisting of the three commandants appointed by the respective Commanders-in-Chief. This governing body became better known as the Allied Kommandatura and was located in a building taken over from an insurance company on Kaiserwerther Strasse, deep in the American Sector. As Colonel-General Berzarin, the Soviet commandant, had been killed in a traffic accident on June 16, his place was taken at the first meeting by Colonel-General A. V. Gorbatov (Third Shock Army).

Our comparison was taken in 1991, shortly after the building had been handed back to its original owners.

The Sectors were established using the districts of Greater Berlin as defined by the German law of April 27, 1920. To the Soviet Union went the north-eastern part comprising Pankow, Prenzlauer Berg, Mitte, Weissensee, Horst Wessel (which now reverted to Friedrichshain), Lichtenberg, Treptow and Köpenick. The north-west was assigned to Great Britain: Reinickendorf, Wedding, Tiergarten, Charlottenburg, Spandau and Wilmersdorf. The United States received the remaining boroughs of Zehlendorf, Steglitz, Schöneberg, Kreuzberg, Tempelhof and Neukölln.

four nations, although the French had yet to have a sector allocated them. Unfortunately the Western Allies agreed that the regulations and ordinances already made by the Soviets would remain in force until further notice, an act that would seriously handicap their future deliberations.

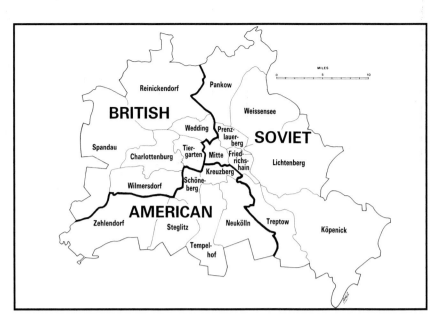

However, the 1944 protocol avoided addressing one major issue: the right of access to Berlin across the Soviet Zone. At the time, the British had not expected that the Zones would be sealed off from one another, and the Americans believed the simple right to be in Berlin carried with it the automatic right of access. Another miscalculation by the Western Allies was the acceptance of all the regulations which the Soviets had imposed on Berlin during the previous two months — endorsed in Order No. 1 of the Allied Kommandatura *(centre)* issued on

July 11. *Left:* The Press photographs taken that July endeavoured to portray the concord between the Allies, and the Four Powers (France was given her own Zone at the Potsdam Conference) administered the city from this building until the Soviets walked out on July 1, 1948. The Western Allies continued to hold meetings there until October 2, 1990, with offices and a place at the table permanently reserved for the Russians who never came to the building again. *Right:* 'Two Powers' in 1991. Your Editor with the power behind the throne.

The formal occupation of the city by the Four Powers officially began with the first meeting held at Kaiserwerther Strasse on Wednesday, July 11. As Colonel Howley, the deputy American commandant stated later, by agreeing to the acceptance of the Soviet ordinances already in place, 'we acquiesced to Russian control of Berlin'. Thereafter, it became impossible to change any of the officials already appointed to run things Soviet style in the western sectors, including the police force. The outward signs of the Four Power status were already evident on the streets as notices were erected where roads crossed the sector boundaries. The following day a ceremony was held at the junction of the British and Soviet Sectors when Field-Marshal Montgomery, the British Commander-in-Chief, invested Marshals Zhukov and Rokossovsky of the 1st and 2nd Byelorussian Fronts with the Order of the Bath (GCB and KCB respectively).

General Eisenhower had already conferred the Legion of Merit on Marshal Zhukov in Berlin on June 5, acting on behalf of the government of the United States. Stalin had reciprocated five days later when Zhukov presented Eisenhower and Montgomery with the Soviet Order of Victory in a ceremony at American headquarters in Frankfurt-am-Main. *Left:* Now it was the turn of the British government who had included OBEs for the Marshal's deputies, Colonel-Generals Sokolovsky and Melinus. *Right: After the Battle* researcher Roger Bell stands in for the long-forgotten military policeman.

As regards the choice of a suitable venue, Zhukov says that he put the onus on Montgomery. Zhukov records that the Field-Marshal replied: 'Soviet troops dealt the coup de main at the Brandenburg Gate where they hoisted the Red Flag over the Reichstag. I believe this is the right place to present you with the British decorations honouring the merits of the Soviet troops you commanded.' Prior to the issue of the awards, Marshal Zhukov was invited to inspect a Guard of Honour provided by the 1st Battalion, Grenadier Guards. The picture was taken by Fred Ramage, a Fleet Street war correspondent/photographer with Associated Press, who had driven over 1,200 miles in six days in April covering the advance.

Meanwhile, preparations were proceeding apace for the Potsdam Conference, as Lavrenti Beria, Head of the NKVD reported to Joseph Stalin and Vlatislav Molotov, the Soviet Foreign Minister on July 2 in curious style:

'The NKVD of the USSR reports on the completion of the preparation of the

Left: **Although the parade was held west of the Brandenburg Gate facing the Reichstag, the two traffic islands and tramlines actually lay in the Soviet Sector as the borough boundary between British-occupied Tiergarten and Soviet-controlled** Mitte ran along the edge of the pavement so even the tanks are in the east! *Right:* **When the Wall was erected in 1961, this spot fell within the East German security zone and was left untouched for thirty years.**

measures for the preparation for the reception and accommodation of the forthcoming conference. 62 houses (10,000 square metres) have been prepared and a two-storey detached house for Comrade Stalin with 15 rooms, an open veranda, and an attic (400 square metres). This house stands on its own and is fully equipped. There is a post and telegraph office. There are stocks of game, fowl, gastronomic goods and groceries as well as other produce and drinks. Establishments have been set up seven kilometres from Potsdam with cattle and chicken farms, and market gardens, as well as two bakeries. The whole staff is from Moscow. There are two special airports available. As guards there are seven regiments of NKVD troops and 1,500 ordinary troops available. The guard is organised in three rings. The chief of the bodyguard at the detached house is Lieutenant-General Vlassik. The guard of the conference centre is under Kruglov.

Even the places where the posts for the Russian traffic signs had stood in 1945 were unrepaired when the area became accessible again in 1989.

That same day, the first low-level aerial obliques were taken by another Associated Press photographer, Henry Griffin, in an L-4 Cub. By now these locations should be familiar, so we will leave readers to pick out the salient features themselves.

This picture is undated, so may not have been taken with the others on July 12. It looks extremely unlikely that it was as there are no signs of the medal parade on the Hindenburgplatz or even the preparations for it.

Our helicopter shots were taken in October 1991 with Sergeant Steve Benco of the Army Air Corps at the controls.

The following day — Friday, July 13 — the 7th Armoured Division held its own parade at which the salute was taken by its commander, now British Commandant in Berlin, Major-General Lewis Lyne. Other units were represented — this is the RAF Regiment — but this was considered a 'private' victory march for the Desert Rats. The saluting base was a new one on the northern side of the Charlottenburger Chaussee west of the Victory Monument and in line with the Hansaviertel church.

Zhukov claims that it was the Russians who, after holding their own parade in Moscow on June 24, first proposed that a quadripartite victory parade should take place in Berlin at which the salute should be taken by the Commanders-in-Chief of the Soviet, American, British and French forces. However, the quadripartite Berlin parade did not materialise until September, when it assumed the dual purpose of celebrating victory over Japan as well as Germany.

> On this occasion, the termination of Combined Command, I welcome the opportunity to express my gratitude and admiration to the people of the Allied Nations in Europe whose fighting forces and nationals have contributed so effectively to victory.
>
> United in a common cause, the men and women of Belgium, Czechoslovakia, Denmark, France, Luxembourg, Netherlands and Norway joined with the British Commonwealth of Nations and the United States of America to form a truly Allied team, which in conjunction with the mighty Red Army, smashed and obliterated the Nazi aggressors. I pay tribute to every individual who gave so freely and unselfishly to the limit of his or her ability. Their achievements in the cause for which they fought will be indelibly inscribed in the pages of history and cherished in the hearts of all freedom-loving people.
>
> It is my fervent hope and prayer that the unparalleled unity which has been achieved among the Allied Nations in war will be a source of inspiration for, and point the way to, a permanent and lasting peace.
>
> DWIGHT D. EISENHOWER, JULY 14, 1945

July 13 was also a landmark day in another respect as it marked the disbandment of SHAEF at midnight. Both Eisenhower and Montgomery believed that a combined headquarters with the retention of a Supreme Commander would be the best method of governing Western Germany, but these proposals had been overruled by the Combined Chiefs-of-Staff. SHAEF was effectively superseded by the Allied Control Council on July 1 but General Eisenhower, then in the United States, requested that formal disbandment be held over until he returned to his Frankfurt headquarters to bid farewell to his staff. *Left:* When Eisenhower returned to Berlin on July 20, he was acting in his position as the United States Commander-in-Chief. On the right is his deputy, General Lucius D. Clay. (There was a small measure of historic continuity when the SHAEF shoulder patch was adopted for the US Army in Europe.)

At the beginning of June, Churchill had set out his guidelines for the forthcoming Three Power Conference — the third in the series which had begun with Teheran in November 1943, followed by Yalta in February 1945. 'I propose "Terminal" as the code-word for the conference', minuted Churchill, stressing that 'we are in Berlin by right, on terms of absolute equality and not as the guests of the Russians'. Nevertheless, it was the Russians who were the only ones in a position to provide suitable facilities as Zhukov explains: 'A group of top-ranking officials from the Foreign Affairs Commissariat arrived to make preparations for the forthcoming conference. I explained to them that there was no suitable accommodation in Berlin for the conference of the Heads of Government. I suggested they look over the area of Potsdam. Potsdam was also badly damaged, and it was difficult to accommodate the delegations there. The only big building in Potsdam that remained intact was the Palace of the German Crown Prince. It had enough room for meetings and for the work of numerous experts and advisers. The heads of delegations, foreign ministers and principal advisers and experts could be well quartered in Babelsberg (outside Potsdam) which had remained practically undamaged. Before the war it had been the residence of high-ranking government officials, generals and other prominent Nazi leaders. The suburb was made up of a large number of two-storyed villas amid thick greenery and flowers. Moscow approved our proposal to start preparations for the conference in the Potsdam area. Consent to hold the conference there was also given by the British and the Americans. There was a rush to put the territories, the premises and the driveways in order. Numerous squads and units of engineers had to be assigned for this job. Work continued almost round the clock. By July 10 everything was ready and the premises were almost fully equipped. Merit should go to the officers of the rear services who accomplished a great deal of work in very little time. A particularly hard task fell to the Chief of the Quartermaster's Division, Colonel G. D. Kosoglyad.'

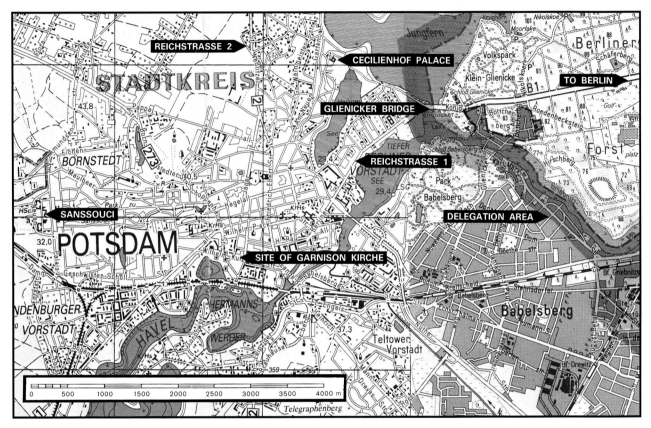

'Inside the palace itself 36 rooms and a conference hall with three separate entrances were given a major repair,' explained Marshal Zhukov. 'The Americans requested that the premises set aside for the President and his staff be finished in blue, the British, for Churchill, in pink. The Soviet quarters were finished in white. In the Neuer Garten, countless flower-beds were laid and up to 10,000 flowers and hundreds of decorative trees were planted. The meetings were held in the biggest room of the palace, in the middle of which stood a round, well-polished table. It is an interesting point that we were unable to find a round table of the size we needed in Berlin. It had to be made urgently in Moscow at the Lux furniture factory and brought to Potsdam.' In this photo, the table has arrived and the chairs are being given a final polish by a Russian girl under the watchful eye of a British military policeman — an official picture released for publication in the London evening papers on July 16.

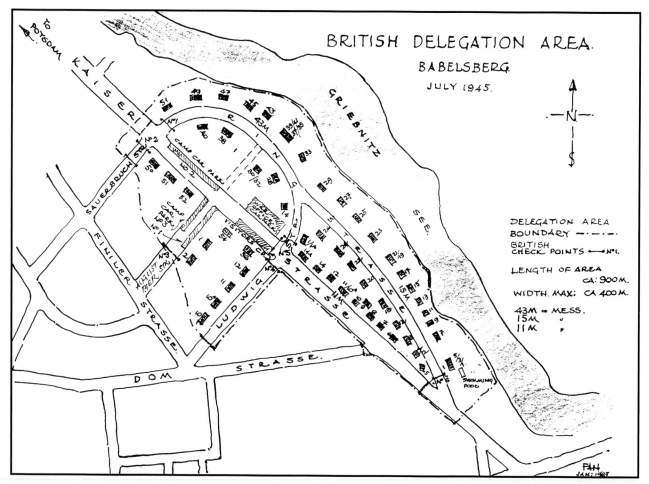

The British compound at Babelsberg, as compiled by Major Freddie Newton, who was responsible for the British facilities. *Ringstrasse, north-east side.* (1/3/5) Main delegation telephone exchange Delegation Foreign Office Signals Communications Centre and Bag Room. (7–11) Delegation staff (now demolished). (13) Delegation staff. (15) Delegation staff mess. (17) Delegation staff. (19/21) Rt Hon. Anthony Eden, personal staff and mess. (23) Known as 'No. 10'. The Prime Minster (Rt Hon. Winston Churchill — later Rt Hon. C. R. Clement Attlee); Mary Churchill, ATS; PM's personal staff; map room and map room staff (RN, Army and RAF); PM's mess. (25–27) Delegation staff. (33) Rt Hon. C. R. Clement Attlee; personal staff and mess. (35–39) Delegation staff. (43) Delegation Administrative Office and staff; delegation senior officers' and officials' mess; VIP entertainment room. (45–47) Delegation staff. *Ringstrasse, south-east side.* (2/4) Delegation staff. (8) General Sir Hastings Ismay; Major-General L. C. Hollis; Field-Marshal Sir Henry Maitland-Wilson. (12) Marshal of the RAF Sir Charles Portal; Air Commodore Sanderson; personal staff. (18) Lord Cherwell (PM's physician); delegation staff. (20) Sir Alexander Cadogan;

Sir A. Clark-Kerr; Foreign Office delegation staff; Sir William Strang; Sir Walter Monkton. (22–24) Admiral of the Fleet Sir Andrew Cunningham (First Sea Lord); personal and supporting naval staff. (26) Field-Marshal Sir Alan Brooke (CIGS); Lieutenant-General Sir James Gammell; Major-General W. D. A. Williams; personal and supporting military staff and some civil servants. (28) Delegation staff. (30/32) Major F. A. Newton, RE, and staff 42 Works Section, RE (now demolished). (38) Royal Marine orderlies. (40) ATS, typists and Women's Services. *Ludwig-strasse.* (1/1A) Field-Marshal Sir Harold Alexander; Major-General R. S. Airey; Major-General R. Laycock; personal staff. (10) HQ 4th (Lines of Communication) Sub Area staff. (10a) HQ 4th (Lines of Communication) Sub Area staff. (11) HQ 4th (Lines of Communication) Sub Area 'A' mess. (12) HQ 4th (Lines of Communication) Sub Area staff. *August-Bier-Strasse.* (1–2) Senior military and civilian personnel. *Kaiserstrasse.* (10A/11) Delegation staff mess. (15) 105 Provost Company, CMP. (52) 84 General Hospital, RAMC. (Others) Junior military and civilian personnel. (President Truman's residence was at No. 2 Kaiserstrasse, with Generalissimo Stalin at No. 27.)

Left: Site of the main checkpoint (No. 3) on August-Bier-Strasse and, *right*, Checkpoint No. 1 at the beginning of Ringstrasse leading to the Prime Minister's residence. Churchill arrived in

Berlin on Sunday, July 15, having flown with his daughter, Mary, from Bordeaux after a ten-day break, in good time for the first session on Tuesday.

'A special train has been prepared. The route is 1,923 kilometres *(sic)* long (1,095 through the USSR, 594 through Poland and 270 through Germany). The route has been secured by 17,000 NKVD troops and 1,515 ordinary troops. There are between 6 and 15 men on guard for every kilometre of track. Eight NKVD armoured trains will form an escort.

'A two-storey building has been prepared for Molotov (11 rooms). There are 55 houses for the delegation, of which eight are fully detached.'

The Soviets had allocated houses to all three delegations in Babelsberg, a select residential area for successful businessmen and film stars from the nearby UFA film studios, but had omitted to allocate accommodation for the Allied troops needed to administer their delegations' areas. For instance, the British administrative support provided by Brigadier O. M. Wales's 4th Lines of Communication Sub Area were allocated 56 houses, all in a good state of repair and guarded by Soviet troops, but then had to negotiate space for themselves, which was eventually found in part of the UFA film studio area.

The Soviets maintained a strict control of all the routes linking the delegations' residential areas with the conference centre in the Cecilienhof and the nearby airfield at Kladow in the British Sector (later known as RAF Gatow) for the use of which special passes were issued. Closer inspection by the British team revealed that many of the houses were not suitably equipped for the purpose required of them and a considerable amount of preparatory work and

With the new influx of VIP visitors, all wanted to see the sights in Berlin — meaning the Reichstag and Chancellery. This picture shows the three British Chiefs-of-Staff, Field-Marshal Sir Alan Brooke (Chief of the Imperial General Staff), Marshal of the RAF Sir Charles Portal (Chief of the Air Staff), and the First Sea Lord, Admiral of the Fleet Sir Andrew Cunningham, walking through the arched rear entrance of the Reichstag. 'I was very impressed by the degree of destruction,' wrote the CIGS in his diary. 'We went to the Reichstag and from there to the Chancellery. It was possible to imagine the tragedies that had occurred there only some two and a half months ago: Hitler's study in ruins, with his marble top writing table upside down, the Gestapo HQ opposite and the scene of all their last struggles. In one part of the apartments, masses of Iron Crosses on the floor and also medal ribbons. On the way up I was handed a German decoration in its box by a Russian private soldier. In fact the whole afternoon seemed like a dream and I found it hard to believe that after all these years I was driving through Berlin.'

In the post-war reconstruction, the vehicle ramp has been replaced by steps.

adjustment was still required. The most important failings to be corrected were the electricity supply, which was found to be limited and liable to interruption, the water supply, which was adequate but unsuitable for drinking purposes, and the domestic sewage system, which proved totally inadequate for the numbers concentrated in what were intended merely as family houses.

Above: **The Prime Minister with Foreign Secretary Anthony Eden, arriving at the Reichstag accompanied by Churchill's interpreter, Major A. H. Birse, and his Scotland Yard bodyguard, Inspector W. H. Thompson perched on the rear seats.** *Right:* **Mary has now joined her father, walking along the rear of the Reichstag.**

The principals arrived on July 15, two days ahead of the conference. Prime Minister Winston Churchill was exhausted, having just finished fighting the British General Election, whose results were still unknown. Both Truman and Churchill ventured out into Berlin before the conference began, Truman to review his 2nd Armored Division, which was drawn up for inspection along the Avus in massive array. Churchill visited the ruins of the Reichstag and the Reichskanzlei, and even went down into Hitler's bunker before going on to open a new club for warrant officers and sergeants on the Kurfürstendamm. He was quickly recognised wherever he went, and at the latter location was actually applauded by some German passers-by to his obvious embarrassment.

Right: **In this comparison taken in 1990 the Wall on the far bank has yet to be demolished.**

At the Chancellery, the group emerges through the shattered French windows of Hitler's office.

Above: **Picking their way carefully over the debris in the garden, the party walks over to the Führerbunker. 'Our Russian guides then took us to Hitler's air raid shelter', wrote Churchill. 'I went down to the bottom and saw the room in which he and his mistress had committed suicide, and when we came up** again they showed us the place where his body had been burned' *(below left).* **Churchill was then offered one of the damaged chairs from the bunker while he waited** *(below right)* **beside the observation tower for his daughter and Mr Eden to come up from the bunker.**

Left: **The Prime Minister passes the bomb crater in the Rundersaal before emerging** *right* **through the Ehrenhof doorway. Ten years later, Churchill set down his recollections of the day: 'On July 16 both the President and I made separate tours of Berlin. The city was nothing but a chaos of ruins. No notice** had of course been given of our visit and the streets had only the ordinary passers-by. In the square in front of the Chancellery there was however a considerable crowd ... I walked about among them; except for one old man who shook his head disapprovingly, they all began to cheer.'

Left: **The Cecilienhof, the palace commissioned by Wilhelm II as the permanent residence of Crown Prince William of Hohenzollern, was erected between 1913 and 1917, and named after the Crown Princess Cecilie. The Kaiser abdicated and left Germany** in November 1918 but the ex-Crown Prince returned in 1923 and lived in the palace with his family until the spring of 1945.
Right: **The Soviet delegation was allocated the former writing room of the Crown Princess for use as a private study.**

The business of the conference centered primarily on the future of Germany, accepting economic unity as a principle. There was much argument over war reparations, the Soviet Union, having demanded $10,000,000,000 at Yalta, had to be reminded that this amount had only been agreed in relation to other claims and that it was now obvious that Germany would never be able to meet them all in full. Nevertheless, it was agreed that a quarter of the reparations actually taken from the Western Zones would be allocated to the Soviet Union, who would have full reparation rights in their own Zone, which was already being stripped.

Despite the change of government occurring in the middle of the meeting, the other participants were astounded to see no change of advisers or policy in the British representation. Unfortunately, this position, with all Churchill's warnings to the Americans, still failed to combat the Soviet position over Poland, which the Americans in their anti-imperialist sentiments failed to comprehend. Consequently, the basic cause for which Britain had gone to war in 1939, the freedom of Poland from foreign domination, was ignored by the other victors, who allowed the Soviets to continue to control Poland.

Over the nine days between July 17 and July 25, when Churchill had to return to Britain for the results of the General Election which had been held three weeks earlier, there were nine plenary meetings between the three leaders. *Above:* **According to Eden (sitting to the Prime Minister's right), Churchill was not at his best at the opening session on Tuesday afternoon: 'He [Churchill] had read no brief and was confused and woolly and verbose about the new Council of Foreign Ministers.' Major Birse, the interpreter, sits to Churchill's left beside the Deputy Prime Minister, Clement Attlee. President Truman has his back to the camera.**

The American delegation was given the Crown Prince's smoking room *(left),* **while the British were allocated the library** *(right).*

The third day. Truman and Stalin greet each other, watched by Attlee. 'The third and fourth meetings of the Potsdam Conference were occupied with a variety of questions,' wrote Churchill, 'none of which were pushed to any definite conclusions. Stalin wanted the United Nations to break off all relations with Franco "and help the democratic forces in Spain" to establish a régime "agreeable to the Spanish people". I resisted this suggestion, and eventually the subject was dismissed. The disposal of the German Navy and Merchant Marine, peace terms for Italy, and the Allied occupation of Vienna and Austria also raised discussion without reaching any result. Most of the problems were remitted to our Foreign Secretaries for examination and report. My own policy was to let these points accumulate and then bring matters to a head after the result of our election was known.'

The American and British sides kept dragging out these talks. During the round table discussions with Truman and Churchill, Stalin had to make several rather sharp observations on the different size of the losses borne by the Soviet Union and by its Allies in the war and on the right of our country to demand appropriate compensation.

The first stage of the conference proceeded in a strained atmosphere. The Soviet delegation came up against a united front and a preconcerted stand by the US and Britain. Not all the questions were easily resolved. The most aggressively-minded participant there was Winston Churchill. Yet Stalin was usually able quickly to convince him, in rather calm tones, that he erred in his approach to the questions under discussion. Probably due to his then limited diplomatic experience, Truman seldom entered into sharp political discussion, giving priority to Churchill.

GEORGI ZHUKOV, 1974

The discussions were difficult, as the Russians were out to get all they could in the way of territory and reparations and insisted on the very big concessions which they had got at Teheran and Yalta. We sought to get a reasonable settlement which would allow Germany some prospect of becoming, in time, a member of the European community of nations. We were also acutely aware of the combination of Russian old-time and Communist modern Imperialism which threatened the freedom of Europe. I thought that the Americans had an insufficient appreciation of this danger and indeed of the whole European situation. They suspected us of being old-time Imperialists, and were inclined to think of Russia and America as two big boys who could settle things amicably between them. This was no doubt partly due to the fact that Roosevelt had managed to get on fairly good terms with Stalin at Yalta.

CLEMENT ATTLEE, 1954

On Friday, July 20 (significantly, the first anniversary of the attempt against Hitler's life), President Truman attended the inauguration of the US Control Council headquarters which had been established in the ex-Luftwaffe Luftgaukommando III barracks on Krönprinzen Allee. Present were the Commander-in-Chief, General Eisenhower, Henry L, Stimson, US Secretary for War, and other high-ranking officers including General Bradley and Lieutenant General George S. Patton, Commanding General Third Army. The flag was the same one which had flown over Washington when war had been declared in 1941, and which had since been raised over Casablanca, Algiers and Rome. Its next scheduled port of call was Tokyo. Also present was General Lucius D. Clay, the Deputy Military Governor, later to take over from Eisenhower as the American C-in-C. 'While the soldier is schooled against emotion,' wrote Clay, 'I have never forgotten that short ceremony as our flag rose to the staff. When in later days anyone suggested the possibility of

our departure from Berlin before, of our own choice, we left a free Berlin, I could not help thinking that no one who had seen our flag raised by right of victory but dedicated to the preservation of freedom and peace could possibly see it withdrawn until peace and freedom had been established.' The preservation of this particular flag had been instigated by a congressman from Texas, Morrie Maverick, who had quickly seized the flag on December 7, 1941 and had a resolution passed that it should be flown over each of the enemy capitals when defeated. However, after its debut in Tokyo, it appears that the flag disappeared until, by an amazing coincidence, it was discovered two years later by Colonel Barnie Oldfield in the drawer of a desk to which he had been assigned in the Pentagon press section in Washington. Oldfield had been in Berlin in 1945 and knew the history of the flag, so he was charged with organising its return to the Capitol with all due dignity in the spring of 1948.

To symbolise the post-war rôle played by General Clay in Berlin, shortly after his death in 1979 the barracks were renamed US Army HQ Clay Compound. Also, as a token of gratitude by the people of Berlin for the Airlift, Krönprinzen Allee was changed

to Clayallee by the city authorities on June 19, 1949. With the re-unification of Germany, two new flagpoles were erected in 1990 so that the German national flag could be flown alongside the Stars and Stripes.

Above: Also on Friday came the inspection of the 2nd Armored Division drawn up in impressive array on the northbound track of the AVUS (see page 32). Mr Stimson rides in the leading half-track beside the diminutive figure of the 2nd Armored Division commander, General John Collier, and General Patton. *Below left:* The British Chiefs-of-Staff had been invited by General George C. Marshall to inspect the division on July 18. Brooke described it as a 'most impressive sight,' commenting that 'the efficiency of the equipment left a greater mark on one than the physique and turn-out of the men.' With them in the lead half-track are Admiral Cunningham, Admiral Ernest King, C-in-C of the US Navy, Major-General Floyd Parks, General Collier and Field-Marshal Sir Henry Maitland Wilson, Head of the British Joint Staff Mission in Washington. *Below right:* Patton and Collier on a job well done.

Now the E51 autobahn, the parade was held just north of the Spanische Allee turn-off. The first post-war race on the AVUS was held in July 1951.

Saturday was a busy day with more ceremonial but, surprisingly, Churchill devotes no space in his memoirs to describe the British victory parade — rather unusual bearing in mind it was the culmination of all he had worked for over the previous five years. One possible explanation is given by his Private Secretary: 'It struck me,' recalled John Peck later, 'and perhaps others as well, although nothing was said, as decidedly odd that Winston Churchill, the great war leader but for whom we should never have been in Berlin at all, got a markedly less vociferous cheer than Mr Attlee, who, however great his contribution in the Coalition, had not hitherto made any marked personal impact upon the fighting forces.' The Prime Minister first reviewed the parade of the 7th Armoured Division drawn up on the Charlottenburger Chaussee between the Monument and the Brandenburg Gate in a half-track accompanied by Field-Marshals Sir Bernard Montgomery and Sir Alan Brooke, and Major-General Lyne. Inspector Thompson, hand constantly on the butt of his pistol, is again in evidence.

This picture gives a good idea of the position of the Soviet saluting base erected in May for their earlier parade.

Above left: The British saluting base was located in a similar position to that of the Desert Rats parade on the 13th; just in front of the ruined Kaiser-Friedrich Gedächtniskirche seen in the background. *Above right:* We pinpointed the exact spot by reference to the manhole and gutter drain. *Right:* Prominent of the notables in the front row were Montgomery, Brooke, Lyne, Cunningham, Portal, Alexander, King, Marshall and General Henry H. Arnold, US Army Air Force commander. Mr Attlee described how 'We attended an impressive parade of our troops in the Unter den Linden *(sic)*. One of our interpreters elicited from some Russian officers, who were looking on, that the things which struck them most were the way in which Churchill and I walked about without any guards and the fact that the uniform of our officers was so little different from that of the men.' *Below:* Cromwells and Quads approach the saluting base. Altogether 10,000 men were on parade, including contingents from the Royal Navy, led by the band of the Royal Marines (Chatham Division), and the Royal Air Force.

During the course of the conference all three leaders did their best to out-vie the others with the entertainment at dinners provided in their villas. Truman, as chairman of the conference, was the first host and provided a violinist and pianist to entertain his guests during the meal. Stalin's turn came next, doubling the number of musicians. Churchill was not to be outdone and blasted them with the Central Band of the Royal Air Force, but his attention to detail in such matters is shown by the special table he had assembled for his dinner party, whose dimensions he personally checked well beforehand to ensure that there was adequate space for each guest and no obstructing table legs before them.

To the affront of the British hosts, and especially the Scots Guards providing a Guard of Honour, Stalin was preceded by two truck-loads of NKVD guards, who ignored the security measures already in operation and surrounded the house and the Guard of Honour. Then when Stalin arrived in his armoured limousine he was tightly surrounded by high ranking officers, who only parted briefly to let Stalin be greeted by Churchill.

President Truman too had a bullet-proof car, in his case preceded and followed by armoured jeeps and festooned with an FBI escort, who would fan out aggressively every time he stopped, all contrasting sharply with the Prime Minister's modest escort of a single plain-clothes detective.

When the first 'Protocol on Zones of Occupation' had been signed in London in September 1944, Germany had been divided into three Zones and Berlin into three Sectors, giving six city boroughs each to the British and Americans and eight to the Soviets. No provision had been made for a French Zone although at the Yalta Conference in January 1945, Stalin had indicated that he had no objection to France being included provided her zone (and sector) came from territory designated to Great Britain and/or the United States. At the Potsdam Conference the Americans insisted that the French Sector in Berlin must be made up of territory jointly given up by all three powers, but the Russians refused to agree.

On his way back to Potsdam Churchill travelled via the AVUS to review the men and machines of the 'Hell on Wheels' Division before attending the fifth session of the conference. In the two meetings held that weekend, the fate of Poland was sealed. The lack of agreement over the final frontiers, which the Soviets had arbitrarily shifted westwards, meant that the prime reason for Britain and France declaring war in 1939 was not achieved and the liberty of Poland, which had meant so much six years earlier, and for which Churchill had fought so hard at Teheran and Yalta, was lost. After the seventh session on Monday, Churchill hosted Stalin and Truman to an evening reception at 'No. 10'. *Below:* When we tracked down No. 23 Ringstrasse in 1991, it was undergoing restoration work and we were amazed to be told that we were the first British visitors they had ever seen!

The pictures taken that evening were all smiles, belying the underlying differences which were building up behind the scenes.

On July 25, Churchill returned to England to learn the results of the General Election. Incomprehensibly to Stalin, Churchill had lost and it was the far less impressive figure of Clement Attlee that replaced him at the conference table for the last few days.

The matter of the French Sector was not resolved until July 26 when the British announced that they were prepared to give the French two of their boroughs (Reinickendorf and Wedding in the north-west). Everyone quickly agreed but the net result was that while the British Sector was reduced to four boroughs, the American and Soviet Sectors remained at six and eight respectively. The exclusion of the French from the conference also proved a sore point in future Allied relations.

Churchill had announced at the seventh session on Monday that it would be necessary for himself and Mr Attlee to return to London on Wednesday so they could be there when the results of the General Election were announced on Thursday. He said that they would attend the Wednesday morning session before leaving and that they planned to be back for the session on Friday afternoon. But it was not to be. By lunch-time on Thursday — July 26, 1945 — Churchill knew that his party had been soundly beaten at the polls. Churchill himself had been re-elected and still remained Prime Minister, and it was well within his constitutional right to have returned to Potsdam to see the conference through. However, by nightfall Churchill had resigned and the burden to continue the negotiations fell on Attlee. Delaying his return until Saturday, Attlee's colleague for the remainder of the conference was the new Foreign Secretary, Ernest Bevin. *Above:* 'Our arrival created something of a sensation,' wrote Attlee. 'Our American friends were surprised to find that there was no change in our official advisers and that I had even taken over, as my Principal Private Secretary, Leslie Rowan, who had been serving Churchill in the same capacity. Molotov kept saying, "But you said the election would be a close thing and now you have a big majority." I said, "Yes, we could not tell what would be the result." But he kept repeating the same phrase. He could not understand why we did not know the result. I am sure he thought that Churchill would have "fixed" the Election and that the change-over by democratic process was a great shock to him.'

Left: The final day — Wednesday, August 1. The Potsdam Agreement was signed by Stalin, Truman and Attlee at thirty minutes past midnight after the thirteenth session. *Right:* The room has been preserved just as it was left on August 2, 1945.

The official end-of-conference publicity picture was taken on the terrace of the palace before the final meeting. Rear rank, L–R: Fleet Admiral William D. Leahy (the President's Chief of Staff); Ernest Bevin (British Foreign Secretary); J. F. Byrnes (US Secretary of State) and V. M. Molotov (People's Commissar of Foreign Affairs).

While the discussions at Potsdam were still going on, the first executive meeting of the Allied Control Council, for the governing of Germany as a whole, took place on July 30. Few large buildings remained undamaged in Berlin, but the Kammergericht on Potsdamer Strasse (in the American Sector), where Roland Freisler had held his trials in 1944, was chosen to host future meetings of the four military governors. *Right:* The flags of the four powers were officially raised in the presence of the Commanders-in-Chief (see pages 286–287) on August 3, when troops of the US 82nd Airborne Division provided a Guard of Honor.

The conference broke up on August 2 and Stalin returned to Moscow over his carefully guarded route, never to venture outside his own frontiers again.

The Potsdam Declaration published the same day, wrapping up this final high-powered meeting of the war-time Allies, did surprisingly little but agree to a system of reparations and define the new border with Poland along the Oder-Neisse river line, which meant that the German populations of East Prussia, Pomerania, East Brandenburg, and Silesia would have to be evacuated and resettled within the boundaries of a much smaller Germany.

The Potsdam Conference, however, gave authority to the Allied Control Commission, which held its first meeting on August 10 in the same room in the Prussian Appeal Court building in the von Kleist Park off the Potsdamer Strasse where Freisler had held his trials of those involved in the July 20 plot. Unfortunately, the French had taken umbrage at being excluded from the Potsdam meetings and proceeded to be awkward about accepting the decisions taken there regarding the Commission's tasks, Général Marie-Pierre Koenig regularly vetoing the proposals for the establishment of central economic agencies as they were introduced, thus preventing the treatment of Germany as a single economic unit.

The meetings were held in Freisler's old courtroom — this is a typical sitting photographed in 1946.

The Allies relinquished the building on February 6, 1991 with the closure of the Four Power Berlin Air Safety Centre.

Above: Soviet soldiers in a requisitioned landau drive past the ruins of the Neue Wache on the Unter den Linden. Traffic signs indicate the way to the Reichstag, Potsdam and the Havel.

Below: Today landaus have resumed their original rôle as transport for tourists. Comparison taken in August 1990 before the NVA Guard of Honour was withdrawn.

Above: The symbol of Berlin — the Brandenburg Gate — pictured in August 1945 surrounded by the detritus of war including an SS Kübelwagen. *Below:* Today it is the detritus of the Nationale Volksarmee which is displayed for sale on the same spot as young entrepreneurs from East Berlin set up their stalls of memorabilia from the former communist era.

Brigadier General Frank Howley, deputy to General Parks, says that it was Parks, not Zhukov, who proposed the international victory parade to celebrate V-J Day although he adds that the Soviet commander was all for it. 'In fact,' wrote Howley, 'the Russian Supreme Commander felt the parade was so important that General Eisenhower, Field-Marshal Montgomery, and General Koenig should be invited to Berlin. Zhukov also suggested that someone should make a speech. It was pretty obvious who was going to do the orating. Not Eisenhower, to be sure. Not Montgomery. Not Koenig. They weren't even invited to speak. Zhukov announced that he would make the speech himself.' General Howley explains that 'a committee was formed and, after petty squabbles and minor delays, the details of the celebration were settled. The parade was to be a spectacle to impress the Allies as well as the Germans ... and each nation was limited to one thousand soldiers and not more than one hundred vehicles.'

That was one of the strangest parades I ever saw on the European continent. Few Berliners turned out, understandably being unable to digest an Allied victory demonstration at that dismal point in German history. Eisenhower, Montgomery, and Koenig were unable to attend, but thousands of Allied soldiers lined Unter den Linden as spectators.

Zhukov was there in all his glory. He wore robin's egg blue trousers, with yellow stripes, topped off with a dark green blouse and a bright red sash. Across his chest, and almost down below his hips, hung so many decorations that a special brass plate had to be worn to house this immense collection, giving the appearance of being riveted to the Russian's chest. The decorations included the highest in the Soviet Union, as well as many from the Allies. Zhukov is a big man, with a big, broad chest, but there was no room left. In an emergency, he had hung one decoration, a gold saucer affair, on his right hip.

One dazzled GI blurted out, 'That's the God-damnest Roxy doorman I've ever seen!' when Zhukov appeared.

General Eisenhower sent the spectacular General George S. Patton to represent him at the celebration. Patton, too, was a magnificent spectacle — but in another way. He was dressed in a simple battle jacket, with a few ribbons, but his gleaming boots and polished helmet outshone all Zhukov's medals. As far as I can remember, nobody else on the platform attracted the slightest attention.

Zhukov planted himself in the center of the platform, jealously guarding his position, and each time Patton shifted his feet the Russian eyed him nervously, then moved nearer the front of the platform. When he did so, Patton inched up to him. In the end, Zhukov's rather expansive stomach was hanging indelicately over the rail while Patton stood, grim and soldier-like, beside him.

The less said about Zhukov's speech the better. He was never drearier. The only bright spot in the entire monologue

However, on August 22, Field-Marshal Montgomery suffered two broken vertebrae when his personal aircraft crashed after the engine cut out as it was preparing to land at the headquarters of the 3rd Canadian Division. The Field-Marshal was badly shaken-up and bruised and, although he does not say as much in his memoirs, his accident was no doubt one of the reasons why he, and thus his French and American counterparts, failed to attend the parade.

Their places were taken by Lieutenant-General Sir Brian Robertson, Général Louis Koeltz, and General Patton.

was Margaret Bourke-White, the photographer, whose flashing skirts and silk-stockinged legs completely distracted the usually stoic Russian Supreme Commander when she knelt in front of the reviewing stand to take his picture.

The parade was impressive and the Russians had arranged their customary surprise. Each nation paraded its best troops. The 82nd Airborne, with white gloves through their shoulder straps, white parachute silk scarves, and polished guns slung over their backs, looked very dressy, not at all like the sky devils of Normandy. The French scout cars performed the neat trick of turning turrets in salute; the British marched along, taking it all in the day's work.

As for vehicles, the Western powers were content to parade with light armored cars and other comparatively light equipment. There the Russians had us. With a dreadful clanking of steel treads against concrete, one hundred giant, new Stalin tanks rumbled into view and rolled down the historic street past the reviewing stand. All Unter den Linden was dwarfed. As they passed in review, the shiny muzzles of their guns pointed up to the sky.

Patton watched the Russian tanks narrowly. Finally, turning to General Nares, the British commandant, who was staring, fascinated, at this display of Soviet might, he whispered, 'They look good enough tanks, but don't worry. If they start shooting, I'm on your side.'

One more recollection of the parade helped me keep my sanity in those insane days. When the British light tanks passed, following the Russian juggernauts, a young, blonde major, with a mustache turned up at the edges and the nonchalance of a handsome rogue out of Kipling, barked his command, 'Eyes right!'

He snapped his head to the right and looked straight into the eyes of a pretty little French WAC in the reviewing stand. The Major gave her a broad wink, then turned up the corner of his mouth and pulled a poker face as he passed the wondering Zhukov.

A parade's a parade, I said to myself, Zhukovs come and go — but a pretty girl is a joy for ever.

BRIGADIER GENERAL FRANK HOWLEY, 1950

There was nothing Patton liked more than a parade, yet this was the last he was to see as commander of his beloved Third Army. Pat Merle-Smith overheard his converstion with Zhukov on the stand as the huge Joseph Stalin tanks rumbled by. 'My dear General Patton,' he heard Zhukov remark, 'you see that tank, it carries a cannon which can throw a shell seven miles.' Patton answered, 'Indeed? Well, my dear Marshal Zhukov, let me tell you this, if any of my gunners started firing at your people before they had closed to less than seven hundred yards I'd have them court-martialled for cowardice.' It's a nice story — in the Patton mould — and it is said that Zhukov was stunned into silence, but for Patton it was another nail in his coffin. Patton was never politically expedient and when this statement was followed up by thoughtless remarks at a Press conference two weeks later, Eisenhower removed him, relegating Patton to command a largely 'paper' Fifteenth Army.

Meanwhile, the Soviets had men working day and night to complete their permanent war memorial in the Tiergarten for its scheduled inauguration on November 11. The plot contained the mass graves of the 2,200 Soviet soldiers killed in the storming of the Reichstag, and was so located as to be astride the former Siegesallee and aligned parallel to the Charlottenburger Chaussee, avoiding the tunnels which still existed from the U-Bahn extension to Hitler's Volkshalle.

But in this overall setting Berlin had become an island, even further isolated until the single railway bridge across the Elbe near Magdeburg was repaired and reopened to traffic at the end of July. The conquerors got on with their task of putting some order into the chaos they had inherited. In this they were hampered by the lack of German manpower, virtually all fit, surviving men of military age having been shut up in prisoner-of-war camps, so it was the women, the famous 'Trümmerfrauen' (rubble women) that cleared the debris and cleaned the bricks for the reconstruction of the city. A vital role was played by the town majors liaising with the borough administrations in all the fine details that the desperate poverty of those early days entailed.

How concerned the British were for their charges can be seen with Operation 'Stork', which was initiated in October 1945 and provided for 50,000 child-

This picture was taken in 1962 and shows the guardhouse subsequently erected behind the monument. (See also page 242.)

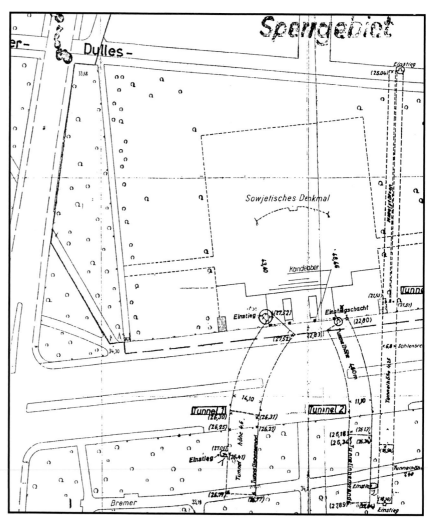

All four Allies participated in the official unveiling of the Reichstag War Memorial by Marshal Zhukov on November 11,

the British providing a Guard of Honour from the 2nd Battalion, The Devonshire Regiment.

ren from the British Sector, together with 10,000 mothers, teachers, etcetera, to spend the winter in camps at Oldenburg, Aurich and Osnabrück away from the city, which they knew would be a tough, cold one for those that had to stay. Buses brought the children from various collection points to the Avus, where they formed up in convoy under military escort with doctors and ambulances in attendance. Once they were safely through the Soviet Zone they stopped at Alversdorf for a midday meal, were given a postcard each to send back to their parents announcing their safe arrival, and then spent the night there before going on by train to their camps the next day. When those children returned the following spring they had gained an average increase of 15 lbs in weight.

The construction of the Soviet War Memorial was completed in November 1945 in a Tiergarten already stripped of trees needed for firewood that first cold post-war winter, to be replaced the following spring by allotments growing precious food.

On October 31, William Shirer, the American broadcaster who had left Berlin in December 1941, returned to the city for the first time in four years. One of the first sights he described was the memorial where 'hundreds of workmen were labouring like beavers behind an enormous scaffolding'. A week later came Armistice Day — 'cold, gray and drizzly', when 'the Russians unveiled the mammoth monument . . . you could almost hear Hitler's Bolshevik-hating bones rattling in the grave.'

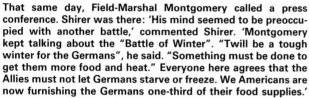

That same day, Field-Marshal Montgomery called a press conference. Shirer was there: 'His mind seemed to be preoccupied with another battle,' commented Shirer. 'Montgomery kept talking about the "Battle of Winter". "Twill be a tough winter for the Germans", he said. "Something must be done to get them more food and heat." Everyone here agrees that the Allies must not let Germans starve or freeze. We Americans are now furnishing the Germans one-third of their food supplies.'

Although Monty took several months to fully recover from the injuries he suffered from his accident, he was still able to carry out his duties. Here he inspects the 1st Royal Tank Regiment (of which he was Colonel Commandant) just a month after his accident. *Left:* The regiment then occupied the barracks built for I/Luftgau-Nachrichten-Regiment 3 at Kladow (near Gatow airfield), whose final British occupants in 1992 *(right)* were the 1st Battalion, Royal Welch Fusiliers.

The lack of food naturally brought about a black market system in which in this case cigarettes became the common currency. There was considerable lawlessness in the city with former slave labourers, stateless persons, deserters and the like at large. Crime was rife until the reformed Berlin police were first armed early in 1946, following a period in which in any one month 40 to 50 murders and about 10,000 burglaries and 1,000 major robberies were committed.

One of the prisons in civil use in the British Sector during the first two years of the occupation was the former military prison on Wilhelmstrasse in Spandau. Several executions by guillotine were carried out there, reluctantly witnessed by officers of the Public Safety Branch of the British Military Government, which was responsible for the law and order aspects of the sector.

On August 16, 1946, the four Commandants presented the city authorities with a draft constitution for adoption following elections to be held in the October. That summer the Russians proposed that the Communist Party and the Social Democrats should merge as the Socialist Unity Party (SED), hoping thereby to gain Communist domination over a broader spectrum and to convince the electorate that they supported a united Germany. However, the sceptical Berliners thought otherwise. The

Centre: **Shady transactions outside the Reichstag, July 1945. A flourishing black market is pictured here beside the Reichstag with a GI, undoubtedly well stocked up with chocolate and cigarettes, bartering with German civilians. The Russian is most probably more interested in watches.** *Right:* **Shady transactions outside the Reichstag, July 1990. A beautiful comparison as the wheel turns full circle. Russian equipment is now offered to tourists as Roger 'Bellski' takes on the rôle of Soviet soldier.**

Shirer also returned to the Chancellery ... and remembered: 'How many times had I stood opposite on the curb and watched the comings and goings of the great! They would drive up in their black super-Mercédès cars, the fat bemedalled Göring, the snake-like little Goebbels, though he lived just across the street, the arrogant, stupid Ribbentrop, though he lived a mere hundred yards down the street — these and Hess and the drunkard Ley and the debauched-looking little Funk with the small eyes of a pig and the sadist Himmler and the other swashbuckling party hacks and then the generals, their necks stiff even when they dismounted from a car, one eye inevitably squeezing a monocle, their uniforms immaculately pressed. They would come, be saluted by the guard of honor, and pass within this building to plot their wars and their conquests. Today, I reflected, standing there in front of the Chancellery's ruins, they are all dead or in jail. This building too, in whose stately rooms they worked out so confidently and cold-bloodedly their obscene designs, is, like them, smashed forever. Germany, their land, which they wanted to rule the world, is smashed too. It will not for a long time recover, and perhaps never.'

autumn elections drew a 92 per cent turn-out of the eligible electorate. The Socialist SPD came out top with 48.7 percent of the vote, followed by the Conservative CDU with 22.2 per cent, the Communist SED with 19.8 per cent and the Liberal LDP with 9.3 per cent. The results were a bitter set-back for the Communists, for even in the Soviet Sector the SED had only gained 21 percent of the vote. All the tricks used by them in the build-up to the election, like handing out free shoes to the children and cigarettes to the workers in

Top left: **The view across the street to where Shirer would have stood with the press corps in the days of Hitler.** *Top right:* **The Wilhelmplatz 1945 with the burned-out Ministry of the Interior.** *Right:* **The building still stands, hidden behind the apartment blocks still under construction in 1991.**

Shirer: 'And yet what suffering they caused on this planet, these German men, before an aroused world turned them back and smashed through to hunt them out and kill them or capture them! How many millions dead, killed and murdered? How many maimed and broken? How many homes in ashes? And yes — *how* the lives of even those who survive? For even though the fighting has stopped, the peoples of Europe this winter are hungry and cold, and a million or so of them probably will die. All because of what these evil, stupid little men — in this building before it was smashed — did.'

Though my time has been much too short, I guess I have found out some of the things I came here to find out: what happened after I left — indeed, first of all what went on in secret during the tumultuous years I was here — and then what the physical damage has been and the moral damage and finally the state of the German spirit after defeat and collapse.

There is so much more I could learn if I could linger on. The picture is so black. Are there no shadings? Could I not find some? Are there no 'Good Germans,' for instance, on which to build one's hopes? Ah, surely! Was there not the poet Adam Kuckhoff, who did not give in? Who was convicted of 'high treason'? Who was hanged on the gallows at Plötzensee on the morning of August 5, 1943? Who, before he was led away, wrote his wife, Greta, one of the most moving poems and one of the most courageous letters ever penned by man? Yes, there was Kuckhoff and the poet Bonhoeffer and others in this sad land who gave their lives in the name of human decency.

But amidst these ruins I do not hear their names. Was the sacrifice of these few of no account? Is it not rather the spirit of Hitler and Himmler that is rising again from the debris? Is it not their deaths and their deeds that count among these tragic people? And are the Germans not already waiting to follow another diabolical Führer to still another destruction? Alas, so it seems to me.

The German people, I fear, have not — by a hell of a long way — learned the lessons of this terrible war. They have no sense of guilt and are sorry only that they were beaten and must now suffer the consequences. They are sorry only for themselves; not at all for those they murdered and tortured and tried to wipe off this earth.

Tomorrow I shall leave Berlin — perhaps for the last time. I am weary of the Berlin story I started to chronicle so long ago, which has been the core of my life for more than a decade. I was lucky, though, that it turned out to be the most important story of my generation, starting, almost unnoticed, here in this city and in the end engulfing the world, uprooting the lives of the mechanic in Stalingrad, the farmer near Cedar Rapids, Iowa, and the sheep-grower in Australia on the other side of the planet.

I am weary and have had enough of it. Surely there must be something less ugly, not so brutal and evil, that I can concentrate on in the remaining years. The sprawling, crazy, wonderful land of America, certainly. My family, which I hardly know, the children whom I have scarcely seen. And perhaps poetry and music and the theater and, above all, Peace.

WILLIAM SHIRER,
END OF A BERLIN DIARY,
NOVEMBER 15, 1945

Probably the best interior shot of Hitler's bunker was taken that October by the US Signal Corps of a party from the Secretary of the Interior's Office inspecting the reception area. L–R: Alton Jones, Mr S. Richardson, Robert E. Hardwicke and Joseph P. Zook. The smoke-blackened walls and furniture are very evident. The doorway to the conference room shows up clearly, as does the breathing apparatus set mentioned in the Soviet report on page 246. However, when compared with the picture on page 256, something odd appears to have happened to the furniture as the table and chairs have reversed their positions!

Left: **The underground system was functioning over an ever-increasing area as tracks were cleared of debris and damage repaired, although many sections were open to the sky like this stretch on Tauentzien Strasse. However, the whole of Berlin's railway system remained under Soviet (and later East Berlin)** control right up to 1990, even where it ran through the Western Sectors. *Right:* **As trains began to run below ground, overhead the US 78th Cavalry, riding some of Germany's finest bloodstock, brought a vision of the 'Old West' to Berlin. Both pictures were taken within a week of each other in 1946.**

their Sector, and then supplying fresh fruit and vegetables to the Western Sectors to try to demonstrate how much better conditions would be under them, but then curtailing the electricity supply to demonstrate their power; all this had been in vain. The only thing left to them was to force the Western Allies out of the city one way or another, and for this they would adopt terror tactics.

The NKVD had moved into Pankow behind the advancing troops in April 1945 and immediately commenced operating in accordance with Moscow's instructions. Their activities not only involved tracking down former Nazi officials but extended to all those who opposed a communist take-over. People were dragged from their houses during the night or kidnapped off the streets in all sectors of the city. The old Nazi concentration camps at Oranienburg, Ravensbrück and Buchenwald were reopened to NKVD victims, including children, and tens of thousands of these hapless prisoners succumbed to sickness and malnutrition. Others were deported to labour camps in the Soviet Union, their fate unknown to those they left behind.

The winter that followed was one of the coldest ever, bringing much suffering to the population, 700,000 of whom were dependent upon public funds for survival. The acute shortage of fuel meant that more than 1,000 companies had to close down and their workers laid off. Some 11,000 people died of cold within the city and over 40,000 had to be treated for hypothermia.

Centre: **The sector boundary crossed Tauentzien Strasse along the line of Nürnberger Strasse, crossing from left to right. The platoon is returning from the British borough of Tiergarten, and is beginning a formal march through American Schöneberg.**

In August 1945, the International Military Tribunal was established by the Four Powers holding its opening session in Berlin. However, because a suitable building could not be found in the city, the actual trials were switched to Nuremberg where both the court and adjacent prison were still intact.

The trials opened on November 20 with 20 defendants arraigned in the dock. Bormann was being tried 'in absentia' as at that time it was not accepted by the tribunal that he had died in Berlin. Already 200,000 notices had been posted throughout the occupied zones to notify Bormann of his impending trial.

Restoring the lines of communication. *Above:* **Major-General Nares, the British military commandant, breaks the tape with his staff car on the Bailey bridge built by 672 Army Troops Company, Royal Engineers, to take the Frey Bridge traffic while the latter is being rebuilt. Started on December 10, 1945, the bridge took until January 24 to complete as the Soviets insisted on a minimum 15-foot clearance to enable the passage of barge traffic underneath. The Frey Bridge had been held by the Hitlerjugend Regiment in the vain hope that General Wenck's Twelfth Army would break through to Berlin by that route. Although not directly attacked, for the Havel formed the boundary between Marshal Zhukov's 1st Byelorussian Front and Marshal Koniev's 1st Ukrainian Front, the Hitlerjugend Regiment's positions were repeatedly shelled and they suffered heavy casualties in consequence. The Germans deliberately refrained from blowing the bridge, but at the last minute a chance Soviet shell hit the demolition chamber and destroyed the bridge. The Bailey bridge was so placed as to enable unimpeded reconstruction of the original bridge, which was completed in 1951.** *Below:* **The site of the western end of the Bailey bridge, which crossed the Havel diagonally to join the Heerstrasse in line with the tallest trees on the opposite bank. The rebuilt Frey Bridge can be seen on the left.**

On November 30, 1945, the Air Corridor Agreement was approved by the four-power Allied Control Commission — the only formal agreement ever concluded by the Soviet Union granting the Western Allies unrestricted access — in this case by air along three 'corridors' — to Berlin. The agreement had largely come about by the persistence of air force personnel in pushing their case, but the same vigorous action was not pursued for the right of access on the ground. The land corridor for road traffic was the Hannover–Berlin autobahn which entered the Soviet Zone of Germany at Helmstedt at Checkpoint 'Apha' to reach the American Sector of Berlin at Dreilinden, called Checkpoint 'Bravo' by the Allies. *Left:* Major-General Hon. Ian Erskine, Provost Marshal of the Corps of Military Police, is pictured at the Allied checkpoint on February 8, 1946.

By 1946 the large majority of the fighting men who had first occupied the city had gone. Demobilisation had denuded the military structure of its wartime personnel at all levels as the civil servants took over the task of administering occupied Germany. General Eisenhower had been succeeded by General Joseph T. McNarney in November 1945 and Marshal Zhukov returned to Moscow in April 1946, having been replaced by General Vassili Sokolovsky. In May 1946, Field-Marshal Montgomery returned to London to become CIGS, his 21st Army Group having already been renamed the British Army of the Rhine.

Also leaving was Richard Brett-Smith who so aptly coloured the scene for us back in July 1945:

'I left Berlin as I had come to it, in my armoured car. It was 10th March 1946 when we drove for the last time over the cobbled streets of Spandau and through the outskirts of Berlin to the autobahn. It was raining and trying to snow.

'Somewhere in Spandau we had got tied up in the usual traffic block, and so my car had been halted for a minute or two. It was then that I heard, coming from some battered tenement and

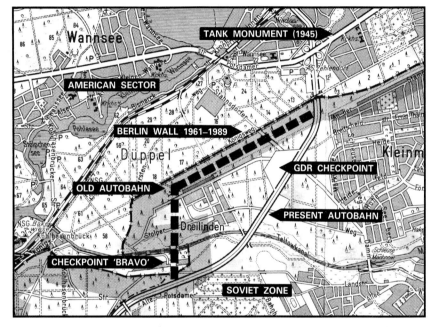

Above: In 1969 the autobahn was re-routed to the east, cutting out the dog-leg over the Teltow Canal which caused the sector boundary to be crossed twice. *Top right:* The site of the old Checkpoint 'Bravo' is now a caravan park, the original unused stretch of the autobahn *below right* being slowly reclaimed by nature.

And the spoils of war. Two months after the Russians took this photograph *(left)* of political officers addressing their men beside the Victory Column on May 2, 1945, French troops had entered Berlin and placed the Tricolour on the 48-foot gilded figure of Victory. As we have explained earlier, the Siegessäule celebrated German victories over the Danes in 1864, the Austrians in 1866 and the French in 1870-71. *Right:* The west-facing panel depicted the first Sedan battle in 1870 (on the left-hand side) leading into the triumphal German entry into Paris in 1871 on the right.

The French were without a sector in Berlin when they arrived at the beginning of July, and the Soviets insisted that any territory given to the French must be provided from the American and British Sectors only. Britain had already given up the Rhine Palatinate and the Saar, and the United States part of Baden-Würtemberg, to provide the French with an occupation zone in Germany proper, and at Potsdam the US insisted that any territory for a French Sector in Berlin must be relinquished equally by the three powers. Both the Soviet Union and the United States refused to budge from their declared positions and it was left to Britain to break the deadlock by graciously donating their boroughs of Reinickendorf and Wedding in north-west Berlin to create a French Sector. However, the monument still remained within the British Sector and in 1946 the French requested that the bronze plaques be removed for transportation to Paris as spoils of victory. Napoleon would surely have approved of the idea as the Quadriga taken in 1806 had been surrendered back in 1814, and the former prize was now not only shot to pieces but inaccessible within the Soviet Sector. Major Freddie Newton, RE, who we last heard of organising the facilities at Potsdam, was tasked with examining the feasibility of the French request. After he ascertained the weight of the plaques at about 6½ tons each, they were duly removed and transported to Paris.

The original intention was to melt down the bronze to re-cast statues which had been purloined by the Germans during the Occupation, but in the end the plaques were put on display in the courtyard of Les Invalides. However, from the 1950s on, Berlin had been pressing for their return, but it was not until January 1984, with the city's 750th birthday celebrations looming three years hence, that the issue was finally resolved.

played on a wheezy gramophone, Strauss' *Voices of Spring*. It was so wildly unsuitable that I nearly laughed. My hands were already frozen, and there was nothing springlike about frosty Spandau.

'But as we drove on, leaving the lilting waltz behind us, I seemed still to hear it dancing out from every ruined house that we passed. Perhaps after all it was not so unsuitable, for it taught me something I had long known but never before put into words. Berlin was indestructible. Stalin had been righter than he knew when he said that Hitlers might come and go but the German people and the German State would go on for ever. He should have said it of himself and of Berlin as well.

'The column picked up speed as we began to draw clear of Berlin. We were going back to West Germany. It would be safer — and duller — than Berlin. But each of us was taking in his heart something of the city and perhaps many of us were leaving behind something in its keeping for ever.

'Someone shouted to me as we bowled along opposite Dahlem and Zehlendorf to look back to the *Funkturm*, which always stands out like a silver mast for the traveller reaching or leaving Berlin.

'But I did not turn my head to look towards the heart of Berlin, for it was time to leave. Something had ended. I knew that though I would come back in later years and recognise a city, never again would I set foot in the same Berlin that I had come to know as a familiar, never again would I set eyes upon the grey city.'

After visiting Berlin, the French Minister of Defence, M. Charles Hernu, announced on January 13 that the plaques were to be returned without a counter-exchange (the return of three French cannon had been demanded), and the four plaques were flown back to the French airport at Tegel the following month. Here they are seen being examined by the French President, François Mitterand, and the Mayor of West Berlin, Eberhard Diepgen, in Schöneberg town hall.

In the Soviet Sector, 1947 saw the end of the Führerbunker. *Left:* American business executives touring the occupied zones of Germany to promote economic recovery are shown the bunker in April 1947, and, *right*, American newspaper reporters pictured the following month looking at the spot from where Colonel Klimenko's men disinterred Hitler's remains (compare with the picture at the bottom of page 280).

In June 1947, the Municipal Assembly elected Ernst Reuter, a former Communist and Spartacist, as Oberbürgermeister, or Lord Mayor. However, the new Soviet Commandant, General Alexander Kotikov, vetoed this appointment at a meeting of the Allied Kommandatura, and the other Commandants were obliged to accept this obstruction in order to continue the system previously agreed between them. The elected Deputy, 60-year-old Louise Schroeder, was obliged to stand in as Acting Oberbürgermeister during one of Berlin's most difficult periods of history, but Reuter continued to dominate the political scene.

Meanwhile, American attempts to promote economic and political recovery in Europe were meeting strong Soviet resistance. In February 1948 the Western Allies agreed to go ahead and combine their zones into a single economic and democratically political unit,

At the same time the Reichstag battlefield was being cleared by Trümmerfrauen and also by black marketeers as a punishment under the law.

Left: French officers take one last look. On December 11, 1947, Soviet engineers set off charges to demolish the stairway and seal the entrances. The Russians refused photography of the actual explosion, this shot, *right*, being taken three days later.

On January 1, 1947, for economic purposes, the American and British Zones in West Germany had been merged as continuing Russian vetoes in the Allied Control Council had made it plain that the Soviet Union was not prepared to co-operate in the running of the country. Within a year, curbs were being placed on inter-zonal traffic, attempts being made by the Soviets to board and inspect military trains, and a concerted propaganda campaign begun against the Western Allies. Material published in the West was banned in the Soviet Zone and the Russians spread rumours that the three Western Allies were about to pull out of Berlin. The two incidents depicted here both occurred in Berlin in the early part of 1948 involving British soldiers *(left)* and the American military *(right)* as relations deteriorated between East and West. On March 5, General Clay warned Washington that something was about to happen: 'For many months, based on logical analysis, I have felt and held that war was unlikely for at least two years. Within the last few weeks I have felt a subtle change in Soviet attitude which I cannot define but which now gives me a feeling that it may come with dramatic suddenness. I cannot support this change in my own thinking with any data or outward evidence in relationships other than to describe it as a feeling of a new tenseness in every Soviet individual with whom we have had official relations. I am unable to submit any official report in the absence of supporting data, but my feeling is real. You may advise the Chief of Staff [General Bradley] of this for whatever it may be worth if you feel it advisable.' Two weeks later the Soviets broke with the Allied Control Council, followed by a walk-out from the Berlin Kommandatura on June 16. Concurrent with the Russian departure, the three Western Allies introduced currency reform to eliminate the situation whereby the Soviets were printing, from a set of duplicate printing plates, whatever amount of Reichsmarks they wanted, which were then redeemable at the US Treasury at a fixed parity against the dollar.

a decision that so enraged the Russians that they walked out of the Allied Control Council on March 20, ending all administrative unity in the country, and on June 16 they also withdrew from the city's Allied Kommandatura.

The joint discussions on currency reform, an essential prerequisite to economic reform, and which had failed to achieve Soviet agreement, were thus abandoned and the Allies decided to go ahead on their own, replacing the old Reichsmark with the Deutsche-Mark in their zones with effect from June 20. The Soviets then followed with their own currency reform two days later. As Berlin had not been included in the original Allied plan, the Soviets tried to introduce their new currency to the city, thereby incorporating Berlin into the economic structure of the Soviet Zone. However, the Allies had anticipated this move and within a day were able to issue their new currency in their sectors, despite all Soviet attempts to render it illegal. This economic tie with the West further alienated the Soviets, who decided to bring even more pressure to bear, with the aim of eliminating what they saw as an hostile enclave within their zone.

The nicer side of currency reform. A young lady demonstrates the best hiding place for the new Western money, called 'Deutsche-Marks', when entering the Soviet Sector.

On July 18, 1947, an American DC-3 approached Berlin from the south and landed at RAF Gatow late in the afternoon. From it emerged seven men, escorted by armed guards, who quickly directed their prisoners to a waiting bus with blacked-out windows. Then, escorted by Jeeps and armoured cars, the convoy drove east towards Wilhelmstrasse 23 in the Spandau district.

There, in 1876, the Kaiser had erected a formidable military prison, built of red brick, with cells for a total of 600 prisoners. Later it became a civil prison but under Hitler it was used both for military prisoners awaiting trial and

For a moment we must stop here while we look at one important aspect of the life of Berlin in which the Four Powers did continue to co-operate throughout the Cold War. Although the trial of the major Nazi war criminals had been carried out in Nuremberg for reasons already explained, the incarceration of those sentenced to various terms of imprisonment was to take place in Berlin under the joint supervision of Great Britain, France, the United States and the Soviet Union. The prison selected was located in the borough of Spandau on the Wilhelmstrasse — not to be confused with the other street of the same name although the choice was not without its touch of irony. This picture was released six days after the seven arrived in July 1947. The person responsible for preparing the prison was our old friend, Major Freddie Newton.

for political prisoners in transit to concentration camps. Now — and for the next 40 years — it was to perform a new rôle as a prison for the seven men of the Nazi hierarchy convicted by the Nurem-

berg Military Tribunal to varying terms of imprisonment.

Responsibility for guarding the prisoners was to be split between the Four Occupying Powers: the British taking

Right from the start publicity was strictly controlled and these were the only photographs officially released showing the interior of Spandau Prison beyond the watch towers and barbed wire. Built for 600, it was now to house just seven men, guarded by a force ten times as great. From 1966 to 1987 it was occupied by just one prisoner — Rudolf Hess.

Prisoner No. 1. Baldur von Schirach, 40 years old. Former Reich Youth Leader and Gauleiter of Vienna, sentenced to 20 years imprisonment.

Prisoner No. 2. Grossadmiral Karl Dönitz, 55 years old. Hitler's successor as Head of State, and previous longtime U-Boat C-in-C, sentenced to 10 years.

Prisoner No. 3. Konstantin Freiherr von Neurath, 74 years old. Hitler's first Foreign Minister, later Reichs Protector in Prague, to serve 15 years.

charge in January, May and September; the French in February, June and October; the Soviets in March, July and November; and the Americans in April, August and December.

Six watch towers stood at intervals around the wall with its electrified barbed wire fence, and at night the whole area was floodlit. The exterior guard of 32 armed soldiers was reinforced within the building by 18 warders plus ancillary staff, making a total of 78 persons directly involved: a ratio to the prisoners of more than 10 to 1.

Executive power at Spandau was given to the Directors of the Four Powers, who enforced the strict and onerous regime which had been laid down by the Control Commission at Nuremberg. The following is an extract:

'The prisoners must salute officers, warders and senior staff with marks of respect. They must obey all orders and regulations without hesitation, even when these appear to them to be unjust. They must answer honestly all questions addressed to them. The prisoners may approach an officer or warder only if ordered to do so or if they wish to make a request.

'The discipline of the institution provides that prisoners should adopt a standing position. The prisoner must salute an officer, an official or a warder by standing to attention or by passing him in an upright posture. The prisoner must at the same time remove his headgear.

'On admission, the prisoner will undress completely and his body will be carefully searched. The search, which will be in the presence of the Directorate, will be carried out by four warders. All parts of the body, including the anus, will be searched for articles which might be smuggled into the institution.

'Prisoners will be locked up and guarded in accordance with the verdict of the Nuremberg IMT. They will be addressed by their convict's number; in no circumstances by name. Imprisonment will be in the form of solitary

Prisoner No. 4. Grossadmiral Dr Erich Raeder, 71 years old. Chief of the Kriegsmarine, sentenced to imprisonment for life.

Prisoner No. 5. Albert Speer, 42 years old. Hitler's architect who went on to become Minister of Armaments on the death of Fritz Todt in 1942. Sentenced to 20 years.

Prisoner No. 6. Walter Funk, 56 years old. Former Reich Minister of Economics and President of the Reichsbank. He was given life imprisonment.

Prisoner No. 7. Rudolf Hess, 53 years old. Hitler's deputy and a Reich Minister until his defection to Britain in May 1941. Sentenced to life imprisonment.

The ritual of the monthly changing of the guard. This early picture dates from April 1953 as the Russians hand over to the Americans. The following month the duty would be given to the British and then to the French, this same rotation being maintained year in, year out, for exactly 40 years from August 1947 to August 1987.

confinement. The cells will be isolated, but work, religious services and walks will be carried out together.

'When awakened, the prisoner will rise immediately and make his bed. He will then strip to the waist, wash, brush his teeth and rinse his mouth. Clothing, shoes and the cell, including furniture, will be cleaned in the time provided for this purpose and in the prescribed manner. Making a noise, shouting, whistling and even approaching the window are forbidden.

'The prisoners may not talk or asso- ciate with one another, nor with other persons except with special permission from the Directorate. The prisoner may not have in his possession any articles without permission. If he should find something, he must hand it over to the warder immediately. Equipment, cloth-

It had long been decided by the Four Powers that when the last prisoner died — whoever that was — the prison would be demolished to avoid it becoming a shrine to Nazism. Rudolf Hess, serving a true 'life' imprisonment, lived to the ripe old age of 93. After he died in August 1987, Spandau was razed and the rubble buried at RAF Gatow, leaving only the two mature chestnut trees which stood either side of the gateway to mark its passing.

ing and all articles belonging to the institution are to be treated with care, and used only for the prescribed purposes.

'The Directorate will establish a plan for daily activities, but in principle work will be carried out every day except Sundays and public holidays.'

Because of their age and health, von Neurath, Raeder and Funk were released early in 1954, 1955 and 1957 respectively. Dönitz served his full term of ten years and was released in 1956. At midnight on September 30, 1966, Speer and von Schirach were released, at the end of their sentences, leaving Rudolf Hess the sole inmate.

During the next twenty years there were many calls for his release on humanitarian grounds, and much pressure was brought to bear on the three Western Allies to arbitrarily release Hess during one of their periods of tenure of the prison. Following a suicide attempt in February 1977, conditions for the lone prisoner were gradually ameliorated, the original regulations being dropped in practice so that eventually Hess was able to roam at will within the confines of the cell block and the garden, and, among other amenities, he was provided with television.

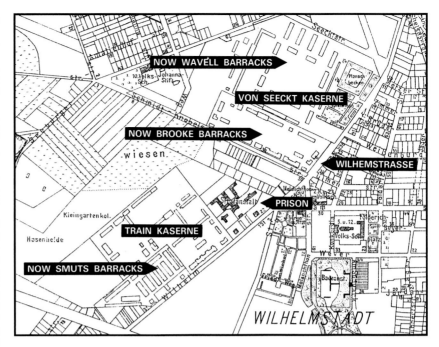

As a former military prison, it was ideally situated alongside former German Army barracks, which had been renamed Wavell, Brooke and Smuts Barracks. Von Neurath, Raeder and Funk were released before their time was up but Dönitz, Speer and von Schirach served their full terms, leaving Hess the sole inmate after October 1, 1966.

Endless campaigns were mounted to secure his release on humanitarian grounds, pressure being put on the United Kingdom government to arbitrarily release Hess during one of the British periods of tenure. However, what people did not realise was that even when the British were guarding the perimeter, personnel from the other three nations would

always be present inside the prison itself, precluding any independent action. More violent means to draw attention to the prison, illustrated by these 'scene of crime' pictures from the files of the army's Special Investigation Branch, show the damage caused to the officers' mess by an explosion caused by intruders on October 23, 1986.

Throughout the forty years that the prison was in use, all four governors would meet weekly, even when another nation was on guard duty. This picture of the French to Soviet handover on July 1, 1984, features our author, Tony Le Tissier, who was the British Governor at the time Hess committed suicide in August 1987. L–R: Lieutenant-Colonel Savin (Soviet Governor); Lieutenant-Colonel Tony Le Tissier (British Governor); adjutant, 2nd Battalion Royal Irish Rangers; Lieutenant-Colonel Durofeyev (Commander, Karlshorst Garrison, Berlin); M. Michel Planet (French Governor); Mr Darold Keane (US Governor).

Bouts of ill-health led to him being transferred to the nearby British Military Hospital in Dickensweg, Charlottenburg, on several occasions, but each time he was returned to Spandau.

In April 1987 Hess celebrated his 93rd birthday — it was to be his last — for late in the afternoon of August 17 it was announced that Hess had died. Delay in the issue of subsequent announcements on behalf of the Four Powers by the spokesman for the British Military Government led to considerable speculation being aroused about the circumstances of the death. However, these delays were due to the eventuality of suicide not having been catered for in their preliminary planning and agreements, and the need to clear the text of the announcements with all four capitals.

Following a post-mortem examination conducted in the British Military Hospital, the body was flown by RAF Hercules to an American airstrip at Grafenwöhr in Bavaria, where the Directorate then handed it over to Hess's family for burial. His son, Wolf Rüdiger Hess, elected to have a second autopsy performed by a German pathologist in Munich. It was intended to bury Hess in the family grave, at Wunsiedel, north-east of Bayreuth, but due to pro-Nazi demonstrations it was decided to inter him at a secret location until a quiet opportunity presented itself for the proper burial, which did not take place until March 17, 1988.

The same day that Hess died, the British Military Government issued a statement announcing that 'in accordance with the decision of the representatives of Great Britain, France, the USA and the USSR, the Allied prison administration will be permanently terminated and the prison will be demolished.'

Work began immediately. On August 20 the American guard stood down, to be replaced by a caretaker detachment of the King's Own Scottish Borderers. Demolition was completed by the end of the year, the rubble being buried on Gatow ranges. The prison site was then redeveloped as The Britannia Centre, a community centre for the British garrison that included a cinema and a NAAFI superstore.

The suicide. Because of the need to clear every press statement with London, Washington, Paris and Moscow, the first official communiqué was not issued until nearly 24 hours had elapsed. It said that Hess had attempted to take his own life. He walked in the prison yard and then sat in 'a small cottage in the garden' with a prison warder (it was the Americans' month for guard duty). His escort left him alone for a few minutes and when he returned 'found Hess with an electrical cord around his neck'. However, the fact that the communiqué ended with speculation on whether 'this suicide attempt was the actual cause of death', and that the Russians had expressly disapproved of the statement, fuelled controversy as to whether there was an official cover-up. On September 17, 1987, the Four Powers issued a final statement: 'Investigations have confirmed that on

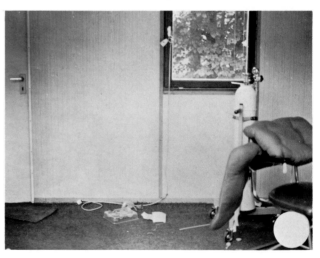

17 August Rudolf Hess hanged himself from a window catch in a small summer house in the prison garden, using an electrical extension cord which had for some time been kept in the summer house for use in connection with a reading lamp. Attempts were made to revive him and he was then rushed to the British Military Hospital where, after further unsuccessful attempts to resuscitate him, he was pronounced dead at 1610.' Hess never repented of his Nazi beliefs, so perhaps like Hitler, Goebbels — and Göring who took over the deputy leadership after Hess arrived in Britain — suicide was the right way out for the last of the Nazi bigwigs. (Readers interested in learning more of Hess's last flight to Britain, his capture and the years which followed are referred to *After the Battle* Nos. 58 and 66, and Tony's forthcoming book, *Farewell to Spandau*.)

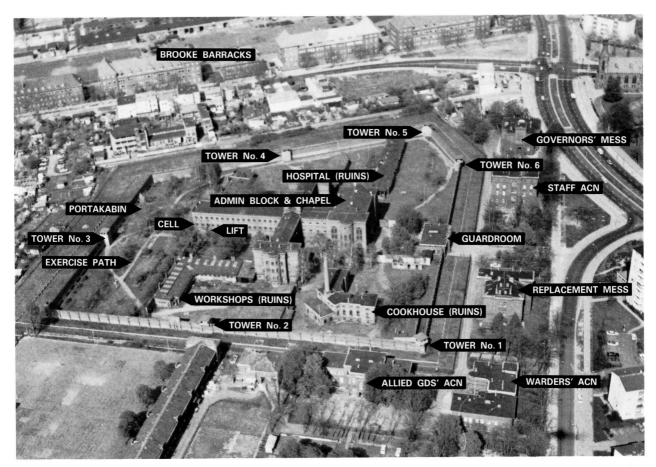

The prison itself was totally demolished, including the perimeter wall, and the rubble buried on the British gunnery ranges at Gatow. The two horse chestnuts beside the prison gatehouse were retained in the grounds of the new Britannia Centre which was constructed to serve the British garrison in Berlin. As well as a NAAFI, a cinema was included in the complex with the apt name of Jerboa Cinema — a trace back to the days of the Desert Rats in 1945. The officers' mess and other administrative buildings along Wilhelmstrasse were renovated and adapted for use by the garrison's social services.

The Berlin Airlift

Checkpoint 'Alpha' at Helmstedt where the autobahn entered the Soviet Zone of Germany. From here it was just over 100 miles to Checkpoint 'Bravo' outside Berlin.

The Soviets had already been interfering with the vital traffic lifelines to the west since the beginning of the year, when on June 24, 1948, they abruptly cut all road and rail connections on the pretext of 'technical difficulties', and cut the electrical supply generated in the East, causing particular hardship to hospitals and forcing many commercial enterprises to close. At this point the Western Sectors held only enough food for 36 days and coal for 45 days.

The sole remaining supply route available was by air, and on June 26 the largest airlift in history began. What at first were national efforts designed merely to sustain their respective garrisons under the British title of Operation

The road link was vulnerable to interference by the Soviets and the first trouble began on March 20, 1948, when restrictions were imposed on autobahn traffic, limiting four vehicles per hour through the Russian checkpoint at Helmstedt. Civilian freight on the rail lines to Berlin from Hamburg and Nuremberg was halted on April 3 with individual clearances being demanded on the sole remaining railway line between Helmstedt and Berlin. The 'Little Blockade', as it was later called, ended with the total severance of all road and rail links at 6.00 a.m. on June 24.

Checkpoint 'Bravo' lay at the Berlin end of the autobahn — we saw it in its first location on page 339. After the autobahn at Dreilinden was re-routed, the Soviets moved their tank monument and re-erected it beside the new stretch of road (above) as a continuing symbol of the victory of the Red Army in 1945. This particular picture was taken in 1965 during a subsequent closure of the autobahn by the East Germans showing a British military police vehicle by-passing the stalled traffic to reassert the right of free access to the city.

'Knicker', later to be changed briefly to 'Carter Paterson' then 'Plainfare', and the American title 'Vittles', then rapidly expanded into a vast combined operation catering for the basic needs of the entire population of the Western Sectors.

Fortunately, the Soviets had previously agreed to the establishment of three air corridors over their zone to Berlin from Hamburg, Hannover and Frankfurt-Main, each being 20 miles (32 kilometres) wide and culminating in the Berlin Control Zone, a circular area twenty miles in radius centred on the Allied Control Council building, from where the quadripartite Berlin Air Safety Centre would operate. The Soviets were keen to participate in this organisation in order to learn more about Western air traffic control methods (although the actual air traffic control by radar was in fact handled separately) and continued to co-operate in air safety even during the worst parts of the Cold War.

The only precedent of a sustained airlift of any magnitude had been the Second World War 'over the Hump' supply of American and Chinese forces in China from airbases in Assam. This had lasted three years and carried at the most 72,000 tons per month between a variety of airfields at either end, a situation that allowed a considerable degree of operational flexibilty in adverse weather conditions. Such circumstances failed to apply to Berlin, where weather conditions frequently intervened and more than double that tonnage would be required as a bare minimum.

The idea of an airlift apparently came from US Army Lieutenant General Albert Wedemeyer, who had himself served in China at the receiving end and saw the feasibility of its application to Berlin. He suggested this to General Clay, who ordered the 61st Troop Carrier Group at Rhein-Main to test the practicality of air supply to Berlin with their 25 Douglas C-47s from April 2 onwards.

On April 5, an indication of what

On Thursday, June 24, the future of Berlin hung in the balance. Faced with multiple threats including the severance of supplies of electricity and water, the American military government was divided over what response should be made to the overt Soviet action. The faint-hearted advocated that the city should be abandoned, but when the mayor, Ernst Reuter, assured General Clay *(above)* that the Berliners could hold out with air supply alone, Clay ordered the airlift to begin.

Soviet reactions to such a move might be occurred when a Vickers Viking of British European Airways on a scheduled passenger flight to Berlin was buzzed by a Yak-3 fighter, whose pilot miscalculated in turning to make a second pass and smashed into the airliner, killing himself and the ten passengers and crew on the civilian aircraft.

The possibility of armed conflict with the overwhelming air superiority available to the Russians, caused the Americans to discreetly prepare operational air strips and stockpile munitions for the protection of their supply routes across Germany from their Bremerhaven enclave. The British also took the precaution of ordering eight Hawker Tempest fighter-bombers to Gatow on June 22 for escorting RAF transports across the Soviet Zone if necessary, but these were

withdrawn on July 14 when it became clear that the Soviets had no intention of direct interference with air traffic.

On June 24, the day the Soviets began their blockade, Wedemeyer, as Director of Plans and Operations, flew to London with Major General William Draper, the Under Secretary for the Army. Opinion in Washington among President Truman's advisers was divided although Truman himself was determined to stand up to the Russians. The Americans wanted to sound out the British government's reaction to the crisis. They were surprised to learn that the British had already decided to make a stand in Berlin and had started flying in supplies to their garrison, believing that the Soviets were simply out to make a gesture and would not maintain their blockade for long.

The following day, the first C-47s, flying in from the American Zone, arrived at Tempelhof loaded with food.

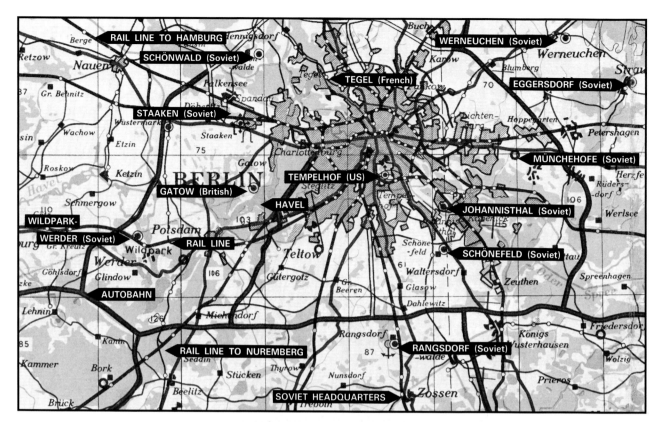

Although Berlin was surrounded by air-fields, only two were available for use by the Western Allies: at Tempelhof in the American Sector and Gatow in the British. However, as the RAF still possessed a number of wartime-vintage Sunderlands, a third option was to land on the Havel lake in the British Sector, and a new airfield was constructed in the French Sector at Tegel.

The British government's attitude helped to turn the waverers in Washington, and Wedemeyer recommended that Major General William H. Tunner USAF, who had been in charge of the 'over the Hump' airlift from Assam to China during the last year of the war and brought big business methods and efficiency to this kind of operation, be put in charge. Tunner eventually received the appointment at the end of July and immediately started to sort out the 'cowboy operation' that he found in which accidents were taking place through the sheer exhaustion of aircrew and ground staff working in hastily improvised conditions.

The Western Sectors' basic requirements were calculated at 4,500 tons per day, as opposed to more than 13,000 tons normally imported by road, rail and canal.

Centre: By the time the Americans took over Tempelhof, battle damage had been compounded by deliberate demolition by the Russians before they pulled out, which left most of the underground facilities unusable. The Germans had also enclosed the huge open hangar in front of the terminal. *Right:* The airfield remained in USAF hands until 1990, when the administration passed to the Berliner Flughafen Gesellschaft, prior to the US finally handing it over in 1992.

Tempelhof was still only grass in 1945, but by 1948 American engineers had laid a Pierced Steel Plank (PSP) runway to facilitate use by heavier aircraft. This C-82 Packet came to grief on December 14 that year due to a burst tyre.

When the airlift began the Americans had only two troop carrier groups of C-47s, which were brought up to a total strength of 110 aircraft by calling in all those loaned out as personal transports to VIPs. The C-47 was known commercially as the DC-3 and to the RAF as the Dakota; it had two engines, flew at 170 miles per hour and had a payload of just over three tons. The RAF had about 60 of the same type and some 50 four-engined Avro Yorks which could carry ten tons at nearly 300 miles per hour. Overall, therefore, the Anglo-American carrying capacity was only about 700 tons per day. The French were unable to help, being heavily engaged in Indo-China and having very few aircraft left in Europe.

This capacity was soon increased by the Americans replacing their C-47s with C-54s, otherwise known as DC-4s or Skymasters, with four engines and the ability to transport ten tons at 180 miles per hour. The British also introduced larger aircraft, bringing in more of their Yorks, in addition to some fuel tankers and a variety of aircraft hired commercially on contract. A total of 103 civilian aircraft were eventually engaged in the British effort overall, although no more than 47 operated at any one time. (One of these entrepreneurs was Fred Laker, who was reputed to go round his only aircraft checking with a screwdriver between flights to keep it going. He went on to found Laker Airways, which was finally put out of business by British Airways in the 1980s.) Then on July 5, ten RAF Short Sunderland flying-boats started a shuttle service from Finkenwerder on the River Elbe near Hamburg to the Havel lake close to Gatow. They could carry four and a half tons of cargo and their internal anti-corrosive treatment enabled them to bring in salt, which was a dangerous cargo for normal aircraft. They were also used to ship out passengers and manufactured items from Berlin. In all, these flying-boats flew over 1,000 sorties, bringing in 4,500 tons of food and evacuating 1,113 under-nourished children.

The Americans augmented their fleet with nine DC-4s from Pan-Am, which were already operating in Germany under Captain Jack Bennett, who eventually was able to claim that he had flown more hours than any other pilot in the airlift. They also had the services of a USAF C-97 Stratofreighter for a while until it was damaged in a landing accident. This aircraft, with its 25-ton capacity, proved very useful in importing heavy, awkward loads, such as bulldozers to assist with the construction of an additional airfield at Tegel. Machinery was also brought in to build a new power station (to be named after Ernst Reuter) in Siemensstadt.

However, it was not simply a matter of getting together sufficient aircraft to achieve the required daily tonnage. Keeping them flying meant having adequate aircrew, maintenance personnel, support facilities and spares to back them up. More ground personnel of all kinds were needed — meteorologists, radio and radar operators, technical and construction engineers, mechanics and drivers, clerks, cooks and medical staff. Further, meticulous planning and staff work was required in order to achieve the maximum effectiveness of all aspects of the operation, which were kept under constant review. Time and motion experts played an important part in keeping maximum utilisation of men and machinery.

At the western end of the American operation lay the former Luftwaffe bases of Wiesbaden and Rhein-Main at Frankfurt which the US Air Force had already built up into what they called 'the aerial gateway to Europe', being the European terminal of the Military Air Transport Service (MATS). Tempelhof (above) was 267 miles as the crow flies, but air safety dictated that aircraft flew in via the southern corridor, and out using the central one, making a round trip of over 600 miles.

The need to fly by dead reckoning, and strict discipline in all weathers, often only on instruments, imposed a heavy strain on the aircrews. The ground staff were equally hard worked in maintaining this round-the-clock operation, not least the Displaced Persons recruited as labourers for the loading teams.

All the despatching airfields needed drastic overhauls to bring them up to the necessary operational standard and increased capacity, with the extension of their runways and taxiways, hard-standings, hangars, workshops, loading and unloading facilities, and fuelling facilities and equipment, as well as an immediate updating of all lighting and communications equipment. A ground approach system was required to talk pilots down in bad weather and directional beacons improved to enable precise navigation to and from Berlin.

At first there were only two airfields available to the Allies in Berlin, Tempelhof in the US Sector and Gatow in the British. Tempelhof had been designed as Berlin's principal pre-war airport and consisted of a magnificent multi-storey terminal building, shaped in ground plan like an eagle, and with an overhanging roof over the apron that enabled aircraft to load and unload their passengers under cover. It even had seven storeys below ground, where a Messerschmitt aircraft factory had operated during the war. However, the airfield itself was severely limited for modern aircraft, being closely surrounded by tall apartment blocks, fac-

Hemmed in by housing and factories, Tempelhof obviously had its restrictions, but Gatow *(above)* was surrounded by open countryside. The nearest RAF bases in the British Zone were at Fassberg and Celle, each about 150 miles from Berlin, making the RAF round trip via the northern and central corridors 50 per cent shorter than the American route which enabled the RAF to fit in more sorties per day.

tories and chimneys and therefore, with the acute housing shortage, incapable of expansion to allow a safer landing approach. The Americans had improved the grass landing strip by laying a runway of pierced steel planking (PSP) 5,000 feet long and 120 wide, which they had connected to the apron with a concrete taxiway.

Gatow had been developed as the Luftwaffe's main training academy and had also been used as a fighter base during the war. Again it was merely a grass landing strip, so the RAF had laid a PSP runway 4,500 feet long as early as 1945, but this had proved inadequate in practice so a concrete runway designed to take medium-sized aircraft had been

October 1991 and a Hercules approaches Gatow — still an RAF base — but also now used by the Army Air Corps. Save for new married quarters and schools, and one or two modern additions to the installations, RAF Gatow remains exactly how it was built for the Luftwaffe.

commenced in 1947 with a view to being able to supply the British garrison by air in time of crisis.

In west Germany the principal American airfields were at Rhein-Main and Wiesbaden, with the British at Wunstorf, and by flying in on the southern and northern corridors and out on the central corridor, this gave round trips of 603 and 320 miles respectively. This disparity between the distance of Berlin from the British and the American Zones was demonstrated in the fact that two planes operating out of the British Zone could do the work of three of the same type operating out of the American Zone. Similarly, when comparing aircraft capacities, two C-54s operating out of the British Zone could do the job of nine C-47s operating out of the American zone so clearly the British Zone provided the opportunity for a more effective service.

The chartering of civilian aircraft by the RAF led to overcrowding at Wunstorf, so Fassberg airfield north of Celle was rapidly prepared with PSP to take all the RAF and civilian Dakotas from the end of the July. A month later the airfield at Fassberg was handed over to the USAF, which brought in 40 C-54s, and all the British Dakotas moved north to Lübeck. Then on October 5 the civilian Dakotas were separated from the RAF squadrons and sent to Hamburg's civil airport of Fühlsbüttel, and at about this time the RAF were reinforced by twelve Royal Australian Air Force, ten South African Air Force and three Royal New Zealand Air Force aircrews with their aircraft.

As an indication of how things were originally organised, the RAF airfield at Wunstorf near Hannover, on which the main British effort was based, had two concrete runways and perimeter tracks but was mainly grass. To accommodate the heavier Yorks in any numbers, a considerable extension with PSP had been needed. Before the Yorks joined

Initially, the USAF and RAF operated independently of each other, the French being unable to make any sizeable contribution as their air force was then heavily committed to the war in Indo-China. General Clay had expected to have to maintain the lift for a few weeks at the most to gain negotiating time with the Russians but, when the blockade showed no sign of relaxing, and with winter just around the corner, things had to move into top gear. General William H. Tunner, who had masterminded the wartime airlift to China and was now deputy of MATS, was flown in from Washington to take charge. Ultimately the RAF and USAF operations were combined, with American aircraft flying from the British bases. Here a C-54 Skymaster taxies into Gatow for unloading, while an Avro York prepares to take off.

in, the Dakotas were spaced at six minute intervals by day and fifteen at night. This was based on the timings then needed to unload the aircraft at Gatow but was later improved as better techniques and equipment were introduced.

The difference in speeds between these two types of aircraft also brought problems in traffic control. The inward and outward routes along the central corridor were kept as far apart as possible and the different aircraft types were separated in altitude, but there was still a danger of collisions in the ascent and descent phases.

Eventually the traffic was so organised that all aircraft, regardless of type, arrived at regular four minute intervals. Turnaround time at Gatow for the Dakotas was reduced to 20 minutes, but at Wunstorf, where refuelling was necessary in order to keep the aircraft's load-carrying capacity at the maximum, refuelling and maintenance extended the time to 45 minutes. For the Yorks this was 40-45 minutes and two and a half hours respectively.

For their C-54s, the Americans evolved a system whereby the ten-ton aircraft cargos were pre-packed on ten-ton trailers in the order and correct

Civilian aircraft were also brought into play. This Avro 691 Lancastrian 3 was an ex-RAF aircraft (TX282) which had been modified as a passenger carrier named *Star Guide* (G-AGWL). In 1949, Flight Refuelling Ltd took it over for bulk fuel transport.

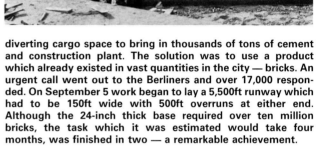

Work had already begun on laying down a concrete runway at Gatow and to provide another strip on the grass at Tempelhof. However, it was obvious that to be able to deliver sufficient supplies of food and fuel to keep the western part of the city going throughout the winter, a third airfield would be needed. An ideal site presented itself in the French Sector at Tegel where a former German anti-aircraft training area, flat and unobstructed, lay abandoned. The French agreed to the Americans building a new airfield, yet there could be no question of diverting cargo space to bring in thousands of tons of cement and construction plant. The solution was to use a product which already existed in vast quantities in the city — bricks. An urgent call went out to the Berliners and over 17,000 responded. On September 5 work began to lay a 5,500ft runway which had to be 150ft wide with 500ft overruns at either end. Although the 24-inch thick base required over ten million bricks, the task which it was estimated would take four months, was finished in two — a remarkable achievement.

weight distribution required for loading the aircraft. The trailers were then matched up with empty aircraft as they arrived, and the loads transferred and strapped down within the aircraft in 20 minutes flat. Unloading took only 13 minutes.

By the end of August the daily target tonnage had been exceeded by 500 tons with over 5,000 tons being delivered every 24 hours. Then in October, in anticipation of another severe winter, the basic requirement was raised to 5,620 tons per day.

It was not until October 15 that the independent British and American efforts were amalgamated in a Combined Airlift Task Force which had been set up at Wiesbaden under Major General Tunner's command, with Air Commodore J. W. F. Merer of the RAF as his deputy.

In November, the British began operating Handley Page Hastings transports out of Schleswigland, near the Danish border, where the Halton tankers (converted Halifax bombers) were also based. These four-engined aircraft had an airspeed of 300 miles per hour and could carry eight tons of liquid fuel-stuffs. A further development was the transfer on December 15 of the USAF C-54s of the 317th Troop Carrier Wing from Wiesbaden to the airfield at Celle in the British Zone.

On December 15, 1948, Tegel became operational as West Berlin's third airfield with a runway of 5,500 feet, having been constructed in the French Sector in just two months by American engineers using German labour, mainly female. Two Soviet radio transmitter masts obstructing the approaches to the new airport were blown up on the instructions of Général Ganeval, the

The runway that Berliners built to help their own salvation remains a remarkable 'living' memorial to their labours. When commercial operations were switched from Tempelhof to Tegel in September 1975, which then became Berlin's main link with the outside world, it was a fitting gesture that the USAF Art Collection should transfer this painting by Dick Kramer to the new main concourse as a fitting reminder to present-day travellers as to how — and why — the airport was born.

French Commandant who, when asked by Major-General Kotikov how he could so such a thing, replied simply: 'With dynamite, of course!' However, one outcome was that the French were obliged to return to Russian control the district of Stolpe, just outside the city boundary, which had been hitherto reserved for the French as a possible airfield site.

The airlift was not without its mishaps. On September 19 a York crashed due to engine failure during a night take-off and all five crew members were killed, and on November 19 a Dakota crashed in the Soviet Zone with the loss of three aircrew and a soldier who was being flown out on compassionate leave. A second Dakota crash occurred in severe turbulence just inside the Soviet Zone on January 24 as it was about to land at Lübeck with three crew and 22 passengers aboard. The signaller and seven passsengers were killed. In all, 73 Allied personnel and five German civilians were to lose their lives in the airlift.

However, despite misgivings, none of this was due to the Soviet harassment experienced by many pilots during the course of the airlift, particularly in early 1949. Soviet fighter aircraft would make mock attacks on the transports, or carry out firing practice on towed or ground targets in close proximity. Sometimes anti-aircraft guns fired close to but never actually at the transports, or seachlights were switched on in an attempt to dazzle the pilots.

One ploy that did win the hearts and minds of Berliners was introduced by Lieutenant Gail Halverson, who started dropping sweets and chewing gum on handkerchief parachutes to the children watching the aircraft landing. His action was soon copied by many other American pilots, much to the delight of the beleaguered population.

The constant comings and goings over the city inspired youngsters to watch the aerial activity from numerous vantage points, especially around the more accessible airfield at Tempelhof. Their interest and enthusiasm was also increased in another way which probably did more in its way to focus a spotlight on the Berlin Airlift and give it worldwide publicity. Lieutenant Gail S. Halverson, one of the pilots who became known to every child in Berlin as the 'Schokolade Flieger', explains: 'Down in Africa and Italy all through the war, and in South American cities since the war ended, I always got snowed under by kids swarming around wanting gum and candy and, naturally, cigarettes. I don't smoke or drink, so I can't indulge their wilder vices, but usually I have candy and gum in my pockets. Well, I'm telling now about Berlin. I got in the middle of all these kids and what do you think happened? None of them jerked at my pants or threatened to knock my block off. They wanted to hold a polite conversation and try out their English on me. Their English is about as bad as my German. After about an hour, in which I gained considerable stature as an airlift pilot, I noticed something was missing. I couldn't put my finger on it, but it nagged me. And finally I realised what it was. Those kids hadn't begged for a single thing. It took another hour of crossbreeding our languages to find out it wasn't lack of candy-hunger that held them back; they just lacked the brass other kids have. So I told them to be down at the end of the runway next day, and I'd drop them some gum and candy. That night I tied up some candy bars and gum in handkerchiefs and had my chief sling them out on a signal from me next day.'

The daily drop was made over the cemetery on the north side of Tempelhof and that Christmas Lieutenant Halverson received over 4,000 letters from his young fans. 'Day by day, the crowds of kids waiting for the drop got bigger,' recalled Halverson, 'and day by day my supply of old shirts, GI sheets and old shorts, all of which I used for parachutes, got smaller.'

CEMETERY

COLUMBIAHAUS

THIRD REICH EAGLE

MEMORIAL ERECTED HERE

Tempelhof at the height of the airlift. Hemmed in by buildings, the 400-foot chimney of a nearby brewery was an additional landing hazard that even Göring failed to get demolished way back in the days of the Luftwaffe!

All Soviet attempts to coerce the inhabitants and force an Allied withdrawal from the city failed. In the initial stages, about 20,000 out of the 2,000,000 inhabitants are believed to have succumbed to Soviet blandishments to purchase their rations in the eastern part of the city, but many of these later reverted. In demonstration against the Soviet machinations, on September 9, 1948, Ernst Reuter was able to summon a crowd of 300,000 in front of the Reichstag, when he called on the peoples of the world not to abandon the city in its hour of need.

Attempts by international relief agencies to get supplies to Berlin through the Soviet Zone were blocked, and even the Swedish Red Cross's deliveries of supplies for 20,000 needy children in the city, which had been in operation since the beginning of the military occupation, were now denied to the Western Sectors. As a consequence, the Swedes called off their support in disgust.

The Soviets meanwhile were losing whatever sympathetic international reputation they may have had with this blockade and, furthermore, the counter-blockade imposed by the Allies was beginning to hurt. The British had immediately stopped coal and steel deliveries to the Soviet Zone, and further restrictions on trade had been imposed by the British-American Bizonal Economic Commission. It was then revealed by American intelligence sources that, from a conference convened with East German economic experts at Karlshorst by the Soviet Military Governor of Germany, Marshal Vassili D. Sokolovsky (who had

been Zhukov's deputy in the battle for the city), it was evident there had been no prior consultation with them about the implications of imposing the blockade. The whole matter was proving an utter disaster for the Communist cause.

Early in 1949 discussions started in the United Nations, culminating in an offer by the Soviets to lift their blockade of Berlin if the Four Powers' Foreign

Ministers could meet to discuss the question of currency reform. This was eventually agreed on May 4, with the lifting of the blockade to come into effect at 0001 hours, May 12, 1949.

May 12 was celebrated as a public holiday in the Western Sectors. The lights came on again as the Soviets allowed the electric current to come through, and the crowds assembled to meet the first convoys driving up the autobahn. Nevertheless, the airlift was maintained until the end of September to build up an adequate stockpile of supplies against the possibility of a renewal of the blockade by the Soviets, who continued to make life awkward.

The statistics of the eleven-month blockade were impressive. Percentage-wise, the USAF had contributed 76.7 per cent of the overall capacity, with the RAF 17 per cent and British civil aviation 6.3 per cent. All told, 2,325,809 tons were delivered by air to Berlin between June 1948 and September 1949, of which 1,586,500 tons were coal. Food supplies totalled 538,016 tons with fuel oils 92,282 tons.

But the success of the airlift could also be measured in more human terms, for there was not one single case of death from either starvation or cold recorded in the city during that winter of 1948-49. During the same period, the USAF had flown out 1,500 tuberculosis patients and the RAF 15,426 children to foster homes in western Germany in an airborne continuation of Operation 'Stork' started in 1945.

However, the major result of this demonstration by the Western Allies in standing up to communist bullying had been to change their status from occupying to protecting powers, and to expedite the democratic process in western Germany with the Federal Republic (FDR) being founded on May 23, 1949.

Having survived the winter, it must have been obvious to the Soviets by the spring of 1949 that their attempt to strangle the Western Sectors had failed. A counter-blockade against the Soviet Zone introduced by the Allies helped bring the Russians to their senses and the land restrictions were finally lifted on May 12. Nevertheless, the planes continued the shuttle, building up stocks for another four months. This is the last USAF C-54 of the airlift being honoured by a flypast on September 30 — the official end of the emergency. The tally of 1,738,572.7 tons represented 76.7 per cent of the total Allied contribution of 2,325,809 tons airlifted into Berlin.

Two years after the airlift finished, a memorial was unveiled to the 73 Allied airmen and five Germans killed in crashes during the operation. A site was chosen in front of the Third Reich terminal building, which still sported the Nazi eagle on its roof (see page 193), the segment of park in the south-east corner of the square having been dedicated 'Platz der Luftbrücke' (Air Bridge Square) the previous summer. Eduard Ludwig designed the memorial to represent the three air corridors running to the West, the monument facing in the same direction. Over 80,000 people attended the unveiling which took place on July 10, 1951.

Thirty-four years later, the car park directly in front of the terminal was renamed 'Eagle Square' after the Nazi emblem which had been removed from the roof in 1962. The eagle, which had been designed by the architect, Ernst Sagebiel (who was also responsible for drawing up the plans for Göring's Air Ministry), and modelled by sculptor Walter Lemtke, had been taken to America where it was given to the museum of the United States Military Academy at West Point. In August 1985, the head alone was brought back to the city by the United States Air Force 'to be shared with the people of Berlin'.

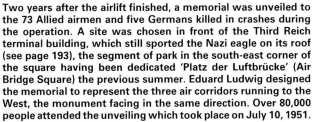

In 1949, the military occupation of Germany came to an end. It formally ended in the Soviet Zone on May 30 with the adoption by the People's Council of the Constitution for the German Democratic Republic (Deutsche Demokratische Republik), and in the Western Zones with the creation of the Federal Republic of Germany (Bundesrepublik Deutschland) on September 21. As far as Berlin was concerned, the status quo remained, although West Berlin was permitted to send observers to the FRG parliament sitting in Bonn, while East Berlin was incorporated as the capital of the GDR in August 1950. *Top:* Potsdamer Platz — crossroads between East and West. The station in the foreground lies in the British Sector, while the Columbushaus on the far corner is on the Soviet side. In the background on the right, further down Hermann-Göring-Strasse, is the Reichs Chancellery, about to be demolished.

During the course of the airlift there had been a distinct polarisation in the political situation in Berlin. Following the constant disruption of the city parliament by communist-directed mobs during the summer of 1948, which the police of the Soviet Sector did nothing to prevent, in early September the members voted to move to Schöneberg town hall in the American Sector. It was these disruptions that had caused Ernst Reuter to call on public support and brought about the massive meeting outside the Reichstag on September 9, but a few weeks later the SED were able to rally similarly large numbers at another rally in the east.

The Communists then convened an 'Extraordinary Municipal Assembly', which appointed a new City Council acceptable to the Soviet authorities, whereupon the freely-elected City Council was also obliged to move to West Berlin. The Communists tried to impose a boycott of the next elections due in December 1948, but 86.7 per

The Birth of the Republics

cent of the electorate turned out and voted Ernst Reuter Governing Mayor, an appointment the Soviets could no longer block with their veto, having moved out of the Allied Kommandatura.

The legal complexities of Berlin's status now began. Although the Soviets no longer took part in the joint ruling process, they continued to regard the whole of Greater Berlin as a entity apart from the rest of the Soviet Zone. Following the creation of the Federal

Republic in May 1949, the German Democratic Republic (GDR) was established in the Soviet Zone on October 7 that year, and its original constitution reflected this view, even though its governing functions took place in the Soviet Sector of the city. Although the Basic Law of the Federal Republic included Berlin as one of its states, the Western Allies did not permit integration of the city into the Federation, reserving certain rights to ensure their ability to continue to defend Berlin.

Forty years have passed and one now looks out on the wasteland which divided East and West after the Wall was built. Although the Wall has gone, the same station entrance is still sealed, awaiting the rebirth of Potsdamer Platz Station.

Left: **The piecemeal demolition of the Chancellery had been going on since 1947 to provide materials for the construction of** the second Soviet war memorial in Berlin to be located in Treptow Park *(right)*, on the western bank of the River Spree.

Ripped apart, baring its innards, the final remnants were brought down in 1949. On the right, the end of the famous double doorway to the Ehrenmal. Small-gauge railway track was used extensively in Berlin to clear rubble.

The design of the cemetery included ramps either side of the central memorial which, when clad with red marble from the Chancellery, were to simulate two huge Red Flags. This picture shows the situation in June 1948.

Top: **The memorial was unveiled on May 8, 1949 — the fourth anniversary of the surrender. The effect when completed was quite stunning with the two enormous red marble flags, dipped in salute, and the five symbolic graves — the graves of the 3,200 Soviet soldiers actually buried here lie under the trees on either side, except for a general, a colonel, a captain and a soldier specially interred upright in a small grave in the foreground.** *Left:* **On either side of this viewpoint are the statues of two Soviet soldiers, one old, one young, kneeling in homage to their fallen comrades.**

Above: The conical mound at the far end contains mosaics depicting a similar theme and is surmounted by a symbolic statue of a Soviet soldier holding a young female child in his arms whilst smashing a swastika at his feet with a sword. This was inspired by the story of Colour Sergeant Nikolai Masalov crossing the Landwehr Canal to rescue a child from its dead mother before the attack (see text page 226). *Right:* Soviet Premier Nikolai A. Bulganin and Communist Party Secretary Nikita S. Kruschev visiting the memorial on July 24, 1955 with GDR Premier Otto Grotewohl.

The third Soviet war cemetery in Berlin is in the northern borough of Pankow, across which the 12th Guards Corps and 79th Corps fought their way to victory. Soviet soldiers wore a small capsule around their necks in which a piece of paper gave their identity. In many cases this soon disintegrated after burial, but officers were more easily identified when disinterred from field graves as they were usually buried in pairs in wardrobes taken from nearby houses. Those that fell in the northern suburbs lie in huge mass graves at Pankow surrounded by smaller plots in the Soviet style.

Despite having been deprived of its hinterland, thanks to the Marshall Aid Plan and increasing support from the Federal Republic, the economic situation in the Western Sectors of Berlin gradually began to improve, and by 1956 production had regained the pre-war output levels of twenty years earlier. Allied to this was a massive rebuilding programme for the provision of housing to replace that destroyed during the war.

In 1953, an international architectural competition was held in the Western Sectors which resulted in the reconstruction of the Hansaviertel in the Tiergarten in which 53 architects took part, creating 20 apartment blocks, 50 houses and all the necessary infrastructure, and incorporating the original two churches in that area. The associated 'Interbau' exhibition attracted even more international visitors than the 1936 Olympics had done. Le Corbusier's contribution was too large for the Hansaviertel, so his massive 'Unité d'Habitation', 17 stories high and planned to accommodate 1,200 people, was built near the Olympic Stadium instead.

The clearing of debris from the city continued and it was not until 1957 that

Memorials were also being constructed on the lines of advance to the capital. This is Müncheberg where the last of the German lines of defence was breached on April 19, 1945.

the last of the 'Trümmerfrauen', the women who sorted out and cleaned bricks, girders and wooden beams for re-use, was seen. Two-thirds of the six million cubic metres of debris resulting from the war was used to form the 'Teufelsberg' hill in the north-eastern

corner of the Grunewald, while other artificial hills were formed in the Hasenheide next to Tempelhof Airport and elsewhere, as well as over the remains of the Flak-towers at Humboldthain and Friedrichshain in the Soviet Sector.

Meanwhile, all over the city, ruins were being pulled down and sites cleared for redevelopment. On November 6, 1950, the Schloss was razed in the Soviet Sector — more in this case because of its imperial associations with the Second Reich (see page 6). The following March, the Krolloper in the British Sector was demolished as a political symbol of the Third Reich.

Above: In 1951 the Communist Party was also revering its dead. On January 14, the 32nd anniversary of the deaths of Karl Liebknecht and Rosa Luxemburg, a ceremony was held at the Gedenkstätte der Sozialisten in Friedrichsfelde where the remains of the faithful were interred in the circular wall around the shrine. Original gravestones or new plaques *(right)* record those buried within, while the 'holy of holies' surround the central memorial *(below)*. The top ten are: Karl Liebknecht and Rosa Luxemburg (15.1.1919); Franz Mehring (28.1.1919); John Schehr (1.2.1934); Franz Künstler (10.9.1942); Ernst Thälmann (18.8.1944); Rudolf Breitscheid (24.8.1944); Wilhelm Pieck (7.9.1960); Walter Ulbricht (1.8.1973); and Otto Grotewohl (21.9.1984).

What with all the martyrs and marchers, there really was very little difference between the regime ousted in 1945 and the one which replaced it. This picture could have come right out of the pages of the Third Reich instead of being taken in 1951. Save for the fact that the shirts were blue, the Communist Youth Movement — the Freie Deutsche Jugend — appeared no different from the Hitlerjugend on their May Day parade down the Unter den Linden. 'Forward with Stalin' reads the banner . . . yet something seems wrong. The equestrian statue of Frederick II is missing, having been removed the previous year and set up at Sanssouci (see map page 313) in 1963. By 1980, the East Germans had had second thoughts and Rauch's 'Old Fritz' returned to his rightful place outside the Kronprinzen Palais. The old Prussian State Library is on the right.

As we have seen, Grosse Frankfurter Strasse and Frankfurter Allee were smashed to pieces by the end of the war, so it was here that the fledgling GDR decided to lay the 'foundation stone' to its showpiece to socialism. *Above:* The street had been renamed Stalinallee on December 21, 1949, whereupon every building was torn down, the carriageways widened, and Soviet-style apartment blocks erected along its entire length *(right)*, complete with lanterns à la Albert Speer.

In 1952 the GDR had begun reconstruction of the former Frankfurter Allee in true Soviet architectural style as 'the greatest, widely visible symbol of our policy of peace and the improvement in conditions for all our population', according to GDR President, Wilhelm Pieck. This was at first called Stalinallee but the name was changed to Karl-Marx-Allee in October 1961 in the wake of the condemnation of Stalin by the Soviet Premier, Nikita Kruschev.

And it was here, before work had been completed, that the uprising of June 17, 1953 against the Communist government originated among the construction workers. Already the measures introduced by the new regime had led to ever-increasing numbers of people leaving the Soviet Zone, and by the beginning of the year the average monthly loss was 20 to 30,000. On March 5 Stalin died, and by the end of the month the figure had escalated to nearly 60,000. The death of the leader of the communist world spurred on those who dared to oppose, the catalyst being the demand for increased production on May 14 by the East German government. *Below:* Stalin was succeeded by Kruschev but it was not until 1961 that he finally discredited the former Generalissimo. Stalin fell from grace and with him went his statue which stood in front of 70e Strausberger Platz.

The cavernous shops lining the ground floor frontage of these buildings have now largely been taken over by Western businesses since the unification, but the façades and apartments above require urgent attention after years of neglect.

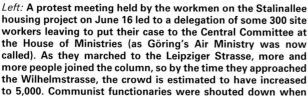

Left: **A protest meeting held by the workmen on the Stalinallee housing project on June 16 led to a delegation of some 300 site workers leaving to put their case to the Central Committee at the House of Ministries (as Göring's Air Ministry was now called). As they marched to the Leipziger Strasse, more and more people joined the column, so by the time they approached the Wilhelmstrasse, the crowd is estimated to have increased to 5,000. Communist functionaries were shouted down when**

they attempted to reason with the workers over the new production targets, and by nightfall a full-scale revolt was under way. The Soviet military were then deployed in support of the puppet East German regime which showed itself incapable of handling the situation and the following morning saw Red Army T-34s once again rolling down the streets of central Berlin. *Right:* **This barricade protected by tanks and artillery has been set up on Leipziger Strasse beside the old Air Ministry.**

On June 16, 1953, a call by the East German government for a doubling of effort with no increase in wages led to a strike on the Stalinallee construction site. Thousands of workers converged in a march on the Ministries' building (Göring's former Air Ministry) to protest to the SED leadership, calling for the resignation of the government and free elections, but the SED leaders, Otto Grotewohl and Walter Ulbricht, lacked the courage to face them. News of this event spread throughout the GDR and next day strikes and demonstrations occurred in 270 different locations. The SED could not cope. At 1300 hours the Soviet Commandant declared a state of emergency and called in tanks to disperse the demonstrators. The East Berlin uprising was crushed during the course of the afternoon, but not before the Red Flag had been torn down from the Brandenburg Gate. It is suspected that about 260 demonstrators and 100 policemen were killed that day. Even though some Soviet troops fired on the crowds, it is known that some refused to do so and were subsequently court-martialled and possibly executed for failure to carry out their orders. A wave of arrests then followed.

In the Western sector, this revolt against the communist authorities was commemorated by the renaming of the former Charlottenburger Chaussee (the East-West-Axis), the Strasse des 17. Juni.

Following Stalin's death, Soviet policy was, as Kruschev explained, to 'accept the division of Germany as a fait accompli which it might be undesirable for either side to try to change'. As far as the three Western Commandants were concerned, their first public announcement was to deny any complicity in the uprising, and it was only later that protests were made over the Soviet involvement. *Right:* **British military police guard the Soviet memorial against any backlash from West Berliners.**

Battle of Berlin, Part Two. With smoke rising from the area of the Stalinallee in the distance on the left, Soviet panzers manoeuvre on the Pariser Platz. The corner of Wilhelmstrasse is in the centre. The ruin of the Adlon Hotel has virtually gone, but the massive bulk of the brand new Soviet Union Embassy rises further down Unter den Linden, recently replanted with young lime trees.

David and Goliath fight it out on Potsdamer Platz. Eight years on from 1945, the Panzerfausts and anti-tank guns have given way to sticks and stones. The following day, after the attempted uprising had been put down, the West Berlin Mayor, Ernst Reuter, broadcast his epitaph: 'A people cannot be held in submission in the long run, with martial law and bayonets and tanks; and it would be terrible if the graves, which are already deep enough, should be made deeper. What I saw today at the Potsdamer Platz of these wastes, this dead, empty city, reminded me of my first impression at the end of 1946 in that terrible winter when I first returned to Berlin and saw the Tiergarten. A man's heart could have stopped, and it could stop today as we see this city murdered by the forces of history with which we have all been torn.'

Left: And it was also the end of the Columbushaus, now a state-owned communist store called the Handelsorganisation, fired by the demonstrators. *Above:* The scene of the battle in 1991 following the demise of the Wall which bisected the road at this point. From here, the Leipziger Strasse now takes a different course to join the old Potsdamer Strasse at the bridge.

One of the anomalies of the East-West situation in Berlin was that the railway system within the city was still under the overall control of the authorities in the East. This involved the state railways, still known as the Deutsche Reichsbahn, and the city's S-Bahn. To a large extent the West Berliners boycotted the S-Bahn, so that in the end only two lines were in operation; the north-south stretch from Frohnau to Lichtenrade, which closed down shortly before the collapse of the GDR but has since been revived, and the vital shuttle service connecting the Friedrichstrasse, Zoologische Garten and Charlottenburg railway stations, which provided a link between East and West Berlin subject to the usual GDR passport, customs and financial controls, and was extensively used by GDR old age pensioners visiting the West. The S-Bahn system in both parts of the city became so run down that the city authorities are now spending vast sums on rebuilding its stations and tracks in the hope that the West Berliners can be re-educated in its use and so help to relieve the city's traffic problems. The Zoologischer Garten Station became West Berlin's main station, each of the Western Allies having their own termini for their military trains, the French at Tegel, the British at Charlottenburg and the Americans at Lichterfelde West. Most of the ruined stations like the Alexander Bahnhof *(above)* in the Soviet Sector were repaired or rebuilt, but others fell foul of the border restrictions.

The Lehrter main-line station in the British borough of Tiergarten had been one of the assembly points for refugees in the immediate post-war period *(left)*. However, the closure of the rail line out of Berlin to Hamburg meant that the station no longer had a purpose, and it was shut on August 28, 1951. *Right:* Later the buildings were demolished, the site being used as a road freight transport depot, but this area is now all scheduled for redevelopment.

Left: The tracks were ripped up, leaving only the S-Bahn station in the background of our comparison *right*, taken from the bridge on Moabit looking towards the bridge under Invalidenstrasse (near where Bormann committed suicide).

Left: The Anhalter Station in the US Sector was closed by the Russian-controlled railway management on May 18, 1952, together with the Potsdamer Station (bottom) to bypass the Western sectors. Walter Ulbricht, the GDR's deputy premier, described it as 'a 'measure to prevent American interference' with East German rail traffic which would henceforth be routed around Berlin on the outer ring. The station was in such a damaged state that the West Berlin authorities decided to demolish it in the interests of safety, leaving a small portion of the façade as a memorial to the bombing (see page 86). The site was then used for various funfairs and open air exhibitions over the years and has now been cleaned up (see page 160).

Although the GDR's Deutsche Reichsbahn controlled the railways running through Berlin, a number of West Berlin railway enthusiasts continued to work for the organisation, giving problems over rates of pay and pensions occasionally leading to strike action, in which the rôle of the Reichsbahn traffic police operating in the Western Sectors was particularly sensitive. Right: Believe it or not, this is the comparison! Although the station building was demolished, the platforms still survive. Below left: The severed stanchions which once supported the platform canopy can still be traced in the undergrowth. Below right: Although the track has been lifted, piles of sleepers lie in wild confusion.

We have seen the Potsdamer Station at the end of the war on pages 228-229. It, too, was closed due to Communist action in 1952. Left: Here we show it in its pre-war glory and right as a

construction site in 1991. During the division of the city Bernburger Strasse was extended across the centre of the site, but traffic has since reverted to Stresemannstrasse.

Berlin during the Cold War evokes memories of George Smiley and Harry Palmer but, as they say, truth is often stranger than fiction. The operation carried out successfully by British and American intelligence organisations in 1954-55 to tap into main telephone cables in East Berlin and eavesdrop on Soviet and East German communications was certainly worthy of the most exciting novel or spy film. Five years earlier, MI6 had carried out a similar telephone tapping intercept against the Russians in Vienna (another city also occupied by the Four Powers under military government) with great success. Now, using a diagram of the Berlin telephone lines obtained by the CIA, a new combined operation with the British was to be code-named 'Gold' (Operation 'Prince' to the British Secret Intelligence Service). The tunnel was to be dug in Alt Glienicke in south-east Berlin where the American and Soviet Sectors adjoined close to the Schönefelder Chaussee, alongside which land-lines ran to the Soviet HQ at Karlshorst. The tunnel would have to be at least 500 yards long to reach from the American side to the road so a cover operation was put in motion to build a radar station within a few yards of the sector boundary, ostensibly to keep a check on the nearby Soviet airfield at Johannisthal. Such a move would not be looked on as suspicious as it was part and parcel of the activities of both East and West to keep the other side under observation. The official CIA report states that the responsibility was to '(1) procure a site and drive a tunnel to a point beneath the target cables. (2) be responsible for the recording of all signals produced. (3) process in Washington all of the telegraphic material received from the project.' SIS would '(1) drive a vertical shaft from the tunnel's end to the targets. (2) effect the cable taps and deliver a usable signal to the head of the tunnel for recording; and (3) provide a center to process the voice recordings from the site.'

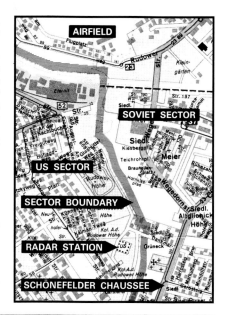

To prevent any possibility of subsidence, the 78-inch diameter tunnel was dug 20 feet below ground (leaving 13½ feet of solid earth above), and lined with steel segments. It was to run 1,476 feet and, as the report explains: 'No one had ever tunnelled under clandestine conditions with the expectation of hitting a target two inches in diameter and 18 inches below a main German/Soviet highway'. Precise measurements were obtained by two agents faking a breakdown on the road and

leaving behind a tiny radar reflector. The work began in August 1954 using a hydraulically-operated steel ring which was pressed forward as the earth was removed. The excavated spoil was then packed into wooden crates to make it look as if technical equipment for the radar station was being moved. The tunnelling took seven months before the British began installing the switchgear, which included 600 tape recorders, in the masking radar building.

The work was finished on February 25, 1955. 'Vapor barriers were erected,' says the CIA report, 'and, in addition, a heavy "anti-personnel" door of steel and concrete was constructed to seal off the tunnel some 15 yards from its terminal end. This door bore the following inscription neatly lettered in German and Cyrillic: "Entry is forbidden by order of the Commanding General". It was reasoned that this sign might give pause to Soviet and/or German officials and gain time. From the

beginning it was realised that the duration of the operation was finite' and that 'considerable thought was given to the posture the US Government would adopt upon the tunnel's discovery.' That discovery came eleven months and eleven days later on April 21, 1956,. The Soviets decided to make capital out of the event and the world's press, as well as thousands of East Germans, were allowed to inspect the installation as an indictment of Allied perfidy.

Berlin's unique position during the Cold War period led in the 1950s to the Berliners beginning to call their city the 'Agentensumpf', or the spy swamp. This state of affairs began with the arrival of the NKVD in 1945, when the latter set up their base in Pankow, and continued on the Soviet side with the establishment of a KGB headquarters at Karlshorst. The Western Allies subsequently brought along their own intelligence agencies, such as the American Central Intelligence Agency (CIA) and the British Secret Intelligence Service (SIS), otherwise known as MI6, and the French SDECE, all of whom revelled in the unusual opportunities that the Berlin situation provided.

One of the most famous episodes of this period was Operation 'Gold' as it was named by the Americans, or 'Prince' by the British, in which a joint CIA and SIS team drove a tunnel between the American and Soviet Sectors to intercept East German and Soviet communications. The scheme was agreed in December 1953 and, under cover of the establishment of a US Air Force radar station, a seven-foot diameter tunnel was dug 24 feet below ground for some 1,800 feet to a point suggested by General Reinhard Gehlen of the Federal German Intelligence Service where the main communication cables ran alongside the main road from Berlin to Schönefeld airport in the Soviet Sector. The lines in question were successfully tapped in April 1955 and the traffic on them automatically taped, the tapes being sent back to the UK and USA, where specially formed teams of experts proceeded to analyse them. The volume and consequent amount of work involved was enormous. It was indeed a gold mine and it continued to produce

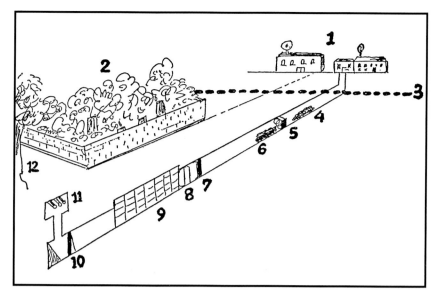

The KGB even published an illustrated 'guide' in June 1956 which included this sketch. (1) American radar station at Rudow. (2) Rudow Cemetery. (3) Border between West and East Berlin. (4) Sandbags. (5) Barbed-wire entanglement. (6) Sandbags. (7) First steel door. (8) Air-conditioning unit. (9) Amplifiers. (10) Second steel door. (11) Shaft to Soviet telephone lines. (12) Schönefelder Chaussee.

intelligence for almost a year until East German engineers began digging near their end of the tunnel and exposed it. The Soviets and East Germans expressed their fury at this penetration of their secret communications and invited journalists and thousands of their own people to view this concrete evidence of the perfidiousness of the West

However, in December 1960, with some of the material obtained from the tunnel still being analysed, it was suddenly revealed (through the defection of a Polish intelligence officer) that the SIS secretary of the joint committee that had examined the feasibility of the

project, and studied and planned the tunnel, had in fact been a Soviet agent! Consequently the Soviets had been given ample warning and time to arrange to bypass the target area and set up their own special team to occupy and mislead Western intelligence resources. Further, this agent, George Blake, had gone on to persuade his superiors that he offer himself as a double agent for the Soviets, thus justifying his frequent contacts with them and in effect becoming a triple agent. In this manner it was estimated that he was also able to betray some forty western agents in eastern Europe before he returned to

The Glienicker 'spy swap bridge' near Potsdam — the same one illustrated on page 197 — which formed the crossing point between the American Sector of Berlin at Wannsee and the Soviet Zone of Germany (see map page 313).

the UK from Berlin in April 1959. He was then posted to Beirut, from where he was eventually recalled and arrested.

Blake was born in Holland with the name of Behar and had volunteered to become a Soviet agent when he was a prisoner in Korea. As a youngster, he had played a minor role in the Dutch resistance before fleeing to England in 1943. He then joined the Royal Navy, having first changed his name to Blake. He was commissioned in 1944 and worked with the Dutch Section of the Special Operations Executive (SOE) for a while and then, because of his linguistic talents, was transferred as an interpreter to work at the Supreme Headquarters Allied Expeditionary Force (SHAEF). At the end of the war he was posted to Hamburg where he was involved in collating technical information about the German Navy, and then became involved in checking Soviet infiltration into the British Zone, which prompted him to start learning Russian. He was then recruited by the SIS, who first sent him to Cambridge University to study Russian, and then to Seoul under consular cover to found a new SIS station there. He, with the remainder of the legation, was captured by the North Koreans in 1950 and spent nearly three years in 'captivity' before being returned to the west via Moscow. After a spell of leave he was employed in London before being transferred to the Berlin station.

At his trial for offences under the Official Secrets Act, Blake admitted to have betrayed to the Soviets every secret that had crossed his desk since his return to duty in September 1953, and was sentenced to a total of 42 years' imprisonment. Although it was anticipated that the KGB would try to recover their agent somehow or other, his daring escape from Wormwood Scrubs on the evening of October 22, 1966, was actually engineered with the help of a friendly Irish fellow-prisoner about to be released, and a rope ladder

with knitting needle rungs was thrown over the perimeter wall at the critical moment. Blake was allegedly then sheltered by Michael Randle and Pat Pottle, two members of the Committee of 100, a left-wing radical group, and in due course was smuggled out of the country to East Germany in the Irishman's Dormobile camper.

The value and prestige given to their agents by the KGB was such that eventually an exchange system was evolved, where the Glienicker Bridge connecting Potsdam with the American Sector provided a suitable venue. The first such event took place on February 10, 1962, when the atomic spy, Colonel Rudolf Abel, was exchanged for the American U-2 pilot, Gary Powers, who had been shot down over the Soviet Union in May 1960. In May 1985 four East German spies were exchanged for 23 American agents and then on February 11, 1986, a further five East German spies were exchanged for two western agents and the Soviet Civil Rights activist, Anatoly Scharansky.

Understandably, the exchanges took place in secret away from the prying eyes of the press, so that photographs of the early transfers are not available. These pictures show the last deal between East and West on February 11, 1986 when Anatoly Scharansky 'came in from the cold'.

The paraphernalia of the crossing point was done away with on November 10, 1989.

Many East Berliners continued to work in the Western Sectors, thereby benefiting from the currency exchange rates, although the communist authorities tried to discourage this as much as possible as the obvious disparity of conditions between the two halves of the city grew.

The open boundaries of the Western Sectors meant that the free part of the city was open to inspection by visitors from the Soviet Zone, many of whom had family connections anyway. The result was a steady drain of persons seeking political and economic refuge in the West, particularly via Berlin, where 675,000 refugees were registered up to the end of 1952, and a further 330,000 in 1953.

This haemorrhage of East German citizens continued unabated throughout the 1950s, most of them being of prime working age. The effect on the East German economy, which was still paying off reparations to the USSR, was catastrophic, and so the Soviet Union was called upon to intervene, thus bringing about what is now known as the Second Berlin Crisis. On November 10, 1958, Kruschev made a statement in Moscow demanding that the Western Powers: 'should relinquish the remains of the occupation regime in Berlin, thus facilitating the normalisation of the situation in the capital of the GDR.' This was accompanied by hints that he intended to hand over to the German Democratic Republic certain functions in Berlin still exercised by the Soviets.

This was pursued on November 27 with notes to the Western Allies demanding the withdrawal of their troops and the conversion of West Berlin into an independent political unit. The idea of the Western Sectors becoming a 'free city' failed to appeal to the Western Allies, who saw that it would only be a matter of time before the Communists would effect a complete take-over. The Soviets set a six-month time limit for the withdrawal of the Western Allies, failing which they would carry out the 'planned measures through an agreement with the GDR', giving the latter full sovereignty over its territory 'on land, on water and in the air.'

The Western Allies countered the following month with a declaration by the North Atlantic Council, which administers NATO, saying: 'the denunciation by the Soviet Union of the inter-Allied rights on Berlin can in no way deprive the other parties of their rights or relieve the Soviet Union of its obligations.'

An attempt was made to resolve the various problems with a conference of Foreign Ministers at Geneva from May 11 to June 20 and again from July 13 to August 5, 1959, but to no avail. However, the six-month limit was discreetly allowed to elapse. A summit conference between the Four Powers was due to be held in Paris in June 1960, but Kruschev used the U-2 incident to call it off.

The East German authorities then experimented with various measures restricting the movement of West Berliners and West Germans into East

Fifteen years after the end of the Second World War . . .

Berlin. Firstly, they required West Germans to obtain a permit to enter, then they refused to recognise the validity of West German passports issued to Berliners for travel purposes through their territory, insisting on the use of the locally-issued Berlin identity card. Allied protests to the Soviet authorities were rejected as interference with East German sovereignty.

In his report to the American people on July 25, 1961, President John F. Kennedy summed up the position of the Allies in what was recognised as a firm and resolute declaration of Western policy on Berlin:

'We are there as a result of our victory over Nazi Germany — and our basic rights to be there, deriving from that victory, include both our presence in West Berlin and the enjoyment of access across East Germany. These rights have been repeatedly confirmed and recognized in special agreements with the Soviet Union. Berlin is not a part of East Germany, but a separate territory under the control of the Allied Powers. Thus our rights there are clear and deep-rooted. But in addition to those rights is our commitment to sustain — and defend, if need be — the opportunity for more than two million people to determine their own future and choose their own way of life . . . We cannot and will not permit the Communists to drive us out of Berlin, either gradually or by force, for the fulfilment of our pledge to that city is essential to the morale and security of Western Germany, to the unity of Western Europe, and to the faith of the entire Free World.'

. . . on Victory Day, May 8, 1960, the GDR dedicated the repaired Neue Wache as a 'Memorial to the Victims of Fascism and Militarism', with a permanent honour guard provided by East Germany's Nationale Volksarmee.

The Second Berlin Crisis was set in motion by the East German leader, Walter Ulbricht, during the night of Saturday, August 12, 1961. In an effort to stem the massive drain of skilled workers from East to West — over 2½ million since 1949 — with its disastrous effect on the East German economy, workmen and border troops began a massive operation to seal off East Berlin. Although there was already an outer security fence between the Western Sectors and East Germany, it was now intended to seal off the border between the Soviet Sector of Berlin and the three Allied Sectors along a distance of nearly 30 miles as it zigzagged along the old borough boundaries. Initial operations that night and during Sunday centred on closing off numerous side streets with temporary fences and barbed wire barricades. For many in East Berlin, the decision whether to try to escape before it was too late came to a head during the following week. The first actual border guard made a break for it on Tuesday.

The Berlin Wall

As night fell on Saturday, August 12, 1961, a day on which over 4,000 people had registered as refugees at the Marienborn centre, the highest daily count yet recorded, senior commanders of East German military and police units were briefed on an operation that had been planned with such secrecy that its execution achieved complete surprise. At midnight their units were alerted and at 0200 hours on Sunday, August 13, some 40,000 men started sealing off the Soviet Sector from the Western Sectors of Berlin, setting off a shock wave across the western world.

A preliminary to this operation had been the appointment of Marshal Koniev to command the Group of Soviet Forces in Germany (GSFG) on August 10, an appointment that would normally have been regarded as being beneath his seniority were it not for the seriousness of the situation. Although

The famous picture of the escape was taken by Peter Liebing, although the guard in question was not named. *Above:* Ten years later, a press conference was held at the Hotel am Steinplatz in Charlottenburg to mark the tenth anniversary of the division of the city, at which Conrad Schumann posed for pictures beside the original photo.

the Soviet Union was prepared to back the GDR, neither it nor the Western Allies were prepared to go to war over the issue, and therefore a reliable hand was needed to maintain a tight grip while both sides cautiously experimented with their moves and counter-moves.

Left: Schumann's jump for freedom took place on the corner of Ruppiner Strasse and Bernauer Strasse in the French Sector. Our 1991 comparison looks somewhat different due to the foreshortening effect of the telephoto lens and the subsequent demolition of buildings close to the Soviet side of the sector boundary.

376

The focus of attention that Sunday was naturally at the Brandenberg Gate which was sealed by a phalanx of border guards (Grenzpolizei) and water cannon manned by the Volkspolizei — the people's police force nicknamed the 'Vopos'. British military police in turn sealed off the Strasse des 17. Juni to prevent West Berliners exacerbating the situation.

The Soviets began by openly deploying units from about two divisions in a loose ring around the city, ready to intervene if necessary. The Western Sectors' external boundary with the Soviet Zone had already been wired off and was known as 'The Wire' to the Allied garrisons, but the internal boundary with the Soviet Sector, an erratic composition of former parish boundaries linked into district boundaries, was 28.5 miles (45.9 kilometres) long. The materials required for the first stage of the operation — a rapid wiring backed by armed troops and police — had already been stockpiled supposedly for construction projects, as had materials for the more substantial barrier to follow, which would eventually evolve into 'The Wall' proper.

The timing of the operation, a quiet summer weekend with the leaders of the Western Allies all off on breaks of one kind or another, could not have been better chosen. The first reports from taxi drivers and then from alerted newsmen, of unusual activity in East Berlin, took a long time to percolate through to the higher echelons. Even when the enormity of the act was finally perceived, the lack of a positive Allied response astounded the outraged Berliners and led them to believe that they had been betrayed. Fears of what the future might hold led to some 300 people a day leaving the city.

August 1990. The division of Berlin lasted nearly 30 years but even after the Wall had been demolished, British military police continued to patrol the sector boundary until Unification.

The lack of an immediate, positive, and resolute response from the Western Allies both dismayed and outraged West Berliners who sensed that they were about to be abandoned. West Berlin's mayor, Willy Brandt, called a mass demonstration for Wednesday afternoon outside Schöneberg Town Hall, seat of the West Berlin civilian administration. Upwards of a quarter of a million people packed Rudolf-Wilde-Platz (later John F. Kennedy Platz) to express their anger and frustration.

All the East German measures had been conducted scrupulously within the boundaries of the Soviet Sector with no encroachment into the western side. Consequently it was the Tuesday before the Allied Commandants delivered a protest to the Soviet Commandant based on the illegal deployment of East German troops in the Soviet Sector. This was countered with a remark to the effect that the Soviets did not interfere in the affairs of the GDR!

However, the fury of the Berliners and Willy Brandt, their Governing Mayor, at the lack of Allied response and what appeared to be a tacit acceptance of the authority of the GDR in East Berlin, could not be ignored. President Kennedy therefore decided to send Vice President Lyndon Johnson, together with General Clay, to try and restore morale in the city. Clay had by now retired from the Army, and was active in politics in support of Kennedy's rival in the presidency campaign, but his heroic image with the Berliners from the days of the airlift made him an immediate choice as Kennedy's personal representative in the city, even though his natural irrascibilty was hardly conducive to popularity with others of his countrymen or their allies engaged with the same problem.

Caught by surprise, the Allies did not even present their formal protest to the Soviet commandant, Colonel Andrei Solovyev, until Tuesday — a full two days after the first barbed wire went up. The only British military response that week was to erect a barbed wire fence of their own around the Soviet War Memorial, and mount their own external guard to protect it from the angry populace.

Three thousand miles away in Washington, America's new president of just six months, John F. Kennedy, was wavering as to how to respond in the face of conflicting proposals from his advisers. His commanders in the front line in Germany were demanding a quick response, and a show of strength to counter the East German action, though Kennedy believed it equally important to boost the morale of the citizens in the beleaguered city. In the end his decision was twofold: first to despatch the one man he knew the Berliners would trust: General Lucius

Clay — the hero of the 1948 blockade. The general had already volunteered his services but because Clay was a Republican, active in supporting Kennedy's rival in the recent election, the President performed a neat balancing act for home consumption by sending his Vice President, Lyndon Johnson, along with him. *Left:* On Saturday (August 19), General Clay was greeted at Tempelhof by Willy Brandt and the Vice President of the House of Deputies, Edith Lowka. *Right:* Lyndon Johnson gives his speech of assurance from the steps of the town hall.

The arrival of Johnson and Clay on September 19 achieved exactly what was expected of them. They were greeted with frenzied celebration wherever they went. In his speech to the crowd outside Rathaus Schöneberg Johnson said: 'To the survival and the creative future of this city, we Americans have pledged in effect what our ancestors pledged in forming the United States — our lives, our fortunes and our sacred honor. The President wants you to know and I want you to know that the pledge he has given to the freedom of West Berlin and to the rights of Western access to Berlin is firm . . . This island does not stand alone.'

The only military gesture allowed at this stage was the despatch of 1,500 troops by road to reinforce the American garrison and the delivery by rail of some additional British armoured cars and scout cars to help patrol 'The Wire'. However, British troops also placed barbed wire around the Soviet War Memorial in the Tiergarten after the guard reliefs arriving by bus had been stoned by angry crowds.

Meanwhile the reinforcement and consolidation of 'The Wall' continued. The 88 crossing points previously in use were reduced to only 13 with differentiations between those that could be used by West Berliners and West Germans. Only one rail connection was allowed, that to Friedrichstrasse S-Bahn Station, where the platform was sealed off and passengers processed through a series of tiny cells. For the Western

The second part of Kennedy's plan was to send 1,500 armed troops of the First Battle Group of the 8th Infantry Division — the 'Golden Arrow' Division which had fought across France and into the Hürtgen Forest in 1944, and crossed the Elbe in the final stages of the war. In six columns, each of 250 men, they rolled down the autobahn and reached the city shortly after midday on Sunday to be greeted by Clay, Johnson and Brandt on a hastily-built reviewing stand. Later that day, Berliners were treated to a stirring military parade along the Kurfürstendamm.

Late on Thursday (17th), East German workmen had appeared on the Potsdamer Platz with loads of concrete blocks and began to build the Berlin Wall proper to replace the wire barricade thrown up on Sunday. This is the same S-Bahn entrance that we saw on page 360 — now sealed. Note the absence of the Columbushaus on the far corner — we can now see right across the Tiergarten to the Reichstag.

Allies, whose right to circulate freely throughout the city was now in contest, only the Friedrichstrasse crossing point became available. Here the American military police established Checkpoint 'Charlie', and were later joined by Royal Military Police and Gendarmerie colleagues to supervise their national traffic to and fro. (The name 'Charlie' arose out of the alphabetical sequence given to the Checkpoints 'Alpha' and 'Bravo' at the Helmstedt and Berlin ends of the autobahn corridor connecting Berlin with the Federal Republic.)

Freedom of passage through 'Charlie' for entitled Allied personnel had to be forcibly demonstrated on October 22

Although the US Army's wartime Sherman tanks had given way to Pattons, and personnel carriers had replaced half-tracks, the picture of the Garand-armed GI staring out across no man's land brought back the aura of World War II. In actual fact Zimmerstrasse, which crosses in front of the soldier, lay in the Soviet Sector, the line of the boundary running along the edge of the buildings on this side of the street. This checkpoint between the American and Soviet Sectors on Friedrichstrasse was designated by the East Germans as the only crossing point for Allied personnel (and foreigners), and so became the focus of attention even though there were another twelve checkpoints in Berlin, quickly reduced to seven, allocated to either West Germans or Berliners. Being the third control point between Allied West Germany and Soviet East Berlin, it was given the next letter in the phonetic code: 'Charlie'.

when an American diplomat and his wife set off in their officially registered car to attend the opera in East Berlin. The East German officials refused to allow them through unless they showed

their passports, an act which was contrary to the US Mission's current instructions. The American military police saw what was happening and informed General Clay, who ordered a

There were several probes by the Americans. In this incident using civilian vehicles at Checkpoint 'Charlie', East German guards detained a car trying to enter the Soviet Sector without

showing any papers. In a show of force, the US Army brought up M48A1 Pattons and M59 APCs which had immediate effect: the vehicle was released and allowed to drive on.

Things really came to a head on Sunday, October 22, when Allan Lightner, the senior US civilian official in Berlin, drove with his wife to spend the evening at the opera in the Soviet Sector. At Checkpoint 'Charlie', their Volkswagen, bearing American number plates, was stopped and they were asked to show their passports before entering East Berlin. Following standing instruction for official American personnel, Mr Lightner refused. While his car was held up, the Americans called up four tanks and armed GIs went forward to escort the Volkswagen through to demonstrate the right of free access. Although a principle had been established by force, the following day the East Germans announced that in future only uniformed Allied personnel would be allowed to enter without showing documentation. The British acquiesced to this demand but General Clay was determined that the US would not back down. A series of test entries were then made using civilian cars *(right and below)*, each time the vehicle was stopped it was escorted a few hundred yards into the Soviet Sector by Jeeps.

platoon of infantry, four medium tanks and two armoured personnel carriers forward to Checkpoint 'Charlie'. An officer then went forward to request the East Germans to let the diplomat and his wife through. When this request was refused, the officer sent the diplomat's wife back on foot then brought up two squads of infantry with rifles at the ready and escorted the diplomat through in his car. The East Germans made no move to stop them and the procession moved solemnly and slowly some distance into East Berlin before returning. This diplomat was then joined by a colleague and the two set off once again through the checkpoint, only to be stopped with a demand for passports. The diplomats signalled up their military escort and repeated the earlier performance, again without hindrance.

Then on Wednesday, October 25, with presidential approval, Clay sent two army officers across in civilian clothes in a civilian car with American Forces' registration plates. The East Germans turned them back for refusing to show their passports so three Jeeploads of armed infantry came forward to escort them through. Again the East Germans made no effort to stop them. Half an hour later ten American M-48 tanks and two armoured personnel carriers took up positions near Checkpoint 'Charlie', attracting a crowd of journalists. Then followed a series of test entries that day and the next, using civilian clothes and cars, each rejection by the East Germans being overrun with Jeep escorts.

Right: **Today 'Charlie' has, in the words of Douglas Hurd, Britain's Foreign Minister, at the dismantling ceremony on June 22, 1990, 'come in from the cold', the sector boundary signboard having been retained as part of a display on the Berlin Wall mounted by the Checkpoint 'Charlie' Museum. In the background, Stadtmitte U-Bahn Station, Krukenberg's command post in April 1945.**

The second night 33 Soviet tanks appeared and parked conspicuously near the Brandenburg Gate, the first appearance of Soviet armour in the city since the 1953 uprising. On the third day ten of these Soviet tanks faced the American tanks down Friedrichstrasse only a hundred yards apart. It was a dangerous confrontation over an issue that few could understand. The British, for instance, had authorised the showing of identity documents for personnel in civilian clothing from the beginning but now uniform became essential wear. Certainly neither government in this American-Soviet exchange was prepared to go to war over the matter, and

The Soviets likewise sent their military attaché through into the American Sector but more to assess US military strength in the area. On Thursday (26th) Soviet armour was brought up and deployed next to Göring's old Air Ministry while ten tanks were sent forward to the crossing point. On Friday, October 27, 1961, American and Soviet tanks drawn up on opposite sides of Checkpoint 'Charlie' faced each other on full alert. The world held its breath . . . and waited.

on the Saturday morning the Soviet tanks withdrew, followed soon afterwards by the Americans.

In the subsequent exchange of protests, the principle of only Allied troops in uniform being allowed through without showing proof of identity was established, diplomats and wives of entitled personnel having to display — but not hand over for examination — their

identity documents. However, Clay had won the major issue of freedom of access and circulation in East Berlin, with which the Soviets could only concur as they themselves needed to maintain reciprocal rights in the Western Sectors, and had proved conclusively that the Soviets had by no means relinquished their control over the GDR and East Berlin.

After 16 hours of muzzle-to-muzzle confrontation, both sides withdrew their armour on Saturday morning. As far as the Americans were concerned, they had stood their ground, forcing the Soviets to reveal that they were openly backing the creation of the Berlin Wall. *Left:* In later years, the facilities for

inspection on the Soviet side were greatly enlarged to cater for the increase in foreign traffic. The Allies accepted the Inspection of documents by the East Germans for their civilians but henceforth insisted that their military personnel wear uniform in the Soviet Sector.

The only other crossing point made available to Allied personnel and non-Germans was further up Friedrichstrasse at the S-Bahn station where foot passengers were processed through a tight security system. Trains left a sealed-off platform for Lehrter Stadtbahnhof in the British Sector, while the U-Bahn connected direct with the Humboldthain and Anhalter stations in the other Weatern Sectors. All the intermediate stations, like Potsdamer Platz *(left)*, were sealed. Armed guards were then stationed on the platforms to ensure that the through trains did not stop. *Right:* In the early days, some Volkspolizei in Berlin were reluctant to fire on would-be escapers. Consequently, Grenzpolizei from other areas were drafted in, in the belief that they would be less squeamish in shooting their own countrymen. This picture was taken at Alexanderplatz.

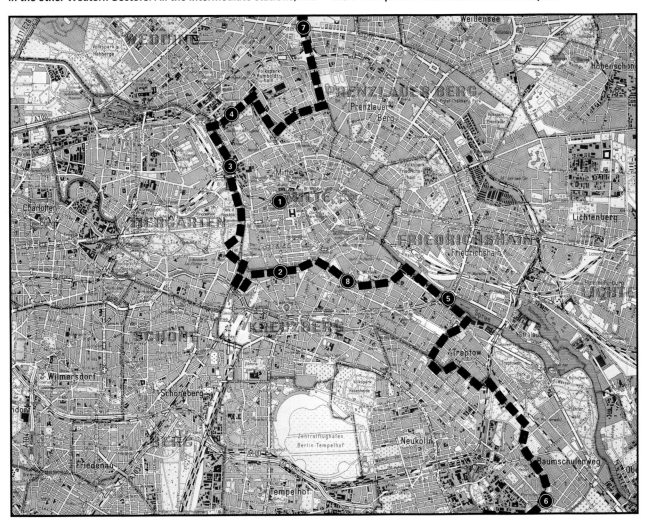

The first twelve crossing points were reduced to seven by the GDR on August 23, seemingly as a protest against General Clay's arrival in Berlin. Apart from the two Friedrichstrasse crossing points (1 and 2), Invalidenstrasse (3), Chausseestrasse (4), the Oberbaumbrücke (5) and Sonnenallee (6) were reserved solely for West Berliners, while the checkpoints on Bornholmer Strasse (7) and Prinzenstrasse (8) (also called Heinrich-Heine-Strasse) were for exclusive use by West Germans.

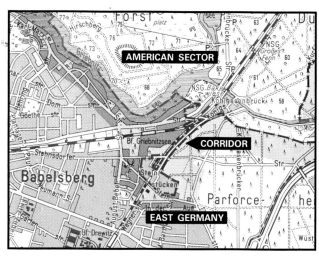

The route of the wall, along the old borough boundaries gave scant regard to geographical anomalies, which led to a number of problem areas, exploited by the GDR. Steinstücken near Babelsberg belonged to West Berlin but lay totally isolated south of the wall. General Clay resisted pressure by the East Germans to isolate the hapless residents by initiating a helicopter lifeline *(left)*. This lasted for ten years until an agreement was reached in December 1971 to provide a road along a fenced corridor to Zehlendorf *(right)* and this was opened on August 29, 1972.

Another distinctive issue arose out of the efforts by the GDR to take over the exclave of Steinstücken, on the southern boundary of the American Sector, where the East German authorities had been harassing the 300 families living there with increasing intensity since August 13. Clay's proposed solution was to force a way through to the exclave with two companies of infantry, but the military hierarchy was already appalled by his dangerously belligerent attitude and refused to allow their troops to take part. Instead Clay flew in by helicopter to reassure the residents and then stationed three military policemen there on a helicopter link.

There were several other exclaves belonging to Berlin, some of which were exchanged in due course to alleviate territorial problems on the border. For instance a schoolboy living in the Eiskeller area at the north-western tip of Spandau required a British military escort to and from school on the single track linking that area with the rest of the district, and the maintenance of a permanent military police presence.

In the British Sector, a 'Wire' patrol of the 1st Battalion, The Cheshire Regiment, checks activity at the Staaken crossing point on the Heerstrasse, the only alternative exit to the West other than the autobahn, although not available to the Allies.

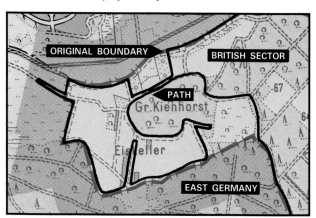

Right in the north-east corner of the British Sector lay another border problem, also not solved until 1972. The route taken by 12-year-old Erwin Schabe on his way to school lay right alongside the boundary along a narrow path in the Eiskeller. Following harassment by the Volkspolizei, the boy was provided with a unique armed escort to and from school.

384

A more amazing border anomaly also lay in the British Sector but this time right in the centre of Berlin. When the GDR erected the Wall along the Hermann-Göring-Strasse, instead of running a dog-leg around the awkwardly-shaped triangle of derelict land where the Columbushaus had once stood, they just continued the wall in a straight line. Thus the so-called 'Lenne Triangle' lay abandoned in West Berlin although it was still nominally part of the Soviet Sector. It was finally purchased by the West Berlin Senate in 1988. This picture was taken in 1962 on the first anniversary of the erection of the Wall.

Later some exclaves further out were exchanged to enable the linking neck of land in the Eiskeller to be widened. An earlier exchange of land involved the surrender of the suburb of Staaken in exchange for a wedge of Kreis Potsdam that had hitherto severed the land connection between Gatow and Kladow villages with Spandau. (Staaken was promptly restored to Spandau after Unification.) However, the so-called 'Lenne Triangle' west of Potsdamer Platz, which the East Germans had not bothered to enclose because of its awkward shape (although wired off from the public), was eventually sold to the West Berlin Senate for a prohibitive sum in July 1988.

Left: At the time the Wall went up, West Berlin's top expert on military explosives was Gerhard Raebiger, seen here with his assistant, Walter Braun, having just defused a 4,000lb RAF blast bomb. *Right:* The Lenné Triangle had never been cleared of unexploded bombs, so after West Berlin took over the land, a bomb disposal team had to spend several weeks clearing the site. The Senate had paid the equivalent of an extortionate DM500 million (£175 million) in cash and kind for the old bombsite but had they been a little more patient and waited for the Wall to collapse, they could have got it for nothing!

For over 1,000 metres, Bernauer Strasse in the 'French' borough of Wedding formed the boundary with 'Soviet' Prenzlauer Berg. The actual dividing line ran along the southern pavement leaving the street itself in the French Sector. *Left:* This 'pre-

Wall' picture was taken at the junction with Brunnenstrasse during the earlier troubles in June 1953. *Right:* The present day comparison shows how buildings along Bernauer Strasse on the Soviet side were later demolished to clear a free fire zone.

The first person killed while trying to breach the border controls was Rudolf Urban who fell to his death on August 19 while trying to jump from an upstairs window of No. 1 Bernauer Strasse. During the first weeks, numerous people attempted to escape from buildings on the south side as the French Sector technically began right outside their front doors. West Berlin firemen with safety nets were able to break the fall of most of those who jumped but some fell heavily and were injured. By

the end of August, two people had been killed. Dozens had attempted to escape but on Sunday, September 24, the Vopos moved in and ordered the two thousand people remaining to evacuate their homes. The empty buildings were then sealed with their doorways and windows facing Bernauer Strasse bricked up. The road was then walled across at its eastern end where it met Eberswalder Strasse, but grim crosses lining the pavement continued to commemorate the victims.

By the first week of October four more people had died on the street. *Above left:* On September 25, Olga Segler, an 80-year-old grandmother, waited until her daughter and three grandchildren had safely got across the street before she jumped from the second floor of her home at No. 34. Although the firemen were ready, she landed badly and broke her wrist. The shock of her escapade was too much for her and she died the following day. This memorial was erected on the spot where she fell. *Top right:* Bernd Lünser lost his life on October 4 together with an unnamed man who were both shot by Volkspolizei outside No. 44 as they were attempting to escape by abseiling down a washing line.

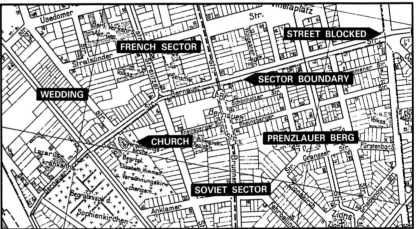

On February 12, 1962, the Soviets started harassing civilian air traffic, firstly by announcing that they were taking over the corridors at certain times of the day for their military aircraft, then reserving certain altitudes for themselves. They then started buzzing the airliners with their fighter aircraft and began dropping metal foil to disrupt the radar. At night they even tried to blind the pilots with searchlights. The Allied response was to put fighter aircraft on the alert in Western Germany, to fly military transport aircraft in those parts of the corridors the Soviets were claiming for their exclusive use, and to maintain their own civilian

It was ironic that the Versöhnungskirche (Church of Reconciliation) was not only unable to live up to the high ideals of its creators, but its position south of the boundary led to it being cut off from its former congregation, the majority of whom came from Wedding. When the East Germans built a second, inner wall to enclose the so called 'death strip', it stood isolated and abandoned in no man's land.

As far as West Berliners were concerned, General Clay was doing an excellent job championing and upholding their cause and demonstrating, in no uncertain way, that he was prepared to use force if necessary. However, behind the scenes, his moves at Checkpoint 'Charlie', and on the autobahn, where he had introduced armed patrols, were viewed as highly provocative, bearing in mind that Berlin could never be defended against an all-out Russian attack. The US Army Commander in Germany, General Bruce Clarke, was up in arms as was General Lauris Norstad, the Supreme Allied Commander, Europe, who had been kept completely in the dark. A rift began to grow between Clay and Washington where the general's cavalier

actions were considered highly dangerous. *Left:* In February, two of the Kennedy brothers, Robert, the Attorney General, and Edward, (later Senator for Massachusetts) paid a visit to the city when Robert promised that 'we will stand by you' and that 'an armed attack on West Berlin would be considered the same thing as an armed attack on Chicago, New York, London or Paris.' *Right:* However, young Edward didn't improve matters when he visited East Berlin via the Friedrichstrasse checkpoint at which he acquiesced to the border checks and willingly allowed the East Germans to examine his passport. We are told that the President, who was still not ready to recognise the GDR, was not at all happy!

air services despite this extremely dangerous provocation. It was not until Lord Home, the British Foreign Minister, told his Soviet counterpart in no uncertain terms what he thought of a government that could order steps that might make an aircraft crash, that the Soviets abandoned these measures. Shortly afterwards, his mission accomplished, General Clay left Berlin.

Just over a year after the erection of the Wall an incident occurred that shocked the world as a demonstration of the GDR's brutal policy towards would-be defectors from their country. On August 17, 1962, two young construction workers tried to escape over the Wall in broad daylight not far from Checkpoint 'Charlie' and were fired at by the guards. One got over safely but

the other, 18-year-old Peter Fechter, was seriously wounded in the gunfire and fell back on the wrong side of the Wall. The guards then stood around and watched him die for nearly an hour without making any effort to help him, all in full view of the Western press and a large crowd of spectators. The anger this incident caused led to five days of demonstrations and rioting in Berlin.

Three months later, General Clay's mission was deemed fulfilled and he was withdrawn in May 1962, much to the distress of West Berliners, who, knowing little of the behind-the-scenes wranglings, looked on him as their guardian angel.

On August 17 that year — just two days after the first anniversary of the erection of the Wall, an event which itself had seen mass demonstrations — came the killing of Peter Fechter. No other death on the Wall, before or after, had the impact of this incident where an escaper was shot and left to bleed to death in front of hundreds of horrified West Berliners. It happened in Zimmerstrasse just a few yards east of Checkpoint 'Charlie', where the Wall stood on the southern side of the street leaving the roadway itself to form the death strip on the Soviet side. Peter Fechter and his friend, Helmut Kulbeick, were both employed on a building site in the East and, wearing their working clothes, they were able to enter a building near the Wall unchallenged. From here they pulled aside the barbed wire around a boarded-up first floor window, dropped down on the side facing the West, and sprinted across to Zimmerstrasse. Helmut managed to climb the Wall but Peter was caught by a burst of automatic gun-fire from a concealed position in a derelict building overlooking the area.

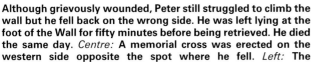

Although grievously wounded, Peter still struggled to climb the wall but he fell back on the wrong side. He was left lying at the foot of the Wall for fifty minutes before being retrieved. He died the same day. *Centre:* A memorial cross was erected on the western side opposite the spot where he fell. *Left:* The observation post on the first floor of the old newspaper building from where he had been shot can be seen directly behind. *Right:* The building was demolished two years later. Today with the Wall demolished, Zimmerstrasse is once again open to traffic but Peter's memorial has been retained.

In June 1963, President Kennedy visited Berlin in another demonstration of support. With the President was General Clay who, Kennedy promised 'will come again if needed'. *Left:* At the Hindenburgplatz, red cloth banners blanked off the arches of the Gate: to stop Kennedy looking into East Berlin or to hide him from its people? *Right:* Two decades later. A thoughtful President Aleksandr Gorbatov looks westwards from the East German viewing platform on April 16, 1986.

The following year saw the memorable morale-boosting visit by the US President John F. Kennedy. This was the occasion on which he emphasised his solidarity with West Berliners in his speech outside the Schöneberg town hall on June 26: 'All free men, wherever they may live, are citizens of Berlin, and therefore, as a free man, I take pride in the words: Ich bin ein Berliner.'

When completed, the Wall enclosing the Western Sectors of Berlin was 100 miles long, of which 61 miles consisted of concrete slabs. There were 30 miles of metal fencing and three miles of barbed wire, the rest being improvised with existing obstacles. Out of 193 roads crossing this boundary, only nine rigidly controlled routes remained. Backing this system were 231 look-out posts and towers, 132 bunkers, 214 dog runs, 63 miles of anti-vehicle ditches, 72 miles of electrified fencing and 71 miles of patrol roads.

The President, escorted by Brigadier General Frederick O. Hartell, the commander of the US Berlin Brigade, visits the control point on Friedrichstrasse.

Left: Another viewing platform had been specially erected on the corner of Zimmerstrasse. Peter Fechter's memorial lies 200 metres or so behind the cameraman. *Right:* Today an outdoor display illustrates the various types of construction used for the Wall. The final version, comprising 3.6-metre (approximately 12 ft) high pre-cast, reinforced concrete segments topped by an anti-climb cylinder to stop a person getting a grip even when standing on the shoulders of another, can be seen on the left.

It was not until December 17, 1963, after seven preliminary meetings, that the so-called Pass Agreement was concluded enabling West Berliners to visit the other half of the city. More than 730,000 West Berliners took immediate advantage of this concession over that Christmas season. GDR policy, fully supported by the Soviet Union, was aimed at gaining international recognition as a sovereign state and at trying to sever existing relationships between the Western Sectors and the Federal Republic. To this end, they repeatedly described the city as an 'independent political entity' and the ties with the Federal Republic as being 'contrary to international law', but the Western Allies equally persistently, refused to give way.

The GDR also repeatedly interfered with the means of access to West Berlin. For instance, when the Federal Parliament decided to hold a plenary session in Berlin in April 1965, the GDR refused access to members on the road and rail transit routes. The next step took place in June 1968 when the GDR demanded the use of passports and visas for travel on these transit routes. The Federal Government was then obliged to refund the cost of these visas to their citizens as an encouragement to continue travelling by these means. However, the delays and treatment encountered at the hands of the East German authorities resulted in many refusing to travel other than by air, until the Quadripartite Agreement enabled an easing of the situation to come into effect the following year.

This Quadripartite Agreement of September 3, 1971, arose out of the Four Powers' search for a solution to the problems of avoiding nuclear conflict, as demonstrated by the Cuban crisis of 1962, and a gradual acceptance of the 'status quo' in Europe, as demonstrated by the Soviet invasion of Czechoslovakia in 1968 and the inability of the West to intervene. In a visit to Berlin on February 27, 1969, US President Richard Nixon suggested to the Soviets, in a speech, that together they should seek an end to tensions, to which the Soviets responded by suggesting they talk about it. Thus a deal came to be struck that accepted official recognition of the GDR in exchange for better human contacts between the two Germanys. The latter followed this up with an agreement on transit traffic signed between them on December 17, followed by the Berlin Senate coming to an arrangement with the GDR on travel and visitor traffic for West Berliners on December 20. These measures were then approved by the ambassadors of the Four Powers on June 3, 1972 as the Final Protocol to the Quadripartite Agreement, setting a relatively stable pattern for the foreseeable future.

One outcome was the re-establishment in August 1972 of a road link to Steinstücken, the exclave cut off from the American Sector in the south. Another was an agreement between the GDR and the Federal Government for the resurfacing of the Berlin-Helmstedt autobahn by the former at the latter's

Throughout the 1960s, repeated attempts were made by the East Germans to interrupt traffic on the autobahn link with the West. This picture shows a typical incident in 1965 with members of the Nationale Volksarmee erecting barriers on the access slip road at Checkpoint 'Bravo' at Dreilinden.

Those first ten years were the worst as the East German authorities pressed by every means at their disposal to gain recognition by the West. The situation only eased on the signing of the Quadripartite Agreement by the Four Powers in September 1971 in which the West agreed to officially recognise the GDR in exchange for a more humane relationship between the two Germanys. By that time, although hundreds had managed to escape to the West, 65 people had died in the attempt within the city itself (and many more elsewhere along the Iron Curtain frontier).

After the Four Power Agreement, killings reduced dramatically and, in the twenty years which followed, only 13 people lost their lives attempting to reach the West via Berlin before the barriers finally came down.

expense, which was completed in 1979. Rail links were also improved. In 1973 the GDR gained the international recognition it so badly wanted through admittance to the United Nations. The following year the two Germanys exchanged permanent representations, as opposed to embassies, in their capitals and the Western Allies appointed embassies on the understanding that their presence in the Eastern Sector of Berlin did not imply its recognition as the capital of the GDR.

The severance from the Soviet Sector had already caused a loss of some seven percent of the labour force in West Berlin, some 60,000 jobs, a deficiency that increased as the city's industrial capacity grew. This shortage was eventually met by the importation of foreign workers from Greece, Turkey and Yugoslavia. The initial concept was to import just young bachelor workers who would stay for a while and then return home suitably enriched to found new lives in their own countries. However, although it worked in this manner for some, and many benefited by learning new skills and acquiring the German work ethic, others started summoning their families to join them. In this way, a large Turkish community became established in Berlin, taking over many of the more menial tasks. By the 1980s the problems encountered with this community, with German-educated children upholding Moslem customs, and growing competition for jobs, sparked off inter-racial tensions.

The fact that deaths went down after 1971 was also indicative of the gradual improvement in the construction of the Wall making it virtually impregnable. *Left:* **This could be considered the Mark I version — a rather rough mixture of concrete slabs and blocks topped with strands of barbed wire. This section bisected Elsenstrasse in Treptow. We are looking across Heidelberger Strasse running left and right. Vopos on the Wall and a West Berlin Bereitschaftspolizei equipped with a Wehrmacht-pattern steel helmet and an American M1 Carbine.** *Right:* **This is another example of how buildings close to the Wall on the eastern side were all cleared.**

Comparisons of pictures taken soon after the Wall went up are mostly a disappointment because of the subsequent demolitions to create a wide, unobstructed, security zone right round Berlin.

Perhaps the most dramatic spectacle was provided by the Wall in front of the Brandenburg Gate. Although it was lower than the norm at this point, it was heavily reinforced with the intention of creating an anti-tank barrier. The death strip and patrol road leading towards Potsdamer Platz can be seen beyond in this March 1976 picture, which pre-dates both the modernisation of the Wall the following year and the 1980s redevelopment of Otto-Grotewohl-Strasse (as the former Wilhelmstrasse had been renamed). The East-West boundary in fact followed the line of the pavement curbs on the west side of Ebertstrasse (the old Hermann-Göring-Strasse) and Hindenburgplatz, hence the precautionary railings. The British Army maintained an observation post in the south-eastern tower of the Reichstag from where this picture was taken.

LENNE TRIANGLE

The zone between Ebertstrasse and Otto-Grotewohl-Strasse was nearly 250 metres wide, encompassing the majority of the Voss-strasse, the whole of the Leipziger and Potsdamer Platz. The site of the Führerbunker was marked by a grassy knoll.

The Mark II Berlin Wall was a little more sophisticated, built of concrete panels slotted between concrete posts. The main departure was the replacement of the barbed wire on the top, which could, of course, provide handholds, albeit painful ones.

Meanwhile, the late 1960s saw political unrest among the students of Berlin, based upon long-overdue university reform but also focusing on social injustices in the Federal Republic and American involvement in Vietnam, and led to some violent episodes. Many of these students were West Germans avoiding compulsory military service in the Federal Republic by living in Berlin, a point which added edge to their protests. At the same time it annoyed those who looked upon the Americans as their protectors and preferred to regard the defence of democracy against communism in Vietnam as similar to their own situation. This situation faded with the turn of the decade but the Kreuzberg district continued to remain a focus for all kinds of social dissidents with regular outbursts of unrest.

In 1976, the East Germans started rebuilding the Wall outwards from the Brandenburg Gate, replacing a system of concrete slabs slotted between concrete posts and capped by a concrete cylinder with self-standing, prefabricated vertical sections whose metal reinforcements were welded together. The Wall in front of the Brandenburg Gate was constructed differently in the form of a flat-topped arc slightly lower than the rest and designed to serve as an anti-tank barrier.

This formidable system was manned by an equally formidable organisation with the Headquarters Berlin Border Command Centre located at Karlshorst,

a signals battalion at Klein Machnow to the south of Berlin and supporting units, including a chemical warfare battalion and an assault crossing company, at Gross Glienicke west of Kladow. The regiment specialising in manning the crossing points had its headquarters in Niederschönhausen, and the two training regiments, Nos. 39 and 40 were stationed at Rahnsdorf and Oranienburg respectively. There were then no less than six border guard regiments deployed around the Western Sectors, No. 33 based at Treptow, No. 34 at Gross Glienicke, No. 35 at Rummelsburg, No. 38 at Hennigsdorf, No. 42 at Blankenfelde and No. 44 at Babelsberg.

In 1976 the Mark III Wall was introduced. This was formed from purpose-built, L-shaped sections of reinforced concrete, each metre-wide section being welded to the next to provide a smooth, continuous surface. These pictures were both taken outside the front door of the Gestapo headquarters on Prinz-

Albrecht-Strasse and show how the Wall was set back from the actual boundary to permit the East Germans working space on the Western side without infringing the territory of the Allied Sector concerned. The remains of the lamp-post, cut off at ground level, helped pinpoint the exact spot.

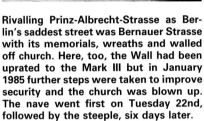

Rivalling Prinz-Albrecht-Strasse as Berlin's saddest street was Bernauer Strasse with its memorials, wreaths and walled off church. Here, too, the Wall had been uprated to the Mark III but in January 1985 further steps were taken to improve security and the church was blown up. The nave went first on Tuesday 22nd, followed by the steeple, six days later.

The Wall had turned the Western Sectors into an island, a situation that promptly gave rise to a popular weekly cabaret programme put out by radio in the American Sector (RIAS) with the title 'Die Insulaner' ('The Islanders'). However, with substantial subsidies from the Federal Government and the security provided by the Western Allies Berlin prospered generally. The Wall remained a cultural shock to all those who came across it for the first time, even those West Germans who were familiar enough with it through the news media, but the inhabitants grew to live with it. Where it was more easily accessible from the western side without interference from the border guards, it became a convenient hoarding for graffiti artists and others.

Following the signing of the Quadripartite Agreement, the threat posed by the presence of some 350,000 Soviet troops in the immediate vicinity faded from most people's minds, and visits by various heads of state, above all those of the Allies, brought messages of reassurance and support. For instance, Queen Elizabeth II visited Berlin in 1965, 1976 and 1987, on each occasion taking the salute at the annual Queen's Birthday Parade held on the Maifeld before thousands of Berliners, as well as visiting other parts of the city.

The French and Americans too held their national day parades and there was also an Allied Forces Day parade held annually on the Strasse des 17. Juni, all attended by vast numbers of the public. The monthly guard changeovers at the Allied prison at Spandau also continued to attract the attention of tourists until the death of the last inmate, Rudolf Hess, in August 1987.

Bernauer Strasse was also the location of the most successful escape of all. *Left:* In January 1964, three girls escaped from East Berlin via this tunnel, being inspected by West Berlin police. Later the Communists dynamited the tunnel on their side of the Wall. *Right:* Nine months later, 57 people escaped from another tunnel leading from an outside toilet behind No. 55 Strelitzer Strasse, under the death strip and across Bernauer Strasse to exit in a bakery at No. 96 — a distance of 145 metres. The building had been rented by an escape committee of 36 young students who disposed of the soil in its rooms.

In Bernauer Strasse, Operation 'Tokyo' went according to plan. The diggers worked in eight-hour shifts. They lit the tunnel by tapping the mains and they talked by telephone to a look-out on a nearby roof-top. Vopos took out sound detectors during the silence. The look-out warned the diggers. The Vopos found nothing.

The tunnel went down to 40ft below ground; the bore was 3ft and a bosun's chair on a pulley was installed to bring up the passengers as they arrived. It started from a disused bakery on the French Sector side of Bernauer Strasse, ran four hundred feet along a tunnel that had been blocked in by the Vopos after a previous escape bid. Then it went on. It was aimed at a back yard in 55 Strelitzer Strasse, behind the Wall. It finished up under an outside privy in a back yard. The ramshackle shanty gave enough cover for the passengers to enter unnoticed from the 'reception centre' set up in the dark porch of the house.

The tunnel entrance was reached through a hole in the ground inside the privy. The tunnellers used a field 'phone to announce crossings and they sent telegrams in code to prepare prospective passengers. Couriers with West German passports that allowed them to be abroad in East Berlin, went to guide them to the tunnel. Half the passage money was paid in advance, the rest was due on delivery or by instalments. There should have been fifty-eight passengers: thirty-two women and girls, twenty-three men, and three children. But one girl missed the trip. Her mother was worried about her safety. She said she could go only if the courier promised to marry her, and he wouldn't. So she didn't.

It was a cold clear night. Grepos with dogs made their ceaseless patrols. The couriers began bringing the passengers after dark, in ones and twos. And the passenger entered the house, reached the back yard and went down. One woman saw the Grepos patrolling on Strelitzer Strasse and she panicked. She tried to run away, but the courier grabbed her arm and forced her to go on. No one panicked in the tunnel, but many nearly did. It was a grim journey.

Fifteen to thirty minutes crawling through the mud. There was water in places. There was light but not much. Air, but not much. Often there were two and three or more in the tunnel at one time. By midnight twenty-eight were safely through, and the escapes stopped for the night.

On Sunday after dark they started again. By midnight the last few were crawling through the tunnel, elbows squelching in the mud. Two students waited at the tunnel entrance at the back yard. It was dark. Two men came in. The students could just see them and thought they were passengers. It was not unknown for tunnel organisers to accommodate last-minute passengers. It was all money. One of the men had a flashlight. He didn't flash it once as they'd all done. He turned it on and kept it on. One of the students said: 'Are you mad. Switch that off and get going.' The man said he had a third passenger waiting outside and he would fetch him. After five minutes he wasn't back so the students got ready to leave. Then the two men returned, accompanied by a third one. The students noticed that the third man was wearing a uniform under a civilian top coat. They heard a whispered order: 'Load the pistol.' There was the tell-tale click. The students backed into the tunnel. There was a stampede. Shots were fired. One of the students had a pistol. He fired it in the dark, to where the shots were coming from. They escaped back to West Berlin. 'Operation Tokyo' was over, with fifty-seven rescued. The third man, Grepo Egon Schultz, lay dead with a bullet through his chest. Whether he'd been shot by the student with a pistol or died in a random hail of bullets no one knew. Whether the East Berlin police had just chanced on the tunnel, or been led there by an informer — an SSD man planted among the diggers or the passengers, no one knew either. In the morning East Germany threatened to scrap the agreement on East Berlin passes because of the shooting of Egon Schultz.

PIERRE GALANTE,
THE BERLIN WALL, 1965

The presence of the Wall and the desire for freedom by the people trapped behind it led to a wide range of daring and inventive escape attempts, some on personal initiative and some organised as commercial ventures. Not all the latter were honest, for the business attracted the attention of the underworld, and the criminal elements became so dangerous that the West Berlin government eventually had to crack down on them. Students would do anything to help during the early years, and the various intelligence agencies also became heavily involved in the escape organisations, which were also frequently penetrated by East German agents.

Tunnels proved to be the most effective, one known as 'Tunnel 57' because that number of people escaped by that means. This tunnel, dug by students, was 140 yards long, extending from a bakery in the Bernauer Strasse to an outside toilet in a house in East Berlin. Unfortunately the tunnel was discovered when one of the organisers mistook an East German soldier for an escapee, realised his mistake and shot him before getting away through the tunnel chased by border guards. Another tunnel leading from a tomb in an East Berlin graveyard was revealed when a woman left her child's pram nearby.

One man who had a contract to deliver frozen meat to West Berlin succeeded in smuggling out his wife, sister-in-law and her husband, together with their eleven children, all of whom had been previously heavily doped, hidden among the frozen carcases.

Special compartments built into cars became a favourite method, one of the

Yet another tunnel on Bernauer Strasse being dug out by East Berlin guards actually working in the death strip in February 1971.

most ingenious being the conversion of an Isetta 'bubble car', in which the petrol tank was removed and replaced with one taking just four litres. Nine people were smuggled out one at a time this way until the ruse was discovered when an elderly woman shifted position, causing the car to move up and down without any apparent reason.

Another use of a car was devised by Hans-Peter Meixner, who selected an Austin-Healey Sprite to smuggle his fiancée and her mother across by removing the windshield and driving under the closed barriers. He first found

a suitable piece of ground on which to practise the necessary manoeuvring and the final acceleration to get through the checkpoint with heads ducked.

A really dangerous method was used successfully by Wolfgang Eulitz, who strapped his fiancée to the underside of his Skoda which had Irish number plates. Other escapes were effected in the early days by disguising cars as Allied vehicles and copying Allied uniforms for those inside. One escapee simply walked through the Friedrichstrasse checkpoint in a home-made copy of an American uniform.

The finishing touches are put to the reconstruction of Brunnenstrasse in 1990.

A lift maintenance engineer employed in what had been Göring's Air Ministry building evolved an escape for himself and his family by adopting the idea of a ski-resort chair-lift from the roof of the building the short distance across the Wall. Working in cooperation with some students in West Berlin, he selected a position on the roof that was out of sight of the watchtowers. When all was ready, one of the students short-circuited the border lights in the area and the engineer threw across a hammer coated in luminous paint, to which he had attached a strong nylon cord. The students then attached a cable to this, which the engineer hauled up to the roof and attached to a special frame that he had constructed. All three then took it in turns to slide down the cable on special harnesses. A similar method was used sometime later when a bow and arrow was utilised to get a line across the Wall, allowing two persons to escape on a steel cable.

Another memorable incident occurred on September 13, 1964, again near Checkpoint 'Charlie', when Michael Meyer, aged 21, made a dash for freedom. He was fired at but managed the first wire fence and crawled on to the second, still under fire, and was hit as he reached the Wall. The two guards involved caught up with him and trained their weapons on him, but a young American military policeman, Private Hans Puhl, saw what was happening from a second-storey window and decided to intervene. In the meantime the guards began pulling Meyer away, but when they saw two West Berlin policemen watching them, they dropped Meyer and ran for cover. Meyer used this opportunity to make another attempt to escape but was hit five times by fire from the guards before the West Berlin policemen put down some covering fire which, however, failed to stop the guards attempting to pull Meyer away once more. Puhl threw a tear-gas grenade over the Wall, forcing them to withdraw slightly, and then climbed over with the help of a couple of civilians. Puhl pointed his pistol at the guards and told Meyer to lie still while

Left: **A famous escape in 1965 was via a chair lift from the roof of the Haus der Ministerium. The cable ran diagonally over Prinz-Albrecht-Strasse to the waste ground beyond.** *Above:* **That was in the days of the Mark I Wall — the Mark III version has been preserved at this point.**

the wire on top of the Wall was being cut by volunteers behind him. Other guards in a trench 100 yards away started firing at Puhl, fortunately without hitting him, as a rope was thrown over and Meyer was hauled to safety. Meyer was immediately taken to hospital, where he made a rapid recovery.

Escape of a different sort. On May 6, 1987, a suicide attempt by a 26-year-old man from West Berlin. Driving at the Wall was not a rarity — this was the sixth crash of its kind in the previous year. Although the car has smashed into the western side, the police in the picture investigating the incident are East German, for the British Sector ended on the edge of the pavement opposite.

Water formed a 'moat' in front of or behind several stretches of the Wall. The sweeping curve of the Spree between the Reichstag and the Humboldthafen provided one 'window' of opportunity although guarded by patrol boats. *Left:* This picture was taken on February 14, 1989, as a man is pulled back from the southern embankment within inches of freedom.

Right: Subsequently, the Royal Engineers installed swimming pool type ladders in the water to give any future escapers a chance of climbing out of the river. The East Germans promptly objected because the rungs protruded a few inches into their territory. This ladder can still be seen near the Reichstag although the watch tower has gone.

One of the last escape attempts to attract world attention took place early in 1989, when three young men burst through the obstacles on the northern bank of the Spree opposite the Reichstag in a heavy truck. They then jumped into the river and started swimming across. Two got safely across but the third was pulled out of the river with a boathook on to a border guard boat when he already had his arms on the southern embankment ready to lift himself out of the water. This was witnessed by numerous spectators, one of whom took the photograph reproduced above. British sappers later set up a series of swimming pool type ladders interspersed with hanging grabropes along the first 100 metres of the embankment from where the Sector boundary along the river began. This led to a round of protests with the Soviet Embassy in East Berlin, for the latter could argue that the inter-Sector boundary at this point was the water's edge into which the ladders projected. This discussion dragged on with no change in the situation until the collapse of the GDR made the whole matter superfluous, but in the meantime protests at a higher had level secured the early release of this man from captivity.

Escape by air was also tried, a major effort being a large home-made balloon that brought a family across the inner German border, but a smaller version led to tragedy in March 1989 when a potential escapee, trying out his balloon prior to taking his wife out with him on the plank suspend below, plunged to his death. It is thought that the balloon rose too high over the city and that the cold forced him to release his grip.

Two microlights found abandoned outside the Reichstag one morning in early 1989 revealed the means whereby their pilots had each rescued a person from East Berlin, having smuggled the aircraft into Berlin, assembled them and completed their task during the night. Hijacking or stealing aircraft by Polish refugees to land at Tempelhof, the only airfield shown on Warsaw Pact maps, became such a frequent event that a Polish national airlines representative once commented wryly, as he passed through the old passenger halls with their Pan-Am, Air France and British Airways hoardings, that LOT was the only regular user not represented. The Berliners themselves dubbed LOT in their argot 'Landet Och im Tempelhof' ('We also land at Tempelhof'). All these aircraft were later collected by their owners.

There was always the possibility of crossing the 'moat' by the 'drawbridge'. *Left:* This picture was taken in happier times in 1937 showing an historical pageant passing the mediaeval-style Oberbaumbrücke which crosses the Spree in Kreuzberg. This bridge became one of the authorised crossing points (for

West Berliners) — the paraphernalia of the partially-dismantled Wall sealing the bridge still remaining to be seen. The river at this point was the scene of two attempted escapes in the 1960s, both of which ended in tragedy with the deaths of those concerned: Anton Walzer and Hans Räwel.

The orders for guards to shoot escapers has been regarded as illegal in the Federal Republic, to the extent that one guard that escaped and subsequently was found to have been involved in a shooting incident was tried for murder and sentenced to fifteen months imprisonment. Fritz Hanke had shot at a man trying to swim across the icy Teltow Canal in January 1963 and himself defected before the body was recovered. Hanke's trial was used by the East German authorities as an object lesson to their border guards, 2,200 of whom had already defected in the first two years following the erection of the Wall. The orders read: 'If suspicious persons are in the vicinity of the border, order them first to stop. If they continue in the direction of the border fire two warning shots into the air. If this measure fails, shoot low to wound. If this fails shoot to kill.' In all, the Wall was to result in the death of 258 people attempting to cross it, a further ten from drowning and also the lives of 25 border guards.

At the time of writing, the whole matter is under scrutiny by a special commission. Around twenty culprit border guards have already been identified for trial although the main problem is bringing to justice those persons responsible for the issue and enforced implementation of the orders. So far, some leading personalities in the former GDR system responsible for the issue of these orders have been arrested, including Erich Honecker in July 1992.

BERLIN WALL DEATHS

	Date	Name	Location
1	19 Aug 61	Rudolf Urban	Bernauer Strasse 1
2	22 Aug 61	Ida Siekmann	Bernauer Strasse 48
3	24 Aug 61	Günter Litfin	Humboldthafen
4	29 Aug 61	Unknown Man	Teltow Canal
5	Sep 61	Axel Brückner†	Border zone
6	25 Sep 61	Olga Segler	Bernauer Strasse 34
7	4 Oct 61	Bernd Lünser	Bernauer Strasse 44
8	4 Oct 61	Unknown Man	Bernauer Strasse 44
9	5 Oct 61	Udo Düllick	River Spree near Oberbaum Bridge
10	5 Oct 61	Unknown Man	River Spree near Oberbaum Bridge
11	13 Oct 61	Unknown Man	Potsdam/Babelsberg railway
12	14 Oct 61	Werner Probst	River Spree near Schilling Bridge
13	18 Oct 61	Unknown Man	Potsdam/Babelsberg railway
14	27 Oct 61	Unknown Man	S-Bahn Wilhelmsruh
15	31 Oct 61	Unknown Man	Potsdam/Babelsberg railway
16	17 Nov 61	Unknown Man	River Spree (actual location unknown)
17	Nov 61	Lothar Lehmann*	Havel Lake near Sacrow
18	9 Dec 61	Dieter Wohlfahrt	Corner Bergstrasse/Hauptstrasse, Staaken
19	10 Dec 61	Ingo Krüger	River Spree, near Reichstag
20	10 Feb 62	Dorit Schmiel	Wilhelmsruher Damm, Rosenthal
21	27 Mar 62	Heinz Jercha	Heidelberger Strasse 35 (tunnel)
22	9–11 Apr 62	Phillip Held	River Spree, Osthafen
23	18 Apr 62	Klaus Brueske	Heinrich-Heine-Strasse crossing point
24	14 Apr 62	Peter Böhme*	Kohlhasenbrück, Wannsee
25	29 Apr 62	Horst Frank	Klemkestrasse, Pankow
26	27 May 62	Lutz Haberland	Humboldthafen
27	5 Jun 62	Axel Hannemann	River Spree near Reichstag
28	11 Jun 62	Erna Kelm	River Havel near Sacrow
29	22 Jun 62	Unknown Man	Teltow Canal, Treptow
30	28 Jun 62	Siegfried Noffke	Sebastianstrasse 81, Mitte/Kreuzberg (tunnel)
31	29 Jul 62	Unknown Man	Eiskeller exclave, north Spandau
32	17 Aug 62	Peter Fechter	Zimmerstrasse, Mitte
33	23 Aug 62	Hans-Dieter Wesa	Böse S-Bahn Bridge, Pankow
34	4 Sep 62	Ernst Mundt	Bernauer Strasse
35	8 Oct 62	Anton Walzer	River Spree near Oberbaum Bridge
36	Nov 62	Ottfried Reck	S-Bahn tunnel
37	Nov 62	Unknown Person	River Spree near Reichstag

* Nationale Volksarmee   † Volkspolizei

Général Jean-Pierre Liron, the commandant of the French Sector, attends a wreath-laying at the memorial in Bernauer Strasse on April 5, 1984. Dorit Schmiel, the 20th to die in Berlin, was shot while trying to escape into the French Sector with four others, while Ottfried Reck and a companion were caught and shot by border guards in an S-Bahn tunnel air duct, Reck being killed.

What first began as individual memorials in the streets where the deaths occurred, has now given way to formal groups of commemorative crosses. These particular ones have been set up beside the Reichstag where seven people were killed attempting to escape. The last was Manfred Gertzki, shot from an NVA patrol boat while trying to swim across the Spree on April 27, 1973. For example, Rudolf Urban, whose name appears on the cross on the right, and who was the first to die, lost his life in Bernauer Strasse some two kilometres to the north-east, but these crosses were meant to represent the whole tragedy.

38	6 Dec 62	Unknown Man	Griebnitzsee
39	6 Dec 62	Unknown Man	Griebnitzsee
40	1 Jan 63	Hans Räwel	River Spree near Oberbaum Bridge
41	15 Jan 63	Horst Kutscher	Alt Glienicke
42	23–4 Jan 63	Peter Kreitloff (or Kreitlow)	Niederneuendorf (north of Spandau)
43	Mar 63	Wolf-Olaf Muszinski	River Spree *(exact location unknown)*
44	16 Apr 63	Unknown Person	Teltow Canal, Teltow
45	16 Apr 63	Unknown Person	River Spree, near Reichstag
46	26 Apr 63	Unknown Person	Teltow Canal, Teltow
47	4 Nov 63	Klaus Schröter	River Spree, near Reichstag
48	25 Nov 63	Dietmar Schulz	Near Böse S-Bahn Bridge, Pankow
49	13 Dec 63	Dieter Berger	Teltow Canal, Johannisthal
50	25 Dec 63	Paul Schultz	Treptow/Kreuzberg boundary
51	5 May 64	Adolf Philipp	Staaken
52	22 Jun 64	Unknown Man	Invaliden Cemetery, Mitte
53	26 Nov 64	Hans-Joachim Wolff	Teltow Canal, Treptow
54	19 Jan 65	Unknown Man	River Spree near Schilling Bridge
55	4 Mar 65	Christian Buttkus	Klein Machnow
56	15 Jun 65	Hermann Döbler	Teltow Canal, Dreilinden
57	25 Nov 65	Heinz Sokolowski	Clara-Zetkin-Strasse, near Reichstag
58	26 Dec 65	Heinz Schöneberger	Heinrich-Heine-Strasse crossing point
59	7 Feb 66	Willi Block	Finkenkruger Weg, Staaken
60	25 Apr 66	Michael Kollender	Teltow Canal, Neukölln
61	29 Apr 66	Paul Stretz	Spandauer Schiffahrts Canal, Mitte
62	29 Aug 66	Heinz Schmidt	Spandauer Schiffahrts Canal, Mitte
63	27 Jan 67	Max Willi Sahmland	Teltow Canal, Johannisthal
64	15 Nov 68	Unknown Person	Schlosspark Babelsberg
65	24 Jul 71	Werner Kühl	Teltow Canal, Johannisthal/Treptow
66	1 Jan 72	Horst Kullack	Lichtenrade boundary
67	7 Mar 72	Klaus Schulze	Eiskeller exclave, north Spandau
68	27 Apr 73	Manfred Gertzki	River Spree near Reichstag
69	5 Jan 74	Burkhard Niehring*	Border zone
70	22 Nov 80	Marinetta Jirkowski	Hohen Neuendorf/Frohnau
71	4 June 82	Lothar Fritz Freie	Bornholmer Strasse
72	Oct/Nov 84	Peter Böcker (or Boecker)	Frontier zone, West Berlin
73	1 Dec 84	Unknown Person	Near Wollankstrasse, Pankow
74	21 Nov 86	Manfred Mäder ?	Near Puderstrasse, Treptow
75	24 Nov 86	Unknown Person	Hohen Neuendorf/Frohnau
76	12 Feb 87	Lutz Schmidt	Neukölln/Treptow border
77	5 Feb 89	Chris Gueffroy	Neukölln/Treptow border
78	8 Mar 89	Winfried Freudenberg	Balloon over West Berlin

The complete list of names reproduced here was compiled by the authors of *Der Salzgitter Report* published in 1991. This book, by Heiner Sauer and Hans-Otto Plumeyer, summarises the evidence of GDR crimes against humanity collated by the Salzgitter team, which was disbanded in June 1990. Although incomplete, this evidence, supplemented by that of witnesses coming forward since unification, plus access to hitherto secret files, has already enabled the trials of some of the border guards involved to take place. However, many would prefer to have the persons responsible for the shooting orders on trial.

PART V
UNIFICATION

40 JAHRE
DDR

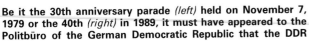
Be it the 30th anniversary parade *(left)* held on November 7, 1979 or the 40th *(right)* in 1989, it must have appeared to the Politbüro of the German Democratic Republic that the DDR would last for ever. At least the hardware did not appear to change: these are the SPW 70s of the 'Hans Beimler' Truppenteil (combat group).

The Collapse of the German Democratic Republic

On October 7, 1989 the German Democratic Republic celebrated its 40th anniversary in East Berlin with a parade before a huge crowd of spectators on Karl-Marx-Allee. Erich Honecker proudly took the salute, surrounded by the leading members of his government and the SED ranged in strict order of protocol on the tribune. His guest of honour was the President of the Soviet Union, Mikhail Gorbachev. In his speech, Herr Honecker boasted of the regime's achievements, its stable society and dynamically expanding economy. Following his usual theme, he accused his conceived enemies — 'international reactionary forces' — of attempting to confuse the people and sowing seeds of doubt about socialism, saying that any problems would be solved by socialist means.

The armed forces of the GDR then marched past to the music of massed bands, followed by their wheeled and tracked fighting vehicles, in an impressive display of military might. Then came the massed worker and youth delegations dutifully waving their flags and banners.

Viewed uncritically on television, this celebration appeared to be just another typical display of triumphant communism. In fact it was all a vast sham. The measures that had created this Stalinist state had also fossilised it and its leader-

ship, and the structure was so badly cracked and eroded that its survival was now only a matter of days. Mass demonstrations were taking place all over the country and even on the fringes of the official celebration. Cosseted by their Ministry of State Security, otherwise known as the Stasi, the ageing

Previous pages: **Officer students and cadets of the Offiziershochschule (Officers' High School) of the Volksmarine (People's Navy) 'Karl Liebknecht' march past the saluting base on Karl-Marx-Allee at the parade held on October 7, 1989.** *Above:* **The reviewing stand stood here, just to the left of the Hotel Berolina, and only a few yards from the site of the building where Horst Wessel was shot in 1930.**

The 'Felix Dzierzynski' Wacht Regiment on Unter den Linden on October 7, 1989.

leadership could not see that the system they had dutifully brought about in the Marxist-Leninist mould could no longer stand up to the reality of the outside world. Gorbachev knew this and told them so, but his warnings fell on deaf ears.

One aspect of this sham was that some of the items of military ironware on display were actually wooden copies exact in every visual detail down to the last centimetre. The immaculately turned-out troops came from filthy, run-down barracks with only two shower heads per company and hot water available only on Fridays. Taking part was the 7,000-strong 'Felix Dzierzynski' Regiment, named after the founder of the Cheka, the Soviet secret police, which also provided the honour guards for the Neue Wache on the Unter den Linden, yet even they were no better off, even though they formed the main recruiting ground for the Stasi.

On guard at the Neue Wache. *Left:* The guard turns out on July 21, 1941 for the Croatian leader, Marshal Slavko Kvaternik. On the left, the commandant of Berlin, Generalleutnant Paul von Hase. *Right:* July 21, 1990 for the tourists.

One aspect the communist world loved was the 'then and now' comparison to demonstrate the achievements of the regime. However, they always ignored what had gone before and this sequence provides an excellent example. *Right:* Our picture, not published by the GDR, shows the Spree running behind the Royal Palace and the Dom (cathedral) with the equestrian statue of the Great Elector, Friedrich Wilhelm (1640-1688) on the Kurfürsten Bridge in the foreground.

Nevertheless, for Honecker this parade marked the culmination of his career. Born in the Saarland in 1912, he had been a convinced and dedicated communist from the time he joined the Communist Youth Federation at the age of 14, followed by the KPD three years later. Recognising his qualities, the Party sent him to Moscow for extensive training. On his return he was

An effigy of Stalin replaces the Great Elector outside the ruined palace on May Day in 1953.

Above: Released by the official East German press agency, Allgemeiner Deutscher Nachtrichtendienst, in August 1979: the same view across the Kurfürsten Bridge after the battle in 1945. The bridge is where the right wing of the Fifth Shock Army crossed the Spree on April 30. The Great Elector's statue had been removed from its pedestal for safety, but it sank in an overloaded barge in Tegel Harbour during transit. It was retrieved in 1949 and placed in its present location in the centre of the courtyard at Schloss Charlottenburg three years later.

employed as a youth leader until the Nazis came to power in 1933 and he was forced to go underground. The Gestapo caught up with him two years later and subjected him to a lengthy period of brutal interrogation before having him convicted on a charge of 'preparation for high treason', for which he received a ten-year jail sentence. The Russians released him from Brandenburg prison in 1945 and he immediately set to work founding the Freie Deutsche Jugend (FDJ) as a successor to the Hitler Youth

Triumph of the Deutsche Demokratische Republik. ADN's 1979 comparison with the '180-metre long and 85-metre wide Palast der Republik', but was its bronze glass an improvement on the ornate stonework of the old Royal Castle?

Typical propaganda shots from the 1970s. Here we see the delights of the high-rise apartment block — GDR style.

movement. His success in this task led to his being elected to the Politbüro as head of state security in 1958, in which capacity he became directly responsible for the construction of the Wall in 1963 and the security instructions relating to it.

Honecker went on to inherit the GDR as Party Secretary from Walter Ulbricht in May 1971, when the latter stepped down, unable to take any more pressure from the Soviet Union to accept some measure of détente with the Federal Republic in response to 'Ostpolitik'. This was at a time of great changes in East-West relations, including the signing of the Quadripartite Agreement, and although Honecker was to make some concessions to meet this new situation, he, too, in turn was to become fossilised in his attitudes.

The GDR remained a country econo-

mically overshadowed by its West German neighbour, but nevertheless the strongest representative of the Soviet Bloc in terms of per-capita productivity. It was often said in the late 1970s and early 1980s that only the Germans could have made an equal success of both democracy and communism. However, this situation meant that the GDR was constantly having to compare itself with Western Germany, and for the SED to justify its system of government with its people.

Acceptance into the United Nations and international recognition by the Western Allies brought significant advances in national status, which Honecker then sought to increase with success in international sport. The country was scoured for talent and the selected few virtually force-fed with training and dietary regimes to a pitch

at which they could barely fail to bring home the coveted Olympic gold medals. The successes in this field sponsored a modicum of national pride, which Honecker further promoted by reviving suitable elements of Prussian and Saxon history. For instance, the famous statue of Frederick the Great was restored to its place on the Unter den Linden, and even Bismarck obtained a favourable mention in the history books for having introduced extensive welfare legislation into the newly-industrialised Prussia (although his success in uniting Germany was deliberately ignored as being too provocative).

The 750th anniversary of Berlin in 1987 was celebrated in great style, all the GDR's building resources having been concentrated in the city for the previous five years in carrying out massive modernisation programmes, to

Children's playground — 1945 and 1979 — when one was told that the rebuilt Leninallee behind had its name changed yet again to Ho-Chi-Minh-Strasse!

Erich Honecker: 'The development of the productive forces and socialist relations of production have enabled our people to attain a standard of living without precedent in their history.' *Above:* **Shops 1945 and 1979; the truth when it emerged ten years later was somewhat different.**

the detriment of the rest of the country. One minor aspect of this was the smartening up of the Friedrichstrasse crossing point and the establishment of new boutiques and restaurants around the corner on Leipziger Strasse.

Nevertheless, merely to keep his economy afloat, Honecker had to obtain considerable support from the Federal Republic by one means or another, mostly given in exchange for concessions relating to movement between Berlin and West Germany, and to visiting rights between citizens of the two countries. The latter brought the dangers of exposure of GDR citizens to the Western economy and thus increased the pressure of internal dissent. In order to relieve this pressure, Honecker allowed the release of certain dissidents from time to time. For instance, in the mid-1970s many promising artists, such as the singer Wolfgang Biermann, the writer Rainer Kunze and the actor Manfred Krug, were deprived of their citizenship and forced to leave, as happened to the peace activists in the late 1980s.

The most scandalous means of obtaining hard currency used by the GDR was by the sale of political prisoners to the Federal government at prices varying from DM 50,000 to DM 100,000 each, depending on their individual skills. Between 1963 and 1989 some 33,000 political prisoners were released in this manner through the GDR's intermediary, Dr Wolfgang Vogel, a confidant of Honecker's, who acquired considerable personal wealth in his dealings with the West. At Christmas 1964 some prisoners were even swapped for oranges in order to provide an otherwise unobtainable treat for East German citizens. As soon as one of these major transactions had occurred, it was a simple matter for the Stasi to refill their prisons with anyone who failed to meet the demands of the state without complaint or question.

Showpiece of East Berlin — Leipziger Strasse ruined in 1945, rebuilt by 1979.

The Stasi had been developed to a degree at which it was later calculated that one person in five must have been directly connected. Through its ramifications, it duplicated every political office. It controlled the appointment of all business managers and directors of concerns and offices, and far outbid the Gestapo in its meticulous documentation of the citizenry and their activities.

It was a monstrous cancerous growth, every member, apart from the most senior, being expected to recruit another 25 each year, and dominating every aspect of activity within the GDR. Created in 1950 as 'The Sword and Shield' of the revolution, it was estimated by West German intelligence to have had some 100,000 full-time employees and another 500,000 paid informers, although some of its branches were so secret that it is doubtful if the actual total numbers involved will ever be known.

In 1985 the organisation was militarised, its members given military training and expected to maintain their weapons and equipment at close hand in their offices ready to repel an invasion from the West. At the same time their instructions made them even more paranoic about security and they were constantly obliged to display their zeal, ever fearful of being denounced by their own colleagues.

Over 2,000 were employed just opening and checking mail, another 1,000 eavesdropped on and sometimes recorded telephone conversations. Others listened to what was being said in queues, in cafés and public places. In all, the Stasi kept files on some six million Germans. Stasi-Zentrale, the main headquarters in Berlin, occupied a complete block off Frankfurter Allee under the pseudonym of the 'Oscar-Ziethen-Krankenhaus-Polyklinik', the recognised heading used in correspondence with subordinate posts. This

Far from a showpiece: the Ministry of State Security — the Staatssicherheitsdienstes — better known as the 'Stasi'. This block on Frankfurter Allee concealed the headquarters for the whole of the GDR's secret police organisation. Since Unification, the building has been taken over by the Deutsche Reichsbahn.

massive complex was the workplace for 33,000 Stasi personnel, including the Minister for State Security, Erich Mielke, and contained not only the clinic, but also a databank, files galore, barracks, an ammunition bunker and a completely sealed-in prison for 200 prisoners with tiger-cages for the isolated exercise of the inmates.

Another vast complex further out on the same avenue accommodated the local Berlin headquarters. Emergency Stasi command posts were located in bunkers outside all the fourteen district capitals as well as the Wandlitz complex north of Berlin, where the SED leadership were provided secure seclusion from the normal population. Throughout the country, the Stasi had over 2,000 apartments at its disposal, prisons, weapons, aircraft, speedboats, road transport of all kinds, communications, holiday homes, and so on.

The effect of this organisation on the normal citizen was to make him adopt a double life. Outside a circle of trusted acquaintances no opinions or comments could be expressed, so public attitudes tended to be tense and discourteous, whereas in the trusted group a degree of relaxation could be found. For the Stasi to have a file on you, or for you to have been imprisoned at some stage, meant the end of one's career in this Socialist paradise. One consequence of these constraints on society was a high degree of drunkeness among the lesser-privileged workers, for whom subsidised rents, clothing and foodstuffs, and a surplus, money-absorbing, supply of shoddy consumer goods were not enough to satisfy their demands for a better life.

Through the Stasi the SED leadership were able to sponsor terrorist activities by providing instructors overseas, as

Further along lies the local Berlin HQ of the Stasi.

409

well as training, weapons, munitions and safe havens within the GDR. The Red Army Faction, which was responsible for the assassination of several leading German industrialists over the years, was sponsored in this manner.

In addition, the Stasi operated a vast espionage service penetrating all parts of political and industrial life in Western Germany, both on its own account and on behalf of the KGB. Its members even outnumbered the true diplomats and business representatives in the GDR's missions abroad.

Confident of its own ability to control the situation in perpetuity, and trusting no one, not even its own personnel, the Stasi reported only to the Politbüro, but in such a manner that the ageing leadership failed to read the portents.

With their specially sealed off compound at Wandlitz; their special shops and supplies of Western goods unobtainable by the normal population; their country and seaside resorts; virtually unlimited funds and their ability to travel world-wide; their private hunting areas and other privileges to distance them from the common people, the SED leaders standing on the saluting dais were utterly divorced in their privileged isolation from the reality of a disintegrating state, whose achievements, disguised by false statistics, amounted to the despoilation of the landscape and ecological ruin on an unprecedented scale. Their blind adherence to the Stalinist principles of total central control and decision making, with the execution of their directives to be carried out by the lower echelons without question, whatever the cost, had stultified all attempts at criticism or open discussion that might have led to a more satisfactory outcome. Now the economy was effectively bankrupt, relying on West German financial support of DM 4 billion a year while supplying an East European market that could never provide a return in hard currency.

In 1974 the GDR's constitution was amended to read 'The German Democratic Republic is for ever and irrevocably allied with the Union of Soviet Socialist Republics' but the shining

The Central Committee of the Sozialistische Einheitspartei Deutschlands (the East German Communist Party) elected Erich Honecker to the position of First Secretary in 1971. *Above:* **By 1976, the same year when the People's Chamber elected him Chairman of the Council of State, Honecker's future seemed assured, with the GDR recognised around the world, having been admitted to the United Nations in 1973.**

Chairman Honecker forged links throughout the Communist world, giving the impression of a benign statesman but in reality having adopted the rôle of a dictator. *Above:* **With Marshal Tito of Yugoslavia.** *Below left:* **With Todor Zhivkov, General Secretary of the Central Committee of the Bulgarian Communist Party and,** *below right,* **greeting Nicolae Ceauşescu, head of the Romanian Communist Party.**

example of the Soviet Union rebounded on the GDR leadership when President Gorbachev introduced 'glasnost' and 'perestroika', something with which these elderly men, frozen within their Stalinistic mould, could not reconcile themselves. Soviet publications spreading these dangerous new ideas, such as *Sputnik*, were banned from the GDR.

However, unable to control the air waves, they could only try to compete with their own television and radio channels. At first only the border areas and the central area around Berlin could receive Western television, but then, to appease the people living in the Leipzig area, it was brought in by cable. The people living in the Dresden area could not receive the signals either because of natural geographical conditions, and there the curiosity about the West was the strongest. Lacking the strong political direction of the GDR's services, the Western networks broadcast more accurate news and current affairs programmes directed at their West German audiences. This open portrayal of both the good and bad features of life in the West enabled the East German audiences to compare and decide for themselves, an aspect that a special GDR programme 'Der Schwarze Kanal' was unable to combat effectively.

However, in 1989, Gorbachev's ideas eventually penetrated through to the people of the GDR, most of whom were now thoroughly discontented with their lot. The legal means of emigration had been eased to some extent in response to popular demand, and it was anticipated that some 90,000 exit permits would be issued in 1989 and another 1,500,000 people under retirement age would be allowed to visit relations in the West. Then on May 2, 1989, Hungary opened part of its border with Austria, and East Germans started streaming in that direction. At first those that were caught by the Hungarian authorities were returned with their passports duly

For ten years, Honecker reigned supreme, cheek-by-jowl with his Soviet masters whose armed forces were firmly entrenched in the GDR. The possibility of German reunification appeared less and less likely, that is, until Mikhail Gorbachev came on the scene as the new General Secretary of the Communist Party of the Soviet Union. Here at the 11th SED Congress held in Berlin in April 1986, it is all smiles as Honecker is re-elected as General Secretary of the Party.

marked for the attention of the Stasi. However by July 1 there were 25,000 East Germans filling the refugee camps in Hungary, and on August 9 the Hungarian border authorities abandoned this practice as the sheer volume of people attempting to flee to the West overwhelmed them and their sympathies. By August 20 border controls had been relaxed to the extent that a group of some 300-500 East Germans were able to cross into Austria without hindrance on the pretext of holding a picnic near the border.

Meanwhile on June 5 the communists were defeated by the Solidarity Movement in the Polish general elections, opening another avenue of escape to the East Germans. In August, West German embassies in Prague, Budapest and Warsaw were besieged by hundreds seeking passports, and at various stages these embassies were forced to close their doors temporarily, as did the Permanent Representation Office in East Berlin, being totally unable to cope with the demands being made on them.

Having established a seemingly secure position behind the protection of the Iron Curtain, Honecker's world began to fall apart in the middle of 1989 when, in May, János Kádár *(below left)*, General Secretary of the Hungarian Socialist Workers'

Party, opened his country's border with Austria. *Below right:* Another chink in the Iron Curtain came the following month when the Communists in Poland under the State Chairman, General Jaruzelski, were defeated by Solidarity.

Crisis in Berlin, October 1989. What would have been unthinkable in earlier years, now became a reality as 'people power' began to assert itself in East Germany. Taking a hint from the Chinese, Honecker's immediate reaction was to order the demonstrators to be put down with the utmost ruthlessness. However, with power inexorably slipping from his grasp, this time it was *he* who was backed into a corner, and on October 19 he was forced out of office. *Above:* Five days later, with the State on the run, members of the 'Felix Dzierzynski' Wacht Regiment formed the thin grey line protecting the Staatsratsgebäude where Liebknecht's famous balcony (page 26) was once again in the spotlight of revolution.

On August 24 the GDR government gave permission for 108 of their citizens to leave the embassy in Budapest for the West as 'an exceptional humanitarian measure that in no way constitutes a precedent' but this was followed by another similar concession in September when the GDR laid on five special trains to evacuate 4,000 from the Prague Embassy, only to have 15,000 taking advantage of this means of exit. In an attempt to stop the flow, the GDR then imposed visas on travel to Czechoslovakia, all to no avail, for by the beginning of October there were another 3,000 encamped at the Prague Embassy. The GDR laid on special trains for their evacuation but again this misfired, for as the sealed trains carrying 'irresponsible, anti-social traitors and criminals' passed through Dresden and Halle, they were besieged by many thousands more trying to get aboard. Furthermore, these demonstrations began calling for a change of government.

Indeed the situation within the GDR with tens of thousands missing from their normal places of work — 240,000 by the end of the year — was little short of catastrophic. The army had to be called in to keep essential transport, food delivery and hospital services going, and the government even considered hiring 80,000 Chinese to augment the existing contract workforce of 100,000 Africans and Asians hired from their socialist governments as virtual slave labour. All these circumstances only exacerbated the social unrest within the country.

The new 'fall guy' was Honecker's 'crown prince', Egon Krenz, formerly the SED Minister for State Security and member of the Politbüro. However, by now it was impossible to stop the rot. The East Germans had suddenly realised that there was strength in numbers and that demonstrations of hundreds of thousands of people were more powerful than anything in the armoury of the State.

The largest demonstration took place on November 4 on the Alexanderplatz. The banner reads: 'In spring the vote was fixed. In summer China congratulated (on its action in suppressing the democratic movement at Tiananmen Square). In the autumn a few things were corrected but the SED government has shot its bolt.'

The churches, which had long been tolerated by the government as a kind of safety valve that could be kept under close observation, provided meeting points for the various dissident factions that emerged and now attracted vast numbers to their meetings, which would then depart to form mass demonstrations in the streets against the government. The 5.00 p.m. Monday 'peace prayers' held in the St Nicholas Church in Leipzig led to vast regular demonstrations in this manner, evoking the cry 'We are the people!' In Berlin it was the Gethsemane Church off Schönhauser Allee that provided the nucleus. At first the police and the Stasi put down these demonstrations with great brutality, making numerous arrests. The government had only recently sent a delegation led by Egon Krenz to congratulate the Chinese government on its brutal repression of the students on Tiananmen Square, so many feared that similar methods might be adopted.

They were correct. Honecker issued instructions for the army and police to be mobilised to disperse the expected massive anti-government demonstration in Leipzig on October 9 with the utmost force. Live ammunition was issued, local hospitals alerted and collecting points for the dead prepared for the expected civilian casualties. Egon Krenz, as head of internal and external security, was despatched by air to supervise the action but, fortunately, on the way down the army's Chief of Staff

managed to convince him that the plan was totally unacceptable, and so the demonstration was allowed to pass off comparatively peacefully.

On October 19 Honecker officially resigned, along with two other members of the Politbüro, Mittag and Hermann, responsible for economics and the media respectively. After two days of in-fighting, Honecker was replaced by Krenz in a palace coup with Moscow's approval. However, Krenz's background was too well-known to inspire any confidence in the prospects of genuine reform under his leadership, and the exodus continued.

Meanwhile, the opposition parties were forming and growing in strength. The SPD, which had been forcibly merged into the SED in 1946, split to seek an independent rôle. The New Forum evolved as a political entity; the surviving Liberal Democrats and the CDU sought to exert themselves. Then on October 26 round table talks on the Polish model were held in several cities, in each case in response to demonstrations by tens of thousands of people.

The government continued to waver, reluctant to abandon either its powers or its principles. Margot Honecker and Harry Tisch, head of the trade union movement, 'resigned' from the Polit-

buro. Krenz went to Moscow to consult with Gorbachev, bringing back nothing but vague promises of free travel. Removal of the wall was out of the question, he said, as he swore loyalty to Communism and the Warsaw Pact.

The demonstrations also continued, increasing in size. On November 4 half a million people demonstrated in East Berlin. Next day new travel regulations were announced, requiring thirty day's notice for the provision of a travel visa, although this could still be denied for security reasons. Unimpressed, half a million demonstrated in Leipzig on November 6 calling for free elections and an end to communist domination. At the first press conference ever to be held in the GDR, it was announced that the Council of Ministers had resigned. Next day so did Prime Minister Stoph and his Cabinet. On November 8, Hans Modrow was appointed Prime Minister in his place by the SED's reconstituted Central Committee of half 'die-hard' and half 'liberal' delegates, which also reinstated Krenz in post when he made the gesture of resigning. The same day Federal Chancellor Helmut Kohl declared that the Federal Republic was prepared to provide financial assistance to the GDR, but only on the basis of free elections.

On November 9, the opening of the Wall came about in a most curious manner. That evening during the course of the GDR's second press conference, the spokesman was passed a note, which he immediately read out, saying that the government had agreed to allow full freedom of travel. Within minutes people started converging on the checkpoints asking to be allowed through to the West. The guards had clearly received no instructions on this matter, but the statement about freedom of travel was undeniable and the pressure was such that they eventually opened the barriers and let the people through. From both sides, Berliners converged on the crossing points to celebrate this great event in their history. Strangers hugged and kissed each other, invited each other to their homes, opened bottles of champagne and danced in the streets.

A day the world believed could never happen. Where in 1961, Walter Ulbricht had built the Berlin Wall to halt the exodus of East Germans to the West, now in 1989 Egon Krenz took completely the opposite view to gamble on a free travel policy to stop the exodus. On the evening of November 9 — Germany's traditional date for holding important events, viz. Philipp Scheidemann proclaiming the Republic in 1918 (page 25); Hitler and his Putsch in 1923; and Crystal Night in 1938 (page 111) — SED Politburo member, Günter Schabowski, *(left)* announced the immediate opening of the GDR border with the Federal Republic and West Berlin. The gamble was that with no restrictions, people would feel confident to return to the East. And this was exactly what happened with the vast majority who crossed over that evening happy just to visit the West and then return home again.

The scenes that night were, as one Berliner commented, 'like those of another planet'. The Wall, which had divided the city for more than a generation, suddenly came tumbling down. People simply could not believe the impossible had come true.

'In the most dramatic breach yet of the Iron Curtain, which has divided Europe since the Second World War, East Germany last night announced that it is throwing open all its border points and will lift virtually all restrictions on its citizens' freedom to travel. The Berlin Wall, which has been the ultimate symbol of the division lof Germany since 1961, thus becomes little more than a museum piece. . . . The raising of the Iron Curtain from Stettin to Trieste, which Winston Churchill denounced at Fulton, Missouri, in 1946, is now almost complete. With the borders of Germany, Hungary, and Yugoslavia open, only Czechoslovakia maintains restrictions on a limited scale. . . . On hearing the news, MPs in Bonn's parliament launched into a rousing and emotional rendition of the national anthem.'
The Daily Telegraph. Friday, November 10, 1989

After that first night, when crossings were limited to the seven official checkpoints, additional access was provided by physically removing whole sections of the Wall. On Saturday, November 11, nine new crossing points were announced to cater for the huge crowds expected to visit West Berlin that weekend.

Above left: One significant location was at the end of Bernauer Strasse (see map page 387) where the Wall which crossed the street was demolished by Saturday (11th). *Above right:* Another was in the Potsdamer Platz, opened up at 8.00 a.m. on Sunday. All gave ready access to public transport.

Clearly this was the end of the GDR and events towards unification with the Federal Republic began to occur with ever-increasing speed. Hans Modrow's new Cabinet pledged itself to the reform of the country. On November 28, Chancellor Kohl's call for a German confederation set the path for the future. Again within days the SED Central Committee and the Politbüro resigned, and with them went Egon Krenz, the last of the SED leadership, under whom 1.8 million had applied to leave the GDR that year.

On December 19, Chancellor Kohl met Modrow in Dresden, where they agreed to work for a German confederation. Modrow further agreed that visas for visiting West Germans would be dropped from Christmas. Three days later the Wall either side of the Bran-

Left: Glienicker Bridge had been opened from 6.00 p.m. on the 10th, Kirchhainer Damm being the second crossing point opened up that Friday. Other crossing points followed at Puschkinallee (Saturday 1.00 p.m.); Wollankstrasse (Monday

8.00 a.m.); Falkenseer Chaussee (Monday 6.00 p.m.); with Stubenrauchstrasse and Philipp-Müller-Strasse both open from 8.00 a.m. on Tuesday (14th). *Right:* 'Spy-Swap' bridge today — a location of high drama ever since 1945.

However, the one special place, which for Berliners — East and West — would mark the real uniting of both parts of the city was still firmly closed. As one woman commented: 'Next to the Brandenburg Gate, all the other crossings are side entrances. It's only when they open up here that people will truly feel the Wall has gone.' The area had already seen some ugly scenes that first weekend as border guards reacted in the only way they knew how — with water cannon. The wide, flat top of the anti-tank wall had been 'captured' by the demonstrators on Thursday evening, (see *The Daily Telegraph* on page 415) but later regained by the Grenzpolizei *(above)* but the debate about opening the Gate was to go on for several weeks.

denburg Gate was formally opened and people streamed through in both directions, some like Chancellor Kohl and Governing Mayor Walter Momper symbolically walking through the arches, enjoying the moment despite a steady downpour. Despite all the damage already inflicted on the Wall by those chipping away at it to obtain their own souvenirs, the anti-tank arc in front of the Gate remained to provide a spectator platform for an enthusiastic audience to this event. At the end of the year, the Quadriga above the Brandenburg Gate suffered damage when revellers stormed it during the New Year period and it was later removed for restoration and repair.

Chancellor Kohl now discreetly set up various task forces to examine the problems of unification with a view to achieving as smooth and rapid a takeover as possible. The problems were immense, the first consideration being that of currency reform. GDR industry had been largely worked to death, over-exploited, inefficiently conducted and poorly co-ordinated, with no regard for short or long term environmental or safety consequences.

Finally, on December 19, it was announced by Hans Modrow (who had replaced Egon Krenz on November 13) that the Gate would be opened by Christmas. On Friday, December 22, the

West German Chancellor, Helmut Kohl, walked through a gap opened by the NVA to be greeted by Hans Modrow to the tumultuous cheers of thousands of Berliners.

417

At the end of January 1990, Modrow formed a new government with a complete cross-section of the parties represented, and called for early elections. Two weeks later he went to Bonn for discussions and agreed that currency union should be implemented as soon as possible. However he was unable to get the DM 15 million in immediate aid that he wanted, for the West Germans insisted on this help being dependent on the holding of free elections in the GDR. These were held on March 18 and produced a landslide victory for the Conservative Alliance of the Christian

By New Year's Eve, the city really had something to celebrate, and celebrate it did with a crowd of around half a million people packed around the floodlit symbol of Berlin — united after 28 years.

Democrats (CDU), Democratic Socialists (DSU) and Democratic Awakening, which gained 47.7 percent of the vote. De Maizière took over as Prime Minister with a Cabinet that included SPD and Liberal Party representatives with the majority Conservative Alliance. In the middle of May agreement on currency, economic and social unification was reached and brought into effect on July 1.

Meanwhile, in February, US President George Bush had given his blessing to the unification of Germany and the incorporation of the new country into NATO, a position supported by France and the United Kingdom. Nevertheless the approval of the Russians was still required. Chancellor Kohl and Foreign Minister Genscher went to see President Gorbachev in the Ukraine in mid-July and were agreeably

Left: **Unfortunately, things got out of hand and one person was killed when scaffolding collapsed on the eastern side; another 50 people were injured.** *Right:* **East German experts and police inspect the damage to the Quadriga inflicted by revellers who** had managed to climb to the top. Three months later, the whole sculpture was dismantled and lowered to the ground to be repaired and restored in time for the 200th anniversary of the opening of the Gate due to be held in August 1991.

Back in November, in his annual 'state of the nation' address to the West German Parliament, Chancellor Kohl had stated that there was 'less reason than ever' to accept the long term division of Germany. Suddenly what had once seemed an impossible dream to decades of German chancellors — re-unification — now appeared a distinct possibility, and on November 8 Kohl promised massive aid to East Germany if the regime would renounce its power monopoly and agree to free elections. The speed of change was frightening with the Stasi headquarters having been sacked on January 15 and the demolition of the first 300-yard stretch of Wall the following week. To maintain an element of sovereignty, it was replaced by a five-foot fence although the authorities acknowledged that its life would be short. *Right:* On February 19, squads of military engineers began tearing down the most significant part of the Wall: the two-mile stretch dividing the Reichstag from the Brandenburg Gate, down past the Potsdamer Platz to Check-point 'Charlie'. By now 'unification' as it was now being termed, was firmly on the top of the political agenda. One sticking point was Chancellor Kohl's insistence that he was not in a position to accept Germany's eastern frontier with Poland but, by June, both West and East Germany pledged never to try to regain land lost to Poland after the war. Both countries also agreed to merge their economies which, in reality, meant the replacement of the Ost-Mark by the Deutsche-Mark from July 1. *Below:* Meanwhile the Foreign Ministers of the four wartime Allies, together with those of the two Germanys, were in conference in Berlin to pave the way for German reunification. On Friday June 22, the Ministers attended the ceremonial dismantling of Checkpoint 'Charlie' — the pre-fabricated building being craned away for storage at RAF Gatow, pending its display at some future date by the German Historical Museum.

surprised at his ready assent to the establishment of a sovereign, united Germany, despite the adverse comments being expressed in the Soviet Union. This meeting was followed by the 'Four-plus-Two' talks in Berlin, attended by the Foreign Ministers of the Four Powers and the two Germanys, which tidied up the details and came to the conclusion that no formal peace treaty with Germany was necessary. The delegates then assisted in the symbolic removal of Checkpoint 'Charlie'.

As the summer of 1990 progressed, the GDR Parliament, the Volks-kammer, decided to disband the constituent 14 districts into which the country had been divided by the communists and reinstate the original five counties, or Länder, as the framework for the general election to be held on October 14. However, by August 23, the growing appreciation of the extent of damage inflicted on the GDR by the SED regime was such that the Volkskammer decided on bringing forward the date for unification with the Federal Republic to October 3, instead of December 1 as previously intended. Consequently on August 31, Federal Interior Minister, Wolfgang Schäuble, and GDR State Secretary, Günther Krause, signed the unification treaty, which incorporated a clause resolving problems over the differences in the abortion laws between the two countries. It was further agreed that the Stasi files should be kept in the East under the supervision of a special commission.

At the same time the West Berlin city parliament decided to change the city constitution and election laws to enable a joint election for both parts of the city to be held on December 2. Western city districts were twinned with Eastern ones, exchanging staff in preparation for reuniting the city as one combined

SECTOR COMMANDANTS OF BERLIN
American Sector

11.7.1945 Floyd L. Parks	1954-1955 George Honnen	1971-1974 William W. Cobb
1945-1946 Roy Baker	1955-1957 Charles L. Dasher	1974-1975 Sam S. Walker
1946-1947 Frank A. Kesting	1957-1959 Barksdale Hamlett	1975-1978 Joseph C. McDonough
1947 Cornelius E. Ryan	1959-1961 Ralph M. Osborne	1978-1981 Calvert P. Benedict
1947 William Hesketh	1961-1963 Albert Watson II	1981-1984 James G. Boatner
1947-1949 Frank L. Howley	1963-1964 James H. Polk	1984-1988 John H. Mitchell
1949-1951 Maxwell D. Taylor	1964-1967 John F. Franklin Jr.	1988-1990 Raymond G. Haddock
1951-1953 Lemuel Mathewson	1967-1970 Robert G. Fergusson	
1953–1954 Thomas S. Timberman	1970-1971 George M. Seignious II	

British Sector

5.7.1945 Lewis O. Lyne	1956-1959 Francis D. Rome	1973-1975 D. W. Scott-Barrett
1945-1947 Eric P. Nares	1959-1962 Sir Rohan Delacombe	1975-1978 Roy M. F. Redgrave
1947-1949 Edwin O. Herbert	1962 Claude T. H. Dunbar	1978-1980 Robert F. Richardson
1949-1951 Geoffrey K. Bourne	1962-1966 Sir David Peel Yates	1980-1983 J. David F. Mostyn
1951-1954 Cyril F. C. Coleman	1966-1968 Sir John Nelson	1983-1985 Bernard C. Gordon Lennox
1954-1955 William P. Oliver	1968-1970 F. J. C. Bowes-Lyon	1985-1989 Patrick G. Brooking
1955-1956 Robert C. Cottrell-Hill	1970-1973 The Earl Cathcart	1989-1990 Robert J. S. Corbett

French Sector

11.7.1945 Jeoffrey de Beauchêne	1958-1962 Jean Lacomme	1975-1977 Jacques Mangin
1946 Charles Lançon	1962-1964 Edouard K. Toulouse	1977-1980 Bernard d'Astorg
1946-1950 Jean Ganeval	1964-1967 François Binoche	1980-1984 Jean Pierre Liron
1950-1952 Pierre Carolet	1967-1970 Bernard Huchet de Quenetain	1984-1985 Oliver de Gabory
1953-1954 Pierre Manceaux-Démiau	1970-1973 Maurice Routier	1985-1987 Paul Cavarrot
1955-1958 Amédée Gèze	1973-1975 Camille Metzler	1987-1990 François Cann

Soviet Sector

28.4.1945 Nikolai E. Berzarin	1946-1950 Alexander G. Kotikov	1956-1958 Andrei S. Tschamov
1945 Aleksandr V. Gorbatov	1950-1953 Sergei A.Dengin	1958-1961 Nikolai F. Sacharov
1945-1946 D. S. Smirnov	1953-1956 Pavel T. Dibrova	1961-1962 Andrei J. Solovyev

On September 27 it was goodbye to Checkpoint 'Bravo' as the commandants of the Western Sectors (the Soviets had officially renounced the appointment of sector commandant back in 1962) shook hands in front of the control point at Dreilinden. L-R: Major General Raymond G. Haddock (USA); Major-General Robert Corbett (UK) and Général François Cann of France.

Throughout the summer of 1990, intensive negotiations took place to prepare the way for unifying the two countries. By September, after seven months of talks, the Soviet Union withdrew the last of its objections to the terms of the proposed Treaty on the Final Settlement when it accepted £4 billion of West German aid to finance the resettlement of its occupation troops in East Germany. With communist regimes collapsing across Europe, and the Soviet Union itself in trouble on the home front, it had been forced to agree to the inevitable end of the GDR, for there was no doubt that 'unification' really spelt 'take-over' by the Federal Republic. *Above:* At the signing ceremony for the 'Four-plus-Two' treaty held in Moscow on September 12, Edouard Shevardnadze, the Soviet Foreign Minister, declared: 'Today we drew a line under the Second World War and started the clock of a new era.' *Right:* Twelve days later, West German President, Richard von Weizsäcker, signed the document sealing the reunification of East and West Germany.

administrative element, with the new Oberbürgermeister of East Berlin, Tino Schwierzina, functioning in public virtually as Governing Mayor Walter Momper's deputy.

During September 1990, the unification treaty was ratified by both parliaments, and the final meeting on the 'Four-plus-Two' talks held in Moscow gave its seal of approval.

On October 2, the three Western Commandants, their Ministers and members of all the Allied Kommandatura committees held their final sessions in that building before lowering their national flags for the last time. They then proceeded to Rathaus Schöneberg, where the British Commandant, Major-General Robert Corbett (the British being in the chair for that month), addressed the assembled city parliament, officially handing over all the Allied rights and responsibilities that had held the Western Sectors together for some 45 years. Later that afternoon the Governing Mayor held a reception for a large number of the Western Allies in the foyer of the Philharmonie in appreciation of the Allied contribution.

Unification was to begin from Wednesday, October 3. Earlier the previous day, the flags outside the Allied Kommandantura on Kaiserswerther Strasse were lowered for the last time, Allied occupation rights in Berlin formally coming to an end at midnight on October 2.

Berlin united as never before. As the city awaited the unification ceremony which was to restore the two countries to one, 25,000 athletes from 61 nations arrived for the Berlin Marathon which, for the first time, passed through both halves of the city.

The day ended in mass celebrations in front of the Brandenburg Gate and the Reichstag building, where a large German flag was hoisted at midnight in honour of the unification to the accompaniment of a firework display and the playing of the national anthem, followed by Beethoven's 'Ode to Joy' and Elgar's 'Land of Hope and Glory'.

Two days later the focus of attention was on the steps of the Reichstag where the first Chancellor of a united Germany for 45 years saluted a crowd estimated at around one million. With Chancellor Kohl and his wife Hannelore is, left, Foreign Minister Hans-Dietrich Genscher and, right, President von Weizsäcker.

The reunification of Germany — the dream come true — and achieved with a spirit of co-operation and goodwill.

The huge Fahne der Einheit — the Unification Flag — is raised on the specially erected flagpole as President von Weizsäcker declares that 'In free self-determination, we will complete Germany's unity and freedom. For our task we are aware of our responsibility towards God and the people. We want to serve peace and the world in a united Europe.'

423

Postscript

The decision of the Federal Parliament of June 20, 1991, that Berlin should become the capital of the new united Germany has vindicated the stance taken by the Western Allies since the end of the Second World War. It also means that the city is now in the throes of change at a scale not experienced since the reparations taken from the French after the Franco-Prussian Wars of the last century. Then the city, little changed in size from the time of Frederick the Great, expanded under Emperor Wilhelm II into the second-largest city in Europe.

The garrions of the Western Allies are still present as the only viable counterweight to the withdrawing Soviet forces, and it is presumed that once these have all gone there will then be room for the Federal government ministries to transfer their staffs from Bonn. This forthcoming move, together with that of the Federal Parliament, Berlin's nomination as the German candidate for the 2000 AD Olympic Games, and the sudden focus of the larger German companies on placing their prestige head offices in the city, has brought about a spate of development planning that will inevitably bring some major changes in the city centre, especially in those areas so recently dominated by the Wall. To help cope

Left: **Then — December 12, 1932. The opening of the last session of the Reichstag before the building was put to the torch in February 1933.** *Right:* **Now — October 4, 1990. The opening of the first session of the new parliament of the reunited Germany. Having been restored in modern style, the same debating chamber lacks the character and stature of Paul Wallot's original Hall of the Imperial Diet. (See also page 44.) However, this first meeting was merely a symbolic gesture, extra chairs having been brought in specially for the occasion to accommodate all the deputies. It was not until June 1991 that Berlin was confirmed as the new capital, making the Reichstag building once again the official home of the German Parliament.**

with the massive increase in vehicular traffic that the ending of Berlin's island-like isolation has brought about, the S-Bahn, which, being East German run, was shunned by West Berliners for decades, is now being extensively rebuilt and modernised, and other public transport systems developed to encourage their use on a 'park and ride' basis.

However, the city authorities have announced their intention to adhere to the present basic outline of spoke-like lines of development from the city centre so that the intervening natural divisions of woods, lakes and fields that enhance the city will remain.

The visitor to the city — and the tourist trade has also increased dramatically — will find plenty of visual and other attractions to make the trip worthwhile, or 'Eine Reise wert', as the Berliners would say.

Berlin's fortifications of the late 17th century have long since been merged into later generations of development, although the elevated S-Bahn on the northern side of the river roughly fol-

lows the line of the star-patterned ramparts and moat. Those of a century later, however, are still discernible running south of the Brandenburg Gate along the lines of Ebertstrasse and Stresemannstrasse to the Hallesches Tor and then along the line of the elevated stretch of U-Bahn leading to the Oberbaum Bridge across the Spree. North of the river, the lines of Lichtenberger Strasse, Wilhelm-Pieck-Strasse and Motzstrasse serve a similar purpose.

The Schloss, the Royal Palace forming the heart of the old city on the island between the Spree and the adjacent canal, was torn down by the SED government after the Second World War but the section containing the balcony from which Karl Liebknecht proclaimed a 'Free Socialist Republic' was retained in the Staatsrat building on Karl-Marx-Platz. The Volkskammer, or parliament building, which replaced part of the Schloss site, is now closed because of asbestos contamination problems, but the Marstall, or Royal Stables, still stands nearby.

Left: **The creation of the new Germany has now been memorialised with the replacement of the wooden flagpole outside the Reichstag, on which the Unification Flag was hoisted, with this** massive steel mast. *Right:* **At the other end of Unter den Linden, the East German Volkskammer parliament building is closed, its title and symbol expunged from the stonework.**

Significant remains on the Reichstag battlefield. *Left:* Until the mid-1980s, the Moltke Bridge still bore its scars and the evidence of the repaired span was clearly visible. *Right:* Now the statuary and stonework have been beautifully restored, but one of the smashed dragons has been preserved on the northern bank, near the spot where the Soviet attack began.

Close by, the Schloss Bridge leads into Unter den Linden. Here the magnificent statue of Frederick the Great stands midst a corner of Berlin one can associate with his concept of a centre for art and science based on what was once called the Forum Fredericum (now Bebelplatz), with its Alte Bibliothek (Old Library), St Hedwig's Roman Catholic Cathedral and the Opera House. Across the street, the Zeughaus (Armoury) and the Humboldt University building, originally a palace for his brother, are also associated with Frederick the Great. The Neue Wache, where until recently members of the 'Felix Dzierzynski' Regiment performed their exaggerated goose-stepping drill, is now to be taken over by the Bundeswehr's Guard Battalion as a national shrine in its post-First World War form as a memorial to German war dead.

Outside the city walls, but within the Greater Berlin boundaries of 1920, relics of Frederick the Great can be found in the Schloss Charlottenburg and the palace's administrative enclave of Lietzow to the south-east, where the parish church has an interesting cemetery. Little village churches and single-storied hostelries can still be found in places such as Rixdorf (Neukölln) and Dahlem, where Pastor Dr Martin Niemöller once preached in defiance of the Nazi regime.

The Reichstag building on the banks of the Spree has witnessed and survived the political upheavals of the 20th century, serving as a symbol and focal point of Germany's recent history. Burned, gutted, patched and repaired, minus its dome and about to be gutted yet again to accommodate the Federal Parliament as the Bundestag building, it surely will still be referred to popularly as the Reichstag. At the moment it contains a most interesting museum of German political history with considerable attention to the Nazi era. Outside symbolic crosses draw attention to some of those who died trying to escape from East Berlin and across the river a remaining section of the Wall records the numbers of those who died in the attempt year by year.

It is still possible to walk the Reichstag battlefield starting from the point on Alt Moabit where 79th Corps's scouts first spotted the building. The Moltke Bridge has recently been extensively repaired, but if one descends to the embankment on the north-western corner the shattered remains of the figure that previously stood at the south-western end continues to bear testimony to the violence of the battle. The famous photograph taken from the corner house that was the initial objective of tanks crossing the bridge under intensive fire is on display nearby. The site of the actual window is marked by a stone carved with a shield.

The Swiss Consulate General remains as the only relic of the diplomats' quarter. Just beyond it is the concrete, bunker-like building that marked the central strip of the southern end of Alsenstrasse. The layout of streets on the western side of Moltkestrasse still display the outlines of the Ministry of the Interior building ('Himmler's House'), although the whole area has reverted to parkland.

Pock-marked blocks of stone from the bridge still line the road to the Swiss Consulate, all that remains of the diplomatic quarter.

As one approaches the front of the Reichstag, the figure surmounting the Soviet War Memorial can be seen above the trees of the Tiergarten on the right. The memorial was handed over by the Soviets to the German authorities on December 22, 1990, with the guard-room behind set out as a museum to its previous use.

Some sights will never be seen again in Berlin . . . like the impressive parades held by the Soviet Army at the Soviet War Memorial on the Reichstag battlefield. Both these march pasts were held in 1978: the first *(left)* on the occasion of Soviet Army Day on February 23, being the Soviet Army's 60th anniversary, and the second one *(right)* on May 8 on the 33rd anniversary of the Victory over Fascism. The Soviet guard was withdrawn in December 1990 when the memorial was assigned to the safe keeping of the German authorities. Since then it has been possible to inspect the tombs and artillery pieces firsthand . . . though not by vehicle! This enterprising driver ascended the steps on December 29, 1987.

The artillery piece is a 152mm gun-howitzer of 1937 (ML-20), and the plaque is one of two commemorating a cross-section of holders of the 'Hero of the Soviet Union' Award killed during the course of the overall battle from April 14 onwards naming a colonel, a Guards lieutenant-colonel, a major, a Guards lieutenant and a guardsman.

The Siegessäule, or Victory Column, still stands on the Grosser-Stern where Speer moved it from outside the Reichstag, together with the statues of Bismarck, Moltke and Roon. The bronze plaques, each weighing six tons, around the base of the Column were removed by the French authorities after the war and were later seen at Les Invalides in Paris. They were returned and replaced in time for the city's 750th anniversary celebrations in 1987. The Neue Siegesallee, on which Speer re-assigned the statues of German heroes commissioned by Wilhelm I from the old Siegesallee in preparation for constructing the planned North-South-Axis, has been re-named the Grosser-Stern-Allee, and the surviving statues can now be found in the Lapidarium on the north bank of the Landwehr Canal next to the Schöneberger Bridge.

The original Siegesallee photographed in its heyday back at the turn of the century.

Relocated by Albert Speer after he moved the Victory Column, the 'New' Siegesallee ran south-east through the Tiergarten from the monument's new position on the Grosser Stern. This picture shows it as it appeared in 1945.

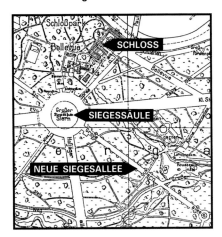

After the war, all the statues were removed by the British Army and buried in the grounds of Schloss Bellevue, north of the Siegessäule. Years later they were dug up and those that remain can now be seen on display in the Lapidarium *(right)*.

We have now seen the symbol of Berlin come full circle although whereas in 1945 its arches were open to traffic, this is not seen as a solution to east-west city communication problems in the 1990s. Anyway, it makes a nice comparison of film crews in July 1945 *(left)* and in October 1990 *(right)*. The

scaffolding we saw on page 11 had to be specially removed for the unification celebrations and the Gate looked rather bare on the night of October 2 without its four-horse chariot. Victoria was replaced the following year, having been repaired and converted to her pre-war configuration.

Close by, the Quadriga has been repaired and restored on the top of the Brandenburg Gate with its old symbols of the pre-communist era. The arches of the Gate are too narrow for modern traffic and a solution to the problem this poses has yet to be resolved.

Around the corner on what was Wilhelmstrasse, but is still named Otto-Grotewohl-Strasse, the former government quarter was extensively covered with prefabricated apartment blocks built during the late 1980s. During the construction phase, the East Germans

uncovered the Führerbunker, and partial access was possible through the former underground passageway to the Vorbunker. *After the Battle* managed to briefly secure access in April 1988 despite belated attempts by the East German Foreign Ministry to deny visits

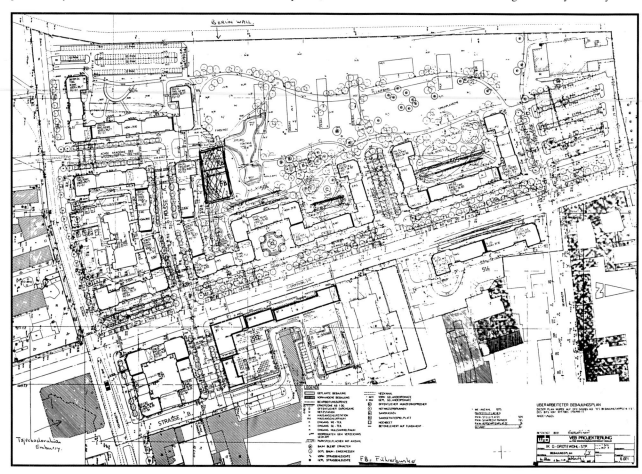

Three years prior to the reunification, at a time when the city was still firmly divided, the East German VEB Projekterung agency was working on the redevelopment of the lower end of the Wilhelmstrasse, including that portion of the Voss-strasse lying east of the Wall. This plan was smuggled out to us by Dutch journalist Tom Posch when we learned that the construction work would involve uncovering the Führerbunker. Although its precise location was not indicated on the plan, the

site engineer drew in its approximate position to show how the blocks of flats had been fitted in around its massive bulk. We had to refrain from publishing the drawing when we covered the story in *After the Battle* No. 61, published in August 1988, in order to protect our source, as the East German Foreign Ministry was putting pressure on Tom and threatening him with arrest next time he came to Berlin if he published anything concerning the bunker.

to Westerners. From May to October that year contractors toiled to demolish the roof of the Führerbunker, which would otherwise have protruded several feet above the new ground level surrounding the new blocks of flats. There was possibly a more profound reason

Tom initially visited the site early in April 1988 under the pretext of reporting on the construction of the showpiece apartment blocks. The roof of the Führerbunker (in the foreground) and Vorbunker had been exposed, but the interior was full of water and he arranged to return two weeks later by which time, he was told, the East Berlin Fire Brigade would have installed pumps and reduced the water level. In this picture, we are looking due east with the remaining part of the old Nazi Propaganda Ministry in the background.

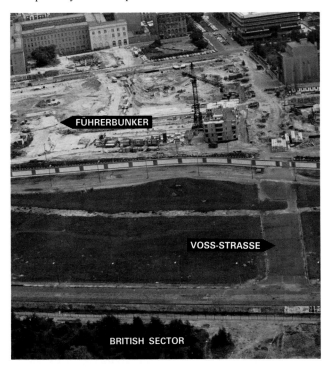

Left: **At the same time, the Army Air Corps kindly took pictures for us of the whole building site looking from the British Sector as helicopters were not permitted to fly over the Wall as they were not specifically mentioned in the Four Power agreements drawn up in 1945. (Fixed-wing aircraft could cross into the Soviet Sector, and this right was periodically maintained using**

a Chipmunk based at RAF Gatow.) The inner wall had been moved westwards to give more area for the redevelopment, (compare this picture with that on page 393 taken in 1961). *Right:* **In October 1991, Sergeant Benco circles Voss-strasse for this comparison. Two further bunker sites discovered in 1990 are indicated.**

In these two pictures we are looking south across the Chancellery garden towards the Prussian State Ministry building which still stands on Leipziger Strasse. *Above:* Taken in 1959, with the garden of the old Foreign Office in the foreground, the Chancellery has gone, leaving the shattered observation tower and bunker exit still lying askew following the attempt to blow it up in 1947 (page 342). The solitary building on the left is Vossstrasse 33/35 which still stands. *Below:* Today, with development of the 'Chancellery Gardens' estate virtually complete, the remains of Hitler's bunker are about to be paved over.

BURIED FÜHRERBUNKER

So what was found in the bunker and what is left today? When Tom returned to the building site later in April 1988 — still without official permission — he entered via the exposed tunnel entrance to the Vorbunker (see plan page 246).

for the vast effort expended to obliterate the bunker: that politically the Communist government could not be seen to be preserving in any way the most important relic left in Berlin associated with the Third Reich era.

With the opening of the Wall and the downfall of the regime, all building work stopped on the site. As the main structure of the bunker is still intact below ground, and the whole of the former 'death strip' area is now designated as the new hub of German government activity in Berlin, one must await future developments in this quarter with interest.

Left: **Stains on the walls of the Vorbunker indicated the fluctuating water level, the sandy site being only 700-odd** metres from the River Spree. *Right:* **Rusting bunk beds in the Goebbels' quarters spoke louder than words.**

Tom picked up two nice relics: a fragment from a vegetarian menu with one intriguing item — 'Salat Eva' — and a rusted helmet.

Left: **And so down the stairs to the Führerbunker.** *Right:* Unfortunately, when Tom reached the bottom corridor, he found the entrance into the holy of holies choked with rubble brought down by the demolition. *Below:* **The garden exit was** also blocked. The stairway by which sightseers had descended at the end of the war had gone, although the stairwell shaft itself remained at the end of the roof slab. To the left of this the bodies were burned.

Because the bunker would have protruded some three metres above the new ground level, demolition of its roof was begun in May 1988. *Top left:* The method adopted was to drill a line of holes about two feet apart all along one edge. Charges would then be inserted and a daily 'blow' would blast off a sliver of concrete from the roof slab. *Top right:* After each explosion, the tangle of reinforcing rods had to be cut away with blow-torches so that by August all that remained to mark the Vorbunker was a massive pile of twisted metal. Work then started on the Führerbunker. *Above:* As the work progressed, it was possible to look in under the roof slab at the water-filled rooms below, which were slowly being filled with rubble as the roof was collapsed. *Centre and right:* A 'then and now' of a different sort as your Editor stands more or less on top of Hitler's conference room — in August 1988 and August 1990. Thus, the walls and floor of the bunker still remain virtually intact below ground.

In 1990, more underground rooms were discovered beneath the former death strip during work being carried out to clear it of ordnance left over from the war. *Above:* In March, one of the basement rooms of the Chancellery was exposed through a hole in its roof (14 on the plan on page 244). Before it was sealed, some West Berlin youngsters managed to enter and leave their mark. Voss-strasse can be seen behind the crane with part of the Wall, as yet undemolished, in the distance.

More interesting, was another bunker complex found a little further to the north-west in June. This time the graffiti was genuinely of the period, and the find received considerable publicity in Britain (though not in Germany), coming as it did on the eve of the Pink Floyd concert entitled 'The Wall'. Dr Alfred Kernd'l (left), an archaeological expert at Schloss Charlotten-burg, is pictured with the group before exploring the rooms which have been identified as those once used by drivers at the Chancellery (17 on the plan). On July 1, 1992 it was announced that the city's senate had been asked to grant a preservation order on bunker complex beneath the Chancellery site which is destined to be redeveloped as a new government quarter.

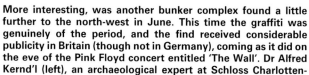

In 1990, during clearance work on the death strip for a symbolic pop concert to be held to celebrate the demolition of the Wall, numerous firearms and munitions were found. Just off the Vossstrasse an opening was also discovered to another bunker — later sealed, but scheduled for preservation at the time of writing, once part of the underground quarters used by Leibstandarte drivers attached to the Chancellery.

Marble from Speer's Reichs Chancellery was used during the building of the Soviet Embassy on Unter den Linden and in the construction of their various war memorials, as well as the plaques bearing the names of their formations and units that distinguished themselves in the battle for the city on a wall of the room in which the German unconditional surrender was signed at Karlshorst — now the Soviet Army Museum. The green carpet is also said to have come from the Chancellery.

Wilhelmplatz — the open square which originally flanked the Chancellery on its eastern side — was largely built upon by the East German authorities, but part of Goebbels's Propaganda Ministry, formerly used by the GDR's press and information service, still stands between Otto-Grotewohl-Strasse and Mauerstrasse.

A little further down Otto-Grotewohl-Strasse Göring's Air Ministry

'The Wall' concert held in July 1990 was held to raise money for the Fund of Disaster Relief, and it involved the building of an 80-foot-high imitation wall of polystyrene blocks which was to be symbolically destroyed during the performance. Meanwhile, the real Wall was undergoing a battering from all and sundry as everyone from former Presidents to ordinary tourists sought to get a piece of their own. The constant hammering could be heard all along the Wall, the souvenir hunters being dubbed 'woodpeckers'. Ronald Reagan attacked the Wall that September.

lately housed a consortium of GDR ministries and currently various Federal government agencies, beyond which the site of the Gestapo headquarters has been adapted into a memorial to their victims with a small museum. The cross street leading to Checkpoint 'Charlie' beyond where the Wall used to stand, has been resurfaced and re-opened to traffic. At the latter site, samples of the Wall and the various constructions and devices used have been set out as an open-air exhibition by the Checkpoint 'Charlie' Museum. The actual East German checkpoint on Friedrichstrasse has since been completely cleared and now serves as a car park.

Below left: **Checkpoint 'Charlie' is destined to remain a firm tourist attraction. Although the GDR buildings were dismantled early in 1991, the control tower** *(below right)* **has been retained as part of the museum display.** *Right:* **The stumps of the steel supports for the doorway, through which one entered East Berlin, can be seen torched off at ground level.**

Not far away the remaining façade of the Anhalter railway station serves as a memorial to the bombing. Next to it is a massive concrete bunker that was intended as a civilian air raid shelter (see page 129), but was taken over by the SS when the fighting reached that area. The sites of the Anhalter and adjacent Potsdamer railway stations, both demolished by the city authorities after the war, remain prime sites for the future development of the city centre.

The twisting embankments of the Landwehr Canal serve to remind one of Colonel-General Chuikov's assault from the south, although the former harbour in the centre has been filled in with rubble and converted into a park (page 225). Further to the west the OKH headquarters building (page 278), from where General Weidling conducted the defence of the city, still stands on the former Tirpitzufer (now Reichpietschufer). The side street — then the Bendlerstrasse but now renamed Stauffenbergstrasse in honour of the leader of the abortive July 1944 coup — leads to the entrance to the courtyard where the plotters were executed by firing squad. Now it is laid out as a memorial to their death (page 167) and a fitting backdrop to the Museum of the Resistance

The Flak-towers that provided the backbone of the defence have gone although not without some difficulty.

'Charlie' has also become one of the many venues where the bric-a-brac of the East is offered for sale. The atmosphere is cosmopolitan as entrepreneurs from all walks of life attempt to make a fast buck out of selling pieces from the Wall (or Mauer as it is called in German), uniforms, flags, medals, badges, and equipment of all kinds from the armed forces of East Germany and the Soviet Union. One is told that anything from a button to a Kalashnikov is available at a price. In this shot, the bargaining — in Russian — is between a Soviet Army wife and an American serviceman over the price for an officer's hat.

The Wall will also remain one of Berlin's lasting attractions. As the L-shaped reinforced concrete sections of the Mark III version were stockpiled ready for recycling as hardcore, the dates of manufacture stamped on the bases became visible.

One of the plants where the slabs were manufactured stands abandoned east of the city near Rüdersdorf. Complete with double fencing and watch-towers, the work-force comprised civilian prisoners bussed in daily.

Several sections of Wall have been preserved. *Left:* On Bernauer Strasse, this piece of land has been earmarked for a

Berlin Wall memorial. *Right:* Memorial to Günter Litfin, killed trying to swim across the Humboldthafen on August 24, 1961.

The recommissioning of the closed stations near the Wall went on simultaneously with its demolition. Here on Pariser Platz, another favoured spot for the stallholders, a Turkish immigrant has set up shop beside Unter den Linden S-Bahn Station.

All were blown up but, whereas the two Zoo bunkers in the Tiergarten were completely cleared, the Friedrichshain pair are buried under the piles of rubble known as the Bunkerberg and the Kleine Bunkerberg. The main tower at the Humboldthain forms the prop for the Humboldthöhe pile of rubble, but still exposes its northern face across the dry moat of railway cuttings that made it so impregnable.

However there are several vast passive air raid shelters still to be seen in Berlin, one bridged by an apartment block straddling Winterfeldstrasse (page 129) and visible off Potsdamer Strasse on the right as one approaches Heinrich-von-Kleist Park. In the latter stands the Allied Control Council building (pages 168, 286–287, and 327), which also contained the Berlin Air Safety Centre.

Despite all Albert Speer's efforts to transform the face of Berlin according to Hitler's master plan, little of his work remains today apart from his lines of distinctive lamp-posts leading down from Theodor-Heuss-Platz to where the S-Bahn crosses the widened East-West-Axis at the western end of the Tiergarten. This stretch of the road incorporates the area especially widened in time for Hitler's 50th birthday parade.

Speer's East-West Axis — the setting for the last Allied Forces Day parade held on June 18, 1989. It would have been fitting if a final stand-down march past could have been held by the four Allies — now reconciled — before the troops are finally withdrawn in 1994-95. The ideal date would be the 50th anniversary of the quadripartite parade in September 1945 when the troops could have marched off into the sunset . . . As it stands, they will, like all old soldiers, simply fade away.

Other interesting buildings of Speer's period, although not designed by him, can be found close by in the form of the embassies specially constructed for fellow fascist countries in suitable national style. These are the Spanish Embassy in Lichtensteinallee, now occupied as a consulate and due to be renovated as an embassy, as is the Italian Embassy in Tiergartenstrasse (page 84), while its Japanese neighbour was only recently completely rebuilt in the original style. However, Speer's contribution to March's Olympic Stadium is perhaps the most significant in its solid screen

Left: **The Spanish Embassy stands on Lichtensteinallee with the majority of its windows still bricked up from wartime days.** *Right:* **The Hermann-Göring-Kaserne, currently the Quartier Napoléon, has been earmarked for the Federal Ministry of Defence when the French headquarters is disbanded.**

walls and consequent durability that may well encompass the Olympics in the year 2000.

The Wehrkreis III headquarters buildings of that period can be found on the Hohenzollerndamm (No. 144) just south of the Stadt-Autobahn-Ring but now house the AEG central offices, while the former Luftwaffe Luftgaukommando III headquarters further

down on Clayallee (No. 170) now serve as the American headquarters. Not far off is the insurance company building on Kaiserwerther Strasse that was used as the Allied Kommandatura. The old Hermann-Göring-Kaserne on the Kurt-Schumacher-Damm provides the French with their headquarters as the Quartier Napoléon until such time as the Germans take over the barracks.

The impressive entrance hall to the US headquarters building in the Clay Compound. It was debated whether the American Embassy should take over the building when the military pull out, but it was considered that its location at the southern end of Clayallee was too far from the city centre. The GI is Sergeant Thomas E. Love of Company E, 3rd Infantry Regiment.

Two kilometres to the west of Clayallee, on the edge of Grunewald Forest, lies the small back street of Wasserkäfersteig. At the end of the road stands what appears to be an ordinary suburban villa, typical of the area; that is, apart from the barbed wire fence and armed guard at the gate. Still under American control at the time of writing (May 1992), this is the Berlin Document Center — the depository of millions of captured personal records covering members of the Nazi Party and its affiliated organisations. Located below ground in a massive two-storey bunker that the Nazis once used for telephone tapping, it became the central location for files and records uncovered by Allied troops throughout Germany. In all, the collection totals over 10 million Nazi party membership cards; 660,000 SS files, with detailed family trees for about 300,000 SS officers and wives; 400,000 SA records, and over 2½ million items of Party correspondence. In all, the priceless collection totals between 25 and 30 million items. Also included are hundreds of files containing the records of those who were tried for opposing the Party.

Agreement to transfer control of the archive to the West German government was reached in 1980 after microfilming the contents for the US National Archives. However, one understands that political considerations over pending investigations of suspected Nazi war criminals has delayed the transfer as the records are in regular use by the US Justice Department's Office of Special Investigation.

Further out in Zehlendorf, at Nos. 56/58 Am Grossen Wannsee, stands another significant part of the Nazi story in Berlin, for this was the house where the infamous 'Wannsee Conference' was held on January 20, 1942. Chaired by Heydrich, the meeting was held to inform senior officials of the 'Final Solution of the Jewish Question' — believed to have been the turning point from the indiscriminate mass executions carried out thus far into the creation of a sophisticated killing machine to exterminate the Jewish race. It was Heydrich's intention to promote himself as the chief executive but, as we have seen, he was assassinated four months later, his place being taken by Himmler. The house was used as a children's holiday home until January 1992 when, after many years of lobbying by Jewish interests, a permanent exhibition and library was opened to the public — Germany's first specific memorial to the 'Holocaust'.

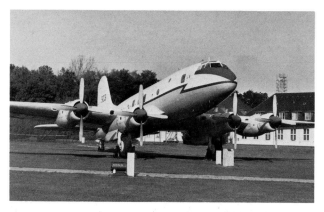

Left: **At RAF Gatow, a Hastings, TG503, is displayed to commemorate the part the aircraft type played in the Berlin Airlift.** *Right:* **In 1980, a genuine survivor of the Airlift, A65-69 of the** Royal Australian Air Force, was flown to Berlin as a gift of the Australian government. It is pictured during a temporary display beside the Invalidenstrasse in 1991.

Other evidence of Third Reich military structures will be found in the form of the buildings at the Royal Air Force station at Gatow and the hospital opposite, which between them used to accommodate the Luftwaffe's main academies. The boathouse at the British Berlin Yacht Club on the banks of the Havel below the station entrance was built to take the boats that conveyed Göring and his guests between the airfield and his residence on Schwanenwerder island opposite. The actual building was demolished after the war, but that of Goebbels still remains on the island and now houses the world-famous Aspen Institute.

Beyond Gatow at Kladow, Sacrower Strasse 144, the spacious British-occupied Montgomery Barracks on the so-called Hüttengrund, also dates back to the Third Reich and was originally the home of a Luftwaffe signals regiment.

Back in Spandau on Wilhelmstrasse (not to be confused with the street of that name already mentioned) the site of Spandau Allied Prison currently serves as The Britannia Centre, the shopping and welfare centre for the British forces in Berlin. Although the prison and its walls have gone, the external buildings have been preserved and renovated, the northernmost one along the street having been the original Governor's residence and used by the Allied Governors as their mess.

Nearby is the Schulenburg Bridge, the route by which the 7th Armoured Division crossed the Havel on July 4, 1945, and also one of the two bridges used in the German breakout of May 1/2, the other being the Schloss Bridge connecting Stresow with the old part of Spandau. South of there, the Frey Bridge was rebuilt after the Second World War, spanning the Havel on the Heerstrasse, up which the Wehrmacht used to march from the Döberitz training area to participate in Hitler's parades. Between this bridge and the next one to the east is the wooded stretch of Pichelswerder, where the Hitler Youth Regiment suffered dire casualties in the rôle imposed on them by Hitler of holding it open for Wenck's relieving army.

Further up the Heerstrasse can be found the British Commonwealth War Cemetery (page 136) with its endless rows of airmen's gravestones showing some of the cost of the aerial Battle of Berlin. The complex of apartment blocks immediately across the Heerstrasse is said to be the biggest of its kind in Europe, but pales into insignificance with the Corbusier building that towers above the junction of the Heerstrasse with Reichssportfeldstrasse.

The straight stretch of the Heerstrasse between Scholzplatz and the Theodor-Heuss-Platz was the route taken by Colonel Dragunski's 55th Guards Tank Brigade after they had come up through the Grunewald covering Marshal Koniev's right flank in his bid for the Reichstag. Turning off right onto the Jafféstrasse one sees on the right-hand side the electronic surveillance installations on the 300-foot-high Teufelsberg, Berlin's largest mound of rubble, before passing the Deutschlandhalle, in which Hanna Reitsch once flew an early version of a helicopter (page 82). In front of this are the backs of the stands facing the inner end of the Avus. This was built in the period 1913 to 1921 (page 32) and once provided the fastest racing track in the world, 18.4 kilometres long, and was eventually connected to the autobahn net in 1940. The Soviets avoided using it in their approach up the Grunewald, but President Harry Truman reviewed the 2nd Armored Division there in July 1945 (page 321) while in Berlin for the Potsdam Conference.

Midnight on February 29, 1992 saw the end of another facet of RAF life in Berlin when No. 26 Signals Unit at Teufelsberg was shut down after operating continuously from the artificial hill since moving there from Gatow in October 1972. It was in the early 1960s that the US Army approached the British authorities for permission to use the mound of rubble — the largest in Berlin — as an elevated platform for the establishment of a radio intercept station. The Americans were allowed on the hill in the presence of a small RAF and British Army unit, and accommodated in wooden huts. These gave way to the major construction of permanent buildings in 1969-71 when the 120-metre-high Rohde & Schwarz mast was added. With the Cold War in Germany coming to a sudden end in the autumn of 1989, there was no longer any need for a sophisticated listening station, and the base was run down. The fate of this site remains uncertain.

The first . . . and the last. One cannot help but feel a little nostalgic for the fast-disappearing trappings of the Soviet presence which for so long dominated the scene in Berlin. The conflict for the city remains one of the Red Army's greatest battle honours and one hopes that the care it lavished on its cemeteries and monuments will be maintained for historical reasons, if nothing else. *Centre:* This plaque marks the HQ of the first Soviet military governor, Colonel-General Berzarin (the spelling is the Germanised version), on Frankfurter Allee (page 274). *Above:* The first tank into Berlin. We saw this T-34 in its original location on page 294 and after it was moved to its new location beside the autobahn on page 350. It was inaugurated on a new plinth *(left)* on October 5, 1969 but removed following severe vandalisation early in 1991.

Driving on down the Avus one comes to the former Allied Checkpoint 'Bravo' spanning the roadway just short of the city boundary. A few yards further down is the pedestal on which Koniev's first tank into the city used to stand after vandalism had forced its removal from its original site in Zehlendorf. The tank, whose turret was still capable of being rotated, was removed early in 1991 by the Soviets with financial assistance from the Berlin Lions Club 'Alexanderplatz', who funded the hiring of a crane. Some joker has since replaced it with a luggage loader painted a shocking pink. Then one comes to the abandoned East German checkpoint at Dreilinden lying off the autobahn to the right. Today all traffic, not just the Allies, follows the direct route past the deserted Soviet checkpoint and across the Teltow Canal, which proved such a formidable obstacle in the struggle for the city in 1945.

Babelsberg, once Germany's Hollywood, is now a sadly dilapidated suburb of Potsdam, the houses that once accommodated the Soviet, British and American delegations in style now ruined by neglect over the intervening years. Moving along Virchowstrasse today, it is hard to believe that Churchill and then Attlee once slept here at No. 23. The nearby film studios where the support echelon was located is still in use.

The parts of the Cecilienhof, where the Potsdam Conference took place, are open to the public, the rest of the building being used as an hotel. Pots-dam itself invites attention for its past with many attractive, if now tatty buildings, but particularly for Frederick the Great's Sanssouci Palace in the splendid Sanssouci Park, which also contains the Orangerie, his father's Neues Palais with its delightful Schloss Theater, the charming Charlottenhof Palace and many other buildings of interest in the imposing landscape designed by the famous Lenné.

Lenin (page 208) lost his head in December 1991. Now we are told that the square is due to be renamed United Nations Platz.

Another statue lost to Berlin — although reclaimed as stolen property — was the lsted lion (pages 15 and 63) now back in Denmark at the Royal Arsenal Museum.

Frederick the Great, who ruled Prussia from 1740 to 1786, led his small provincial kingdom to dominate the former loose collection of states, and with his diplomatic and military achievements transformed Prussia into Europe's leading power.

When he died on August 17, 1786, contrary to his desire to be laid to rest in his magnificent palace of Sanssouci in Potsdam, he was buried instead in Potsdam's Garrison Church. There he lay until Hitler issued instructions that Germany's heritage must be protected against the risk of destruction from enemy bombing. Art treasures by the thousand were being stored in mine

And so to the greatest restitution of them all — the return of the mortal remains of two German kings to Berlin. The main media attention was focussed on Frederick the Great, the second Prussian king who had been born in Berlin in 1712. *Left:* **This statue of him stood in Letschin until 1945 when the little Oderbruch village was captured by the Russians during their advance on Berlin (page 181). In 1990, it was restored once again to the village square. The king had died in Sanssouci Palace at Potsdam on August 17, 1786 but his dying wish to be buried in his palace alongside his beloved whippets was never fulfilled and instead he was laid to rest in the crypt** *(right)* **of the Garrison Church in the town itself. As we have seen, 247 years later the church was selected by a latter day 'emperor', Adolf Hitler, for his own 'crowning' by President von Hindenburg in 1933.**

shafts and the coffins containing the remains of Germany's revered dead — Frederick the Great, his father, Frederick William I, the Soldier King, together with those of President Paul von Hindenburg and his wife, removed from their graves at Tannenberg in East Prussia, were taken to Bernterode, 40 kilometres east of Kassel and walled up in a 2,000-foot-deep salt mine.

Hitler's concern for the preservation of Germany's heritage led to the remains of Frederick and his father, Frederick William I, together with those of von Hindenburg and his wife, being taken to a salt mine 40 kilometres east of Kassel.

The US First Army overran the area and seven soldiers inspecting the mine for ammunition noticed fresh mortar in a corridor. They broke down the five-foot-thick wall and the secret shrine was revealed. The coffins were surrounded by over two hundred regimental banners, many dating from the Prussian wars, and other treasures including the Hohenzollern crown.

The mine at Bernterode was captured by the US First Army which found it contained upwards of 40,000 tons of explosives and ammunition stored in the 23 kilometres of galleries. A quarter of a mile from the lift shaft, a squad from an ordnance depot came across a masonry wall built into the side of the main corridor. The mortar was still fresh so they made an opening and, after tunnelling through some five feet, they exposed a padlocked door. Breaking through, they entered a section divided into bays filled with paintings, boxes and tapestries and hung with colourful banners. Sergeant Travers posted his men to guard the treasure and hurried back to report the find. After inspecting the haul, his commanding officer realised its importance and notified the Monuments, Fine Arts and Archives Unit.

Captain Walter Hancock was sent to investigate: 'Crawling through the opening into the hidden room, I was at once forcibly struck with the realisation that this was no ordinary depository of works of art,' wrote the famous American sculptor after the war. 'The place had the aspect of a shrine. The symmetry of the plan, a central passageway with three compartments on either side connecting two large end bays; the dramatic display of the splendid banners, hung in deep rows over the caskets and stacked with decorative effect in the corners; the presence of the caskets themselves; all suggested the setting for a modern pagan ritual. Hardly stopping to gasp, I turned to examine the caskets. In each of the three compartments on the right of the central passageway was a wooden coffin, placed parallel to the partitions. In the last compartment on the left, a great metal casket lay perpendicular to the partitions. It bore no decoration of any kind — merely the label "Friedrich der Grosse". There were two hundred and twenty-five regimental banners dating from the early Prussian wars and including many of the First World War. All were unfurled, contributing to the gorgeous display. I next turned my attention to three boxes ... the contents proved to be the regalia used in the coronation of Frederick William the First and Sophie Charlotte in 1713. The jewels had been removed from the crowns (left), according to the identifying label, "for honourable sale". There was the Great Seal in a silver and gold box, showing Frederick William enthroned; the huge plumed "Totenhelm" (centre), first used in the funeral of the Great Kurfürst in 1688; the sword given to the Kurfürst Albrecht Achilles by the Pope in 1460; as well as the Reich Sword, made for Prince Albrecht of Prussia in 1540 (right).'

Walter Hancock explained that 'to the lid of each coffin a label had been fastened wth Scotch tape. Hastily scrawled in reddish crayon, these read, "Feldmarschall von Hindenburg", "Frau von Hindenburg", "Friedrich Wilhelm Ier, der Soldaten König". Hitler's wreath was placed upon this casket — the Führer's tribute to the Soldier King *(right)*.'

The coffins and regimental banners were removed to the castle of Marburg an der Lahn for safe keeping. There they remained for fourteen months until plans for their disposition could be resolved. The problem of restitution was handled by an American monuments officer, Everitt Parker Lesley, who consulted the Crown Prince at the family castle at Hechingen near Stuttgart. The main problem was that of finding a suitable Protestant setting for the remains since only the Sigmaringen branch of the Hohenzollerns was Catholic. Finally, Frederick and Son were transferred to the fairytale Hohenzollern Castle in Baden Würtemburg, but von Hindenburg, who had been buried with much pomp in the presence of Hitler at the Tannenberg Memorial in East Prussia in 1933, still lies buried in the Chapel at St Elizabeth's Church in Marburg. the first Gothic church built in Germany.

The month following German reunification in 1990, Prince Louis Ferdinand von Hohenzollern announced that Frederick's dying wish was to be carried out: 'to be buried at Sanssouci with dignity and without pomp, circumstance and the slightest ceremony'. Frederick the Great's reburial in Potsdam was scheduled for midnight on August 17, 1991, exactly 205 years after his death. The day before, his coffin, and that of his father, Frederick William I, was taken from the castle on the 500-mile journey to Potsdam with a Bundeswehr Guard of Honour. Chancellor Kohl's decision to attend the ceremony was met with considerable criticism from the Social Democrats, church leaders, and from anti-militarist demonstrators. The thousands of sightseers and live television coverage also hardly accorded with Frederick's dying wish 'not to be put on show for the vain curiosity of the people'!

'The actual work of packing and hoisting consumed four days and ended on V-E Day. The caskets were the last to be hoisted. We arranged to leave Frederick the Great until the very end, as the great weight and size of his casket might have caused some trouble. His father and Frau von Hindenburg, being the lightest, were sent aloft first. I then rode up in the carriage with the Field Marshal. Meanwhile a radio installed in the office alongside the shaft entrance poured forth patriotic speeches and music in celebration of the Victory in Europe. Finally the ready signal came and we started hoisting as slowly as the engines would turn. By one of the most whimsical of all coincidences ever arranged by the ironic Fates, the radio at this instant began playing the *Star Spangled Banner*. And then, just as the casket of the greatest of the Prussian kings rose to the earth's surface, the tune changed to *God Save the King*. Early the next morning our convoy of eight trucks and two jeeps started on its journey toward a place of safekeeping.' *Right:* Hohenzollern Castle — post-war resting place for Friedericus Rex.

Seen from afar, the reburial, coming close on the heels of the re-establishment of Berlin as the capital of Germany, was interpreted as a portent of the desire to recreate former glories. Close at hand, Chancellor Kohl described the event merely as a symbol of Germany's democratic revolution. Either way, it provides a fitting conclusion for our journey through time — not quite the whole of the 205 years since Frederick was first laid to rest at Potsdam, but throughout the most turbulent years of Berlin's history.

Father and son — the Soldier King and Der Grosse — near the end of their 500-kilometre journey from Bavaria to Berlin. From the 18th century to the 20th — after two centuries his last wish finally honoured at the beautiful Sanssouci Palace at Potsdam.

Index

COMPILED BY PETER B. GUNN

Note: Page numbers in *italics* refer to illustrations

Whatever the period, in peace or war, the Brandenburger Tor is central to Berlin's history. *Above:* Pre-war parade of the 'People's Car'. *Opposite:* Soviet forces on the Gate in 1945.

The Allies enter Berlin. *Above:* **The Red Army crosses the Spree under fire in April 1945.**

French forces pass a succinct slogan: 'When you retreat, death marches to Berlin'.

A Sherman of the US 2nd Armored Division surrounded by curious Berliners.

Troops who took part in the British victory parade relax beneath a Soviet hoarding depicting the Big Three.

The war is over. Appreciation is extended to the men of the Red Army for deliverance.

The big clear-up begins. Conservation of materials was paramount.

'Rubble women' operate a human chain of buckets to salvage re-usable debris in the Kaiserdamm, July 1945.

Female construction workers are each rewarded with a five-metre length of cloth.

468

The field of battle in July 1945. The guns stand as silent sentinels of the bitter and bloody battle for the Reichstag.

Counting the cost. All told, the Soviets suffered over 300,000 casualties in the capture of Berlin. Here three American WACS, Corporal Kathryn Knutson, Sergeant Mabel Schweter and **Pfc Doris Gedney, from the 1st Allied Airborne Army HQ Detachment — the first American unit in Berlin — are shown the graves of two Soviet soldiers beside Berliner Strasse.**

Photographic Credits

Aral: 442 bottom left.
Acme-British: 254 centre, 257 top and bottom,
258 top and bottom, 305 top, 308 centre, 370 top left.
Allgemeiner Deutscher Nachrichtendienst, Berlin (ADN):
19 bottom left, 30 top left, bottom left and right,
35 bottom, 46 bottom, 57 bottom right, 128 bottom left,
152 bottom left,
158 top left, centre left and bottom left,
159 top left and centre, 173 top, 177 top, 188 both,
189 top, 194 top, 195 top and bottom left, 197 top,
208 top, 209 top, 212 both, 215 top and centre left and
right, 219 top, 222 bottom left and right, 223 top left,
228 top right, 231 bottom left,
237 centre and bottom centre, 238 bottom right, 246,
264 top, 277 centre right, 286 top and bottom left,
308 top, 317 bottom left, 331 bottom, 342 centre,
361 bottom, 362 top and right, 363 top right, 364 bottom left,
365 top, 375 bottom, 388 top right, 402–403,
404 top left and right, 406 centre left and bottom,
407 all, 408 all, 426 top left and right, 427 centre,
434 top left and right, 441 top left, 467.
Associated Press, London: 46 top, 70 bottom left,
79 top left, 111 bottom left, 225 centre and bottom left,
226 top left, 254 bottom, 309 top, 310,
342 bottom right, 344 bottom, 349 top, 359 top left,
371 top left, 372 centre left and bottom right, 385 top,
390 centre, 391 top, 398 bottom, 416 bottom left,
421 top, 435 top left.
Author: 425 top left, 426 centre left and right.
Bild und Heimat: 318 top and bottom.
Richard Brett-Smith: 294 bottom left.
British Army Public Information: 348 top,
384 centre and bottom right.
Charles Brown: 354 top, 355 bottom,
356 top left and right.
Bulloz Photographic: 8–9.
Bundesarchiv, Koblenz: 65 top left.
Camera Press: 304 bottom, 390 top left.
Checkpoint 'Charlie' Museum: 392 centre bottom.
Cotton Coulson: 387 bottom.
Michael Davis: 431 top.
ECP Armées, Paris: 19 centre, 122 top, 124 bottom,
220 bottom left, 248 top, 293 centre,
301 top and bottom, 307 bottom left, 328 top,
333 top and centre, 394 top right, 400, 438 top right,
455.
Elmar Widmann: 124 top right, 205 bottom.
Fotoservice Axel Springer: 399 top left.
Gedenkstätte Deutscher Widerstand: 164 top left,
165 top left and centre, 166 top left and bottom left,
167 top left and centre row.
German Tourist Board: 444 bottom right.
John Giles: 387 top left and right, 389 centre, 395 top left.
Hulton Picture Company, London: 109 bottom right.
Walter Hancock: 442 bottom right, 443 all,
444 top and bottom left.
John Hearne: 85 top right.
Imperial War Museum, London: 44 bottom left,
80 bottom right, 81 bottom right,
127 bottom left and right, 131 top, 132 bottom, 133 top,
134 top, 135 bottom, 137 top, 138, 139, 203 top right,
236 top right, 237 top left, 298 centre,
299 top left and bottom left, 304 top, 308 bottom left,
309 centre left, 312 top, 315 top, 316, 317, 319 bottom,
322 top, 323 top left, 324 top and bottom,
325 top and bottom, 326 top, 338 top,
339 top and bottom, 352 centre, 370 centre left, 458.
Keele University (Air Photo Library): 68 bottom left,
125 bottom right, 204 top.
Keystone: 334 top left.
Landesbildstelle, Berlin: 17 bottom, 18 bottom left,
23 top, 24 top, 29 top and centre, 32 top left,
centre right and bottom left, 34 top left, 35 top left,
36 bottom left, 37 top left, 39 bottom left, 40-41,
44 top left and top right, 45 top left, 50 top, 51 top left,
56 top, 58 bottom left, 78 centre, 82 bottom left,
84 centre, 87 top left and bottom,
88 centre left and right, 89 top left,
90 top left and bottom, 91 bottom,
92 top left and top right, 95 top left,
centre and bottom left, 111 top centre, 120 bottom,
122 bottom left, 129 top left, top right and centre,
130 top, 132 top, 136 top and bottom, 144 top,
145 top left, bottom left and right,
147 top and bottom left, 148 centre, 152 top,
153 top left and centre, 154 centre left, 155 top right,
169 centre, 189 bottom left, 194 centre, 197 centre,
201 bottom, 204 bottom, 205 top and centre, 214 both,
216 both, 217 both, 218 bottom left, 222 centre,
224 top left and right, 232 top left and bottom left,
236 top left, 237 top right and bottom right,
242 top left and bottom, 243 top left, 270 bottom,
292 top, 306 centre, 327 centre, 332 bottom,
333 bottom, 335 bottom right, 340 top and centre, 341,
342 bottom left, 343 top, 346 top, 351 top,
353 top and bottom, 356 bottom, 357 top and 358 bottom,
361 centre left and right, 364 bottom right,
367 top left and right and centre, 368 all,
369 centre and bottom left, 371 bottom left,
372 centre right and bottom left, 374 top and centre,
376 top and centre, 378 all, 386 top left,
388 bottom left and right, 391 centre, 392 top left,
393 top, 394 top left, 396 both, 397 top,
405 top and centre, 406 centre right, 413,
427 bottom right, 430 top, 437 centre and bottom,

Two of 'our' combat photographers, Bill Vandivert, left, of *Life* magazine who took the picture on page 259 with Fred Ramage — see page 309.

439 top left, right and centre, 440 bottom, 445 both,
446–447.
D. Lang: 178 bottom right.
N. Leonhard: 66 bottom left.
Clifforde Mark: 92 centre left, 152 centre, 203 top left,
221 bottom left, 251 top, 300 top left, 370 bottom left,
469.
Margret Nissen: 66 bottom right.
Jan Norgård: 441 bottom right.
Nuremburg Stadtarchiv: 107 top.
Jürgens Ost+Europa Photo: 412 top and bottom.
Günter Peters: 416 top left.
Popperfoto, London: 140 top, 419 bottom.
Tom Posch: 429 top, 431 centre left and right, 432 all,
433 top left and right.
Press Association: 420, 421 centre and bottom,
422 top and centre, 423, 424 top right.
Pressefoto Mrotzkowski: 417 top.
**Preussischer Kulturbesitz (Deutsche
Staatsbibliothek), Berlin:** 61 top, 68 top centre,
74 bottom left, 108 bottom left, 156 top left and right.
Progress Publishers: 174 top centre and right.
R. Raiber: 163 bottom.
Royal Air Force Museum, Hendon: 89 bottom right.
Royal Engineers: 223 centre and bottom.
RV Reise-und Vekehrsverlag, Stuttgart-Munich: 32 centre,
68 bottom right, 157 top right.
**Der Senator für Stadtentwicklung um
Umweltschutz, Berlin:** 31 centre, 47 centre left,
108 centre, 213 centre.
Andreas Schoelzel: 414 both, 418 top.
Schöning & Schmidt: 393 bottom.
Senatsverwaltung für Bau-und Wohnungswesen V:
313 centre, 339 centre, 383 bottom, 384 top right.
Sovfoto: 2–3, 173 bottom, 187, 191 both, 192 top, 193,
198 all, 199 all, 206 all, 210, 211, 218 top, 221 top,
224 centre left, 227 centre and bottom, 231 top,
233 top and bottom, 234 top, 235 top, 237 bottom left,
238 top, 240 bottom, 241 all, 244 top,
265 top and bottom, 268, 269 top left and bottom, 272,

274 top and bottom left, 275 top left, centre and
bottom left, 278 top and centre, 279, 280, 281, 282
bottom, 289 bottom, 290, 291, 292 centre, 302, 320, 340
top left, 367 bottom left, 449, 452, 460.
Special Investigation Branch, RMP: 347, 348 bottom.
Süddeutscher Verlag, Munich: 21 top, 29 bottom left,
39 centre, 64 top right, 66 centre, 74 bottom right.
Bildarchiv Tagesspiegel: 417 bottom left and right.
Tass: 220 top, 235 bottom, 238 bottom left, 239 all,
240 top left, 273, 390 top right.
Time Life: 259.
Ullstein Bilderdienst, Berlin: 25 bottom left,
27 top and bottom left, 37 bottom left,
47 centre right and bottom left, 64 top left, 66 top left,
69 centre right, 86 top, 106 top, 156 bottom,
267 top and centre.
Maria Ulrich: 434 centre left and right,
bottom left and right.
US Army/Signal Corps: 10 top, 57 bottom left, 67 top,
94 top left, 126 top left, top right and centre,
133 centre bottom, 143 bottom, 149 top, 150 top,
151 bottom, 154 top, 155 bottom right, 157 bottom,
159 bottom, 160 top, 161 top, 201 top, 222 top,
229 top left and centre, 245 top, 249 both, 253 top,
262 top, 263 top left and bottom left, 276 top,
277 top and centre left, 278 bottom left, 282 top,
283 top, 284, 285 top and bottom left, 286–287,
289 top and centre, 293 top left and bottom, 294 top,
295 top, 296, 297, 300 centre, 303, 312 bottom,
318 centre, 319 top, 320, 321, 322 bottom,
323 centre and bottom, 327 top, 331 top, 334 centre,
335 top right, 336, 337, 342 top, 343 bottom, 358 top,
394 bottom left, 456, 471, 472.
United States Military Community Activity: 438 bottom.
Wiener Library, London: 111 top left.
Zenit Bildagentur: 416 top right.

Photographs not listed were supplied by the **Historical
Research Unit** and the **Bellarchiv**. All present-day photographs (including aerials) copyright **After the Battle**.